BLAMING THE JEWS

STUDIES IN ANTISEMITISM

Alvin H. Rosenfeld, editor

BLAMING THE JEWS

Politics and Delusion

—⁓—

BERNARD HARRISON

INDIANA UNIVERSITY PRESS

This book is a publication of

Indiana University Press
Office of Scholarly Publishing
Herman B Wells Library 350
1320 East 10th Street
Bloomington, Indiana 47405 USA

iupress.org

Manufactured in the United States of America

Library of Congress Cataloging-in-Publication Data

Names: Harrison, Bernard, 1933- author.
Title: Blaming the Jews : politics and delusion / Bernard Harrison.
Description: Bloomington, Indiana : Indiana University Press, [2020] | Series: Studies in antisemitism | Includes bibliographical references and index.
Identifiers: LCCN 2020007441 (print) | LCCN 2020007442 (ebook) | ISBN 9780253049902 (hardback) | ISBN 9780253049919 (paperback) | ISBN 9780253049926 (ebook)
Subjects: LCSH: Antisemitism—History—21st century. | Arab-Israeli conflict—Influence.
Classification: LCC DS145 .H376 2020 (print) | LCC DS145 (ebook) | DDC 305.892/40905—dc23
LC record available at https://lccn.loc.gov/2020007441
LC ebook record available at https://lccn.loc.gov/2020007442

1 2 3 4 5 25 24 23 22 21 20

For Alvin H. Rosenfeld

Antisemitism frequently charges Jews with conspiring to harm humanity, and it is often used to blame Jews for "why things go wrong."

—INTERNATIONAL HOLOCAUST REMEMBRANCE ALLIANCE (IHRA) DEFINITION OF ANTISEMITISM

CONTENTS

PREFACE

A DECADE AGO, RAEL JEAN Isaac published a review of an earlier book of mine on antisemitism. Her review was generally approving, though it also contained some sharp and well-deserved criticisms, with which I now find myself wholly in agreement. Isaac's (2009) review concludes:

> Harrison focuses on today's left wing, and does a fine job of showing how it has come about that "the 'anti-racist' liberal left finds itself currently up to its neck in the oldest form of racism." But at the end of the day we are left with the larger question—one hopes Harrison will one day turn his formidable analytic talents to it—"Why, over time, do so many different roads, left, right, religious, anti-religious, lead to anti-Semitism?" If nothing else it speaks to the poverty of the human imagination that it comes back endlessly to the same imaginary demons and, impervious to reason or logic, sinks into the same familiar collective madness.

The present book is my attempt, more than a decade later, to do what Isaac asked of me: to answer the above taxing but entirely legitimate question. I have returned, in this new book, to many of the issues of contemporary antisemitism that dominated the first. But this time, I have tried to set them in the wider context of a new account of what antisemitism is, of the functions it serves in non-Jewish politics and culture, and of why it has enjoyed the protean power it has displayed over the centuries to continually re-create itself in an extraordinary variety of political and religious contexts.

A non-Jew such as myself would have found it difficult to even address these questions without an immense amount of sympathetic help from friends and colleagues, Jewish and non-Jewish. Those from whom I have learned most include Edward Alexander, David Conway, Anthony Julius, Lesley Klaff, Michael Krausz, Matthias Kuentzel, Deborah Lipstadt, Kenneth Marcus, Cynthia Ozick, Alvin Rosenfeld, Abigail Rosenthal, Tammi Rossman-Benjamin, and Kenneth Waltzer. The critical comments of my wife, Dorothy Harrison, who read the final version of the manuscript in its entirety, led me to excise a number of tediously overwritten passages, which must once have seemed good to me but no longer did so when seen through her eyes. Others from whose advice the book has gained much include Jonathan Campbell, Amy Elman, the late Ilan Gur-Zeev, David Hirsh, Alan Johnson, Peter Hacker, Menachem Kellner, Michael Leffell, David Patterson, Steve Rich, Leona Toker, Stephen Riley, Alan Tapper, and Elhanan Yakira. Any remaining errors, from which they and many others have not succeeded in saving me, are entirely my own.

Katelyn Klingler did a splendid job of ridding the manuscript of a host of typos and minor infelicities. To her, to those mentioned above whom I have consulted in person, and to the many more whose books and essays have helped me see new complexities or turn new corners in the discussion, my heartfelt gratitude is due.

BLAMING THE JEWS

—ᴗᴗ—

INTRODUCTION

Left-wing anti-racists should think more about the fact that anti-Semitism is both a form of racism and a prejudice with its own specific characteristics.

—Dave Rich, *The Left's Jewish Problem*

I

In recent years, Western countries have seen a sharp increase in both the incidence of antisemitic material on the web, social media, and elsewhere, and in actual attacks on Jews. In 2015, according to the *Guardian* newspaper, antisemitic incidents doubled over the previous year, reaching the highest level ever recorded in Britain. One of the incidents reported by the paper concerns a leaflet found among Israeli produce in a supermarket. It showed an image of the Israeli flag with the caption "The flag of Zionist racist scum," and it read, "Deny the Holocaust? Of course there was a holocaust. What a pity Adolf and Co didn't manage to finish the job properly!" Another involved an "identifiably Jewish man, cycling to synagogue, knocked off his bicycle, and when on the ground kicked, by a group of youths."[1]

Also in Britain, 2016 saw a series of accusations of antisemitism in the Labour Party. This began with a highly publicized row among members of the Oxford University Labour Club, with allegations of a "poisonous" atmosphere, including constant reference to Jewish students as "Zionists" or "Zios." In the words of the *Independent* newspaper, the club

became embroiled in an anti-Semitism row following the resignation of one of its chairs after the club decided to endorse Israel Apartheid Week in February.

1

Co-chair Alex Chalmers, a student at Oxford's Oriel College, issued a
strongly-worded statement on his Facebook page at the time in which he
said he was stepping down from his position because a large proportion
of both OULC and the student left in Oxford "have some kind of problem
with Jews."

Despite highlighting the benefits he received during his time with the
OULC over the past two terms, Mr Chalmers said the club was becoming
"increasingly riven by factional splits." He added: "Despite its avowed
commitment to liberation, the attitudes of certain members of the club
towards certain disadvantaged groups was becoming poisonous."[2]

In due course, as a result of the dependence of modern political life on social
media, which lend extraordinary volume and publicity to the kind of remark
formerly confined to sympathetic ears in smoke-filled rooms, the row spread to
the Labour Party itself. By the middle of 2016, "up to twenty Labour members,
including one MP [Member of Parliament] had been suspended or expelled due
to alleged anti-Semitism and the party had conducted three different enquiries
into anti-Semitism within its ranks."[3]

In the United States, concerns about campus antisemitism echoing those
voiced at Oxford have been heard for a number of years in connection with the
Boycott, Divestment and Sanctions (BDS) movement, aimed at "delegitimizing" Israel, that unites left-wing faculty with left and pro-Palestinian student
groups. "In the U.S. more than 1,000 scholars on more than 300 college and
university campuses across the country have endorsed an academic boycott of
Israel."[4] In faculty members' hands, the debate remains largely academic. But in
the hands of students, the debate often becomes angry, violent, and threatening
to Jews, as we shall see at more length in chapter 14.

> Professors who use their university positions and university resources
> to promote campaigns to harm or dismantle the Jewish state and who
> encourage students to do the same, can contribute to the creation of a hostile
> and threatening environment for many Jewish students, who report feeling
> emotionally harassed and intimidated by their professors and isolated from
> their fellow students. Moreover, in light of the fact that no other racial, ethnic
> or religious group is currently being subjected by faculty to such pervasive
> harassment and intimidation, Jewish students experience this flagrant double
> standard as a kind of institutional discrimination that is antisemitic in effect
> if not in intent.[5]

Worse has occurred in France. The most newsworthy event of this kind in
2015 took place in early January when, coincidentally with the Charlie Hebdo

massacres, an Islamist terrorist killed four shoppers—Yoav Hattab, Yohan Cohen, Philippe Braham, and François-Michel Saada—at a kosher supermarket in Paris. But that event, even then, formed part of a general pattern. According to the watchdog Service de Protection de la Communauté Juive (SPCJ), as reported in the *International Business Times*, 508 antisemitic incidents took place between January and May of that year. Almost a quarter of these were violent; the bulk of the rest took the form of death threats.

The same article reports the Conseil Représentatif des Institutions Juives de France (CRIF) as having issued a statement to the effect that the SPCJ findings represent a small fraction of actual attacks in France, which, according to it, have reached "appalling levels."[6]

The rise of attacks on Jews to these levels, moreover, has occurred very recently and very rapidly. "In France, for example, there had only been one recorded incident of anti-Semitic violence in 1998, but there were nine in 1999 accelerating to 116 in 2000 and 725 in 2002 (when 80% of all racist violence in France was directed against Jews)."[7]

Unsurprisingly, emigration has reached correspondingly high levels among France's five hundred thousand Jews, many of whom are already refugees from persecution in the Near East. The number of French Jews emigrating to Israel between January and August 2015 was 5,100—25 percent more than the number (4,000) doing so in the same period in 2014.[8]

In Germany also, antisemitism has been growing again. In late 2019 Cardinal Reinhard Marx, archbishop of Munich and Freising, pledging that "Jews and Christians will never separate again," warned against the renewed rise of anti-Jewish feeling. "He stressed that he was 'very worried' about the direction society is heading because there are 'more and more blogs and ideologies from people that cannot be taught, who indulge in conspiracy theories and soon unite as a sounding board for . . . slogans of antisemitism.' Marx went on to explain that the religious component of antisemitism is also playing a role in its rise."[9]

The Jew hatred of the 1930s, apparently, is up and running again. It appears that Europe and—to an admittedly lesser degree—the United States, are once again frightening places, and at times dangerous ones, in which to be a Jew.

II

These developments have made it fashionable since the turn of the century to talk and write of a "new antisemitism." Four things are "new" about it. First, it is not coming exclusively from the far-right websites and political groups

across the Western world that continue to promote, and to glory in, antisemitism of highly traditional kinds. In addition, it now comes from groups on the
political left and liberal left. Second, it is almost wholly motivated by hostility
to the State of Israel. Third, those accused of it, unlike traditional antisemites
of the political right, are generally extremely concerned to deny the justice of
the accusation. They wish it to be understood that they are not hostile to *Jews*
as such but merely to Zionism, and to Jews merely to the extent that the latter
are Zionists—or in the terminology of Labour's young ladies and gentlemen
at Oxford, "Zios"—Jewish supporters, that is to say, of the right of the State
of Israel to exist as a Jewish state. For the most part, they also argue that
the accusation itself is politically disingenuous: a mere diversionary tactic
designed to silence criticism of the evils perpetrated by Israel in the context
of its long war with the Palestinians. Fourth, and perhaps most importantly,
as a result of the attractions for the left of the new antisemitism (if antisemitism is in fact what it is), antisemitism has ceased to be a *socially marginal*
phenomenon in the Western world. For half a century after the end of World
War II, the recollection of the Holocaust made it socially suicidal to express
open hostility to Jews, even when deeply felt. Antisemitism became in those
years the province of an obscure minority of nasty little people who spent
their time circulating nasty little pamphlets read only in their immediate
circle. Since 2001, commentators without number have recorded the growth
of a climate of opinion, not merely in sections of the media widely regarded
as pillars of left liberal respectability—the BBC, the *New York Times*, the *New
Statesman*, the *London Review of Books*—but at innumerable middle-class
dinner tables, within whose bounds it is no longer unacceptable to be rude
about "the Jews."

   The tone of this new liberal-left open season on Israel and its Jewish supporters was caught early on, in 2001, by a remark attributed to the French ambassador to the United Kingdom. According to Tom Gross, writing close to the
time in the *National Review*,[10] the affair began when Barbara Amiel, a columnist
in the London *Daily Telegraph*,

> revealed that at a reception at her house, the ambassador of "a major EU
> country" told guests that the current troubles in the world were all because of
> "that shitty little country Israel."
>   "Why," he asked, "should the world be in danger of World War Three
> because of those people?"
>   Within 24 hours, the British *Guardian* newspaper identified the
> ambassador in question as Daniel Bernard, France's man in London and one

of President Chirac's closest confidants. (While Bernard has not admitted using these exact words, he hasn't clearly denied doing so either.)

Several conservative columnists in the United States (where are those who profess to be liberal?) have condemned the ambassador for his "crude anti-Semitic remarks."

What has not been properly noted in the U.S. media is that in the British and French media, it is not the French ambassador or anti-Semites who are being condemned, as one would expect, but Barbara Amiel and "those people." As for Israel, it seems to be open season.

A piece in the *Independent*, for example, by one of the paper's regular columnists (titled "I'm fed up being called an anti-Semite," by Deborah Orr, December 21, 2001) described Israel as "shitty" and "little" no fewer than four times.

"Anti-Semitism is disliking all Jews, anywhere, and anti-Zionism is just disliking the existence of Israel and opposing those who support it," explains Orr. "This may be an academic rather than a practical distinction," she continues, "and one which has no connection with holding the honest view that in my experience Israel is shitty and little."

III

It seems clear that Tom Gross, in this report, is of one mind with those he mentions as condemning the "crude anti-Semitic remarks" of Daniel Bernard. But is it—as he records Deborah Orr as complaining—*in fact* antisemitic to "dislike the existence of Israel," and if so, why?

The difficulty of answering these questions is elegantly and simply exposed in an article published in the "Magazine" section of the BBC Television News website for April 29, 2016. The article, titled "What's the Difference between Antisemitism and Anti-Zionism," begins, "The UK Labour Party has been at the centre of a row over anti-semitism, including its relationship to anti-Zionism. What do these two terms actually mean?" It then answers its own question by offering two definitions, heralded by bullet points intended, no doubt, to set the definitions off as sufficiently authoritative to be beyond further debate.

- Anti-Semitism is "hostility and prejudice directed against Jewish people" (OED).
- Zionism refers to the movement to create a Jewish state in the Middle East, roughly corresponding to the historical state of Israel, and thus support for the modern state of Israel. Anti-Zionism opposes that.

If one takes these definitions at face value, it becomes very difficult to see how a mere anti-*Zionist* could, in reason, be accused of anti*semitism*. According to the BBC's definition, "anti-Semitism" is the name of an *emotion*, one of "hostility and prejudice" (that is to say, unreasoning dislike), directed against "Jewish people" per se. Anti-*Zionism*, on the other hand, is a (presumably reasoned) political position of opposition, not to "Jewish people" in general, but simply to the existence of the State of Israel. Unsurprisingly, therefore, the subsequent article is sympathetic to Ken Livingstone, Vicki Kirby, Gerry Downing, and others at that time recently expelled from the Labour Party, and generally skeptical concerning the validity of the accusations of antisemitism brought against them. The piece concludes with the following respectably anodyne verdict that echoes very much in line with the BBC's standard editorial stance of sympathy for the Labour Party, and more generally for liberal opinion on Israel, in the face of right-wing accusations of Jew hatred: "Few would deny there are anti-Semites who call themselves anti-Zionists, or that it's possible to criticise Israel without being a racist or a bigot. But agreement on how exactly the two relate appears elusive."

In effect, this BBC guide to the dispute comes to much the same conclusion as the report by the Labour politician Shami (shortly afterward Baroness) Chakrabarti into antisemitism in the party: that while "hostility and prejudice against Jewish people" may be present in a minority of individual Labour members, such hostilities are not shared by the vast majority of Labour opponents of Israel.

IV

Is the anti-Zionism now popular in liberal-left circles across the Western world, then, actually antisemitic or not? If so, in what ways and to what extent? These are among the central questions that I propose to address in this book.

On the face of it, as we have just seen, much depends on what one takes antisemitism to consist in—on what phenomena one takes the word to cover. On the definition above, tagged "OED" (Oxford English Dictionary) by the BBC's unnamed journalist, matters are simple enough: "antisemitism" is the name of an *emotional state*: of "hostility and prejudice" toward individual Jews *considered as Jews*. Reasoned political opposition toward the continued existence of a state is surely to be distinguished from unreasoning hostility toward individual Jews, even when the state in question happens to be a Jewish state. Hence, anti-Zionism cannot in the nature of things be considered antisemitic; QED.

But are matters as simple as that? I was at first unable to locate the definition that the BBC cites with the tag "OED" in any of the various shorter print editions of that dictionary accessible to me. The mystery was solved when it was pointed out to me[11] that the BBC's definition comes from the *online* version of the OED and is in fact the first definition that appears in the online entry. The definition given in the complete, and therefore presumably definitive, print version of the OED[12] is rather different. It reads, in part (omitting examples of usage): "**Anti-Semitism.** Theory, action or practice directed against the Jews. Hence anti-Semite, one who is hostile or opposed to the Jews, anti-Semitic."

According to this longer and more considered definition, antisemitism, though it may consist of individual hostility to Jews, can take other forms. In particular, it can take the form of *practices, actions,* or *theories.* These are all, as it happens, things characteristic of collective or political life. Political parties— and for that matter, citizens committed to a common liberal political or moral outlook—evidently can and do subscribe to *theories,* engage in *practices,* or put into effect *actions*—all of which, according to the full OED definition, may be (or may not be; it remains to be seen, case by case) *antisemitic.*

In light of the complete OED's more considered definition, then, the simple retort to the BBC's and Baroness Chakrabarti's suggestion, that—in effect— anti*semitism* is one thing and anti-*Zionism* another, would seem to be that what the term *antisemitism* covers in everyday English is not *one thing* but rather *a variety of things.*

v

Of the OED's triad—theory, action, practice—the most important is, plainly, theory. In politics, after all, theory, in the form of an analysis of how society functions, and hence of how it might for the best be changed or conserved, is a major factor both in the direction of day-to-day political practice and in the choice of favored outcomes.

It seems equally clear that antisemitism is in one of its standard forms a theory. It is the theory, or political fantasy, that Jews are conspiratorially organized to exercise secret control over the world in order to pervert the energies of non-Jewish society into the service of sinister Jewish ends. Antisemitism of this type peddles, among many other delusive notions, the idea that "the Jews" are the real agents behind vast and dangerous forces threatening world peace.

In pursuit of that thought, let us return for a moment to Ambassador Bernard's unwise remarks at Barbara Amiel's reception. While the phrase "that shitty little country Israel" might be considered undiplomatic, I do not, myself, find it particularly *antisemitic*. One might be led to say the same thing of England, or even of France, neither of them particularly large tracts of territory by global standards, and both of them well equipped with local habits and customs highly irritating to foreigners, doubtless including some ambassadorial ones.

What I do find antisemitic about Bernard's remarks, and profoundly so, is the *thing he then went on to say*, which practically no contributor to the chorus of indignation at the time seems to have noticed. Once again I cite Gross's report: "'Why,' he asked, 'should the world be in danger of World War Three because of those people?'"

On the sour breath of this question can be detected the authentic odor of antisemitism in the mode of theory, or better, political fantasy. At the point when it was asked, in 2001, there was as compared to many moments in the preceding half-century little need to worry about an outbreak of "World War Three." So far as any dangers to peace existed in embryo, they involved powers far greater than Israel and conflicts for the most part remote from the Middle East: the possibility of a nuclear exchange between India and Pakistan over Kashmir, of a recrudescence of the recent wars in the territories of the former Yugoslavia, the threat posed by a nuclear-armed North Korea, and so on. But to Jacques Chirac's ambassador to London, these perfectly genuine threats to world peace paled into insignificance beside the imaginary one posed by "those people": the Jews.

Antisemitism of this kind, the kind that poses as an explanatory theory about who really possesses the power to determine world events, is among other things, the lethal kind—the kind that accounts for the Holocaust. One does not, after all, set out to extirpate a people from the face of the earth because one happens to dislike or despise them on an individual basis. One takes such a step because one sees them as constituting, collectively, a threat so serious that it can be countered in no other way than by their total removal from the world scene. Hitler and his circle did not set the Final Solution in motion because they viewed Jews individually as a tribe of hucksters and vulgarians given to pushing their noses into social circles in which they neither belonged nor were welcome. They did so because they seriously believed the real enemy of the Third Reich to be not America, or the British Empire, or the Soviet Union but the vast Jewish conspiracy that, they supposed, secretly controlled these—only seemingly independent—powers through its control of world capitalism.

As we shall see, it is nowadays widely believed in mainstream liberal circles that that kind of antisemitism was a delusion peculiar to the German National Socialist Party—one that largely disappeared with its fall and survives today only in a few obscure neo-Nazi groupuscules. Those who believe this believe in consequence that the only kind of antisemitism we need to bother about

nowadays is what I shall call—to distinguish it from the theoretical kind—
"social" antisemitism: the kind that indeed consists, in the words of the BBC's
version of the OED, in "hostility and prejudice directed against Jewish people"
taken individually. It is this that persuades them, as we have just seen, that the
anti-*Zionism* currently so popular on the liberal left of Western politics can have
nothing to do with anti*semitism*.

It is often asserted, both by Jews and by others, that social antisemitism has
greatly declined in Western societies over the seventy years that have elapsed
since the end of World War II. That is broadly—though somewhat patchily—
true. What I shall argue in this book, however, is that social antisemitism is
by no means the only kind we have to worry about today. As I shall show in
what follows—and as many others have noted—antisemitism as a political
fantasy concerning the mysterious, demonic, and conspiratorial power of "the
Jews" to determine world events has enjoyed a political rebirth since September 2001. All that has changed is that "Zionism"—understanding by that term
the State of Israel together with its *Jewish* supporters (though not, as we shall
see, its far more numerous *non-Jewish* ones)—has taken over, in effect, the role
traditionally assigned in antisemitic theory to the world Jewish conspiracy.
In that new form, antisemitism as a delusive political theory is once again as
active in the political life of the West as it has been at any time over the past
two millennia.

Unfortunately, that political rebirth has taken place chiefly on the left. The
left has, of course, its own traditions of antisemitic theorizing. These theories
were specific to the left and in any case not particularly active or influential
during the greater part of the twentieth century. But what the French ambassador's remark exemplifies, as we shall see in what follows, is a straightforward
transfer from one end of the political spectrum to the other of what used to be
the exclusively right-wing fantasy that the Jews are to be blamed for most of
the evils besetting the world and, among other things, for being the main force
pushing the world toward war.

In short, I shall argue in this book that those who presently complain of a
revival of antisemitism in sections of the British Labour Party, in American
academia, and for that matter in the wider drift of liberal opinion in the Western world do not for a moment, *pace* the BBC, suppose that problem to consist
only in the entertaining, by individuals who may or may not happen to be on
the left, of private attitudes of "hostility and prejudice" toward anybody who
happens to be Jewish.

On the contrary, they take it to consist *also*, and most importantly, in a revival, largely on the left this time, of antisemitic *theory*: of belief in the ancient
fantasy of a collective Jewish threat to non-Jewish interests.

In the minds of the believers, that threat consists primarily in the supposed hidden conspiratorial power of the Jewish community to dominate world events; the commitment of the community to the exercise of darkly demonic powers in the service of purely sectional Jewish interests; and more seriously still, in what believers imagine to be the collective recalcitrance of the Jewish community toward the very moral and political values that believers find most reasonable and compelling.

VI

The subject of the book is that fantasy: its extraordinary persistence over the centuries; its remarkable ability to transform and adapt itself, like some strange virus of the mind, in order to speak afresh to the concerns and anxieties generated by new historical circumstances; the functions it serves in non-Jewish culture and political life; and finally the reasons for its extraordinary recrudescence in liberal-left circles in the twenty-first century.

If we are to get clear about the nature of the recurrent delusion that "the Jews are to blame" for what are virtually always in reality failures and deficiencies of the non-Jewish world, we need to examine that delusion's nature and content in relation to other kinds of prejudice, including other forms of antisemitic prejudice. This is the business of part I of this book: "Varieties of Antisemitism."

Chapter 3, "Problems of Definition," addresses these questions directly. But because questions of definition are best approached on the back of concrete and clearly described examples, chapters 1 and 2 introduce the formal arguments of chapter 3 by offering two real-life examples of political discourse dominated by very different versions of the fantasy, the first taken from the Charter of the Islamist organization Hamas, the second drawn from American academic debate about the uniqueness of the Holocaust.

Part II—"Why the Jews?"—addresses the question of why the strange collection of beliefs constituting what I shall here call "political antisemitism" should have attached itself to the Jews, rather than to any other diasporic people.

The first four chapters (6–9) of part III return to the question of whether "anti-Zionism" and BDS are antisemitic movements, and if so, in what ways and to what extent. They argue that the burden of proof should be shifted from questions of motive to questions of fact. If antisemitism can manifest as fraudulent theory, then the issue of antisemitism in political discourse comes to turn, not on the motives or emotional dispositions of those who disseminate it, but on the alignment, or lack of it, between discourse and fact. If the various accounts of the nature and history of Israel on which the two movements depend for their ideological legitimacy are simply and straightforwardly true, then, indeed, we are dealing with legitimate political criticism. If, on the other hand, they systematically defy belief, to the extent of representing merely the results of a sustained attempt to cut, stretch, and deform the facts to fit the procrustean bed provided by the traditional categories of antisemitic theory, then the latter is the enterprise to which they belong, and there's an end of the matter. This therefore becomes the central issue addressed in these chapters.

Those active in anti-Zionism and BDS are, almost without exception, academics, students, or university-educated people employed in politics, the arts, charitable organizations, or public service. If, as I argue, political antisemitism is an inextricable element in both, then that fact alone raises the larger question, already opened in part II, of why, in the history of the West over many centuries, antisemitism of the theoretical, pseudo-explanatory kind has exercised such a hold over the minds of intellectuals. That question occupies chapter 10.

Chapter 10 serves, among other things, to provide, after the long intervening discussion in part III of the history and politics of the Israeli-Palestinian dispute, a bridge between part II and part IV ("Judaism Defaced"), and thus to return the argument of the book from the narrow concerns of chapters 6–9 to the wider issues of the nature and functions of political antisemitism across the centuries broached in chapters 1–5.

Antisemitism as a delusive theory concerning the collective power and guilt of the Jews usually includes one or more items drawn from a small collection of equally ill-founded beliefs concerning the nature of the Jewish religion and outlook itself. The business of part IV (chapters 11–13) is to examine in some detail the three most salient of these beliefs. According to the first of these, Judaism, the supposedly crabbed fabric of grotesque medieval absurdities and rationalizations to which observant Jews are widely supposed to cling with irrational fanaticism, is a primitive religion, a religion of vengeance rather than love, long since superseded by the "new covenant" of Christianity or the rise of Islam. According to the second, the religious and moral law (halakah) at the center of Judaism is a tissue of absurd and arbitrary rules to which the observant Jew abandons his power to direct his own life according to his own reason. The function of these laws is, it is supposed, merely to bind Jews into a closed community in moral isolation from the rest of the human race; a community, whose crabbed "particularism," according to the third of the beliefs to be examined in part IV, stands in stark contrast to the generous universalism characteristic of both Christianity and the moral philosophies of the Enlightenment.

There is much more charged by antisemites to the account of the Jews, but these three historically prominent accusations will do to be going on with. They are childish and, for anyone with the least acquaintance with actual Jewish life and thought, childishly easy to refute. But without a clear sense of what makes them absurd, it is difficult to emancipate the mind fully from the influence of antisemitic fantasy in its role as a body of pseudo-explanatory theory.

Finally, it is a main contention of this book that the fantasy of exceptional Jewish power and guilt, while a good deal more harmful to Jews than to non-Jews, is also harmful to non-Jews. It corrupts institutions and political parties, encourages bad political and administrative decisions, sometimes at the highest level, and generally darkens counsel. These matters are touched on, more cursorily, no doubt, than they deserve, in the three chapters of part V ("Anti-semitism as a Problem for Non-Jews") that conclude the book.

Ten years ago, I published one of the earliest books to appear on "the new antisemitism."[13] In that book, I argued, among other things, that the primary, the originating habitat of antisemitism is not, or not only, the individual mind but in addition and more centrally, the public consciousness manifest in what I there called climates of opinion. The implication of that shift of focus, I suggested, was that we should move from treating antisemitism as a quirk of individual psychopathology to treating it as a type of social or cultural pathology, and therefore as something for which responsibility, and at least the basic tools required for understanding and resistance, may reasonably be regarded as generally shared.

The object of the present book is, in effect, to take up that thought again but this time to develop it a good deal further and more systematically than was possible in 2006. It is not merely that my thoughts on these matters have changed and developed a good deal over the intervening years. Over the past decade, a substantial academic and extra-academic literature of remarkably high quality has grown up around the topic, the work of a formidable collection of academics and media commentators, not to mention major political figures of the calibre of Manuel Valls, until recently prime minister of France, Irwin Cotler, lately attorney general of Canada, or the former Soviet dissident and later Israeli cabinet minister Natan Sharansky in Israel. To this recent body of work, either to borrow or to dissent, I shall be making constant and extensive reference in what follows. If that to any extent proves helpful in making this literature better known to the general reading public, I shall be well content.

NOTES

1. Robert Booth, "Antisemitic Attacks in UK at Highest Levels Ever Recorded," *The Guardian*, Thursday, February 5, 2015, https://www.theguardian.com/world/2015/feb/05/antisemitic-attacks-uk-community-security-trust-britain-jewish-population.
2. Aftab Ali, "Oxford University Labour Club Co-chair, Alex Chalmers, Resigns Amid Anti-Semitism Row," *The Independent*, Wednesday February 17, 2016, https://www.independent.co.uk/student/news/oxford-university-labour-club-co-chair-alex-chalmers-resigns-amid-anti-semitism-row-a6878826.html.
3. Rich 2016, 239.
4. Rossman-Benjamin 2015, 218.
5. Rossman-Benjamin 2015, 230–31.
6. Michael Kaplan, "Attacks on France's Jews Surge amid Concerns of Rising Anti-Semitism in Europe," *International Business Times*, July 13, 2015, https://www.ibtimes.com/attacks-frances-jews-surge-amid-concerns-rising-anti-semitism-europe-2006003.
7. Marcus 2015, 148, citing Wistrich, *Lethal Obsession*, 323–24.
8. Itamar Eichner, "French Immigration to Israel Surges in Summer of 2015," *Ynet News.com*, June 17, 2015, https://www.ynetnews.com/articles/0,7340,L-4669430,00.html.
9. Ilanit Chernick, "German Cardinal: Antisemitism Is an Attack on Us All," *Jerusalem Post*, November 4, 2019, https://www.jpost.com/Diaspora/Antisemitism/German-Cardinal-Antisemitism-is-an-attack-on-us-all-606821.
10. Tom Gross, "A Shitty Little Country," *National Review*, January 10, 2002, http://www.nationalreview.com/comment/comment-gross011002.shtml.
11. By one of my Indiana University Press editors, Katelyn Klingler, to whom my thanks are due.
12. *The Compact Oxford English Dictionary*, 2nd ed. (London: BCA, by arrangement with Oxford University Press, 1994), 60. Complete text reproduced micrographically.
13. Harrison 2006.

PART I

VARIETIES OF ANTISEMITISM

HAMAS ADDRESSES
THE JEWISH QUESTION

To take only the subject of the Jews: it would be difficult to find a form of
bad reasoning about them which has not been heard in conversation or been
admitted to the dignity of print.

—George Eliot, *Impressions of Theophrastus Such*

NAZI ANTISEMITISM IN ARAB DRESS

The prewar German National Socialist Party made itself notorious, as we all
know, for promoting the kind of antisemitism with which this book will be
mainly concerned: the kind that sees a Jewish conspiracy at the root of every
non-Jewish reverse and holds that the inimical influence of the Jews, or Zionism, can only be countered by getting rid of them, or it, altogether.

It is common to hear it said today that that kind of antisemitism died as a
serious political force with the final defeat of Nazism in 1945 and nowadays
survives in the Western world only among tiny neofascist groups with neither
the numerical strength nor the political influence to revive it.

Despite the undeniable frequency and savagery of Islamist assaults on individual Jews and on Jewish institutions and property, one commonly also hears
it said that there is in the Islamic world no equivalent to Western antisemitism,
of this or any other kind. In the same vein, it is widely assumed in the more bien-
pensant liberal and left-leaning sections of the media that Muslim opposition to
Jews, far from being antisemitic, is wholly political in nature, stemming purely
from resentment against the threat to Muslim interests posed by the establishment and continued existence of the State of Israel.

I shall be arguing at length in this book that both these claims are false. Argument starved of concrete instances, however, soon becomes vapid and overformal. It seems appropriate to begin, therefore, with two chapters offering instances of both the survival and the influence today of exactly the kind of antisemitism popularized by the Nazis. The present chapter will contrast the overt antisemitism of an Islamist organization with the covert but not dissimilar implications of a Eurobarometer poll. Chapter 2 will examine an American academic debate ostensibly concerned with the "scholarly" issue of the uniqueness of the Holocaust.

Hamas, the Islamist[1] organization that at present controls Gaza, is a branch of the Muslim Brotherhood (the Society of Muslim Brothers, *Jama'at al-ikhwan al-muslimin*), an organization founded in 1928 in Egypt by the charismatic preacher Hassan al-Banna. A leading scholar of Islamic antisemitism has this to say of the latter: "The significance of this organization goes far beyond Egypt. For today's global Islamist movement the Muslim Brothers are what the Bolsheviks were for the Communist movement of the 1920s: the ideological reference point and organizational core which decisively inspired all the subsequent tendencies and continues to do so to this day."[2]

Hamas currently enjoys support in the West both among elements of the Muslim community and in those parts of the left whose dislike of the United States and Israel allows their sympathizers to overlook the utter moral and intellectual incompatibility of leading elements of Hamas's outlook with values they themselves profess in other contexts. Those elements include religious fanaticism, support of suicide bombing (including the use of children as suicide bombers), rabid misogyny, hatred of gays, and in general, the contempt of Hamas and similar Islamist organizations for everything in which the Western left has traditionally believed, including human rights, democracy, and socialism. Blatant political opportunism of this kind is widely considered to extend at time of writing to the current leadership of the British Labour Party. "In 2009, when Jeremy Corbyn [recently the leader of the Labour Party in parliamentary opposition—BH] invited 'friends' from Hezbollah and Hamas to speak in Parliament, he said of Hamas: 'The idea that an organization that is dedicated towards the good of the Palestinian people, and bringing about long-term peace and social justice and political justice in the whole region should be labelled as a terrorist organization by the British government is really a big, big historical mistake.'"[3]

In addition to its other unsavory characteristics, Hamas has traditionally advertised its commitment to a type of antisemitism differing in no significant respect from that espoused by the Nazis. Article 22 of the movement's 1988 charter, or covenant, contains the following passage:

> For a long time, the enemies [the Jews] have been planning, skilfully [sic] and with precision, for the achievement of what they have attained. They took into consideration the causes affecting the current of events. They strived to amass great and substantive material wealth which they devoted to the realisation of their dream. With their money, they took control of the world media, news agencies, the press, publishing houses, broadcasting stations, and others. With their money they stirred revolutions in various parts of the world with the purpose of achieving their interests and reaping the fruit therein. They were behind the French Revolution, the Communist revolution and most of the revolutions we heard and hear about, here and there. With their money they formed secret societies, such as Freemasons, Rotary Clubs, the Lions and others in different parts of the world for the purpose of sabotaging societies and achieving Zionist interests. With their money they were able to control imperialistic countries and instigate them to colonize many countries in order to enable them to exploit their resources and spread corruption there.
>
> You may speak as much as you want about regional and world wars. They were behind World War I, when they were able to destroy the Islamic Caliphate, making financial gains and controlling resources. They obtained the Balfour Declaration, formed the League of Nations through which they could rule the world. They were behind World War II, through which they made huge financial gains by trading in armaments, and paved the way for the establishment of their state. It was they who instigated the replacement of the League of Nations with the United Nations and the Security Council to enable them to rule the world through them. There is no war going on anywhere, without having their finger in it.[4]

The 1988 Hamas covenant makes a good starting point for our purposes, not least because of the refreshing openness with which it parades views that in the West tend, except in the relative anonymity of the street or social media, to be expressed only in ways designed to disguise their real nature. The above passage from Article 22 serves to illustrate, with bracing directness, the bulk of what we shall find in this book to be leading components of antisemitism considered not as a mere matter of personal contempt or dislike but as a body of pseudo-explanatory theory capable of directing the political outlook of believers.

First, it asserts the Jews to be the deliberate authors of evil on a world scale. In this case, it construes them as the unique and sole cause of *every* war and *every* revolution that has taken place since 1793. Second, it takes Jews to be conspiratorially organized in the pursuit of these appalling aims. It assumes there to exist, in other words, a coherent system of Jewish "control" extending across the whole world. Third, it asserts this system of control to be occult, wrapped in a degree of secrecy sufficient to render it in practice utterly inscrutable and hence inviolable, operating beneath or "behind" all the apparently (but only *apparently*) non-Jewish institutions, great and small, from the media to the United Nations to the Lions Club, that appear (but only *appear*) each to exercise an influence independent of the others over what happens in the world. This extraordinary web of Jewish influence is exercised through the mysterious power of money. This makes it terrifyingly opaque to any form of scrutiny available to non-Jews and thus to any form of control that might be exercised over Jewish power by non-Jewish political institutions. All of these (except, inexplicably, for those constituted by the antisemite and his friends) are anyway themselves totally under the control of the Jews. Fourth, the passage powerfully conveys the impression that *the world would be to all intents and purposes perfect*—no wars, no revolutions, the Islamic Caliphate that expired at the end of World War I still in existence—*if only the Jews did not exist*. That, together with the first three claims, strictly entails the remaining contention of this type of antisemitism: that the only viable way of restoring the world to that happy state is to remove, to eliminate, in the last analysis to exterminate the Jewish people in its entirety.

EUROPEAN ECHOES

The Hamas charter of 1988, echoing in detail as it does the main claims of prewar Nazi antisemitism, might seem so extreme in this respect as to justify the consoling belief that antisemitism—at least *that* kind of antisemitism—is essentially dead in Europe.

That would be a mistake. In 2003, the European Union (EU) commissioned Gallup to carry out a public opinion poll aimed at discovering what European citizens considered to be the main threat to world peace. The results were startling enough to cause concern around the world:

> A Flash Eurobarometer survey carried out in October 2003 for the European Commission in the fifteen member states of the EU found that nearly 60 percent of European citizens believe Israel poses the biggest threat to world peace. Iran is considered the second biggest threat, North Korea the third and the United States the fourth. The survey was carried out by EOS Gallup Europe.

The European Commission survey asked the public in all 15 member states to look at a list of countries and say which they considered potential threats to peace. Israel was selected by a majority in almost all the EU member states, with 74% of Dutch citizens putting the country at the top of the list as a threat to peace and 69% of Austrian citizens. Italy is the only country where opinions are divided with 48% of respondents confirming that they perceive Israel as a threat to peace in the world and 46% of the opposite opinion.

In all member states, with the exception of Italy, the majority of citizens believe Israel presents a threat to peace in the world with "yes" results in the EU as a whole as 59%. Iran, North Korea and America were all selected by 53% as a threat. The survey also listed Iraq, Afghanistan, Saudi Arabia, Libya, Pakistan, China and Russia as potential threats.[5]

What makes these results startling is the extent to which they reveal European opinion to be in accord, in certain important respects, with the outlook so ingenuously presented in Article 22 of the 1988 Hamas covenant. It is not clear from the terms of the Eurobarometer poll whether what was "deemed . . . a threat to world peace" was, in the minds of the assenting 59 percent, the policies of the government of Israel or the very existence of the State of Israel itself. Given the democratic cast of Israeli politics, however, that is perhaps a distinction without a difference.

Either way, to consider "Israel" *the* single most important threat to world peace is, necessarily, to consider it a very considerable force for evil in the world. While some Jews on the left share this view, a large number of Jews do not. It is in any case a commonly held view that most, if not all, Jews support Israel. It follows that it is a very short step from considering Israel to be the main threat to world peace to regarding Jews in general as supporters of evil—or at the very least, as people who place Jewish interests above the interests of humankind at large.

It follows that for those Europeans who view Israel as the chief threat to world peace, the general support for Israel manifested by a number of Western nations, with the United States at their head, cannot but seem intrinsically puzzling. The puzzle would be easily solved if one could regard the United States as acting in this respect not in the interests of its non-Jewish citizens but at the behest of an absurdly minuscule but nevertheless wealthy and entrenched Jewish lobby, conspiratorially active behind the scenes of conventional politics. And, indeed, suggestions of this kind have been, and still are, widely promoted by at least notionally respectable voices in the West.[6] For those with any clear sense of the evils of war, and the importance of avoiding it, the conclusion to be drawn from these considerations can only be the one drawn by the authors of the Hamas covenant—and for that matter, as we noted in the introduction by a senior French diplomat—that the world would be a much better, because a much safer, place if only the Jews and their wretched national state did not exist. The eliminationist consequences of this conclusion are too volcanic in their implications to be explicitly stated or examined in the West—at present. Nevertheless, they hang in the air.

Setting the 2003 Eurobarometer poll and Article 22 of the 1988 Hamas charter alongside each other reveals a further characteristic of antisemitism, shared by all versions of it in all ages. The beliefs on which it rests and in which it trades are one and all delusive. Not only that, they are delusive in the more radical of two senses attaching to that term. Someone may be deluded in the sense that he or she believes something that might have been true but happens not to be true. Thus, I may deludedly believe that my glasses are at my bedside. And indeed they might well have been, although in fact they are on the kitchen table, where I have quite forgotten having left them earlier in the day. More seriously, someone may be deluded in the second of my two senses, in that he or she believes something that could not possibly be the case. This is the condition of those who believe the world to be flat or hollow, either possibility being inconsistent with elementary and exhaustively confirmed laws of physics. The philosopher J. L. Austin caught the distinction between the two types of delusion in a happy phrase when he spoke of its being "plain boring" to hear, from certain philosophers, "the constant repetition of things that are not true, and sometimes not even faintly sensible."[7] The beliefs cherished by antisemites, like those cherished by flat-earthers and hollow-earthers, fall characteristically into the second category—that of the not only false but also "not even faintly sensible."

A case in point is that of the celebrated blood libel, the medieval belief that Jews, as a matter of religious duty, are constrained to abduct and kill gentile children in order to add their blood to the dough of the Passover matzo (accusations of this kind were brought in law as late as 1911).[8] While an individual Jewish lunatic, or for that matter a gentile one, might do such a thing, it is not something that Jews might do as a matter of religious duty, for the simple reason that the consumption of blood, from any source and in any form, is expressly forbidden to observant Jews by the laws of kashruth (the dietary laws). Explaining the disappearance of a gentile child by suggesting that Jews might have killed the child in order to mix its blood with the Passover matzo is thus on a par with explaining the disappearance of a cow by suggesting that Hindus might have slaughtered it in order to make a religious offering of roast beef in the temple. These are not things that "might have happened, though thank goodness they have not." The belief that either even *might have* occurred is a delusion in the second of the above two senses: a mere confusion of thought, a maggot of the mind.

The same is true of the central contention of Article 22 of the Hamas charter, that the Jews control every apparently non-Jewish institution in the world, from the United Nations to the Rotary Club, and do so in the service of an organized pursuit of world domination. One might argue against these concerns that the Jews, of all people, given their general character, hardly seem best placed to conduct a world conspiracy of the kind envisaged. For one thing, such a project would require, on the part of those conducting it, an unusual degree of willingness to subordinate rationally grounded dissent to the demands of political unity, and such willingness is not something that, with the best will in the world, one readily associates with Jews. "Argument is the life of Judaism," say the rabbis, to which the Jewish man in the street notoriously responds, spreading his hands, "Two Jews, three opinions." But to argue in that way would be tacitly to grant to the authors of Article 22 that if they are deluded, it is only in the first sense: to grant, in other words that it remains a real possibility, though one happily unrealized on grounds of incapacity, that the Jews *might* be in secret control of the world. But why should anyone grant the reality of such a possibility when plainly it savors of lunacy! The Jews are, indeed, not in control of the world but *that* they are not is not a mere consequence of their *not being up to the job*. Rather, it is a consequence of the evident fact that nobody, no nation, no state, no movement—not the United States, not international socialism, nor anybody else—*could* conceivably be up to such a job. Humanity is manifestly too diverse, economically, politically, socially, and ideologically, for any unified control of it to be feasible. In even envisaging such a possibility, we, like the authors of Article 22, have strayed into cloud cuckoo land.

What about the famous Eurobarometer poll that created such a stir in the world press in 2003? Might the majorities that fingered Israel as the greatest threat to peace in the world have been, and be, then and now, right about that?

One needs for a start to ask what the vague phrase "threat to peace in the world" is supposed to mean. Are we talking about peace in the Middle East, or are we speculating about World War III?

Let us begin with peace in the region. In fact, the Middle East has been convulsed by an endless series of wars since 1948. Some of these have involved Israel, but these, as I will argue in chapters 7 and 8, have been brief, minor, and from Israel's standpoint, overwhelmingly defensive in character. The others, all very much more enduring and far more serious both in terms of loss of life and destruction of property and infrastructure—from the Iran-Iraq War of 1980, which lasted eight years and devastated both countries, to the more recent but equally enduring and even more destructive wars in Iraq, Syria, and Yemen—have arisen entirely out of conflict between the major Muslim regional powers, motivated in part by rival territorial claims and in part by the religious conflict between Sunni and Shi'a Islam, and having in either case virtually nothing to do with Israel.

Israel, in short, has hardly shown itself in practice to constitute even *a* major, let alone *the* major, threat to peace in the region. And this is hardly to be wondered at, given that the main object of the State of Israel since its foundation has been to provide a safe space within stable frontiers for Jews (not to mention several other groups recently subject to abuse of quasi-genocidal proportions under neighboring regimes) to inhabit in freedom from persecution. This has been manifest in the readiness of Israel to exchange land for peace—by the withdrawal from the Sinai Peninsula after the 1967 war, in the unilateral withdrawal from the Gaza Strip under Ariel Sharon, and in the readiness of Israeli politicians to engage in repeated negotiations aiming at the creation of a Palestinian state in the West Bank. A state with as its main aim security within *any* borders capable of securing an agreed and enforceable peace can hardly be said intelligibly to "threaten peace" with its neighbors—unless of course its neighbors would wish, if they could, to destroy it. The latter condition certainly holds true in Israel's case; however, that can scarcely justify blaming *Israel* for any resulting breaches of the peace.

Leaving aside war and peace in the region, then, are there any grounds for crediting the existence of a Jewish state in Israel with the potential to set off World War III?

Serious debate on that question has mainly concerned Israel's nuclear options. Israel is widely believed to have possessed an effective nuclear deterrent since just before the 1967 war. Israeli government policy, however, has always been to neither confirm nor deny that it possesses nuclear weapons, although it does affirm that it will never be the first to use them. The most serious and widely believed book on the issue is Avner Cohen's 1998 *Israel and the Bomb*.[9] Cohen, who has written widely on a range of moral and political issues concerning nuclear deterrence and proliferation, argues against Israel's policy of secrecy concerning its nuclear abilities, on the grounds that it is undemocratic, violates the public's right to know, undermines the principle of public accountability, and hinders the effort to achieve internationally recognized and accepted norms for the control of nuclear weapons. However, even were one to admit the force of these charges, they by no means suffice to identify Israel's possession of nuclear weapons as any more likely to lead to World War III than the possession of nuclear weapons by other countries, such as Russia, the

United States, Britain, France, China, India, Pakistan, and North Korea—the last three of which are not even signatories to the Non-Proliferation Treaty of 1968–70.

That is not, perhaps, the end of the matter. In 1991, the celebrated Washington-based investigative journalist Seymour M. Hersh published a book called *The Samson Option*, largely based on information supplied by Ari Ben-Menashe, a former Israeli government employee who claimed to have worked for Israeli intelligence.[10] It explores the idea that Israel might be ready and willing to launch a devastating nuclear strike on an enemy state, possibly Iran, in the event of its suffering an attack so great as to threaten its survival as a Jewish state. The thought expressed in the book's title is that Israel would in this respect be harking back to the celebration, in the Book of Judges, of Samson's final act of pulling down the pillars of the temple of Dagon, crushing both himself and all the Philistines.

In 2011, the same idea was explored again by the American journalist Ron Rosenbaum in a book titled *How the End Begins: The Road to a Nuclear World War III*.[11] The tone and the quality of Rosenbaum's reasoning can be gauged by the following extract: "A Samson option is made possible by the fact that even if Israel has been obliterated, it can be sure that its dolphin-class nuclear submarines cruising the Red Sea, the Indian Ocean, and the Persian Gulf, at depths impervious to detection, can carry out a genocidal-scale retaliation virtually anywhere in the world.... [The policy] presupposes a rage on the part of post-second Holocaust survivors in possession of nuclear weapons determined to reduce the entire temple of civilisation to ashes for having complacently allowed two Holocausts to be inflicted on our people."[12]

The second half of this passage argues that the policy outlined in the first "presupposes" a willingness to "reduce the entire temple of civilization to ashes," that in turn can only issue from a rage so great as to be peculiar to those who have survived a Holocaust and hence to be something that only a Jew could possibly feel. This, of course, echoes several themes of antisemitism as a pseudo-explanatory theory: that the Jews are a uniquely vengeful people, that Jews care nothing for the sufferings of non-Jews, and so on.

But this is absurd, because the policy complained of has nothing to do with rage of any kind, let alone the rage, if such there be, peculiar to Holocaust survivors. The possession of some means of ensuring the possibility of delivering a devastating blow to a nuclear aggressor *even after* a first strike by that aggressor is essential to the policy of mutual assured deterrence, which is why nuclear powers, such as the United States, Britain, France, and Russia, take steps, including the deployment of nuclear-armed submarines, to secure the possibility of such a blow independently of the continued territorial integrity of the nation wielding it. That is just a feature of where we sit in the modern world. If nuclear deterrence is to work, that is how it must be organized. To give a spuriously Jewish tinge to the policy by labeling it a "Samson option" is to employ the most debased kind of political rhetoric to mislead those whose critical powers lag behind their credulity.

Where does that leave Israel's putative ability to start a World War III, assuming that to be the issue on which the 2003 Eurobarometer poll was endeavoring to test opinion? It leaves it nowhere for a very simple reason. A World War is by definition a war between major powers. Israel, like all the other actors in the continuing drama of Middle Eastern politics, is a very minor power indeed. How, after all, could a nation of seven million, occupying a tiny scrap of land at the far end of the Mediterranean, pose at any time even *a* threat, let alone *the main threat* to world peace, if by that phrase one means to invoke the possibility of a World War III? Posing such threats is the privilege of major players in the game of world politics. One needs to be Russia, or China, or the United States to pose *in those terms* a "threat to world peace." The minnows of the world order—Denmark, Switzerland, the Netherlands, Israel—while they may be in a position to defend themselves against aggression (as Switzerland and Israel, for example, certainly are) are not in any kind of position to pose a threat to anyone: they simply lack the firepower (and if it comes to that, the resources of cannon fodder) available to more populous nations. The nations of the Middle East have in any case been for two centuries, and are at present, subject to extensive interference by major powers in their tormented affairs. That interference has caused untold suffering to the inhabitants of the region. But it has not led to any major conflict between the major powers concerned—at present the United States and Russia—and shows no sign of doing so.

Once again, in short, we are dealing with a set of implicitly antisemitic claims based, as such claims always appear to be, not merely on factual error but on a rooted inability to distinguish between what is factually possible and what Austin called "not even faintly sensible." Such claims deal in dreamwork: more specifically, in the dream that the wounds of an imperfect world might suddenly and magically be comprehensively healed, *if only the Jews could somehow be got rid of.*

A QUALIFIED RECANTATION

In 2017, Hamas issued a new charter[13] that contains nothing—or almost nothing—corresponding to Article 22 of the 1988 charter. This matters little for the concerns of the present chapter, since antisemitic theorizing along much the same lines, as we know from the work of Matthias Küntzel and others able to read Arabic- and Farsi-language sources, is nowadays entirely commonplace throughout the Middle East. I chose Article 28 of the 1988 Charter for discussion merely because it offers a convenient English-language source for such thinking. It is interesting, however, that what has replaced it in the 2017 charter corresponds closely to the current discourse of Western "anti-Zionism." Central to that discourse, as we saw in the introduction, is the idea that hatred of Zionism and Zionists can be sharply distinguished from hatred of Jews and that only the latter constitutes "antisemitism." Article 16 of the new charter reads: "Hamas affirms that its conflict is with the Zionist project not with the Jews because of their religion. Hamas does not wage a struggle against the Jews because they are Jewish but wages a struggle against the Zionists who occupy Palestine. Yet, it is the Zionists who constantly identify Judaism and the Jews with their own colonial project and illegal entity."

The last sentence attempts to shift the blame for any idea that the Jews are responsible for the existence of Israel to the Zionists themselves. The suggestion here is that *if* there are Jews who accept in its entirety Hamas's analysis of the origins and nature of Israel and are prepared to agree inter alia that "the Zionist project is a racist, aggressive, colonial and expansionist project based in seizing the properties of others" (Article 14), *then* Hamas has no quarrel with *those Jews*. This stance, as we shall see later, has been characteristic of Western antisemitism since at least the French Revolution and remains popular on the left today. However, it is clearly an assertion of Jew hatred, not a renunciation of it.

It is not the case, anyway, that the vision of the Jews as secretly in charge of the world, and as capable of employing vast hidden powers to subvert non-Jewish interests, so clearly set out in the 1988 charter, has been entirely expunged from the 2017 version. In Article 15, we learn that "the Zionist project" is not confined to the setting-up of a Jewish state in Palestine but threatens the peace and security, not only of the entire Muslim world but also that of humanity in general. The article reads: "The Zionist project does not target the Palestinian people alone; it is the enemy of the Arab and Islamic Ummah posing a grave threat to its security and interests. It is also hostile to the Ummah's aspirations for unity, renaissance and liberation and has been the major source of its troubles. The Zionist project also poses a danger to international security and peace and to mankind and its interests and stability."

The parallels between this and Article 28 of the 1988 version make it tempting to suggest that "the Zionist project" is here merely functioning as politically correct code for "the Jews." That impression is confirmed when one learns from Article 17 of the 2017 version, ostensibly containing a further attempt to distance Hamas from the antisemitism so roundly embraced in the 1988 charter, that the Zionist project is able to summon the Western powers to its assistance. "Hamas is of the view that the Jewish problem, anti-Semitism and the persecution of the Jews are phenomena fundamentally linked to European history and not to the history of the Arabs and the Muslims or to their heritage. The Zionist movement, which was able with the help of Western powers to occupy Palestine, is the most dangerous form of settlement occupation, which has already disappeared from much of the world and must disappear from Palestine."

The 2017 charter does not, as the 1988 version did, call for the slaughter of Jews wherever they live in the world. However, the difficulty of establishing who is a Zionist (Any Jew who supports Israel? Any non-Jew who supports Israel?) makes it difficult to establish precisely who remains outside the range of the license to kill claimed in Article 25 of the 2017 charter: "Resisting the occupation with all means and methods is a legitimate right guaranteed by divine laws and by international norms and laws. At the heart of these lies armed resistance, which is regarded as the strategic choice for protecting the principles and the rights of the Palestinian people."

"All means and methods" have, as actually implemented, included successful attempts on civilian lives by means ranging from rocket attacks from the Gaza zone, suicide bombings, the use of cars and lorries to run down pedestrians in the street, casual stabbings, and more. All of these, according to "international laws and norms," constitute war crimes. However, the 2017 charter offers no prospect of these ending at any point short of the complete destruction of Israel "from the river to the sea." International attempts to resolve the crisis have of course since 1948 involved the creation of a Palestinian state coexisting with Israel. Hamas, though in the 2017 charter it professes itself prepared to accept such a state—described in Article 20 in terms that could hardly survive any actual negotiation—makes it clear that it would regard such a development not as a solution but at most as a halfway house to the total destruction of Israel.

> Hamas believes that no part of the land of Palestine shall be compromised or conceded, irrespective of the causes, the circumstances and the pressures and no matter how long the occupation lasts. Hamas rejects any alternative to the full and complete liberation of Palestine, from the river to the sea. However, without compromising its rejection of the Zionist entity and without relinquishing any Palestinian rights, Hamas considers the establishment

of a fully sovereign and independent Palestinian state, with Jerusalem as its capital along the lines of the 4th of June 1967, with the return of the refugees and the displaced to their homes from which they were expelled, to be a formula of national consensus.

Reading through this new charter, it is difficult not to agree with "Robert F.," who posted the following comment on the Middleeasteye.net website:

I suppose the major difference between this Hamas Charter and the previous one is that the previous one called for the slaughter of the Jews no matter where they live, whether in Israel or anywhere else in the world. It was profoundly anti-Semitic. It was profoundly Nazi.

The present new Hamas Charter does not contain this language. But the omission is in the interest of legitimating themselves in the world of diplomacy. Nothing has changed. They still educate their children to hate and murder Jews. However, Hamas has learned a valuable lesson from the Europeans. If you want to hate Jews, call them "Zionists" rather than Jews and it becomes politically correct in some circles.

We shall have occasion in later chapters to reflect at length on the pros and cons of his concluding remarks.

NOTES

1. I really do mean "Islamist" and not "Islamic." Those who think that to be a Muslim is necessarily to be infected with Jew hatred would do well to spend a little time in the company of websites such as http://arabsforisrael.blogspot.co.uk. A Google search for "Muslim/Arab friends of Israel" will turn up many more such sites representing both groups and individuals.

2. Küntzel 2007, 7–8.

3. Rich 2016, 174–75.

4. Transcribed from the library of documents in law, history, and diplomacy maintained by Avalon Project of the Yale Law School and available at their website: http://avalon.law.yale.edu/20th_century/hamas.asp.

5. Arjan El Fassed, "EU Poll: 'Israel Poses Biggest Threat to World Peace,'" *Electronic Intifada*, November 3, 2003, https://electronicintifada.net/content/eu-poll-israel-poses-biggest-threat-world-peace/4860.

6. See, for instance, John J. Mearsheimer and Stephen M. Walt, *The Israel Lobby and U.S. Foreign Policy* (New York: Farrar, Straus and Giroux, 2008).

7. Austin 1962, 5.

8. For an excellent recent study of the long history of the blood libel, see Rose 2015.

9. Cohen 1998.
10. Hersh 1991.
11. Rosenbaum 2011.
12. Rosenbaum 2011, 141–42.
13. The 2017 version of the charter is available in full at the website of Middle East Eye: http://www.middleeasteye.net/news/hamas-charter-1637794876.

TWO

—⟶⟶—

"PROFITING" FROM THE HOLOCAUST

There is [in Holocaust Studies] a distinct danger of escaping from the
reality of the Nazi regime and its consequences into a nebulous general
humanism, where all persecutions become holocausts, and where a general
and meaningless condemnation of evil helps to establish a curtain between
oneself and the real world. This escapism must of course be fought.

— Yehuda Bauer, *The Holocaust in Historical Perspective*

PRELIMINARIES

My second example of antisemitism operating as a type of pseudo-explanatory
political fantasy moves from European polls and Islamist rodomontade to the
groves of American academe. It concerns the long-running dispute over the
question of whether the Holocaust was a "unique" event. This has divided academic opinion since roughly the start of the 1990s. An excellent account that
surveys its various stages and its main contributors can be found in an out-
standing new book by Gavriel Rosenfeld.[1] My concern in this chapter will not
be to contribute to this debate but rather to question the intellectual and moral
solidity of some of the assumptions underlying it.

Several features of the uniqueness debate mark it out from the general run of
academic or scholarly controversies. There is, for instance, the unusual degree
of acrimony with which it has frequently been conducted. Another curious

---

An earlier and rather different version of this chapter appears under the title "The Uniqueness
Debate Revisited" in A. H. Rosenfeld 2015.

feature of the debate is its power to unite academic solemnity at one extreme with political scurrility at the other. The academic end of this spectrum of opinion has for almost twenty years found rich expression in Alan S. Rosenbaum's voluminous anthology, *Is the Holocaust Unique? Perspectives in Comparative Genocide*, which has now run into three editions, the first in 1996, the most recent in 2009.[2] The other, scurrilous extreme can be encountered in the spatter of openly antisemitic and Holocaust-denying websites that can be located by typing the words *Was the Holocaust Unique?* into a search engine.

As putatively academic debates go, this one has proven unusually free, even in the present age of "culture wars," from the disinterested objectivity popularly associated with the academy. On the contrary, it has been remarkable from the outset for the incessant and resolute grinding of political axes that has accompanied its various phases. In addition, it has been widely characterized, by journalistic and academic observers alike, as a dialogue of the deaf, or more accurately a collection of such dialogues, in which participants characteristically argue, not so much against one another, as past one another.

QUESTIONS OF MEANING

At its most abstract level, the dispute turns on the question of whether the terms *Holocaust* and *genocide* are general terms like *horse* or proper names like *Aristotle* or *Bismarck*: whether, in short, given the nature of the thing named, there can be in principle more than one such thing.

When such abstruse philosophical issues become the focus of high emotions and pitched battles among nonphilosophers, there is generally a reason. In this case, the reason is itself philosophical. One of my teachers at the University of Michigan in the late 1950s was the late C. L. Stevenson. Stevenson was, and remains, famous for his book *Ethics and Language*, a monument of American Pragmatism that is still read, though not as widely as it ought to be. Chapter 9 concerns what he calls persuasive definitions. For Stevenson, the meaning of a moral term—for example, *freedom*—has two components. First, there is a factual description, a statement of what constitutes a free society. Then, second, there is the emotional aura that surrounds the word; in the case of *murder*, say, a negative, disapproving one; in the case of *freedom*, a positive, approving one.

Stevenson takes from Hume the thought that these two components of meaning can be made, on occasion, to shift independently of each other. A term like *freedom* or *murder* thus becomes an instrument of political or moral persuasion to the extent that one can get people to accept a shift in the descriptive meaning of the term, while leaving its emotional aura unchanged. If one can persuade people, for instance, that abortion counts descriptively as murder, then the bleakly negative emotional aura surrounding the term *murder* can be successfully displaced onto the term *abortion*. If one can persuade people to accept that part of being free, descriptively speaking, is to possess a legally enforceable right to demand that the state provide one with medical care, then with luck, the warm emotional aura surrounding the term *freedom* can be displaced onto the idea of state provision of medical care. As Stevenson puts it, "our language abounds with words which, like 'culture,' have both a vague descriptive meaning and a rich emotive meaning. The descriptive meaning of them all is subject to constant redefinition. The words are prizes which each man seeks to bestow on the qualities of his own choice."[3]

THE CONTESTED POSITIONS

An understanding of Stevenson's distinction, it seems to me, is essential to making sense of the uniqueness debate. The debate exists only because the intense emotive auras surrounding the words *Holocaust* and *genocide* have become covetable enough for the words themselves to become "prizes" in exactly the sense that Stevenson here exposes.[4] What turns a word into a prize for political debate, he suggests, are the evaluative and associative structures that constitute its "emotive meaning." In the case of *Holocaust* and *genocide*, these include horror and revulsion against the perpetrators, on the one hand, and on the other, sympathy and fellow feeling for the victims.

These, of course, are responses of a kind that all of us would wish acts of mass murder to evoke. And recent history offers many episodes of mass murder, including many felt, by the communities involved, to be inadequately recognized or condemned. This has led some to seek redress for that situation in what Charles Stevenson would have called a persuasive redefinition of the terms *Holocaust* and *genocide*.

If—such people feel—the *descriptive* meaning of those terms could only be redefined in such a way as to make them capture descriptively *any* episode of mass killing, then the *emotive* meaning of the words, the responses of pity and horror indelibly associated with them, would transfer over to a multitude of eminently deserving cases in exactly the manner described by Stevenson.

The trouble, from the point of view of those who think like this, is that both *Holocaust* and *genocide* are uniquely linked in their origins with one specific episode of mass murder. And that episode has generally been supposed to stand in a unique relationship to one particular people—namely, the Jews.

For the emotive connotations of the terms to transfer smoothly to other
episodes of mass murder involving other, non-Jewish groups, that link must be
broken. To a degree, it has been broken in the case of the term *genocide*. Significant ambiguities attend the word *genocide*, as they do all the contested terms in
the uniqueness debate. It remains contestable, for instance, whether for an act
of genocide to have occurred the people in question must have undergone total
extermination or "merely" have endured persecution *aiming* at total extermination, or at the very least, at extensive loss of life. Equally, people disagree over
whether it can be appropriate to speak of "cultural genocide," where the people
of a nation, or some of them, remain extant but where everything that gave their
nation its original character, as a special human group, has been systematically extirpated. But on any of these readings of the term, historical instances
both Jewish and non-Jewish can be found. Among cases of more or less total
extermination (by systematic hunting among other things), one might cite
the Tasmanian and Western Australian aboriginals. As survivors of cultural
genocide, one might cite the Inca or the inhabitants of a few mountain villages
in Portugal of whom I once read, remnants of campaigns of persecution and
forced conversion of Jews in earlier centuries, who know that they once were,
or were descended from, Jews, but know nothing of Jewish religion or culture.

Genocide, then, has become, for better or worse, a general term. There can
be—have been—genocides other than the Holocaust. The term *Holocaust*, on
the other hand, remains obstinately possessed, in common usage, of the logical
characteristics of a proper name. A proper name, such as *Bismarck* or *Gandhi*,
names a single individual; in the case of those names, an individual person; in
the case of the term *Holocaust*, an individual act of mass murder—namely, the
Nazi destruction of the bulk of European Jewry between 1933 and 1945.

The uniqueness controversy has concerned, for the most part, the issue of
whether that link—the link between the term *Holocaust* and a specific act of
mass murder—can and should also be broken. Some—David E. Stannard,
Ward Churchill, Norman Finkelstein, the late Tony Judt in some of his writings, and many others—consider that there is nothing about the murderous
events commonly denominated by the term *Holocaust* that links those events
specifically to the *Jewishness* of their Jewish victims. According to such views,
Holocaust becomes to all intents and purposes a synonym for *genocide* and
shares all the ambiguities as well as the resulting subordination to a multitude
of political uses that have come to characterize the latter term.

The thought is that what happened to the Jewish victims of the Nazis has also
happened to large numbers of non-Jewish victims, whose sufferings, it is then
alleged, are diminished and obscured by the concentration in commemorative

activities, including museums and educational programs, on the sufferings of the Jews. Should we not, such reasoners suggest, universalize our conception of the Holocaust by recognizing that what made it a *crime against humanity* was that its victims, irrespective of whether they were Jews or gentile Germans, Poles, or Soviet prisoners of war, were *human beings*? And does not that eminently humane and reasonable shift of perspective, they conclude, commit one to seeing the Holocaust not as something confined to World War II or to Europe but as a type of human aberration that has had, and continues to have, many exemplars, from the starvation in the Ukraine brought about by Stalin's policy of forced collectivization in the 1930s, to the Cambodian massacres under Pol Pot, or to Srebrenica, or for that matter, to the history of Palestine since 1948?

Against this way of reconceiving the Holocaust, a broad spectrum of scholars, whose Jewish representatives include Elie Wiesel, Yehuda Bauer, Emil Fackenheim, Lucy Dawidowicz, Steven Katz, Deborah Lipstadt, Daniel Goldhagen, and latterly Alvin Rosenfeld,[5] have in general retorted that one cannot universalize the Holocaust without de-Judaizing it in ways utterly false to the historical record. The basic thrust of their objections is that to treat the Holocaust as a crime against humanity rather than against the Jews is not only to render its nature and origins impossible to understand, except in terms of some vague and explanatorily vacuous notion of evil or "the darkness of the human heart." It is to erase Jews and Jewishness from the historical record in a manner entirely agreeable to, and indeed reminiscent of, the ideology of National Socialism.

THE JEWS AS PUTATIVELY JEALOUS "PROPRIETORS" OF THE HOLOCAUST

Given the seemingly progressive and humanitarian note characteristically struck by opponents of the uniqueness claim, such as Native American historians David E. Stannard or Ward Churchill, it might appear surprising that their views should attract the promoters of openly antisemitic, revisionist, and white supremacist websites.[6] Codoh.com, for example, the website of a Holocaust-denial group calling itself the Committee for Open Debate on the Holocaust, currently carries a 1996 essay by Stannard, titled "The Dangers of Calling the Holocaust Unique," despite the fact that in that piece Stannard expressly dissociates himself at the outset from both Holocaust denial and antisemitism.

What strikes one about these caveats on Stannard's part, however, is that the internal logic of the enterprise of universalizing—and thus necessarily de-Judaizing—the Holocaust itself works to defeat any such attempt at dissociation. Arguments involving what Stevenson called persuasive definition are, by

their nature, arguments about *ownership*, even though the asset whose ownership they contest is no more than a word—or to be more accurate, the emotional connotations of a word. From the perspective of those questioning the
singularity of the Holocaust—the perspective, that is to say, of the putatively
disinherited—the attempt to defend the singularity of the Holocaust, especially when conducted by Jewish writers, can hardly be perceived otherwise
than as an attempt to assert a *proprietary* claim to the word and its emotional
connotations and thus as an attempt to exclude other abused groups from enjoyment of any benefit that might accrue to them in consequence of the horror
and sympathy widely evoked by the very word *Holocaust*.

Furthermore, once the notion of *ownership* has been introduced into the
debate—as it must be if the debate is to get off the ground at all—it can hardly
fail to evoke by association a familiar range of antisemitic stereotypes. There
is, for a start, that of the obstinately "particularist" Jew with no interest in anybody's suffering but his own, attached passionately to his own community but
chillingly unresponsive to wider humanitarian causes. Then, more darkly, there
is the stereotype of the Jew as owner of assets that should not by rights belong
to him at all; of the Jew who uses his legendary business abilities in underhand
ways that baffle the simple blond gentile to acquire suspiciously vast assets of
just the kind to afford him the means of exercising secret and illegitimate kinds
of control over non-Jews. More darkly still, there is the stereotype of the Jew
who controls Hollywood or controls Wall Street—and who also, it now appears,
"controls" the history of World War II. And finally—one could extend the list
further, but an end must be made somewhere—there is the stereotype of the
Jew who, whenever anyone attempts to reclaim his ill-gotten assets in order
to put them at the service of a wider suffering humanity, uses the craven and
dishonest cry of antisemitism to smear and obscure the sterling nobility of his
opponents' motives.

These stereotypes, and others related to them, have no particular political
constituency. Historically important as they are, they can equally be found
nowadays, figuring, though usually in ways less overtly expressed, as much in
the public discourse of far-left political groupings as in that of movements on
the far right.[7] And as we are about to see, they can also be found in putatively
academic writing.

THE POLITICS OF MISPLACED UNIVERSALISM

It will be useful in further developing that last claim to examine in some detail
a specific contribution to the uniqueness debate—namely, David E. Stannard's

lengthy closing contribution to the Rosenbaum volume,[8] "Uniqueness as Denial: The Politics of Genocide Scholarship."[9]

First, though, a further question of definition needs to be got out of the way.
It is customary in academic controversy for all parties to agree at the outset on
common definitions of the main terms that define the debate if for no other
reason than to ensure that they are at least arguing about the same things. One
of the oddest things about the uniqueness debate is the cheerful indifference
shown by most of its participants to this elementary requirement. The terms
Holocaust and *genocide*, for instance, appear to take on whatever meaning happens to suit the changing dialectical needs of each participant, as the moving
sands of debate shift under him or her.

Such ambiguities extend to the term *unique* itself, where they are even less
helpful to the cause of rational debate. Wittgenstein, criticizing the philosophical use of the term *simple* to characterize a supposed class of metaphysical
entities, pointed out that the term means little until we specify what kind of
simplicity we have in mind. The term *unique* behaves in much the same way: in
any given context, that is to say, the question "Is X unique?" remains unanswer-
able, even in principle, until we answer the further question, "In what respect?"
Moby-Dick, for instance, may be unique in respect of being a novel about a
whaling skipper called Ahab but is not unique in respect of being a novel by
Melville.

It matters, therefore, whether the parties to the uniqueness debate specify *in
the same way* the respect in which uniqueness is to be attributed to, or denied of,
the Holocaust. And the briefest acquaintance with the main documents in the
debate is sufficient to reveal that they do not. The specifically Jewish defenders
of the uniqueness claim, singled out for attack by Stannard, with one accord
take the Holocaust to have been unique *in respect of the criteria used to select its
victims for destruction*. A typical statement of this kind occurs in Elie Wiesel's
response to the presentation of the Congressional Gold Medal, on April 19,
1985: "I have learned that the Holocaust was a uniquely Jewish event, albeit with
universal implications. Not all victims were Jews, but all Jews were victims."
Elsewhere Wiesel expands on this judgment as follows: "I believe the Holocaust was a unique event. For the very first time in history . . . a Jew was
condemned to die not because of what beliefs he held . . . but because of who
he was. For the very first time, a birth certificate became a death certificate."[10]

For Yehuda Bauer, again what made the Holocaust a "totally new reality"
was "the unique quality *of Nazi Jew-hatred*": "The *unique quality of Nazi Jew-
hatred* was something so surprising, so outside of the experience of the civilized world, that the Jewish leadership, as well as the Jewish people, could not

comprehend it.... The post-Holocaust generation has difficulty understanding this basic psychological barrier to action on the part of Jews—and non-Jews— during the Nazi period. We already know what happened, they, who lived at that time, did not. For them it was *a totally new reality* that was unfolding before their shocked eyes and paralysed minds."[11] Stannard, on the other hand, takes what is fundamentally at issue in the uniqueness debate to be, as he puts it, "the uniqueness *of Jewish suffering.*"[12] For Stannard, the claim that the Holocaust was unique equates, that is to say, with the claim that the Holocaust was unique *in respect of the quantity of suffering experienced by its Jewish victims;* a quantity of suffering that he alleges to be considered, not merely by his selected Jewish opponents, but by a wide spectrum of non-Jewish opinion, to have been grossly in excess of the quantity of suffering experienced by *any* other people, in *any* other of the numerous episodes of mass murder that have occurred in world history.

Stannard in effect takes this extraordinary proposition to be at present accepted, and accepted as undeniable, moreover, by the bulk of informed opinion. Commenting on the fact that more is heard of the Holocaust than of the far more prolonged and numerically destructive processes of near-extermination that overtook the native peoples of the Americas following the arrival of the Europeans, and having ironically discounted the obvious explanation, that the victims of the latter destruction were nonwhite, he adds:

> For those who might find such overt racial distinctions distasteful and preferably avoided, however, a more "reasonable" explanation exists for the grossly differential responses that are so commonplace regarding the American and the Nazi Holocausts. This explanation simply denies that there is any comparability between the Nazi violence against the Jews and the Euro-American violence against the Western Hemisphere's native peoples. *In fact, in most quarters it is held as beyond dispute that the attempted destruction of the Jews in Nazi-controlled Europe was unique, unprecedented and categorically incommensurable—not only with the torment endured by the indigenous peoples of North and South America, but also with the sufferings of any people at any time in any place during the entire history of humanity.*[13]

This claim for the uniqueness of the Holocaust does not, on the face of it, appear to be the claim that Wiesel, Bauer, Lipstadt, and other Jewish defenders of the uniqueness of the Holocaust wish to advance. *Their* claim is merely that the Holocaust has a Jewish dimension that is essential to understanding it and that is lost sight of when one universalizes and hence de-Judaizes the word *Holocaust.* There is no inconsistency between claiming that and granting that other, even vaster episodes of mass murder have killed more people. So Stannard's proposed counterclaim is, it would seem, not a *counter*claim at all but merely an adroit change of ground. With such blank disparities of meaning and intention at its heart, it is surely small wonder that the uniqueness debate should have struck many observers as a dialogue of the deaf, between antagonists who argue not with but past one another.

But failure to grasp what it is that troubles his Jewish opponents is clearly not the only thing wrong with Stannard's argument at this point. The claim that Stannard takes to be "in most quarters beyond dispute"—that the sufferings of Jewish victims of the Holocaust were greater *in sum* than (those of) *any people at any time in any place during the entire history of humanity*—is surely too vaunting in its generality to be seriously held by anyone, Jewish or non-Jewish, in his or her right mind. And even more fundamentally, how are sufferings to be quantified in any way capable of giving a clear meaning to a comparative judgment of any kind, let alone that kind? How could anyone in his or her senses assent to a proposal not only as absurdly overgeneral, but as ludicrously underdefined as that?

BLAMING THE JEWS

Nevertheless, this is the claim Stannard takes to be "in most quarters . . . beyond dispute." And he takes its supposedly wide acceptance to be the outcome of "hegemonic" activity on the part of the Jews, those practiced pullers of wool over the eyes of honest but simple gentiles. "This rarely examined, taken-for-granted assumption on the part of so many did not appear out of thin air. On the contrary, it is the hegemonic product of many years of strenuous intellectual labor by a handful of Jewish scholars and writers who have dedicated much if not all of their professional lives to the advancement of this exclusivist idea."[14]

Folded together in the above sentence are two of the characteristic motifs of traditional antisemitism, together with a new one that has taken hold since the turn of the present century. First, there is the motif of Jewish "exclusivism," or as it is more usually phrased, particularism, of which we shall have more to say in chapter 13. This is the idea that Jews are exclusively concerned with the welfare of their own community to the exclusion of any wider humanitarian goal or concern.

Second, there is the motif of secret, behind-the-scenes Jewish control of the non-Jewish world implicit in the adjective *hegemonic*. A tiny group of Jewish scholars, through "strenuous intellectual labour" occupying—obsessively it is

to be supposed—"much if not all" of "professional lives" that might, by implication, have been better spent, has, according to Stannard, succeeded in establishing the hegemony over a multitude of non-Jewish minds of the idea that Jewish
suffering in the Holocaust was incomparably worse than, and so by implication,
should be held to *matter* more than, the sum total of *all other* human suffering,
"of any people at any time in any place during the entire history of humanity."

Finally, if Stannard's "handful of Jewish scholars and writers" actually believed what he says they believe, then irrespective of their success in getting
others to believe it, they would be not unreasonable targets for the third, ancient trope of antisemitism, recently popular again, that I mentioned above:
that the Jews believe Jewish blood, Jewish suffering, to be worth more than the
blood and suffering of non-Jews.

It would be surprising if this last claim were actually true, since "it is fundamental to the whole Jewish *Weltanschauung* that no life is more valuable than
any other. In the words of the Talmud: 'What makes you think your blood is
redder?' 'Perhaps his blood is redder'" (*Pesanhim* 25b).[15] Nevertheless, the *canard* that Jewish blood per se *is* held by the Jews to be redder than non-Jewish
blood has of late become part of the stock in trade of revisionist and antisemitic
propaganda around the world. The following, from the American antisemitic
website *The Resistance Report*, is typical: "The Holocaust was crafted for two
purposes. (1) To justify wiping Palestine off the map so that Jews can have a
homeland there. (2) As a propaganda weapon to fool Gentiles into believing
that Jews suffered more than any other people in the world." Setting aside the
relatively urbane and academic style of Stannard's paper, it is not easy to see
any difference in *content* between the above piece of gutter antisemitism and
the following remark of Stannard's, à propos his observation that although a
given revolution may display characteristics peculiar to it, no one would deny
that all revolutions are *revolutions*, or consider one so special in nature as to
require a special, capitalized word to designate it: "This has not been done,
because to do so would be to depart from the world of scholarship and enter
the world of propaganda and group hagiography—which in fact quite clearly
is what Holocaust uniqueness proponents are up to: elevating the Jewish experience to a singular and exclusive hierarchical category, thereby reducing
all other genocides to a thoroughly lesser and wholly separate substratum of
classification."[16]

And the impression can only be deepened when this is followed up a page
later with a passage asserting the classic antisemitic interpretation of Jewish
"chosenness," not as chosenness to obey a stricter moral law than others but
as an assertion of superiority over all other peoples: "We are concerned with a

small industry of Holocaust hagiographers arguing for the uniqueness of the
Jewish experience with all the energy and ingenuity of theological zealots. For
that is what they are: zealots who believe literally that they and their religious
fellows are, in the words of Deuteronomy 7:6, 'a special people . . . above all
people that are on the face of the earth,' interpreting in the only way thus possible their own community's encounter with mass death."[17]

A major motif of antisemitic propaganda has always been the myth of the
Jewish conspiracy. In all versions of the myth, a tiny Jewish elite motivated by a
belief in the innate superiority of Jew over non-Jew exerts overwhelmingly disproportionate power over non-Jewish societies. Stannard's thesis follows that
pattern. A "small industry of Holocaust hagiographers," composed of "zealots"
who supposedly interpret Deuteronomy 7:6 in a way lacking not only any basis
in Jewish tradition but any textual basis in Deuteronomy 7 read as a whole, have
succeeded, remarkably enough, in persuading the non-Jewish world that the
sufferings of Jews in the Holocaust vastly outweigh all non-Jewish sufferings
since the beginning of time. In consequence, the bulk of non-Jewish opinion
has been led to consider the sufferings of non-Jewish groups in genocide after
genocide as of little or no consequence by contrast with those endured by European Jews between 1933 and 1945.

As many contributors to the uniqueness debate pointed out at the time,[18] the
last claim in particular appears to stand reality on its head. The term *genocide*
and the concept itself, not to mention the genocide convention and the Universal Declaration of Human Rights, adopted by the United Nations General
Assembly in 1948, owe their origins not merely to the climate of alarm created
by the destruction of European Jewry between 1933 and 1945, but to the work of
one particular man: a Polish-Jewish lawyer by the name of Raphael Lemkin,[19]
whose struggle to establish the latter legal instruments was by no means motivated solely by Jewish concerns. "Born in relatively comfortable circumstances
in 1900 on a farm belonging to his parents in Eastern Poland, Lemkin grew up
deeply troubled by the numerous and vicious acts of antisemitism committed around him, as well as by other, more distant but no less appalling acts of
barbarity of which the most notable was the massacre by the Turks in 1915 of a
million or so Armenians."[20]

In 1948, I was a politically aware British fifteen-year-old. At that point, the
Armenian genocide of 1915–17 had sunk entirely from European consciousness
(I certainly recall no mention of it at the time or for many years afterward).
At the same time, no general consciousness existed of the full extent of the
destruction visited upon non-European peoples, in the Americas and else-
where, by European expansion and colonialism from the late Middle Ages

onward. All of that was still for the most part seen, I seem to recall, as it had been for the preceding two centuries as part of the onward march of civiliza- tion. The publication, in 1966, of Alan Moorhead's *The Fatal Impact*, which cat- aloged the ill effects, including massive losses of native populations through the introduction of alien diseases and weapons of warfare, consequent upon European invasion of the South Pacific from the mid-eighteenth century on- ward, marks, to my recollection, the first point at which the complacencies of Whig history in that respect began to be seriously doubted by large numbers of educated people.

I would therefore be inclined to say—*pace* Stannard's blank assertion to the contrary—that far from it being the case that opinion has been distracted from the sufferings of non-Jewish groups through the effort of "Holocaust hagiog- raphers" to exalt the sufferings of Jews above those of others, the post–World War II awareness of the historical prevalence of genocide arose largely as a consequence of the Shoah, and did so to a considerable extent through the work of Jewish pioneers, among whom the now largely forgotten Lemkin was perhaps the most prominent.

As a result of their work, there has been since the 1960s, at least, no lack of consciousness among Western intellectuals of the long history of genocide to be laid at the door of European colonialism. To finger a supposed group of Jew- ish zealots, as Stannard does, as responsible for an entirely nonexistent lack of concern is evidently absurd. Equally evidently, it is antisemitic.

Since the Holocaust, the malignant absurdities of antisemitic calumny have tended—though with some surprising exceptions—to encounter, for obvious reasons, a less receptive mass audience than they did, say, in the 1930s and earlier. For that reason no doubt, antisemitic discourse tends nowadays to be marked by a tendency to conclude each Judeophobic harangue with a complaint to the effect that innocent folk who merely attempt to tell the truth about the Jews always get accused of antisemitism, with a view to shutting them up. Here is a move of that type from the website The Resistance Report: "They want us to think that they are always innocent and powerless, and anyone who disagrees with or hates even one Jew must be anti-Semitic. Yet if I say I hate White racists, does that make me anti-White? If not, then how does it make me anti-Semitic to say I hate Jewish racists? It doesn't, but they don't want you to know that." And here is the equivalent move in Professor Stannard's essay: "In short, if you disagree with Deborah Lipstadt that the Jewish suffering in the Holocaust was unique, you are, by definition—and like David Duke—a crypto-Nazi. Need- less to say, such intellectual thuggery usually has its intended chilling effect on further discussion."[21]

IN SEARCH OF TEXTUAL EVIDENCE

But does Deborah Lipstadt, or anyone else in Stannard's chosen band of Jewish "zealots," actually *say*, either in so many words or via some plausibly paraphrasable circumlocution, that what was unique about the Holocaust was the *suffering* it involved, taken—in terms of some suitable modulus—quantitatively?

Manifestly, Stannard stands in need of textual evidence to back up a claim like that. It is nowhere to be found in his essay. In its place, we find repeated and forceful, but entirely unargued, assertions of the pair of implausible assumptions we have already repeatedly encountered. The first is that non-Jewish Holocaust scholars who regard the Holocaust as without parallel (and there are, after all, plenty of them) do so only because of pressure from Jewish "Holocaust hagiographers." The second is that the only sense in which the Holocaust could intelligibly be deemed unique or unparalleled is in respect of the quantity of suffering (assuming suffering, as distinct from number of persons killed, to be quantifiable) endured by its Jewish victims.

Once these deeply dubious suggestions have been introduced into the unwary reader's mind—essentially by blank assertion alone—the remaining bulk of the essay is taken up with an attempt, in itself unexceptionable enough though frequently cursory, to show that in a range of other genocides, from the Ottoman massacres of Armenians between 1915 and 1917 to the accelerating destruction of the native peoples of the Americas in the decades and centuries following 1492, the sum total of the suffering endured, estimated by a variety of criteria (all of them conceptually parasitic on the idea of counting the dead) may be reasonably supposed to have been as great or greater than that endured by the sum total of Jewish victims of the Holocaust.

There is, though, one point late in the essay at which something at least resembling textual evidence is offered, with reference to an essay by Edward Alexander of the University of Washington.

> According to uniqueness advocate Edward Alexander, for instance, the experience of the Holocaust provided "a Jewish claim to a specific suffering that was of the 'highest,' the most distinguished grade available." Even to mention the genocidal agonies suffered by others, either during the Holocaust or at other times and places is, Alexander says, "to plunder the moral capital which the Jewish people, through its unparalleled suffering in World War II, had unwittingly accumulated." One of the most ghastly amassments of genocidal suffering ever experienced is thereby made the literal equivalent for its victims of a great bounty of jealously guarded "capital" or wealth. It is unlikely that there exists any

more forthright expression than this of what Irving Louis Horowitz calls Holocaust "moral bookkeeping."[22]

Stannard here equips Alexander, who happens to be Jewish, with the character and motives of Shylock: the pitiless Jew who not only considers the sufferings of Jews "higher" and more "distinguished" than those of the non-Jew but who can think in no other terms than those of ownership, possession, wealth, and "capital" to describe human suffering, even the sufferings of his own tribe, and who "jealously guards" both the word *Holocaust* and the thing itself as uniquely Jewish *possessions*.

It thus becomes rather an important question whether Alexander's text, considered in extenso, will actually bear this thrillingly accusatory interpretation. Alas, when the context of Alexander's remarks is restored, the heightened colors so easily bestowed by selective citation fade, as happens in such cases, into the light of common day. The distinction between "high" and "low" as applied to Jewish concerns, it turns out, is not Alexander's at all but George Eliot's, and the attaching of central significance to suffering, in Alexander's opinion, not to be Jewish but rather Christian in character. Here is the full sentence in context: "The uniqueness of Jewish suffering and of the Jewish catastrophe during the Second World War had no sooner been defined than it was called into question, by Jews as well as by Christians. The fact and the idea of suffering are central in Christianity, whose ethical values are based on the idea of a community of suffering. Many Christians also believe that, as Mary Ann Evans, later known as George Eliot, wrote in 1848, 'Everything specifically Jewish is of a low grade.' Yet here was a specific suffering that was of the 'highest,' the most distinguished grade imaginable."[23] Alexander's response to Eliot is ironic, which is why the word *highest* is in scare quotes. His point is that whatever nineteenth-century Christians may have thought concerning the low-grade nature of any concern specifically involving the Jews, the Holocaust, whatever else it has done, has at least rendered impossible that kind of airily patronizing dismissal. The point has, in short, no bearing whatsoever on the *meaning* of uniqueness. Nor can the phrase *the uniqueness of Jewish suffering* be taken, as Stannard seems to imagine, to align Alexander's understanding of the term *uniqueness* with his own. What Alexander, like other Jewish commentators, takes the uniqueness of the Holocaust to consist of, as he makes clear in the first paragraph of the essay concerned, is not the supposedly "incomparable" *extent* of Jewish suffering but rather *the nature of the criteria by which its victims were selected.*

The Jews held a unique position in the Nazi world because they alone, of all the peoples subject to German rule, had been marked for total destruction, not for anything they had done or failed to do, but because they had been born of three Jewish grandparents. Their guilt lay exclusively in having been born. Although only Jews could be guilty of being Jewish, the centrality of the Jews in the mental and political universe of the Nazis established a universal principle that involved every single person in German-ruled Europe: in order to be granted the fundamental human right, the right to live, one had to prove that he was not a Jew.[24]

That leaves Stannard with nothing to brandish but the phrase *moral capital*, which he takes, by implication, to convict Alexander—in a manner at the very least, highly redolent of one of the central motifs of traditional gutter antisemitism—of a willingness to see everything, including the sufferings of his fellow Jews, in light of a "possession," of "capital," and of "wealth." I have no access to the original Midstream version of Alexander's article, and I cannot locate the phrase, beginning "plunder the moral capital," that Stannard cites, in either of the versions of the essay that Alexander later reprinted (in *The Holocaust and the War of Ideas*[25] and *The Jewish Idea and Its Enemies*). But that hardly matters, since the phrase "moral capital," expressing much the same thought, recurs, anyway, in a passage in the version of the article included in *The Jewish Idea and Its Enemies*. In this passage, Alexander discusses the tendency, in recounting and dramatizing the diary of Anne Frank for popular consumption, to downplay, in the interests of giving the work a "universal significance," its author's references to her own and her family's Jewishness as the cause of their predicament. "Cut free from her Jewish moorings, improperly understood by her own people, Anne Frank has become available for appropriation by those who have a sounder appreciation of the worth of moral capital, and know how to lay claim to sovereignty over it when the question of sovereignty has been left open."[26]

I think it is clear from context that the term *moral capital* refers here, not as Stannard insists, to *quantity of suffering*, Jewish or otherwise, but rather to the recognition of the *causal role played by their Jewishness in the selection for persecution* of the Jewish victims of the Holocaust. In short, for Alexander, as for Bauer, Lipstadt, Rosenfeld, and other Jewish (and many non-Jewish) defenders of the uniqueness of the Holocaust, it is *general recognition of the fact that Jews, unlike other victims of Nazi atrocity, were killed just for being Jews* that constitutes the "national asset" of which would-be universalizers and de-Judaizers of the Holocaust wish to deprive the Jewish people.

WHO OWNS WHICH ASPECTS OF THE HOLOCAUST?

If Alexander and Stannard agree about nothing else, they agree that the uniqueness debate was, and is, a debate about *ownership*. I want to conclude, therefore, by confronting this question afresh and head-on. Who does "own" the Holocaust: the Jews alone or all the victims of Nazi atrocity, of whatever kind or nation, or maybe all of suffering humanity? Evidently, one cannot answer that question without also confronting the central question of the uniqueness debate: *was the Jewish experience of the Holocaust unique?*

I have argued, with a nod to Wittgenstein, that the question of whether something X is or is not unique becomes answerable only if one has specified the characteristic or characteristics *in respect of which* uniqueness, for purposes of present discussion, is to be predicated of X.

So let's make the question a little more complex by way of making the discussion a little more interesting and maybe somewhat increasing the proportion of light over heat. *In what respects* was the Holocaust unique, and in what respects was it not unique? And to whom—to the Jewish people or to others—does *the Holocaust considered in each of these respects* "belong"?

Bringing into play the notion that a thing can be unique in one respect and not in another opens up two possibilities that, simple and obvious as they are, appear so far as I am aware to be new to the debate. The first is that the Holocaust might turn out to have been unique among genocides in some respects and not unique in others. The second is that the respects in which it *was* unique, while they might turn out to "belong to the Jews," might just as well turn out to belong to others—that is to say, to the non-Jewish part of humanity. I believe, for reasons that I shall now set before you, that this second possibility is in fact the case.

Much has been made in the uniqueness debate, not only by David E. Stannard but also by many other contributors, of the uniqueness claim as a pretended attempt by Jews to exalt themselves above all other persecuted peoples since the beginning of time in respect of the supposed uniqueness of their *suffering*. One of the reasons why the bulk of Jewish (and for that matter non-Jewish) scholars have in fact made no such claim is, no doubt, that it would be an impossible claim to defend. Equally, I take it, the reason why those, like Stannard, hostile to the idea that the Jewish experience of the Nazi persecution was *in any sense* unique, emphasize the aspect of the Holocaust *as suffering* to the exclusion of all other aspects, is that by doing so, they think to position themselves on strong ground.

Both sides are right, at least about this! Sadly, there is seldom anything unique about suffering. However great, however abominable the present form it takes, however satanically ingenious the modes of its present infliction, as bad or worse can generally be found in the long panorama of human barbarity.

But the proper conclusion to be drawn from this truth is not Stannard's. Suppose we agree with Stannard, for the sake of argument, that the Holocaust may be said to belong to the Jews *under the aspect of suffering*. In that case, it belongs to them under an aspect that, far from dividing them from the rest of suffering humanity, unites them to it. No distinction arises between Jews and members of other nations *in that respect*. As victims of *suffering*, we may all weep together.

But what about other aspects of the Holocaust? What in particular about its aspect as a persecution conducted against the members of a certain people *for no other reason than that they were members of that people*, and therefore, in logic, even if not always in practice, directed *against every member of that nation without exception*?

Here, the Holocaust does seem to me, as it has to many others, Jewish and non-Jewish, including all of Stannard's "small industry of Holocaust hagiographers," to have been unique.

But under that aspect, the aspect of *persecution upon the sole ground of birth*, the Holocaust in no way belongs to the Jews. It belongs to *the rest of us*, to non-Jews—that is to say, simply because the *project* of extermination on the sole ground of membership by birth of a given people *has no Jewish component*. It took its rise and, in the course of time, arrived at the moment of its attempted implementation *entirely within gentile circles*.

We seem forced to conclude, in short, that what belongs to the Jews, where the Holocaust is concerned—that is to say, suffering so vast as not in practice to be remotely imaginable *or quantifiable*—is *not* the thing that makes the Holocaust unique. It is rather what makes it part of the common human inheritance of distress. On the other hand, what *does* make the Holocaust unique—namely, the nature of the grounds upon which it was conceived and set in motion—is in no sense "the property of the Jews." On the contrary, if it is part of any "inheritance," the heritage of which it forms a part is not the Jewish heritage but the gentile heritage. As a property bequeathed by history it belongs, in other words, not to the Jews but, as the French say, to *nous autres*, to the rest of us: to non-Jews.

Every attempt to secure the "prize" of the term *Holocaust* for another oppressed group, however deserving of sympathy *expressed in other terms*, therefore carries with it the risk of losing touch with the uniqueness of the Holocaust *as crime*. Here it is worth quoting at length Pascal Bruckner:

> In other words the Shoah has become a monstrous object of covetous lust. . . .
> From this comes the frenzied effort to gain admission to this very closed
> club and the desire to dislodge those who are already part of it. Consider this
> circa-2005 statement by Sir Iqbal Sacranie, secretary general of the Muslim
> Council of Great Britain until 2006, who proposed replacing Holocaust
> Memorial Day with Genocide Day: "The message of the Holocaust was 'never
> again' and for that message to have practical effect on the world community
> it has to be inclusive. We can never have double standards in terms of human

life. Muslims feel hurt and excluded that their lives are not equally valuable
to those lives lost in the Holocaust time." In short, and to put it bluntly, it is
now time to change victims. In the contest for world title of best outcast, the
Muslim must replace the Jew, all the more so because the latter not only failed
to live up to his status but because he has himself become, with the creation
of the state of Israel, an oppressor. In short, the idealization of the Jews has
paved the way for his later vilification, or, to put it differently, the Judaization
of the Muslims necessarily leads to the Nazification of the Israelis.[27]

Once again, it apparently needs to be said, the crime committed by the pros-
ecutors of the Holocaust was that of treating a birth certificate as equivalent
to a death warrant. It was not that of regarding the death of one person as less
valuable (whatever that may mean) than the death of another. To think that
it was *is to forget*. And with forgetfulness comes the possibility of repetition:
perhaps this time not in the shape of a further destruction of the Jews but in
that of some other group.

CONCLUSION: HOLOCAUST MEMORY AS
BOTH DUTY AND PRUDENCE

That is the ultimate reason why Stannard and others who think like him are
wrong to suppose that we can do without the term *Holocaust* understood as
a singular term—a proper name referring uniquely to the destruction of European Jewry between 1933 and 1945. We need it because it is essential to the
work of Holocaust memory that includes museums, such as the United States
Holocaust Museum in Washington, DC, along with Holocaust Days, research
groups, university and school courses, books and articles.

The place occupied by the Jews in the imagination of both Christians and
Muslims being what it is, it might still be asked: But why should all this effort
be put into remembering the sufferings of the Jews, when others have suffered
as much or more without being accorded this kind of attention?

The answer I have offered here—to repeat it one last time—is that what such
things serve to keep alive is not the (alleged) uniqueness of the *suffering* inflicted
in the Holocaust but rather the (actual) uniqueness of the Holocaust *as political
crime*. The Holocaust was a unique and (for the moment at least) uniquely European crime because it was the first moment in history at which an entire people
was willed to destruction merely to save the credit of a political fantasy.[28] No
doubt we, who as non-Jews belong to nations the bulk of whose citizens are non-
Jews, ought to remember these things *as a duty to the Jews*. But non-Jews like
myself, and no doubt many of my readers, also stand under a duty of prudence

of which I shall have more to say in chapters 14–16: *a duty to ourselves as non-Jews* to remember these things. While the Jewish world suffered the consequences of the Holocaust, it was the non-Jewish world, its mythic structures, its resources of secular political messianism, that originated and contrived it. But the bulk of non-Jews who were in no way a party to Hitler's war against the Jews, except through lack of vigilance, also paid a price for that lack of vigilance. Antisemitism is certainly part of what drew converts to the Nazi Party, and so part of what served to bring Hitler to power. Hence, antisemitism lay causally at the root of many millions of non-Jewish as well as Jewish deaths. Antisemitism, as long as it remains alive, will continue to retain the power it then demonstrated, to blind many to the demonic character of messianic politics until it is too late.

That is why "the Holocaust industry," as Norman Finkelstein derisively calls it, is not, as he and others like Stannard have wished to persuade us, a specifically *Jewish* enterprise. It is an enterprise that serves all of us, one that we should pursue with all the industry we can muster, because it is in everyone's interest, the interest of all citizens of the free world, Jewish and non-Jewish, to remember the specific nature and origins of the Holocaust *as a crime*. To lose that memory, at the behest of a sophistical universalism, is to lose a precious bulwark against the perennial power of spurious moralizing to betray society into the bloody hands of political messianism.

CONCLUDING POSTSCRIPT

The most troubling thing about this chapter, to me, is the fact that it needed to be written. Its origins go back to a talk I gave to a university audience in Seattle in 2011. The discussion inevitably turned to the topic of the Holocaust, at which point a former colleague in the audience whom, as a literary critic, I knew to be widely read and deeply insightful, and as a man, utterly devoid of any form of bigotry, raised the question whether commemoration of the Holocaust, dreadful as was the extent and nature of the suffering the Holocaust involved, and understandable as is the Jewish desire to see that suffering commemorated, was not nowadays serving to deflect attention from the sufferings—considerable, even if not *as* considerable—of other, non-Jewish groups.

In my reply, I made on the hoof the obvious point that I have been laboring in this chapter. The object of Holocaust commemoration was not, I said, to perpetuate the memory of Jewish *suffering*, suffering being the property of no particular people, but inseparable per se from the experience of humanity in general. Rather, I suggested the object of Holocaust commemoration was to perpetuate the memory of a crime unique not in *the amount of suffering it caused* but rather *in its nature: as murder inflicted on grounds of ancestry alone.* The task of commemoration, I said, was to perpetuate among other things the memory of the nature of that crime, of its historic unfolding and bleak fruition, and of the essential and central part played in that process by an irrational hatred of Jews—a hatred that survived the downfall of the Third Reich and remains with us today.

I should not have thought that there was much deserving to be thought original, or even surprising, about *that* as a reply: a host of Jewish writers and thinkers, after all, have said as much. But my reply seemed to strike my ex-colleague as astonishing—as unheard of in its startling originality, in short as some sort of thunderbolt. "Well, that may be a good point," he said, "but I have to say it's new to me. Who says this? Where did you read it? Where is it in print? I'd like the reference."

I had to tell him, lamely, that so far as I knew it was not in print anywhere, at least precisely in that form—that I had just said it off the cuff, for no better reason than that it had happened to occur to me just at that moment, on my feet, in the stress of discussion. On the other hand, the nature of his response was such as to have made me think it, since then, eminently worthwhile to say it again and this time in print.

What was puzzling and a little distressing to me about this exchange was that my reply should have seemed so new and surprising to my former colleague. On the one hand, he is a man of both goodwill and high intelligence. On the other hand, the point that struck him as so original and unheard of is, I would have thought, once stated, not only obvious but trivially and unanswerably so. The distinction between the nature of a crime and the suffering it produces is in itself, after all, neither obscure nor difficult to grasp. The idea that the Jews use the extent of their sufferings in the Holocaust to obscure and devalue the sufferings of others remains plausible, as we have seen, only as long as that distinction can be ignored or somehow made to seem irrelevant.

So what could explain my colleague's surprise? I in no way suspect him of conscious antisemitism. On the other hand, I do think him deeply sensitive, like all good literary scholars, to the subtleties of Western culture. And lurking deeply in that culture is the conviction that Judaism is a deeply particularist culture. Bound up with that conviction is the subordinate and plainly fatuously antisemitic proposition that the Jews characteristically use their sufferings to gain illicit advantages over non-Jews. One can find that proposition assumed as axiomatic in a host of literary sources. It can be found, for example, in Alphonse Daudet's Algerian sketch "À Milianah" in which Daudet says of the plight of an elderly Jew struck and injured by a French settler in a dispute over land, "a large indemnity is alone capable of curing him; so don't take him to the doctor, take him to the man of business."[29]

Any mind that, however unconsciously, takes as axiomatic the proposition that Jews use their sufferings as a lever to gain advantage will naturally be inclined to pass with dizzying speed, without touching ground at any intervening point, from it to the closely allied thought that the "Holocaust industry" offers a case in point.

It is when thought moves like that, too fast, too easily, over rails locked into one position by long cultural familiarity, that we are led to overlook obvious distinctions and the possibilities of alternative interpretation opened up by them. I should like to think that this is not the explanation of my colleague's ability, and that of others since, to find "original" and "surprising" the arguments presented in this chapter. But sadly, I think that that probably *is* the explanation.

NOTES

1. See G. D. Rosenfeld 2014, 78–121.
2. Rosenbaum 2009.
3. Stevenson 1944, 212–13.
4. For an excellent examination, complementary to the present chapter, of the operation of this principle in current political discourse, see Pascal Bruckner, "Antisemitism and Islamophobia: The Inversion of the Debt," in A. H. Rosenfeld 2015, 7–20.
5. See A. H. Rosenfeld 2011; Harrison 2011.
6. Including, for instance, those of CODOH (Committee for Open Debate on the Holocaust), Davidduke.com, Focal Point Publications (a site devoted to the writings of David Irving), and jewwatch.com.
7. See Harrison 2006, chap. 2 and passim.
8. A. S. Rosenbaum 2009.
9. David E. Stannard, "Uniqueness as Denial: The Politics of Genocide Scholarship," in A. S. Rosenbaum 2009, 295–340.
10. Both citations from the section "Wiesel Resources" on the PBS website, www.pbs.org/eliewiesel/resources/.
11. Bauer 1978, 7.
12. Stannard in A. S. Rosenbaum 2009, 301, emphasis mine.
13. Stannard in A. S. Rosenbaum 2009, 299, emphasis mine.
14. Stannard in A. S. Rosenbaum 2009, 299.
15. Gershon Weiler, "The Jewish Establishment," *New York Review of Books*, letters section, March 17, 1966, https://www.nybooks.com/articles/1966/03/17/the-jewish-establishment-3/.

16. Stannard in A. S. Rosenbaum 2009, 324.

17. Stannard in A. S. Rosenbaum 2009, 325.

18. See, for example, Samantha Power, "To *Suffer* by Comparison," *Daedalus* 2 (Spring 1999): 31–66; Alan Steinweis, "The Auschwitz Analogy: Holocaust Memory and American Debates over Intervention in Bosnia and Kosovo in the 1990s," *Holocaust and Genocide Studies* (Fall 2005): 276–89; John Torpey, "Making Whole What Has Been Smashed: Reflections on Reparations," *Journal of Modern History* (June 2001): 333–58. Further instances to be found in A. H. Rosenfeld (2015).

19. See Cooper 2015.

20. Conway 2015.

21. Stannard in A. S. Rosenbaum 2009, 300.

22. Stannard in A. S. Rosenbaum 2009, 325.

23. Edward Alexander, "Stealing the Holocaust," in Alexander 1998, 101 (originally published in *Midstream: A Monthly Jewish Review*, November 1980).

24. Alexander 1998, 99.

25. Alexander 1994.

26. Alexander 1994, 102.

27. See endnote 5. The passage cited here is from p. 16.

28. Several of the essays in the A. S. Rosenbaum (2009) volume, including one by Professor Ben Kiernan, director of the Genocide Studies Program at Yale, explore the question of possible analogies between the Holocaust and other genocides. Am I committed to regarding this as an illegitimate activity? Clearly not. The only claim I am committed to is that Holocaust is rendered unique, whatever analogies may exist between it and other episodes of mass killing, interesting as those may be, by the strange but clearly causally determining relationship subsisting between it and the uniquely European system of politically active myth and delusion concerning the Jews.

29. Alphonse Daudet, *Lettres de mon moulin* (Paris: Le Livre de Poche Classique, 1994), 154 (the translation in the text is mine): "Une forte indemnité est seule capable de le guérir; aussi ne le mène-t-on pas chez le médecin, mais chez l'agent d'affaires."

THREE

—⁓⁓—

QUESTIONS OF DEFINITION

Nowadays virtually everyone is opposed to anti-Semitism although no-one
agrees about what it means to be anti-Semitic.

—Kenneth L. Marcus, *The Definition of Anti-Semitism*

A BASIC DEFINITION

Within limits, it is possible to say or to show what one means by a term merely
by indicating the sort of thing it applies to: "That is a trombone," "These animals are what we call monkeys." Up to this point in the book, so far as I can be
said to have explained the meaning of the term *antisemitism*, I have done so in
roughly that way. I have offered examples—in chapter 1, an extract from the
1988 Hamas charter; in chapter 2, a modern resurrection of the ancient canard
that Jews cherish their sufferings as a means of defrauding others—chosen in
the expectation that they will seem to the reader as patently antisemitic as they
do to me. And I have suggested that both represent, in different ways, a late-
twentieth-century recrudescence of a type of antisemitism—antisemitism as
a political fantasy, in the form of a pseudo-explanatory theory of the real force
controlling world events—widely supposed to have died with the Third Reich.

It is now time to attempt to give that claim more substance by moving from
mere exemplification to analysis and the exact definition of terms. Explaining
the meanings of words by appeal to examples doubtless has its uses. Yet as Plato
strove to show us, it also has its limits. Sooner or later, we must face the question
Socrates never tires of posing to overconfident young Athenians: "No doubt

53

this is an N, maybe *that* is, too; but what *makes* them both Ns? What, that is to
say, does 'N,' in general terms, *mean?*" Nor are these Socratic questions mere
toys of philosophical or lexicographical debate. If rational discussion of a topic
is to proceed without needless, purely verbal misunderstandings—if sound
legal or political responses to a given pattern of abuse are to be devised—then
formal definitions of terms are indispensable. In this chapter, we shall see what
can be done to provide one for the term *antisemitism*.

On the simplest, most basic level, a formal definition is easy to provide:

Definition 1. *Antisemitism is prejudice against Jews.*

If we supplement this with Gordon Allport's shrewd definition of *prejudice*
as "thinking ill of others *without sufficient warrant*"[1] and give due regard also to
the evident power of prejudice to express itself equally in thought, word, and
act, we get

Definition 2. *Antisemitism is thinking, speaking, or acting injuriously toward
Jews without sufficient warrant.*

It might seem possible to object to this definition on the grounds that it
makes a mistake in logic. The objection would be that since it treats lack of
cognitive warrant as conceptually built into the notion of antisemitism, it must
entail, absurdly, that if a statement is antisemitic, it is not merely false but *necessarily* false.[2] But the objection is itself logically mistaken. All that Allport's
definition says is that a true statement can't be a prejudiced one. It certainly
follows from that as a matter of conceptual necessity, that a statement expressing prejudice must be false; but it in no way follows that *the statement in question* must be *necessarily* or *conceptually* false. Any kind of falsehood will do,
including simple contingent falsehood. It is also the case, of course, that many
statements manifesting prejudice fail of truth because they are too confused
for it to be possible to form any clear idea of what, in concrete terms, their truth
would involve. But that is another matter.

PROBLEMS OF INTENTION

There is, in a sense, nothing wrong with definition 2. It does much of what we
ask a definition in a good dictionary to do. That is, it tells us clearly, simply, and
correctly what the term *antisemitism* means in English. Over and above that, it
explains why at least some things deserve to be so regarded. The contention of
the authors of the Hamas charter, for instance, that "the Jews," in the service of
sinister ends, secretly control the media, publishing, business clubs, and so on,

around the world, is antisemitic by the terms of definition 2: on the one hand because the accusation it levels is defamatory, and on the other hand because the absurdity of the idea that such a conspiracy could be operated by the Jews, or for that matter anybody else, not merely affords the accusation insufficient warrant but deprives it of any conceivable foothold in reality. It is equally clear by the terms of definition 2 that the central claim of Stannard's essay—that a handful of Jewish scholars and writers have bamboozled the world into the delusion that Jewish suffering in the Holocaust outranks all other human suffering since the beginning of time—also qualifies as antisemitic. On the one hand, it is injurious, amounting to the claim that Jews purposefully exaggerate their sufferings in order to defraud others of the sympathy that should by rights be theirs. On the other hand, it fails of sufficient warrant by virtue, first, of its mendacity and second, of its absurdity. No Jewish—or non-Jewish—scholar of the Holocaust has ever, in sober fact, claimed that the suffering endured by Jews at the hands of the Nazis and their sympathizers outweighs all other human suffering for the simple reason that the claim itself, given the unquantifiable nature of suffering, is empty of meaning.

Nevertheless, definition 2 will not do as it stands. One of the things we demand of a definition of a term N is that it resolve disputes in cases where people disagree about whether some particular thing is or is not an N. In this respect, the examples of Stannard and the Hamas convention might seem to show definition 2 in a favorable light (this is one of the reasons why I chose them, rather than others, to open the discussion). Unfortunately, there are a great many other disputed cases in which it fails that challenge—or fails it, at least, in the absence of further, supplementary clauses and/or explications of kinds yet to be determined. An extended discussion of cases of this kind, and of the problems of definition to which they bear witness, is to be found in Kenneth L. Marcus's indispensable *The Definition of Anti-Semitism*.[3]

One important category of cases throws into relief the weaknesses of the opening clause of definition 2: the clause, that is to say, that identifies antisemitism as "thinking, speaking, or acting injuriously *toward Jews*." Hostility toward Jews need not be antisemitic in character. For instance, it may in no way reflect antisemitism if people living in a quiet suburb object to the opening of a synagogue on the grounds that they fear a resulting increase in cars vying for scarce parking places at certain busy times of the weekend. It may be, for instance, that they object with equal vigor, and for the same reasons, to the opening of an already existing Catholic school for parent/pupil activities on a Saturday morning. In such a case, one is not closing one's eyes to Jew hatred if one concludes that residents don't, after all, want the area to be *judenfrei*.

They just want it to be free of the kinds of social activity that they see as dis-
rupting the peace of the neighborhood on Saturday mornings.

To exclude such cases, Marcus notes, Charles Glock and Rodney Stark[4]
suggest defining antisemitism "not [as] the hatred of persons who happen to
be Jews, but rather the hatred of persons *because* they are Jews."[5] In effect this
yields

> Definition 3. *Antisemitism is thinking, speaking, or acting injuriously toward
> Jews without sufficient warrant,* **because they are Jews**.

If we wish to screen out cases like that of the tranquility-loving neighborhood, it is hard to see how we can avoid adopting this or some equivalent reformulation of definition 2. But to take that route is, as Kenneth Marcus shows,
to risk arriving at a definition that can serve to disguise rather than expose the
true incidence of antisemitism.

A specific case will serve to display both the nature and the extent of the
problem. Now famous in France, it is that of the murder of Ilan Halimi. In
January 2006, a French Muslim gang calling itself Les Barbares (The Barbar-
ians) kidnapped a young French Jew, Halimi, torturing him over a three-
week period before abandoning him in a wood near a train station to which
he crawled before dying of his wounds. The French police, along with public
officials at levels up to and including that of the office of the Minister of the
Interior, were at some pains to deny any suggestion that the attack was antisemitic in character, in effect justifying this stand by appeal to what one
might term the Glock/Stark Amendment. They accepted, that is to say, as-
surances by the leader of Les Barbares, Youssuf Fofana, that Halimi had not
been targeted *because he was a Jew* but merely because the gang believed Jews
in general to be rich. Halimi's injuries were certainly savage enough to suggest
far greater interest on the part of the gang in torturing their victim than in
making money from him. Despite this, however, the French public authorities, including the then interior minister and subsequent president Nicolas
Sarkozy, continued for a considerable time to insist that Halimi had been the
victim not of an antisemitic attack but merely of a kidnapping gone wrong.
They revised this stance only when another member of the Barbares confessed
that the gang had burned Halimi on the forehead with a cigarette *because he
was a Jew*.

This case neatly displays the main problem with definition 3, that its termi-
nal clause makes the question of whether an act is or is not antisemitic *appear
to depend on the motives, goals, or intentions of its perpetrator*. It makes an act's
status as antisemitic or non-antisemitic depend on issues regarding which the

perpetrator himself is generally supposed to enjoy the determining voice. If the perpetrators are prepared, like Fofana's unreliable colleague, to vaunt their antisemitism, then well and good. If, on the other hand (in tune with the majority of Western antisemites at the moment), they wish to disguise it, they need only equip their conduct with some plausible motive allowing them to admit freely to hostility toward Jews while absolving themselves of hostility to Jews *because they are Jews.*

IS *ANTISEMITISM* A GENUINE CONCEPT?

The successive difficulties encountered by the above three opening stabs at a definition might prompt one to wonder whether the enterprise itself is misconceived. Does the term *antisemitism,* when it comes down to it, express any clear notion susceptible of *definition* in the first place? There is a strain of reputable opinion in the social sciences that thinks not. I am thinking in particular here of the late Gavin Langmuir (1924–2005), a distinguished and influential Stanford medieval historian widely celebrated for his work on the history of medieval Jewish-Christian relations. In his *Towards a Definition of Antisemitism,* Langmuir (1990) makes the sound point that the very term *antisemitism* is of very recent vintage and is inseparably bound up with a body of nineteenth-century German theorizing, quasi-anthropological in character, that can now, many think, be regarded as effectively defunct. "'Antisemitism' was invented about 1873 by Wilhelm Marr to describe the policy towards Jews based on 'racism' that he and others advocated. . . . As elaborated in the Aryan myth, it maintained that Jews were a race and that, not only were they, like other races, inferior to the Aryan race, but also that Jews were the most dangerous of those inferior races."[6]

If *Rassentheorie* of that type is for us nowadays, as Langmuir hopes, merely another forgotten essay in pseudoscience, and if the original meaning of antisemitism—as, roughly speaking, "hostility to Jews considered as an inferior and dangerous race"—was so bound up with "Aryan myth" as to be reasonably supposed to have died with it, then what residual meaning, if any, can we nowadays suppose to attach to the term?

There is an answer to this question, not infrequently canvassed by Jewish commentators (in chap. 4 we shall find Dennis Prager and Joseph Telushkin offering a version of it) from which Langmuir strongly dissents.[7] "Although [various] adjectives [are often used to] distinguish different rationalisations for the hostility, the noun 'antisemitism' still implies a constancy in the basic cause and quality of hostility against Jews at any one time. . . . Like the Aryan myth, this conception of 'antisemitism' depends, I would argue, on the fallacy of misplaced concreteness or illicit reification, in this case on the unproven assumption that for centuries, and despite innumerable changes on both sides, there has been a distinctive kind of reaction of non-Jews directed only at Jews that corresponds to the concept evoked by the word 'antisemitism.'"[8]

In effect, Langmuir argues that in Jewish hands this story frequently becomes little more than an inversion of the Aryan myth. "What makes that fallacy attractive to many people, I would suggest, is their prior assumption that, whether by divine choice or otherwise, there has always been something uniquely valuable in Jewishness, because Jews have always incorporated and preserved uniquely superior values. They then assume that the resolute and enduring expression of those unique values by Jews has aroused a correspondingly unique type of hostility against them as bearers of that unique quality throughout their existence."[9]

Langmuir's objection to this way of looking at things is, on the one hand, that it is in principle as viciously "ethnocentric" as the Aryan myth itself, and on the other hand, more interestingly to my mind, that it has served, unhelpfully, to focus the attention of many theorists of antisemitism on Jews and Jewish culture instead of, more usefully, on non-Jews and non-Jewish culture.

> Such a perspective might fairly be called ethnocentric; and, not surprisingly, those who accept it have not felt any need to examine non-Jews carefully to see whether the quality of their hostility to Jews has in fact been unique and unchanging. Yet the quality of hostility against Jews cannot be determined by premises about Jews, for it is a characteristic of the mentality of non-Jews, not of Jews, and it is determined, not by the objective reality of Jews, but by what the symbol "Jews" has signified to non-Jews. Moreover, the kind of hostility evoked has not been directed only against Jews.[10]

Three claims are being advanced in the brief passage to which these two citations belong. They are (1) that the idea that there is something "uniquely valuable in Jewishness" is both false and ethnocentric (that is, presumably, as racially condescending as the Aryan myth itself); (2) that for an understanding of antisemitism we must look not to the nature of "Jewishness" but to the mentality and culture of non-Jews; (3) that, when so examined, hostility to Jews turns out to possess no feature unique to it; no feature, that is to say, that is not equally manifested by hostility directed against other groups.

Of these three claims, (2), I shall argue, is in the main true; (1) and (3) false. So far as (2) goes, I am in entire agreement with Langmuir. That antisemitism is a fundamentally non-Jewish phenomenon and that its nature and incidence are determined not by objective reality, Jewish or otherwise, but by a system of political fantasies internal to non-Jewish culture, are among the more central conclusions argued for in the present work.

By contrast, (1) seems to me not only unhappily expressed but factually mistaken. To anyone with an ear for antisemitic discourse, some of Langmuir's more dismissive phrases—"whether by divine choice or otherwise," "uniquely superior values," "ethnocentric"—must seem themselves dismally redolent of "what the symbol 'Jews' has signified to non-Jews." Any persistent and fair-minded student of Judaism and Jewish culture will find that both embody a multitude of insights and styles of conduct both valuable in themselves and unique to those traditions. The difficulty with envisaging *antisemitism* as a *response* to what is "uniquely valuable in Jewishness" is merely that the aspects of Jewishness that a dispassionate observer might wish to regard as falling under that rubric are for the most part unknown and invisible to non-Jews.

The only argument that Langmuir offers for claim (3)—that there is no such thing as the "distinctive kind of reaction of non-Jews directed only at Jews" that supposedly "corresponds to the concept evoked by the word 'antisemitism'"—is, unless I misread him, that antisemitism is not "determined by the objective reality of Jews" but by "what the symbol 'Jews' has signified to non-Jews," and hence cannot be a reaction by non-Jews to the "uniquely superior values" supposedly manifested by and within Judaism.

From a logical point of view, unfortunately, this is a non sequitur. Given the massive ignorance of Judaism and Jewishness prevalent among non-Jews, it is indeed unlikely that any non-Jew ever became an antisemite out of chagrin at the perceived "superiority" of Jewish "values." However, it is scarcely more plausible that the meaning, for non-Jews, of "the symbol 'Jews'" could have developed in a manner entirely unaffected by "the objective reality of Jews." In chapters 4 and 5, I shall suggest some ways in which certain objective features of Jewish conduct—features deriving ultimately, moreover, if not from non-Jewish *hatred of*, then at least from Jewish *attachment to*, "Jewish values"—may, *pace* Langmuir, have played a rather decisive role in the development of the myth of "the Jews."

Nevertheless, weak as the argument is, Langmuir considers himself licensed by it to conclude that the hostility directed against Jews by non-Jews is over-whelmingly of a kind that "has not been directed only against Jews." It follows, for Langmuir, that we stand in no need of a definition of antisemitism, because the term is used, confusedly, to describe kinds of hatred by no means uniquely experienced by Jews for which perfectly good and well-defined terms are already in use among social scientists, namely, *xenophobia* and *ethnic prejudice*, both of which invoke "the idea of an instinctive hostility towards strange— little-known and differently constituted—outgroups."[11]

In summary, Langmuir thinks that whereas talk of antisemitism postulates a special form of hatred solely directed toward and solely experienced by Jews, there exist in fact no empirical grounds for supposing that anything of the sort actually exists.

Despite this sobering conclusion, Langmuir remains prepared to grant that xenophobia toward Jews, although no different in its essential nature from xenophobia toward blacks, Muslims, Roma, or other groups, does display one unusual feature specific to it. Langmuir considers, and here I agree with him, that for the most part *xenophobic* hatred is "realistic hostility," meaning by that "that well-nigh universal xenophobic hostility which uses the real conduct of some members of an outgroup to symbolize a social menace."[12]

Resentments of this kind, he thinks, often share "a kernel of truth." Langmuir also allows, however, for "a new kind of stereotype, which I shall call chimerical [having] no kernel of truth [but depicting] imaginary monsters."[13] And he suggests that what is unusual about xenophobic hostility toward Jews is that it involves, to a greater degree than other forms of xenophobia, "socially significant chimerical hostility."[14] Here, perhaps, and only here, he thinks, is there a legitimate role for the term *antisemitism* to play. Social scientists, he concludes, should

> free "antisemitism" from its racist, ethnocentric or religious implications
> and use it only for what can be distinguished empirically as an unusual
> kind of human hostility directed at Jews. If we do so, we may then be able
> to distinguish more accurately between two very different kinds of threats
> to Jews. On the one hand there are situations in which Jews, like any other
> major group, are confronted with realistic hostility, or with that well-nigh
> universal xenophobic hostility which uses the real conduct of some members
> of an outgroup to symbolize a social menace. On the other hand, there
> may still be situations in which Jewish existence is much more seriously
> endangered because real Jews have been irrationally converted in the minds
> of many into a symbol, "the Jews," a symbol whose meaning does not depend
> on the empirical characteristics of Jews yet justifies their total elimination
> from the earth.[15]

Fully chimerical hatred of Jews, however, Langmuir takes to be a late and aberrant development, commencing in the twelfth century with "the first European accusation of Jewish ritual murder . . . created in Norwich about 1150 by the cumulative irrationality of a superstitious insignificant priest and his wife, a mendacious Jewish apostate, and an unimportant monk who sought to overcome his sense of inferiority."[16]

For this reason, Langmuir considers that the term *antisemitism* is misused to describe earlier hostility to Jews. In view of the turn that my own argument will take later in this chapter, however, it is worth recording in passing that Langmuir's sense of chimerical accusation as a late and relatively marginal ingredient in xenophobia directed against Jews is contested by other scholars, who note many earlier examples of chimerical beliefs concerning Jews going back as far as the first-century Greek rhetorician Apollonius Molon and including ninth-century beliefs to the effect that Jewish men menstruate and pray to Satan.[17]

IDEOLOGY VERSUS INDIVIDUAL PSYCHOLOGY

Suppose for the sake of argument that we were simply to disregard Langmuir's arguments for the conclusion there is no distinctive type of non-Jewish hostility experienced only by Jews and side instead with the many Jews and others who have always believed that the term *antisemitism does* mark a distinctive form of hostility encountered only by Jews. Would that get us any further toward a definition of the term?

No, because either choice commits us to thinking of antisemitism as a *form of hostility*. Hostility, after all, is a *psychological state*. And if *that* is *what antisemitism is*, then its site, its habitation, as it were, is the individual mind: the mind of the antisemite. And here, a further problem confronts us. *Ideologies* are *not* inhabitants of the individual mind. Marxism or liberalism, for instance, is not simply the sum of what happens to be believed about politics by individual Marxists or liberals. An ideology comes to more than is contained in the mind of any of its individual adherents. It has an internal structure, a logic of its own that none of its adherents at a given point in history may fully comprehend. An ideology is a *cultural*, not a *psychological*, entity in roughly the sense in which history, or physics, or the romantic movement are cultural rather than psychological entities.

The problem confronting us now is that there are many reasons for regarding antisemitism *both* as a form of animosity *and* as an ideology. By purporting to offer, among other things, a systematic account of how the world is secretly governed, antisemitism takes on a significance for believers far transcending any merely personal ground of animosity or contempt. As Kenneth Marcus puts it, "As an ideology, it [antisemitism] provides a way to make sense of the entire world and all of history, not just the relatively small territory occupied by the descendants of Jacob."[18]

At the same time Marcus, as I read him, continues throughout his book to share the founding assumption of Langmuir (and indeed of most other writers on the topic) that *what* we are trying to clarify in seeking a definition of the term *antisemitism* is the nature of a *state of mind*: an enduring *psychological disposition*, that is to say, characteristic of a certain class of *individuals*, namely, antisemites. Unless I badly misread him, that seems certainly to be the underlying premise of the following passage, which sets the tone for his opening chapter, "Attitude, Behavior and Ideology": "The bewildering array of definitions of anti-Semitism—and the resulting difficulty in understanding cases like Ilan Halimi's—arises because people are trying to define different phenomena. To some, anti-Semitism is an attitude, to others a form of conduct, and to still others an ideology or pathology. The differences reflect the varying qualities that people find most important or troublesome about anti-Semitism: the way that anti-Semites feel about Jews, the things they do to Jews, or the mindset that makes them think and act as they do."[19]

The word that I find most troubling in this passage, for reasons that I have just explained, is of course *mindset*. A *mindset* is, at least to my conceptual ear, a complex state of some individual mind. An *ideology*, on the other hand, is not a constituent of any *individual mind* but rather a constituent of a *culture*. The prospects for a unitary definition seem at this point even worse than Marcus suggests. It is not just that the mind of the individual antisemite is a bafflingly complex place but that antisemitism, in at least one major mode in which it manifests itself, as ideology, altogether transcends the mind of the individual antisemite.

The great merit of Marcus's book, as I see it, consists not so much in providing a definition of *antisemitism* as in providing an invaluable conspectus, on which I have leaned heavily in the foregoing, of the difficulties attending the attempt to formulate one. He does, it is true, contend that "the chief lessons of the preceding chapters can in fact be reduced to a single general definition"[20] as follows: "Anti-Semitism is a set of negative attitudes, ideologies and practices directed at Jews as Jews, individually or collectively, based upon and sustained by a repetitive and potentially self-fulfilling latent structure of hostile erroneous beliefs and assumptions that flow from the application of double standards towards Jews as a collectivity, manifested culturally in myth, ideology, folklore, and imagery, and urging various forms of restriction, exclusion, and suppression."[21]

But he readily concedes that this may be less a definition than a handy summary of the results of prior discussion: "The precise terms of the definition may be less important than the thinking that went into it. In this sense the broader definition consists of this entire volume and not just the one sentence in which its message is encapsulated."[22]

We might reasonably be challenged to show whether we can do any better. This challenge I shall now—cautiously and with a sense of the attendant difficulties sharpened, I hope, by the discussion up to this point—attempt to meet. Before getting on with the business of this chapter, though, there is one last question to be raised concerning the nature of definition itself.

ARE DEFINITIONS INVENTED OR DISCOVERED?

"Some readers," Marcus notes, "may be inclined to dismiss definitional questions as a matter of arbitrary linguistic conventions that may be selected, revised, or replaced at will and with little consequence."[23] And indeed they may. It is not uncommon, particularly among the more hardheaded media commentators, to think that there can be no objective standard of correctness for definitions and that therefore all definition, per se, is tendentious.

But is that necessarily so? Who or what determines the meaning of terms? Is it merely human stipulation? Or is it, to put it grandly, the nature of things? Philosophers have frequently tended to opt for one or the other of these stories to the exclusion of the other. There is a case to be made, however, for regarding the fabrication of meaning as a joint enterprise in which both play a part. Consider, for example, the biological term of art *species*. A species is a group of individual organisms capable of mating to produce fertile offspring. So much is stipulation: the term *species* means *that* because that is what biologists have collectively decreed that it should mean. Knowing the meaning of species in that sense is, in effect, a matter of knowing what language game (*Sprachspiel*: Wittgenstein's term) we human beings have chosen to play with the word: in this case, the game of sorting organisms into groups satisfying that (stipulative) requirement. However, knowing the meaning of a term can also mean knowing how to single out instances of the kinds of thing to which the term applies. And at this point, nature enters the picture. We can't, in other words, just *stipulate* that this or that arbitrary collection of individual organisms shall be held to constitute a species. It only constitutes a *species* if all its members are capable of interacting sexually to produce fertile offspring. And whether a particular group of organisms meets that specification is clearly a factual question: something to be determined not by arbitrary stipulation but by empirical inquiry.

TWO TYPES OF PREJUDICE

Is something of the sort also true of that other abstract term *antisemitism*? I think that it is. But to see what precisely, we need to go back a step and consider a more fundamental term: *prejudice*. Let us avail ourselves, as we did earlier, of Gordon Allport's shrewd definition:

D_0. Prejudice is thinking ill of others without sufficient warrant.

So far, everything is indeed "just a matter of arbitrary stipulation." D_0 just records how we English speakers have decided to use (or better, fallen into the habit of using) the term *prejudice*. But now, by analogy with the question "Which collections of organisms as a matter of fact *satisfy* the definition of a species?" we can ask, "Which human phenomena turn out as a matter of fact to *satisfy* D_0?" At this point, just as in the other case, we pass abruptly from stipulation to empirical inquiry. And very little reflection on the passing scene is enough to dislodge the thought that there are two general kinds of phenomena (no doubt among others) that do so. I shall label them, respectively, *social prejudice* and *political prejudice*.[24]

By "social prejudice" I have in mind roughly the sort of thing that Langmuir labels "xenophobia" or "ethnic prejudice": that is to say, prejudice on the part of members of a dominant social group in society against people they consider to be foreigners, aliens, interlopers, upstarts, lower-class vulgarians, or in some other way inferior. Emotionally speaking, it is driven by *contempt*, and its goal is *social exclusion*. Its object, that is, is to prevent members of the despised out-group as far as possible from participating in the life of decent society: the society, that is to say, of which members of the dominant in-group consider themselves to be the representatives and guardians.

Social prejudice is characteristically directed not against *collective entities* but against *individuals*. It operates, as logicians like to say, *distributively*. The contempt of the Englishman who despises West Indians, for instance, tends to be focused on West Indians taken, as it were, *one by one* as individuals; it is not, or not primarily, focused on the West Indian *community*. Indeed, he may not even grasp that there is such a thing. He does not, that is, find the individual West Indian contemptible because the latter is a member of a despicable *community* but because of what he *is as an individual*. On the contrary, if he is in any way allergic to the West Indian community, it will be because it appears to him merely as a rabble of independently despicable individuals.

A further feature of social prejudice is that fear, except very occasionally, in the context of special concerns over matters such as competition over employment, property values, or some immediate threat of physical violence, plays very little part in it. Contempt, after all, tends to drive out fear. We kick into the gutter with confidence those we despise on social grounds because our very contempt for them persuades us that these miserable persons, inferior as they are, are far from possessing either the means or the temerity to fight back.

Social prejudice is apt to justify itself by appeal to what social scientists call *stereotypes*: disagreeable or contemptible features supposedly shared by all members of the despised group or class. According to such stereotypes, Scots are sanctimonious and incorrigibly mean, Englishmen arrogant and inscrutable, women (as Virginia Woolf makes the socially uneasy and resentfully misogynist young Cambridge don Charles Tansley say in *To the Lighthouse*) "can't write, can't paint." According to others, money has a way of sticking to Jewish fingers and Jews themselves a habit of becoming dominant, to a degree out of keeping with their numbers in society, in such professions as law, medicine, and academia, while West Indians are equally widely perceived as leading *ganja*-soaked, noisy, and disorganized lives, and so on.

It is important to notice that contrary to common opinion but in line with Langmuir's account of xenophobia, what is wrong with such stereotypes is not that they are false, or at least false *in the sense of having not the slightest grain of truth in them*. There has to be more than a grain of truth in all of them for the simple reason that one cannot intelligibly despise an individual for qualities that he or she simply does not possess. Contempt, to give itself something on which to brood resentfully, has to fasten on something with at least some tenuous connection with reality. Hence, for social prejudice against these groups to get off the ground, there have to be at least *some* ludicrously bad women writers and painters; at least *some* self-righteous, penny-pinching Scots; at least *some* noticeable Jewish presence in the professions over and above what might be accounted for by strict statistical parity in terms of population numbers; at least *some* Jews with a remarkable capacity for money making; at least *some* West Indians with a marked love of marijuana and wild parties; and so on.

What is wrong with the stereotypes on which social prejudice feeds is not that they fail of—at least partial—*truth* but rather that they lack the *generality* that they claim for themselves. On the one hand, there are plenty of West Indians, Jews, women, Scots, and Englishmen who fail utterly to conform to the usual stereotypes. On the other hand, there are always, equally, plenty of people around who conform exactly to one or other of them but who happen, unfortunately, not to be Jews, West Indians, Scots, Englishmen, or women as the case may be. Sober, productively employed West Indians are in fact as common as marijuana-puffing white party animals. Writers as good as Virginia Woolf or Cynthia Ozick happen to be female; ones as bad as Jeffrey Archer happen to be male. Curiously enough, the two least financially astute persons I have encountered in my life happened both to be Jews, while on the other hand, the impressive houses of gentile pop stars, footballers, television celebrities, industrial magnates, and bankers to whose stalwartly non-Jewish fingers, unsullied by the least contact with a tallit or a siddur, money has displayed a truly remarkable capacity to stick, can be found all over what the British call the home counties. And while the presence of Jews in the liberal professions may indeed be out of proportion to the relative size of their community, so is that of a number of other groups, including beneficiaries of a private education, Londoners, British Hindus, and children of the professional class. No doubt there are cultural reasons for these disparities, but rather than disparaging them, discontent might be better devoted to inquiring into them with a view to reproducing them in communities—such as that of beneficiaries of a British state education—at present comparatively disadvantaged in these respects.

I turn now to the second type of phenomenon that satisfies D_o: political prejudice. Political prejudice differs from social prejudice in a number of respects, three of which seem to me more fundamental than the rest. The first is that it is directed—in the first instance at least—not against *individuals* but against *collective entities*, real or imaginary. Second, it is driven emotionally not by *contempt* but by *fear* of the collectivity in question. Third, this fear is both supported and inculcated by a complex, theory-laden narrative that purports to explain why the collectivity in question is to be feared.

The difference between social and political prejudice can readily be exemplified in common life. One example is to be found in the differing forms taken by the anti-Catholic prejudice that used to be not uncommon in England. *Social prejudice* against Catholics involves dislike of individual Catholics as superstitious, idol worshipping, Jesuitical, and priest-ridden hypocrites incapable of thinking for themselves—and for all these reasons, not at all the sort of person one finds it pleasant to be forced into contact with in daily life or to have brought home to the house by one's less fastidious children.[25] Someone *politically* prejudiced against Catholics, on the other hand, may find individual Catholics amusing, enjoy playing chess with a Jesuit friend, and so forth but entertain a holy fear of the hidden power of the Catholic Church and of such organizations as Opus Dei, concerning whose sinister machinations he or she will be prepared to inform in some detail anyone prepared to listen.

To conclude, the defining contrasts between social and political prejudice can be briefly summarized as follows:

C_1. Social prejudice targets individuals; political prejudice targets collectivities.

C_2. Social prejudice is driven emotionally by contempt, political prejudice by fear.

C_3. Social prejudice justifies itself merely by appeal to a range of contemptuous stereotypes to which individuals of the despised group are held to conform. Political prejudice, by contrast, embodies some complex, theoretically elaborated narrative explaining why the targeted group, considered as an organized whole, is to be feared.

SOCIAL VERSUS POLITICAL ANTISEMITISM

Prejudice against Jews can also come in either or both of these two forms. Social prejudice against Jews—*social* antisemitism—sees *individual* Jews as, inter alia, greasy, hook nosed, money grubbing, noisy, overfamiliar, and overemotional alien vulgarians, too clever, moreover, for their own good: as thoroughly disgusting types, that is to say, with whom no English gentleman, however sadly short of the money that sticks so miraculously to Jewish fingers, would wish to associate either himself or his family. Such an evocation of the mind of the social antisemite is, like my earlier evocation of anti-Catholic animus, to some extent parodic; yet it does to a degree serve to capture both the content and the essential silliness of the thing. English literature and letters offer plenty of actual examples no less startling in their inanity.[26]

Political antisemitism on the other hand can in principle cohabit easily with friendship toward and even a high moral regard for *individual* Jews (the cant phrase, "Some of my best friends are Jews," uttered by a political antisemite, may at times express no more than the truth, that is to say). This is the case because political antisemitism is driven not by *contempt* for Jews *as individuals* but by *fear* concerning the supposed "threat" posed by the Jewish people *considered as an organized community.*

Like other forms of political prejudice, political antisemitism disposes of a complex, theoretically elaborated *explanatory account* of what is to be feared from "the Jews" and why it is to be feared. The character of the beliefs that give it substance and direction are, however, as we have already seen in chapters 1 and 2, far stranger and far less in accord with any remotely plausible reading of reality than those that direct any other form of political prejudice.

I have in mind here generalized forms of the beliefs that in chapter 1, we found openly exposed in article 22 of the 1988 Hamas covenant and in chapter 2 covertly active in the debate over the uniqueness of the Holocaust. In neither case are the various indictments of the Jews we encountered in those chapters original, either to Hamas or to the American academics to be found on one wing of the uniqueness debate. On the contrary, versions of its main clauses can be found directing antisemitic discourse at most periods over the entire twenty centuries of the Common Era. The bulk of these variants can be assimilated to the following five claims:

PA$_1$. The obsessive concern of Jews with their own interests and their indifference or contempt for the interests of non-Jews make them directly and solely responsible for human suffering on a scale far exceeding anything that can be alleged against any other human group, and in particular for whatever specific evil or evils (SEs) most concern this or that concrete version of political antisemitism.

PA$_2$. The Jewish community is conspiratorially organized in the pursuit of its self-seeking and heinous goals to an extent that gives it demonic powers not to be suspected from the weak and harmless appearance of its individual members.

PA$_3$. Through the efficacy of its conspiratorial organization and through its quasi-miraculous ability to acquire and manage money, the Jewish community has been able to acquire secret control over most of the main social, commercial, political, and governmental institutions of non-Jewish society.

PA$_4$. Given the secret control exercised by world Jewry over (only apparently) non-Jewish institutions and given the obsessive concern of the Jewish community with its own interests to the exclusion of those of non-Jews, it is simply not feasible to remedy the evils occasioned by the presence of the Jews in non-Jewish society (and in particular SE) by any means short of the *total elimination* of the Jews.

PA$_5$. Since the evils that the Jews do in the world (and in particular SE) owe their existence solely to Jewish wickedness, the elimination of the Jews will cause those evils to cease without the need for any further action on the part of non-Jews, whose world will, in the nature of things, return forthwith to the perfect state of order natural to it, from which it would never have lapsed had it not been for the mischievous interventions of the Jews.

It is to be noticed that these five beliefs are not logically independent but mutually entail and confirm one another, composing a hermetically self-enclosed and internally defended vision of reality. PA_4, for instance, follows necessarily from the conjunction of PA_1 with PA_3, as does PA_5 from PA_1. Any doubts that the convert to political antisemitism may entertain concerning the difficulty of finding evidence of Jewish wickedness outside specifically antisemitic websites or newspapers of the type of the Nazi *Der Stürmer* can be countered by appeal to PA_2 and PA_3. In Kenneth Marcus's words noted earlier, "As an ideology it [antisemitism] provides a way to make sense of the entire world and all of history, not just the relatively small territory occupied by the descendants of Jacob."[27]

Political antisemitism thus, while it shares the fundamental characteristics of political prejudice mentioned earlier, adds several further characteristics of its own. The first is that unlike the stereotypes that masquerade as knowledge for the socially prejudiced and the heightened allegations of plot and conspiracy that direct some types of political prejudice (anti-Catholic prejudice in sixteenth-century England offers a good example of the latter), the above five founding claims of political *antisemitism* have in them *not even the grain of truth that such stereotypes possess*. The Jewish community, as anybody at all closely acquainted with it knows perfectly well, is far too small and far too divided in historical, cultural, political, and religious terms to be remotely capable of marshalling the darkly secret and demonic power in the service of evil attributed to it by claims (1)–(5). All five claims are, not to put too fine a point on it, *wholly* delusive. In terms of Langmuir's vocabulary as noted earlier, they are *chimerical*.

Nevertheless, versions of (1)–(5) differing only in the specific nature of the concrete evils assigned to collective Jewish agency in one period or another, from well poisoning or religiously sanctioned child murder, to organizing the Russian Revolution or determining the outcome of World War I in favor of the Allies, have commanded unwavering belief from large numbers of otherwise sane people over many centuries. The Jews, moreover, would appear to be the only minority or diasporic group of which this extraordinary combination of claims has ever been asserted.

A second characteristic in terms of which political antisemitism differs sharply both from social prejudice and other forms of political prejudice is that the goal that it pursues is neither merely the *exclusion* of individual Jews from "decent" society nor merely the *political defeat or neutralization* of a feared collective entity sought for the most part by other forms of political prejudice.

Political antisemitism, given its belief in the demonic power of world Jewry to preserve the Jewish conspiracy from outside scrutiny, cannot, short of doubting its own principles, avoid the conclusion that the only way to deal with the Jews is to remove them wholesale from the scene. Political antisemitism, that is to say, unlike other forms of political prejudice, is *essentially* eliminative in character.

A third feature to be noted is that it is political antisemitism—antisemitism masquerading as a universally explanatory worldview—and not social antisemitism, that is the *potentially lethal* form of Judeophobia. Social antisemitism is not eliminative. Consisting as it does merely in contempt for Jews *as individuals* nourished by more or less feeble stereotypes, it tends to present the Jewish *collectivity* less as a source of *threat* than as a source of indulgent comedy: a little world populated by Jewish mothers, gefilte fish, klezmer music, and demented dietary restrictions. In itself, it can no more provide a motive for *eliminating* the Jews than blackface minstrel shows could have provided a motive for *eliminating* the harmlessly brainless, banjo-strumming blacks who populated such entertainments. Genocide has fear as its necessary precondition. Contempt, as we noted earlier, tends to drive out fear. For genocide to become a possibility, we need a wide diffusion of the outlook noted by Sartre in the French writer and antisemite Louis-Ferdinand Céline (1894–1961):

> Anti-Semitism is . . . a form of Manichaeism. It explains the course of the world by the struggle of the principle of Good and the principle of Evil. Between these two principles no reconciliation is conceivable; one of them must triumph and the other be annihilated. Look at Céline: his vision of the universe is catastrophic. The Jew is everywhere, the earth is lost, it is up to the Aryan not to compromise . . . the anti-Semite does not have recourse to Manichaeism as a secondary principle of explanation. It is the original choice he makes of Manichaeism which explains and conditions anti-Semitism.[28]

Political antisemitism, now, both articulates and encourages exactly that type of Manichaean panic.

Finally, it is to be noted that if social antisemitism is the antisemitism of unthinking bigots, then political antisemitism, by contrast, is very much the thinking person's version of Judeophobia. One can become a *social* antisemite without doing anything as demanding as reading or thinking—become one, perhaps, as the result of no more than a bad personal experience at the hands of a real Jew. Political antisemitism, on the other hand, given its rich and specific conceptual and doctrinal content, cannot simply materialize out of the thin air of that sort of bad experience. One can become a *political* antisemite

QUESTIONS OF DEFINITION 71

only through a process of intellectual conversion, of reading, of listening to speeches, of thinking things out until it comes to seem to one, in the burst of enlightenment characteristic of conversion experiences, whether by having been talked into it or by having talked oneself into it, that the Jews are at the root of everything evil in the world. It is no doubt for this reason that as we shall see in chapters 5 and 10, while *social* antisemitism is the antisemitism of the common man, *political* antisemitism—the lethal, the eliminative kind, in other words—is and has always been peculiarly a disease of intellectuals.

SOME PROBLEMS OF DEFINITION REVISITED

It is time to ask ourselves whether the distinction between social and political antisemitism, as we have here developed it, can help to resolve some of the problems of definition we encountered in above sections of the present chapter.

In the light of the above arguments, it might seem tempting to agree with Kenneth Marcus that "the bewildering array of definitions of anti-Semitism . . . arises because people are trying to define different phenomena." But in fact that way of putting it misdescribes the problem. The problem is not that we are dealing with a single *concept*, "antisemitism," which happens, for some mysterious reason, to be exemplified by a range of "phenomena" too diverse and mutually incompatible to permit a single definition. Rather, it is that the *word* "antisemitism," as we use it in discourse, covers a family of distinct though closely related *concepts*. In the most general terms, the word *antisemitism* picks out the concept of hostility lacking in cognitive warrant toward Jews. *In virtue of that definition*, however, the word ranges in addition over (at least) the two subordinate concepts we have distinguished as those of *social antisemitism* and *political antisemitism*. It is in the nature of concepts to rank themselves into hierarchies of this kind, and definition must proceed accordingly. In legal terms, one would hardly expect the definition of *tort* to include within itself the definitions of terms for individual torts. In scientific terms, it would be equally futile to expect the definition of the term *element* to include the content of the definitions of terms such as *hydrogen, strontium*, and so on, naming specific elements.

In much the same way, once we have a grip on the idea that the term *antisemitism* might correspond not to a single concept but to a hierarchically organized family of concepts, it becomes possible to envisage the possibility that the apparent incompatibility of phenomena associated with the term might disappear as a result of partitioning them between different members of the family of concepts it covers. Might there not be, for instance, phenomena closely associated with social antisemitism but not at all with political antisemitism, and vice versa?

A natural place to begin exploring this suggestion might be Gavin Langmuir's distinction between kinds of xenophobic hostility whose stated grounds share a "kernel of truth" and those he calls "chimerical hostility" whose grounds are entirely delusive. If we have argued correctly, then both of these types of hostility are characteristic of antisemitism—but of entirely different types of antisemitism. What Langmuir calls, following a consensus among social scientists, xenophobia or ethnic prejudice on the one hand is characteristic of what we have here distinguished as *social* or *racist* antisemitism. What Langmuir calls "chimerical hatred" of Jews on the other hand is characteristic of what we have here distinguished as *political* antisemitism.

However, because Langmuir treats antisemitism as a name for a single concept requiring a single definition, rather than as a name for a family of differently definable concepts, he is led to treat chimerical hatred as a sort of odd, not easily explicable adjunct to what is for the most part a standard type of xenophobia: in effect, an unusually factually baseless variety of stereotype. This not only leads him to fail to grasp the full oddity, the extraordinary *strangeness*, of antisemitism in its political, ideological version. It also leads him to reject as "fallacious" the idea that there has ever existed such a thing as "a distinctive kind of reaction of non-Jews directed only at Jews that corresponds to the concept evoked by the word 'antisemitism.'" It now appears, if we have argued correctly, that *political* antisemitism constitutes exactly that: a distinctive type of hostile reaction by non-Jews to Jews *and to no other group*. Moreover, it is one that has been central in organizing lethal hatred of Jews across a period far longer than the one Langmuir assigns to "chimerical hostility." As we shall see in later chapters, while the *specific* accusations offered in support of those fundamental beliefs—in the absolute commitment to evil of the Jewish community, in the community's quasi-demonic power, in its conspiratorial character, and so on—have displayed a bewildering and protean power to reinvent themselves in new forms as the centuries pass, the fundamental beliefs themselves have remained effectively unchanged in Europe since late antiquity. Their persistence offers an explanation for the curious proneness of Jew hatred, relative to hatred of other groups, to express itself in the terms that Langmuir labels "chimerical": the blood libel, the supposed capacity of Jewish males to menstruate, the alleged Jewish control not only of major branches of the United States government but also of the Lions or Kiwanis, and so on. If one has *already* accepted that the Jewish people is collectively committed to demonic goals and that it is conspiratorially organized in systematically impenetrable ways, then there is no reason why anything alleged of these abominable people should not be true and no reason to demand evidence for any of it, since in any case the quasi-supernatural efficiency of the Jewish conspiracy can be relied on to have ensured that any evidence that might have been available has been ruthlessly suppressed.

Dropping the idea that antisemitism names a single, unified kind, rather than a small number of distinct (though hierarchically related) kinds, may equally shed light on the issue, one that bulks large in Kenneth Marcus's discussion, of whether antisemitism is to be understood as a type of personal animosity or as a species of ideology. The answer suggested by the present analysis is that neither understanding is false but that each applies to a quite different version of antisemitism. Social antisemitism is indeed a form of personal animosity applied to individual Jews and grounded in hostile or derisive stereotypes. Political antisemitism, by contrast, is an ideology—one offering a comprehensive explanation of any of a wide range of non-Jewish discontents in terms of the malignity, not so much of individual Jews, as of the Jewish *collectivity* conceived as vested, in virtue of its conspiratorial organization, with quasi-demonic powers.

If this is correct, then we have to regard ourselves as dealing under the label *antisemitism* not merely with more than one kind of phenomenon but with more than one kind of antisemite and hence with more than one kind of "antisemitic mentality." Certainly, those antisemites whom I have encountered personally and listened to over the past sixty years or so have fallen fairly consistently into two quite sharply distinguished types that correspond with the categories of *social* versus *political* prejudice distinguished earlier. In one group, there is the barroom blowhard with an antipathy to any Jew he encounters based on the usual stereotypes. He finds Jews, that is, vulgar, pushy, money grubbing, prone to "get above themselves," given to insinuating themselves into social milieus that should by rights have rejected them, and to using their undoubted cleverness to obtain positions of influence that should by rights belong to "our sort." And that is not all that is wrong with Jews, he is very willing to tell you sotto voce. They are also constantly on the lookout for any advantage to be gained by complaining about the supposed injustices under which they suffer.

In the other group, one finds people obsessed not with despised traits of individual Jews but with the alarming nature of the threats posed by "the Jews"— the imagined Jewish collectivity—to whatever causes or values the speaker happens to hold dear. The two sets of concerns may overlap in the minds of some antisemitic individuals, but equally, they may not. In the thinking of

the first group, emotional dispositions—animosity, resentment, contempt—
dominate, and ideology plays very little part. In the thinking of the second
group, ideology is the main factor, the nerve of the obsession. Hence, members
of this group, unlike members of the first, tend to be anxious to assure one that
they nourish no personal antipathy toward individual Jews, and indeed that
"some of their best friends are Jews."

These two branches of antisemitism, it seems to me, require very different treatment if we are either to understand or to deal with them. With the
first, we are dealing with very familiar kinds of xenophobia based on dislike
and exclusion and supported in the individual mind by appeal to stereotypes
whose irrationality consists, as we have already argued (in partial conformity
with Langmuir) not in lacking a kernel of truth but rather in lacking the generality claimed for them. Although it may be common in this or that social
group, we are dealing here with a type of antisemitism essentially rooted in
the individual mind in the sense that what this kind of antisemite *has against*
Jews is to be explained in terms of the individual's own tastes, self-image,
and group allegiances. For such an antisemite, his dislike of Jews plays no
particular *explanatory* function in his larger worldview and connects with
no large concerns of public or political morality. While this kind of casual,
stereotype-buttressed animosity may lead the antisemite to wish to *exclude*
Jews from groups or clubs to which he and his friends belong, there is nothing
about it that could give him a reason for wishing to *eliminate* Jews from society
or from the world.

With the second branch, political antisemitism, matters are very different. Here, we are dealing not with merely personal prejudices, seated in the
individual mind, but with a *cultural formation*: a body of wholly delusive but
supposedly explanatory beliefs, claiming, in Marcus's telling phrase, to "make
sense of the entire world and all its history," not just the tiny part of it actually
occupied by the Jews. Like many other cultural formations, it is equipped with
a public presence, a complex internal logic, a long history, and a substantial
body of literature. These, as with other cultural formations, give it the power
to transmit itself to new believers by standard processes of gradually increasing familiarity leading eventually to conversion. Its internal logic commits its
converts to demanding not merely the exclusion or disadvantaging of Jews but
the outright elimination of Jewish influence, whether by the literal destruction
of the Jewish people or by the destruction of Jewish institutions such as the
State of Israel.

The influences exerted by political antisemitism over minds susceptible
to it are thus very different from those exerted by antisemitism entertained

as a merely social prejudice. Political antisemitism affords a potent means of constructing "the Jew" as the enemy of whatever values the political antisemite happens to regard as central to national or human progress. It is thus very easy for a mind so influenced to give anti-Jewish hostility a mask of seeming moral virtue, and thus to justify as *moral demands*, actions and emotions that under any other circumstances it would recognize as prejudice and persecution.

To reach an understanding of a phenomenon of this kind, it is plainly not enough to confine our attention to the psychology of individual minds or even to individual minds viewed as expressive of group loyalties and hostilities. What requires explanation is the strange permanence of political antisemitism as an element in European *culture*. It has displayed, after all, a remarkable power to reinvent itself in the radically different conditions presented by successive periods of European history and to attach itself as a strange kind of bolt-on addition, somewhat in the manner of a virus attaching itself to the biochemical systems of a living cell, to systems of belief as radically diverse as medieval Christianity, British imperialism, nineteenth-century German nationalism, and Soviet communism. This power of attraction and renewal can only be explained if political antisemitism offers to its supporters and disseminators some political or cultural advantage sufficiently important to offset its essential absurdity. We need at the very least to ask ourselves, as we shall do in chapters 4 and 5, what that role might be: to attempt at least, that is, to understand political antisemitism in terms of what one might term its *cultural functions*. We need also to ask why such an extraordinary and grandiose tissue of delusions should have attached itself in the first place to, of all people, the Jews: a small, immensely useful but demonstrably disorganized and largely powerless tribe. In the same vein, we need to ask ourselves why and how a system of manifestly delusive beliefs should have come to influence over many centuries the minds of a long list of major European intellectuals, from Voltaire to George Bernard Shaw, and from Luther to T. S. Eliot. That last question is really too vast for a book of this nature. Preliminary sketches toward an answer will be found, however, in chapters 4, 5, 10, and 11–13.

In conclusion, several further consequences of distinguishing clearly between social and political antisemitism deserve our attention.

Earlier in the chapter, in "Problems of Intention," we noted that to define antisemitism reasonably enough as unwarranted hostility to Jews *because they are Jews* creates problems when it comes to identifying acts or discourse as antisemitic. It does so because, as we observed there, it seems to make the issue of whether what someone says or does is antisemitic dependent on that person's intentions or motives in saying or doing it: that is, upon questions

concerning whose truth or falsity the speaker or actor himself may be said to
have the determining voice. What we need to note at this point is that while
this remains true of social antisemitism, where what is ultimately at stake is
the existence of personal feelings of animosity, it is not true of political antisemitism. In the latter case, what makes someone an antisemite is not his or
her *feelings* or private inward disposition toward Jews but public participation
in a cultural formation involving the originating or diffusing of material in the
form of slogans, pamphlets, posters, demonstrations, newspaper articles, and
so on, the antisemitic character of which is readily discernible from its *content*.
What made Julius Streicher's newspaper *Der Stürmer* antisemitic and its editor an antisemite, that is to say, is not the character of Streicher's *consciousness*
or his *feelings* toward Jews but the evident manner in which the content of the
paper served to recapitulate, embroider, and reinforce the familiar tropes and
doctrines of political antisemitism.

This means in turn, as we shall see in the chapters 6–9, that drawing a clear
distinction between social and political antisemitism becomes crucial when it
comes to determining whether opposition to Israel is to be construed as legitimate political criticism or antisemitic defamation. In dealing with the forest
of vexed questions that arise at that point, the best guide available to date is
perhaps Natan Sharansky's 3-D Test[29] for distinguishing between mere criticism of Israel and antisemitism. This was originally floated by Sharansky in a
short piece in the *Jerusalem Post*[30] but has since become extremely influential.
According to Sharansky, antisemitic hostility toward Israel is distinguished
by the employment of three techniques: *demonization, double standards, and
delegitimization.*

The increasing frequency of occurrence of all three techniques, since the
late 1960s, in public debate concerning Israel in the West, is undeniable. The
reasons why this should be so are unclear, given their relative absence from
critical debate concerning other nations—China, North Korea, Iran, Syria,
Turkey, Saudi Arabia, say—whose political condition might, on the face of it,
be expected to provoke, if anything, more stringent kinds of political critique
from a left-wing standpoint than Israel.

I suggest that both the relative absence of Sharansky's three Ds from other
debates and their relative frequency in debate concerning Israel are explicable
as a consequence of the gradual penetration of that debate by a revived version
of political antisemitism. "Demonization"—the attribution to Israel of a level of
political savagery, contempt for human rights, and so forth, in excess of that of
which *any other nation on earth* can supposedly be accused—revives in a new

but still wholly chimerical form the ancient belief in the Jewish community's absolute commitment to evil. Double standards are a necessary accessory to any attempt to advance the vision of Israel as a "demonic" nation, because that claim cannot, as we shall see in chapters 6–9, rationally survive any serious comparison between Israel's record with regard to respect for human rights, the rule of law, the rules of war, and so forth, and that of a multitude of other nations. "Delegitimization," finally, is merely a new manifestation of the conviction, built into the quasi-logical internal structure of political antisemitism in the ways we have examined, that the only way to get rid of the putative threat constituted by the Jewish collectivity is altogether to remove that collectivity's capacity to interfere in human affairs, either by the destruction of its members or, failing that, by the destruction of any organized polity it may have succeeded in establishing.

THE HALIMI CASE: A SECOND LOOK

As Kenneth Marcus notes, the French legal and political authorities, when they found themselves confronted with the torture and death of Ilan Halimi, went to considerable lengths to deny that Halimi had been the victim of an antisemitic attack. Instead, they preferred the theory that he had simply been the victim of an attempted kidnapping that went wrong. It was only when one of the attackers confessed that Halimi had been treated in a certain way "because he was a Jew" that the latter interpretation was widely held to have collapsed.

This way of reevaluating the crime presupposes, as Marcus points out, that antisemitism consists of the antisemite's possession of a certain kind of inward mental disposition toward Jews: consists of something, that is to say, very easy for the antisemite to disguise and ascribable with anything approaching certainty only on the basis of an avowal by the antisemite himself. But as we have seen, this is only true for social antisemitism. Political antisemitism is an ideology with a cultural and therefore collective presence. It is a group phenomenon rather than an individual one.

It is relevant to the Halimi murder, therefore, that the attack was carried out by a group. The perpetrators pretended at first to have been interested in money, rather than in the fact that Halimi was a Jew. In the case of a mugging by an individual mugger, where what was clearly at stake was the victim's watch or wallet or iPhone, the fact that the victim happened to be wearing a kippah would not necessarily make the attack an antisemitic one. One would need to have become familiar, over an extended period, with the character and conversation of that particular mugger before one could say with any certainty whether the presence of the kippah had played any part in leading the mugger to choose that victim rather than another.

The fact that we are dealing, in the case of Les Barbares, with a concerted group action, blocks the transfer of that reasoning. There must, in their case, have been some motive to which the whole of the group subscribed and that must have been discussed among them. By employing the usual methods of comparing the independent stories of different group members with one another and with what actually took place, the truth of matters of this kind is rather easier to come at than the truth about what took place in the mind of an individual mugger in the split second of choosing a victim (was it, say, the kippah or the Rolex that weighed heaviest in the scale of that momentary decision?).

Fofana, the group's leader, admitted from the outset that Halimi had been targeted because he was Jewish. He claimed, however, that the object had been to demand ransom for him "from his synagogue." But if money had been the object, was that object not defeated by the torture and still more by the eventual abandonment of Halimi? If the motive of money is discounted for that reason, what possible motives are we left with? Sadism is one possible answer; extreme resentment is another. If pure sadism had been the motive, it would have been equally well served by choosing a non-Jew. What about resentment? If that had been social resentment, the supposed resentment of the poor, despised *Maghrebin* immigrant against the wealth and indifference of white French society, then the same argument applies. Why not choose just any white Frenchman to torture? Why choose a Jew particularly?

The only remaining option for the inquiry, it seems to me, is that the motive was antisemitic resentment. Political antisemitism of the classical European variety is now no longer a solely European delusion but is also very widespread in the present-day Muslim world. And in the peculiar demonology of political antisemitism, "the Jew" figures as the fons et origo of everything that is to be resented in this world. Therefore, for people in the grip of antisemitic delusion, to torture and kill a Jew, any Jew, is to direct one's anger at the *real thing*, as it were, the ultimate fount of all that is not working, all that is poor, miserable, and contemptible in the lives of the killers.

At the time of writing (early 2018), following the massive attacks of 2015–16 on French and Christian targets in Paris, Nice, and Sainte-Étienne-du-Rouvray, it seems less likely that if a case like Halimi's were to occur today, the French authorities would attempt to pass it off as a kidnapping gone wrong. But there is doubtless still some way to go before people finally grasp that in order to understand such things from the inside, we need to recognize, as the French authorities in 2006 clearly did not, the sad fact that political anti-semitism, antisemitism of exactly the type formerly disseminated by the Nazi magazine *Der Stürmer*, is once more becoming as widespread in the world as it was in prewar Central Europe. Moreover, we are still far from a widespread understanding that this is a far more dangerous phenomenon in its power to provoke and to its devotees to justify senseless extreme violence than its milder and far less lethal congener, social or racist antisemitism.

CONCLUSION: THE DEFINITION OF ANTISEMITISM

In conclusion, it may be useful to summarize the foregoing arguments in a formal definition of the term *antisemitism* as follows:

Antisemitism is thinking, speaking, or acting injuriously toward Jews, with-out sufficient warrant, because they are Jews. It has two main variants; *social* or *racist antisemitism*, and *political antisemitism*.

Social antisemitism is a form of *xenophobia* or *racism*. It targets individual Jews, whom it represents, as in the case of racism directed against other groups, in terms of stereotypes lacking widespread applicability but possessing a kernel of truth. It aims at the exclusion of Jews from the society of those prejudiced against them.

Political antisemitism is a *cultural formation* in the form of a delusive *system of beliefs* claiming the power to explain a wide variety of human social and political phenomena. It targets Jews (or "*the* Jews") considered as a *collectivity*. Against the Jewish collectivity, it asserts (in their most general form consis-tently over the past two millennia) a range of entirely delusive accusations, among them an absolute commitment to evil, conspiratorial organization of an essentially impenetrable kind, and vast power to harm any non-Jewish so-ciety that harbors Jews. These beliefs necessarily commit devotees of political antisemitism—as the only means, as they see it, of saving the world from Jew-ish iniquity—to pursuing the goal, not merely of *excluding* Jews from non-Jewish society but of altogether *eliminating from the world* either the entire Jewish community or at the very least any organized political entity that it may succeed in setting up.

In the next two chapters, we shall look into two obvious issues raised by this definition. We shall first ask what functions political antisemitism serves in non-Jewish culture and politics, and second, why *the Jews*, of all people, should have become the subject of the extraordinary collection of delusive beliefs that together make up the content of political antisemitism.

NOTES

1. Allport 1954.

2. I am grateful to my friend David Conway for pointing out the possibility of this objection. I am not sure that it is one that would occur to many readers, but it still seems worthwhile putting it out of court early in the argument.

3. Marcus 2015. One of the virtues of this book is its author's wide practical knowledge of the legal and constitutional difficulties obstructing the defense of American Jews against antisemitism in the new forms that it began to assume toward the end of the twentieth century. Marcus is an eminent lawyer and academic, who has served as staff director of the US Commission on Civil Rights and who is at present president of the Louis D. Brandeis Center for Human Rights Under Law, which he founded.

4. Glock and Stark 1966, 102.

5. Marcus 2015, 120.

6. Langmuir 1990, 311.

7. Prager and Telushkin 2003.

8. Langmuir 1990, 314–15.

9. Langmuir 1990, 315.

10. Langmuir 1990, 315.

11. Langmuir 1990, 321.

12. Langmuir 1990, 352.

13. Langmuir 1990, 306.

14. This and the preceding two citations, Langmuir 1990, 351.

15. Langmuir 1990, 351–52.

16. Langmuir 1990, 307.

17. Marcus 2015, 98. The works Marcus cites in this connection are Georg Christoph Berger Waldenegg, *Antisemitismus: "Eine gefährliche Vokabel"? Diagnose eines Wortes* (Vienna: Böhlau, 2001), and Léon Poliakov, *The History of Antisemitism*, vol. 1, *From the Time of Christ to the Court Jews*, trans. Richard Howard (New York: Vanguard, 1974).

18. Marcus 2015, 192.

19. Marcus 2015, 35.

20. Marcus 2015, 193.

21. Marcus 2015, 193–94.

22. Marcus 2015, 193.

23. Marcus 2015, 6.

24. Earlier, less developed versions of this distinction are to be found in Harrison 2006 and 2013 (see especially pp. 14–17).

25. I should explain, perhaps, for the benefit of the nervous reader who may feel his or her "safe space" to be infringed by these words, that I was baptized and brought up a Catholic.

26. Many of them collected in Cheyette 1993.

27. Marcus 2015, 193.

28. Sartre 1948, 41.

29. Marcus 2015, 155–59.

30. Natan Sharansky, "Anti-Semitism in 3D," *Jerusalem Post*, February 23, 2004. Retrieved from: https://www.swuconnect.com/insys/npoflow.v.2 /_assets/pdfs/flyers/sharanskyAntisemitism.pdf.

PART II

WHY THE JEWS?

FOUR

—꿈—

THE DISEASE METAPHOR

Within the history of the peoples of Europe the history of the Jews is not treated as circumstantially as their intervention in European affairs would actually merit, because within this history they are experienced as a sort of disease, and anomaly, and no one wants to put a disease on the same level as normal life.

—Ludwig Wittgenstein, *Culture and Value*

WHAT KIND OF QUESTION? WHAT KIND OF ANSWER?

In the last chapter, we arrived at a formal definition of the kind of antisemitism— political antisemitism—with which this book is concerned. But that definition raises as many questions as it answers. Political antisemitism in its most general form attributes a range of extraordinary accusations, delusive but profoundly political in character, uniquely to the Jews.[1] Supposedly, they are an absolutely depraved people, consumed by hatred of humanity, conspiratorially organized in the pursuit of world domination, and occupied in exercising secret control over the economic, political, and cultural life of non-Jews in an extraordinary variety of sectors, ranging from world finance to American foreign policy, and from Hollywood to revolutionary politics.

But one might ask, *why the Jews?* These dreamlike terrors neither have histor-ically been nor are today evoked by any of the other alien diasporas—Gypsies, Cathars, Huguenots; more recently the Irish, the British, the Armenians, the Turks, the Chinese, or the Sikhs—that have spilled, over the centuries, into one

85

or another European country. Why has the suspicion of the Other natural to most human cultures never resulted, in their case, in anything like the baroque growth of fantastic indictments, from the blood libel to the alleged direction by the "Israel lobby" of American foreign policy, that fulgurates perpetually and unstoppably around the Jews?

A skeptical reader might well object, "Wait a minute. You say 'perpetually.' But that seems to foreclose the discussion by introducing the assumption that antisemitism is a single, unitary phenomenon that persists unchanged across centuries. And that would seem to presume in turn that there must be a single, unitary answer to the question 'Why the Jews?' But is that necessarily so? Why shouldn't there be many different reasons, varying over time and having little in common, why from time to time Jews have found themselves the objects of persecution?"

On the face of it, that is a good question. One theorist of antisemitism who took this line was the late Hannah Arendt. It is not irrelevant, however, that her reasons for doing so were connected with her belief that Jews themselves must bear some responsibility for the twentieth-century version of the phenomenon. In *The Origins of Totalitarianism*,[2] she takes nineteenth- and twentieth-century antisemitism to be strongly causally linked to "'specifically Jewish functions' related to commerce and economic circulation that developed in the modern nation-state."[3] If that is the case, of course, then attempts to understand modern antisemitism by relating it to past outbreaks of prejudice against Jews, outbreaks occurring in ages yet to see the rise of economic structures specific to the modern nation-state, are both pointless and misleading. Arendt viewed all such claims as instances, as she put it, of the fallacy of "eternal antisemitism."

It cannot be doubted that the proportion of Jewish *individuals* involved in banking and the professions in pre–World War II central Europe was greater than the proportion of Jews in the community. Walter Laqueur estimates that in the 1920s, while Jews in Hungary amounted to 6 percent of the population, Jews made up "about half of Hungary's lawyers and physicians, and more than half of the banks and leading industries were in Jewish hands,"[4] while "half of the doctors in Vienna, and more than half in Warsaw were of Jewish origin."[5] But individual representation has no tendency to support the antisemite's central contention that the nation is under threat from Jewish influence unless one supplements these figures concerning individual participation with belief in the long tradition of ideological fantasy ascribing to this tiny and relatively powerless people, both the collective will to damage non-Jewish interests and the *collective* power to put such aims into practice.

The force of Arendt's argument is greatly weakened, that is to say, if her analysis of the causal roots of modern antisemitism, with its attendant demonstration of the "coresponsibility" of the Jews, cannot be shown to be independent of the idea that the interests that each and every *individual* Jew has primarily at heart are not those of the country of which he is a citizen but those of a vast Jewish conspiracy in which he functions merely as a humble but faithful foot soldier. David Nirenberg has recently pursued this line of criticism of Arendt.

> It was in their special commitment to bourgeois capitalism that [according to Arendt] the Jews were "co-responsible" for the reality to which they fell victim. "[All] economic statistics prove that the German Jews belonged not to the German people, but at most to its bourgeoisie."[6]

> It is a bit surprising that Arendt so often drew the necessary statistics from work produced by Nazi economists in support of party propaganda. It was, for example, to the "fighting scholarship" of Walter Frank and his "Reichsinstitut for the history of the New Germany" that she owed her indictment of the Rothschilds and other nineteenth-century Jewish bankers as "reactionary," "parasites upon a corrupt body."[7] But even if her statistics had been less obviously partial and partisan, their selection out of the world's infinite sea of significance would still be shaped by what her conceptual framework encouraged her to recognize as meaningful. In this case her negative view of "bourgeois capitalism" and its role in the nation state, the ease with which she was willing to assume that Judaism was essentially bound to money, her insistence on the "co-responsibility" of the Jews for the economic order within which they function: these were among the a priori ideological commitments that structured her selection and interpretation of "facts" about the Jews.[8]

In this drily telling passage, the thought fatal to Arendt's antiuniversalism is ultimately the one expressed by its final sentence. The problem for Arendt is not whether a viable distinction can be drawn between a "people" and "its bourgeoisie," or even whether there are sound arguments for regarding "bourgeois capitalism" as hostile to the interests of either "the nation-state" or its "people." The problem is rather that of showing what on earth the fact that a high but by no means dominating proportion of individuals engaged in carrying forward the affairs of bourgeois capitalism happen to be *Jews* has to do with any of these vast and imponderable questions.

Nevertheless, to Arendt—and not only to Arendt but also to a very large number of influential German and European figures of the preceding two centuries—much and quite possibly everything concerning the fate of modern Europe hinges on the Jews.

Moreover and more puzzlingly still, similarly disproportionate estimates of the historic importance of this tiny and scattered people had at the start of the modern era already haunted Europe for a millennium and a half.

Contrary to our initial objector, and to Arendt, in other words, we have uncovered what begins to look like a unitary phenomenon consistent across centuries: namely, the strange and persisting obsession of European culture with fingering the Jews as the most ready explanation for its self-perceived defeats and distresses, *however diverse the latter*. The question "Why the Jews?" now becomes the question, "Why this obsession, this rooted cultural fixation?"

Dennis Prager and Joseph Telushkin, the authors of the best recent book on the question "Why the Jews?" offer closely related reasons for taking that question to demand a unitary, universal answer, rather than a collection of answers specific to times and places.

> To ignore or deny that there is an ultimate cause for antisemitism contradicts both common-sense and history. Antisemitism has existed too long, and in too many disparate cultures, to ignore the problem of ultimate cause and/or to claim that new or indigenous factors are responsible every time it erupts. Factors specific to a given society help account for the manner or time in which antisemitism erupts. But they do not explain its genesis—why antisemitism at all? To cite but one example: the depressed economy in Germany in the 1920s and 1930s helps to explain why and when the Nazis came to power, but it does not explain why Nazis hated Jews, let alone why they wanted to murder every Jew. Economic depressions alone do not explain gas chambers.

> The very consistency of the passions Jews have aroused demands a consistent explanation. Ancient Egyptians, Greeks, and Romans, mediaeval and many modern Christians and Muslims, and Nazis and Communists have perhaps only one thing in common: they have all, at some point, counted the Jews as their enemy, often their greatest enemy. Why?[9]

Prager and Telushkin note the paucity of scholarly attempts to arrive at a unitary answer to the question "Why the Jews?" understood as we have so far suggested.

> Why such hatred and fear of a people who never constituted more than a small minority among those who most hated and feared them? Why, nearly always and nearly everywhere, the Jews?

Many answers have been offered by scholars. These include, most commonly, economic factors, the need for scapegoats, ethnic hatred, xenophobia, resentment of Jewish affluence and professional success, and religious bigotry. But ultimately these answers do not explain antisemitism; they only explain what factors have *exacerbated* it and caused it to erupt in a given circumstances. None accounts for the universality, depth and persistence of antisemitism. In fact, we have encountered virtually no study of this phenomenon that even attempts to offer a universal explanation of Jew-hatred. Nearly every study of antisemitism consists almost solely of historical narrative, thus seeming to indicate that no universal reason for antisemitism exists.[10]

In the dozen or so years since 2003, things have improved a little in the last of the respects they mention but possibly not in ways that would have satisfied Prager and Telushkin. What they see as important is not only the issue of universal versus piecemeal explanations of antisemitism. There is also the issue of "Judaizing" versus "de-Judaizing" explanations. They contend that "the traditional Jewish view that the Jews were hated because of Jewish factors" is the correct one.[11] And they reject "modern attempts to dejudaize Jew-hatred, to attribute it to economic, social and political factors, and universalise it as merely another instance of bigotry, [that are] as opposed to the facts of Jewish history as they are to the historical Jewish understanding of antisemitism."[12] It is a problem for Prager and Telushkin, therefore, that the most impressive recent attempt to construct a universal answer to the question "Why the Jews?"—David Nirenberg's "anti-Judaism"—offers in important respects a conspicuously "de-Judaizing" one.

Nirenberg's central claim, with which I broadly agree, is that anti-Judaism is by no means an irrational hiatus in the edifice of Western thought and culture but rather an essential element in the construction of that edifice. This sets him, of course, entirely at odds with Arendt. "Her pithy mockery of approaches that looked to the long history of ideas about Judaism to understand modern ideologies—she dubbed these approaches 'Eternal Anti-Semitism'—could serve as an ironic title for my own book."[13] At the same time, Nirenberg sees both the inception and the subsequent luxuriant development of the Western obsession with Jews and Judaism as minimally dependent on knowledge of or even contact with actual Jews. On the contrary, Nirenberg argues, what has rooted the obsession in Western culture is the fact that certain—for the most part hostile—stereotypes concerning Jews and Judaism have come to afford a means of conceptually articulating a range of issues having little to do with

actual Jews or with the actual nature of Judaism but much to do with certain
enduring problems and stresses internal to Western culture itself.

Thus, Nirenberg argues that Luther initially has recourse to the concept of
Judaism as a means both of opposing and of conceptually bundling together
various versions of nascent Protestantism more radical than his own, such as
the Sabbatarianism of Oswald Glaid.[14] All these people could in one way or
another be classed—by other Protestant Christians—as "Judaizers." And of
course the effects of such metaphors, once introduced, are hard to keep within
bounds.

> For Luther, however, the sectarian struggle was not only against Christian
> "Judaizers," but also against "real" Jews. He seems to have experienced
> the rise of Biblicist groups like Glaid's as a wave of Jewish proselytism [for
> which, as Nirenberg later argues, no shred of historical evidence exists—BH]
> endangering entire provinces of Christendom. His own treatise aimed at
> such groups, "Against the Sabbatarians" of 1538, began with the claim that
> Jewish missionaries were converting Christians to Sabbath observance and
> circumcision. The treatise therefore took the form of a question "Whom
> should we believe more, the true, trustworthy God or the false, lying Jews?"
> His answer extended for thirty printed pages of polemic against the Jews,
> pages that flowed directly into "On the Jews and their Lies" and his other
> "cruel" works of 1543.[15]

What sets Nirenberg in opposition to Arendt is his concern as a historian of
ideas to trace the interwoven continuity, across centuries, of such conceptually
and polemically motivated deployments of the concepts "Jew" and "Judaism"
among non-Jews, most often people with no inward understanding of Judaism
or for that matter much in the way of contact with "real Jews."

What sets him in opposition to Prager and Telushkin, on the other hand,
is the gap his methodology as a historian of ideas introduces between, on the
one hand, the consequences for real Jews of the salience of the notions Jew and
Judaism in *non-Jewish* theological, cultural, and political debate and, on the
other hand, the absence of any very evident causal link between those consequences and anything plausibly identifiable as a real characteristic of real Jews.
As Nirenberg trenchantly puts it,

> I am not interested in contributing to arguments, so often dominated by
> apologetics and anachronism, about whether Martin Luther was an anti-
> Semite or an architect of the Holocaust. My point is simply that Luther's
> reconceptualization of the ways in which language mediates between
> God and creation was achieved by thinking with, about, and against Jews

and Judaism. Insofar as these reconfigurations diminished the utility and heightened the dangers Jews posed to the Christian world, they had the potential to transform figures of Judaism and their fates. How powerful this potential might be, and what work it might perform in the future, were not Luther's to control. In the event, his teachings woke into startled ferocity the long slumbering debate about the place of letter, law and work in the Christian world. The conflict raged far beyond the borders of the Bible, invaded many provinces of human thought and action, and ensured that the spectre of Judaism would stalk battlefields in which scarcely a real Jew was left alive.[16]

Are we to choose Nirenberg's approach to the explanation of antisemitism over Prager and Telushkin's or vice versa? Neither, at least exclusively, I would like to think. I shall argue here that both answer to certain aspects of the truth. Nirenberg powerfully confirms my own sense that the actual content of political antisemitism is both deeply delusive and profoundly divorced from engagement with the actual nature of Judaism or the actual character of any real Jewish community. At the same time, it seems to me that Nirenberg's methods as a historian, sound and skillfully deployed as for the most part they are, work to deepen that divorce more than is entirely plausible. Could a largely un-Jewish Judaism have come to seem to non-Jews over many centuries to constitute as salient a key to the understanding of the world as Nirenberg plausibly makes it out to have been, if "real" Jews and "real" Judaism had not possessed aspects and characteristics capable of renewing and reinforcing, among non-Jews encountering them, the sense of threat and hostility diffused by the imaginary construct?

Such doubts tend to revive the claim central to Prager and Telushkin's argument: "Antisemitism is, as Jews have always regarded it: a response to Jews"[17]—that is to say, to "real" Jews committed to the actual outlook known as Judaism, not to imaginary Jews supposedly actuated by some mishmash of fundamentally non-Jewish concerns arbitrarily baptized by their enemies with the name "Judaism."

What aspects of "real" Judaism might make it particularly repugnant to its enemies? Prager and Telushkin consider the following to be fundamental:

1. Jewish monotheism has challenged the legitimacy of the religious beliefs of others.
2. The affirmation of national identity by Jews has "intensified antisemitic passions among those who viewed this identity as threatening their own nationalism."[18]

3. "[The] doctrine of the Jews' divine election ['chosenness'] has been a major cause of antisemitism."[19]

4. "From its earliest days, *the raison d'être* of Judaism has been to change the world for the better (in the words of an ancient Jewish prayer recited daily, 'to repair the world [*tikkun olam*] under the rule of God'). This attempt to change the world, to challenge the gods, religious or secular, of the societies around them, and to make moral demands upon others (even when not done expressly in the name of Judaism) has constantly been a source of tension."[20]

5. "As a result of the Jews' commitment to Judaism, they have led higher-quality lives than their neighbours in almost every society in which they have lived. For example, Jews have nearly always been better educated; Jewish family life has usually been more stable; Jews aided one another more than their non-Jewish neighbours aided each other; and Jewish men have been less likely to become drunk, beat their wives, or abandon their children. . . . This higher quality of life among Jews, which, as we shall show, directly results from Judaism, has, as one would expect, provoked profound envy and hostility among non-Jews."[21]

I have two worries, of rather different kinds, concerning this list. The first worry is logical and methodological. Prager and Telushkin begin by demanding a unitary, universal explanation of antisemitism, in opposition to those theorists who claim, like Arendt, that the causes of antisemitism change from age to age: that eternal antisemitism is a fabrication. My worry here is simply that the above list of five putative causes of antisemitism is too diverse, too heterogeneous, to figure as the required unitary account.

The second worry concerns the individual entries and whether any of them possess much in the way of explanatory power given the extraordinary, not to say bizarre, character of the attitudes and events they are supposed to explain.

For a start, I can confirm as a non-Jew that the higher quality of Jewish life, in precisely the respects cited by Prager and Telushkin, is quite often remarked on by non-Jews. I recently came across a fellow non-Jew, brought up in the East End of London, who does remember as a child in the 1930s hearing this being cited as one among a litany of grudges against the Jews. Yet until I met her, I would have had to say that I myself had never heard it cited except, in tones of approval, by people one would tend to identify as pro-Jewish rather than the reverse. Of the other four allegedly rebarbative features of Judaism, three (monotheism, national identity, commitment to the improvement of life in this world) are widely shared with non-Jewish sects, national entities, and political movements of many kinds. If such commitments were sufficient to explain the kinds of murderous resentment that Jews have endured, why have not those other groups found themselves similarly afflicted?

That leaves us with "chosenness." Plenty of casual conversations as well as a brief tour of antisemitic websites will confirm that there is quite a widespread belief among non-Jews to the effect that Jews consider themselves "better than other people." Equally, people who hold that belief do quite often connect it with the idea that Jews regard themselves as the "chosen people." But how far will this take us as an explanation? Whatever the accuracy of such beliefs, arrogance and social exclusiveness are scarcely the exclusive property of the Jews. Supercilious snobbery in the non-Jewish world, however, never evokes the bizarre set of responses characteristic of political antisemitism. For the latter, therefore, we must seek some other explanation.

That is what I propose to attempt in the remainder of this chapter and the next. My object is to locate an answer to the question "Why the Jews?" that mediates between the positions of Prager and Telushkin on the one hand and David Nirenberg on the other hand.

To be acceptable, that answer should, on the one hand, satisfy two plausible demands of Prager and Telushkin. It should (1) be universal, that is to say, unitary across time, and (2) consist *at some fundamental level* in a response to "real" Jews and/or Judaism. On the other hand, it should be such as to leave unchallenged David Nirenberg's equally plausible and superbly argued account of the centrality to Western culture of an enduring engagement with a range of essentially Eurocentric delusions concerning Judaism and its adherents.

SOME CONDITIONS OF ADEQUACY

The answer I have in mind is, as we shall see, a complex one. It lacks the elegant simplicity and evidence to inspection that compel immediate assent. If it is to carry conviction, that can only be because it manages to meet criteria of adequacy that require it to explain things otherwise difficult to make sense of: things that any adequate answer to the question "Why the Jews?" ought to be capable of explaining.

What might those things, or at any rate some of them, be? For a start, any decent explanation of political antisemitism, at least of the kind we are after, ought to be capable of explaining why the content of political antisemitism is for the most part delusive, if political antisemitism is in any sense a response to real Jews or real Judaism.

Second, an adequate account ought to be up to explaining why the fear and resentment channeled by political antisemitism target the Jews considered as a collectivity, rather than Jews as individuals: why, for example, people terrified by the supposed threat posed by Jews can sometimes say, and even say truthfully, that "some of their best friends" are Jews.

Third, if the discourse of "anti-Judaism" has been as widespread and historically recurrent as Nirenberg shows it to have been, then neither its persistence nor its ability to arise over and over again, in new forms and in very different sets of historical circumstances, can plausibly be accounted for merely in terms of cultural inertia. There must, that is to say, be some advantage or advantages accruing to those who find it expedient either to adopt or to reinvent it. A decent explanation of political antisemitism ought, therefore, to offer some account of what those advantages might be.

Fourth, an adequate answer to the question "Why the Jews?" ought to be capable of addressing the curious fact that while social antisemitism has displayed the appeal to a broad social constituency characteristic of other kinds of *social* prejudice—prejudice against blacks, say, or against Asians, or the Irish— *political* antisemitism has found its main constituency among intellectuals. (I use the term *intellectual* here not only in the broad sense that includes the clergy, and other highly educated groups in Western societies but also, and crucially, in the narrow sense that restricts the term to writers, theologians, philosophers, political theorists, and others exercising major kinds of influence over the content and development of Western culture.) Why, in short, should *political* antisemitism, from John Chrysostom to Luther, Voltaire to Marx, Wagner to Shaw, Wells to Eliot, have displayed so compelling a hold over the minds of deeply thoughtful people, people highly educated by the standards of their day?[22]

A fifth question is that of the connection between antisemitism of both kinds and *adherence to Judaism*. Why, throughout most of the history of antisemitism, up until the invention, in the nineteenth and twentieth century, of the idea that the Jews constitute a biologically determinate *race* (rather than— like the English, say—a racially heterogeneous but religiously and culturally coherent *people*), has it generally been possible for a Jew to avoid persecution and in effect cease to be regarded as a Jew simply by converting and abandoning Judaism?

A sixth, closely related question is this: Why, when ordinary social prejudice strives only to maintain the despised outsider in an inferior social position, should political antisemitism appear to its adherents to require the *elimination* of the Jews, whether by conversion, emigration, or extermination?

A further question concerns the strange combination of stability and variability displayed over the centuries by the content of antisemitic belief. On the one hand, certain very general beliefs, as that "the Jews are faithful only to one another and to their own laws, and are otherwise enemies of all humankind" remain constant from Haman to Goebbels. Once such generalized grounds of resentment descend into concrete specificity, on the other hand, the charges historically leveled seem bizarrely arbitrary. These charges range from child murder to well poisoning; from the imagined consumption of gentile blood in the Passover matzo (despite the fact that the consumption of blood per se is forbidden to Jews by the laws of kashruth) to the murder of gentiles for their body parts; from usury in pursuit of private interest to usury in support of (hated but non-Jewish) kings and states; from obstinacy in avoiding contact with others in order to hug to themselves a despised religion to threatening the Judaization of the non-Jewish majority faith; from secret control of states of whose citizens they comprise a minuscule minority to plotting to subvert the very states they supposedly control; from responsibility for the rise of capitalism to responsibility for its overthrow. The dreamlike heterogeneity displayed by these alleged depravities of the Jews is matched only by their internal incoherence.

Eighth and finally, there is the question to what strange processes political antisemitism owes its power to shift its constituency over time from one end of the political spectrum to the other. Prior to the eighteenth century, principled, political hostility to the Jews was largely associated with the church. In the later decades of that century, it became equally strongly associated with the Enlightenment in its revolutionary phase. In the nineteenth century, hostility shifted back to an association with social and religious conservatism but then in the second half of the century began to acquire equally powerful links with the rising forces of socialist reform. The first half of the twentieth century, on the one hand, saw political antisemitism take on new and this time even more savagely lethal forms in the hands of fascists and nationalists. The second half and the opening years of the twenty-first century, on the other hand, saw it shift its constituency yet again to become a standard element in the discourse of "progressives" and internationalists.

These eight questions are no doubt far from exhausting the puzzling features of political antisemitism. Nevertheless, if we can devise an answer to the question "Why the Jews?" capable of throwing useful light on even this modest collection of puzzles, we shall not have done badly. Let us, therefore, proceed to the chain of arguments that it is the main business of this chapter and the next to elaborate.

SEEING "THE JEWS" AS "A DISEASE"

Recently, in a paper on the causes of the Holocaust by the German sociologist
and economist Gunnar Heinsohn (more specifically, on the motives underlying Adolf Hitler's desire to get rid of the Jews), I came across the following
communication from Hitler to Martin Bormann, dated February 3, 1945:[23]

> I have never been of the opinion that the Chinese or Japanese, for example,
> are racially inferior. Both belong to old cultures and I admit that their
> culture is superior to ours.... I even believe that I will find it all the easier
> to come to an understanding with the Chinese and the Japanese, the more
> they persevere in their racial pride.... Our Nordic racial consciousness is
> only aggressive towards the Jewish race. *We use the term Jewish race merely
> for reasons of linguistic convenience, for in the real sense of the word, and from a
> genetic point of view there is no Jewish race.* Present circumstances force upon
> us this characterization of the group of common race and *intellect*, to which
> all the Jews of the world profess their loyalty, regardless of the nationality
> identified in the passport of each individual. This group of persons we
> designate as the Jewish race.... The Jewish race is above all a *community of
> the spirit*.... *Spiritual race is of a more solid and more durable kind than natural
> race.* Wherever he goes the Jew remains a Jew ... presenting sad *proof of the
> superiority of the "spirit" over the flesh.*[24]

Heinsohn argues, from this and other textual evidence, that Hitler's antisemitism was not *racially* based (a judgment that I, as I have argued elsewhere,
would be inclined to extend to antisemitism in general).[25] Rather, Hitler believed that the Jews must be eliminated as the only way of eliminating *the
malign spiritual influence* of Jewish culture. In what was this malign influence
supposed to consist? Heinsohn marshals persuasive textual evidence to suggest that in Hitler's mind, it consisted in the insinuation into European culture
of ethical principles, notably that of the sanctity of life, which had sapped the
capacity of the Nordic race (as it had historically sapped, Hitler seems to have
believed, that of the nations of the ancient world) to achieve their goals through
the merciless destruction both of enemy combatants and of entire enemy peoples. Three of the passages Heinsohn cites in support of this reading of Hitler's
motives are particularly telling. The first comes from an account by the Nazi
leader of Danzig, Hermann Rausching, of conversations with Hitler at the start
of the 1930s. Rausching represents Hitler as having said,

> We terminate a wrong path of mankind. *The tables of Mount Sinai have lost
> their validity. Conscience is a Jewish invention.* ... It is our duty to depopulate,

just as it is our duty to provide appropriate care to the German population.... What do I mean by depopulation, you will ask. Do I intend to eliminate entire peoples? Yes, more or less. That is where it will lead to.... Natural instinct commands every living being not only to defeat the enemy but to destroy him. In earlier ages there existed *the good right of the victor to exterminate whole tribes, whole nations*.[26]

The second, from Hitler's table talk, records his belief that the Germans lost World War I only because Jewish ethical inhibitions rendered them unable to pursue their aims with the absolute ferocity that he supposes (arguably falsely, given the actual outcome of such tactics in World War II) would have brought victory in its train: "We experienced it during the World War: the only country that was religious was Germany, and that was the country that lost."[27]

The third supporting passage, dating from August 7, 1920, records Hitler's conviction that it is because the Jew is, spiritually speaking, a *disease* of Western civilization that he must be treated as such: "Do not think that you can fight a disease without killing the causative agent, without destroying the bacillus, and do not think that you can fight racial tuberculosis without seeing to it that the nation is freed from the causative agent of racial tuberculosis. The influence of Judaism will never fade as long as its agent, the Jew, has not been removed from our midst."[28]

Heinsohn has two aims in his essay: first, to elucidate Hitler's motives as a means of challenging the common view that the Holocaust is simply "inexplicable" and second, to defend the idea that the Holocaust was indeed, in some sense, an utterly new and historically unique event. His proposal is that that what made the Holocaust unique—or "uniquely unique" as he puts it—was that "it was a genocide for the purpose of reinstalling the right to genocide."[29] Hitler wished to abrogate the doctrine of the sanctity of life that he considered the Jews to have introduced to Western civilization and to reestablish a supposedly ancient right to kill without limit in the service of national or racial self-interest: a right extending from the killing of the handicapped and the infanticide of surplus or unwanted children to the wholesale massacre of enemy populations.

The textual evidence that Heinsohn marshals, here and elsewhere, goes far to persuade me that he has much to teach us about the outlook and reasoning both of Hitler and of the party he founded. The main doubt I have concerning the paper under discussion is that it suggests the conclusion that if the Holocaust was indeed unique, it was so mainly because it was the sole creation of one man, Hitler, whose reason for hating the Jews—that they had introduced into Western culture the principle of the sanctity of life—was so singular as to be essentially sui generis.

That this is a direction in which Heinsohn wishes to move is evidenced by the fact that he quotes with approval the following sentence from an article in the *New Yorker* strongly criticizing Daniel Goldhagen's (1996) *Hitler's Willing Executioners: Ordinary Germans and the Holocaust*: "Hitler was the culprit who gave all the other culprits their chance."[30]

The doubts I feel concerning this are fueled by the fact that aside from the issue of the sanctity of life, Hitler's thoughts on the Jews, as Heinsohn develops and documents them, seem not to have been in the least singular but entirely consonant with the broad current of European antisemitism as that had developed during the previous century. Take, for example, the thought that the Jews are the source of a spiritual disease that cannot be cured without getting rid of the causative agents through which the body—the body politic in this case—is continually reinfected. We find the philosopher Ludwig Wittgenstein committing to his notebook in 1931 an observation very much along these lines, which he plainly regards as so familiar an aspect of the history of the Jews in Europe as to go almost without saying.

> Within the history of the peoples of Europe the history of the Jews is not treated so circumstantially as their intervention in European affairs would actually merit, because within this history they are experienced as a sort of disease, and anomaly, & nobody wants to put a disease on the same level as normal life. (& nobody wants to speak of a disease as though it had the same rights as healthy bodily processes [even painful ones]).
>
> We may say: people can only regard this tumour as a natural part of the body if their whole feeling for the body changes (if the whole national feeling for the body changes). Otherwise the best they can do is *put up with it*.
>
> You may expect an individual man to display this sort of tolerance or else to disregard such things; but you cannot expect this of a nation, because it is precisely not disregarding such things that makes it a nation. I.e. there is a contradiction in expecting someone *both* to retain the aesthetic feeling of his body and *also* to make the tumour welcome.[31]

Let us look more closely at these remarks. When both Wittgenstein and Hitler proclaim, in an eerily harmonious chorus, that Jews cannot but be regarded by a nation as a disease, neither, it seems to me, can be regarded as making an empirical claim. Rather, as David Nirenberg's historical analysis of what he calls "anti-Judaism" would suggest, both are exploring the internal logical structure of a complex myth. Wittgenstein says at one point in the passage cited earlier that one cannot expect a nation to tolerate the diseased state constituted

by the presence of Jews, because "it is only a nation by virtue of not disregarding such things." Not merely does this fail as an observation capable of
persuading by its conformity with empirical evidence; it is not even faintly
sensible. Why should the Jews be regarded as the agents of a spiritual disease
fatal to the integrity of a nation, or perhaps as constituting the disease itself,
when no European nation possesses historically the cultural and spiritual integrity presumed by these remarks of Wittgenstein's? Why do the French not
regard the Basques or the Bretons, or the English the Welsh, or the Scots the
Orcadians or the Hebrideans as carriers of a spiritual disease? Perhaps it is because, in Wittgenstein's terms, the former do not constitute (or perhaps do not
yet constitute) nations or "real nations"? But if that is Wittgenstein's answer,
then it becomes clear that we are dealing here at best with a pair of arbitrary
redefinitions of the terms *disease* and *nation*. Neither the experience of the Jew
as a sort of disease nor the nation that must, according to Wittgenstein, "experience" Jews in this way are, in short, *empirical realities*. Rather, they are merely
correlative poles within the arbitrary structure of mutually defining notions
that serve to constitute the metaphor of "the Jew" as a form of cultural disease:
notions provided with the appearance of sense and reference, that is to say, not
by their correspondence with anything real but merely by the conventionally
established relationships in which they stand to one another.

THE "DISEASE" METAPHOR AND ITS MOTIVATION

The analogy between the healthy state and the healthy human person is a common enough trope of Western political philosophy. Plato begins it with the
analogy between the city and the soul in book 4 of the *Republic*. Analogies
between the organization of the state and that of the body are to be found
throughout the subsequent history of Western thought, in Cicero, John of Salis-
bury, Hobbes, Herbert Spencer, and many others. The idea that the healthy
state is analogous to the healthy body is commonplace in such thinking, and
since the analogical "organs" of the state are necessarily made up of subsets of
its citizens, it is also commonplace for the deranged state to be explained in
terms of the moral derangement of the citizens who make up such groupings.
In *Hamlet*, Marcellus's "Something is rotten in the state of Denmark" is directly
motivated by Claudius's drunken revelry: the state is rotten not least because
of the bodily vices of its present king.

   In the bulk of such analogies, however, the individuals who constitute
the disease of the state are in the full sense citizens of the state whose health
their activities threaten. This is of course exceptionally true of Claudius, who,

whatever his vices, is not merely *a* Dane but *the* Dane. Those citizens whose conduct threatens the health of the Platonic ideal city are Greeks and citizens like anybody else. When the Jews are, as Wittgenstein puts it, "experienced as a disease," that is no longer the case. It is essential to the metaphor as a trope of antisemitism that the Jew, whatever his passport may say, is not a "real" citizen of the country that he affects as his own but an alien interloper.

This changes the whole force of the metaphor. It is no longer a matter, as it were, of an illness *native to* the body of the state: something analogous, say, to a failing heart valve or an ankle sprained through the foolhardiness of its owner. Rather, it is a matter of an invasion by some organism altogether alien to the body or institution it invades—as if the Jews were analogous to an infection of bacilli or trypanosomes in the bloodstream, or to rats in the walls of a hospital. T. S. Eliot's poem "Burbank with a Baedeker, Bleistein with a Cigar" famously contains an expression of the latter image that many have found offensive: "The rats are underneath the piles. / The Jew is underneath the lot."

That is, the function of the metaphor is no longer to dramatize the idea that some flaw *native to the state* needs to be set right. On the contrary, its function is to dramatize the idea that the *state in itself is without flaw*: or would be *if it were not for the activities of people who, while they may seem to belong to it as citizens, are in fact wholly alien to it.*

The third of the questions raised in the last section but one was, in effect, cui bono: who benefits or profits from spreading the message of political anti-semitism? The answer suggested by the foregoing thoughts would seem to be, anyone who has a vested interest in representing the social problems and vices of the age, not as inherent in the societies they disfigure but rather as due to an alien infestation that as such is capable of cure, provided only that sufficiently vigorous measures are taken against it. And if one looks around for people who might satisfy that description, it is tempting to locate them within any ruling group with a vested interest in preventing popular discontent from impacting it or its members.

Certainly, such an analysis seems to fit the National Socialist Party in the period 1933–45. On the one hand, there is the need to project both the party and the Third Reich as the expression of everything that is healthy, strong, energetic, and masculine in the German *volk*. On the other hand, there is the equally pressing need to represent any acts of the party to which domestic ob-jections might be raised, up to and including war, as measures made necessary by the need to protect the Aryan moral and spiritual purity of the nation against a malign alien force striving constantly to corrupt them: to wit, international Jewry and the world Jewish conspiracy. Hitler's speeches abound in images of the Jews as disease: "All that which is for men a source of higher life . . . is for the Jew merely the means to an end, namely, the satisfaction of his lust for power and money. . . . His action will result in the tuberculosis of peoples."[32] "For hundreds of years, Germany was good enough to receive these elements [the Jews], although they possessed nothing except infectious political and physical diseases."[33]

National Socialism was, of course, only one among the many European movements, over the entire period separating us from the ancient world, that have based their claims to power upon a claim to possess a unique capacity to restore society to political, social, and spiritual health. All such movements share with Nazism the need to explain away tendencies in society (private property, for instance, or working-class unrest, or religious dissent) that on the one hand can be made to seem inconsistent with whatever notion of social health the movement in question exists to peddle but that on the other hand are far too deeply rooted in the fabric of everyday human life to suit the political and ideological convenience of the movement.

Therefore, if our analysis of the functions of the metaphor of the Jews as disease is correct, then we should expect the discourse of political antisemitism to appear tempting to any movement aiming at political, social, moral, or spiritual renovation, when that movement finds itself faced with the need to explain away, as *externally* imposed, social phenomena threatening to its program of redemption that are in fact wholly *internal* to the society it proposes to redeem.

And that, in fact, is what we find. We have already noted one such example, drawn from Nirenberg: Luther's transition from seeing Protestant "Judaizers" as a threat to his own conception of reformation to seeing real Jews as the real source of that threat. In the case of the philosophes—Montesquieu, Voltaire, Rousseau, Diderot, whose ideas led to the French Revolution—Nirenberg's discussion is similarly suggestive. He notes that at a time when actual Jewish settlement in France was negligible, the terms *Jews* and *Judaism* occur with remarkable frequency in the discourse of the philosophes. Nirenberg suggests acutely that the *idea* of "Jews" and "Jewishness," even in the absence of actual exemplars of either, served the philosophes as a means of conceptualizing the limits of their conception of Enlightenment. In the imagination of the philosophes, Nirenberg argues, the Jews, in their extraordinary resistance to conversion, and the strength of their commitment to what was seen as an antiquated and obscurantist superstition, represented the limits of the power of reason to "regenerate" humankind.[34] For Montesquieu in *The Spirit of the Laws*, the consequence of the medieval Christian forcing of Jews into the credit market had been that "commerce passed to a nation covered with infamy and soon was distinguished only by the most frightful usury, monopolies, the raising of subsidies and all dishonest means of acquiring money."[35]

Nirenberg comments as follows on these antique speculations:

> Because the Jews were generally imagined as the most fanatically irrational segment of the species (indeed, as the very origins of fanatical irrationality), they provided the perfect proving ground for the powers of Enlightenment. Perfect because Enlightenment won either way. If even the Jews could be "regenerated" then there were no limits to the emancipatory powers of Enlightenment anthropology. But if they could not, it simply meant that reason had reached the boundaries of its authority, *and that the Jews lay on the other side* [italics mine—BH]. For philosophes bent on exploring the boundaries of their anthropology, the Jews were a "limit case," an example whose pursuit charts the extremes of a concept. In this case the limits were those of humanity, and the question "Can the Jews be regenerated?" was also the question "Are the Jews human?" In the words of the lawyer Pierre-Louis Lacretelle in his legal brief of 1776 on behalf of the Jews of Metz, "The real question in this case . . . is whether Jews are men." Or as the philosophes more often put it "Is the Jew more a human or a Jew?"[36]

It will be evident how neatly the argument I have been developing in the preceding pages fits with these remarks of Nirenberg's. If one is committed to the regeneration of humanity, then if humanity, for its part, seems obstinately committed to resisting the proffered regeneration, for example through its obdurate resistance to reason or its devotion to making money, things look bleak. But if irrational fanaticism and cupidity can be seen as vices *leaking into humanity from a source located beyond its borders*, then immediately things look brighter, the prospects for regeneration more realistic. Blaming such things on the Jews, that is to say, has the useful result of allowing one the luxury of regarding non-Jewish society as, if not altogether healthy, then at least as not suffering from a disease *inherent in it*, and so as capable of being restored to whatever counts for a given tribe of political theorists as health.

The same interplay of myth and interest is to be found in more recent examples. Bryan Cheyette's *Constructions of "the Jew" in English Literature and Society: Racial Representations, 1875–1945* is a mine of such instances.[37] Chayette shows how George Bernard Shaw (1912), for example, in his preface to *Androcles and the Lion* finds it convenient to articulate the political distinction he wishes to draw between "socialism" and "materialism" in terms of a more general and quasi-religious distinction between "baptism" and "circumcision." "Throughout his Preface to this play Shaw contrasts the universalist world of 'baptism' with the particularist world of 'circumcision' which reinforces the binary opposition between a socialist Jesus and a materialist Jewry or, as he puts it elsewhere in the Preface, 'God and Mammon.' Shaw defines a 'Christian' as someone who 'to this day' is 'in religion a Jew initiated in baptism instead of circumcision' (483) and, at the same time, points to the need to 'make Christ a Christian' and 'melt the Jew out of him' (487)."[38]

Shaw's political interests in the play, in other words, are in forging a link between Christianity and the socialism just at that point beginning to achieve a foothold in British politics. Britain was at that historical moment an overwhelmingly Christian country; yet it was also a country in which a large majority of people of all classes, while certainly Christian in religion, were sharply opposed to socialism in politics. It is therefore to the advantage of Shaw's political project to be able to represent a commitment to Christianity as in some sense *intrinsically a commitment to socialism.*

To achieve that effect, Shaw needs some way of associating the denial of socialism with a denial of Christianity. This is the work done for him by the myth of "materialist Jewry." The myth works for him in two closely connected ways. By allowing him to equate the distinction between baptism and circumcision with that between God and Mammon, it allows Shaw on the one hand to suggest that socialism is the natural *political* home for the vast majority of his Christian fellow citizens. But on the other hand, that equation allows him in addition to *defame opposition to socialism* by associating it with a marginal and despised group: a group, moreover, not only placed by its religion beyond the limits of Christian society but also offering through the mythic association of Jews with money, a permanent source of infection of the baptized Christian world by the world of circumcision with its insidious fidelity to the forces of Mammon.

At this comparatively early stage in Shaw's thinking, the disease metaphor shows its face in a more or less explicit form in the phrase "melt the Jew out of him"—as if what were required to cure Christian/socialist society of the infection represented by the forces of Mammon/circumcision were somehow analogous to relieving a cold by sitting in a sauna or steam room. But as the century wears on, both the disease analogy and its implications become more explicitly realized in Shaw's writing.

Shaw, in his later plays, both stressed the pernicious nature of non-universal racial, national or religious particularisms and continued, with added stridency, to suggest "eugenic" means of ending such differences. His Preface to *On the Rocks* (1933), in this regard, was to state blandly that "extermination must be put on a scientific basis if it is ever to be carried out humanely and apologetically as well as thoroughly" (574). Shaw, just as problematically, was to apply this Edwardian eugenicism to the rise of Nazi Germany. In a letter to Beatrice Webb in 1938, Shaw declared that:

> We ought to tackle the Jewish question by admitting the right of states to make eugenic experiments by weeding out any strains they think undesirable, but insisting that they should do it as humanely as they can afford to, and not shock civilization by such misdemeanours as the expulsion and robbery of Einstein.

Shaw's letter, rather worryingly, constructs Jews as a potentially "undesirable" "strain" who might, at any time, be thought to be outside of established nation states.[39]

A couple more cases may suffice to exemplify the extraordinary degree of presence, amounting in effect to near omnipresence in intellectual debate concerning the redemption of society from this or that social evil, *both* of the disease metaphor itself, *and* of the characteristic devices of projection and self-deception that the metaphor both dominates and serves.

The first of these cases concerns a well-known passage, italicized below, in *After Strange Gods*, a book that the poet T. S. Eliot published in 1934, but unsurprisingly, refused to republish, at least as a whole, after World War II. The book discusses the prospects for a society based on the Christian and Catholic orthodoxy that Eliot had long embraced. "The population should be homogenous; where two or more cultures exist in the same place they are likely either to be fiercely self-conscious or both to become adulterate. What is still more important is unity of religious backgrounds; *and reasons of race and religion combine to make any large number of free-thinking Jews undesirable.* There must be a proper balance between urban and rural, industrial and agricultural development. And a spirit of excessive tolerance is to be deprecated."[40]

Much ink has been expended over the question of whether Eliot was an antisemite.[41] That question, for better or worse, I propose to leave on one side. The question that interests me here is a different one—namely, what could have induced a man of Eliot's intellectual capacity to imagine for a moment that the words italicized above could constitute a remotely sensible addendum to the sentence that contains them?

A number of references in Eliot's poetry of the period—"Sweeney among the Nightingales," "Burbank with a Baedeker, Bleistein with a Cigar," "Geron-tion," and "The Waste Land," among them—combine to create the impression that for Eliot at the time, images of the Jew functioned as a powerful poetic

image of the destructive forces of materialism and religious and cultural confusion that that poetry locates at the heart of contemporary Western civilization. An obvious way of exonerating Eliot from the charge of antisemitism
would be, indeed, to point out that we are dealing here merely with poetic
imagery and hence only with culturally embedded *images* of "the Jew" rather
than with real Jews. Poems, that is to say, being poems and not manifestos,
cannot be read straightforwardly as expressions of beliefs or attitudes held by
their authors.

On the other hand, *After Strange Gods* is precisely that: a manifesto. Here,
Eliot *is* talking about actual Jews and their impact on society as he conceives it.
We are here, then, entitled to read him quite straightforwardly as contending
that the activities of "free-thinking Jews" are inimical to the life of the kind of
conservative Christian commonwealth that Eliot wishes to see restored. The
reason, according to Eliot, is that the presence of "any large number of free-
thinking Jews" is inconsistent with the (non-Jewish) cultural and religious
homogeneity that must be preserved if there is to be any return to a society
soundly based on conservative Christian values. To which, I suppose, a natural
skepticism must in all honesty return the answer: "What homogeneity?" The
passage echoes, that is to say, with the hollow clap of stable doors closing a
century and a half too late, long after the horses of cultural and religious homogeneity in the non-Jewish Western world have definitively fled. The opponents
Eliot's ideas have actually to confront, in other words, are not free-thinking
Jews, whose numbers in proportion were very far from large even in the 1930s,
but the inconceivably greater numbers of free-thinking ex-Christians who, following Hume and Voltaire, will accept neither Eliot's politics nor his Christianity and whom it is far too late to cow into silence, let alone submission, merely
by the avoidance of "excessive tolerance."

The function of *Jews* per se in Eliot's discourse, as in that of Shaw, Luther, or
the philosophes, is in other words to create a delusive appearance of non-Jewish
unity in support of certain ideas by exporting, or in Freudian terms projecting,
a disturbingly domestic disunity onto a reassuringly external and putatively
alien source. If—*if only*—the *Jews* were the problem, then the politics of Eliot
and those of his political mentor Charles Maurras would be assured of success.
That, I submit, is what explains the presence of "free-thinking Jews," otherwise
hardly rationally explicable, in the passage cited above.

Now for one final example of the technique of neutralizing the threat
to entrenched theoretical positions posed by inconvenient facts about the
non-Jewish world, by exporting, or projecting, those facts onto the shoulders of the Jews. This one concerns Holocaust denial—known in French as

négationnisme—on the part of elements of the French left in the concluding quarter of the twentieth century. The best-known figures here are Paul Rassinier (1906–67), whose widely influential writings were instrumental in making Holocaust denial a live political issue in France, and later in the period, Robert Faurisson, a former literary scholar at the University of Lyon, famous for having attracted ambiguously phrased support from no less stalwart a pillar of the American left than Noam Chomsky. Faurisson received support in publishing and popularizing his views from *La vielle taupe* (The Old Mole—the name comes from Hamlet's remark concerning his father's ghost, as recycled by Hegel to refer to the "underground" progress of Spirit), a Parisian bookshop and publishing firm run by one Pierre Guillaume, for whom it represented a continuation of his involvement in the French political upheavals of the 1960s, culminating in the "May events" of 1968.

A fascinating report on this obscure movement based on, among other things, a lengthy interview with Guillaume himself was recently published by the Israeli philosopher Elhanan Yakira.[42] I shall concentrate here on what Yakira has to say about the ideological and (in a certain sense) moral considerations motivating Rassinier.

Yakira notes that Rassinier held throughout his life "pacifist and proto-anarchist views."[43] As a young man, he joined the Communist Party. As a member of the Resistance during the early stages of World War II, he was captured by the Gestapo, tortured, and sent first to Buchenwald and then, along with thousands of other slave laborers, to Dora, a work camp for the construction of the V1 and V2 rockets. At the end of the war, he enjoyed a brief political career as a member of the Socialist Party in which capacity he was elected for a time to the National Assembly. From 1948 onward, however, he began to publish a series of books whose object was to deny that the Holocaust had taken place. What Yakira makes clear is that this project was motivated directly by Rassinier's lifelong anarcho-pacifism.

> Rassinier was particularly opposed to efforts to present a Manichaean view of the modern world, to depict Nazi Germany as the incarnation of absolute evil and what had been done in the concentration camps as uniquely wicked.[44] ... According to him, Nazi concentration camps were not really a unique historical phenomenon. Not only did they not differ from Soviet camps; they did not differ from French penal institutions either: a camp is a camp, as we were to hear fifty years later from various self-styled progressive writers. It is merely an expression, more or less severe according to circumstances, of the essence of the state as such, not just of the Nazi

SS state or even the totalitarian state. For Rassinier, the underlying logic
of the essence of the state is the logic of war and enslavement. The task of
the intellectual of the left, especially one who himself as witnessed such
events, is, on the one hand, to warn against the Manichaeism that places
all the blame on one side, thus provoking war, and, on the other hand, to
strip the other side of its claim to moral superiority. It is war itself that is the
absolute evil, not one warmongering party or another.[45]

Plainly, the facts concerning the near extermination of the Jews of Europe
between 1933 and 1945 are incompatible with this account, both as an account of
reality and as an assessment of the duties of the intellectual. But the response of
the likes of Rassinier, Faurisson, and *La vielle taupe* is not to modify their position but to attempt to neutralize the threat to their ideological stance posed by
the Holocaust by recasting the latter as a tissue of Jewish lies. As Yakira justly
observes, "Reflecting on the story of Rassinier's life and reading his writings are
a lesson in the genesis of a perversion and in the mechanisms by which ideology
can triumph over reality."[46]

What I have been attempting to show in this chapter is that the entire history of political antisemitism consists of a series of such "triumphs," achieved
through the operation of just such mechanisms. In the next chapter, I shall
return to the second main question before us: What is it about the Jews, of all
the nations of Europe, that has made them so fatally convenient as a means to
such triumphs?

NOTES

1. The present version of this chapter has profited greatly from comments on
an earlier draft by Cynthia Ozick and Professor Alvin Rosenfeld.
2. Arendt 1976.
3. Nirenberg 2013, 463.
4. Laqueur 2008, 110.
5. Laqueur 2008, 157.
6. Arendt 2007, 463.
7. Arendt 2007, 95–99.
8. Nirenberg 2013, 463.
9. Prager and Telushkin 2003, 7.
10. Prager and Telushkin 2003, 6–7.
11. Prager and Telushkin 2003, 7.
12. Prager and Telushkin 2003, 7.
13. Nirenberg 2013, 464.

14. Nirenberg 2013, 263f.

15. Nirenberg 2013, 264.

16. Nirenberg 2013, 267.

17. Prager and Telushkin 2003, 11.

18. Prager and Telushkin 2003, 8.

19. Prager and Telushkin 2003, 8.

20. Prager and Telushkin 2003, 8–9.

21. Prager and Telushkin 2003, 9.

22. See, e.g., Elhanan Yakira, "Virtuous Antisemitism," in A. H. Rosenfeld 2015. Yakira (2010) is excellent on this phenomenon in postwar intellectual life in France, while encyclopedic studies of its influence in British intellectual circles can be found in Julius (2010) and Cheyette (1993).

23. Heinsohn 2000.

24. Heinsohn 2000, 412. The citation is H. Trevor-Roper and A François-Poncet, eds., *Hitlers politisches Testament: Die Bormann Diktate vom Februar und April 1945* (Hamburg: Albrecht Knaus, 1981), 66, 68, 69. The italics are Heinsohn's.

25. Harrison 2013.

26. Heinsohn 2000, 418. The italics are again Heinsohn's. The citation is H. Rauschning, *Gespräche mit Hitler* [1938] (Vienna: Europaverlag, 1988), 189, 210, 129ff.

27. Heinsohn 2000, 419. The citation is H. Picker, *Hitlers Tischgespräche in Führerhauptquartier* [1951] (Stuttgart: Seewald, 1976), 77.

28. Heinsohn 2000, 424. The citation is, E. Jäckel and A. Kuhn, eds., *Hitler, Sämtliche Aufzeichnungen 1905–1924* (Stuttgart: Deutsche Verlags-Anstalt, 1980).

29. Heinsohn 2000, 425.

30. Heinsohn 2000, 414. The reference is to C. James, "The Much Lauded Revisionist Study of the Holocaust [by Goldhagen] Goes Too Far," *The New Yorker*, April 22, 1996, 7.

31. Wittgenstein 1980, 20e.

32. Hitler, "Letter on the Jewish Question," September 16, 1919.

33. Hitler, "Speech before the Reichstag," January 30, 1939.

34. Nirenberg 2013, 343–52.

35. Montesquieu, *De l'esprit des lois* (1755). Reprint, Paris: Belles Lettres (1958), bk. 21, chap. 20, 121–22, cited in Nirenberg 2013, 345–46.

36. Nirenberg 2013, 350–51, emphasis mine. See, in Nirenberg, note 38 for the references for his included citations.

37. Cheyette 1993.

38. Cheyette 1993, 113–14. The page references to Shaw are to volume 4 of the Bodley Head edition of *Androcles and the Lion* (London, 1972).

39. Cheyette 1993, 115. The reference for the preface to *On the Rocks* is to the Bodley Head *Collected Plays with Their Prefaces*, edited by D. H. Laurence; that for Shaw's letter to Beatrice Webb is to D. H. Laurence, ed., *Collected Letters 1926–1950* (London: Reinhardt, 1988), 493.

40. Eliot 1934, 19–20, emphasis mine.

41. See, in particular here, Julius 1993, and the extensive subsequent controversy that it unleashed.

42. Yakira 2010. Pages 1–15 are particularly relevant to the present discussion.

43. Yakira 2010, 5.

44. Yakira 2010, 6.

45. Yakira 2010, 7.

46. Yakira 2010, 11.

FIVE

AN OBSTINATE PEOPLE

The Second Commandment is . . . expressive of one of the essential ideals
of Judaism, and like most of the essential ideals of Judaism—consider in
this light the institution of the Sabbath—it is uniquely antithetical to the
practices and premises of the pre-Judaic and non-Judaic world. In short, it is
the Jewish idiom . . . that is, in its deepest strain dissenting, contradictory,
frequently irreconcilable. . . . What is antithetical goes against the grain of
the world at large.

—Cynthia Ozick, "Literature as Idol: Harold Bloom"

TWO CONCEPTS OF SOCIAL HOMOGENEITY

In the last chapter, I argued that the attraction of political antisemitism, for
those tempted by it, is always that it offers a means of preserving the fiction,
relative to a given society, of what Eliot called a "homogenous culture." It does
so by representing whatever quarrels threaten the desired homogeneity as conflicts not *within* that society but rather *between* that society and an alien and
parasitic community ensconced within it in the manner of a disease agent in
an otherwise healthy body.

Two immediate objections to this analysis suggest themselves: namely,
(1) that it merely repeats a familiar explanation of antisemitism as collective

---

The present version of this chapter owes much to criticism of previous drafts at the hands of
Professors Alvin Rosenfeld, Abigail Rosenthal, and David Conway.

scapegoating and (2) that it offers no explanation of why *the Jews*, in particular, should for so long and with such consistency have been represented in the light of a disease. If "homogeneity" is supposed to be the issue, then surely almost any society will contain a number of small, dissident, or diasporic communities sufficiently distinct in their outlook and practices to be deemed, not altogether unreasonably, to threaten the homogeneity of the matrix society they inhabit. Why is it that among such groups, only the Jews—rather than, say, the Amish, the Gypsies, Cajuns, Methodists, or Mormons—have been seen as presenting a major threat to the homogeneity of society, as distinct from a minor and sometimes irritating irregularity in a prevailing landscape of social uniformity? Why is it only around the Jews that the extraordinary delusions of political antisemitism—delusions of vast and malign power, conspiratorial plotting, hidden control of non-Jewish institutions in the service of Jewish world domination—should have sedimented and accreted? Both objections deserve answers. It will be the business of this chapter to offer some.

We need to begin, perhaps, by distinguishing two senses of the term *homogeneous*. On the one hand, there is what one might call *natural homogeneity*— the actual set of customs, character traits, ingrained beliefs, and styles of conduct that naturally develop over time in any community separated from others by distance, language, or natural boundaries. On the other hand, there is what one might call *project-driven homogeneity*. Project-driven homogeneity is the kind required for the successful implementation of a project for the reform of a society or a collection of societies. Natural homogeneity is quite insufficient for such purposes because the whole point of such a project is precisely to transcend natural homogeneity by inducing masses of people to *reconceive their identity*, no longer in the terms offered by the commonplace and familiar habits and ways of thinking they have been, and perhaps would still prefer to be, accustomed to but rather in the terms offered and constituted *by the project*.

Such projects can take many forms. The welding of nations together to form components of larger political structures, imperial or federal as the case may be, is an obvious example, as is the imposition of a new religion: the successive Christianization, first of the Roman Empire and then of Europe as a whole, for instance; or the seventh-century imposition of Islam on large parts of the Near East. The major projects of political transformation that have racked modern Europe—the French Revolution, fascism, Nazism, communism—also plainly fall into this category. Then again, there are moments when a significant body of opinion within a nation begins to see that nation as having a special mission in the world, whose implementation should both inspire and absorb the major energies of the nation as a homogeneous whole. Examples of this last phenomenon, both significantly associated with antisemitism, are to be found in the Germany of the 1880s and 1890s, and in Britain toward the turn of the century, at the zenith of the British Empire. The historian Albert Lindemann notes how, in the last couple of decades of the nineteenth century, "Germans were gaining a new respect among nations; admiration for things German and imitation of German models spread throughout Europe. . . . As noted, many Germans were inclined to see world historical significance in the establishment of the German Reich; it represented a turning point in modern history. Even more grandiosely, some German nationalists believed the new Reich was the expression of divine purpose, an affirmation of the mission of the German spirit in the modern world."[1]

Similarly, at the end of the nineteenth century, it was commonplace among parts of the English governing and cultural elites to envisage the identity of the nation in imperial terms—to think of England as the mother nation of a vast empire, a nation charged with the historic duty of leading the numerous and largely uncivilized peoples whom it had brought successively and, at the time it seemed, permanently under the shelter of its imperial mantle toward the kind of civilization it represented. It was equally commonplace to displace the darker elements of this process onto the shoulders of "Jewish financiers."

The earlier displacement of the "immoral" aspects of British Imperialism onto a racialized construction of Jewishness was, by the turn of the century, a widely circulated strand of contemporary Liberal and Socialist pro-Boer opinion. After the abortive Jameson Raid against Kruger's Boer Republic in 1895, many pro-Boers regarded the inevitable full-scale conflict as "a war fostered by Jews for Jewish gain." Prominent "Jewish financiers" based in South Africa were represented as a "conspiracy" which, according to H. M. Hyndman's *Justice*, the journal of the Social Democratic Federation, were planning to create "an Anglo-Hebraic empire stretching from Egypt to cape Colony and from Beira to Sierra Leone."[2]

PROJECT-DRIVEN HOMOGENEITY AND THE JEWS

So much, then, for the distinction between natural and project-driven homogeneity. The suggestion I propose to develop in this chapter can now be put very briefly. It is that the kinds of hostility, contempt, and social exclusion that go to make up "ethnic prejudice," to use Langmuir's term, represent a negative reaction against people whose manners, habits, or appearance are perceived as *offending against natural homogeneity.* Political antisemitism, on the other hand, I shall argue, is in essence a hostile reaction against people perceived as *offending against this or that enterprise of project-driven homogeneity* and is unique to the Jews because, for reasons that I shall hope to uncover later in the chapter, only the Jews are perceived by non-Jews prejudiced against them as offending in this way.

I will begin with the first type of reaction. Obedience to the demands of natural homogeneity involves dressing, thinking, and behaving *like everybody else* on pain of attracting dislike, contempt, and hostility. Of course there are many, many groups that fail this test, from blacks to the Amish, from Virginia Woolf (who complained that passers-by in London in the early years of the century laughed openly at her for the way she dressed) to homosexuals—and of course, the Jews, especially Haredi Jews, whose dress, particularly such things as side curls (*payot*) or fringes (*tzitzit*) I have often found to attract vocal, quasi-moral disapproval from fellow non-Jews.

But however high the tide of hostility against people perceived as different in such ways may run in certain quarters and however permeated this hostility may be with contempt, it is generally innocent of the kind of fear, not to say panic, characteristic of political antisemitism. However much ordinary people with a leaning toward racism or ethnic prejudice may loathe Mormons, or West Indians, or the Welsh, or vegetarians, that is to say, they never imagine society to be *seriously at threat* from such people. They never think of them as constituting a "disease" against which we should all be on our guard because, like an actual disease, it may prove stronger than the recuperative powers of the body upon which it has once taken hold.

I want to suggest that this is because those who feel social contempt feel it from a position of superiority founded both in their own perceived normality and in the sense that those who think as they do constitute the overwhelming majority. This latter belief may of course be mistaken, but it is strongly felt nevertheless, and it preserves the mere racist from imagining that whatever group of outsiders he or she despises might constitute a serious threat to the very identity, the homogeneity, of the society he or she takes himself or herself to represent.

The sublime complacency of the merely *social* antisemite regarding any possible threat that the Jews might pose to natural homogeneity makes it hard to explain the panic felt by successive generations of *political* antisemites faced with what they imagine to be the unstoppable, because conspiratorial infiltration of society by the Jews together with the related worry that the Jews threaten the very *identity* of non-Jewish society (the kind of panic that Sartre detects in the antisemitism of Céline, for instance).

To recur to a couple of examples of such panic that we addressed in the last chapter: why should T. S. Eliot have found "freethinking *Jews*" (my italics) more of a threat to a Christian polity than the vastly more numerous and influential class of non-Jewish freethinkers? Why should Hitler, believing that in World War I "the only country that was religious was Germany, and that was the country that lost," pass with sublime illogic to the conclusion that therefore *Jews* (in Germany at the time a tiny minority, half a million strong, the vast majority of whom were resolutely secular and profoundly pro-German) must be got rid of, rather than to the conclusion that ridding Germany of the baleful influence of religion must primarily entail ridding it of Christians?

Some very odd concatenation of ideas is plainly at work in the minds of people who talk like this. What are we to make of it? Unless the repeated choice of the Jews as the focus for such fears, by people of extraordinarily diverse beliefs interests and political orientations, is to be regarded as defeating any possibility of rational explanation, that choice must—*pace* David Nirenberg—be motivated by some characteristic exhibited by actual Jews. Yet at the same time, Nirenberg is surely correct to insist that at most periods of history, including the present, non-Jews (including and especially antisemitic ones) have possessed very little understanding of what motivates actual Jews or of what Judaism in its various forms actually involves. It seems, then, that what we are looking for—paradoxically enough—is some characteristic of actual, real-life Jews that is (1) apparent, even glaringly apparent, to non-Jews, that is (2) felt by non-Jews not only to require explanation but to be actually explained by the various beliefs about Jews that go to make up the armory of political antisemitism—but that can in reality be explained (3) only by appeal to features of Judaism and Jewish culture that are for the most part invisible to non-Jews, including antisemitic ones!

I want to suggest that that characteristic is to be found in the rooted refusal exhibited over the centuries, by an irreducible core of the Jewish people, to accept and internalize *at the price of total assimilation and the final abandonment of both Judaism and Jewish nationhood* any of the schemes of *project-driven homogeneity* that have successively seized the mass imagination of the West over the past two millennia. The crime of the Jews has consisted, to put it bluntly, in persisting obstinately in remaining Jewish, when all about them were engaged in abandoning all particular group loyalties in favor of Roman citizenship, or Christianity, or service to the values of the Enlightenment, or to the civilizing mission of one or another nation, or to the supposedly redemptive power of one or another revolution.

THE JEWISH REFUSAL TO DISAPPEAR

Let us look more closely at why this refusal to assimilate totally and vanish utterly into the non-Jewish mass might be capable of provoking enough alarm and dismay in certain quarters to give wings to the disease metaphor. Western European civilization has for the past two millennia been characterized by a succession of religious or political upheavals, each of which has allowed a dominant culture of the day to define itself in positive terms against a range of hostile or putatively inferior forces either external or internal to the continent. Thus, Hellenistic and later Roman culture defined themselves in terms of the contrast between the Hellene or the Roman citizen and the barbarian. Later still, Christendom defines itself in terms of the contrast between Christianity on the one hand and on the other hand paganism abroad and heresy at home. The rise of what one might loosely term modernity from the mid-seventeenth century onward involved, on the one hand, the gradual displacement of Christian uniformity at the hands of science and critical rationality but also on the other hand, the rise of a series of more or less messianic ideologies serving, among other things, the same function of marking a boundary between the civilized and the outsider (or his reprobate domestic representatives). These include more or less coherent systems of thought, such as Marxism, fascism, or the ideas of the philosophes from Rousseau onward that provided the intellectual and moral basis for the French Revolution, as well as the eclectic mishmash of ideas promoted for several generations since World War II by a variety of "hard-left," "progressive," or "anticapitalist" groups or groupuscules.

All of these movements have tended to be both profoundly triumphalist and profoundly insecure. All of them have been at least technically universalist in the sense of imagining themselves as representing the future for all humankind, or at the very least for all Europeans, or all members of a given nation. All of them could be regarded as articulating this aspiration in terms of an offer: the offer of Roman citizenship, or of salvation and eternal life, or in the case of the various messianic movements sprung out of modernity, of participation in the putatively inevitable march of history toward the golden future of humankind or of the nation.

Given the universalist ambitions of each such movement, the ability of its supporters to continue believing in the validity of its messianic claims will inevitably depend to a great extent on the movement's success in persuading or forcing individuals or groups to accept the offer in terms of which it defines itself and, by accepting that offer, to accept also the need to define *themselves* in future in the terms offered by this new version of project-driven homogeneity. The ultimate criterion of success in the enterprise of establishing a new order in Europe has thus always been the willingness of new groups of converts to abandon their former views or culture, to throw in their lot *unreservedly* with the movement—of Roman civilization, or Christendom, or the proletarian revolution, or whatever it may be—and in consequence to cease to exist as a recognizably separate group; to vanish like a drop of water into the larger ocean of the movement.

I would propose, then, that what has primarily fitted the Jewish people, in the eyes of non-Jewish antisemites, for their perennial role as the unique presumed locus of alien malignancy, has been simply their refusal to accept any of the grand offers—the poisoned chalices, if you like—extended to them by Western civilization in any of its successive guises, and their consequent failure to dissolve into the majority community of the day and to cease, in so doing, to exist as a recognizably distinct group. The perceived bad taste—to the palates of some non-Jews—of this perennial rejection of the most generous offers of dissolution by total assimilation has been much aggravated by the perceived sense—that the majority of observant Jews cannot seem to help reinforcing by numerous dropped hints—that their reason for refusing to become ("just like anybody else") Roman citizens, say, or Christians, or the ideal individuals subject only to the general will beloved of Rousseau and such French revolutionary theorists as Clermont-Tonnerre, or Marxists, or fascists, is that they as Jews feel themselves already to possess something better, something more worthwhile than any of the political goodies on offer at the tables of the mighty, and wish, thank you very much, to hold on to it.

I don't mean, of course, that Jews have never *in some senses* assimilated and in large numbers. In terms of modernity, for instance, the numbers of eminent Jewish intellectuals, scientists, and writers, including Nobel prize winners— numbers quite out of proportion to the size of the total Jewish community—is a measure of the extent to which Jews have responded, since Spinoza, to the purely intellectual advances that begin with the Enlightenment.[3] The point I am laboring, however, is a political rather than a purely cultural one. It is that since antiquity the Jews have successfully resisted the *total* assimilation that has relegated innumerable other minority cultures to the history books, have succeeded in doing so despite enduring repeated and frequently catastrophic persecutions, and have done so for reasons that although (or perhaps even because) they remain opaque to most non-Jews, have been uneasily perceived in some non-Jewish quarters as implying some cloudy, half-grasped but possibly profound devaluation of and contempt for the most cherished illusions of the majority culture.

Where does this leave the Jews? It leaves them, in a sense, out of the game. That is because in all of the great revolutionary convulsions that have overtaken the Western world, the Jews (or some fraction of them substantial enough to be taken by hostile non-Jewish opinion to represent the response of the community as a whole), bending a skeptical eye on the world-changing and life-changing offers being made to them, have answered in effect, "No. Thank you but no. We have, and always have had, something better of our own."

THE JEWISH—AND THE NON-JEWISH—PROBLEM

Choosing this status of permanent refusal of full assimilation into whatever has been the dominant culture and ideology of the day has always left the Jews in a difficult position. But one should not overlook the fact that the position in which this refusal has always left at least some supporters of the dominant culture of the day has also had its difficulties. I can perhaps suggest what I have in mind by comparing two speeches, both made at turning points in Jewish history. The first, recorded by Titus Flavius Josephus in *The Jewish War*, was made in the summer of AD 66 by the tetrarch Marcus Julius Agrippa to the people of Jerusalem in an attempt to persuade them to step back from revolt against Rome.

The second, made on December 21, 1789, to the revolutionary French National Assembly by a representative of the liberal nobility of Paris, Count Stanislas-Marie-Adélaïde de Clermont-Tonnerre, had as its object the liberal aim of justifying the universal extension of political and civil rights to groups, including actors, executioners, and the Jews, who had been excluded from a wide range of such rights prior to 1789. Each speech makes powerful moral claims of a general nature for the regime each defends. Each argues powerfully for the extension to and the acceptance by the Jews of certain rights originating within that regime. Each ends, nevertheless, by arguing that the refusal of those rights and correlative identities on the part of the Jews—their insistence, that is to say, on retaining what they take to be essential aspects of their Jewishness— *cannot but threaten equally essential aspects of the regime.* In effect, the Jewish refusal of the regime's offers of inclusion threatens the fundamental moral and political credentials of the regime in a manner sufficient not merely to render all such offers of inclusion nugatory but also to necessitate a reaction, on the part of the regime, of violent and totalizing rejection of the Jews as a people.

The background to Agrippa's speech, in Josephus's account, includes an event extraordinary in terms of the normal procedures of Roman rule. The procurator of Judaea, Pilate, having been appointed by the Roman emperor Tiberius, takes the normal step of conveying to Jerusalem the usual portrait statues of the emperor, known as *signa*. These, of course, outrage the Halakhic proscription against the setting up of graven images, and large numbers of people from the city, joined by even larger number from the surrounding countryside, gather in public to demand the removal of the *signa*. Pilate summons a large number of those concerned to an audience and has them surrounded by soldiers in full armor three deep. He then tells the Jews that they have a choice: they can either accept the *signa* or be cut to pieces. At this, the Jews in a body fall to the ground "as though by agreement" and bare their necks, shouting that they are ready to be killed (to make a kiddush hashem, a sanctification of the name of God: in Jewish terms a martyrdom) rather than deviate from the law. Amazed, Pilate gives in and orders the removal of the *signa* forthwith. Rome has, in short, suffered a significant moral defeat at the hands of the Jews, one that has called into question a standardized procedure for demonstrating, in effect, both its power and its right to rule.

For a people as small and defenseless as the Jews, faced with the might of Rome, provocative behavior of this kind was plainly, from a practical point of view, madness. This, on one level, is the burden of Agrippa's speech. Far stronger nations, as devoted to their former freedom and far better provided with natural defenses than the Jews, have been conquered by Rome and now form part of the empire against which some among the Jews now propose to rebel: how can such a project end in anything but disaster? There is, however, a second strand of feeling that runs through the speech: an undercurrent of puzzlement. Why should the Jews, alone among all these far greater nations, *wish* to rebel? For the fact of the matter is, according to Agrippa, that the general contentment of the subject nations with the Roman status quo is manifest in the very small size of the military garrisons needed to ensure the continuation of Roman power across the vast extent of the empire.

> Consider the defences of the Britons, you who feel so sure of the defences of Jerusalem. They are surrounded by the Ocean and inhabit an island as big as this continent; yet the Romans crossed the sea and enslaved them, and four legions keep that huge island quiet.... [Again, take Africa.] This third of the whole world, whose nations could hardly be counted, bounded by the Atlantic and the Pillars of Hercules, and supporting the millions of Ethiopia as far as the Indian Ocean, is subdued in its entirety; and apart from the regular crops which for eight months of the year feed the entire population of Rome, these people pay tribute of every kind, and for the needs of the Empire

willingly submit to taxation, and unlike you they take no offence when given orders, though only a single legion is quartered in their midst.[4]

There is much more along the same lines. The sense of this strand in the speech is that there is no need for the Romans to garrison their empire other than very thinly because Roman rule is too little oppressive, and too advantageous to those subject to it, for revolt to be a rational option. It makes sense, in other words, to see this strand in Agrippa's speech as appealing to a generally shared belief in an overall conformity of interests between the empire and those it rules, that in turn supports a vast network of interest groups operating at every level of society above that of the slave. For the Jews to stand alone against that belief is thus to threaten it. If one people is prepared to rebel and against such overwhelming odds, why not others?

The conclusion of Agrippa's speech is that such a threat is intolerable—in effect, that the offer of Roman citizenship cannot be lightly refused.

> Possibly some of you suppose that you are making war in accordance with agreed rules, and that when the Romans have won they will be kind to you, and will not think of making you an example to other nations by burning down your Holy City and destroying your entire race. I tell you, not even if you survive will you find a place of refuge, since every people recognises the lordship of Rome, or fears that it will have to do so. Again, the danger threatens not only ourselves here but also those who live in other cities; for there is not a region in the world without its Jewish colony. All these, if you go to war, will be massacred by your opponents, and through the folly of a few men every city will run with Jewish blood. . . . Spare the Temple and preserve for your use the sanctuary with its sacred treasures. For the Romans will no longer keep their hands off when they have captured these, since for sparing them hitherto they have received no thanks at all.[5]

The speech of Clermont-Tonnerre to the French National Assembly, some seventeen hundred years later, runs eerily parallel to Agrippa's in the sequence of stages it follows, from an evocation of Republican reason and liberality, to the extension of an offer to the Jews, an offer too reasonable, too advantageous to be refused, and finally to a threat of total expulsion should the Jews rashly choose to refuse it.

The speech begins by welcoming the "consecration" of "the rights of man and citizen" by these rights having been placed by the assembly "at the head of the French constitution."[6] It then announces its purpose to be that of defending a draft of a decree whose purpose is to establish "the principle that professions and religious creed can never become reasons for ineligibility [for the enjoyment of such rights]."

The occupations concerned are those of actors and executioners: the putatively excluded religions are Protestantism and Judaism. So far as the latter are
concerned, Clermont-Tonnerre adopts the liberal position that differences of
doctrinal belief of the type that divide Catholics and Protestants are in themselves of no interest to the state, whose sole legitimate interest is in the morality
advocated by this or that religious sect. There follows a passage that rebuts a
range of supposed objections to the morality of the Jews. "This people, they
say, is not sociable. They are commanded to loan at usurious rates; they cannot
be joined with us either by marriage or by the bonds of social interchange; our
food is forbidden to them; our tables prohibited, our armies will never have
Jews serving in the defence of the fatherland."

Clermont-Tonnerre's way with these complaints is brisk: "the worst of these
reproaches is unjust, the others are only specious." Jewish usury is a consequence of non-Jewish laws. Dietary laws and restrictions of marriage are trivial
in themselves and unlikely to prove resistant to liberal institutions. "No doubt
these religious oddities will disappear, and if they do survive the impact of
philosophy and of finally being true citizens and sociable men, they are not
infractions to which the law can or should pertain."

These remarks give an impression of tolerant liberalism. The combination
of tolerance and dismissive contempt for Jewish "oddities" that they express
is, indeed, wholly characteristic of a certain type of liberal outlook, both
then and now. But these liberal pieties give place to a harsher note in the final paragraph of the speech in which Clermont-Tonnerre finally confronts
what one might reasonably consider to constitute the essential core of Jewish
identity: the fidelity of Jews qua Jews to the notions of divine commandment
and observance: to halakah (law) as established by the processes of rabbinic
interpretive debate.

> But, they say to me, the Jews have their own judges and laws. I respond that
> it is your fault, and you should not allow it. We must refuse everything to
> the Jews as a nation and accord everything to Jews as individuals. We must
> withdraw recognition from their judges; they should only have our judges.
> We must refuse legal protection to the maintenance of the so-called laws of
> their Judaic organization; they should not be allowed to form in the state
> either a political body or an order. They must be citizens individually. But,
> some will say to me, they do not want to be citizens. Well then, if they do
> not want to be citizens they should say so, and then, we should banish them.
> It is repugnant to have in the state an association of non-citizens, and a
> nation within the nation. . . . In short, Sirs, the presumed status of every man
> resident in a country is to be a citizen.

We are dealing with more than a shift of tone here. Both of these speeches on the "Jewish problem," one from the commencement of the closing centuries of classical civilization, the other dating from the beginnings of our present conception of modernity, display a common structure. Each begins by displaying a genial, even benevolent, tolerance of Jewish religious oddity. In Clermont-Tonnerre's case, the absurd commitments to dietary and marital restrictions will not, he imagines, long survive the entry of the Jews into a fully accepting civil society. Agrippa for his part reminds his hearers that Rome is quite ready to respect the services of the temple and the observance of the Sabbath, though neither, as he jokingly twits his audience, could survive the day-by-day conduct of a war against Rome.[7]

At the end of each speech, however, this tone of gently mocking invitation to inclusion shifts abruptly to one of radical, indeed totalizing, exclusion. In effect, the offer becomes a threat: Either join with us in our common project—the project of Roman civilization, or that of a civil society of individual citizens owing no other allegiance than to the state—*or we will utterly destroy you*, either literally or by an equally total expulsion.

There is a certain disproportion in these threats. They seem too extreme to match the apparent political gravity of those they oppose. There were, for example, at the time Clermont-Tonnerre was speaking, no more than forty thousand Jews in France, most of them resident in the half-German province of Alsace. Why should it be important, or indeed worth the trouble, to expel from France this handful for rejecting the offer to become citizens rather than subjects, when France at the time included a number of vastly larger but equally rejectionist groups, including a large part of the population of the Vendée? Similarly, why should the Roman reaction to Jewish revolt as envisaged by Agrippa extend to "burning down your Holy City and *destroying your entire race*" (emphasis mine); a destruction not to be confined, apparently, to Jerusalem or Palestine but extending to the massacre of Jews in every city of the Roman world. General massacre, as distinct from partial enslavement and general economic exploitation, was only very rarely, in fact, how the Romans treated conquered peoples.

What is it that makes a people as numerically insignificant as the Jews such a problem for these two orators, engaged as they are in the service of far vaster, world-changing political projects? The only plausible answer, it seems to me, is that for both speakers, the Jews represent not so much a practical problem as a problem of principle. Clermont-Tonnerre is clearly right to regard the idea of a civil society as an association of individuals, each equally subject to a common law, as central to the revolution at that point in the early stages of finding its feet in France. That idea, then newly minted, descends from a well-known passage in Rousseau's (1762) *Du contrat social*: "It is therefore essential, if the general will is to be able to express itself, that there should be no partial society within the State, and that each citizen should think only his own thoughts: which was indeed the sublime and unique system established by the divine Lycurgus. But if there are partial societies, it is best that they should be as many as possible and to prevent them from being unequal, as was done by Solon, Numa, and Servius."[8]

The threat that Clermont-Tonnerre sees the Jews as posing to this ideal is inseparable from Jewishness per se—that is to say, from Judaism itself. An observant Jew cannot stand alone, as a naked individual, thinking "only his own thoughts" before the legislative machinery of the revolutionary French state, conceived in Rousseau's terms as manifesting the general will. He or she cannot, because an observant Jew is committed by his or her Judaism not merely to the observance of a body of law, the halakah, deferring to no such theoretical origins but to membership in a community altogether distinct from and far older than any version of the French state, whose institutional functions, exercised through the processes of Rabbinic interpretation, include law making.

Judaism so conceived being, for those reasons, systematically and in principle incompatible with the political theory of the philosophes, the only possible response to it, so far as Clermont-Tonnerre sees it, must be to get rid of it. Being a liberal, he wishes to see this achieved as far as possible by separating Jews from their Judaism one by one to the extent that they can be induced as individuals to accept the offer of citizenship. For the irreconcilable remainder, the only option logically consistent with the unity and homogeneity of revolutionary political institutions must in principle be exile, and good riddance.

Marcus Julius Agrippa also sees the Jews as irreconcilables but in a simpler sense. He sees them as disturbing the peaceful imperial order that relies for its continuation, with a minimal exercise of Roman military expenditure, on the general acceptance of Roman rule as burdensome only in minor and inessential ways. If the Jews can accustom themselves to accepting Roman rule in the same spirit as other, far more powerful and warlike peoples have done, well and good: if not, then they become a threat to the established order. And since that threat arises not from the particular circumstances of Palestine but from religious commitments common to all Jews, the threat that Jewish recalcitrance poses can only, logically, be met by the general destruction of the Jewish people wherever they are settled throughout the empire.

The outlook common to Agrippa and Clermont-Tonnerre might thus be summarized as follows. "We represent a political order that promises vast benefit to humankind, and whose success depends upon general belief in its founding principles and acceptance of its political machinery. We offer Jews the opportunity of joining as equal participants in the work of building that order. If they accept that offer, well and good; if they refuse it, however, they reveal themselves, by that refusal, as constituting a permanent threat to the unity and homogeneity of opinion that the success of the project requires; and, given the importance of the project, must expect to be dealt with accordingly."

We set out in this chapter primarily to explain a curious *duality* exhibited by Jew hatred alone and unmatched in hatred of other groups. On the one hand, Jews have attracted contempt, like many other minority groups, on account of their mere otherness in dress or conduct—in effect, as I put it earlier, on account of offenses against the *natural homogeneity* of the societies in which they have found themselves. But they have *also*—this time suffering a form of prejudice unlike any suffered by any other minority group—found themselves the object of the extraordinary system of delusive beliefs characteristic of *political* antisemitism, together with the fear integral to that system of delusions: a fear sufficiently intense to express itself in the characterization of the Jewish people as constituting, or carrying, a *disease of society*.

My suggestion is that the perception of the Jews as posing a *threat* to society, or as constituting or carrying a *disease* of society, is felt in the first instance in connection with the incompatibility felt in certain quarters to subsist between, on the one hand, the existence not of *individual* Jews but of the Jewish *community*, and on the other hand, the requirements of one or another system of *project-driven homogeneity*. As in both the Agrippa and the Clermont-Tonnere cases, so in others, wherever political antisemitism has gathered strength as a strand in Western societies, it is because the terms on which the Jewish *community* exists and operates have been felt to be incompatible with demands for new kinds of homogeneity associated with political or cultural movements whose success requires an appeal beyond the familiar values and habits constituting the *natural* homogeneity of the society. By their nature, such movements necessarily appeal to some form of intellectually imagined and therefore essentially *invented* homogeneity. They therefore demand and require for their success *mass conversion to some new set of beliefs and habits*: the wholesale creation of a "new" Germany, a "new" France, a "new" Europe.

The threat Jews pose to all such projects is that for reasons internal to the nature of Judaism to be examined more closely in part 4, Jews find it difficult if not impossible to join, at least en masse, big battalions marching to the beat of non-Jewish drums, whether the battalions in question be those of Roman civilization, Christianity, liberalism in its revolutionary phase, fascism, communism, progressive opinion, or whatever. The sense, among non-Jews, that Jews are as a group stonily resistant to *mass* conversion is ancient and widespread enough to have found literary expression as an accepted commonplace, as in the well-known lines from Marvell's *To His Coy Mistress*:

> Had we but world enough and time,
> This coyness, lady, were no crime.
> We would sit down, and think which way
> To walk, and pass our long love's day.
> Thou by the Indian Ganges' side
> Shouldst rubies find; I by the tide
> Of Humber would complain. I would
> Love you ten years before the flood,
> And you should, if you please, refuse
> Till the conversion of the Jews.

This commonplace sense that Jews as a group will invariably prove blankly inaccessible as recruits to whatever movement happens to have captured the mass enthusiasm of a given time and place is of course accentuated by the more obvious markers of Jewish difference, from the laws of kashruth and the observance of Shabbat to such things as yarmulkes, or the *payot, tzitzit,* or *shtreimlach* affected by Haredi Jews—all of them opaque to the non-Jewish mind in ways that envelop them in a frequently absurd aura of strangeness and mystery.

The resulting combination of perceived strangeness and perceived irreconcilability, I suggest, is what leads, in minds disposed both to political enthusiasm and to the rooted proneness to self-deception that is so often its accompaniment, to the pattern of ideas so ably cataloged by David Nirenberg. Such minds naturally wish to believe that the virtues of whatever political or religious movement happen to agitate them make that movement capable in principle of attracting the allegiance of the vast majority of their fellow citizens. Dissent therefore presents a problem. Jewish dissent is part of that problem. But Jewish dissent offers a possible route to the resolution of the far more serious problem of non-Jewish dissent. To open up that route it is only necessary to see the possibility of *identifying the two* and thus of representing *all* dissent as the *kind* of dissent to be expected from people who are not "really" fellow citizens, or perhaps even fellow human beings, in the first place! Once that step is taken, it is easy to progress to the further thought that the dissent that so troubles the politically committed is not merely Jewish in character but *is actually dissent encouraged and organized by the Jews.* And that in turn suggests the conclusion that upon the removal of the Jewish community—however that might be achieved—the remainder of the population, healed of the Jewish "disease" because no longer subject to the disturbing influences formerly emanating from the pool of morbidity constituted by the Jewish community, might well be happy to fall into line behind whatever banner the ideologues in question happen to be waving.

As we shall see in later chapters, this basic structure of delusion is once again operating powerfully in the minds of today's anti-Zionists. It is—or would be if it were admitted—a standing embarrassment for those parts of the Western left hostile to Israel that support and sympathy for Israel comes overwhelmingly, not from the small and divided Jewish communities of the West but from the broad masses of non-Jews of political persuasions opposed to the left. That is why in universities and elsewhere at the moment the hostility of anti-Zionists, as we shall see in chapter 14, is virtually exclusively directed against *Jewish* supporters of Israel. The object is to create the entirely misleading impression that support for Israel is a new Jewish conspiracy and that non-Jewish opinion, on this issue at least, is overwhelmingly behind a hard left whose increasingly fascist methods and outlook are in actual fact increasingly draining it of support.

Around this basic structure of self-regarding delusion in any age, I suggest, the remaining themes or topoi of political antisemitism swiftly accumulate. The process is aided, among other things, by the mere survival of the Jews and of Judaism as a more or less coherent religious-cum-national culture in the face of repeated and horrific acts of persecution. To minds in which heat predominates over light, this suggests that the Jews cannot possibly *really* be as weak as they appear. Their apparent helplessness in the face of persecution must therefore be a mere front, a ploy to throw the antisemite off the scent by concealing their actual power, the actual extent to which the tentacles of Jewish control have been insinuated into the leading institutions of the societies in which they only seemingly constitute a rejected and marginalized presence. The mythology of Jewish conspiracy certainly takes a part of its force, if not all of it, from reflections as demented as these.

THE SOURCES OF JEWISH COHESION

The reality underlying these fevered speculations is that over several millennia, the last two spent in diaspora as a collection of mostly small and isolated communities spread across the nations of Europe, the Americas, and the Muslim world, the Jewish people has demonstrated extraordinary powers of cohesion and tenacity.

At the same time, conversion and assimilation have over the past two millennia constantly threatened the continued existence of the Jews as a recognizably distinct community. Intermarriage and forced conversion have also taken
their toll. But most probably, the majority of conversions have been deliberate
and unforced. At every period prior to the invention of the nineteenth- and
twentieth-century obsession with race, after all, it has been possible for Jews
to escape the burdens consequent upon being born Jewish simply by converting to Christianity or to Islam. And many have done so. When German Jews
in the 1860s were given the opportunity to enter fully into civil society, very
large numbers took advantage of it to abandon all connection with Judaism.
The same process occurred in Russia half a century later. The Choftez Chaim,
a leader of East European orthodox Jewry during the interwar years, in his 1930
book *Chizuk Ha-Emunah* (Strengthening the faith), laments, "The sanctity
of the Holy Torah is declining from day to day at a frightening pace. The new
generation is growing up without Torah and faith. They are becoming wayward
children who deny Hashem [God] and his Torah."[9]

Similarly elevated rates of assimilation on the part of American and British
Jews are equally familiar today and equally a source of concern to those Jews
who like the Choftez Chaim remain persuaded of the value of their traditions.
According to a survey of American Jews conducted in 2013 by the Washington,
DC–based Pew Research Center:

> The percentage of U.S. adults who say they are Jewish when asked about
> their religion has declined by about half since the late 1950s, and currently
> is a little less than 2%. Meanwhile the number of Americans with direct
> Jewish ancestry or upbringing who consider themselves Jewish, yet describe
> themselves as atheist, agnostic, or having no particular religion, appears to be
> rising, and is now about 0.5% of the U.S. adult population. . . . [Whereas] 93%
> of Jews in the aging Greatest Generation [i.e., those born 1914–27] identify
> as Jewish on the basis of religion [and] just 7% describe themselves as having
> no religion . . . among Jews in the youngest generation of U.S. adults –the
> Millennials—68% identify as Jews by religion while 32% describe themselves
> as having no religion, and identify as Jewish on the basis of ancestry, ethnicity
> or culture.

Similar demographic trends have been reported for British Jews.

Such trends naturally fuel concerns among Jews themselves that the Jewish
community, despite its persistence into the present, might now be facing final
dissolution into the matrix community. In moods of pessimism, indeed, Jewish
observers are sometimes inclined to wonder whether the tendency of Jews to

leave the faith once the pressures of antisemitism relax might not imply that the continued existence and coherence of the Jewish community, rather than arising from resistance to those pressures, might rather be a consequence of them.[10] Nor is that worry of recent origin. Theodore Herzl himself, according to Dan Cohn-Sherbok,[11] remarked that "it is only pressure that forces us back to the parent stem" and warned that "if our Christian hosts were to leave us in peace for two generations, the Jewish people would merge into surrounding races." This idea—that Jewishness—and with it the very possibility of identifying as a Jew *is itself an artefact of antisemitism*, was taken up and put into circulation among intellectuals after World War II by Jean-Paul Sartre in his pamphlet *Réflexions sur la question juive* (Paris: Gallimard, 1946), published in English as *Antisemite and Jew*.[12] The essay is pro-Jewish, if only nominally so, in blaming the corruption of Jewish consciousness not on Jewish culture and ways of thought (for Sartre, there are, in effect, no such things) but on non-Jewish antisemitism. Sartre argues, in effect, that the category "Jew" is an entirely unreal and artificial one and that Jews are brought into existence as a recognizable group solely by the refusal of non-Jews guided by antisemitic sentiment (which Sartre considers irrational) to permit them to assimilate. As the current Wikipedia page on the essay neatly puts it in French, "C'est le regard d'autrui qui fait du Juif, un Juif" ("It is the gaze of others that makes a Jew a Jew"). It is not so much, that is to say, that the sudden disappearance of antisemitism would make Jews suddenly turn into non-Jews but rather that its sudden disappearance would result in its becoming evident that *there never were any Jews in the first place!* So much for three millennia of Jewish history, for vast tracts of talmudic learning, for Jewish literature from Buber's *Hasidic Tales* to the novels of Saul Bellow or Cynthia Ozick, and for God knows how many kiddush hashem (acts of Jewish martyrdom), individual and collective.

If Herzl and Sartre were correct about this, then the argument of the present chapter would plainly collapse. If the resistance of Jews to conversion and assimilation is *entirely* an artefact of antisemitism, then that resistance can hardly serve as part of the *explanation* of antisemitism—unless, as Sartre (not Herzl) suggests, antisemitism and the coherence of the Jewish community stand in a reciprocal and mutually sustaining causal relationship to each other, with the result that if this plainly profoundly unhealthy relationship were to be somehow disrupted, Jews and antisemites would both simultaneously cease to exist.

How plausible, then, is Herzl's suggestion that "only pressure forces us back to the parent stem"? It is certainly plausible that hostility to what people believe tends to strengthen their commitment to their beliefs. But it is hardly plausible to imagine that people might continue in a belief, let alone in a commitment to a complex pattern of observance, *solely* because others oppose it. And it is to this second, deeply implausible option to which Herzl and Sartre have nailed their flag.

Moreover, there are plenty of historical counterinstances to Herzl's prediction that "if our Christian hosts were to leave us in peace for two generations, the Jewish people would merge into surrounding races." During the entirety of the fifteenth century in Poland, for instance, Jews were largely able to live in peace with their fellow citizens, but the result was not that the Jewish community gradually dissolved into the Polish Catholic masses surrounding it but that the Jewish population increased tenfold from 15,000 to 150,000.

What about the elevated rates of contemporary assimilation revealed by surveys such as the one by the Pew Research Center cited above? Do these provide empirical support for the Herzl/Sartre claim that the presence of serious levels of antisemitism is necessary to sustain Jewish culture and religion in existence? Clearly not. If true, the Herzl/Sartre thesis would predict vertiginous levels of assimilation in the absence of the pressures from antisemitic hostility that are allegedly all that forces Jews "back to the parent stem." And the rates of assimilation noted by the Pew survey are hardly vertiginous. That survey, in any case, concerns only the religious commitments of contemporary Jews, whereas what the Herzl/Sartre thesis requires is that the bulk of citizens of Jewish descent, in the absence of pressure from antisemitism should rapidly—"within two generations"—cease to maintain any further connection on any level with their former Jewish identity. What the Pew survey tells us, on the contrary, is that amid all the contrary pressures of modern life, almost 70 percent of *millennials*, of all people, identify as Jews, not merely culturally or socially, but *by religion*! I cannot begin to imagine the delight of the Archbishop of Canterbury if anything approaching that many British millennials of Anglican descent were to be found by surveys to identify themselves as members of the Church of England. It does not sound, in other words, as if the American Jewish community, after several generations of freedom from antisemitic pressure, is at present anywhere close to dissolution into the non-Jewish majority.

These results strongly suggest, indeed, that what I have been calling the Herzl/Sartre thesis, that Jewish religion and practice have no intrinsic power to attract and retain the adherence of Jews, is simply false. A recent article in *The Atlantic* confirms the attractions, not just of Judaism but of Jewish orthodoxy, for young American Jews who may not have come from orthodox families.

> On a typical Friday night in Houston, many young people are out drinking at bars or curled up watching Netflix, grateful to be done with the obligations

of the workweek. But in a few Houston homes, Jews in their 20s and 30s have opted to fill these evenings with a different kind of obligation: strictly observing Shabbat, or the Jewish Sabbath. This means no texting, no music, no use of electronics, no driving, no meeting last-minute deadlines, no carrying objects outside of a few hundred square yards. It is a choice to embrace ritual over leisure, a sacrifice of freedom in behavior, diet, and dress for an ancient set of rules.

On its face, this seems like a generation-defying choice. Young Americans are moving away from traditional religious observance in large numbers, and Jews are no exception. Roughly a third of Jews born after 1980 think of their Judaism as a matter of identity or ancestry, rather than as a religion, according to Pew.

But even the young Jews who gravitate toward Orthodoxy, rather than away from it, are still making individual choices about their beliefs and practices, picking among rituals and crafting lifestyles that fit their environments. And rules and rituals seem to have appeal. A greater proportion of Jews in their 20s and early 30s identify as Orthodox than do Jews over the age of 50; the opposite is true of every other Jewish movement. Many of these young people were likely raised Orthodox and have chosen to keep the traditions of their upbringing. But a small portion are *baalei teshuva*, a Jewish concept drawn from the Hebrew word for "return": it denotes those who have become Orthodox as a way of "returning" to God. Like the rest of their generation, they are largely nonconformists—just traditionally minded, rule-bound nonconformists.[13]

A further difficulty for the Herzl/Sartre thesis is that the memory of ancestral Jewishness in those formerly forced to convert, and with it the desire to reconvert, can be powerful enough, it seems, to survive centuries. Forced conversion to Christianity of the large medieval Jewish minorities in Spain and Portugal began in the fifteenth century. Many of these people continued to practice Judaism in secret and became known for that reason by the pejorative term Marrano. With the end of fascist rule in the Iberian Peninsula and the weakening of the power of the church, a few of these communities have finally openly reasserted their Jewishness.[14] Descendants of Iberian Marranos in Iberia and the Americas, known in Hebrew as *Anousim*, are known to number nowadays about four times the present Jewish world population, and movements among these people with the aim of returning to full membership of the world Jewish community have existed for a number of years.[15]

The main argument of this chapter, then, can be summarized as follows. Jewish communities have, over millennia of diaspora, proved capable of maintaining their identity and coherence against formidable and at times formidably

effective pressures inclining them to abandon Judaism and merge untraceably into the matrix community. To the representatives of major non-Jewish
projects of political, social, or religious redemption, and especially to the intellectual leaders and originators of such projects, this remarkable power of
resistance to the forces of assimilation identifies the Jews on the one hand as
a threat and on the other hand as an opportunity. It identifies them as a threat
because such projects require a total renovation of society, and therefore total
acceptance (in effect, total assimilation into the project) on the part of all its
citizens, whether non-Jewish or Jewish. It identifies the Jews as an opportunity
because it opens the possibility of representing non-Jewish rejection of the aims
and methods of the project as exclusively Jewish rejection, and thus as rejection
coming not from within the body of non-Jewish society, but from a group easily
represented as alien and external to the non-Jewish world.

DEFAMING JUDAISM

It is commonplace for explanations to reveal further problems. So it is in the
present case. Explaining antisemitism in terms of the strange phenomenon of
resistance over many centuries to *total* assimilation and disappearance into
matrix communities, even in the face of assimilationist forces as powerful and
as partially successful as those at work in nineteenth-century Germany or Russia, or in present-day America or Britain, requires one to provide some further
explanation of these remarkable powers of collective obduracy themselves.

A natural and obvious explanation for these phenomena would be that Judaism and the various Jewish cultures to which it has given rise over the centuries
in different parts of the world have offered their adherents satisfactions and
sources of strength, not willingly or easily abandoned, into whose nature it
might be worth inquiring. And that is the explanation I shall offer here.

The explanations formulated over the centuries by non-Jewish Western culture in its successive phases, however, have followed a very different pattern.
Non-Jewish voices have tended to see the extraordinary ability of the Jewish
community to withstand and survive persecution as issuing not from any intellectual or moral merit discoverable in Judaism or Jewish culture but rather from
the intellectual and moral defects supposedly evident in both. Judaism has
been represented in many Christian circles since Tertullian as an outmoded
and superseded religion founded in vengeance rather than Christian love. In
the same manner, Jews themselves were, and sometimes are still, regarded by
many Christians as a people whose constant offenses against God led to the
final destruction of their temple, the divine abrogation of their covenant and
their preservation from absolute destruction only in order that they might serve

to Christians as a constant example of the reward visited by God against those who rebel against his commandments.[16]

For the philosophes, as in chapter 4 we found Nirenberg noting, the continued fidelity of Jews to what was perceived as the outmoded medieval nonsense of their religion, along with their consequent failure to fall in with the emancipatory forces of liberal modernity, was an index not of Jewish strength but of a degree of Jewish stupidity and irrationality sufficient to call into question their humanity. For the philosopher Immanuel Kant, arguing in the same vein, Jewish morality, founded in the idea of observance of divine commandment (mitzvah) was no more than a mechanical slavery to tradition, lacking the elements of individual responsibility and independent rational inquiry essential to genuine morality. Similarly, the survival of Jews as a people, a nation, has been attributed not to any positive merit to be found in the Jewish conception of nationhood but rather to Jewish *particularism*; the supposed rejection by Jews of any concern or moral responsibility for non-Jews: a rejection founded supposedly in the absurd conceit of Jews in imagining themselves chosen by God above the rest of humanity.

Plainly, none of these claims go very far to explain the survival of the Jews. Indeed, were they an accurate representation of Judaism and Jewish culture, it would be hard to see how either could have survived. But it is not the function of these claims to explain what it is that has afforded the Jews the strength to survive centuries of persecution as a coherent people with a distinct culture. Their function is rather to explain, on behalf of this or that dominant culture and in ways flattering to its triumphalism, why the Jews, alone among minority groups, fail so persistently to respond to incentives or for that matter to threats designed to induce them to abandon the curious practices and attachments that, inexplicably to the outsider, obstruct their progress toward total assimilation. The "explanation" they advance is that the obstinacy of the Jews derives not from any merit in the sectional culture and practices to which they cling with such tenacity but rather from the supposed fact that this culture and these practices have corrupted Jewish minds and hearts to a degree that makes it impossible for these benighted people to recognize and admit the manifest superiority of non-Jewish culture and practices (whatever form those may take at a given historical moment).

Arguments of this sort, which endeavor to explain Jewish survival and resistance to assimilation without attributing merit of any kind to Judaism and the Jewish cultures to which it has given rise, form an essential element of political antisemitism in all its historically successive versions. These arguments do so not only because they serve to explain an otherwise embarrassing degree of Jewish tenacity and success in resisting assimilation but also because they provide additional support for the central contention of political antisemitism, that whatever is Jewish is, and is *therefore*, essentially corrupt, degraded, and malign, hostile both to reason, to religion rightly understood, and to the progress of (non-Jewish) humankind. Since political antisemitism in all its forms provides the central topic of this book, we cannot therefore avoid examining this aspect of it. We shall do so in part 4: "Judaism Defaced."

HOW TO SQUARE NIRENBERG'S INSIGHTS WITH THOSE OF PRAGER AND TELUSHKIN

It is time to return to a question left unanswered in chapter 4. There, I promised the reader an answer to the question of what has made the Jews, alone among dispersed and despised minority groups, subject to the unique collection of bizarre fantasies of fear and hatred that form the content of political antisemitism. And I promised, too, that it would be an answer capable of meeting what might appear at first sight to be contradictory demands. On the one hand, I promised that it would satisfy Prager and Telushkin's demands (a) that it be "universal," that is to say, unitary across time and (b) that it consist at some fundamental level in a response to "real" Jews—to actual, nonimaginary Jewish characteristics and behavior. On the other hand, I promised it would nevertheless honor David Nirenberg's compelling demonstration of the extent to which Western antisemitism has consisted historically in a long engagement not with actual Jews but with a range of delusions concerning Jews and Judaism motivated essentially by considerations internal to non-Jewish Western culture itself.

I have done my best in the present chapter to fulfill these perhaps somewhat vaunting promises. I have argued that what the Jews have done, to draw upon themselves the storm of essentially delusional hatred cataloged by Nirenberg, Cheyette, Yakira, and many others is basically two things. First, they have had the bad taste to refuse, to some considerable extent, each and every one of the glowing offers made to them by Western culture in its various phases. Second, they have had the even worse taste to survive as a religion and as a people, over an astonishingly long span of time, all attempts—including attempts at outright genocide—to deal with this obstinacy by removing them from the world scene. At bottom, the crime of the Jews, if I am right, has been to deny far stronger but insecure cultures the reassuring tribute of dissolving into them and vanishing.

Here, then, we have, I suggest, the unitary ground of antisemitism, the same from century to century, that Prager and Telushkin seek, and whose existence Hannah Arendt and others have denied. I have tried to demonstrate its dreary consistency across millennial gulfs of time by indicating the manner in which it structures discourses as temporally remote from one another as those of Agrippa and Clermont-Tonnerre.

I have suggested further that this regrettable tendency of the Jews to arouse the bitter ire of would-be redeemers of society by refusing the proffered redemption can only plausibly be regarded as arising from central characteristics of Judaism that render it both a major source of satisfaction and a major source of strength to Jews. I leave to part 4 the task of establishing, or at least suggesting, what some of these sources of satisfaction and strength might be.

This latter commitment plainly compels me to agree with Prager and Telushkin that antisemitism is a response not, as Hannah Arendt thought, to a shifting range of historically accidental features of Jewish life, such as the "specific Jewish functions" in relations to commerce and economic life she considered important in modern Europe, but *to Judaism itself*: to the actual conduct, that is to say, of actual Jews imbued with the spirit of Judaism.

But—in favor of Nirenberg again—the possibility that the historic obstinacy of the Jews *may have its roots in essential characteristics of Judaism* need not, and in practice does not, entail that it is *to those characteristics of Judaism* that antisemites are reacting.

As Nirenberg abundantly demonstrates, antisemites generally have always displayed complete ignorance of how the internal logic of Judaism is structured or of how that internal structure might motivate the obstinacy of the Jews. It is purely to the obstinacy itself that they respond. It is precisely *because* they have no internal grasp of the considerations from which it arises and that render it reasonable that political antisemites have had no option but to invent delusive "reasons" for what seems to them the infuriating, inexplicably stony-hearted unwillingness of the Jews to accept conversion, and with it their putatively "inevitable" dissolution into whatever matrix culture momentarily holds sway, and regards itself as possessing the key to the future of humankind. The resulting reasons range, as we have seen, from pure malignancy to the myth of the Jews as a tightly knit conspiracy aiming at world domination.

In this way, my suggestion, sympathetic as it is to Prager and Telushkin's demands, turns out also to be, as promised, entirely friendly to Nirenberg's more austere analysis.

CONDITIONS OF ADEQUACY

Does that suggestion also satisfy the conditions of adequacy proposed in the section of chapter 4 titled "Some Conditions of Adequacy" for any successful explanation of why the Jews, rather than other minority groups, should have

attracted the strange collection of delusional beliefs that make up the substance
of political antisemitism?

Let us take those conditions in order. With the first we have already dealt.
We have shown, that is to say, how political antisemitism can be *both* a response to "real" Jews and Judaism *and at the same time* a farrago of nonsense
and delusion.

It will be easier to show how the second and third conditions are met if we
skip initially to the fourth. That required an adequate answer to the question
"Why the Jews?" to explain why political antisemitism, as distinct from the
milder social variant, has been devised and propagated mainly by intellectuals.
The answer suggested by the present account is that political antisemitism is a
response to perceived Jewish obstinacy in the face of demands for *project-driven*
rather than *natural* homogeneity. Such demands invariably originate within a
theologically, politically, or socially aware intelligentsia, whose members regard themselves as in some sense ultimately responsible for the health and
future of society. The sad litany of major figures of this type who have found, in
the refusal of Jewish culture to dissolve of its own accord into conformity with
one or another intellectually sponsored social or religious "ideal," grounds for
seeking in one way or another to eliminate that culture, is therefore, according
to the present account, exactly what we should expect.

The same considerations allow our account to meet the second of the criteria of adequacy we distinguished, by explaining why *political* antisemitism, as
distinct from *social* antisemitism, targets the Jews *as a collectivity* rather than
as individuals. It does so, according to me, because the threat to intellectually
sponsored ideals of society, whether in the shape of the Third Reich, or Soviet
communism, or the radical liberalism of the French Revolution, is a threat
presented not by this or that *individual* Jew but by the simple persistence, the
refusal to assimilate and disappear, of the Jewish community as a whole.

The third condition requires an adequate account to offer an explanation
of the *recurrence* of political antisemitism, one that would go beyond mere cultural inertia. The thought behind this condition is that political antisemitism
could not recur as it does, from century to century, each time in a form slightly
altered to answer to the political problems and circumstances of the day, *unless it served some common purpose in the varying economies of ends and means of
the very diverse groups that over time have fondled and promulgated it*. Cui bono?
Who profits? And how?

Here again, our account may serve to shed some light. Intellectual politics
idealizes unanimity. Since the beginnings of the Enlightenment in particular,
speculative programs of social regeneration have tended to cast themselves in

increasingly radically universalist terms as programs for the renovation of the nation or even of humankind *as a whole*. In practice, the self-appointed revolutionaries invariably confront opposition ranging from the determined to the violent from within whatever putative human community they address. There are two great advantages to be gained, however, beyond those we distinguished earlier on, from representing this opposition as coming from a marginalized, "alien" group within that community, particularly if the group in question happens to be, like the Jews, too weak to offer much in the way of actual opposition of its own. On the one hand, it can serve usefully to discredit one's opponents; on the other hand, it can be an effective way of rallying support for one's own position to suggest to those undecided that the "real" political choice before them is between the "authentic voice" of the nation (or of humanity) that one takes oneself to represent and an alien conspiracy. Both Hitler and Stalin, the latter, for instance, at the time of the celebrated (Jewish) Doctors' Plot, were adept at using antisemitism to secure this kind of political advantage. And as I suggested earlier in this chapter, the value of the Jewish threat for such purposes by no means belongs solely to the past and to Europe. In later chapters, I shall look more closely at the contemporary instance of the working out of this type of political motivation in the shape of attempts since 2001 by certain progressive journalists and commentators to discredit the stance of anyone, Jewish or non-Jewish, to the right of themselves on Middle Eastern policy by associating it with the putatively sinister and behind the scenes operations supposedly characteristic of the Israel lobby.[17]

Other features of our account allow it to meet the remaining conditions of adequacy we distinguished in chapter 4. Why, prior to the invention of Nazi *Rassentheorie*, was it always possible for a Jew in most cases to avoid further persecution simply by converting, by ceasing to be a Jew? If our account is correct, it is because the political antisemite's quarrel with the Jews was never, until the rise of Nazism, a quarrel with a *race* but with a cultural formation and ultimately with the collection of ideas constitutive of that formation—a quarrel, that is to say, not with Jews as bearers of a certain *supposedly genetic* identity but with Judaism and the Jewish culture it informed.

Again, the account we have offered explains why, whereas ordinary social prejudice seeks merely to exclude, and to reduce the social and economic opportunities open to, the despised outgroup, political antisemitism has characteristically sought the elimination of the Jews, whether by conversion, expulsion, or extermination. The reason chimes, among other things, with Heinsohn's assessment of Hitler's motives. It is that adopting the strategy of projecting internal threats upon a putatively external source *necessarily*, because conceptually, commits one to regarding those who supposedly represent that external source of disorder as collectively constituting a disease, a threat to one or another ideal conception of homogeneous social order from which a pure, ideally united society can only be redeemed by systematically eliminating all the carriers of the disease in question.

Our account also explains—number 7 in our list of conditions of adequacy— the strange combination of stability and variability in the content of political antisemitism. The stable elements are those surrounding the metaphor of disease and consist in one or another version of the idea that, like the elements of a pathological condition, the Jews support one another while behaving in ways fatal to the natural life of whatever social organism they invade. The variable elements, from child murder to the demonstration of undue business acumen, reflect the specific concerns of this or that coterie of political antisemites.

Finally, our account meets the remaining condition of adequacy—number 8 —by explaining why political antisemitism possesses the dizzying power it does to swing, in the recruitment of its adherents, from one end of the political spectrum to the other. If we have argued correctly, political antisemitism is by no means, as is often erroneously supposed, a delusion unique to the political right. It lies in wait for anyone in whom enthusiasm for the radical reform of society along politically sectarian lines has waxed so strong as to outweigh common sense, respect for fact, and most crucially, respect for opposing views. Since that is a condition perennially prevalent in political life, it should come as no surprise that political antisemitism owns no specific constituency but can crop up, from time to time, anywhere in the political spectrum, at either end or in the middle.

JEWISH SELF-BLAME

Ethnic hatreds, durable as some of them have proved to be, tend to weaken and die out as time and change of circumstance erode them. Hatred of the Jews appears at first sight an exception to that rule. It has endured for so many centuries, and when occasionally it dies away, it does so apparently only to rise again rejuvenated in new forms.

It is unsurprising, therefore, that Jews should ask themselves whether there is not some fault of theirs, "something we do," that might justify a hatred so enduring, and otherwise—it might seem—so inexplicable. And to justify *such* a hatred, what "we are doing" must be something very bad indeed.

If we have argued correctly in this and the preceding chapter, these Jewish self-questionings, anguished as they often are, are needless and without foundation. The *durability* of Jew-hatred is a function, not of enduring Jewish iniquity, but of the enduring *utility* of one form of antisemitism, political anti-semitism, to powerful groups in non-Jewish society. Had antisemitism been, as Langmuir and many others have supposed, merely one more form of ethnic prejudice, it might well have died out. Indeed, as surveys show, it is, *in that form*, much weaker in Western societies than formerly. It is *political* antisemitism that possesses the power to revive again endlessly, now on this side of politics, now on that, bringing the old hatreds with it. But what explains that is its per-ceived utility *for non-Jewish purposes*. *Political* antisemitism, in short, is a *totally non-Jewish phenomenon*. It is a response, not to anything any real Jew can be supposed to have done, but to the need of this or that *non-Jewish* movement to explain, in terms of the machinations of an alien force, failures having nothing to do with the Jews and everything to do with its own inadequacies.

If we are right, of course, there is "something that the Jews have done" that, even if it in no way *justifies* political antisemitism, has at any rate exposed them to figuring, in this enduring non-Jewish political syndrome, as the required alien force. But the something in question is merely continuing to exist as an organized community. It is, hence, not only nothing of which Jews should be ashamed, but nothing they could have avoided doing. Jews have followed Moses's injunction and chosen life, that is all. But for the malign purposes and fantasies of political antisemitism, that has been enough.[18]

NEW DIRECTIONS

There, the issues pursued in this and the preceding two chapters must stand— at least for the moment. At this point, the argument of the book will divide. Part 4 ("Judaism Defaced"), chapters 10–12, returns to the questions raised above in the section titled "The Sources of Jewish Cohesion," concerning the various lines of denigration of Judaism and Jewish culture that form, as we have seen, an essential strand in the complex tapestry of political antisemitism.

Before that, in part 3, however, I shall return to some of the questions raised in the introduction by examining to what extent current "anti-Zionist" op-position to the State of Israel, and in particular the politics of the Boycott, Divestment and Sanctions (BDS) movement, can reasonably be criticized as antisemitic and in particular as constituting a new manifestation of political antisemitism.

Finally, part 4 ("Paying the Price") will examine some of the costs imposed, not solely on Jews but also on non-Jews, by the historic attachment, first of Western and now of Islamic culture, to the fantasies of political antisemitism.

NOTES

1. Lindemann 1997, 107.
2. Cheyette 1993, 56–57.
3. I am grateful to Cynthia Ozick for pointing out to me the necessity for this caveat.
4. Josephus 1971, 41–42.
5. Josephus 1971, 43.
6. I have used the version in *The French Revolution and Human Rights: A Brief Documentary History*, trans. and ed. Lynn Hunt (Boston: Bedford, 1996), 86–88.
7. "If you observe the custom of the Sabbath, with its complete cessation of activity, you will promptly be crushed, as were your ancestors by Pompey, who was most active in pressing the siege on the days when the besieged were passive." Josephus 1971, 43.
8. Rousseau 1913, 23.
9. Cited in Bernard Mazam, *With Fury Poured Out: The Message of the Holocaust for Today and Tomorrow* (New York: C.I.S. Publishers, 1995), 51.
10. I am grateful to David Conway for drawing my attention to this issue and for both the quotation from Herzl and the preceding two citations.
11. Dan Cohn-Sherbok, "The Paradoxes of Antisemitism," *Transcripts* 48, no. 52 (2011): 49.
12. Sartre 1948.
13. Emma Green, "Why Orthodox Judaism Is Appealing to So Many Millennials," *The Atlantic*, March 31, 2016, https://www.theatlantic.com/politics /archive/2016/03/orthodox-judaism-millennials/476118/.
14. Gil Kezwer, "Marranos Return to Judaism after 500 Years," http://www .kulanu.org/marranos/kezwer.php.
15. Jack Cohen, "The Desperate Plight of the Bnei Anusim," *Times of Israel*, July 2, 2012, http://blogs.timesofisrael.com/the-desperate-plight-of-the-bnei -anusim/.
16. Nicholls 1993. See especially chapter 5.
17. For an earlier foray in this direction, see Harrison 2006, chap. 9, particularly pp. 194–204.
18. I am grateful to my friend and fellow philosopher Professor Michael Krausz for pointing out to me the need for the argument of this chapter to include this section.

PART III

IS ISRAEL AN "ILLEGITIMATE" STATE?

SIX

—⚉—

ACCUSATION AND NARRATIVE

When the American Studies Association (ASA) endorsed a boycott of Israeli academic institutions, scores of institutions, including over two hundred and fifty university presidents, distanced themselves from the ASA's actions. Some did so in strong language. But almost all framed their argument in terms of the ASA's encroachment upon the sphere protected by the doctrine of academic freedom. . . . Nevertheless, if BDS is anti-Semitic, then criticisms of it for its violations of academic freedom have something of a busting-Al-Capone-for-tax-evasion quality to them.

—Kenneth L. Marcus, *The Definition of Anti-Semitism*

INDIVIDUAL VERSUS INSTITUTIONAL ANTISEMITISM

It is time to return to the question we raised in the introduction, of the extent to which the widespread hostility to Israel observable on the Left of politics in the Western world can reasonably be accused of antisemitism. That antisemitism is indeed to be found on the left is currently widely admitted. The question is, what kind of antisemitism is it? Are we dealing with a few individual antisem-ites whose private dislike of *Jews as such* can be sharply distinguished from the principled commitment of large numbers of left-wing students and activists, trade union members, and media commentators to a "purely political" opposi-tion to Israel? Or are we dealing, on the contrary, with a type of antisemitism primarily rooted not in the minds of individual members of political move-ments but in the processes of theorizing and *prise de position* that constitute the life and being of political movements themselves and thus inseparable from certain current turns that those processes have lately taken on the left? These questions agitate much current political debate. It is questionable, though—and it is doubt on this score that in part motivated me to write this book—whether the bulk of current political debate proceeds on the basis of conceptual resources sophisticated enough to allow them to be usefully addressed. Thus, Dave Rich, whose book on antisemitism in the British Labour Party is one of the best so far produced, is clearly right that "anti-Semitism is both a form of racism and a prejudice with its own characteristics."[1] Yet almost in the same breath, he doubts the possibility of achieving consensus on this or any other aspect of this increasingly bilious debate.

> Ideally, all sides in the Israel/Palestine debate would agree on where the boundary lies between anti-Semitism and criticism of Israel, but experience suggests this may be difficult to achieve. For Israel's supporters, denying its right to exist and opposing the Jewish right to self-determination is unacceptable, and for many, anti-Semitic. Israel's opponents, unsurprisingly, disagree. Even those anti-Zionists who wish to see Israel disappear completely insist that theirs is a political view, unrelated to anti-Jewish prejudice or hatred. Similar disagreements occur over whether it is anti-Semitic to call Israel a racist or apartheid state, or to campaign for it to be boycotted.[2]

Rich offers some suggestions, short of consensus, that he thinks might serve at least to "address some of the fundamental problems that have brought public relations between British Jews and the left to crisis point."[3] These suggestions include "eliminating conspiracy theories about Jews or Zionists from left-wing politics" and "using ordinary political language to criticize [Israel's] policies, rather than language that echoes older anti-Semitic myths about Jews."[4] Clearly, these are sane and valuable proposals, but they fall short of a detailed elaboration of Rich's basic—and entirely right-headed—point: that antisemitism, while in some of its aspects a form of what we nowadays call racism, is in others altogether sui generis, "a prejudice with its own characteristics."

A DOUBLE INQUIRY

What we set out to do in chapter 3 was, in effect, to supply that detailed elaboration by, in effect, embedding Rich's basic and entirely valid distinction within a taxonomy of types of antisemitism. The task of this and the following three chapters is to see what light, if any, that taxonomy can cast on the embattled debate over antisemitism on the contemporary left.

I argued in chapter 3 that *social antisemitism*, the form of antisemitism that can reasonably be regarded as a version of racism, is a *state of mind*: a collection of personal attitudes of contempt and dislike directed against any individual Jew and defended by appeal to stereotypes. The form in which antisemitism appears as sui generis, as "a prejudice with its own characteristics," on the other hand, is *political antisemitism*. What distinguishes political antisemitism from social antisemitism is that the former is not a *state of mind* at all but rather a *cultural formation*. It is not a collection of *attitudes* of any kind but an organized body of pseudo-explanatory theory concerned not with the denigration of Jews *as individuals* but with the supposed centrality of *the Jewish collectivity*, its nature, acts, and influence, to whatever happens to be deplored by the political antisemite in the ongoing course of world events. Bodies of theory of this type are never the product of isolated individual minds. Nor, though they may and do come to dominate the workings of individual minds, is their *basic* habitat the individual mind. They are political constructs, collectively elaborated climates of opinion, and their *basic* habitat—the habitat in which they originate—is the world of organized political debate and activism.

It follows that if there is any truth in the accusation that the left in Western countries at present fosters a political culture intrinsically or institutionally infected with antisemitism, then the kind of antisemitism at stake cannot be social antisemitism. It must, rather, be a new form of, a recrudescence of, political antisemitism.

Can the accusation in that form be driven home? I argued in chapter 3 that political antisemitism in virtually all its historic manifestations has recycled versions of five basic claims. If a given line of political opposition to Israel can be shown to exhibit versions of these traditional claims, standing in their traditional relationships of mutual support and implication to one another, and if they turn out to be essential to the internal coherence of the stance in question and so inseparable from it, then we have reasonable grounds for suspecting that line of opposition to be antisemitic in character.

But a further step is needed to pass from suspicion to certainty. The account of antisemitic prejudice offered in chapter 3 was constructed on the basis of Gordon Allport's definition of prejudice as thinking, speaking, or acting injuriously *with insufficient warrant*. A line of criticism of Israel might thus in principle mimic in its entirety the traditional content and structure of political antisemitism but nevertheless defeat the charge of anti-Jewish prejudice simply in virtue of being true—or in Allport's terms, of enjoying *sufficient warrant* for its critique.

Any examination of current left-wing opposition to Israel designed to settle the issue of whether it exhibits anti-Jewish prejudice must therefore proceed on two levels: one concerned with establishing continuity with the traditional beliefs and explanatory structures of political antisemitism and the other concerned with truth or warrant. Moreover, the two inquiries, by the nature of their interconnection, need to be pursued in tandem. Following that prescription, the present chapter will be largely, but by no means entirely, concerned with the first of these inquiries, the following two chapters largely, but by no means entirely, with the second.

WHAT IS "ILLEGITIMATE" SUPPOSED TO MEAN?

Let us begin with the central claim of present-day anti-Zionism: that Israel is an illegitimate state, one that should never have been founded in the first place. The general tone of this accusation can be gauged from an article published in the British left-wing daily *The Guardian* in January 2001 by one Faisal Bodi, identified by the newspaper simply as "a Muslim journalist."[5] The title, trenchantly enough is "Israel Simply Has No Right to Exist." It begins: "Several years ago, I suggested in my students' union newspaper that Israel shouldn't exist. I also said the sympathy evoked by the Holocaust was a very handy cover for Israeli atrocities. Israel has no right to exist. I know it's a hugely unfashionable thing to say, and one which, given the current parlous state of the peace process, some will also find irresponsible. But it's a fact that I have always considered central to any genuine peace formula."[6] The article concludes by promising "perpetual war" if Israel fails to seek "models of coexistence (with the Arabs) based on equality and the respect for human rights."

Since 2001, the rhetoric of delegitimization has become standard for a wide variety of organizations of anti-Zionist tendency on the left of Western political life. These include the Boycott, Divestment and Sanctions (BDS) campaign, the Durban conferences, the Israel Apartheid Weeks, many human rights and other nongovernmental organizations (NGOs), and sections of major political parties across the world, including the British Labour Party.

The recent popularity of such rhetoric, however, cannot hide its essential strangeness. For a start, the demand that Israel *be declared illegitimate as a state* is unique. Of no other state, in a world not lacking in tyrannous, terminally corrupt, kleptocratic, or otherwise failed states, is such a demand heard.

Still more seriously, as the philosopher Elhanan Yakira has argued, it is not clear what could even be *meant* by describing a *state*, as such, as illegitimate. There is a long tradition of legal and philosophical theory (Bodin, Hobbes, Locke, Rousseau, Weber, and others) concerning the legitimacy of political authority, but what that tradition deals with is the relationship between the state and the citizen. This vast web of learned discussion, as Yakira points out, proposes criteria of many kinds for assessing the legitimacy of a government or a regime but can offer no guidance on the legitimacy of a *state as such*, since it simply presumes the existence of the state as a given. "The frequently heard comparison between Israel and South Africa on the basis of an alleged similarity between the latter's Apartheid regime and what is called 'the Occupation' is questionable. It is so not only because there is not much similarity between the situation that prevailed in South Africa and the situation in Israel, but because the notion of legitimacy is used in Israel's case to negate something that the theory of legitimacy cannot possibly negate or deny: the legitimacy of Israel as a state."[7]

Since existing legal and political theory gives no clue to what the word might mean in such a context, those who wish to characterize Israel as an illegitimate state are thus open to the demand that they explain what they mean by it.

The meaning of characterizing terms—say, *square*, or *woven*, or *paraplegic*— can very often be inferred from explanations of why informed people give for taking such a term to apply to certain objects but not to others. Some clue as to the meaning attached to the characterizing term *illegitimate* by those who deny the legitimacy of Israel as a state might therefore be expected to emerge from the indications they offer of the characteristics they see as differentiating Israel, as a supposedly illegitimate state, from other states that they take to be legitimate.

It turns out that these indications constitute an extraordinarily mixed bag. For many people, the problem is in part that Israel is a *Jewish* state. That issue comes to a head in the fact that Israeli law enshrines a "right of return" for Jews, which makes it easy for Jews from overseas to obtain Israeli citizenship but allows no such right to Arabs. This is a particular bone of contention for the BDS movement. The latter presents itself as a Palestinian movement but was in fact, according to the British sociologist David Hirsh, the creation of activists on the Israeli and British left.

> In the 1970s and 80s the ANC [African National Congress], which positioned itself as the voice of the whole South African nation, called for a boycott of South Africa. Campaigners for the boycott positioned themselves as passive responders to the "call" of the oppressed. The BDS campaign against Israel has, since 2005, tried to position itself in the same way. However in truth, British anti-Israel activists started the boycott campaign and they persuaded people in Palestine to issue the "call." Although neither the Palestinian Authority nor Hamas have issued a "call," the BDS movement says that the "call" was issued by "Palestinian Civil Society."[8]

Be that as it may, one of the demands of the BDS movement has been that
Arab refugees from Israel and their descendants should also be granted the
right to return. In 1948, at the time of the War of Independence, approximately
750,000 Arab inhabitants fled or were driven from Israel—a figure matched
by the number of Jews who deemed it prudent or were forced to leave Arab
countries after 1949. The Jewish refugees were granted citizenship by Israel and
by other countries. The Arab refugees were, on the contrary, denied citizenship by most other Arab states (the exception is Jordan, though even there it
remains unclear how far former Palestinians can rely on their present Jordanian
citizenship[9]) and became permanent residents of refugee camps funded largely
by the United Nations. The descendants of Arabs who left Israel now number
several million. Their return is opposed by Israel on obvious financial and social
grounds and on the ground that their return would inflate Arab numbers in
Israel to a level inconsistent with continued Jewish political autonomy.

Noam Chomsky, the distinguished linguist and a noted polemicist on the
left, has also made this a central plank of his case for the illegitimacy of the Jewish state. In an exchange with Bernard Avishai, he identifies the Jewishness of
Israel as the source of "discriminatory institutions and practices . . . expressed
in the basic legal structure of the state"[10] that together define Israel as the home
of all Jews, wherever they live.

Will the concern of Israel to represent itself as a state for all Jews, wherever
they may actually live, do the work of singling out Israel from other states as
uniquely illegitimate? Paul Bogdanor has this to say about the argument:

> Here is a typical example of the selective morality for which he [Chomsky]
> is infamous. The Armenian constitution seeks "the protection of Armenian
> historical and cultural values located in other countries" and permits
> individuals "of Armenian origin" to acquire citizenship through "a simplified
> procedure." The Lithuanian constitution proclaims: "Everyone who is
> ethnically Lithuanian has the right to settle in Lithuania." The Polish
> constitution stipulates: "Anyone whose Polish origin has been confirmed
> in accordance with statute may settle permanently in Poland." And the
> Ukrainian constitution . . . provides for "the satisfaction of national and
> cultural and linguistic needs of Ukrainians residing beyond the borders of
> the State." Yet Chomsky, obsessed with the dread threat of Jewish national
> independence, does not rail against the existence of these countries. His
> abhorrence of the democratic nation-state is reserved for Israel.[11]

It is worth adding to Bogdanor's remarks that the subsequent refusal of
a right of return to members of a community by which, or on whose behalf,

war was declared, and who left the country at that time—because, to put it bluntly, their side was unlucky or incompetent enough to lose the war—is by no means unique to Israel. Thus, the Greco-Turkish War of 1919–22, begun by Greek nationalists in hopes of extending the boundaries of Greece to include historically Greek and ethnic Greek-inhabited areas in western Anatolia, led to a huge transfer of ethnic Greeks from formerly Greek villages in Turkey, some of which remain uninhabited and decaying to this day. Another instance is provided by the three million Sudeten Germans in whose supposed interest the Nazi government of Germany invaded Czechoslovakia in 1939, but who were expelled en masse by the Czechs in 1945 as a result of Germany's losing World War II and who have not subsequently recovered either Czech citizenship or their lands. A third instance is the vast and bloody exodus of Muslims from India to Pakistan that accompanied the end of the British Raj in 1947. Such events are in fact as common as they are unhappy and are intensely difficult to resolve in any satisfactory way. But no one seriously imagines them to provide grounds for impugning the legitimacy of any of the states concerned, except Israel, or for raising the question whether Turkey, say, or India, or the Czech Republic, have the *right to exist* as states. These cases are sufficient to make right of return issues, whether involving the establishment or the denial of such rights, useless as means of formulating a criterion for separating off Israel as a uniquely illegitimate state.

LEGITIMACY AND "ATROCITY"

A more promising way to justify singling out Israel as a uniquely "illegitimate" state, in the same breath making clear in what the "illegitimacy" of a state is supposed to consist, might be to take up the veiled suggestion of Faisal Bodi, in his 2001 *Guardian* article denying Israel's "right to exist," that Israel is guilty of "atrocities."

It is not hard to find examples of eminent public intellectuals of "anti-Zionist" tendency prepared to take up this suggestion and run with it. Jacqueline Rose, professor of English at Queen Mary College, University of London, catches the general spirit of this line of anti-Zionist rhetoric: "How did one of the most persecuted peoples of the world come to embody some of the worst cruelties of the modern nation-state?"[12]

In the same vein, the late Edward Said was prepared to describe Israel's occupation of the West Bank and (at that time) of Gaza, as "in severity and outright cruelty more than rivaling any other military occupations in modern history."[13]

The trouble with these claims is that events from 1914 to the present day have set the bar of atrocity too high for it to be easily surmounted by a nation as small and as civilized as Israel. Where are the Israeli atrocities capable of standing comparison with those committed by, to name a few, the Pol Pot regime in Cambodia, the Assad regime in Syria, ISIL in Iraq and Syria, or the Nazis, first in Germany and later throughout Europe between 1933 and 1945? And to name these few, after all, is to offer a very short extract indeed from the crowded roll of potential twentieth- and twenty-first-century competitors.

Anti-Zionist writers frequently reveal themselves to be well aware of the difficulty that the vast and terrible perspectives of horror and inhumanity opened up by recent world history have created for this line of criticism of Israel. Such writers deploy various arguments, all of them bad, in the attempt to minimize the rather glaring disparity that exists between the crimes of Israel and those of states and movements whose legitimacy and right to exist are never questioned—many of them, indeed, dear to the anti-Zionist left. Thus, for instance, Jaqueline Rose, in the preface to her *The Question of Zion*, plaintively inquires, "Why is criticism of everybody else a precondition of criticizing Israel?"[14]

If the matter at issue were some specific criticism of Israel—one of the many, say, that we shall consider in detail in the next two chapters—then this remark would express a sane and entirely proper caveat. But if the issue at stake is—as it can hardly not be in the context of a book accusing Israel of embodying "some of the worst cruelties of the modern nation state"—the question of Israel's *right to exist as a state*, and if the reason for denying Israel *legitimacy as a state* is supposed to be that Israel is *off the scale* of human wickedness, then the behavior of everybody else is not some distracting irrelevance but the heart of the matter—in which case, Rose's remark, far from expressing a reasonable caveat, becomes an attempt to change the subject without anybody noticing.

The essential absurdity of any comparison between Israel and major purveyors of atrocity in our time has not, of course, stopped such comparisons becoming a standard element in anti-Zionist discourse. As Dr. Goebbels knew well, constant repetition breeds acceptance, and the idea that there exists some morally significant parallel between Israel and, in particular, the Third Reich is now half a century old—more than old enough, that is to say, to ensure a climate of ready acceptance, among a certain audience, for remarks like those of Rose and Said, when delivered in a tone of blank ex cathedra assertion.

The parallel seems to have originated, in fact, as long ago as 1967, in the invention of the term *Judeo-Nazi* by Yeshayahu Leibowitz (1903–93), a professor of biochemistry and neurophysiology at the Hebrew University—a notable polymath and public intellectual and a figure greatly celebrated by the Israeli left to this day—to describe those on the Israeli right of whose policies he disapproved. In 1993 (in striking contrast to the treatment visited upon dissident intellectuals in the actual Third Reich), he was selected for the Israel Prize, but his remarks beforehand, in an address to the Israel Council for Palestinian Peace in which he called upon Israeli soldiers to refuse orders, created so much outrage that he refused to accept the prize on the grounds that he did not wish to create antagonism when receiving it.

Since Leibowitz's coinage, the idea that Israel is a Nazi state has thriven greatly and has become sufficiently familiar on the left for placards exhibiting the Star of David and the swastika joined by the equal sign (=) to play a standard part in any anti-Zionist street demonstration. Similarly, radical journalism not infrequently plays with the idea that Israel, if not actually at present engaged in genocide against the Palestinians, very soon will be. Thus, according to the journalist Justin Raimondo writing in the web newspaper *Antiwar.com* on August 4, 2014, "History is full of ironies: World War I, marketed to Americans as a 'war to end all wars' paved the way for an even more massive slaughter. The invasion and conquest of Iraq—which was supposed to augur in what George W. Bush hailed as a 'global democratic revolution'—instead ushered in a new era of chaos, bloodshed and tyranny in the region. And in the year 2014 the state of Israel, founded in large part as a reaction to the Holocaust, has embarked on a policy of genocide in Gaza."[15]

Raimondo's argument for the truth of the last sentence is not strong. In the context of his article, it relies, in essence, on a scurrilous op-ed article by another American journalist, Yochanan Gordon, which did indeed advocate the mass butchery of the Gaza population and which appeared on August 1, 2014, in the *Times of Israel* and also in a small New York news sheet, the *Five Towns Jewish Times*, founded, it seems, by Gordon's father. Later that day, the *Five Towns Jewish Times* took down the article, replacing it with an apology altogether rejecting its contents. Later that afternoon, Gordon was banned from further posting on the *Times of Israel* blog, which also issued an apology. Later still, Gordon himself issued an apology.[16]

Under the circumstances, it seems improbable, *pace* Raimondo, that the government of Israel is likely any time soon to take its cue from Yochanan Gordon. In any event, the population of Gaza, for the present, far from being herded down the path trodden in 1933–45 by the Jewish population of Prague or Warsaw, appears robustly attached not merely to life but to conducting an endless small-scale war with Israel. But the article will nevertheless have served, despite all that, to give comfort to a widespread belief in some sort of parallel between Israel and the Nazis that everyone (everyone, at least, inside a certain ideological bubble) knows, or feels, to be somehow basically sound.

The notion that Jews might be just as bad as their Nazi persecutors, *and bad in the same ways*, is certainly exciting enough to sell newspapers in many parts of Europe. For that reason, if for no other, there continue to be occasional eruptions in the popular press of stories promoting it; and this drip feed of nourishment also helps to keep the idea of a valid parallel between Israel and Nazi Germany alive in a range of Western currents of opinion. A well-known example concerns the publication in 2009, in the Swedish tabloid *Aftonbladet* of a story alleging that Israeli troops harvested organs from Palestinians who had died in Israeli custody. According to the exhaustive and fully referenced Wikipedia entry on the resulting controversy, the story was widely condemned abroad as false and inflammatory, and the Swedish government was asked by Israel and various members of the US Congress to denounce it. Stockholm refused, citing freedom of the press and constitutional issues. The Swedish ambassador to Israel, Elisabet Borsiin Bonnier, did condemn the article as "shocking and appalling," but the Swedish government chose not to associate itself with her protest.[17] Inevitably, therefore, and without anything in the way of verification or further support, the allegation has continued to circulate.

The supposed parallel between Israel and the Third Reich has become so familiar, indeed, that some anti-Zionists criticize it for not going nearly far enough. Here is the video journalist Anthony Lawson writing in 2013 on the blog *Intifada: Voice of Palestine*: "I get incensed when so many people—even intelligent commentators like Paul Craig Roberts and Man of the People Roger Waters—insist on comparing Israel to Nazi Germany, when the comparison is quite absurd. Israel's policies are far worse than Nazi Germany's ever were."

And lest one should think that this kind of thing is confined to the madder elements of the blogosphere, here is the present leader of the British Labour Party, Jeremy Corbyn, speaking in 2016 at the launch of a report into alleged antisemitism in his party, cheerfully bracketing Israel not even with the Nazis on the moral spectrum but with Salafist groups such as the Islamic State whose beheadings, mass executions, and persecutions of Christians, Yazidis, and Shiʻite Muslims have brought them global fame as executants of real-life political Grand Guignol: "Our Jewish friends are no more responsible for the actions of Israel or the Netanyahu government than our Muslim friends are for those of various self-styled Islamic states or organisations."[18]

The unbounded hysteria and moral hyperbole of these claims brings into new focus the current political cause they support: "anti-Zionism." The reader will have noticed, and possibly deplored, my occasionally putting the term *anti-Zionism* in quotation marks, as if there were something wrong with the very concept that strives here for expression. My reason for doing so is that there is indeed something wrong with that (putative) concept—namely, that it is no clearer at first sight what "anti-Zionism" could mean in current contexts than it is clear what illegitimate could mean when applied not to a regime or a government but to a nation-state.

Let me amplify that thought. At the start of the twentieth century, it would have been perfectly clear what one meant by "anti-Zionism." In those days, Zionism was the name of a controversial, mainly but not exclusively Jewish movement advocating the creation of a national home for the Jewish people. Its arguments were widely debated in Jewish circles, within which it numbered, in those days, more dissenters, or "anti-Zionists," than supporters.

Since 1948, however, a self-governing Jewish national state, Israel, has existed. In consequence, both Zionism and anti-Zionism, in the senses they bore in 1900, have become terms of purely historical interest. In precisely the same way, while prior to 1922 it would have been possible either to advocate or to resist home rule for Ireland, both positions lapsed into historical irrelevance once an independent and self-governing Irish state had actually come into existence.

After 1922, it would still have been possible for someone to describe himself as "opposed to home rule." But what could he have meant by that? He could not have meant to describe himself as opposed to the *realization of a political project*, because by that point, home rule *as a political project* had become a dead letter, having been overtaken by the march of history. So what political stance, at this point in history, could the expression "opposed to home rule" still be describing? The only thing left for it to describe, it seems to me, is opposition not to the *project* but to the *actuality* of an independent, self-governing state for the Irish people. Political discourse being what it is, the term could only intelligibly have served, after 1922, in the role of a political euphemism, expressing—without quite admitting—a desire to see the results of the Irish war of independence overturned and Ireland reconquered by force of English arms.

Thankfully, revanchism of that sort enjoyed no political resonance in England at the time, and it has enjoyed none since. "Opposed to home rule" therefore remained a term of purely historical reference.

A development of that type does seem to have taken place, however, in the case of the term *anti-Zionism*. Manifestly, it can no longer mean opposed to the *project* of a Jewish national state. The only possible meaning left open to it, therefore, is opposed to the *continued existence* of the Jewish national state. It thus functions as a term of self-description for those who in fact hold not that the present government of Israel is delinquent in ways that world criticism

might serve to change but rather that a self-governing Jewish national state
should never have been allowed to come into existence in the first place and
should therefore be abolished as soon as possible and replaced with a larger,
putatively Arab-majority successor state in which Jews would be merely one
of a number of ethnic and religious minorities.

This is, evidently, a volcanically contentious proposal, analogous to demanding, say, that Pakistan should be abolished and its territory absorbed into an
enlarged India. One of the many problems surrounding it is that the suppression of an existing state, with the extinction of the right of its people to govern
themselves, has never been brought about by any means short of war—nor is
it easy to see how it could be.

It would be fair to say, then, that at present the term *anti-Zionist* serves as a
political fig leaf. By appearing to identify those who brandish it as opponents
merely of a policy or a project, it disguises the fact that today's anti-Zionists
seek the suppression of a successful and self-governing modern state through
the agency of a revanchist war of conquest.

POLITICAL VERSUS SOCIAL ANTISEMITISM

In chapter 3, I suggested that political antisemitism—antisemitism of the kind
that targets the Jewish community as an organized whole rather than Jewish
individuals—offers its adherents a pseudo-explanatory theory that places the
organized Jewish community causally at the heart of world affairs. In chapter
3, I summarized its content as consisting in five claims (PA_1-PA_5). The first of
these credits the Jewish community with causing harm far exceeding anything
that can be alleged against any other human group, while the fifth asserts that it
is not feasible to bring these Jew-contrived abuses to an end in any way short of
altogether eliminating the power of the Jewish community to influence affairs.

On the face of it, as we have just seen, current anti-Zionist discourse on the
left of Western politics offers versions of both these claims. The only Jewish-
majority state in the world, we are told—and that on the authority of public
intellectuals of the repute of Noam Chomsky, Tony Judt, or Edward Said—is
guilty of atrocity on a scale comparable to or greater than any, however vile,
committed by any other actor on the world stage, including the Nazis. We are
told further that these atrocities are inseparable from the nature of Jewish
culture and consciousness—that they take their root in the sense Jews have
of themselves as a chosen people, destined to be "set above others" (Judt) and
thus entitled to write "discriminatory institutions and practices" into "the basic
legal structure of [their] state."[19] We are therefore assured that the only way to

bring the wave of Israeli atrocity to an end is not to induce the Jewish leaders of Israel to mend their ways (that would be impossible—we are dealing with Jews after all) but for Jewish political autonomy in Israel to be brought to an end by the abolition of the (Jewish) state.

Two initial grounds for regarding present-day anti-Zionism as antisemitic thus seem to be met. The anti-Zionist appears to share with the political anti-semite not only the latter's conviction that the Jews, taken collectively, are the authors of atrocity on an extraordinary scale but also his *eliminationism*—his sense that since it is no good reasoning with the Jews, the only thing to be done is to get rid of them. In the anti-Zionist's case, "getting rid of them" means elimi-nating the political autonomy that at present gives this degraded people power to impose its evil rule upon a conquered nation. None of this would constitute *prejudice*, of course (remember Gordon Allport's definition of prejudice) if the anti-Zionist's factual claims happened to be true. From our present perspec-tive, they seem to fall rather a long way short of truth, but of course that might change as we pursue the argument through the remainder of this chapter and the next two.

ISRAEL AS A THREAT TO PEACE

A determined anti-Zionist might claim factual accuracy at the very least for the claim that the existence of a Jewish-majority state in the shape of Israel threat-ens peace in the region and possibly in the world. As we saw in chapter 1, in connection with the 2003 Eurobarometer poll, the belief that something of the sort is the case is by no means confined to the hard left and the BDS movement.

The poll throws no light on why so many of its respondents put Israel first. What it plainly does reveal, however, is that an extraordinarily high proportion of Europeans at that point shared with anti-Zionism and BDS the belief char-acteristic of political antisemitism, that the Jewish state exerts a dominating influence on world affairs out of all proportion to its size. It hardly needs to be pointed out, however, that the belief that Israel could pose any consider-able threat, let alone the chief threat to world peace, could not have had at the time, any more than it could now, any substantial contact with reality. By 2003, when the poll was conducted, Israel had indeed been forced more or less continuously since 1948 to defend its independence in a series of wars. But the wars in question had amounted to little more than a series of small-scale and very local armed skirmishes, none of them lasting more than a few days or weeks. Conversely, none of the major wars that had taken place between 1945 and 2003, including the Korean War (1945–present), the first Indochina War

(1946–54), the Vietnam War (1955–75) the Iran–Iraq War (1980–88), the Gulf War (1990–91), the Yugoslav wars (1991–2001), and the Iraq War of 2003, had had anything whatsoever to do with Israel.

What about Israel's immediate neighborhood? In 2003, it might have seemed possible, if not likely, to envisage a general war in the Middle East arising from a mass attack on Israel by its Arab neighbors on the model of 1947–49, or from an attack by Israel on Iranian nuclear facilities. As things have turned out, the series of devastating wars currently tearing apart Iraq, Syria, and Yemen, with immense accompanying loss of human life, vast displacements of populations, and savage persecution of ancient non-Muslim minorities including Christians and Yazidis, have had nothing in particular to do with Israel either. These wars have had at least three causes. The first is the movement of popular revolt in North Africa and Mesopotamia, known to the Western media as the Arab Spring, against Arab governments perceived by substantial fractions of their own populations as corrupt and oppressive. The second is internecine conflict within the Muslim world: between Sunni and Shi'a, between secular and Islamic liberation movements, and between the collection of Islamist or Salafist movements owing their origins to the Muslim Brotherhood and other, more traditionally minded branches of Islam. The third is the struggle between Shi'a Iran and Sunni Saudi Arabia over which is to become the dominant power in the region. The role of Israel in these titanic clashes has been to sit tight and protect its borders, which the warring parties seem, at time of writing, too fully occupied with attempting to destroy one another to wish to cross.

Part of the case against Israel advanced by anti-Zionists and the BDS movement has always been that the installation of Jewish political autonomy in Israel from 1949 onward, given its supposed power to act as a spark to the tinderbox of Middle Eastern politics, constituted a development dangerous to peace in the immediate region. What subsequent events have done, showing the usual unwillingness of reality to unfold as the politically committed would wish it to do, is to reduce such arguments to matchwood. The Jewish state, far from being in a position to plunge the Middle East, let alone the world into war, has turned out to be entirely marginal to the larger issues of peace and war even in its own immediate neighborhood.

REVIVING THE FEAR OF "JEWISH CONSPIRACY"

As I noted earlier in chapter 1, practical considerations render it hardly reasonable to imagine that a country as small as Israel could be in a position to plunge its region, let alone the world, into war. The limited defensive wars that Israel

has waged and won were all on a scale proportionate to its population and resources of manpower. Conducting a major war, even on the scale of those presently taking place in the Middle East, with the accompanying need to control
and garrison cities and large tracts of territory, would plainly be far beyond the
resources of the appropriately named Israel Defense Forces.

The force of that obvious thought would evidently be much weakened, however, if it could be shown to be the practice of the Jews, considered as a unified and organized collectivity, to augment their otherwise feeble strength by
operating behind the scenes of world affairs to take over and manipulate, by
secret and essentially conspiratorial means, non-Jewish minds and institutions.
Belief in this ancient myth is at present widely assumed to be something the
civilized world has long since outgrown. But is it? We have already, in chapter
2, encountered one modern recrudescence of the hoary canard of a Jewish conspiracy in Professor David Stannard's conviction that a cabal of Jewish scholars
is busily at work inflating the human cost of the Shoah with a view to depriving
other persecuted human groups of the sympathy they would otherwise receive.
Related views have for some years been commonplace among those on the left
who question Israel's right to exist.

The best known and most influential example is to be found in the work of
two American professors of political science: John Mearsheimer, Wendell Harris professor of political science at the University of Chicago, and Stephen Walt,
Robert and Renée Belfer professor of political science in the Kennedy School of
Government at Harvard. Mearsheimer and Walt leaped into public prominence
in March 2006 with an article in the *London Review of Books*, titled "The Israel
Lobby," followed in 2007 by a book, *The Israel Lobby and U.S. Foreign Policy*.[20]
Other authors have since jumped on the bandwagon. As a result, there now
exists a substantial literature on the lobby, all of it ultimately deriving from
Mearsheimer and Walt's work.[21]

A characteristic feature of this literature is that the language deployed in the
very titles of books taking up the baton from Mearsheimer and Walt is entirely
of a piece with that of the historic literature of antisemitism. Such titles and
subtitles include, for instance, *The Host and the Parasite: How Israel's Fifth Column Consumed America*, *The Hidden History of How the US Was Used to Create
Israel*, and *How Israel's Lobby Undermines America's Economy* (see note 21). Such
language reaches back into the rancid conceptual armory of historic Jew hatred
to reanimate themes characteristic of *The Protocols of the Elders of Zion* and, for
that matter, of prewar Nazi antisemitism. It introduces readers to ideas central
to political antisemitism: that Jews are parasites on the life of any community
that offers them sanctuary, that they work secretly to undermine and subvert

non-Jewish economies and institutions, and that they compose a "fifth column" or are in other words agents of a foreign power. Anyone disturbed by them will find much food for thought in Abraham Foxman's excellent, trenchantly argued rebuttal, *The Deadliest Lies: The Israel Lobby and the Myth of Jewish Control*.[22]

Mearsheimer and Walt's *London Review of Books* article aroused a storm of controversy, both in the correspondence columns of that organ and elsewhere. Its intensity and the public importance attributed to it at the time can be gauged by the fact that three months later, in its June 8, 2006, issue, the *New York Review of Books* published a lengthy retrospective of the debate by Michael Massing, titled "The Storm over the Israel Lobby."

Looking back from the perspective of a decade at Mearsheimer and Walt's original article, it would be fair to describe it as advancing two distinct theses: a "core thesis" that defines a set of political circumstances supposedly in need of explanation, and a "framing thesis" that provides the explanation supposedly required. The core thesis advances two claims, which it will be useful to label C_1 and C_2, as follows:[23]

C_1 The support provided by the United States to Israel since 1947 has always been, and remains, contrary to the national interest of the United States.

C_2 The dysfunctionality, in terms of national interest, of US support for Israel is so extreme and so obvious to inspection that some special circumstance, over and above the ordinary workings of politics and opinion-forming in America, must be sought if we are to find any rationally acceptable causal explanation for the inability of successive US administrations, Republican and Democrat alike, to do otherwise than overlook it.

The framing thesis, which gives the essay and subsequent book their titles, is that the special circumstance concerned is to be found in the activities of what Mearsheimer and Walt term "the Israel lobby," a collection of predominantly Jewish organizations of which the American-Israel Public Affairs Committee (AIPAC) is presented as a leading example.

The powers that must be credited to the Israel lobby, if Mearsheimer and Walt's argument is to be accepted at face value, are formidable indeed. They include a supposed ability to induce successive US administrations, *no matter of what political color* and over more than half a century, to act consistently in a manner helpful to Jewish interests but flatly contrary to those of the overwhelmingly non-Jewish nation, the United States, whose interests each of those administrations in its day had solemnly sworn to serve. It would be natural to

dismiss this extraordinary claim as amounting merely to an absurd reanima-
tion of one of the central claims of political antisemitism—that the Jews, for
all their apparent weakness, dispose of demonic powers explicable only by a
formidable talent for conspiracy. If, on the contrary, the claim is to be accepted
as the fruit not of prejudice but of political insight, then some very impressive
and persuasive grounds for doing so are going to be needed.

The grounds actually offered by Mearsheimer and Walt are in effect those
advanced in what I described above as the core thesis of the Israel lobby and
amount in summary to C_1 and C_2 above. They amount, that is to say, to the claim
that American support for Israel since 1949 is so blatantly and evidently incompatible with US national interest as to make it simply inconceivable that successive US administrations would have continued to support Israel had it not been
for the machinations of the Israel lobby. The entire weight of Mearsheimer and
Walt's argument rests on this claim. Will it bear the weight?

As several correspondents in the letter columns of the *London Review of
Books* pointed out, it is not easily believable. One problem lies in the extraordinary account of the workings of American democracy that it requires believers
to accept. If it is *really beyond reasonable doubt* that American support for Israel
betrays American national interest, must we not envisage a level of stupidity
or venality, or both, on the part of innumerable non-Jewish citizens and public
officials, on the face of it people at least as intelligent, honest, and patriotic
as Mearsheimer or Walt, that strains credibility? No doubt the Jews are, as
Churchill thought, a remarkable people. But the American Jewish community
as it emerges from Mearsheimer and Walt's imaginings is a community, we are
asked to believe, capable of setting up a lobbying organization that for more
than half a century has succeeded in reducing the entire American political
establishment to a state of bemused sleepwalking. A community capable of
that is more than "remarkable": it is a creature of fantasy, having more to do
with the dreamwork of comic books or Hollywood than with actual Jews or
Jewish organizations.

Then there is a further question: Is the "national interest" something that
falls into the province of "political scientists"—even eminent ones—to determine? Common sense suggests strongly that it is not. Certain aspects of the
life of a nation-state—its land area, its population, its gross national product
in a given year, are no doubt more or less susceptible to objective determination by academic specialists of one sort or another. But national interest does
not seem to be one of them. The judgment that this or that is "in the national
interest" is always, among other things, a political judgment and hence always
enshrines elements of party-political commitment and acceptability to the

nation at large. Until 2016, in Britain, membership of the European Union (EU) had for forty years been held by all political parties and by a broad consensus of politicians, academics, civil servants, and media commentators to be, broadly speaking, in the national interest. In June of that year, however, a national referendum on membership of the EU, which the government of the day had assumed it would win, was lost, and the country voted roughly 52–48 in favor of national independence. In a matter of months and even before the process of withdrawal had begun, it became an equally accepted matter of political consensus that EU membership, at least in its previous form, was no longer in the national interest.

Reason would suggest, then, that what is perceived as in the national interest depends partly on the shifting terms of debate in the political elite concerning the general direction of policy and, beyond that, on the broad drift of opinion in the country at large. As far as opinion on United States at large goes, pro-Israel sentiment appears to be far more widespread than Mearsheimer and Walt were prepared to allow. Gentile support for the aims of the Israel lobby is, according to them, confined to Christian evangelicals and neo-Conservatives, two groups that at the time were warmly detested by the liberal wing of the Democratic Party, whose outlook Mearsheimer and Walt's essay broadly endorses. A 2016 survey by the respected and nonpartisan Washington, DC, polling organization the Pew Research Center paints a different picture. According to Pew, views of the Israel-Palestine conflict have actually become more polarized in favor of Israel over the past two decades. According to Pew, "In early September 2001, just before the 9/11 terrorist attacks there were only modest partisan and ideological differences in Israeli-Palestinian sympathies." Today, "majorities of conservative Republicans (79%) and moderate and liberal Republicans (65%) say they sympathize more with Israel than with the Palestinians, while just 4% and 13% respectively sympathize more with the Palestinians." Among conservative and moderate Democrats equally, far more (53%) sympathize with Israel than with the Palestinians (19%). Only among liberal Democrats do these numbers shift greatly, with 40 percent sympathizing more with the Palestinians against 33 percent who sympathize more with Israel.

These massive demographic disparities provide a ready explanation for the strength and the political continuity of American support for Israel. The activity of lobbying organizations alone could hardly achieve such levels of support for Israel. And in any case, Jewish lobby groups enjoy, and should enjoy, when it comes down to it, the same right as all the other innumerable lobby groups that populate the American political scene to attempt to further the interests of their constituents.

Leaving aside questions of political demography, is there any objective reason, any reason that prescinds from such questions, for regarding American
support for Israel as contrary to the national interest of the United States? On
the positive side, Israel provides the United States with a reliable ally in the
region, one that shares its central values, of democracy and economic liberalism, as well as a range of others that we shall have reason to consider in the next
chapter. Moreover, the economic success of Israel in a region locally dominated
by economic failure, kleptocracy, Islamist fundamentalism, and religious war
make it a permanent advertisement for the success of those values in securing
the combination of stability, prosperity, and religious toleration at present enjoyed, to put it bluntly, by Israel virtually alone among its immediate neighbors.
To counterbalance these advantages, one would have to believe that hostility to
America, and to the West generally, within the region is virtually entirely a consequence of ongoing hostilities between Israel and the Palestinians and would
end, to be replaced by near-perfect mutual understanding, if Israel could only
be forced to come to an agreement with the Palestinians, preferably through the
end of Jewish settlement in the so-called occupied territories and the creation
of a Palestinian state.

That, of course, has every appearance of constituting a variant of the strand
of political antisemitism we labeled PA_5 in chapter 3: the one that says that since
the present evils that the antisemite feels to surround him are solely the work of
the Jews, they can confidently be expected to evaporate once the Jews are got
rid of. In the present case, might it conceivably be true? Might the departure of
Israel from the world scene, to put it bluntly, in fact produce a significant easing
of tensions between the Islamic world and the West?

A major reason for doubting that—one so well confirmed as to be virtually
uncontroversial—is the extent to which the ingrained antisemitism of Islamist
movements, including the Muslim Brotherhood, al-Qaeda, and ISIL, is interwoven with an equally ingrained anti-Americanism. From the standpoint of
such an outlook, Israel and its dispute with the Palestinians is a minor matter:
America, and with it the supposedly Jew-dominated West as a whole, is the real
enemy and Israel merely one of its subordinate tentacles.

Matthias Küntzel, commenting on the trial in Hamburg (2002–3) of Mounir
el-Motassadeq, a core member of the Hamburg al-Qaeda cell that played a
leading part in organizing 9/11, notes the centrality of this belief not only to
el-Motassadeq's worldview but to that of al-Qaeda itself.

Mottasadeq [a close friend of Mohammed Atta, the leader of the 9/11
hijackers] shared Atta's attitude in believing that a worldwide conspiracy of

Jews exists. According to him, Americans want to dominate the world so that
Jews can pile up capital.

This is, in fact, al Qa'ida's official position, expressed on many occasions
by bin Laden himself. This is apparent, for example, from a closer look at
his *Letter to the American People* of October 2002, where he explains why he
considers the United States to be "the worst civilization witnessed by the
history of mankind." His first reason is that "You are the nation who, rather
than ruling by the Sharia of Allah in its constitution and laws, choose to
invent your own laws as you will and desire." Here we have the very essence
of the Islamist program: away with democratic self-determination! Obey
Allah and his holy law!

. . . However, for his second reason why Americans are "the worst
civilization," bin Laden focuses on the group he believes to be responsible for
all the above machinations. "In all its different forms and disguises, the Jews
have taken control of your economy, through which they have taken control
of your media, and now control all aspects of your life, making you their
servants and achieving their aims at your expense; . . . your law is the law of
rich and wealthy people. . . . Behind them stand the Jews, who control your
politics media and economy."[24]

It hardly needs pointing out how closely bin Laden's view of the state of
America chimes with the presumptions of Mearsheimer and Walt's article and
with those of the literature of the Israel lobby to which it has given rise.

EVADING THE CHARGE OF ANTISEMITISM

Mearsheimer and Walt, along with most Western supporters of anti-Zionism
and BDS, are anxious to rebut the charge of antisemitism frequently leveled by
a chorus of political opponents, Jewish and non-Jewish, on the left as well as the
right.[25] Their first line of defense is to argue that the charge of antisemitism is
simply disingenuous and advanced simply with a view to silencing *all* "criticism
of Israel." "Israel's advocates, when pressed to go beyond mere assertion, claim
that there is a 'new antisemitism,' which they equate with criticism of Israel. In
other words, criticize Israeli policy, and you are by definition an anti-semite."[26]

Other equally distinguished disputants have honored this style of response
with their patronage. In 2006–7, the Indiana University Holocaust scholar Alvin Rosenfeld ignited considerable public controversy by accusing a number of
Jewish public intellectuals, including the late European historian Tony Judt, of
allowing their anti-Zionism to stray into antisemitism. On January 21, 2007, an
article in the *New York Times*, critical of Rosenfeld, contained the following passage: "Mr. Judt said in a telephone interview that he believed the real purpose

of expressing what are, in the last analysis, fundamentally generous and progressive views? That choice, it now appears, following Allport, must ultimately turn on the question of whether the left's favored narrative of Israel as a colonial settler society is, or is not, *warranted*: warranted, that is to say, by the facts concerning the origins and nature of the State of Israel. To this question we shall now turn in chapters 7 and 8.

NOTES

1. Rich 2016, 251–52.
2. Rich 2016, 251.
3. Rich 2016, 251.
4. Rich 2016, 251.
5. Bodi is in fact a well-known British Muslim freelance journalist from Preston, of extreme left-wing views, whose contract with the BBC was terminated later in 2001, because of his "strong views on the Middle East," including the denial of Israel's right to exist. He remains very active in left-wing journalism in Britain.
6. Faisal Bodi, "Israel Simply Has No Right to Exist," *The Guardian*, January 3, 2001, https://www.theguardian.com/world/2001/jan/03/comment .israelandthepalestinians.
7. Elhanan Yakira, "Antisemitism and Anti-Zionism as a Moral Question," in A. H. Rosenfeld 2013, 56.
8. David Hirsh, "Ilan Pappé Admits that BDS Was Not Initiated by a 'Call' from Palestinian Civil Society," *Engage*, August 28, 2016, https://engageonline .wordpress.com/2016/08/28/ilan-pappe-admits-that-bds-was-not-initiated-by -a-call-from-palestinian-civil-society/.
9. See. e.g., "Stateless Again," Human Rights Watch, February 1, 2010, https://www.hrw.org/report/2010/02/01/stateless-again/palestinian-origin -jordanians-deprived-their-nationality.
10. Noam Chomsky and Bernard Avishai, "An Exchange on the Jewish State," *New York Review of Books*, July 17, 1975, https://www.nybooks.com/articles/1975 /07/17/an-exchange-on-the-jewish-state/.
11. Paul Bogdanor, "The Devil State," in Alexander and Bogdanor 2006, 79.
12. Rose 2005, 115–16.
13. "An Exchange on Edward Said and Difference," *Critical Inquiry* 15 (Spring 1989): 641.
14. Rose 2005, xix.
15. Justin Raimondo, "Israel, Genocide and the 'Logic' of Zionism," *Antiwar. com*, August 4, 2014, http://original.antiwar.com/justin/2014/08/03/israel -genocide-and-the-logic-of-zionism/.

16. See Tina Nguyen, "Whoa: Times of Israel Op-Ed Advocates Genocide against Gazans," *mediaite.com*, https://www.mediaite.com/online/whoa-times -of-israel-op-ed-advocates-genocide-against-gazans/.

17. See Wikipedia, "2009 Aftonbladet Israel Controversy."

18. As reported in the London *Daily Telegraph*, July 1, 2016, 9: "Corbyn Savaged after Remarks that Suggest Israel on par with ISIL."

19. Chomsky and Avishai 1975.

20. John J. Mearsheimer and Stephen M. Walt, *The Israel Lobby and U.S. Foreign Policy* (New York: Farrar, Straus and Giroux, 2007).

21. They include Alison Weir, *Against Our Better Judgment: The Hidden History of How the US Was Used to Create Israel* (privately published, 2014); Grant F. Smith, *Big Israel: How Israel's Lobby Moves America*, Institute for Research, Middle East Policy, Inc., 2016; Paul Findley, *They Dare to Speak Out: People and Institutions Confront Israel's Lobby* (Chicago: Lawrence Hill Books, 2003); Grant F. Smith and Michael Scheuer, *Spy Trade: How Israel's Lobby Undermines America's Economy*, Institute for Research, Middle East Policy, Inc., 2009; Greg Felton, *The Host and the Parasite: How Israel's Fifth Column Consumed America* (Crestview, FL: Money Tree Publishing, 2012).

22. Foxman 2007.

23. A longer and more detailed version of the following argument can be found in Harrison 2006, 194–204.

24. Küntzel 2007, 129–30.

25. The website *Engage* (https://engageonline.wordpress.com/about-engage/), for instance, opposes BDS and "anti-Zionism from a left-wing standpoint." Its self-description includes the following, which broadly chimes with the standpoint and arguments of this book: "Engage is a single issue campaign. It focuses on one issue, antisemitism, and is therefore concerned also about the demonization of Israel, and of Jews who don't think of themselves as anti-Zionists. We believe that a new commonsense is emerging that holds Israel to be a central and fundamental evil in the world. We disagree with this notion and we think that it is dangerous. The danger is that this kind of thinking may well lead to, and license, the emergence of a movement that is racist against Jews in general." Quite so. If it comes to that, besides Engage there are plenty of other opponents of the BDS movement on the left, just as there are plenty of anti-Islamist Muslims, many of whom are pro-Israel.

26. John Mearsheimer and Stephen Walt, "The Israel Lobby," *London Review of Books*, March 23, 2006, 8, https://www.lrb.co.uk/the-paper/v28/n06/john -mearsheimer/the-israel-lobby.

27. Hirsh 2018, 6.

28. Mearsheimer and Walt, "The Israel Lobby," 8.

29. Richard Bolchover, "The Absence of Antisemitism in the Marketplace," in Iganski and Kosmin 2003, 267.

30. Neumann 2005, 3.

31. See report in the *Daily Telegraph*, January 24, 2004, 4, https://www
.telegraph.co.uk/news/uknews/1452465/Defiant-MP-sacked-in-suicide-bomber
-row.html.

32. Maxime Rodinson, *Israel: A Colonial-Settler State* (New York: Pathfinder, 1973), 27–28.

33. Rich 2016, 240.

34. Neumann 2005, 3.

35. "Palestinian Civil Society Call for BDS," https://bdsmovement.net/call.

SEVEN

—ᴍᴍ—

NARRATIVE AND REALITY

For the great majority of mankind are satisfied with appearances as though
they were realities, and are often more influenced by the things that seem
than by those that are.

—Niccolò Machiavelli

"ANTI-ZIONISM" AS ANTICOLONIALISM

From the standpoint of "anti-Zionist" and Boycott, Divestment and Sanctions
(BDS)–supporting circles on the left of Western politics, Israel is a "criminal"
and "illegitimate" state, one that does not and never did deserve to exist in the
first place. In chapter 6, we found these claims to rest ultimately, in the minds of
those who accept them, on a closely related political narrative: one that brands
Israel as a "colonial settler state." The job of the present chapter is to determine
how far that narrative corresponds to reality.

The narrative of settler colonialism has a number of components falling
into various categories. It offers a version of the history of the Jewish presence
in Israel, an account—or rather a set of assumptions—concerning the present constitution and nature of the state, an analysis of the reasons behind the
continuing Israel-Palestinian conflict, and a recipe for ending that conflict: the
so-called one-state solution. I will now attempt to summarize these as fairly as
I can, granting as little as possible to the pro-Israel position.

According to the anti-Zionist version of history, Palestine formerly possessed an ethnically and religiously homogeneous indigenous population of

Palestinian Arabs. From the 1880s onward, there occurred a series of influxes of Zionist Jews of European origin. Their attempts to take over the land and establish themselves as a colonial elite provoked local resistance, and in 1948, with the ending of the British Mandate a coalition of neighboring Arab states invaded Palestine with supposedly a view to returning the territory to the control of its indigenous population.

Unfortunately, owing largely to the ease with which the Jews were able to obtain arms from other imperialist powers, the Arab armies lost the war. This defeat, known to the indigenous population as the *Nakba* (the disaster) resulted among other things in the expulsion by the Jews of 750,000 of the former Arab indigenous population, whose lands were seized and who were prevented from returning. The Jewish colonists were thus able to set up, as they had always wished, a state, Israel, in which they exercised the dominant power.

That state has since matched other colonial settler states, such as apartheid South Africa or French Algeria, in treating the remaining indigenous inhabitants as second-class citizens.

In this respect, matters have grown considerably worse since further victories by Israel resulted in the extension of Israeli power over two further tracts of Arab land: the Gaza Strip, and the Occupied Territories between the 1949 limit of conquest (the so-called green line) and the border of Jordan. Israel's continued occupation of these areas, it is claimed, is contrary to international law, as is its policy of building and continuing to build housing for Jewish settlers within the Occupied Territories. Moreover, because Arabs in the Occupied Territories, though greatly outgunned, have continued to defend their rights by armed uprisings against the colonial occupiers and settlers, Israel has adopted a range of policies that it justifies as necessary to protect the security of its citizens but that greatly complicate and impoverish the lives of the Arab population of the Occupied Territories. These include restrictions on entering Israel to work, the building of the so-called security barrier, some stretches of which cut off Arab villages from their own land, along with the building of a road system to serve Jewish settlements that only Israeli citizens are permitted to use. And there are others.

The refusal of the main Palestinian political movements, Fatah and Hamas, to agree to a peace settlement with Israel, it is claimed, in no way reflects the absence of a desire for peace among the oppressed indigenous community but, on the contrary, reflects the refusal of Israel, under increasingly right-wing governments over the past half century, to retreat from its policy of colonial oppression.

On the question of what form peace between Israel and the Palestinians might take, opinions divide. A consensus of center-left and center-right opinion, both in the international community and in Israel itself, has for many years held that a viable settlement should involve what is known as the two-state solution. In its usual form, this envisages an independent Palestinian state coming into being in the West Bank (the Occupied Territories) and the Gaza Strip. One of the main arguments for the illegitimacy of Jewish settlements is that they are inconsistent with the two-state solution. On the left, however, and particularly since the rise of BDS, opinion has moved in favor of a "one-state solution." This has very little support from Western governments or governmental organizations but a considerable amount in certain university and media circles. A good idea, both of what is proposed and of the sort of people who propose it, can be obtained from a recent collection of essays: *After Zionism: One State for Israel and Palestine*, produced by a group of academics and journalists.[1]

Let us now consider what can be said against this view of things, beginning with the question of whether Jews are to be considered "indigenous" to Palestine.

THE ISSUE OF INDIGENEITY

Our common understanding of the concept of colonialism is founded on a range of standard or conceptually speaking "central" examples that include, for example, Australia, North and South America, Polynesia, and Africa south of the Sahara. All these occupy parts of the globe separated—or preserved—from European exploration until at least the late fifteenth century and in some cases very much later. In each of these cases, an indigenous population remained totally unaffected by Europe and indeed ignorant of its existence until one fine day, ships appeared off their shores. These ships in time arrived in greater numbers and in time disgorged European settlers who brought with them new ideas, new diseases, and new weapons and styles of war that in due course allowed them to displace and in some areas such as Australasia and the Caribbean, largely to exterminate the indigenous population and take possession of the land.[2] As an East African friend of mine put it to me at university sixty years ago, "When you arrived, you had the Bible and we had the land. Then, suddenly, we had the Bible and you had the land."

These are the examples to which the anti-Zionist narrative in effect proposes to assimilate the history of the founding of Israel. The following, from Noam Chomsky, catches the essence of many such accounts of the origins of the present conflict: "So there are two national groups which claim national self-determination. One group is the indigenous population, or what's left of it—a lot of it's been expelled or driven out or fled. The other group is the Jewish settlers who came in, originally from Europe, later from other parts of the Middle East and some other places. So there are two groups, the indigenous population and the immigrants and their descendants."[3]

The path of the proposed assimilation is beset with difficulties. To begin with, the history of the eastern Mediterranean has been continuous since antiquity with that of Europe. Syria at the commencement of the Common Era was a province of the Roman Empire and subject to the movement of people within that empire. Over the centuries, Roman rule blended northern European with Mediterranean and North African bloodlines with the majestic indifference to modern notions of "racial" otherness whose results can be seen every night on television at the moment in the faces of the Syrian refugees attempting to flee to Europe.

This mixing of peoples continued until the fall of Byzantine Syria to the nascent forces of Islam in 634–38. The Islamic conquest greatly strengthened the previously negligible Arab presence in Syria but left much of the earlier population in situ. The result was what we would nowadays call a multicultural society with a majority consisting of Arabs and non-Arab converts to Islam ruling over a patchwork of religious and ethnic minorities, including Christians of a variety of confessions, Druse, Yazidi, and Jews. In Palestine, Jews had remained the majority population until the fifth century. Even a millennium later, in the Ottoman era they continued to constitute a substantial minority of about 4 percent, mainly resident in the towns of Jerusalem, Hebron, Nablus, Tiberias, and Safed, in a population 85 percent Muslim and 9 percent Christian.[4] Equally, of course, Jewish minorities, surviving under difficult conditions of institutional disability and occasional persecution, were to be found throughout the medieval Islamic world.

At the end of World War I, following the collapse of the Ottoman Empire, Great Britain acquired a mandate from the League of Nations to assume the temporary government of the territory that had formerly constituted the Ottoman Empire sanjaks of Nablus, Acre, the southern part of the vilayet of Syria, the southern portion of the Beirut vilayet, and the mutasarrifate of Jerusalem, prior to the Armistice of Mudros.

At this point, Palestine was still the remote, poor, and thinly populated region of the Ottoman Empire that it had been for many centuries. For 1920, the British government's *Interim Report on the Civil Administration of Palestine* (1921) records a total population of around 700,000 persons in the whole of Palestine. It estimates that 77,000 of these are Christians, 76,000 Jews, and

the remainder Muslims. Of the Muslims, a small proportion were bedouin
Arabs and the remainder, "although they speak Arabic and are termed Arabs,
are largely of mixed race": representatives, that is to say, of the pre-Islamic
population.

Of the Jewish population at this point, the interim report has this to say:

> The Jewish element of the population numbers 76,000. Almost all have
> entered Palestine during the last 40 years. Prior to 1850 there were in the
> country only a handful of Jews. In the following 30 years a few hundreds
> came to Palestine. Most of them were animated by religious motives; they
> came to pray and to die in the Holy Land, and to be buried in its soil. After
> the persecutions in Russia forty years ago, the movement of the Jews to
> Palestine assumed larger proportions. Jewish agricultural colonies were
> founded. They developed the culture of oranges and gave importance to the
> Jaffa orange trade. They cultivated the vine, and manufactured and exported
> wine. They drained swamps. They planted eucalyptus trees. They practised,
> with modern methods, all the processes of agriculture. There are at the
> present time 64 of these settlements, large and small, with a population of
> some 15,000.[5]

Jews in 1920, that is to say, constituted about 11 percent of the total population of Palestine, a substantial minority. Were they "indigenous"? Some of them
certainly were in the sense of having been resident in Palestine for centuries.
What of the newcomers? They had certainly not arrived, in the manner of the
nineteenth-century European colonizers of Africa or Australasia, as armed in-
vaders. Escaping the pogroms of the 1880s in the Pale of European Russia, they
had immigrated, perfectly legally, to the Ottoman Empire and had purchased
the land on which they established their agricultural enterprises in the open
market, usually at inflated prices, either from absentee Ottoman landlords or
from local peasant owners. In short, they were immigrants rather than colonists, and as Jews, they were joining a community that, while admittedly small,
had as much right to call itself indigenous as any of the other communities then
occupying the land.

There is reason to believe, moreover, that the Jewish community may well
not have been the only one that grew substantially by immigration during the
period of the British Mandate. British rule, together with the modern methods
of agriculture introduced, even under Ottoman rule, by Jewish immigrants
and continued under the mandate, led to a substantial rise in economic activity in Palestine from the turn of the twentieth century. It is a general principle
of economics that increase in economic activity in a given region promotes

immigration to that region. One would expect to discover, therefore, that substantial Arab immigration to the economically progressive areas of Jewish settlement that later became Israel occurred both from within and from outside Palestine in the three decades separating the start of the mandate era from the foundation of Israel.

It is essential to the anti-Zionist/BDS narrative that the vast majority of Arab Palestinians living in Palestine in 1948 were descendants of those living there before 1880, the approximate starting point of modern Jewish immigration to Palestine. Therefore, the question of Arab immigration during the mandate era has become a battleground for ideologically motivated conflict between opposing camps of economists and historians. The most frequently quoted writers whose work broadly supports the anti-Zionist/BDS narrative are the former Israeli government statistician and demographer Roberto Bachi (1909–95)[6] and the American historian and demographer Justin McCarthy.[7] Their critics include the University of Illinois economist Fred M. Gottheil[8] and the leading Israeli demographer Yakov Feitelson.[9]

McCarthy concludes the study cited below as follows: "The vast majority of the Palestinians resident in 1947 were the sons and daughters of those who were living in Palestine *before modern Jewish immigration began.* There is no reason to believe that they were not the sons and daughters of Arabs *who had been in Palestine for many centuries.*"[10]

To this, Gottheil has two fundamental objections. The first is that it is simply economically inconceivable that the increasing economic activity and prosperity created under the mandate would not have attracted Arab immigration to the areas in which it was taking place. Here, he offers much evidence for vast migratory flows in such circumstances, particularly in the third world. Some hard evidence of this kind is available for the Ottoman era and suggests a flow of Arab immigrants even at that period, often from remote parts of the Ottoman Empire. "Demographer U. O. Schmelz's analysis of the Ottoman registration data for 1905 populations of Jerusalem and Hebron *kazas* (Ottoman districts), by place of birth, showed that of those Arab Palestinians born outside their localities of residence, approximately half represented intra-Palestine movement—from areas of low-level economic activity to areas of higher-level activity—while the other half represented Arab immigration into Palestine itself, 43 percent originating in Asia, 39 percent in Africa, and 20 percent in Turkey."[11]

Gottheil's second objection is that since Arab immigration from outside Palestine was illegal in the mandate period; and since McCarthy, like Bachi, bases his study solely on documentary evidence, including censuses and registrations

of births, marriages, and deaths; and since, therefore, neither possess eviden-
tial means of tracing or estimating the volume of such migration, McCarthy's
conclusions amount to little more than ideological wishful thinking. Matters
are complicated here by the fact that the British Foreign Office, ever anxious
to avoid inflaming Arab opinion, took more care to detect and expel Jewish illegal immigrants than Arab ones. Even so, Bachi, using official records, reports
that the Palestinian police actually discovered and expelled nine hundred illegal Arab immigrants per year during the years 1931–45. But Bachi, unlike
McCarthy, notes that "it is hardly credible that illegal movements which were
actually discovered included all the illegal entrances which actually occurred,
or even the majority of them"[12] and concludes in consequence that "in the
present state of knowledge, we have been *unable to even guess* the size of total
immigration."[13]

The most plausible conclusion from these data, it would seem, is that we
are faced in Israel with a conflict not between indigenes and immigrants but
between two communities both containing both indigenes and immigrants.
Doubtless in 1945 there was a higher proportion of indigenes on the Arab side.
But even so, the realities of Palestinian demography, prior to 1945, insofar as
they can be deciphered, appear to afford no easy match with the armed incursions of altogether alien peoples by appeal to which the meaning of the term
colonialism, as we nowadays use it, is standardly explained.

Of course, that might not matter—might not make much difference, say, to
the general adequacy of Chomsky's summary of events cited above—if it were
beyond dispute that Israel came into being through an armed incursion of
European Jews, much as Australia came into being through armed incursions
of British settlers. But is that in fact what happened?

THE ORIGINS OF CONFLICT

One might expect economically progressive Jewish immigrants to a seriously
underdeveloped part of the world to be welcome. And so they frequently
were in the Ottoman Empire, which, despite occasional persecutions, offered throughout the Middle Ages a relatively safe haven for Iberian and
other Jews fleeing persecution. There, they enjoyed freedom from the European restrictions on the professions Jews could practice and even some
degree of communal autonomy under the millet system of administrative
independence for non-Muslim minorities. In general, Jews under Ottoman
rule were frequently able to rise to positions of considerable wealth and
political influence.[14]

In the immediate aftermath of World War I, Palestinian Arab opinion on the merits of Jewish settlement in Palestine was divided. In 1920–21, riots against the Jews broke out in Jerusalem and other cities, and there were armed attacks on three Jewish settlements.[15] A Christian Arab observer describes the Jerusalem riot as follows:

> Afterwards I saw one Hebronite approach a Jewish shoeshine boy, who hid behind a sack in one of the [Old City] wall's corners next to Jaffa Gate, and take his box and beat him [the shoeshine boy] over the head. He screamed and began to run, his head bleeding and the Hebronite left him and returned to the procession. . . . The riot reached its zenith. All shouted, "Muhammad's religion was born with the sword." . . . I immediately walked to the municipal garden. . . . My soul is nauseated and depressed by the madness of mankind.[16]

In the wake of the riots in Jerusalem, however, "the sheikhs of 82 villages around that city and Jaffa issued a statement protesting the demonstrations against the Jews. They claimed to represent 70 percent of the population and expressed allegiance to the British. Among other things, they stated that they did not see any danger in the Zionist settlement. The leaders of the Druze village Daliat al-Carmel, southeast of Haifa, stated that the settlement by Jews would bring great benefit to everyone in the land."[17]

The Druse and Christian minorities in Ottoman and mandate Palestine had, for that matter, as much reason as the Jews to fear Muslim hostility. It is possible, as we shall see later, that there was also some conflict of perceived interest between the fellahin in the villages and Arabs in the towns more open to political ideas filtering in from Europe.

In any event, the land was largely quiet until 1929, when a massacre of Jews took place in Hebron. This resulted in the deaths of more than 65 Jews and the wounding or maiming of many more, and led to the evacuation of all of the 435 survivors by the British authorities. The rioting spread to Safed, where forty-five Jews were murdered. From that point onward through the whole of the 1930s, sporadic terrorist violence continued throughout the Jewish areas of Palestine. The British authorities condemned it, but their appointed spokesman for the Palestinian community, Haj Amin el-Husseini, the grand mufti of Jerusalem, "in trying to defend himself against charges that he incited the pogroms, . . . blamed the victims. Citing the Protocols of the Elders of Zion (a notorious Czarist forgery long used by anti-Semites), Husseini claimed that it was the Jews who attacked the Muslims, . . . [and] characterised the murder of Jewish women, children and students in Hebron as the beginning of a revolt, which continued through the 1930s."[18]

ATTEMPTS AT PARTITION

In 1937, in response to these continued disturbances, the British government, as part of the discharge of its responsibilities under the mandate, published the *Report of the Palestine Royal Commission,* also known as the Peel Report. Taking a line sharply contrary to Chomsky's and other current anti-Zionist accounts of Israel as a "colonial settler" state, the Peel Report recognized that *as a matter of international law,* "the Jewish community was 'in Palestine by right,' and that the effort to 'facilitate the establishment of the Jewish National Home [by increasing Jewish immigration] was a binding international obligation on the Mandatory.'"[19]

The status of this judgment in international law arose from the commitment of the postwar world not to colonialism but to an essentially anticolonial ideal—namely, the ideal of national self-determination. The future of the bulk of the Near East after the collapse of the Ottoman Empire was one of the major problems facing the Allies at the end of World War I. The decisive part played by the United States in the war allowed it to insist that the postwar reorganization of formerly Ottoman lands should be conducted in accordance with the principles of self-determination insisted on by President Woodrow Wilson. Jewish self-determination was merely one of the smaller elements in this program. The Balfour Declaration, which promised not to make Palestine as a whole into a self-governing national home for the Jewish people but merely to establish such a national home in Palestine, was consistent with this Wilsonian approach. It is often supposed to have been a purely British declaration and thus a mere declaration of British national intent without standing in international law. In fact, it sought and received general international approval, first from President Wilson, who issued a statement in 1919 concurring with it in principle, and then from the French and Italian governments, which also approved it.

Consistently with its Wilsonian credentials, the Peel Commission recognized the Arabs as having rights equal to those of the Jews to land and residence in Palestine. But it also saw Muslim hostility to Jews as posing a fatal obstacle to a unitary Palestinian state. It blames the Arab side for the continuing hostilities of the day: "one side put itself, not for the first time, in the wrong by resorting to force, whereas the other side patiently kept the law."[20] And it considered that the position of Jews in a unitary state would in any case be untenable in the long run, since the grand mufti had made it clear that the first goal of a self-governing Muslim-majority state would be to rid Palestine of Jews altogether.[21]

The solution proposed by the commission was therefore a partition of Palestine: something, in other words, identical to the two-state solution that Israel is nowadays generally accused of willfully denying the Palestinians.

Manifestly the problem cannot be solved by giving either the Arabs or the Jews what they want. The answer to the question "Which of them in the end will govern Palestine?" must surely be "neither." We do not think that any fair-minded statesman would suppose, now that the hope of harmony between the races has proved untenable, that Britain ought either to hand over to Arab rule 400,000 Jews ... or that, if the Jews should become a majority, a million or so of Arabs should be handed over to their rule. But, while neither race can justly rule all Palestine, we see no reason why, if it were practicable, each race should not rule part of it.[22]

In 1938, the Woodhead Commission, following the Peel Commission's recommendations, duly put forward a plan for the partition of Palestine. This would have created a small and territorially discontinuous Jewish national home in the north, where Jews, many of them farming on land largely reclaimed and made fertile by their own efforts, were in a majority. This included the towns of Tel Aviv, Haifa, Netanya, and Tiberias but not Safed. The rest—three quarters of the land—was assigned to a territorially continuous Arab state that included many small pockets of Jewish-owned land, which the commission suggested should become the basis for an "exchange of populations."

The leaders of the Jewish Yishuv reluctantly accepted this plan. The Arab Higher Committee, created under the leadership of the mufti, rejected it out of hand, demanding that all of Palestine be placed under Arab control and the bulk of the Jewish population expelled. The mufti, after all, had said in 1936, "There is no place in Palestine for two races. The Jews left Palestine 2000 years ago. Let them go to other parts of the world where there are wide vacant spaces."[23] The mufti's connection with the Axis powers, however, was not calculated to give him and his followers influence with the British. In 1944, by contrast, after repeated requests by leaders of the Yishuv to be allowed to support the war against the Axis, twenty-five thousand to thirty thousand Palestinian Jews volunteered for service in the British army, and the Jewish brigade duly saw service in Italy.

By the end of World War II, however, Britain itself had lost too much, both in manpower and in economic strength, to be able to carry out its responsibilities much longer under the mandate. In 1946, Transjordan, previously part of the mandate, was recognized as an independent state. The following year, an attack took place by the Jewish terrorist group Irgun on the King David Hotel in Jerusalem. This killed ninety-one people, including Britons, Arabs, and Jews, imposing devastating losses on the British administration and completely destroying the part of the hotel in which it was housed.

At this point, Britain announced its intention to retire from its mandated responsibilities in Palestine and passed the problem to the United Nations (UN).

The General Assembly of the UN established the UN Special Committee on Palestine (UNSCOP) to make studies and recommendations. A September 1947 UNSCOP report once again recommended a partition into an Arab and a Jewish state, and on November 29, 1947, the UN adopted a partition resolution sanctioning the creation of a Jewish state, which obtained the necessary two-thirds majority of nations with thirty-three (including the Soviet Union) for, thirteen against, and ten, including Britain, abstaining.[24]

THE WAR OF INDEPENDENCE, 1947–49

On November 30, 1947, immediately following the passing of the partition resolution at the UN, war broke out between the Jews of Palestine and various armed Arab forces. The strongest and best armed of the latter were those of the Arab Higher Committee, headed since its formation in 1936 by Haj Amin Husseini and largely Palestinian Muslim in its support, and those of the Arab Liberation Army (ALA), a force of mainly Syrian volunteers organized by the Arab League and headed by Fawzi al-Qawuqji. Despite the presence of foreign volunteers, the first stage of the War of Independence, which began at this point, is generally regarded as a civil war. It ended badly for the Arabs. "The civil war half of the 1948 war, which ended with the complete destruction of Palestinian Arab military power and the shattering of Palestinian society, began on 30 November 1947 and ended on 14 May 1948, by which time hundreds of thousands of townspeople and villagers had fled or been forcibly displaced from their homes."[25]

Much debate (though "acrimonious controversy" would be a more accurate expression) surrounds the question of how these displacements of population were brought about. One Zionist account used to be that the approximately 750,000 Arabs who left the country during the 1948 war did so because they were following the advice of league leaders, who wished to clear civilians from the country for their own safety and so that they could return once the Jews had been overwhelmed. The default position of anti-Zionism/BDS supporters is that virtually the entire Arab population was expelled by force.

The work of Israeli revisionist historians since the turn of the century suggests that neither of these extreme and ideologically tendentious positions fits the facts. The complex forces at work are evident in the case of the massacre claimed to have taken place on April 9, 1948, at the village of Deir Yassin, which has provided ever since a major component of the anti-Zionist/BDS account and has therefore attracted a vast amount of controversy.

Among other things, this story brings into focus the sharp disagreements on policy, especially military policy, that had arisen within the Yishuv during the mandate era. The main Jewish defense organization was the Haganah, which eventually became the core of the Israel Defense Forces (IDF). But in 1931, its more radical members, who objected to the moderating control exercised over the Haganah by the Jewish political leadership, had split from it to form the Irgun Tsva'i Leumi (National Military Organization), better known as the Irgun. The village of Deir Yassin was attacked and taken by Irgun forces and those of another dissident Jewish paramilitary organization, the Stern Gang (LHI), with the agreement of the Haganah, but with minimal tactical support from it, on April 9, 1948. Almost at once, accusations of atrocities having been committed during the fighting began to be heard.

The story originates in a report in the *New York Times* for April 12, 1948, by Dana Adams Schmidt, which reads: "Dr Hussein Khalidi, secretary of the Palestine Arab Higher Committee, denounced the 'massacre' of 250 Arab men, women, and children, by Irgun Zvai Leumi and the Stern Gang, Zionist terrorist groups, at Deir Yassin on Friday."

One problem with this is that the Palestine committee, and thus its spokesman Hussein Khalidi, was controlled by the rabidly antisemitic mufti of Jerusalem. Even the Israeli historian Benny Morris, a leading member of the broadly left-wing "new historians" group, considers 250 an exaggeration: "Altogether 100–120 villagers (including combatants) died that day—though the IZL (Irgun Zvai Leumi), Haganah, Arab officials and the British almost immediately inflated the number to '254' (or '245') each for their own propagandistic reasons."[26]

The bulk of the population of the village, Morris claims, in accord with other historians, were not harmed once the fighting had subsided. "Most of the villagers either fled, or were trucked through West Jerusalem and dumped at Musrara, outside the Old City Walls."[27] However, Morris does allege a series of specific war crimes: "It quickly emerged that the fighting had been accompanied, and followed, by atrocities. In part, these were apparently triggered by the unexpectedly strong resistance and by the (relatively) high casualties suffered by the attacking force. Some militiamen and unarmed civilians were shot on the spot. A few villagers may have been trucked into Jerusalem and then taken back to Dar Yassin and executed; a group of male prisoners were shot in a nearby quarry; several of those captured were shot in Sheikh Bader, a temporary LHI (Stern Gang) base in West Jerusalem."[28]

Even more seriously, the Arab press soon carried accusations that rape of Arab women, including pregnant women, had taken place at Deir Yassin. In 1998, however, in the course of a BBC documentary TV series, *Israel and the Arabs: The 50 Year Conflict*, a startling admission was made. Hazem Nusseibeh, a member of a prominent Jerusalem family and presently a Jordanian diplomat and author of a number of books, was in 1948 an editor of the Palestine Broadcasting Service's Arabic news. On the BBC program, Nusseibeh recalls a meeting at the Jaffa Gate in Jerusalem with Deir Yassin survivors and, among other Palestinian leaders, Dr. Hussein Khalidi. Asked by Nusseibeh how he should cover the story, Khalidi said, "We must make the most of this." Nusseibeh adds, "So we wrote a press release stating that at Deir Yassin children were murdered, pregnant women were raped, all sorts of atrocities." In the same program, a Deir Yassin resident at the time, Abu Mahmud, tells the BBC "there was no rape. But Khalidi said, we have to say this, so the Arab armies will come to liberate Palestine from the Jews."[29]

In his most recent book, Benny Morris offers some credence to the story of rape, but his evidence for this consists of the report of the town's commander, Yizhak Levy, an officer in the intelligence branch of the Haganah. Levy claims that the accusation was made against Irgun (IZL) by members of the Stern Gang (LHI): "In a follow-up report, Levy said that LHI participants later charged that IZL troops had 'raped a number of girls and murdered them afterwards (we [that is, the HIS—Haganah Intelligence Service] don't know if this is true).'"[30]

Morris, however, does not consider the possibility that both the LHI and Levy, the latter as a Haganah supporter, were briefing against the IZL—a possibility that equally casts doubt on Levy's support for the parallel story of IZL and LHI murders of prisoners, even though it is clear from the attack on the King David Hotel that the IZL were no respecters of civilian life. Indeed, they may have been settling specific scores in this way, despite the fact that the bulk of the population of Deir Yassin appears to have escaped unharmed. (I find, talking to fellow non-Jews, that they share a belief in the extraordinary, not to say unbelievable, cohesiveness of "the Jews" that makes it difficult for them to credit that different Jewish agencies might brief against one another during a war for Jewish survival. To me this is a further consequence of the mild but unquestionable commitment to the main theses of political antisemitism that surfaces so easily during such conversations.)

An important new Hebrew-language book on the battle by Professor Eliezer Tauber of Bar-Ilan University, which cross-references all available Arab, British, and Jewish testimony, appears to confirm the conclusions offered here on the basis of a smaller range of sources.[31] Tauber recognizes that the various paramilitary forces on the Jewish side that actually conducted the battle were militarily incompetent and prone to brief against one another and that the Haganah forces that arrived the next day, though they could at that stage know very little of what had actually happened, were equally not above reporting events in a way designed to discredit the LHI and the IZL. He concludes that no deliberate massacre or rape occurred, and that although civilian deaths were excessive, they were almost entirely the consequence of the ferocity of the house-to-house fighting that took place.

This last tends to confirm the account of the fighting at Deir Yassin given by the Israeli politician Menachem Begin, who was at that time the head of LHI, gives yet another picture of what happened.

> Apart from the military aspect, there is a moral aspect to the story of Dir Yassin. At that village, whose name was publicized throughout the world, both sides suffered heavy casualties. *We had four killed and nearly forty wounded. The number of casualties was nearly forty percent of the total number of attackers. The Arab troops suffered casualties three times as heavy. The fighting was thus very severe.* Yet the hostile propaganda, disseminated throughout the world, deliberately ignored the fact that the civilian population was actually given warning before the battle began. One of our tenders carrying a loud speaker was stationed at the entrance to the village and it exhorted in Arabic all women, children and aged to leave their houses to take shelter on the slope of the hill. By giving this humane warning our fighters threw away the element of complete surprise, and thus increased their own risk in the ensuing battle. A substantial number of the inhabitants obeyed the warning and they were unhurt. A few did not leave their stone houses—perhaps because of the confusion. The fire of the enemy was murderous—to which the number of our casualties bears eloquent testimony. Our men were compelled to fight every house; to overcome the enemy they used large numbers of hand-grenades. And the civilians who had disregarded our warnings suffered inevitable casualties. [32]

Many would think throwing hand grenades into houses containing possible civilian occupants itself constituted an atrocity. If it comes to that, Tauber (see note 31) recounts that the truck carrying the loudspeaker of which Begin speaks ran into a ditch where it sank, taking with it the loudspeaker, whose potentially lifesaving message thus never reached Arab ears. At the same time, inquiry suggests that the use of grenades has become common in house-to-house fighting in all modern wars, often without even an attempt at advance warning, and may therefore possibly fall short, in moral terms, of rape and the murder of prisoners. Begin takes it for granted that these latter accusations were Palestinian fabrications but, curiously, agrees with Hazem Nusseibeh concerning the results of the publicity given to the atrocities, alleged or otherwise, at Deir Yassin. As Begin puts it: "The enemy propaganda was designed to besmirch our name. In the result it helped us. Panic overwhelmed the Arabs of Eretz Israel. Kolonia village, which had previously repulsed every attack of the Haganah, was evacuated overnight and fell without further fighting. Beit-Iksa was also evacuated. These two places overlooked the main road; and their fall, together with the capture of Kastel by the Haganah, made it possible to keep the road open to Jerusalem. In the rest of the country too, the Arabs began to flee in terror, even before they clashed with Jewish forces."[33]

Nusseibeh, more ruefully, confirms in his BBC interview that the atrocity reports did indeed have this effect: "In this interview with the BBC he admits that in 1948 he was instructed by Hussein Khalidi, a prominent Palestinian Arab leader, to fabricate claims of atrocities at Deir Yassin in order to encourage Arab regimes to invade the expected Jewish state. He made this damning admission in explaining why the Arabs failed in the 1948 war. He said '*this was our biggest mistake,*' because Palestinians fled in terror and left the country in huge numbers after hearing the atrocity claims."[34]

The question why so many Arabs fled before the advancing Jewish forces in 1948, even while many others who were overrun in the Jewish advance came to no harm and ended as citizens of Israel,

> remains a subject of continuing debate in the scholarly literature, partly because there are competing preferences for uniform, simplified narratives both within and without the scholarly community. In truth there seem to be multiple causes. The urban Arab elite left early on; the departure of upper-class Arabs, along with professionals and the intelligentsia, delivered an unspoken message that others should leave as well. Some villages were forced out, though the reasons were often strategic. Other villages fled in fear, responding to stories of real, exaggerated or fabricated violence. An Arab strategy of encouraging Palestinian women and children to leave Israel so men would be free to fight predictably backfired when men left with their families.[35]

Ethnic and religious divisions on the Palestinian side, especially between Muslim and Christian Arabs, were also a factor: "Conflicting economic interests, political differences, and social and interdenominational schisms diminished the appetite for fighting, generated successive waves of evacuees, and prevented national co-operation. There was no overarching mutual interest or shared destiny."[36]

At the end of April 1948, the nature of the war changed. As Dr. Khalidi had hoped, the "Arab armies," those of Egypt, Syria, Jordan, Lebanon, and Iraq, had come "to liberate Palestine from the Jews," invading simultaneously from the south, north, and east.

The Jewish population of Palestine had every reason to suppose that losing this phase of the war would mean not only mass expulsion but also implementation of a program of extermination matching the one that had just taken place in Europe. The secretary-general of the Arab League, Abdul Rahman Azzam, had expressly declared that any attempt to establish a Jewish state would lead to "a war of extermination and momentous massacre which will be spoken of like the Mongolian massacre and the Crusades."[37] But even if we discount explicit expressions of intent—of which this was by no means the only one—Jews had plenty of reasons to fear that victory for the Arab armies would in practice lead to a continuation of the Shoah.[38] The anti-Jewish riots of 1920, 1929, and on through the 1930s were in their nature and consequences indistinguishable from the Eastern European pogroms from which many Jewish families had fled to the Ottoman lands. And if more grounds for disquiet were needed, the readiness of Arab forces to massacre civilians was receiving repeated demonstration in incidents such as those at the kibbutz Kfar Etzion and at the Hebrew University on Mount Scopus, Jerusalem. On May 12, 1947, as part of a larger operation, Kfar Etzion was taken by soldiers of the Jordanian Arab Legion, trained and commanded since 1939 by a British officer, Lieutenant-General Sir John Bagot Glubb, known as Glubb Pasha. Benny Morris takes up the tale:

> The bulk of the defenders, more than a hundred men and women, assembled in an open area at the center of Kfar 'Etzion. Arab soldiers "ordered [us] to sit and then stand and raise our hands. One of the Arabs pointed a tommy gun at us, and another wanted to throw a grenade. But others restrained them. Then a photographer with a *kaffiya* arrived and took photographs of us.... An armored car arrived.... When the photographer stopped taking pictures fire was opened up on us from all directions. Those not hit in the initial fusillade ... ran in various directions. Some fled to the [central] bunker. Others took hold of weapons. A mass of Arabs poured into the settlements from all sides and attacked the men in the center of the settlement and in the outposts shouting wildly 'Deir Yassin.'" Almost all of the men and women were murdered.[39]

The Hebrew University massacre had taken place a month earlier. Morris gives the following account:

> On the morning of 13 April, hundreds of militiamen from Jerusalem and surrounding villages, taking revenge for Deir Yassin and the death of 'Abd al-Qadir ... ambushed a ten-vehicle Haganah convoy carrying mostly unarmed Jewish lecturers, students, nurses and doctors on their way to the mountaintop Hadassah Hospital–Hebrew University campus. Ironically, this

convoy was also carrying two IZL fighters wounded at Deir Yassin. During the previous months, the Arabs had left these convoys—which were often accompanied by British armored cars—alone.

But on 13 April there was no British escort. Perhaps, as they later claimed, the British were shorthanded; perhaps they regarded revenge for Deir Yassin as fitting. It was a classic ambush: at 9:30 AM a large mine blew a hole in the road, halting the convoy. The attackers then let loose with light weapons and grenades.... The shooting went on for more than five hours. The defenders' fire slowly tapered off as their ammunition ran out. The ambushers inched toward the buses, eventually dousing them with gasoline and setting them alight. A British column reached the scene at 3:45 PM. But it was too late. By then seventy-eight academics, doctors, students, nurses, and Haganah men were dead, many roasted alive. Only thirty bodies were recovered and buried; the rest had turned to ashes. The Arabs had had their revenge.[40]

It has been a main contention of Israeli revisionist "new historians," particularly Benny Morris, since the 1990s, that the Israeli belief in the "purity of arms" of Jewish forces during the wars of 1947–48 is a fantasy and that "in truth ... the Jews committed far more atrocities than the Arabs and killed far more civilians and POWs in deliberate acts of brutality in the course of 1948."[41] Morris opts for an estimated global figure of around eight hundred. No doubt such things occurred, as in all wars. The evidence Morris offers for particular instances, however, is often based on hearsay, as at the village of Dawayima: "A Mapam [a Marxist/Zionist political party of the day] activist later wrote a complaint, quoting an officer who had reached the village a day or two later." Morris grants, however, that where such things occurred they occurred in defiance of orders: "Three days before, Southern Front had ordered all units 'not to harm the population' (and to desist from looting and to safeguard 'holy sites')" and that attempts at prevention were made on the Israeli side—"Pressure by Mapam ministers resulted in a number of investigations."[42] And he takes the view that if the Arabs committed fewer atrocities than the Jews, that is because their military weakness left them with fewer occasions to do so. "Arab rhetoric may have been more blood curdling and inciteful to atrocity than Jewish public rhetoric—but the war itself afforded the Arabs infinitely fewer opportunities to massacre their foes."[43]

Morris, however, categorically rejects the idea—central, as we have seen, to the anti-Zionist/BDS position—that the crimes committed by Israeli forces in 1947–48 so exceeded those of any other modern war or nation as to render the very existence of Israel illegitimate. In a 2004 interview with Ari Shavit, Morris says, "You have to put things in proportion. These are small war crimes. All told, if we take all the massacres and all the executions of 1948, we come to about 800 who were killed. In comparison to the massacres that were perpetrated in Bosnia, that's peanuts. In comparison to the massacres the Russians perpetrated against the Germans at Stalingrad, that's chicken feed. When you take into account that there was a bloody civil war here and that we lost an entire 1 percent of the population, you find that we behaved very well."[44]

The War of Independence ended formally in 1949, with the signing of armistice agreements with four of the Arab belligerents: Egypt in February, Lebanon in March, Jordan in April, and Syria in July (the Iraqis having refused to enter into armistice negotiations). By that time, the State of Israel was already a year old, having been brought into existence, on the expiry of the British Mandate, by the Declaration of Establishment of the State of Israel proclaimed on May 14, 1948, by David Ben-Gurion. Consistently with the November 29, 1947, UN partition resolution sanctioning the creation of a Jewish state, the new state was accorded de jure recognition at that point and over the following year, first by the Soviet Union and then by the United States and the bulk of UN member states. In May 1949, the admission of Israel to the UN was approved by General Assembly Resolution 273 by a vote of thirty-seven to twelve, with ten abstaining. The result of the war of 1947–48, in other words, far from extinguishing Jewish settlement, had been to bring into being a Jewish state occupying a far larger proportion of cis-Jordanian Palestine than either the Peel Commission or the UNSCOP partition proposals had envisaged.

DIVERGENT DEVELOPMENTS

However, what the war had brought into existence was not a partition in the sense intended by both Peel and UNSCOP: that is, a partition between a Jewish state *and a Palestinian state.* That this did not happen was entirely the fault of the Arab states whose armies Israel had defeated. With the end of hostilities, it became clear that political autonomy for the Arab inhabitants of Palestine had never been among the war aims of the surrounding Arab states. "While the Arab countries were united in their determination to push the Jews out of Palestine, they largely distrusted one another. The one Arab nation with a clear goal was Jordan; it aimed to annex the West Bank. The character of post-war settlements suggests that the Arab countries overall viewed Palestine either as a possible extension of a pan-Arab nation that included Syria and Jordan, or as an opportunity to add to their own sovereign territory. Nothing suggests they aimed to create an independent Arab nation for Palestinians."[45]

The fate of those Palestinians who fled to adjoining Arab nations during the war was thus for the most part bleak. Only Jordan was prepared to offer citizenship to Arab refugees from Palestine. In Gaza (at that time held by Egypt), in Syria, and in Lebanon, the refugees were offered neither nationality nor civil rights. On the thin and fictional excuse that their situation was one that would last only until Israel had been destroyed and the Jews driven from Palestine, the Arab refugees were treated, in effect, as permanently stateless persons. Held in vast refugee camps on the edge of Arab cities, places that offered them neither prosperity nor a future—and that rapidly became dilapidated slums—they became, in effect, wards of the UN and an object of charity for numbers of mostly European nongovernmental organizations. This lamentable situation has endured until the present day. According to a BBC report, in Lebanon in 2008, "Palestinians are barred from 73 professions, and allowed only menial jobs, so they don't upset Lebanon's employment market. They cannot own property or use state health care and many say they face daily discrimination from the authorities."[46]

The standard anti-Zionist position is that the plight of the Palestinian refugees is entirely the fault of Israel. A diametrically opposite view is to be found in the 1972 memoirs of Khalid al-Azm, a former prime minister of Syria: "Since 1948 it is we who demanded the return of the refugees . . . while it is we who made them leave. . . . We brought disaster upon . . . Arab refugees, by inviting them and bringing pressure to bear upon them to leave. . . . We have rendered them dispossessed. . . . We have participated in lowering their moral and social level. . . . Then we exploited them in executing crimes of murder, arson, and throwing bombs upon . . . men, women and children—all this in the service of political purposes."[47]

A very different fate awaited those Palestinian Arabs who did not become refugees. It has become central to the anti-Zionist/BDS position to claim that the goal of Zionism was always the total expulsion of the Arab population from Palestine. Morris, among others, justly points out that this is borne out neither by studies of opinion and debate within the Zionist movement nor by what actually happened.

> The war resulted in the creation of some seven hundred thousand Arab refugees. In part this was a product of the expulsionist elements in the ideology of both sides. By 1948, many in the Zionist leadership accepted the idea and necessity of transfer, and this affected events during the war. But this gradual acceptance was in large part a response to the expulsionist ideology and violent praxis of al-Husseini and his followers

NARRATIVE AND REALITY 189

during the previous two decades. . . . Among the Zionists it was a minor
and secondary element, occasionally entertained and enunciated by key
leaders, including Ben-Gurion and Chaim Witzmann. But it had not been
part of the original Zionist ideology. . . . Only in the mid-1930s and the early
1940s did Zionist leaders clearly advocate the idea—in response to the Arab
Revolt, which killed hundreds of settlers and threatened to destroy the
Yishuv, and Nazi anti-Semitism, which threatened to destroy German, and
then European, Jewry. . . . By contrast, expulsionist thinking and, where it
became possible, behavior, characterised the mainstream of the Palestinian
national movement since its inception. "We will push the Zionists into the
sea—or they will send us back into the desert," the Jaffa Muslim-Christian
Association told the King-Crane Commission as early as 1919.[48]

The absence of any serious commitment to exclusionism in Zionist thinking is confirmed by the fact that a large Arab population, usually estimated
at around 150,000, remained in the territory of Israel at the end of the war:
"By war's end, even though much of the country had been 'cleansed' of Arabs,
other parts of the country—notably central Galilee—were left with substantial
Muslim Arab populations, and towns in the heart of the Jewish coastal strip,
Haifa and Jaffa, were left with an Arab minority. These Arab communities have
since prospered and burgeoned and now constitute about 20 per cent of Israel's
citizenry."[49]

For a time, Israeli Arabs lived under military law, but in 1966, they were
granted full citizenship of Israel with the same civil rights as other citizens and
equal treatment under the law.

The situation was further complicated by the arrival in Israel over the next
few years of a very large proportion of the six hundred thousand to seven hundred thousand Arabic-speaking Jewish citizens of Arab countries, the so-called
Mizrahis or "oriental" Jews, whose position had become impossible as a result
of the defeat of the Arab armies by their coreligionists in Israel. As a consequence of that defeat, Jewish citizens of Arab countries suffered pogroms in
which many hundreds of Jews were killed, bomb attacks, suspensions of civil
rights accompanied by arbitrary arrest and confiscation of property, dismissal
from government employment, and deportation to internment camps. In this
way, Israel acquired a new population, Jewish in religion but Arab in all other
respects. In effect, a transfer of populations had taken place. Later immigration
by other non-European Jewish groups from Abyssinia, North Africa, and elsewhere and of ethnic Russians of Jewish descent but Russian Orthodox religion
has further complicated the demography of the country.

As a result of these events, the standard anti-Zionist/BDS conception of the population of Israel as consisting not only entirely of Jews but entirely of "white" Jews of European descent at that, is very far from the truth. Present-day Israel is in fact a multicultural society exhibiting a degree of ethnic and religious diversity far exceeding that of any European society. According to Israel's Central Bureau of Statistics (CBS), in 2017, 75 percent of the population was Jewish and 20.7 percent Arab, with 4.3 percent of "Others" including non-Arab Christians, Baha'i, and other groups. Of the Jewish population, only 36 percent are of European and American ancestry and the remainder variously of Middle Eastern, Asian, and African descent. Most non-Jewish citizens of Israel are Arab and identify as Muslims, Christians, or Druze. Most Arab Christians are adherents of the Greek Catholic (Melkite) Church, but the Christian community also includes Maronites, Arameans, Assyrians, and Armenians, as well as a thousand-strong community of Copts (whose Arab status is disputed), Protestants, and others.

All citizens of Israel have the vote. In 2015, a range of Arab political parties managed to unite with a view to increasing Israeli Arab representation in the Knesset. As the *Washington Post* noted:

> If polls taken ahead of next week's general election are accurate, Arab Israelis could end up heading the third-largest political faction in Israel's next parliament, giving a voice to the often-sidelined Arab population.
>
> It's a remarkable twist of fate for Israel's 1.7 million Arabs, who make up roughly 20 per cent of the country's population and have never had much political clout.
>
> It could also mean that Israel is the only country in the Middle East where Arab Muslim, Christian, Druse and even Jewish politicians—representing ultra-religious Islamists, uber-secularists, liberals, nationalists, capitalists, socialists and communists, have succeeded in forming a united group.[50]

All citizens of Israel also have equal access to its heath facilities, schools, and universities. Arab access to university education is healthy and increasing, and government funds are set aside to increase it still further in the interests of promoting assimilation.

> The percentage of Arab university students in Israel has risen significantly in recent years, according to a Central Bureau of Statistics report marking the start of the new academic year.
>
> This year, 14.4 per cent of bachelor's degree students will be Arabs, compared with 9.8 per cent in 1999/2000. In that same period, the rate of Arab master's degree candidates rose from only 3.6 per cent to 10.5 per cent this year, while Arab Ph.D. candidates doubled from 2.8 per cent to 5.9 per cent.

The portion of women among Arab higher education students has also risen. In 2000, 61.7 per cent of Arab students were women, while this year the figure is 67.2 per cent. The most significant increase is in the advanced degrees. The percentage of women among Arab master's degree candidates has jumped from 40.9 per cent in 2000 to 71 per cent this year and Ph.D. candidates from 18.3 per cent to 55.4 per cent.

Funding to increase the numbers of ultra-Orthodox and Arabs in higher education currently stands at 214 million shekels ($55,540,000), the bureau said.[51]

Religious freedom is not merely constitutionally but far more importantly, in practice guaranteed to all citizens of Israel. This is in sharp contrast to the rest of the Middle East, where over the past five years, as a result of the series of murderous wars that have engulfed the region since the inception of the Arab Spring, religious persecution, expulsions, burning of churches and mosques, casual massacre, and mass enslavement have become commonplace. It is not by any means true that all of this has been directed against Christians, Yazidis, and other non-Muslim groups. No doubt the vast bulk of the violence has involved intra-Muslim communal conflict between the Sunni and Shi'a branches of Islam. Nevertheless, the persecution of Christians over the past five years, as much earlier of Baha'i in Iran, has been extreme and on the whole under-reported in a largely post-Christian Europe.[52]

All the above groups currently find safety and sanctuary in Israel. Israel, indeed, is the one country in the Middle East in which membership of Christian churches is stable and growing. In 2012, the *Jerusalem Post* reported:

With thousands of Christians celebrating Christmas on Tuesday, a statistical breakdown of the Christian population by the Central Bureau of Statistics found there are currently 158,000 Christians living in the country, representing 2% of the total population. According to the report, approximately 80% of Christians in Israel are Arabs with the remainder mostly immigrants from the former Soviet Union who came to the country under the law of return, which provided for Israeli citizenship if a person has a Jewish grandparent.

Most Christian Arabs live in northern Israel, and the cities with the largest Christian populations are Nazareth, with 22,400; Haifa with 14,400; Jerusalem with 11,700; and Shfar'am with 9,400.

The Christian population is also growing, albeit at a slower rate than other sectors. Christian population growth stands at 1.3%, compared to 1.8% for Jews and 2.5% for Muslims.

The level of Christian education is notable, with 64% of Christian high school students earning a high school diploma, compared to 59% for Jewish Israelis and 48% for Muslims.[53]

Even if one accepts that non-Jewish minorities are protected and that life in Israel is at the moment, for all its citizens, somewhat safer and more prosperous than life elsewhere in the region, might it not still be asked how non-Jewish groups in Israel feel about the dominance exercised by the Jewish majority? Given the origins of the state in intercommunal war, it would not be implausible to suppose that the feelings of non-Jewish citizens toward the Jewish majority might well be, even seventy years later, uniformly hostile and even violently hostile. On such an assumption, one would expect to find the Jewish and non-Jewish communities related to one another merely by the brute fact of physical proximity, without the least trace of what one might call human proximity: no friendships, no common or intercommunal projects, no intercommunal helping hands: in short, a morally featureless landscape of uniform intercommunal animosity and rejection.

The late Edward Said, a Palestinian professor of literature at Columbia and founder of the academic field of postcolonial studies, was a staunch supporter of this view of things: "There are no divisions in the Palestinian population of four million. We all support the PLO [Palestine Liberation Organization]."[54] "Every Palestinian, without significant exception, is up in arms against the Jewish . . . state."[55]

Against the featureless unanimity touted by Said thirty years ago, however, one has to set the very different picture presented by twenty-first-century observers of Israeli society such as Rachel R. Harris, a professor of Israeli and comparative literature at the University of Illinois:

> Proponents of academic and cultural boycotts often attribute a monolithic character to Israeli society; they assume it is entirely Jewish, generally conservative, and that the only minority is a disenfranchised Palestinian population. In fact, Israel is a vibrant and diverse multicultural society. To claim that Arab citizens feel decisively alienated toward the Jewish state and consequently yearn for a one-state solution to the Israeli-Palestinian conflict is to assume that Israeli-Arabs exist in isolation within Israeli society. The boycott camp wants to exchange this supposed Israeli reality for a monolithic Palestinian polity that would, to their mind, justly represent Arab values and identity. The reality is a good deal more complicated. Within the Arab population of Israel there are cultural and generational differences and tensions that reveal major fissures within Palestinian and Arab-Israeli society. A new generation of fiction writers has used this social conflict as a creative source, demonstrating that Arab-Israeli citizens are increasingly integrated into Israeli society, while rejecting time-honoured and patriarchal Arab social systems. . . . [This] . . . is leading to a new hybrid generation of

Arab-Israelis who are creating a third way; neither Zionist nor Palestinian nationalist, but integrated within the complexities of contemporary Israel.[56]

Examples of this new composite Arab identity are not hard to find in the Israeli press at the moment; nor should this surprise one, given the depth and antiquity of some of the "fissures" of which Harris speaks. Israeli Druze, as well as Circassian Muslims, for example, fought on the side of Israel both during and since the War of Independence and chose to remain in Israel at the end of the war. Young people of both communities perform Israeli military service with the IDF. Many Circassians are employed in the security forces, including the border guard, the police, and the Israel Prison Service.[57]

Israeli Arab Muslims are also nowadays to be found in the armed forces, including Major Ala Wahab, from the Galilee village of Reineh, presently the highest-ranking Muslim officer in the IDF, who describes himself as a "Zionist Israeli Arab": "'From the age of zero I was told that Israel stole Palestine from us, but when I was 14 I woke up. I discovered that Jews are not bad,' says Ala Wahab, an operations officer at a key IDF training base, and the highest ranking Arab officer in the Israeli army."[58]

Anett Haskia, a forty-five-year-old Arab Muslim hairdresser, all of whose children volunteered to serve in the IDF, has run for the Knesset as a candidate for Naftali Bennett's right-wing Zionist Home Party. Her own The True Voice organization works to help Arab youth integrate into Israeli society. Essentially, she regards the current Israeli Arab leaders, not to mention the PLO and Hamas, as having over the long term systematically betrayed Palestinian Arab interests.

> I grew up among Jews. Today, I see the hatred they [Israeli Arabs] have. They see Jews as the enemy. Israeli Arab leaders call Israel a fascist state, but all they do is get a lot of money from the state and at the same time denigrate it. And who pays the price? The Arabs. I have to get up and say I don't agree with the Arab members of Knesset who speak in my name. We do want to live in peace. We support the state of Israel. They [the Arab parties] go and lie to us, and together with the extreme left sell us the idea of a single state that won't be Jewish—and it's a big lie.[59]

Related views are held by Father Gabriel Nadaf, a Palestinian Arab priest of the Greek Orthodox communion, whose organization promotes the integration of Christian Arabs into Israeli society and encourages young Christian Arabs to volunteer for IDF service, which many of them increasingly do. Nor is this merely an individual initiative on his part.

Last week, Christian Arab pro-Israel activists held a rally in Yafia, where Nadaf leads a congregation, and reported that this year 94 Christian Arabs signed up for military duty. In the whole of 2010, the comparable number was merely 30.

In their Facebook page the new recruits refer to themselves as "Arabic-speaking Israeli Christians."

They say they live in a democratic Jewish state, see themselves as integrally part of it (Christians pre-date Muslims by centuries) and will not desist from saying so—especially in view of the bitter lot of their co-religionists in Syria, Iraq, the PA and Gaza. Their ambition, they stress, is status of the sort enjoyed by the Druse and Circassians.[60]

A further voice for Jewish-Arab integration in Israel is that of the internationally famous Palestinian Arab journalist Khaled Abu Toameh, winner of many awards, among them the Hudson Institute Award for Courage in Journalism for 2011. The following remarks of his are perhaps particularly relevant at this point in the present argument, since they suggest that Israel may have its uses as a country of refuge, not merely for Jews and Christians but also for Muslims.

Arab journalists and columnists in Israel have been expressing their views about the Egyptian crisis without fear, while their colleagues in Egypt, Jordan and the Palestinian Authority are afraid to speak their mind.

Israel, for example, is one of the few countries in the Middle East where Muslims are permitted to demonstrate in favor of ousted Egyptian President Mohamed Morsi and his Muslim Brotherhood organization.

This is not because Israel supports Morsi or the Muslim Brotherhood; it is because the Muslim protesters know that in a democratic country like Israel they can hold peaceful demonstrations and express their views without having to worry about being targeted by the authorities.

Israel has become a safe place not only for Arab Christians, but also for Muslims who wish to express their opinion away from intimidation and violence.

While pro-Morsi demonstrators are being shot, wounded, arrested and harassed in Egypt, the Palestinian Authority–controlled territories and some Arab countries, in Israel they are free to stage protests and express their views even in the heart of Jerusalem and Tel Aviv.

In Israel, pro-Morsi demonstrators even feel free to chant slogans against Israel and the U.S., and to hoist Hamas flags.[61]

Toameh is by no means alone. There is, for instance, the extraordinary Zoabi family, or clan, numbering around ten thousand, which includes both the fanatically anti-Israel and antisemitic MK (Member of the Knesset) Hanin Zoabi but also the equally violently pro-Israel and pro-Jewish Nahal, principal of a high school in Kfar Nin, near Abula, and a cousin of Hanin. Both Nahal and Mohammed, another relative, have made public statements (for which both incurred death threats) praising Israel and claiming dissent from Hanin's pro-Hamas political stance on the part of many members of the clan.[62] A passionate defense of Israel by another member of the family, Sara Zoab, who describes herself as a "proud Muslim Zionist," can be found on YouTube. I have not space to cover further instances of pro-Israel Arab Muslim opinion, but the briefest search on the internet will uncover many more.

Polls also suggest that Palestinian opinion within Israel is increasingly appreciative of the advantages that the country provides to all its citizens, even if still in some areas haltingly to Arabs, in terms of democratic accountability, the rule of law, access to education, and career opportunities. The main poll that focuses systematically on the Arab community in Israel is the annual Index of Arab-Jewish Relations in Israel, conducted by the University of Israel and the Israel Democracy Institute. According to its December 2014 poll, there is substantial resentment against discrimination in the Arab community. Thirty-nine percent of respondents believe there is discrimination in Israeli institutions, and 53 percent believe equality is only partial, while only 9 percent believe Israeli institutions to be completely equal and fair: results in line with previous polls by the Brookings Institution and others. A large majority of respondents (86%) believe Israeli society to be moderately or very racist toward Arabs, while only 14 percent believe that Israeli society exhibits only a small degree of racism toward Arabs. These results also match those of previous polls. On the other hand, when asked under which type of government, Israeli or Palestinian, they would rather live, 77 percent opted for Israeli government and only 23 percent opted for Palestinian rule. "These results indicate that the vast majority of the community sees itself as a part of Israeli society. Smooha [the Haifa professor charged with overseeing the conduct of the poll] explains that 'the Arabs in Israel over the past 65 years have become stakeholders in Israeli society and have a vested interest in being part of Israel and living here.'"[63]

A still more unexpected response—at least for those whose information derives mainly from such major components of the Western liberal media phalanx as the *New York Times*, *Washington Post*, the BBC, or the British *Guardian* newspaper—emerged from a poll conducted in April 2017 by the Israel Democracy Institute and the Tel Aviv University Peace Index. This poll found Arab opinion about the condition of Israel more positive than Jewish opinion. Where 43.9 percent of Jewish respondents thought the present situation of

Israel "good" or "very good," 57 percent of Arabs felt that way. Optimism was high among both groups, however, with 73 percent of Jews and 61 percent of Arabs optimistic about Israel's future. On the issue that divides the Zoabi clan, 80 percent of Jewish and 51.1 percent of Arab respondents said they felt proud to be Israeli.[64]

These and other poll results offer, I submit, a picture of present community relations in Israel far closer to that offered by Rachel Harris than to the image of absolute estrangement and disconnection offered forty years ago by Said. The poll results suggest two communities moving toward mutual accommodation, if not in process of merging, at least for many or most practical purposes, despite still facing obstacles in the shape of endemic discrimination and consequent mistrust, and hence still with some distance to go.

A CLASH OF NARRATIVES

Was Israel in its origins, then, and is it still a "colonial settler society" morally indistinguishable in its character and institutions from apartheid South Africa as the anti-Zionist/BDS narrative insists?

The problem for that narrative is not merely that the commonplace facts we have presented in this chapter contradict it but also that there emerges from these commonplace observations the outlines of a very different narrative: one of contrary but equally powerful *moral* purport. Left-wing voices sometimes ask, "Why can't the Jews in Israel go back home where they came from?" This is entirely consistent with the narrative of colonialism. Colonists, by the nature of the colonial enterprise, have a home to go back to. But that is because colonialism is, by its nature, *a state enterprise*. A colony is a colony *of a state*. Hence, if the colonial enterprise collapses, the colonists have a state to which they can return. French *colons* in Algeria were able to return to France, Dutch colonists in the Dutch East Indies were able to return to the Netherlands, and so on.

One major difference with Israel is that the Jews were backed by no such state enterprise. Jews in Palestine prior to 1948 arrived there as immigrants, to the Ottoman Empire or the mandate, because they were fleeing persecution. The same is true of the bulk of Jewish immigrants of Middle Eastern, African, and North African origin who entered the country in the immediate aftermath of the country. "Going home" was therefore no more open to these people than it is to many of the refugees from Syria, Afghanistan, and elsewhere in the conflict-ridden Muslim world presently entering Europe.

By the end of the 1930s, all that Jewish immigration had achieved was a number of small areas of Jewish settlement, for the most part on previously unproductive land, scattered across western Palestine, with the main concentration in part of the north of the country. Zionists certainly wanted to establish a Jewish home, with the political autonomy necessary to secure its population from persecution, but the only reason that the setting-up of a Jewish state in Palestine was advocated, first by the Peel Commission and then by UNSCOP, was the perceived need to prevent conflict between Jews and Arabs.

It is important to insist on this last point because of the constant repetition, both on the left and in sections of the Western media, of the absurd proposition that the Jews were "given" Israel by "the Western powers" (or sometimes just "by America") as a sort of consolation prize for having suffered the Holocaust. It ought not to be but is necessary to remind people tempted to think in this way that the Jews in Palestine, as for the most part perfectly legal immigrants under the regulations of the now-defunct Ottoman Empire, had, as international bodies frequently noted at the time, as much right to be there as anybody else. It is also necessary to remember that illegal Jewish immigration during the mandate period was in all probability matched by illegal Arab immigration drawn by the enhanced economic opportunities created by the Jewish presence. Nor had the Jews been given the land they lived on: they had simply bought it, usually at inflated prices, because it was often apparently useless land anyway and because in peasant communities the world over, a fool who wants to buy what is locally considered rubbish presents an opportunity too good to be missed.

In any case, the wider world, in the immediate aftermath of the war, was not as acutely conscious of the Holocaust as it later became. So far as it was considered at all in the immediate aftermath of World War II, it was, to my recollection, generally held to be a horrifying but happily unique aberration of Nazi ideology and therefore unlikely to recur now that Nazism had been decisively dealt with. Issues of "compensation" to Jews, individual and collective, arose only later in the postwar period, after Israel was already in existence.

It was, in fact, the attacks by Arab mobs on Jewish homes and settlements that predisposed international bodies to put forward the various partition proposals of the 1930s and 1940s. This, in essence, provides the answer internationally accepted at the time to the Palestinian leadership's question why the Jews could not be allowed to remain in an Arab-ruled state as the resident minority they had constituted in the Ottoman era. In this sense, the attacks heavily damaged what the rioters perceived as Arab interests. But even at that point, the damage was to a degree recoverable. The partition proposed by the UN General Assembly in 1947, whatever the objections of the Palestinian Arab leadership to its details,[65] would have left both Palestinians and Jews with independent self-governing states, the former very much more extensive than anything likely to

emerge in the future under any conceivable version of the "two-state solution."
It is not absurd to envisage a kind of mini-Switzerland, with two self-governing
cantons, one Palestinian Arab and predominantly Muslim in character, the
other predominantly Jewish, but both with full residence rights for citizens
of each in the other and possibly overarching federal political structures. It is
likely that such an arrangement might have proved immensely economically
and socially advantageous to both sides.

As we know, a different choice was made. It was not made by the leaders of
the Yishuv, who were fully prepared to accept the General Assembly partition
plan. It was made by the Palestinian leadership and by the neighboring Arab
states, and it was a decision in favor of war.

At this point, the notion that the Jews were given Palestine to assuage the
"sense of guilt" for the Holocaust supposedly then felt by the Western nations
(but actually at that moment—or for that matter now, except in Germany—
hardly very deeply felt) encounters another difficulty. Very few people in 1947
seriously expected the Jews to win, not least because of the vastly larger populations and military establishments of the surrounding Arab states and their
implacable and frequently expressed determination to "drive the Jews into the
sea." In effect, the Jews of Palestine were at that point abandoned by the world
and on their own, as a population of "colonists" in the usual sense—*colons*,
that is to say, with the resources of a colonizing European state behind them—
would never have been. The world, including the UN, simply stood back and
waited to see what would happen.

What happened was that the Jews not only won, first against the Palestinians
and then against five invading Arab armies, but also proclaimed the foundation of a small Jewish state occupying still not the whole of mandate Palestine
but even at that point considerably more than the General Assembly partition
plan had proposed. It is at this point, it seems to me, that the Holocaust does
enter the picture, as partly explaining the Jewish victory. No doubt the Arab
armies, as revisionist Israeli historians nowadays never tire of arguing, were
underprepared for a demanding campaign. But the majority of senior Arab
figures involved in the decision, it appears, saw no reason to prepare for one.
"Without doubt, 'cultural misperceptions and racist attitudes towards Jews in
general blinded and entrapped the Arabs,' as one historian has put it."[66] In the
dying days of the Ottoman Empire, one hears, a standing joke concerned a volunteer Jewish detachment in the Turkish army that asked to be provided with
a military escort for the more dangerous parts of a proposed march through
dubiously loyal territory. That no doubt catches the image that many Arabs and
others would have entertained of Jewish military prowess prior to 1947.

Both the Palestinian forces and those of the Arab armies were, however, attacking people who, because they were by no means colonists in the ordinary sense, could by no means retreat to the territory of a nonexistent colonial power. They were attacking members of a people who had suffered, in Europe, first an interminable history of pogroms and persecution and finally wholesale extermination at the hands of a messianic German political movement and its willing servants in half the nations of the continent. Moreover, the Arabs were attacking these people having taken care to threaten them, at length and repeatedly, with renewed extermination should they lose, and to demonstrate the force and seriousness of these threats with actual massacres, preceded by a history of pogroms no different in essence from those suffered in Europe. Having done all this, they failed to prepare adequately for the war, being guided, apparently, by the familiar confidence of the antisemitic thug that with a Jew, unlike with people of one's own sort, one may do anything one pleases without having to pay a price for it.

The history of Palestine from 1880 to 1948 is undoubtedly in many ways a tragic one: a tale of missed opportunities. But is it a history of *colonialism*? It is very hard to see how that narrative is supposed to fit the facts. Colonialism requires a colonial power and an armed incursion by that power, and in this case, there was neither. The narrative that does fit the facts, one far more common in the present century, is that of the conflict between the imperial, centralizing instincts of a dominant power and the thrust toward political autonomy and self-determination on the part of ethnic, religious, or regional minorities within its territory. From this standpoint, the position of Jews in the Arab Middle East is analogous to that of the Kurds in Iraq, Iran, and Turkey, of the Tibetans in the Republic of China, of the Scots in the United Kingdom, of the Catalans or Basques in Spain, or of the Quebecois in Canada. The one difference from these is that the Jews in Palestine managed to make good their claim to self-determination. The wars that followed the collapse of the former Yugoslavia in the 1990s produced a series of such conflicts, equally bloody and with outcomes equally unsatisfactory to some of the participants. In a case that, in effect, mirrors the situation of Palestinian Muslim Arabs in reverse, the Serbs lost the province of Kosovo to its present Albanian, mainly Muslim-majority population, a large proportion of which had immigrated to the province from Albania over the preceding decades of communist rule. All such episodes generate revanchist demands for the recovery of lost territory, which seldom, if ever, succeed.

For such a demand to gain general sympathy, it does indeed need to be shown somehow or other that all the rights in the case are on one side and all the wrongs are on the other side. That, as we saw at the end of the last chapter, is precisely where anti-Zionists of the type of Professor Michael Neumann or Baroness Tonge take their stand. Are we to take them seriously? Is Israel "generally speaking in the wrong in its conflict with the Palestinians," as Neumann puts it, and "the Palestinians . . . generally in the right"? The history of Palestine since the 1880s seems to me to support, if anything, the contrary view. The present existence of Israel, viewed in light of that history, appears to owe far more to Arab intransigence and violence, counterproductive at every stage as those seem to have been from the point of view of what the perpetrators chose to regard as Palestinian interests, than to the Zionist response, which until 1947, appears to have been for the most part purely defensive in character. In 1947–48, the Jews in Palestine felt themselves, on very good evidence, to be facing, to put it bluntly, a repeat performance of the Holocaust, and they did what they had to: no people, after all, can be expected to acquiesce passively in its own extermination while it possesses any means of resisting it. Israeli revisionist historians have very likely shown that the flight of the bulk of the Arab population beyond the areas eventually claimed by Israeli arms was to some degree encouraged by the Israelis; at the same time, nobody denies that many other forces were working in the same direction. Jewish atrocities there may well have been: if so, they were balanced by equally well or better-attested Arab atrocities. And when the fighting stopped, there was no further attempt on the part of the victorious Israelis to get rid of those Arabs who had chosen to stay put: they were allowed to remain and in due course accepted as fellow citizens.

Wars make enemies, create injustices, and fuel lasting resentments; so much is obvious. What current anti-Zionist and BDS campaigns against the legitimacy of Israel require, however, is far more than that. They require it to be demonstrable that Israel is a *uniquely evil* polity, evil enough for the Israelis to be—to *really* be, *literally*, and not just as a matter of mad political rhetoric— "the new Nazis." That is the prevailing assumption of innumerable meetings and demonstrations called for the purpose of denouncing Israel at which the most common banner displayed consists simply of the Star of David and the swastika connected by an "equals" sign.

Alas, for people like Professor Jacqueline Rose, the late Edward Said, and a host of their political epigones, the late-twentieth- and twenty-first-century atrocities that genuinely do recall the Nazi era have no connection whatsoever with Israel. Even if one looks no further than the immediate region, any abuses of which Israel can with any plausibility be accused are left far behind by those committed by the likes of Saddam Hussein, Assad, Daesh, the Taliban, Hamas, or the Iran of the ayatollahs: all far more accomplished actors in the extraordinary theater of cruelty and the absurd into which, with some help from ill-advised Western interventions, large parts of the Islamic world have subsided over the past couple of decades.

Again, can Israel be accused, as is nowadays standardly alleged by sections of the left and by BDS supporters, of running an apartheid state? What was objectionable about apartheid was that only the white population enjoyed the vote and that nonwhite citizens were systematically excluded from facilities and advantages provided for the whites. Nothing of the kind is true of Israel. In line with the attempt by the BDS movement to present itself as a legitimate successor to, and as fighting essentially the same battle as, the anti-apartheid movement in South Africa, the second demand made by the 2004 "call" was that Israel recognize "the fundamental rights of the Arab-Palestinian citizens of Israel to full equality." As the late Emily Budick points out in an excellent essay,

> Such "full equality" by law, for all of its citizens, is already a part of Israeli law. Israeli Arabs (whether or not they identify themselves as Palestinians or Bedouins or Druse, Muslim or Christian or secular Israelis) do by law enjoy full civil rights: they are represented in the parliament, in municipal governments, in professions like medicine, law, and teaching; and at universities throughout Israel and so on and so forth. They own property. They run businesses. Any visit to an Israeli hospital or college campus dispels any notion of what BDS identifies on is home page as "Israeli Apartheid." ... The boycott against South Africa took a position in relation to a country that ... deprived human beings of their citizenship, their basic human rights, equality under the law, and equal access to national resources. This is *not* the case in Israel, despite BDS's and Barghouti's claims to the contrary. ... The appeal to the example of the boycott of South Africa is nothing more than a rhetorical flourish, aimed at bringing the logic of one situation to bear on another, very different situation, which requires a different set of terminologies and a different set of solutions.[67]

Even at this point, however, the argument has not yet reached its conclusion. There remains one shot in the anti-Zionist's locker. It remains open to him or her to maintain that even if the terms *colonialism* and *apartheid* have, in their ordinary sense, no application to the history or present condition of Israel proper, yet they maintain their full force in relation to the conduct of Israel in the "occupied territories" of Gaza and the West Bank, conquered by Israel in the war of 1967.

In the next chapter, we shall examine the intellectual and moral credentials of that claim.

NOTES

1. Loewenstein and Moor 2012.

2. I use the term *exterminate* advisedly and with a full sense of its literal meaning. In 1978, for example, I stood in a bar in Perth listening while a drunken young Australian from up-country boasted at the top of his voice that his grandfather had taken part in "Abo hunts." Later, I discovered—and still have the documentation—that the last recorded such "hunt" in Western Australia took place in 1929. All the members of an Aboriginal band—an extended family—were hunted down and shot, their bodies burned, and the ashes and bone fragments thrown into a pond. The massacre was discovered through the detective work of a clergyman, and the perpetrators received short jail sentences.

3. Chomsky 1992.

4. See Alexander Scholch, "Palestine in Transformation 1856–1882: Studies in Social, Economic and Political Development," Institute of Palestine Studies (1992).

5. *An Interim Report on the Civil Administrations to the League of Nations, June 1921*, text available on the web at EretzYizroel.org and from the United Nations at unispal.un.org.

6. Bachi 1974.

7. McCarthy 1990.

8. Fred M. Gottheil, "Arab Immigration into Pre-State Israel: 1922–1931," *Middle Eastern Studies* 9 (1973): 315–24.

9. Yakov Feitelson, "The Politics of Palestinian Demography," *Middle East Quarterly* (Spring 2009): 51–59.

10. McCarthy 1990, 34.

11. Gottheil, "Arab Immigration into Pre-State Israel." The reference is to U. O. Schmelz, "Population Characteristics of Jerusalem and Hebron Regions according to Ottoman Census of 1905," in Gar G. Gilbar, ed., *Ottoman Palestine: 1800–1914* (Leiden: Brill, 1990), 42.

12. Bachi 1974, 389. See also Gottheil, "Arab Immigration into Pre-State Israel."

13. Bachi 1974, 390. See also Gottheil, "Arab Immigration into Pre-State Israel."

14. G. E. Von Grunebaum, "Eastern Jewry under Islam," *Viator Mediaeval and Renaissance Studies* 2 (1971): 365–72.

15. Cary Nelson, Rachel S. Harris, and Kenneth W. Stein, "A Concise History of Israel," 399 et seq., in Nelson and Brahm 2015.

16. Morris 2001, 95, cited in Dershowitz 2003, 40.

17. Tom Segev, "When Zionism Was an Arab Cause," *Haaretz*, April 2012, https://www.haaretz.com/1.5212073.

18. Dershowitz 2003, 43–44.

19. Dershowitz 2003, 36. The citation is from page 41 of the Peel Report, available in full at, inter alia, www.jewishvirtuallibrary.org/jsource/History /peel1.html.

20. Peel Report, 2.

21. Peel Report, 141.

22. Peel Report, 375–76.

23. Nelson, Harris, and Stein in Nelson and Brahm 2015, 401.

24. Nelson, Harris, and Stein in Nelson and Brahm 2015, 405–6.

25. Morris 2008, 93.

26. Morris 2008, 127.

27. Morris 2008, 127.

28. Morris 2008, 126–27.

29. Maurice Ostrov, "Deir Yasin—Startling Evidence," available on the website of Ostrov, a celebrated *Jerusalem Post* investigative journalist, maurice-ostroff.org, which also carries a link to the BBC video.

30. Morris 2008, 127 (the reference is given in Morris as "Yavne to HIS-AD, 12 April 1948, IDFA 5254/49//372").

31. Tauber 2017. The book is at present available only in Hebrew, but two long and detailed reviews are available on the internet, the first, dated August 7, 2017, at the website of *Mosaic* magazine, the second, dated November 22, 2017, by Dr. Arnon Groiss at the website of BESA (The Begin-Sadat Center for Strategic Studies).

32. Begin 1951, cited in Ostrov, "Deir Yasin," emphasis mine.

33. Begin 1951.

34. Ostrov, "Deir Yasin."

35. Nelson and Brahm 2015, 407.

36. Karsh 2010, 240.

37. The source of this remark of Azzam's was for a time uncertain, but it has now been traced to a 1947 interview with Azzam in the Egyptian newspaper *Akhbar-al-Yom*. See David Barnett and Efraim Karsh, "Azzam's Genocidal Threat," *Middle East Quarterly* 18, no. 4 (Fall 2011): 85–88. Not for the first time in the long war between Efraim Karsh and Benny Morris (who doubted the authenticity of the quote in dispute with Karsh), Karsh wins.

38. For the extraordinary extent, throughout the Arab world, of jihadist fervor aiming at the total destruction of the Jews on religious grounds, see Morris 2008, 394–96.

39. Morris 2008, 170 (reference to quoted passage given in Morris).

40. Morris 2008, 128–29.

41. Morris 2008, 405.

42. This and the preceding two quotations from Morris 2008, 333.

43. Morris 2008, 405.

44. Ari Shavit, "Survival of the Fittest? An Interview with Benny Morris," *Haaretz Friday Magazine*, January 9, 2004, https://www.webcitation.org /5pvy2Rvfw.

45. Nelson and Brahm 2015, 406.

46. Natalya Antelva, "Lebanese Refugees Fear for Future," BBC News channel, December 11, 2008, http://news.bbc.co.uk/1/hi/world/middle_east /7777060.stm.

47. Cited in Dershowitz 2003, 84.

48. Morris 2008, 407–8.

49. Morris 2008, 408.

50. Ruth Eglash, "Israel's Arab Parties Have United for the First Time," *Washington Post*, March 10, 2015, https://www.washingtonpost.com/world /middle_east/israels-sparring-arab-political-parties-have-united-for-the-first -time/2015/03/09/6f6c021a-c660-11e4-bea5-b893e7ac3fb3_story.html.

51. Yarden Skop, "More Arab Students in Israel Attending University in New Academic Year," *Haaretz*, October 15, 2015, https://www.haaretz.com/.premium -more-arab-university-students-in-new-academic-year-1.5409071.

52. A more adequate idea of the extent of persecution of Christians around the world than that offered by the bulk of news outlets, including and especially the BBC, can be obtained from the website and magazine of the Barnabas Fund.

53. Jeremy Sharon, "CBS Report: Christian Population in Israel Growing," *Jerusalem Post*, December 25, 2012, https://www.jpost.com/National-News/CBS -report-Christian-population-in-Israel-growing.

54. Edward Said, *New Leader*, August 11, 1980.

55. Interview (Tunis), December 1988. I owe this and the preceding reference to Edward Alexander.

56. Rachel S. Harris, "No Place Like Home: Arab-Israelis, Contemporary Fiction and an Arab-Hebrew Identity," in Nelson and Brahm 2015, 327.

57. Eléonore Merza, "In Search of a Lost Time: (Re)construction of Identity in the Circassian Diaspora in Israel," *Bulletin du Centre de recherche français à Jérusalem*, 19 (2008), https://journals.openedition.org/bcrfj/5911.

58. Israel Hayom newsletter, September 7, 2012, http://www.israelhayom.com.

59. Interview with Anett Haskia, *The Times of Israel*, February 14, 2017, timesofisrael.com.

60. *Jerusalem Post* editorial, June 26, 2013.

61. Khaled Abu Toameh, "Where Muslims Can Speak Freely in the Middle East," August 22, 2013. Available on the website of the Gatestone Institute, where a large collection of Toameh's articles can be found.

62. Moshe Cohen, "MK Zoabi's Family Say 'She Doesn't Represent Us,'" Israelinternationalnews.com, June 30, 2014, http://www.israelnationalnews.com /News/News.aspx/182333.

63. Itamar Radai, Meir Elran, Yousef Makladeh, and Maya Kornberg, "The Arab Citizens in Israel: Current Trends according to Recent Opinion Polls." Publications of the Institute for National Security Studies (inss.org.il).

64. Stuart Winer, "Israeli Arabs View Country More Positively than Jews, Survey Finds," *Times of Israel*, May 1, 2017, https://www.timesofisrael.com/israeli -arabs-view-country-more-positively-than-jews-survey-finds/.

65. Morris 2008, 64–65. A map of the UN partition proposal occupies page 64.

66. Morris 2008, 183, citing Fawaz Gerges, *Egypt and the 1948 War*, 155; and see Morris 2008, 183–85 for the gap between Arab bluster and military preparedness.

67. Emily Budick, "When a Boycott Is Not Moral Action," in Nelson and Brahm 2015, 95.

EIGHT

—ᴧᴧᴧ—

THE LEGACY OF 1967

It is a precept, or generall rule of Reason, *That every man, ought to endeavour
Peace, as farre as he has hope of obtaining it; and when he cannot obtain it, that
he may seek, and use, all helps and advantages of Warre.* The first branch of
which Rule, containeth the first, and Fundamental Law of Nature, which is,
to *seek Peace, and follow it.* The Second, the summe of the Right of Nature;
which is, *By all means we can, to defend our selves.*

—Thomas Hobbes, *Leviathan*, part 1, chapter 14

DESTRUCTION POSTPONED

The will of the Arab League and the Arab Higher Committee to expel the Jews
(and after them, perhaps, the Christians) from Palestine by "a war of extermination and momentous massacre" did not evaporate with the defeat of 1948.[1]
Since then, Israel has been involved in a succession of short wars and military
actions that "amount, in effect, to one long war that has sometimes paused but
never really stopped."[2] The best known of these little wars, and the one whose
consequences still resonate today, is the brief war (June 5–10) of 1967 between
Israel and Egypt (at that time under the rule of Gamal Abdul Nasser), Syria,
and Jordan.

> When the Soviets erroneously informed Syria and Egypt that Israel was
> amassing troops for an attack in the North, Nasser demanded that the UN
> [United Nations] withdraw from Gaza, Sinai and the Straits of Tiran. The UN
> complied and Nasser blocked the Straits, preventing Israel's access through

the Red Sea to the Gulf of Aqaba, a major trade route. It amounted to an act of war. The public rhetoric that followed—which included calls on Nasser to drive the Jews out of Israel and PLO [Palestine Liberation Organization] chairman Ahmed Shukeri's (1908–1980) boast that "no Jew whatever will survive" in the event of war—evoked memories of the Holocaust for Israelis. When Jordan's King Hussein then flew to Egypt to sign a mutual defense pact, Israel reacted to the threat implied in the military alliance and launched a preemptive strike.[3]

Once again the rhetoric of extermination—deployed not against a peaceful, assimilated, and helpless population as in the case of the Nazis but this time against an armed and vigilant one—proved counterproductive. Within three hours, Israel's preemptive strike had destroyed the Egyptian Air Force on the ground. On land, Israeli forces reached the Suez Canal and occupied the whole of the Sinai Peninsula. When Jordan unwisely entered the war by shelling West Jerusalem and the Ramat David airfield, Israel responded on the ground, capturing East Jerusalem and the West Bank, both of which had been under Jordanian control, though never formally annexed, since 1948. In addition, Israel captured the Golan Heights from Syria and Gaza from Egypt.

The new territories contained a million Palestinians. Unlike the 150,000 who had remained in Israel in 1948, they were not offered full and equal Israeli citizenship but remained for the indefinite future under Israeli martial law. It was a development that provoked strong opposition within Israel itself. The Israeli left saw it as changing the character of Israel from a state based on democracy and the rule of law to an occupying power imposing its rule by force on an unwilling and alien population. For the Israeli right, control of the Jordan River Valley was seen as essential to national security, given the very narrow width of Israel at this point (approximately 11 kilometers) to protect the country from further incursions from the east. There is also the fact that Israel depended at the time for 30 percent of its water supply on three aquifers that recharge under the Judaean Mountains and the desert to the east of Jerusalem.[4]

In any event, Israel's occupation of these areas post-1969 has proved productive of endless political controversy as well as repeated episodes of armed conflict. It provides, among other things, the *ultimate* basis for anti-Zionist and Boycott, Divestment and Sanctions (BDS) attacks on Israel as a "criminal," "colonial settler," and "apartheid" society: ultimate in the sense that if these claims cannot be defended by appeal to Israel's conduct in the Occupied Territories, then, as we have seen in the previous two chapters, they are to all intents and purposes indefensible.

LAND FOR PEACE

On November 22, 1967, the UN Security Council unanimously adopted Resolution 242, which has ever since constituted the internationally accepted basis
for peace negotiations between Israel, the Arab states, and so far less successfully, the Palestinians. Paragraph 1 of the resolution

> affirms that the fulfillment of Charter principles requires the establishment
> of a just and lasting peace in the Middle East which should include the
> application of both the following principles:
>
> (i) Withdrawal of Israeli armed forces from territories occupied in the
>   recent conflict;
> (ii) Termination of all claims or states of belligerency and respect for and
>   acknowledgment of the sovereignty, territorial integrity and political
>   independence of every State in the area and their right to live in peace
>   within secure and recognized boundaries free from threats or acts of
>   force.

Israel's acceptance of Resolution 242 and its willingness to seek agreement
with each Arab state on the basis of that agreement is a matter of history. Acceptance by the Arab states and the various political factions active in the West
Bank and Gaza has been patchy to say the least.

In view of the present widespread support in sections of the European and
American left for the "delegitimization" of Israel and the consequent denial of
its right to exist, it is important to note that Resolution 242, in effect, *enshrines
Israel's right to exist in international law* as a necessary condition of peace. The
wording of Resolution 242 was that proposed by the UK representative at the
UN at that time, Lord Caradon. In a later interview, Caradon, questioned on
precisely this point, replied,

> Well, that's perfectly obvious if you read again the principles of 242, which
> have been accepted by Egypt, Jordan, Syria and Saudi Arabia, and in effect by
> Israel. The provision is that if there is an adequate withdrawal, all states in the
> area must be free to live within secure and recognized boundaries, free from
> force and threat of force. So it is an acceptance that Israel has a right to exist,
> just as they would have a right to their homeland, and have a right to exist.
> This is the essential bargain that we are proposing. It's not a new thing, it's
> been going since 1967.[5]

A series of peace treaties were subsequently signed on this basis but not
before two further brief wars had taken place. In 1969–70, the so-called War
of Attrition along the border between Israel and Egypt caused considerable

damage to cities along the Suez Canal and sent floods of Egyptian refugees into Cairo. There followed the Yom Kippur War of October 6–24, 1973. This involved a coordinated attack by Syrian and Egyptian forces, attacking simultaneously from the north and south during the most sacred holiday of the Judaic religious year. Israel was unprepared, the government of Golda Meir having even ignored a warning from King Hussein of Jordan that the attack was coming. On the Egyptian front, Israel suffered immediate heavy losses in tanks and aircraft from surface-to-air missiles and Soviet antitank missiles, leading to some fear in government circles, during the first of two disastrous days of the war, that the country might be lost. Within days, however, the course of the war changed dramatically. On the southern front, a further attack by Egypt cost it 250 tanks in contrast to the Israeli loss of about 20. Israeli forces were then able to cross the Suez Canal and encircle the Egyptian Third Army. In the north, the Israel Defense Forces (IDF) counterattacked in the Golan Heights and advanced toward Damascus. Israel lost 2,500, but combined, Egyptian and Syrian combat deaths approached 15,000, and the two countries together lost 1,800 tanks and 400 aircraft.

The Yom Kippur War, however, saw the beginnings of a movement toward peace on the basis of Resolution 242. In 1979, following the Camp David Accords of 1978, a series of meetings between Egypt and Israel facilitated by US president Jimmy Carter, Egypt and Israel signed a peace treaty that involved Israel withdrawing its troops and 4,500 civilian inhabitants from the Sinai Peninsula and returning it to Egyptian sovereignty. For its part, Egypt agreed to guarantee freedom of passage through the canal and other waterways while accepting limitations on the armed forces it could place on the Sinai, particularly within twenty to thirty kilometers of Israel.

Fifteen years later, in 1994, a second Arab country, Jordan, signed a peace treaty with Israel that similarly included recognition of Israel, settlement of existing territorial disputes, and agreement not to engage in further military operations.

Jordan and Egypt, however, remain the only two Arab countries with which a peace treaty has proved achievable. Anwar Sadat and Menachem Begin shared the Nobel Peace Prize for 1978. But the reaction in other Arab states was predictably volcanic. Egypt was suspended from the Arab League for ten years, both as a penalty for signing the treaty and as a warning to other Arab states not to contemplate following suit. And in 1981, during an Egyptian victory parade, Anwar Sadat was assassinated.

Peace with the Palestinians has proven more elusive. During the 1980s, a powerful movement for peace and reconciliation emerged in Israel. This, among other things, led to the Oslo Accords of 1993–95. These and the Oslo

Process, which they initiated, created a new relationship between Israel and the PLO. As a result of secret negotiations in Oslo, the PLO for the first time recognized the State of Israel, and Israel in return recognized the PLO as the representative of the Palestinian people and hence as its partner in all future negotiations. The Oslo Accords led to the signing in 1995 of the "Israeli-Palestinian Agreement on the West Bank and the Gaza Strip," which created the Palestinian Authority as an elected body charged with exercising Palestinian self-governance over parts of the West Bank and the Gaza Strip. The West Bank was divided into three parts, Areas A, B, and C. Area A, including the West Bank cities, and Area B, including most Arab towns and villages, were placed under the control of the Palestinian Authority. In Area C (about 60%), which encompasses unpopulated areas, Jewish settlements, and Israeli military outposts, responsibility was to be shared. The Palestinian Authority was to be responsible for health, education, and other public services for Arabs, while Israel was to discharge the same functions for Jews while maintaining control over security and public order. Later, in 1995, the IDF withdrew from Bethlehem, Jenin, Nablus, Qalqila, Ramallah, and Tulkarm. Later still, in 1997, the IDF withdrew from the greater part of Hebron.

These agreements and withdrawals took place against the background of the Palestinian uprising known as the First Intifada, 1987–93.[6] Prior to 1987, the PLO had characteristically concentrated on political agitation, doing little in practical terms to improve the lives of the severely impoverished Arab inhabitants of the West Bank and Gaza, while widespread Israeli border checkpoints made access to Israel difficult. The intifada began with a campaign of civil resistance, strikes, and commercial shutdowns, but it escalated rapidly into stone throwing, hurling Molotov cocktails, and attacks with knives. Israel responded in ways that succeeded only in making things worse.

The Israeli army responded to the uprising with a large show of military strength. On the one hand, this did little to quell the uprising and even less to mitigate the economic damage caused by a series of strikes called by Palestinian organizations. On the other hand, images shown around the world, of young stone throwers operating against tanks, severely damaged Israel's public image. The intifada forced the IDF into a policing role for which it was not trained. In consequence, the IDF's tactical decisions were sometimes entirely counterproductive. Thus, for example, the decision to close down West Bank and Gaza schools and universities during the 1987–88 school year simply sent unsupervised students into the streets.[7]

The First Intifada is estimated to have killed 100 Israeli civilians and 60 IDF personnel and injured more than 1,400 civilians and 1,700 soldiers. On the

Palestinian side, there were 1,800 deaths. However, a number of these people (estimates put the figure between 800–822) were killed by members of Palestinian organizations as alleged Israeli collaborators.[8]

The First Intifada led to a hardening of attitudes on both sides of the Israeli-Palestinian divide. Despite that, in 2000, Ehud Barak, leader of the Israel Labor Party and at that time prime minister of Israel, having defeated Benjamin Netanyahu on a peace platform, met with Yasser Arafat, US president Bill Clinton, and Secretary of State Madeleine Albright at Camp David in hopes of moving ahead to the next stage of the Oslo Accords. It was hoped that this meeting might result in the founding of a Palestinian state. Israel offered to divide Jerusalem, granting the Palestinian Authority sovereignty over the bulk of East Jerusalem neighborhoods, and to cede 84 percent to 90 percent of the West Bank. Arafat demanded control of all of the Old City, including the entirety of the Temple Mount. In addition, he insisted on a right of return for all Palestinians who had left Israel in 1948, *and all their descendants*. Israel has always refused to accept such a right not only because it would in effect turn Israel into an Arab country with a large and, from that point on, defenseless Jewish minority but also because it would imply an acknowledgment of the allegedly criminal nature of the Zionist enterprise and of the State of Israel. In an attempt to resolve the dispute, Barak offered Arafat 90 percent to 95 percent of the West Bank, the acceptance of several thousand Palestinian refugees as citizens of Israel, and the placing of the Temple Mount under UN control. At the same time, he demanded that acceptance of these offers by the Arab side must entail Arab acceptance that the Israeli-Palestinian conflict now be regarded as at an end.

Arafat rejected this last demand and with it all the associated offers, with the result that the negotiations collapsed and the status quo ante in the West Bank remained in force.

Arafat immediately unleashed the Second Intifada. This proved much more costly to Israel than the first, involving as it did a multitude of suicide bombers and attacks with vehicles full of explosives. The dead included Israelis of all religions, Jews, Christians, and Muslims, as well as tourists. Between September 29, 2000, and June 4, 2003, 820 Israelis were killed and nearly 5,000 were wounded. Israeli Arab demonstrations in northern Israel in sympathy with the West Bank led to riots by hundreds of Jews in response. In response, Israel began building a fence to shut off the West Bank and prevent the infiltration of suicide and car bombers into Israel. The fence, constructed of concrete where cross-border gunfire was a possibility, and of multilayered wire elsewhere, has reduced suicide bombings by 80 percent to 90 percent. This was accompanied by a large-scale military operation by the IDF, which assumed control and freedom of action in all parts of the West Bank.

These events persuaded many Israelis that the land-for-peace enterprise, support for which had always come most decisively from the political left, had failed. The Israeli right recovered support, and the conservative government of Ariel Sharon was elected in 2001. The movement toward a two-state solution was not, however, entirely dead. In 2003, Sharon's government as one of its last acts undertook a unilateral withdrawal from the Gaza Strip, ceding it to the control of the Palestinian Authority without demanding any corresponding concessions. Twenty-one Jewish settlements, with a total population of about four thousand, were dismantled with compensation, and the IDF left Gaza, retaining control only over its external communications with the rest of Israel.

Insofar as this policy was intended as a step toward realizing the Oslo project of a final settlement achieved through the creation of a unified self-governing Palestinian political entity, it was not very successful. The main Palestinian party, Fatah, lost the Gaza election of 2006 to the Islamist organization Hamas but refused to surrender power. The result was the so-called Battle of Gaza, June 10–15, 2007. Vicious hostilities between Hamas fighters and the Fatah-controlled National Security Forces erupted, beginning with Hamas militants throwing Mohamed Sweirky, an officer in the elite Palestinian Presidential Guard, from the top of a twelve-story apartment building. On June 14, the new leader of the PLO, Mahmoud Abbas, dissolved the Palestinian-Hamas unity government; on June 15, Hamas completed its control over Gaza, which it has exercised ever since.

Hamas immediately began to use that power to conduct a variety of offensive operations against Israel, mainly by firing rockets (1,500 of which were fired at the Israeli city of Sderot between December 27, 2007, and January 2008, for example), by tunneling into Israel with a view to infiltrating armed fighters, and by smuggling weapons into Gaza. The stress created by these attacks in nearby Israeli towns led Israel in 2008 to launch Operation Cast Lead. This involved aerial bombardment of weapons caches as well as police stations and political and administrative buildings in the densely populated cities of Gaza, Khan Younis, and Rafah, followed by a ground campaign. These actions resulted in a temporary fall in civilian deaths in Israel but no real change in the status quo.

In June 2009, Prime Minister Benjamin Netanyahu made a speech offering a negotiated agreement with the Palestinians, offering the establishment of a demilitarized Palestinian state conditional on the recognition of Israel as a Jewish state. The leadership of the PLO rejected these terms.

With no changes in the status quo and Hamas continuing to fire rockets into southern Israel, the IDF launched Operation Pillar of Defense (November 2012) with the killing of Ahmed Jabari (1960–2012), chief of the military wing of Hamas. Just days before, one hundred rockets had been launched into Israel. During the operation, nearly 1,500 more rockets fell. Egypt mediated a cease-fire, announced a week after the operation began. In December, maintaining its bravura in the face of IDF attacks, Hamas, through its leader Khaled Mishal (1956–), called for Israel's elimination.[9]

In 2014, following a rocket assault from Gaza that reached Tel Aviv and Ben Gurion Airport, the IDF launched a further attack, Operation Protective Edge, in which two thousand Gazans died, at least twenty-three of whom, including alleged Israeli collaborators and street protesters against Hamas, were summarily executed by Hamas,[10] while Israel lost sixty-six soldiers and seven civilians.

QUESTIONS OF WARRANT

The history of relations between Israel and the Palestinians since 1948 is plainly a profoundly unhappy and regrettable one: a history of missed opportunities and human waste. Our business here, however, is to inquire whether it provides adequate warrant, both moral and intellectual, for the main claims of contemporary anti-Zionism, including the BDS movement.

Briefly, these are that Israel, and by extension all those Jews and non-Jews who support it, bear overwhelming responsibility for evils that are so far in excess of those perpetrated by other states and political organizations and that are so intimately related to the nature of Israel as a *Jewish* state as to render morally imperative the replacement of Israel, at least in its present form as a Jewish-majority state, by a majority Muslim Arab state in which political control would pass to the Palestinian Arab community and in which Jews, though they would remain as a minority group, would be deprived of the right to exercise political autonomy.

We argued earlier, in chapter 6, that these claims, when spelled out in detail, appear to embody versions of all the main tenets of political antisemitism. But we also noted, following Gordon Allport's definition of the term *prejudice*, that whether a complaint against X or Y is an expression of prejudice depends conceptually on whether it is warranted by the facts concerning X or Y. Hence, in addressing the question of whether current anti-Zionism embodies a version of political antisemitism, we cannot avoid the issue of whether and how far its claims are warranted.

In chapter 7, we pursued that issue in the context of the political narrative, popular on the left in Western societies, that seeks to represent Israel, both in its origins and in its present-day character, as a colonial settler or apartheid state. And we argued that that narrative is in multiple ways too remote from the facts to withstand serious critical scrutiny.[11]

Similar charges can be, and are, brought against Israel, however, in terms of its treatment of those Palestinian Arabs who left the new country in 1948. We must also consider these claims if we are to arrive at a final verdict on whether and to what extent anti-Zionism and BDS are to be regarded as antisemitic movements.

ISRAEL AND THE "TWO-STATE SOLUTION"

The charges against Israel that arise in connection with its relations, over the past seventy years, with Palestinian Arabs lacking Israeli citizenship are a diverse collection, though for the most part, they focus on relationships between Israel, the West Bank, and Gaza since 1967. One very common charge is that Israel, in contrast to its own concern for Jewish political autonomy, has consistently shown itself unwilling to tolerate the existence of an equally autonomous and self-governing Palestinian state.

This charge fails to square either with the readiness of the Yishuv to accept partition in 1947 or with the willingness of Barak, at a point of political desperation for the Israeli left, to offer Arafat 90 percent to 95 percent of the West Bank as a Palestinian state; nor does it square with Sharon's unilateral withdrawal from the Gaza Strip in 2003–4, leaving it entirely under Palestinian control; or for that matter, with Israel's readiness to exchange the entire Sinai Peninsula for peace in its 1979 negotiations with Egypt. It is also perfectly true, as is often observed by pro-Israel campaigners, that Israel is the only state that has ever shown the slightest interest in conferring a state on the Palestinians. The Hashemite Kingdom of Jordan, for example, was in control of the West Bank for almost twenty years (1948–67) but never in all that time considered offering its Arab inhabitants self-government.

It must be said, moreover, in accordance with Lord Caradon's reading of Resolution 242, that in the phrase "land for peace," the important words are "for peace." One effect, both of the Second Intifada and of the rise to power of Hamas in Gaza, has been to suggest to people skeptical of the validity of the liberal-left worldview, both inside and outside Israel, that Palestinians in the Occupied Territories are no longer interested in paying the price for a state of their own *if that price is to include guaranteeing the future peace and security of*

THE LEGACY OF 1967

Israel as a Jewish state. Unfortunately, recent polls confirm that impression. In 2015, a poll for the Palestine Center for Policy and Survey Research found that only 48 percent of Palestinians support the two-state solution while 51 percent oppose it. The director of the poll, Khalil Shikaki, also notes the existence of widespread anger at the Arab states, "as the overwhelming majority believes that Arabs no longer care about the fate of the Palestinians." Palestinian mistrust of the Arab states has indeed deep roots in the appalling but (in the West) largely unreported treatment meted out to them elsewhere in the Arab world since 1948. This troubled relationship, according to the Palestinian writer and journalist Khaled Abu Toameh and others, has involved sufferings far exceeding anything encountered by Arab residents of the West Bank.[12]

This sense of isolation and lack of sympathy or support in the wider Arab world on the part of the Palestinian Arab population outside Israel proper seems to have fed a mood of desperation unsympathetic to the idea of peace with Israel. More worryingly still, the poll mentioned above showed equal support (35%) for the Fatah party of Mahmoud Abbas, presently in control of the Palestinian Authority in the West Bank, and for Hamas. The author of the Reuters report on the poll, Ali Sawafta, notes also that the poll revealed "deep seated mistrust of Abbas and the Palestinian leadership and growing support for armed conflict with Israel."[13] That mistrust, frequently reported elsewhere, suggests to many in Israel that a Palestinian state in the West Bank, far from assuring peace to Israel, would very soon fall under the control of Hamas, as Gaza has done. Those fears are further exacerbated by the tendency of the Fatah and Hamas leadership to compete in the Arabic-language media in giving an impression of militancy. For instance, in an Arabic-language interview aired on the *State of Politics* program on Palestinian TV, on December 26, 2016, Az-zam al-Ahmed, a Fatah Central Committee member, assures the interviewer that a Palestinian state in the West Bank would simply be a stepping-stone to a Palestinian conquest of all of Israel, taking as his directing analogy the North Vietnamese conquest of South Vietnam.[14]

This toxic cocktail of historic rejection and bloodcurdling rhetoric, together with incessant and frequently lethal attacks on Israeli civilians, has unsurprisingly led Israeli opinion to conclude that lacking a reliable partner, the program of ceding land for peace is for all practical purposes dead—a deeply depressing conclusion that nevertheless at present extends across the bulk of the political spectrum. As a recent Israeli commentator puts it:

> Israelis want peace with their neighbors—there is no doubt in my mind about that. But both the government and the opposition have joined arms in the chorus of despair that there is no partner on the other side. It is amazing to

hear the same chorus of despair on the other side, with the exact same words and the very same discourse regarding the lack of new leadership.

What is needed to break the myth of no partner is for genuine alternative leaders to build the partnership, even if this must be done from the ground up. [But] I do not see alternative leadership when their [the Israeli opposition's] political discourse is only one or two shades lighter than Netanyahu's.[15]

The present impasse is no doubt regrettable, and it is clearly harmful to both sides; however, there appears to be very little factual basis for the widespread tendency in large sections of the Western media to blame that impasse exclusively on Israeli intransigence.

SECURITY BARRIERS

In the absence of a peace agreement with the Palestinian political leadership, Israeli policy, in the almost two decades since the collapse of the Camp David talks in 2000, has turned to piecemeal efforts to contain Palestinian violence by whatever means happen to come to hand. Such means have included, among others, the security wall around large parts of the West Bank and the Israeli blockade of Gaza. These have resulted in substantial decreases in suicide bombings and other attacks within Israel proper. Equally plainly, there is a cost, mainly to the Palestinians, in restricting economic activity. Palestinians resident in the West Bank who travel into Israel to work meet with frequent delays and obstructions. The reservation of certain roads for the sole use of Israeli citizens makes it necessary for West Bank residents to make lengthy detours. The security barrier does not everywhere follow the "green line" that marks the position of the opposing forces at the end of hostilities in 1948, but cuts beyond it at a number of points, primarily to protect Jewish settlements. Palestinian villages find themselves cut off by the barrier from parts of their land. The list of Arab grievances, in other words, is lengthy. To that extent, the building of the West Bank security barrier has been, to say the least, undesirable, since it manifestly does not advance the cause of peace between the two communities.

Still worse is the situation of Gaza. Hamas is a branch of the Muslim Brotherhood, an organization proscribed by the Egyptian government in the aftermath of the civil war that erupted in Egypt in 2013 between supporters and opponents of the Muslim Brotherhood government of Mohamed Morsi. In consequence, Gaza is blockaded from the Egyptian side as well.

The charges leveled against Israel in connection with these barriers tend to focus on two aspects of the policy. The first concerns separation itself.

It is conventional in anti-Zionist circles to refer to the West Bank barrier as the "apartheid wall" and to suggest that its point, in line with the policies of the apartheid regime in South Africa, is really to prevent the allegedly inferior Palestinian population from mingling with the supposedly superior Jewish population of Israel. This, of course, ignores both the fact that those populating the Occupied Territories are not citizens of Israel and the fact that 20 percent to 25 percent of the population of Israel consists of non-Jews, including a large Muslim Arab component, who enjoy the full range of civil rights, including the vote, the right to form political parties, and so on.

A second accusation is that the barriers in effect create ghettos within which economic conditions are far harder and the standard of living much lower than they are in Israel itself. A problem with this charge is that Palestinian Arabs in the West Bank (since the formation in 1994 of the Palestinian Authority in accordance with the provisions of the Oslo Accords of that year between the PLO and the State of Israel) enjoy a large measure of political autonomy in civil matters and even some autonomous control over security-related issues in many Palestinian urban areas. Economic activity in the areas controlled by the Palestinian Authority consists mainly in family-based small business. About half the budget of the Palestinian Authority is supplied by foreign aid; much of it, since 1948, funneled through the United Nations Relief and Works Agency for Palestine Refugees in the Near East (UNRWA). No such organization exists to support the equivalent number of Jewish refugees forced out of Near Eastern countries after 1948, who have simply been absorbed into other countries, notably Israel. Only about 14 percent of the UNRWA budget comes from the Muslim world. "As recently as 1994, Israel contributed more to UNRWA than all Arab countries except Saudi Arabia, Kuwait and Morocco" but since then has contributed mainly through its UN dues.[16] From time to time, however, Israel makes large contributions to balance the Palestinian Authority budget despite the fact that since 40 percent of the Palestinian Authority budget is spent in Gaza, some of that money will inevitably go to support Hamas.[17] Despite the losses incurred from the intifadas, continued individual terror attacks, and the repeated barrages of rockets from Gaza, "Israel provides most of the electric supply for both the West Bank and the Gaza Strip. Approximately half of Gaza's supply is supplied directly from Israel by way of the Israel Electric Corporation (IEC). The remaining supply comes mostly from the Gaza Power Plant, which is funded not by Hamas but by the Palestinian Authority."[18] Israel also provides extensive medical care to Palestinians from both territories. "In 2009 alone, some 10,544 patients and their companions left Gaza for medical treatment inside Israel."[19]

It is also widely admitted that much of the economic weakness of the Palestinian Authority, despite the existence of a UN agency uniquely tasked with
affording it massive financial support, is to be blamed on corruption. As the
British political weekly *The Economist* noted in 2015, "The Palestinian Authority (PA), the limited self-governing body in the occupied territories, has been
plagued by waste, graft and accusations of both since its inception in 1994
following the Oslo Accords. When auditors looked at the books three years
later, they concluded that nearly 40% of the budget had been frittered away.
By 2006, according to the PA's own attorney-general, officials had embezzled
some $700m."[20]

In Gaza, as a result of the Israeli withdrawal in 2003 and the Battle of Gaza
in 2007, Hamas enjoys complete political autonomy, although its relationships
with the Palestinian Authority in the West Bank have been and remain for the
most part hostile. This conflict as well as the use by Hamas of the territory
primarily as a base for rocket and tunnel-based attacks on Israel have naturally damaged the economic life of the enclave and would have done so even
if communication with Israel and the outside world were not limited (though
by no means entirely cut off) by Israeli and Egyptian control of its border. The
economic potential of the Gaza Strip nevertheless remains considerable, and
Israel has, in fact, formally offered to build on that potential for the benefit of
the Palestinian population in exchange for demilitarization. Of this offer, the
Arab journalist and scholar Bassam Tawil had this to say in February 2017:

> The Palestinian Islamic movement Hamas has once again demonstrated its
> priorities: killing Jews. That clearly takes precedence over easing the plight of
> the two million Palestinians living under its rule in the Gaza Strip.
>
> Since Hamas violently seized control of the Gaza Strip in the summer of
> 2007, the conditions of the Palestinians living there have gone from bad to
> worse. Crisis after crisis has hit those under the Hamas rule; electricity and
> water as well as lack of medicine and proper medical care are in dangerously
> short supply.
>
> Disputes between Hamas and the Palestinian Authority have left the
> Gaza Strip dangerously short of fuel, resulting in massive power outages.
> Palestinians there consequently have had to resort to using wood for cooking
> and heating. Hamas, which has brought about three wars that wreaked havoc
> on its people, is unable to provide them with basic needs.
>
> Last week, Hamas received an offer that no sane entity would turn down.
> It is to be noted that the offer did not come from Hamas's friends and allies
> in Iran and the Arab and Islamic world. Rather, the offer, which promises
> to turn the Gaza Strip, where most residents live in the poverty of "refugee
> camps," into "the Singapore of the Middle East," came from Israel.

Specifically, the offer was made by Israeli Defense Minister Avigdor
Lieberman, who proposed building a seaport and an airport, as well as
industrial zones that would help create 40,000 jobs in the Gaza Strip, if
Hamas agreed to demilitarization and to dismantling the tunnels and rocket
systems it has built up.

"The Gazans must understand that Israel, which withdrew from the
Gaza Strip to the last millimeter, is not the source of their suffering—it is
the Hamas leadership, which doesn't take their needs into consideration,"
Lieberman said in a televised message to the residents of the Gaza Strip.
"The moment Hamas gives up its tunnels and rockets, we'll be the first to
invest."

Only Israel has ever made such an offer to Hamas. Such a plan would vastly
improve the living conditions of the Gaza Strip population. All Hamas is
required to do is abandon its weapons and plans to kill Jews, and return the
bodies of missing Israeli soldiers.[21]

Although Lieberman's proposal is hardly likely to meet with any such response from Hamas, it forms part and parcel of a growing sense in Israel that
economics may be the key to ending the present cycle of terrorism and limited
war. As a 2014 op-ed in the *Jewish Journal* puts it,

In the wake of this summer's war between Israel and Hamas, it is evident that
neither party achieved its military or political objectives. And while a cease-
fire is currently in place, fundamental steps to resolve the conflict aren't on
the agenda. Given a history of costly and recurrent armed conflict, it is clear
that both parties are in need of a paradigm shift.

Perhaps it is time to give economics a chance. Both Israelis and
Palestinians would be well served by aggressive efforts in economic
development of the West Bank and Gaza. This idea is not new. In 2013,
U.S. Secretary of State John Kerry proposed a plan to invest $4 billion in
the West Bank. Currently, a sparkling, privately developed Palestinian new
town called Rawabi, replete with amphitheater, piazzas and multiplex theater,
is about to open in the West Bank. Israeli social-impact entrepreneurs are
seeking to bring venture capital and high-tech success to the West Bank.
Discussions are also underway for an economic federation encompassing
Israel, the Palestinian Authority and Jordan that would bolster trade,
tourism, economic development and energy deployment for the benefit of
all three parties.

A broad-based initiative for economic development of the West Bank
and Gaza could take a page out of the post–World War II U.S. Marshall
Plan playbook. The program provided $160 billion (2014 dollars) for the
reconstruction of a war-ravaged Europe. The plan included a rebuilding

of infrastructure and trade, amelioration of hunger and poverty, creation of economic opportunity and suppression of competing Soviet economic doctrines.[22]

In short, whatever the effects may be of the security barriers on the economies of the West Bank and Gaza, there is little reason to believe either that Israel intends these effects *for their own sake* or that it is not prepared to do all it can, consonant with its security needs, to relieve them.

Those who hold that Israel is a criminal state that should not be allowed to exist, at least as a majority-Jewish state, still have two arguments to field. One concerns the alleged inhumanity of Israel's conduct of the three brief actions against Hamas in Gaza since 2006: Operation Cast Lead (2008), Operation Pillar of Defense (2012), and Operation Protective Edge (2014). The other concerns the alleged incompatibility with international law of Israel's continued construction of predominantly Jewish settlements in part of the West Bank. I will consider them in that order.

The three Gaza operations are commonly asserted to have shown criminal disregard for civilian deaths and casualties on the Palestinian side and to have done so because they used disproportionate force against Hamas units operating in the midst of a heavily built and densely populated human landscape. It is to the advantage of anti-Zionism and BDS, which are primarily movements of the extreme or hard left, that such charges are frequently articulated by liberal or centrist media organizations such as the BBC, the *New York Times*, or the *Washington Post*. A number of instances have been collected by two British lawyers and academics, Leslie Klaff and Stephen Riley, in a recent paper:

> For example, on August 23rd 2006, the BBC News website promoted a report by Amnesty International which began: "Amnesty International has accused Israel of war crimes and of deliberately targeting civilian infrastructure." It went on to state the report's conclusions that: "Many of the violations identified in our report are war crimes, including indiscriminate and disproportionate attacks."
> ... Similarly, ... on August 7th, 2014, a BBC World Affairs correspondent produced a film report which quoted a Human Rights Watch representative as saying: "We've seen reports of large amounts of heavy artillery.... The issue is, you know, what are your (sic) targeting policies and when are you going to bring down very heavy attacks on populated areas in an indiscriminate and disproportionate way?"[23]

[In the 2006 conflict, accusations of Israeli war crimes by the BBC] began just eight days into the 2006 Israel-Lebanon War when its News website ran an article headlined: "*UN Warning on Mid-East War Crimes*" and said, "The UN High Commissioner for Human Rights . . . warns that those involved in the spiral of violence between Israel and Lebanon could face war crime charges if they are found to have deliberately attacked civilians."

. . . The BBC has even promoted the claim that Israel's use of disproportionate force involves the *targeted* killing of Palestinian *children*. In October 2014, BBC journalist Kevin Connolly reported on the BBC Radio 4 Today programme the claim of Mustafa Baghouti that "Israel's war crimes included the collective disproportional use of force targeting civilians and targeting children and killing them."[24]

Similar comments have come from senior British politicians: "On 17th July, 2014, the *Guardian* reported comments made by then Deputy Prime Minister, Nick Clegg, that Israel's response to Hamas was 'deliberately disproportionate' and that '[The Israelis] have proved their point.' Israel was 'imposing a disproportionate form of collective punishment' on the citizens of Gaza which was leading to a 'humanitarian crisis' and 'a very great number of deaths.'"[25]

Klaff and Riley conclude that these examples show the UK media (in line with other European media and with sections of the media in the United States) to have promoted, among other things, "the idea that Israel deliberately uses disproportionate or excessive force in order to exact revenge against the Palestinians. This was done in an episode of BBC Radio 5's '5 Live Drive' programme aired on November 14, 2012. The following remarks were made by one of its presenters . . . regarding Operation Pillar of Defence: 'Yeah, you can count up the casualties and see—you know—that Israel always wreaks its revenge, and the revenge it takes is greater than the original—erm—suffering in this war. It does it all the time.'"[26]

To this must be added, on the showing of the above, the promotion of the idea that Israel *deliberately* targets civilians, including children.

Many of the above citations exemplify a left-leaning discourse that certainly, in Dave Rich's phrase, "echoes older anti-Semitic myths about Jews."[27] The ideas involved, that a Jewish state makes it its business *deliberately* to kill enemy children and to exact disproportionate vengeance, of course tap into traditional antisemitic stereotypes. The image of Judaism as a religion of vengeance—represented inter alia by the figure of Shylock in *The Merchant of Venice*—is very ancient in European culture, as is that of Jews as murderers of children. Thus, for instance, the so-called blood libel—absurdly, since the consumption of blood is expressly forbidden by the dietary laws—represents Jews as required by their religion to murder gentile children in order to mix their blood with the meal for the Passover matzo. Such libels are, for that matter, still very much alive in the discourse of sections of both the left and the right across large parts of Europe and the Middle East.[28]

At the same time, as we have consistently argued here, the fact that a given charge echoes the characteristic formulas of a historic form of bigotry does not therefore show it to be false. Our primary purpose, therefore, is to inquire how much substance these charges against Israel actually possess.

When media reports hostile to Israel deploy the term *disproportion*, they generally have in mind one or both of two distinct kinds of inequality: on the one hand, inequality of weaponry, as when one side disposes of air cover, tanks, or armored vehicles, while the other does not; on the other hand, inequality in the number of killed and injured on each side.[29] The trouble with this is that both kinds of inequality are inseparable from war of any kind. On the one hand, one major object of any side in a war is to achieve superiority of weaponry over the other. And on the other hand, it is equally unavoidable that the winning side may, and often will, have suffered far fewer casualties, military and civilian, than the losing side.

The fallacy that what the law of armed conflict understands by the term *proportionality* is a relationship between *numbers of casualties on either side* draws some of its credence from the related belief, also frequently reinforced by journalists, invited experts, and media presenters whenever Israel is in question, that *any civilian death or injury whatsoever* automatically constitutes a war crime. This is not the case. Causing civilian deaths *as such* is not in itself a war crime, again for the obvious reason that civilian deaths are unavoidable in war, especially in modern warfare with its emphasis on airborne attack. UN figures suggest that, on average, the ratio of casualties in close-fought battles in urban and semiurban areas in modern warfare has been three to four civilians for every combatant killed.[30] And even if causing civilian death by military action did per se constitute a war crime, those resulting from military action by Israel in Gaza and Lebanon are dwarfed by the estimated number arising from the long sequence of wars in Iraq, Syria, and Yemen. These conflicts have for the most part involved the ancient intra-Muslim conflict between the Sunni and Shi'a branches of Islam but they have also seen extensive great power intervention from Russia and the coalition of Western nations including the United States and Great Britain. The volunteer organization Iraq Body Count, which collates data from Iraqi Heath Ministry reports, reports of regional morgues, and other reasonably reliable sources, estimates that successive campaigns in Iraq between 2003 and 2017 have led to an overall total of 268,000 violent deaths (including combatants) of which 171,796 to 191,686 were civilian deaths.[31] Other theaters of war in the region have recorded similar or worse figures. What the law of armed conflict actually condemns as a failure to observe proportionality is failure to consider whether the incidental loss of civilian life, civilian injury, or damage to civilian buildings or institutions risked by a given military action *would be excessive or disproportionate in relation to the concrete military advantage anticipated from the action*. As Janina Dill of the Oxford Institute for Ethics, Law, and Armed Conflict explains, "An injury to civilians or damage done to civilian objects as a side-effect of a military operation may be permissible provided that it is proportionate to the military gain to be anticipated from the operation. This principle is considered part of the customary international law, which binds all states. It has become part of the positive law of armed conflict (IHL) with its codification in the First additional Protocol to the Geneva Convention of 1977. Article 51 para 5 states that 'an attack which is expected to cause incidental loss of civilian life, injury to civilians, damage to civilian objects, or a combination thereof which would be excessive in relation to the concrete and direct military advantage anticipated' is prohibited."[32]

The issue of proportionality, at least as regard the international law governing armed conflict, thus reduces to the question: Which of the combatants in Israel's various campaigns since 1967 has done most to observe the above protocol? Powerful support for Israel comes, inter alia, from Col. Richard Kemp's submission to the United Nations Independent Commission of Inquiry on the 2014 Gaza conflict (see endnote 30), Kemp is a distinguished British army officer with long experience both in combat and in intelligence roles involving the monitoring of terrorist groups.

In assessing the military and civilian background to the Gaza conflict, Kemp argues, inter alia:

1. That Israel had no option but to defend its population from armed attack from Gaza;

2. That it chose the form of operation in principle least damaging to civilians, avoiding, for example, the carpet-bombing that has caused so much destruction of civilian infrastructure and loss of civilian life in the Syrian civil war and other recent conflicts in the region, and opting instead for a combination of "precision air and artillery strikes against command and control infrastructure, and a limited ground incursion to locate and destroy . . . tunnels"; and

3. That the location by Hamas of much of its military infrastructure amongst the civilian population of Gaza made it impossible

to neutralize the threat from Hamas without incurring civilian casualties.

Kemp was in a position to witness both the 2008–9 and the 2014 Gaza conflicts in detail and to interview freely many of those involved on the Israeli side, from serving soldiers to senior political and military figures. His conclusions are worth quoting in full.

I have been briefed in detail on the procedures used by the IDF to avoid civilian casualties in Gaza during the 2014 conflict. I previously commented in relation to the 2008–9 Gaza conflict that no army in the history of warfare had taken greater steps than the IDF to minimize harm to civilians in a combat zone. My observations during the 2014 conflict confirmed this. No other army I have served in or alongside or that I have studied and researched has yet taken such precautions. It is in part due to the specific circumstances of the Gaza conflict, which allow the IDF to go to such lengths whereas other armed forces in other situations may not be able to do so.

However, during some operations in Afghanistan, British and US forces adopted some methods developed by the IDF in Gaza. And in November 2014, General Martin Dempsey, Chairman of the US Joint Chiefs of Staff, said that the IDF "went to extraordinary lengths to limit collateral damage and civilian casualties" during the 2014 conflict in Gaza. He revealed that he had sent a delegation of US military officers to Israel to learn about the measures that the IDF took to prevent civilian casualties.[33]

Estimates of the ratio of civilian-to-combatant deaths in Gaza range from 70 percent (Gaza Ministry of Health, under Hamas control) to 48 percent (Meir Amit Intelligence and Terrorism Information Center, an independent research group based in Israel). On either account, in other words, the ratio is markedly lower than in other conflicts. That fact alone suggests that Israel's efforts to keep such deaths to a minimum are effective.

PROPORTIONALITY AND TERROR

On the day-to-day conduct of Hamas and the other terrorist organizations currently representing the population of Gaza, Col. Kemp's verdict echoes that of many other dispassionate observers: "During my time in Israel during this conflict I witnessed what I believe to be a series of war crimes and planned war crimes by Hamas and other Gaza groups, both by missile attack against civilians and by construction of attack tunnels from which to kill and abduct civilians. I am also aware of, but did not witness, Hamas and other groups' use of their own civilian population as human shields."[34]

Use of civilians as human shields by Daesh (ISIL) and many other groups fighting in the present wars in Iraq, Syria, and Yemen has also been widely recorded. These observations serve to underline the evident fact that the choice of terror as a form of warfare makes it automatically and in principle impossible to observe the prohibition of international law regarding proportionality. That choice compels those who make it to dispense, in consistency, with any further concern for civilians of whatever side. Western journalists and media pundits of a certain political persuasion tend to draw a veil over the extent to which suicide bombing, nowadays a favorite, not to say iconic method of conducting terror campaigns around the world, involves in many cases a further level of crime—namely, the corruption and manipulation of the vulnerable, including large numbers of young children—the very crime, in fact, of child-murder, of which Israel is freely accused at present by so many voices on the anti-Zionist, BDS-supporting left.

There is a further relevant difference between Israel and Hamas. Israel is a parliamentary democracy with the rule of law, freedom of speech and assembly, and political opposition fully guaranteed. It therefore has both a motive and the institutional means necessary to learn from outside criticism and to adjust its practice accordingly; and it does. Hamas has neither and does not. In 2009, Richard Goldstone, a former South African supreme court judge and hero of the struggle against apartheid, chaired on behalf of the UN Human Rights Council a fact-finding inquiry into the Gaza war of 2008–9. The conclusions of that report accused both Hamas and Israel of war crimes, in the latter case involving the military use of white phosphorus in populated areas. In 2011, however, Goldstone published a partial recantation of these conclusions, asserting that "if I had known then what I now know, the Goldstone Report would have been a different document."[35] His reasons are in part those contained in the following paragraph:

> Our main recommendation was for each party to investigate, transparently and in good faith, the incidents referred to in our report. McGowan Davis has found that Israel has done this to a significant degree; Hamas has done nothing.
>
> Our report has led to numerous "lessons learned" and policy changes, including the adoption of new Israel Defence Forces procedures for protecting civilians in cases of urban warfare and limiting the use of white phosphorus in civilian areas. The Palestinian Authority established an independent inquiry into our allegations of human rights abuses— assassinations, torture and illegal detentions—perpetrated by Fatah in the West Bank, especially against members of Hamas. Most of these allegations were confirmed by this inquiry. Regrettably, there has been no effort by

Hamas in Gaza to investigate the allegations of its war crimes and possible crimes against humanity.[36]

To those on the extreme left wing of present-day Western politics, it seems, any action whatsoever on the part of groups like Hamas is cleansed of whatever moral or legal opprobrium might otherwise cling to it by its notionally representing resistance against the crimes of Israel. There is, as we have already pointed out, an evident circularity in a position that posits crime on both sides of a moral equation while assigning justification only to one. But there is worse at stake. You cannot at one and the same time romanticize actions that simply brush aside any concern for proportionality, as that is currently understood by international law, *and at the same time accuse others of disregarding it*. At that point, you have lost all moral credibility. And if on top of that the latter accusations turn out to be specious, you have lost all factual credibility as well. But the first step into this morass is the important one. That is most evident in the case of Western self-described liberals, such as the British Liberal Democrat politician Baroness Tonge, who defend suicide bombing as if it were not largely carried out at the expense of the manipulation and murder of children, especially young girls. With this step, like it or not, the soi-disant liberal has opted for the ancient and tempting idea that there are political goals so morally commanding that they justify *anything whatsoever*, however immoral. But that is the point at which the claims of the liberal conscience collapse into incoherence. One cannot, that is, *in the same breath* both condemn the death of children in warfare and exult in their murder for political ends.

THE SETTLEMENTS QUESTION

The establishment of Israeli settlements in the West Bank, the Golan Heights and the Gaza Strip (the latter now all dismantled) as a result of the territorial gains of 1967, has become a major weapon in the armory of those disposed to regard Israel as a criminal or illegitimate state. It is claimed that these settlements are "illegal under international law," that they constitute an obstacle to peace, and they threaten to make a two-state solution to the Israeli-Palestinian solution possible.[37]

The actual facts of the situation are sufficiently complex and the legal basis of the appeal to international law sufficiently flimsy to render all of these claims far less secure than the degree of conviction with which they are held and daily repeated, by politicians, international bodies, academics, nongovernmental and church organizations, and much of the Western media, might tempt one to suppose.

First, a little more history. On July 24, 1922, the Council of the League of Nations, which at that time consisted of fifty-one countries, agreed a mandate for Palestine (not to be confused either with the Balfour Doctrine or the British Mandate) that became operational on September 29, 1923. The Mandate for Palestine created a legal right for Jews to settle anywhere in western Palestine, understanding by that the entire ten thousand square miles between the Jordan River and the Mediterranean. Since the mandate survived the demise of the League of Nations and is implicitly recognized by Article 80 of the United Nations charter, its provisions remain legally valid down to the present day.

As a result, during the period of the British Mandate in the 1920s and 1930s, Jewish settlements came into being throughout the entire area west of the Jordan, including what came to be known post-1948 as the West Bank. In 1948, their inhabitants, fleeing the advance of the Arab armies, evacuated these settlements. Since the areas containing them had not been recovered by the time of the armistice, they remained unoccupied until 1967.

After the 1967 war, Jews began to return to their former areas of settlement beyond the 1948 armistice line (the green line). For strategic reasons, in order to maintain defensible borders for the future, the Labor Party of the time also created twenty-one settlements along the Jordan Valley and the eastern slopes of Samaria. In all, a number of settlements have since been created. They are for the most part not situated in the areas of the West Bank (A and B) including the bulk of Arab towns and villages, assigned to the control of the Palestinian Authority under the Oslo Accords of 1993–95, but in Area C, covering Jewish settlements, uninhabited land, and Israeli military outposts. The Jewish settlements themselves had for the most part been established either on land that had been owned by preexisting Jewish communities prior to 1948, or on desert land that was unowned (i.e., controlled by Jordan but with no private owners) or on land purchased from established owners. There is thus very little to be said for the frequently heard view that land for the settlements has been "confiscated" from Arab owners or that Arabs have been "forced off the land" by Jewish settlement east of the green line. The Arab towns and villages of the West Bank, in Areas A and B, not to mention a number of villages in Area C, remain where they have always stood with their inhabitants.

There are 121 settlements of this kind recognized by the Israeli government, with 350,000 inhabitants, including several towns of considerable size, including Mod'n Illit (55,000), Beitar Illit (42,000), and Ma'ale Adunim (36,000). There are also around one hundred tiny independent settlements not authorized by the government of Israel. Depending on their location and their legal position relative to land ownership, these are often tolerated by the government. But in a number of cases in which settlements have been declared illegal by the Israeli courts, usually on grounds of having been built on Arab-owned land, such settlements have been forcibly dismantled and the settlers evicted by the police and IDF. The tiny hilltop settlement of Amona, demolished in February 2017, is at time of writing the most recent of these cases.[38]

Is there, as is often supposed, a valid basis in international law for considering all the Israeli settlements on land occupied in 1967 as illegal? Although it is frequently asserted that the international community is of one mind on this question, there are dissenters. In 2014, Julie Bishop, the Australian minister for foreign affairs, famously questioned the consensus: "Asked whether she agrees or disagrees with the near-universal view that Israeli settlements anywhere beyond the 1967 lines are illegal under international law, she replied: 'I would like to see which international law has declared them illegal.'"[39]

The argument for the illegality of these settlements under international law rests in fact on the slender basis of one clause—Article 49—in the Fourth Geneva Convention of 1949. Article 49 forbids the transfer of population to occupied territories. It states: "The Occupying Power shall not deport or transfer parts of its own civilian population into the territory it occupies." It was originally intended to forbid both the transfer of the civilian population of one state into the conquered territory of another and the transfer of parts of that population abroad for purposes of forced labor or extermination, as happened to Jews and others in World War II.

One problem with applying Article 49 to the case of the settlements in the West Bank is that neither in 1967 nor at present could the land supposedly occupied be said to constitute part of the territory of another state. Jordan indeed claimed, between 1950 and 1967, to have annexed the area now called the West Bank, but in the absence of any prior Jordanian title to the territory, the international community did not accept this claim as valid. No political entity or state, that is to say, has possessed title or sovereignty over the land since the days of the Ottoman Empire. The West Bank is therefore better regarded, those who think like Julie Bishop would argue, as "disputed" land rather than as land "occupied" in the sense relevant to Article 49. And that has always been Israel's position. Israel could not, that is to say, "return the land to its rightful owners" because there simply is not, nor has there been since the collapse of Ottoman rule, any rightful owner. In effect, the land remains part of what the League of Nations Mandate for Palestine designated as "West Palestine"—that is, part of the area in which Jews have, under the terms of the mandate, a legal right to settle. This they have done, since 1967, on an individual basis. There has been no question, that is to say, of people being "deported or transferred" into the West Bank by Israeli government decree.

Do the settlements, as is often maintained, hinder—or as is even more frequently asserted, tend increasingly to render impossible—any agreement between Israel and Palestine on a two-state solution? Israel's official position has always been that the resolution of the settlement question requires prior agreement on the two-state solution, for the simple reason that until a Palestinian state actually exists and agreed boundaries are finally drawn up, all of the land conquered by Israel in 1967 remains disputed.

At the same time, the issue of the settlements remains intensely politically controversial within Israel itself. An Israeli friend and fellow philosopher, to whom I sent this chapter and the two flanking it for comment, although he found its arguments generally persuasive, disagreed strongly with what I have just said concerning the legitimacy of the settlements. Interestingly, he was prepared to agree with my main point, which is that opposition to the settlements lacks the basis in international law generally attributed to it. His own view, however, is that the movement to build and expand settlements in the West Bank—many of which, he contends, were built in places never previously inhabited by Jews—was from the outset expressly intended by politicians on the Israeli right to subvert any possibility of a Palestinian state being constructed in the future, and that in consequence the settlements, though possibly there may be no legal argument against them, are nevertheless politically and morally indefensible. He himself looks back with dismay to the failure of the Camp David negotiations and continues to believe that Barak was right to hold, even after that failure, that Israel should unilaterally withdraw from some of these settlements. "All in all," he says, "I think that the settlements are one thing on which Israel, alas, cannot be defended. Israel was ready to evacuate many of them in the failed Camp David negotiations, and of course the Arab refusal paved the way to our own extremists."

This last remark well illustrates, as do those of the *Jerusalem Post* journalist Gershon Baskin cited earlier (see note 15), the problems created for the liberal center of Israeli politics by refusal of the Arab leadership to name any conditions for the ending of violence against Israel. The Arab commitment to permanent low-level guerilla war, whatever the costs and whatever the consequences, naturally pushes opinion in Israel to the right and leaves centrist liberals like my friend, who remain perfectly prepared like Barak, to envisage paying a very heavy price for peace, feeling isolated and hopeless. But that, for the moment, is how things stand.

SECURITY AND THE "ONE-STATE SOLUTION"

While it seems clear to many people that guaranteed security for Israel is an essential precondition for any final settlement of the Israeli-Palestinian conflict, there is a persistent tendency among supporters of anti-Zionism/BDS to talk as if the demand for security expressed a quasi-paranoid obsession on the part of Jewish Israelis. What is suggested by such people is that while this obsession may find some support in the twentieth-century sufferings of Jews in Europe, it retains little if any relevance to the conditions of the Middle East or the present day. Part and parcel with this is the idea, increasingly canvassed by academics on the political left and others, that the cause of peace might best be served by the amalgamation of all the territories between the Jordan and the sea into a single state. This is the so-called one-state solution. A fair sample of current opinion among supporters of this project can be found in *After Zionism: One State for Israel and Palestine*, a recent volume of essays by a collection of journalists and academics, edited by two journalists, the Australian Antony Loewenstein and the Palestinian American Ahmed Moor.[40]

The amalgamation of the Arab populations of the West Bank and Gaza with that of present-day Israel into a single state would of course result in a polity in which Jews, since they would compose merely a large minority in a Muslim-majority state, could no longer expect to constitute an independent, politically autonomous community. The one-state version of Israel, even if it continued to bear that name, would no longer, that is to say, be a *Jewish* state.

Effectively, this would reverse the consequences of the War of Independence and give the present leadership of the Palestinians precisely what they have always demanded: a Palestinian state covering the whole of western Palestine. While the international community and a range of nongovernmental organizations have long contended for a two-state solution, with the guiding assumption that this would at least be acceptable to the Palestinians as a basis for ending armed conflict with Israel, it has long been an open secret that there is little support for any such program on the Palestinian side. Schools in the West Bank and Gaza habitually use textbooks that present the ultimate goal of the Palestinian struggle as the reconquest of the whole of Palestine. These books contain maps that label Haifa, Jaffa, and Tiberias as Palestinian cities, relabel Jewish holy sites as Muslim ones, and deny both the historic connection of Jews with Palestine and the presence of a Jewish population in Palestine throughout recent history, preferring to represent Zionism as a colonialist movement involving solely European Jews.[41]

Despite all this, the contributors to *After Zionism* seem for the most part persuaded that there is no reason why Jewish cultural life in an Arab-Muslim-majority successor state to Israel should not continue, unhindered by loss of Jewish political autonomy. One of them, Jeremiah Haber (the pen name of Charles H. Manekin, a professor of philosophy at the University of Maryland), articulates this vision of things as follows:

> Jewish cultural centrality can be a feature of a state whose population is overwhelmingly Israeli Jewish, but it can also be a feature of one "Abrahamic" state from the Jordan to the Mediterranean. Clearly in the latter state, Palestinian Arab culture would also play an equally central role. I would still call that bi-national state a *Jewish* state, indeed *the* Jewish state, though not the *exclusively* Jewish state, because of the centrality of Jewish culture. Yet whatever the configuration of the Jewish state, a civic national cultural identity of all its citizens would also be fostered. Once again one's ethnicity or religion would not be an integral notion of the state's nationalism. It is not likely, for example, that Palestinian Arab Muslims will feel comfortable with adopting a Jewish national identity, because of the religious dissonance, but there is not reasons [*sic*] why they cannot adopt an Israeli or "Abrahamic" nationalism. And indeed, despite the absence of official Israeli national identity, it very much exists today among the 600,000 [*sic*[42]] Palestinian Arab Israelis.[43]

Several obvious aspects of the present situation would seem to challenge the plausibility of any such proposal. Manekin is no doubt broadly correct, as we noted earlier, that an Israeli national identity "exists today among . . . Palestinian Arab Israelis." We offered a number of concrete examples of that phenomenon in chapter 7, and no doubt there are more to be found. But all that that shows is the degree to which Israel has been successful in extending a sense of common community and nationality to its non-Jewish citizens (to put it bluntly, the degree to which it is *not*, and never has been, an apartheid state). And that in turn draws attention to two further salient features of the situation. The first is that Israel is in the full sense a democratic civil society: that is to say, a society based on participatory democracy, with freedom of speech and assembly, and with a wide range of other civil rights, governed by the rule of law. The second is that in all these respects, Israel is unique in the region. In all of the region's Muslim-majority states, authoritarianism cloaked by a thin and well-controlled veneer of democracy has immemorially been the order of the day, along with a widespread contempt for human rights in general and the rights of minorities in particular.

In 2010–11, when most of the essays in *After Zionism* were doubtless in preparation, two events were much in the news: the opening of the so-called Arab

Spring and the Obama administration's attempt at a "resetting" of relations between America and the Islamic world, particularly Iran. The first, in particular,
was widely expected to initiate a historic movement toward the realization of
Western-style political ideals. The opening of an essay by Omar Barghouti, a
Qatari-born resident of Israel and one of the founders of the BDS movement,
calling for a "secular democratic state in historic Palestine," captures the spirit
of these expectations: "The ongoing popular revolutions in the Arab world are
ushering in a new phase, one which may break the rusty but still formidable
imperial and neoliberal fetters that have consciously, systematically, and struc-
turally inhibited human development throughout the Arab region. As well as
its anticipated emancipatory impact, this process of radical transformation, or
what I call a prelude to an Arab resistance, promises to further the struggle for
ethical decolonisation in historic Palestine."[44]

Unfortunately, these hopes have been dashed by events. The Arab Spring,
far from furthering hopes for the spread of civil rights and democracy, has
vastly increased the power and influence of a range of radical Islamist groups
of which ISIL (or Daesh) is the best known. At the same time, the policies of
the Obama administration in relieving Iran to a great extent from sanctions
while withdrawing American power from the region as a whole have merely
allowed the Iranian regime to engage destructively in the series of wars, largely
representing a struggle for power between the Sunni and Shi'a powers, which
have now engulfed the entire region from Libya to Yemen, leading to immense
civilian losses (approaching 500,000 in Syria alone) and producing vast flows
of refugees.

A still greater difficulty for supporters of the one-state solution west of the
Jordan is the level of persecution of minorities, especially Yazidis and Christians (there being no, or very few, Jews left to persecute), but including Shi'as at
the hands of Sunnis and Sunnis at the hands of Shi'as, perpetrated by all sides in
this conflict. The normalizing of minority ethnic and religious persecution on
an everyday basis across the region makes it difficult to believe that the Jewish
population, let alone "Jewish cultural centrality," could survive the collapse of
Israel as a Jewish state. In addition, a major constant in the checkered history
of Palestine since the fall of the Ottoman Empire, has been, as we have seen in
previous chapters, the settled will of the Palestinian Arab leadership to bring
Jewish settlement in Palestine to an end: to "drive the Jews into the sea." There
is abundant published evidence that that remains the purpose of leading figures
in both Hamas and Fatah—a purpose ceaselessly reformulated and affirmed in
Arabic-language speeches and articles even while it is being denied for Western
consumption. Why on earth should Hamas or Fatah, finding that goal finally

within their grasp, relinquish it at the behest of a piping chorus of bien-pensant Western liberal voices in academia and the media?

Another thing worth considering—although it is seldom or never mentioned—is the situation of the 25 percent to 30 percent of Israeli citizens who happen not to be Jewish. Hamas secures itself in power by, among other things, frequent summary executions of those it considers to be spies of or collaborators with Israel. Israel is nowadays awash with people of Palestinian descent who would doubtless, to any competently conducted Hamas investigation, fall into that category. What would their fate be if Israel were to collapse as a Jewish state? Would the international community step in to save them? The international community, if we take that to include Russia, the United States, Great Britain, France, and others, is, as I write, pursuing, against various adversaries in the region, a war—or rather several wars—mainly conducted from the air and hence productive of very large numbers of civilian casualties, while at the same time demonstrating its continued and utter inability to prevent hideous atrocities against Yazidis, Christians, Baha'i, and other minority groups across the region. Why should a further wave of minority deaths do more than prompt a further round of journalistic hand-wringing as impotent as it would be brief?

THE ELEPHANT IN THE DRAWING ROOM

Depressing as these reflections may be, there is one further consideration, once again one very seldom aired in the mainstream Western media, which should make one still more suspicious of the "one-state solution" and its advocates on the anti-Zionist left. In chapter 1, we found Article 22 of the Hamas covenant of 1998 offering a textbook example of the type of antisemitism characteristic of the Nazis: antisemitism considered not as a form of social exclusion, or "ethnic prejudice," to use Langmuir's term, but as a fully elaborated conspiracy theory, one that supposedly offers believers unique insight into how the world is governed and into the central role supposedly played by Jews in its government.

Such views, however, are by no means confined to Hamas or even to related Islamist movements. Over the past century, they have become general and commonplace in Arab society and the Arabic-language media. For example, in 2002, Egyptian satellite television featured a forty-one-episode series based on the czarist forgery *The Protocols of the Elders of Zion*.[45] In 2003, a twenty-nine-part version produced by Syria and the Shi'a armed group Hezbollah followed, in one episode of which the ritual murder of a young Christian boy by two Jews is presented in close-up.

The fascination for Arab intellectuals of the *Protocols* and its dissemination across the Arab world is one major way in which Jew hatred and hatred of Israel is renewed from generation to generation. But as the origins of the *Protocols* might suggest, one needs to be careful when speaking of *Arab* or *Islamic* anti-semitism. There is nothing particularly *Arab* either about the *Protocols* or for that matter about the type of antisemitism manifested in Article 22 of the 1988 Hamas covenant. There are certainly a number of traditional (seventh-century) hadiths attacking the Jews that can be cited in support of both and that are at present incessantly cited in that role by Islamist groups. But these reflect early conflicts in Arabia between Muslim and Jewish tribes that have little to do with European antisemitism, and the type of antisemitism aired in Article 22 is, when it comes down to it, profoundly European. It is, in effect, a colonial export. It is not merely *redolent* of Nazi antisemitism: it is in fact the direct descendant of antisemitic propaganda widely disseminated across the Middle East by the Nazi Reich between 1933 and 1945. The German political scientist Matthias Küntzel is an excellent guide to the way in which Nazi antisemitism successfully penetrated Arab society and to this day remains active in it. His book *Jihad and Jew-Hatred: Islamism, Nazism and the Roots of 9/11*[46] has been widely praised and translated and has won several major literary prizes. Despite that, one has the impression that the importance of the lessons it has to teach has been widely appreciated neither by politicians nor by media pundits in the West. Küntzel examines in great detail and with a wealth of reference to the surviving textual evidence, some of which he unearthed through his own research, the astonishing scope and range of the campaign of diplomacy and propaganda waged after 1933 by the Nazi Reich in its effort to influence Arab opinion. The object of the campaign was not only to undermine British influ-ence in the region but also to do so by swinging Arab opinion behind the Nazi project of a war against the Jews, seen as the hidden controlling force behind liberal capitalism and thus as the chief obstacle to the worldwide progress of European fascism.

Küntzel catalogs the project's successes in giving a profoundly antisemitic turn to the various Arab revolutionary movements stirring at the time. In Egypt, the Muslim Brotherhood, founded in 1928 by the charismatic preacher Hassan al-Banna, based itself on ideas that have since become the founding doctrines of all subsequent Islamist groups, including al-Qaeda and ISIL: that Islam, as the one true religion, deserves world domination and has been de-prived of it only by the success of Western political ideas and social practices in corrupting humankind—ideas and practices that ought therefore to be resisted to the death through jihad. The Muslim Brotherhood's influence in Egypt was

THE LEGACY OF 1967

235

greatly increased by the support of German funds. At the same time, German propagandists went to work to color the brotherhood's anti-Western ideology with Nazi ideas concerning the supposed centrality of the Jews to the corruptions of Western civilization. The German propaganda ministry, operating through the regional headquarters in Jerusalem of the Deutsches Nachrichtenbüro (German News Agency: DNB), whose radio broadcasts found a wide audience across the region, was active in spreading this message throughout the Middle East.

These efforts were highly successful in creating politically influential Arab versions of National Socialism, first in the Syrian People's Party, "which asserted the superiority of Syrians over other peoples and followed Nazi models even in its outward expressions—a swastika-like flag, the open-handed salute, etc.," and later in the Ba'ath Party in both Syria and Iraq.[47]

Another willing convert to Nazism was Amin al-Husseini, a member of a leading Palestinian Arab family who had been mufti of Jerusalem since 1921. As Küntzel notes, this was a personal decision.

> Even if in the 1930s some Arab nationalists saw Germany as an ally against the British without taking a great interest in the nature of the Hitler regime, the Mufti knew what that nature was and was attracted by it for that very reason.
>
> As early as the spring of 1933, he assured the German consul in Jerusalem that "The Muslims inside and outside Palestine welcomed the new regime of Germany and hoped for the extension of the fascist, anti-democratic governmental system to other countries." The youth organization of the party established by the Mufti operated for a time under the name Nazi Scouts. It adopted Hitler Youth-style shorts and leather belts and distributed leaflets emblazoned with Nazi slogans and swastikas.[48]

Husseini's commitment to Nazism and the fidelity to his ideas demonstrated ever since by the leadership of the Palestinians makes it painfully clear why every attempt to partition western Palestine between Arab and Jew between 1920 and 1948 ended in failure. If the machinations of the Jews lie at the heart of the worldwide web of corruption that denies Islam its rightful place in the world, then of course the Jews must be fought, and any proposal to establish a Jewish state in Palestine in particular must be contested to the last bullet and the last man standing.

That analysis, delusional as it is, has served the Palestinians no better than it served the Germans between 1933 and 1945. Belief in nonsense is seldom a sure guide to national success. But such nonsense, as Küntzel and others have abundantly shown, continues to dominate the thinking of Hamas and every other institutional offshoot of the Muslim Brotherhood and for that matter of Fatah (whose leadership remains firmly in the tradition of al-Husseini). Not only that, it has become so standard in the Arabic-language press and media of the region as to powerfully influence the thinking even of people who consider themselves rooted opponents of Islamism. It is ultimately for that reason that the "one-state solution" to the Israel-Palestine conflict remains at the moment and for the foreseeable future a project as fanciful as it is malignant.

NOTES

1. Morris (2008, 13) notes that Muslim suspicions of Christian Arabs as collaborationist persisted throughout the mandate period and "were expressed in slogans . . . such as "After Saturday, Sunday"—that is, that the Muslims would take care of the Christians after they had "sorted out" the Jews." The recent tide of persecution of Christians in Iraq, Syria, Egypt, and Pakistan demonstrates the continuity of these tensions and demonstrates also the familiar tendency of the passions and ways of thinking associated with antisemitism to incite persecutions that, while they begin with the Jews, inevitably pass on unabated beyond them: in the case of the Nazis, for instance, to Slavs, homosexuals, gypsies, the mentally ill, and other varieties of *untermenschen*.

2. Nelson, Harris, and Stern, in Nelson and Brahm 2015, 438.

3. Nelson and Brahm 2015, 415.

4. Wolf 1995, 79.

5. Interview with Lord Caradon, *Journal of Palestine Studies* 5, nos. 3–4 (Spring–Summer 1976): 147.

6. The term *intifada* derives from the Arabic *nafada*, "to shake off" or "get rid of." It is generally rendered in English as "uprising" or "resistance."

7. Nelson and Brahm 2015, 427–28.

8. Human Rights Watch, *Israel, the Occupied West Bank and Gaza Strip, and the Palestinian Authority Territories* 13, no. 4(E) (November 2001): 49.

9. Nelson and Brahm 2015, 437.

10. Ariel Ben Solomon, "Report: Hamas Executes Alleged Spies, Shoots Protesters in Gaza," *Jerusalem Post*, July 29, 2014, https://www.jpost.com/opera tion-protective-edge/report-hamas-executes-alleged-spies-shoots-protesters-in -gaza-369331.

11. See endnote 12.

12. See, for example, Khaled Abu Toameh, "Palestinians of Syria: A Year of Killings and Torture," Gatestone Institute, January 23, 2017, www .gatestoneinstitute.org.

13. Ali Sawafta, "Most Palestinians No Longer Support Two-State Solution," *Reuters*, September 21, 2015.

14. Available on the YouTube channel of Palestinian Media Watch (PMW).

15. Gershon Baskin, "Becoming a Real, Effective Democracy Requires a Real, Effective Opposition," *Jerusalem Post*, March 8, 2017, https://www.jpost .com/Opinion/Becoming-a-real-effective-democracy-requires-a-real-effective -opposition-483638.

16. Jewish Virtual Library.

17. Rory Jones, "Israel Comes to the Aid of the Faltering Palestinian Economy," *Wall Street Journal*, November 16, 2016, https://www.wsj.com/articles /israel-comes-to-the-aid-of-the-faltering-palestinian-economy-1479293954.

18. Aish Report: "Israel's Support of the Palestinian Economy: What You Never Hear about in the Mainstream Media," www.aish.com.

19. "Israel's Support of the Palestinian Economy."

20. "The West Bank Tires of Its Government. Extravagance and Graft Fuel a Growing Disenchantment," *The Economist*, October 3, 2015, economist.com.

21. Bassam Tawil, "The Offer that Turns the Gaza Strip into Singapore," Gatestone Institute, February 21, 2017.

22. Stuart A. Gabriel and Ed Feinstein, "The West Bank and Gaza: Give Economics a Chance," *Jewish Journal*, October 22, 2014, https://jewishjournal .com/opinion/134345/.

23. This report also featured on the BBC News website for five consecutive days under the heading, "Israel's Military Strategy in Gaza under Scrutiny."

24. Lesley Klaff and Stephen Riley, "'Disproportionate' Force and the Media: Misconstruing the Laws of War," *European Journal of Current Legal Issues* 25, no.1 (2019): 14–16, http://shura.shu.ac.uk/22904/3/Klaff%20Disproportionate %27%20force%20and%20the%20media.pdf.

25. Klaff and Riley 2019, 13.

26. Klaff and Riley 2019, 12.

27. Rich 2016, 251.

28. Julius 2010, 69–102.

29. Klaff and Riley 2019.

30. Richard Kemp, "Submission to the United Nations Independent Commission of Inquiry on the 2014 Gaza Conflict," February 20, 2015, https:// richard-kemp.com/submission-to-the-united-nations-independent-commission -of-inquiry-on-the-2014-gaza-conflict/.

31. Figures taken from https://www.iraqbodycount.org. Further information of the same kind covering other conflicts can be found, inter alia, at the website the nonprofit organization AIRWARS (airwars.com).

32. Janina Dill, "Applying the Principle of Proportionality in Combat Operations," Oxford Institute for Ethics, Law, and Armed Conflict Policy Briefing, December 2010. For a fuller discussion, see Stephen

Riley's contribution to Klaff and Riley (endnote 24) in the section titled "Proportionality: International Rules and Principles."

33. Kemp 2015, 6–7.

34. Kemp 2015, 11.

35. Richard Goldstone, "Reconsidering the Goldstone Report on Israel and War Crimes," *Washington Post*, April 1, 2011, https://www.washingtonpost.com/opinions/reconsidering-the-goldstone-report-on-israel-and-war-crimes/2011/04/01/AFg111JC_story.html.

36. Goldstone 2011.

37. Michael Curtis, "Israeli Settlements Are Not Illegal," *American Thinker*, July 9, 2014, https://www.americanthinker.com/articles/2014/07/israeli_settlements_are_not_illegal.html. This excellent short essay provides a sound introduction to the complexities surrounding the issue.

38. See Al Jazeera, February 1, 2017, for a report on this eviction.

39. Raphael Ahren, "Australia FM: Don't Call Settlements Illegal under International Law," *Times of Israel*, January 15, 2014, https://www.timesofisrael.com/australia-fm-dont-call-settlements-illegal-under-international-law/.

40. Antony Loewenstein and Ahmed Moor, *After Zionism: One State for Israel and Palestine* (London: Saqi Books, 2012).

41. See, for example, Bassam Tibi, "Palestinians: We Have a Right to Poison the Minds of Our Children," Gatestone Institute, March 29, 2017.

42. This is presumably a misprint. The Central Bureau of Statistics of Israel gives the Arab population of the country in 2013 as 1,658,000, representing 20.7 percent of the country's population.

43. Jeremiah Haber, "Zionism after Israel," in Loewenstein and Moor 2012, 233–34.

44. Omar Barghouti, "A Secular Democratic State in Historic Palestine: Self-Determination through Ethical Decolonisation," in Loewenstein and Moor 2012, 194.

45. Daniel J. Wakin, "Anti-Semitic 'Elders of Zion' Gets New Life on Egypt TV," *New York Times*, October 26, 2002, https://www.nytimes.com/2002/10/26/world/anti-semitic-elders-of-zion-gets-new-life-on-egypt-tv.html.

46. Küntzel 2007.

47. Küntzel 2007, 26.

48. Küntzel 2007, 28.

NINE
—⁓—

IS "ANTI-ZIONISM" ANTISEMITIC?

Antisemitic anti-Zionism bends the meaning of Israel and Zionism until both become fit receptacles for the tropes, images and ideas of classical antisemitism. In short, *that which the demonologocal Jew once was, demonological Israel now is:* uniquely malevolent, full of blood lust, all-controlling, the hidden hand, tricksy, always acting in bad faith, the obstacle to a better, purer, more spiritual world, uniquely deserving of punishment, and so on.

—Alan Johnson, "The Left and the Jews:
Time for a Rethink," *Fathom Journal*, Autumn 2015

One has to belong to the intelligentsia to believe things like that: no ordinary man could be such a fool.

—George Orwell, *Notes on Nationalism* (1945)

"ANTISEMITIC" IN WHAT SENSE?

It is time to return to the questions we raised in the introduction concerning the anti-Zionism currently popular in left-wing and liberal circles across the Western world, whose most characteristic expression is the Boycott, Divestment and Sanctions (BDS) movement. Both are often said to be antisemitic. Are they antisemitic? And if they are, what kind of antisemitism, exactly, do they display?

Those inclined to answer the first question in the negative are apt to argue, as we saw earlier, that antisemitism is a form of "ethnic prejudice" (Langmuir's term) targeting *individual* Jews and doing so *because they are Jews*. Anti-Zionism, on the other hand, *questions the legitimacy of a state, Israel,* for reasons having to do not with its *Jewishness* but with its history and political character: reasons, therefore, whose character is in no way racist but straightforwardly and unproblematically political.

Against this argument it is commonly urged that anti-Zionist discourse constantly echoes both the tone and the vocabulary of tropes and accusations characteristic of traditional antisemitism. Its talk of an all-powerful "Israel lobby" evokes the ancient myth of Jewish conspiracy. Claims of moral equivalence between the acts of the Nazis and those of Israel reawaken the myth of an absolute Jewish commitment to evil. Accusations that Israeli airstrikes *deliberately* target civilians, including children, for reasons of revenge hark back to the blood libel and to the traditional Christian characterization of Judaism as a religion of vengeance rather than love.

The trouble with objections of this sort is that they present both anti-Zionism and antisemitism as offending not against truth or humanity but merely against civility. They suggest, that is to say, that what is morally offensive about both is merely that they encourage the employment of language whose connotations are offensive or hurtful to many individual Jews.

That suggestion, of course, returns the argument to its starting point. If what is being complained of under the label "antisemitism" is merely *causing offense to Jews,* then the anti-Zionist can reasonably retort that it is surely time Jews grew thicker skins. It may be, the anti-Zionist will insist, that anti-Zionist criticism of Israel from time to time *evokes* or *suggests* stereotypes associated *in other contexts* with antisemitism. But such criticism, conceptually speaking, cannot *itself* be either *intrinsically* racist or *intrinsically* antisemitic in character, since it involves neither contempt nor attitudes of social exclusion directed at *individual Jews* but rather advances straightforwardly political grounds for hostility toward a *state,* namely Israel.

At this point, we find ourselves confronted, as so often in politics, with a dialogue of the deaf. A limited victory on points goes, for the moment, to one side—in this case the anti-Zionist's—leaving the opposing disputant feeling obscurely cheated and haunted by a strong sense that there might well be more to be said if only he could think what!

In public debate, it has not proved easy to move the argument beyond this point of *impasse,* not least because of the widespread feeling that it is difficult if not impossible to attach any clear sense to the notion of antisemitism *as a distinct form of prejudice*: to see it as amounting to anything more than a special form of ordinary ethnic or social prejudice that can equally target blacks, or the Irish, or other ethnic groups and hence is in no way peculiar or specific in its inner nature, structure, or causality to the Jews.

One thing I take myself to have demonstrated by this point in the argument of this book is that this construal of antisemitism, as merely a specific version of ethnic prejudice, is simply erroneous. In chapter 3, I argued that antisemitism is not a single phenomenon. Often, antisemitism does manifest as ethnic prejudice of a type by no means unique to Jews, expressing attitudes of dislike and contempt, as such prejudice invariably does, in terms of a more or less haphazard collection of opprobrious stereotypes.

But antisemitism can also take a very different form: one that *does* appear to be, both historically and at present, unique to Jews. In this version—*political antisemitism*—it is not just a collection of emotional attitudes but a would-be explanatory political theory. As such, it pretends to offer the believer or convert access to startling insights concerning the frighteningly inimical role supposedly played not by this or that individual Jew but by *the Jewish collectivity as a whole* in the direction of world affairs.

Antisemitism as a structured system of mutually supporting beliefs offers a powerful illusion of political understanding. It communicates an intoxicating sense that the scales have fallen from the convert's eyes, that at last he or she is able to penetrate the mystery of how the world is really governed. For that reason, it is far more dangerous than any mere emotional state of inchoate animosity and contempt toward any individual Jew as such could be. Only the fact that the antisemitism of the Nazi Party was of the political type, for instance, can explain the obsession of the party with prosecuting a wholly imaginary war against the Jews even while real adversaries were snatching the future of Germany and Europe from its weakening grasp. The Nazis, that is to say, did not set out to murder six million people in ways wholly irrelevant or deleterious to the German war effort *merely because they disliked or despised* these people; they did so because they imagined that they had serious reasons to be afraid of them. They shared the terrors Sartre memorably ascribed to Louis-Ferdinand Céline: "Look at Céline: his vision of the universe is catastrophic. The Jew is everywhere, the earth is lost, it is up to the Aryan not to compromise, never to make peace."[1]

MAKING NONSENSE BELIEVABLE

I have argued throughout the preceding chapters that the basic ideological elements of political antisemitism—Jewish power, Jewish conspiracy, the Jewish commitment to evil, all the components of the myth of the Jews as a "disease," that is to say—are delusive. I have argued, moreover, that they are delusive not merely in the weak sense of happening not to be true but in the stronger sense of not even being potential candidates for truth. In the graphic phrase of the British philosopher J. L. Austin, they are "not only not true . . . [but] not even faintly sensible."[2] What makes political antisemitism absurd, that is to say, is not that the Jews happen to be incapable of performing the roles it attributes to them but rather that the roles attributed to them are themselves creatures of fantasy. No small, dispersed, and deeply divided nation could conceivably exert the all but magical powers ascribed by political antisemites to the Jews, no conspiracy could conceivably spread its tentacles as wide and as secretly, and so on.

The absurdity of these imaginings raises the question of how anyone, however credulous, can be got to believe such stuff in the first place. The answer is that political antisemitism is never presented or accepted in isolation from other components of some specific non-Jewish political or religious narrative, call it N. The function of political antisemitism, we argued in chapter 5, is to explain why matters in the world are not going as those who put their faith in N would hope and expect them to. The explanation it offers is that matters in the non-Jewish world would in fact be proceeding exactly as N would lead one to expect were it not for the intervention of forces external to that world: namely, those controlled by the Jews. All the characteristic subordinate accusations of political antisemitism—of Jewish malignancy and cunning, of conspiratorial power exercised in the takeover of non-Jewish institutions, and so on—can now be deployed but in versions equipped with enough concrete, and at least seemingly plausible detail, imported from whatever narrative N represents, to conceal their essential absurdity.

This, I shall argue in this and the following chapter, is essentially the process that has taken place in the fabrication of contemporary anti-Zionism, including the BDS movement.

A closely related analysis is offered by the British left-wing social scientist and political theorist Alan Johnson.[3] In a recent and important article, Johnson accuses what he calls the anti-Zionist ideology (AZI) of systematically misrepresenting the factual and historical character of Israel and of its conflict with the Palestinians in order to make both fit a range of preconceived patterns of significance congenial to a certain, primarily Western, political outlook. Johnson's main concern in this paper is to attack a range of writers influential at present most obviously in university and some media circles, for reasons and with consequences that we shall examine in chapter 14. They include Ilan Pappe, Noam Chomsky, Judith Butler, Norman Finkelstein, Yitzhak Laor,

Israel Shahak, Gianni Vattimo, Jacqueline Rose, and others. His claim is that the charges against Israel and the Jews brought by the bulk of these people have their roots not in objective historical analysis but in abstract intellectual theory of one sort or another. The methodology of such theorizing, which by its nature seeks to detect in events some large overall pattern of events favorable to its leading premises, makes it easy to dismiss or simply ignore concrete historical, political, or sociological detail.

As a "notion" within the AZI, Zionism is an ideology and movement of "racial superiority and supremacy" with a relation of "inherent contradiction" to democracy and liberalism, and which is, anyway, based on a calculated fabrication of peoplehood. This conception of Zionism renders it homogeneous; all is essentialised, all is simplified. Judith Butler, for instance, reduces Zionism to nothing but "a violent project of settler colonialism," while Yitzhak Laor attacks the "fundamentally intolerant nature" of a movement that "has no source of legitimation except the old colonial discourse." For Jacqueline Rose, Jewish nationalism is racism, separatism and exclusivism. The Nobel laureate José Saramago tells us that "the great majority" of Israeli Jews exhibit "a contempt and intolerance which, on a practical level, have led to the extreme of *denying any humanity* to the Palestinian people, at times *denying their basic right to existence*." Zionism, then, is understood as a *genocidal* ideology and movement which "expelled, massacred, destroyed and raped" in 1948, conducting an "ethnic cleansing" of the Palestinians. And which could do no other: "Zionist ideology" is an "ethnic ideology" that seeks a "total cleansing" of non-Jews from the land to make possible the complete "Judaisation of Palestine." Israel, Pappe claims, is "preparing an ethnic cleansing in the West bank and a genocide in Gaza," only leaving the Strip in 2005 so it could "bomb freely."

Zionism, then, is understood [by the AZI] in a philosophically *idealist* fashion, with what Karl Marx called an "ahistorical, eternal, fixed and abstract conception." Hirsh complains of the tendency of left-wing anti-Zionism to "explanatory flattening" and "methodological idealism": "In a departure from the method of historical materialism, their analyses of Zionism tend to focus more on Zionism as an idea than on the material factors which underlay its transformation from a minority utopian project into a nation state."[4] The AZI does not engage with those material factors, but only with Zionism as an Idea, conceived autonomously from history. . . .

In the mid-19th century Karl Marx began to talk about "the German ideology" as a way to reassert the earthy claims of materialism against the airy idealism of German philosophy. I think we should talk about the anti-Zionist Ideology so that we can reassert the claims of earthy material history

in the story of Zionism and Israel. The AZI reduces the complex history of
a people (the Jewish people) and the nature of a state (Israel) to the simple
expression of a Bad Idea ("Zionism") and the Bad Men and Bad Women who
pursued it ("the Zionists"). That distorts reality because it excludes key actors
other than "the Zionists"—not least non-Jewish Europeans, Palestinian
Arabs and the surrounding Arab states—and factors other than "the
Zionist Idea"—not least the storm that Herzl saw approaching: the collapse
of European liberalism, the failure of European socialism, the victory of
Stalinism, Fascism and Nazism, and the radicalization of antisemitism
culminating in the Holocaust.

The AZI refuses to let that history *irrupt* within our thinking because to do
so would not serve the interest of delegitimizing Israel.[5]

Elsewhere Johnson extends this analysis to a point at which it coincides with
the argument we have been developing here. The refusal to "let history irrupt
within [the] thinking" of the AZI, he argues, not only serves to promote "a
program for the eradication of actually existing Jewish self-determination,"[6]
nor is it only that the AZI operates "in the murky borderlands where a modern
anti-Zionism of a particularly excessive and obsessive kind commingles easily
with classical antisemitic tropes, images and ideas." The fact of the matter is
that "Antisemitic anti-Zionism bends the meaning of Israel and Zionism out
of shape until both become fit receptacles for the tropes, images and ideas of
classical antisemitism."

POLITICAL ANTISEMITISM AND ITS FRAMING NARRATIVES

Substitute my "political antisemitism" for Johnson's "classical antisemitism"
and the parallel between his analysis and the one pursued in this book becomes
evident. We seem to have located a further distinctive feature differentiating
political antisemitism from antisemitism of the social or "racist" type. Social
antisemitism, as a collection of stereotypes both focusing and expressing dislike of and contempt for Jews, need not be embedded in any very elaborate
framework of ideas to give it credence; it stands, after all, in no need of *credence*,
being simply a collection of emotional attitudes. The social antisemite simply
cannot abide Jews, and there, for him, is an end of the matter.

Political antisemitism is an altogether different kettle of fish. It is never a
mere collection of emotional attitudes. In all its versions, it takes the form of a
studiously elaborated political theory, which makes certain propositions concerning the nature and conduct of the Jewish collectivity central to the explanation of world affairs it pretends to offer. The propositions in question—that
the Jewish collectivity is vastly more powerful than it appears to be, that its

of outspoken denunciations of him and others was to stifle harsh criticism of Israel. 'The link between anti-Zionism and anti-Semitism is newly created,' he said, adding that he fears that 'the two will become so conflated in the mind of the world' that references to anti-Semitism and the Holocaust will come to be seen as 'just a political defence of Israeli policy.'"

And in more recent British debate, the move has become so familiar a shot in the rhetorical lockers of such standard-bearers of the anti-Zionist left as the former mayor of London Ken Livingstone and Jenny Tonge, the Liberal Democrat member of the House of Lords, as to have been derisively baptized the "Livingstone formulation" by the sociologist David Hirsh.[27]

One evident justification for Hirsh's derision is that the retort is a blatant non sequitur. One cannot establish the falsity of an accusation by questioning its motives. The motives of an accuser may indeed be both ulterior and discreditable but for all that his accusations may be true. A second reason is that if that were the motive of the accusers, the accusation would be ludicrously ill-fitted to their purpose. Accusing such people as Judt or Livingstone of antisemitism manifestly has no power either to silence them or to reduce their access to the media. On the contrary, the more noisily accusations make themselves heard, the more avidly publishers and the grander media outlets on the liberal left— the BBC, *London Review of Books*, *New Statesman*, *Guardian*, *New York Times*, and *New York Review of Books*—compete to load the accused with contracts and column inches.

Mearsheimer and Walt, to their credit, do not allow their attempt at a rebuttal of the charge of antisemitism to repose solely on a non sequitur. They supplement it with a factual, sociological claim, occasionally still to be heard, to the effect that talk of a "new" antisemitism, of a "resurgence" of antisemitism, lacks a factual basis and hence can only be disingenuous, since the incidence of antisemitism has for many years been in decline. "Measuring antisemitism is a complicated matter, but the weight of the evidence points in the opposite direction."[28]

This is in one sense true. It is true of one kind of antisemitism—the kind I have been calling here "social" or "racist" antisemitism; the kind that involves contempt and dislike for any individual Jew, coupled with the attempt to exclude Jews from non-Jewish society and to prevent them from enjoying its advantages and rewards. There is, indeed, plenty of sociological evidence that that sort of antisemitism has long been on the decline in Western societies. As Richard Bolchover testifies:

> In the spring of 2002, a time when synagogues were burning across France, and elements of the British media were given over to political pundits

denouncing Zionist "lobbies," London Jews reported that they faced very little antisemitism in the commercial workplace and their businesses.

This was one of the most significant findings from a survey of 3,000 members of the Jewish population of London and the Southeast, conducted by the Institute for Jewish Policy Research in collaboration with the National Centre for Social Research. When asked about perceived levels of antisemitism in the British economy, only 34 respondents thought they had "definitely" or "probably" had "business contacts or orders refused" in the past twelve months.

I and probably most of my Jewish peers in the commercial world would concur with the responses of the vast majority of London's Jews.[29]

What Bolchover is talking about here—desire on the part of non-Jews to exclude Jews in society, in this case the business world—is plainly what we have been calling social antisemitism. And Bolchover confirms Mearsheimer and Walt's sense that this kind of antisemitism, at least in the Western world, is decreasing. But then, there is the other kind: political antisemitism—Jew hatred as a delusive explanatory theory that deals in talk of Jewish conspiracy, of the Jew as secret ruler of the world, as the hidden manipulator behind all wars, and so forth. This, and not the other, is the kind of antisemitism that burns synagogues. The accusations of "antisemitism" that Mearsheimer and Walt, Judt, Chomsky, Livingston, Tonge, and a host of other public figures and "public intellectuals" actually face are accusations of flirting with *that* kind of antisemitism: the kind of which, to put it bluntly, the Nazis were the last open public defenders. Mearsheimer and Walt, Chomsky, and the rest make no attempt to defend themselves against *these* accusations, no doubt for the excellent reason that it is very difficult to see how such a defense could proceed. Instead, their strategy is to attempt to prevent discussion from focusing on political antisemitism by pretending that social antisemitism is the only form that antisemitism can take. One of the main objects of this book is to strip that mask away by demonstrating both the historical ignorance and the conceptual futility of that strategy. One main support of the strategy is, of course, what Hirsh calls "the Livingston Formulation"—the move of claiming that the sole purpose of accusations of antisemitism is to discredit *all* criticisms of Israel. In addition to being a non sequitur, that move suffers from a further and even more damning defect: it presumes that those who raise such accusations do *in fact* do so in respect of *all* criticism of Israel. And that is simply false. To my knowledge, no critic of current anti-Zionism, Jewish or non-Jewish, has or would commit herself or himself to any such preposterous assertion. What is claimed is not, absurdly, *that it is antisemitic not to regard Israel as above criticism*, but merely that *some* claims put forward as "criticism" of Israel in reality embody not so much *criticism* as *defamation*, and antisemitic defamation at that. Of that we shall have more to say in later chapters.

ARGUING IN CIRCLES

A better—at least a more honest—strategy would be to admit the strange re-semblances of doctrine that connect much anti-Zionist and BDS literature with the kind of thing to be found in the prewar Nazi magazine *Der Stürmer* but to argue that the present-day conduct of the Israelis, and of the world Jew-ish community with respect to Israel, have conspired to turn those doctrines from racist fantasies into plain statements of fact. That is the strategy whose intellectual credentials we have now to examine.

Part of what needs to be shown is that the crimes of Israel are so great as to leave progressive people no choice but to assert the illegitimacy of the Jewish state and to advocate its dismantling. What are called "crimes" in this context, or more often "crimes against humanity," are for the most part acts committed by Israel in its long conflict with the Palestinians and claimed as crimes by the Palestinian side and their supporters overseas. They include several alleged massacres of Palestinians during the War of Independence 1947–49, and the refusal to allow Arabs who, for whatever reason, fled the future territory of Israel during that war, to return. Then there is the alleged use of disproportion-ate force by Israel during its wars in Lebanon and the three recent campaigns in Gaza and the fact that Israel, like Egypt, maintains a blockade that greatly restricts passage into and out of Gaza and is said to limit its economic devel-opment. There is the alleged treatment of Palestinians and members of other non-Jewish ethnic groups as "second-class citizens" over whom Israeli Jews are said to have set themselves as a privileged class. Then there is a lengthy list of claimed abuses connected with the "occupied territories" east of the Jordan River over which Israel gained control in the war of 1967 but which it has only partially annexed. It is alleged that Israeli rule over the territories is essentially similar to white South African rule over the various "Bantustans" during the apartheid era: hence, the tendency in anti-Zionist circles to refer to Israel as an "apartheid state." There is the building of the security barrier, known to such critics as the "apartheid wall." Then there is the building of Jewish settlements in the occupied territories, which is widely claimed to contravene international law, and along with that, the building of a separate road system connecting these settlements with one another and with Israel proper on which only Israeli citizens are allowed to drive. Then there is the policy of destroying the homes of Palestinians who engage in terrorist acts against Israel and the shooting dead of Palestinians in the act of committing such attacks. That is merely a general list, and I imagine not a complete one. But one must stop somewhere.

From the standpoint of a supporter of Israel, the obvious reply to these accusations is that both the *Nakba* (the "disaster," as Palestinians opposed to Israel call the defeat of Arab armies in the War of Independence) and its subsequent consequences for the Palestinians were and remain in part the result of decisions by neighboring states and by successive Palestinian political movements, against which the population of Israel has had, since 1947, no recourse but to defend itself. These include the decision on the part of the neighboring Arab states to refuse partition and instead to embark on a war of extermination against Jews in Palestine, and the subsequent determination on the part of Palestinian political organizations, including the Palestine Liberation Organization, Hamas, and many smaller groups, to wage permanent low-level war against the Jewish state with the same ultimate end in view. Hence, the acts of Israel complained of are not crimes but legitimate acts of war conducted in defense of the liberty and security of the country.

To this objection, anti-Zionists and supporters of BDS are apt to reply that neither the Arab world nor the Palestinians can be held to bear any moral responsibility whatsoever for these decisions, which are not only fully explicable but fully justified, as natural and proper responses to the crimes of the Jews.

Plainly, this is to reason in a circle: on the one hand, what makes hostile acts by Israel against the Palestinians crimes is supposed to be that they penalize the innocent; on the other hand, what makes hostile acts by the Palestinians against Israel innocent is supposed to be that they are justified acts of resistance to Israel's crimes.

THE DETERMINING ROLE OF POLITICAL NARRATIVE

It is not, however, sufficient merely to point out the circularity of such a reading of the situation. Many of those committed to it at present are plainly able to detect such elementary errors of reasoning. Here, for instance, is Michael Neumann, a professor of philosophy at Trent University in Canada: "[I] argue that Israel is, generally speaking, in the wrong in its conflict with Palestinians. The Palestinians, I will claim, are generally speaking in the right. There are grey areas in this black-and-white landscape: no doubt the Zionists did something right, and the Palestinians something wrong. But it's definitely the Palestinians, not Israel, who deserve the world's support."[30] Or the British Baroness Tonge, who in 2004 was dropped from the Liberal Democratic front bench in Parliament for saying, at a pro-Palestinian rally in Parliament, "I think if I had to live in that situation—and I say that advisedly—I might well consider becoming one [a suicide bomber] myself."[31]

Given that Palestinian suicide bombers are frequently children, often girls, who have been mentally and morally subverted by political groups, there is a certain irony in the fact that the post of which Tonge's remarks concerning suicide bombers led to her being relieved was that of Liberal Democrat spokesman for the rights of children.

If one wishes to understand what is going on in the minds of people who say things of this kind, however, it is a good idea to set such criticisms—temporarily at least—aside. These are, after all, people holding responsible positions, from university chairs to seats in national legislatures. Baroness Tonge is no doubt perfectly capable of grasping that suicide bombing not only targets noncombatants but involves, as often as not, the corruption and murder of a child or adolescent in the person of the bomber. Equally, Professor Neumann can be relied on, as a professional philosopher, to be aware of the potential circularity of what he is saying. Something, therefore, persuades both of them that such objections are the merest quibbles.

That something can only be some overarching political "narrative": some way of construing the Israeli-Palestinian conflict so general and so persuasive—at least to some minds—as to make it seem evident to those who accept it that Israel is in the wrong *whatever justification it may be able to offer in terms of self-defense*, while the Palestinians are in the right *however abominable their methods of waging war may appear by accepted moral standards to be.* And it is not difficult to identify the narrative into which the history and circumstances of Israel have for some time been predominantly assimilated by the nation's enemies on the left. The favored narrative is that of the long history of European colonialism and its ultimate defeat by colonized indigenous peoples. In 1973, Maxime Rodinson, a French Marxist and professor of Middle Eastern ethnology at the Sorbonne, wrote, "The accusation that Israel is a colonialist phenomenon is advanced by an almost unanimous Arab intelligentsia, whether on the right or the left. It is one case where Marxist theorizing has come forward with the clearest response to the requirements of the 'implicit' ideology of the Third World, and has been most widely accepted." And she offers as an instance the following, from the Egyptian revolutionary Gamal Abdel Nasser, in his *Philosophy of the Revolution*, recounting his reflections as a young officer returning from the war of 1948–49, which led to the founding of Israel: "All this was in natural harmony with the view that experience had drawn in my mind. [The Arab East] comprised a single zone [in which were operating] the same circumstances and the same factors, and even all the same forces arrayed against it. It was obvious that imperialism was the most conspicuous of these forces. And Israel itself was nothing more than one of the consequences of imperialism."[32]

Since those days, the Arab view that Israel is a colonial settler state and the position of the Jews in Israel is no different from that of the Dutch in Indonesia or the French in Vietnam has become the default position of the left in Europe and the United States. To quote Dave Rich, "Since the 1960s, the idea has spread across the left that Zionism is a racist ideology and that Israel is a western colonial implant in the Middle East. It is a short step from this to the idea that Israel should not exist and that its supporters in the West—which includes most Jews—are racists."[33]

One can now see, I think, why people of the caliber of Neumann and Tonge should regard the Israelis as in the wrong *no matter what justification they can allege for their actions* and the Palestinians as in the right *no matter what charges can be brought against them.* They see matters from the perspective of what even Neumann terms "this black-and-white landscape,"[34] because they view the Israelis as representatives of the—morally indefensible—forces of European (or "white") colonialism and the Palestinians as the last contemporary representatives of the—as they believe, morally unchallengeable—revolt of indigenous peoples against the subordination of their interests to those of the colonialist invader.

The same fundamental claim lies at the heart of the BDS movement, which claims to represent Palestinian opinion and to have been "inspired by the South African anti-apartheid movement." The July 9, 2004, "call" from "Palestinian civil society," which founded BDS, makes the following demands of Israel:

1. Ending its occupation and colonization of all Arab lands and dismantling the Wall.
2. Recognizing the fundamental rights of the Arab-Palestinian citizens of Israel to full equality; and
3. Respecting, protecting and promoting the rights of Palestinian refugees to return to their homes and properties as stipulated in UN resolution 194.[35]

Are we to regard the apparent political antisemitism that betrays itself in the views of many on the left as exactly what it appears to be? Or are we on the contrary to regard it as a misleading appearance created by unfortunate ways conspiratorial abilities and resources are so immense as to render non-Jewish political institutions impotent to act against Jewish interests, and so on—are not particularly plausible in themselves. Therefore, if they are to be made sufficiently believable to persuade converts, they must be embedded in some framing narrative sufficiently elaborate to confer the required plausibility upon them. Nazi *rassenlehre* (race theory), with its fantasies of Aryan masculinity, provides an evident instance of such a framing narrative.

But doesn't any political position, it might be asked, demand a "framing narrative"? It is always the case, of course, that from the standpoint of any political outlook, some facts are more awkward than others. Economic liberals find difficulty in explaining away the more obvious injustices occasioned by the operation of free markets; socialists and statists find themselves equally embarrassed to account for the often still more glaring abuses and inequities that are apt to arise within institutions under state control. Any political narrative, therefore, will tend to gloss over or avoid reference to inconvenient truths evident to many outside the particular political bubble from which that narrative emanates. On the other hand, in what we tend to think of as normal politics, distortion, elision, and denial of fact in political discourse remains within reasonable limits for the excellent reason that there is no need for it to go beyond those limits. The reason its protagonists experience no need to go beyond them is because the basic commitments of what we think of as normal politics enjoy fairly high levels of basic plausibility. It is, after all, intrinsically plausible *both* that the free operation of markets is conducive to general prosperity *and* that well-run public services ("well-run," of course, marks the point at which disaster is prone to strike the enthusiast for state control) can very often serve to mitigate or obviate the inequities of the marketplace.

That basic plausibility lapses in the case of political antisemitism for the obvious reason that the basic claims about the Jews that it endeavors to mediate to the unpersuaded are fundamentally incompatible with any account of reality having the slightest pretension to objectivity and accuracy. Any framing narrative capable of affording them plausibility must therefore employ distortion, elision, and denial of fact on a far more ambitious scale than that found in normal political discourse.

"NORMAL" POLITICS OR ANTISEMITIC
DEFAMATION? TWO CRITERIA

The question of whether modern anti-Zionism, including the BDS movement, is antisemitic thus reduces to the following two subordinate questions. Can it be regarded as one of the many political narratives and campaigns that make

246 BLAMING THE JEWS

up the landscape of normal politics? Or does it, on the contrary, merely offer a new framing narrative for the traditional delusions of political antisemitism? Two types of consideration present themselves, it seems to me, as criteria for choosing between the two possibilities. First, considerations of *warrant*: of strength or weakness of empirical support, and quality of reasoning. Does the discourse of modern anti-Zionism operate at a distance from the facts so great as to disqualify it as serious political analysis and locate it, rather, as mendacious special pleading? Second, considerations of *content*: are the conclusions for which modern anti-Zionism argues recognizable as versions of the basic commitments we have found to characterize political antisemitism in its successive historical guises?

Let us now try to apply these criteria. Alan Johnson, in the paper from which I quoted at length above, argues with copious reference to illustrative extracts that a substantial number of intellectually influential anti-Zionists dispense entirely with the need to refer either to history or to present-day political reality by treating Zionism less as a political reality than as an abstract idea of their own devising. In the foregoing three chapters, I have pursued a different but related line of analysis. I began by doing anti-Zionism the honor of assuming it, for the sake of argument, to be a part of the normal political discourse of the left. In this capacity, I considered two major components of the case it presents for the delegitimization of the state of Israel; the first (chapter 7) that the establishment of Israel in the first place was no more than a late episode in the history of European colonialism; the second (chapter 8) that Israel as it exists today is an apartheid society, founded on doctrines of Jewish racial superiority. In so doing, I did my best, in both chapters, not to make matters too difficult for the anti-Zionist but to present both the history and the present condition of Israel, as the phrase goes, "warts and all."

What has emerged from this staged confrontation between the facts and these two endlessly and rancorously repeated anti-Zionist charges is, I submit, that both charges come across as flimsy in the extreme. Neither appears remotely defensible except at a cost in terms of a degree of distortion, elision, and denial of fact unacceptable in (and in fact seldom found in) normal political discourse, however passionate and committed.

The attempt, for example, to fabricate an analogy between Zionism and Nazism, much touted by the British politician and former London mayor Ken Livingstone, and incessantly invoked in left-wing demonstrations by banners exhibiting the Star of David and the swastika joined by an "equals" sign, floats unsupported in the thin air of its supporters' political imaginations, since Israel's record on human rights is in fact vastly better than that of a host of other states, including, in the region, Iraq, Syria, Iran, Saudi Arabia, and others.

Nor is Israel a "colonial settler" state. Its present possession of the greater part of what the League of Nations Mandate described as "Western Palestine" resulted not from a campaign of colonial conquest and settlement but from the day-to-day exigencies of a war that was dominated on the Israeli side by the need to avoid fates—mass expulsion or worse, extermination—which sadly, other minorities in the region have not escaped. Moreover, that war could have been avoided entirely had the Arab Higher Committee and its external Arab allies been prepared, as the Jews were, to accept less than the whole of Western Palestine and opt for a partition. The facts leave one little option but to conclude, therefore, *pace* Michael Neumann, that far from Israel being "generally speaking in the wrong" and the Arabs "generally speaking in the right," the existence of Israel in its present form owes far more to the mindless violence of the Arab leadership than it does to any settled will on the part of the Zionist leadership to take over the whole of Western Palestine for the Jewish national home mandated by the League of Nations. Not only is it the case that, like many major reversals in human affairs, the foundation of Israel within its present borders happened more or less by accident. It is also the case that no amount of sentimental anti-Zionism can clear the Arab leadership of the day of having played a major part in making it happen, through its self-destructive folly in refusing to compromise on anything less than Arab domination of the whole of Western Palestine and through the virulent antisemitism that helped to dictate this strategy.

Similarly, there is no presentable factual basis to the charge that Israel is an apartheid state. There are no institutions in Israel remotely resembling those that defined apartheid in South Africa. For that reason, attempts are generally made to foist such a description onto Israel's occupation of parts of the West Bank and (formerly) Gaza. These attempts ignore the fact that in these territories, Israel is faced not with a body of its own people whom it chooses to treat as second-class citizens but with noncitizens living on land that Israel claims with every ground of justice not to be part of the territory of any existing state but rather disputed territory over which it has had no option but to establish, on grounds of military and national security, belligerent occupation. They ignore also the fact that it was Yasser Arafat who refused, against advice from other Arab voices, an Israeli offer that would have ended the disputed status of the West Bank by creating a Palestinian state covering 85 percent to 95 percent of its extent. They ignore Israel's de facto establishment, by unilateral withdrawal, of what is effectively a Palestinian state in Gaza. Still worse, they ignore the fact that the resulting statelet has become, in effect, an armed camp run by Hamas: an Islamist terrorist group, committed to permanent war with Israel, that has reduced the enclave to poverty and regularly executes real or imagined enemies and collaborators by firing squad.

In actual fact, present-day Israel is a multicultural society based on representative democracy and the rule of law in which freedom of speech and
assembly and the rule of law are guaranteed and which among other things
provides effective and systematic protection to members of Christian and other
non-Jewish minorities subject to appalling levels of violence and persecution
elsewhere in the region. It cannot, as we have seen in chapter 8, even be described as unambiguously in breach of international law given the ambiguities
and obscurities of the small number of specific international resolutions and
conventions habitually brandished in that capacity when any attempt is made
to apply them to the actual circumstances of the Israeli-Palestinian conflict
in more than the most sketchy and hand-waving manner. The destruction of
Israel as a *Jewish* state could not conceivably constitute an event to be welcomed
by "progressive opinion" (so far as the latter term still retains any non-ironic
meaning), since the entire weight of political experience teaches us that neither
its present political virtues nor the bulk of its population would have the slightest chance of surviving that destruction. Rather, it would merely confirm and
secure the descent of the entire region into the bloody anarchy of religious war.

In sum, the putatively factual claims on which present-day "anti-Zionism"
rests can be made plausible only, as I have argued elsewhere,[7] by means of
moral and factual hyperbole, strained analogy, and casual anecdote, the whole
rendered persuasive only by glossing or suppression of context, evasion, and
actual mendacity. Those claims can be successfully advanced in debate, in other
words, only by the methods that those attracted by political antisemitism have
always used in seeking converts—and are compelled in the nature of things to
use, since the alternatives of reason, common sense, and a robust concern for
truth are apt very quickly to erode the charms of their theory.

THE SECOND CRITERION: ANTI-ZIONISM AS A NEW
FRAMING NARRATIVE FOR POLITICAL ANTISEMITISM

Now for criterion number 2. As Alan Johnson also notes, the specific depar-
tures from respect for fact characteristic of modern anti-Zionism are systematically those required, in context, to disguise the implausibility of the basic
traditional commitments of political antisemitism.

The latter, as we noted in chapter 3, are by no means a simple, unstructured
list of anti-Jewish canards but instead form a structured system of mutually
supporting beliefs. As we saw earlier, a leading claim of political antisemitism,
that the Jewish community cannot be rendered harmless by negotiation or
reason but must somehow be eliminated, rests on two further claims central to

political antisemitism. The first is the claim that the *particularism* of the Jews, their obsession with their own affairs, which supposedly entails a complete disregard for the interests of others, makes them the cause of human suffering on a monumental scale to which they are indifferent. The second is the claim that the immense powers of financial manipulation and conspiratorial organization allegedly vested in the Jewish community have allowed it to take control of vast numbers of organizations normally supposed to be under non-Jewish direction and to pervert them to the service of nefarious Jewish purposes. Hence, these organizations can no longer be trusted unless they can be somehow returned to non-Jewish control, something that can only happen, the political antisemite contends, if the Jews and their dark powers can somehow be eliminated.

On the assumption that this happy outcome can be achieved, however, further entailments click into place within the logical structure of the system to assure the believer that then, at last, all will be well. Political antisemitism begins, after all, by offering the convert the assurance that whatever circumstances he finds deplorable in some present order of things are wholly the fault of the Jews. It follows that once the malign power of the Jews has been broken, those circumstances must in the nature of things cease to obtain, and the world return to whatever state is envisaged as normal by the convert: that happy state from which the world would never have strayed in the first place—so political antisemitism assures its converts—but for the influence of Jewish malignancy.

I began this chapter by mentioning the complaint frequently voiced concerning modern anti-Zionism, that despite its claim not to be antisemitic, it is difficult not to detect in its discourse versions of the tropes, images, and ideas of traditional antisemitism. We are now in a position to explain these echoes of the past. Contemporary anti-Zionism not only shares with earlier forms of political antisemitism certain characteristic propositions; it also exhibits an identical internal structure in the way in which it relates these propositions to one another as elements in a delusive but putatively explanatory political theory.

As with other forms of political antisemitism, anti-Zionism is *eliminationist*; its central contention being that the world's sole independent Jewish polity, Israel, is also unique among present-day states in being illegitimate (obscure as that term becomes, as we noted earlier, when applied to a state rather than to a regime) and hence in need of urgent replacement by a successor state—and not just by any kind of successor state but by a specifically *non-Jewish* successor state.

What makes the elimination of Jewish political autonomy urgent and essential, according to the anti-Zionist, here arguing in a manner consistent with earlier versions of political antisemitism, is that the government of Israel (with the entire approval, as the anti-Zionist sees it, of the supposedly exclusively Jewish electorate to whose votes it owes its authority) is guilty of abuses of human rights on a monumental scale. These, we are told, rival or exceed not only those committed by the Nazi regime in Germany or the apartheid regime in South Africa but also those committed anywhere in the world, in any country or under any regime, over the past century.

Why could not the government of Israel be reformed, or made at any rate less iniquitous in its proceedings, by some means short of eliminating Jewish political autonomy—say, through the good offices of the US presidency or the State Department? To this question, the anti-Zionist replies standardly that any such route to remedying the situation has been rendered ineffective by the fact that all the institutions concerned have been taken over by Jewish interests, in this case supposedly operating through the Israel lobby.

Thus, for instance, in an essay published in 2012, half a decade after the joint essay, with Stephen Walt, that introduced the theory of the Israel lobby and its supposedly limitless power, John Mearsheimer continues to assert the incapacity of the institutions of "the most powerful country in the world" to resist the machinations of what used to be known as the Jewish conspiracy. In a passage bemoaning the fact that President Obama had at that point proved less opposed to the continued existence of Israel than some of his supporters felt they had had reason to hope, he has no hesitation in ascribing the debacle to the political impotence of the White House in the face of Jewish opposition:

> The Obama administration needs to come up with a clever strategy for putting pressure on Israel to allow the Palestinians to have their own state. Once the right strategy is found, it should be a relatively easy task to move Israel in the right direction. After all, the United States is the most powerful economy in the world, and should have great leverage over Israel because it gives the Jewish state so much diplomatic and material support.
>
> But this is not going to happen, because no American president can put meaningful pressure on Israel to force it to change its policy toward the Palestinians. The main reason is the Israel lobby, a remarkably powerful interest group that has a profound influence on US Middle East policy.[8]

It is difficult to see what of substance (as distinct from style) separates this account of the Jewish conspiracy—notionally respectable as it is and widely circulated in the Western liberal media—from the one offered in the following passage from a 2008 address to the United Nations General Assembly by the then-president of Iran, Mahmoud Ahmadinejad.

The dignity, integrity and rights of the American and European people are being played with by a small but deceitful number of people called Zionists. Although they are a minuscule minority, they have been dominating an important portion of the financial and monetary centers as well as the political decision-making centers of some European countries and the US in a deceitful, complex and furtive manner. . . . This means that the great people of America and various nations of Europe need to obey the demands and wishes of a small number of acquisitive and invasive people. These great nations are spending their dignity and resources on the crimes and occupations and the threats of the Zionist network against their will.

If one seriously believes, as the majority of anti-Zionists appear to do, in the impotence of the main constitutional institutions of the United States before the "small number of acquisitive and invasive people" involved in the Israel lobby, then there is, of course, no alternative to the political strategy of anti-Zionism/BDS, which consists largely in generating, on university campuses and in sympathetic elements of the world media, propaganda for its own view of Israel. They do so in hopes of converting so many progressive people to that outlook that the power of the Israel lobby may eventually be defeated by sheer force of numbers and Israel swept out of existence, as many on the left appear to believe that the apartheid regime in South Africa was—not by political factors internal to the country, as was in fact the case, but by pressure of "world public opinion."

But if the delegitimization of Israel and a resulting collapse of Jewish political autonomy could be achieved, what would follow? The recent experience of the Western powers in pursuing projects of "regime change" in the Middle East might well make the politically wary query whether the consequences of ending Jewish national sovereignty might not be worse than those of allowing it to continue. Confronted with this question, however, contemporary anti-Zionism turns out to share with other forms of political antisemitism the delusive certainty arising, as we have seen, purely from the internal logic of the theory, that only good consequences can flow from the elimination of Jewish influence from whatever context causes concern to the antisemite.

In the specific case of the anti-Zionist version of political antisemitism, that is to say, the convert necessarily accepts as the condition of his conversion that, in the words of the Canadian philosopher Michael Neumann, "Israel is generally in the wrong in its conflict with Palestinians . . . [while] . . . the Palestinians . . . are generally speaking in the right."[9]

But if that is correct, it must necessarily follow that violence between Jew and Arab in the Middle East is entirely the fault of the Jews. Hence, Arab violence is entirely to be explained as a justified response to Jewish oppression and "theft of Arab land." And hence, all such violence may reasonably be expected to cease entirely once the Jews of Palestine no longer possess an autonomous polity and are thus no longer in a position to act in the ways that have justly caused offense to Palestinian Arabs. Indeed, since the Israel-Palestinian conflict is widely supposed in anti-Zionist circles—and in left-liberal circles generally—to be causally implicated in all the conflicts that have racked the region for the past forty years and to pose in consequence the threat of a new world war, the suppression of Jewish political autonomy in Israel might be expected to set not only the region but the world on a new path of peace and prosperity.

If we can assume these claims to be sound, then, of course we can go further. We can argue (like "Jeremiah Haber," whose essay "Zionism after Israel" we encountered in the previous chapter) that the Jews of Palestine, in seeking political autonomy, have acted as their own worst enemies, since it is perfectly possible to envisage, once current Arab demands for the abolition of Jewish political autonomy have been satisfied, a large and thriving Jewish minority, and a central Jewish presence, in an Arab-dominated successor state to Israel. But unless we entirely absolve Palestinians and the Arab world of any responsibility for the current state of affairs, all these further reasonings fall to the ground.

THE REBIRTH OF ANTISEMITISM AS A PSEUDO-EXPLANATORY THEORY

At this point, it seems to me, the conclusion toward which we have been arguing in the foregoing chapters becomes irresistible. Present-day anti-Zionism, along with the BDS movement, offers no more and no less than a new framing narrative for the ancient delusions of political antisemitism—a further addition to the long series of pseudo-explanatory theories alleging the centrality of the Jews to the discontents of the age that have haunted European civilization for so many centuries. Its essential identity with earlier versions of political antisemitism displays itself on the one hand in parity both of basic theoretical claims and of internal structure, as exhibited in the relations of entailment and mutual support holding between those basic claims and on the other hand in the extraordinary extent of the distortion and elision of fact needed to force reality to fit the procrustean bed of anti-Zionist theory.

Moreover, as we shall argue in the next chapter, the function served by political antisemitism in this new version differs in no way from its function in earlier versions. The job it does is, as always, to explain in a reassuring and face-saving way the embarrassing failure of a would-be transformative religious or political narrative to achieve the dominance in non-Jewish affairs believed by its supporters to be its natural due. The explanation is that it *is* dominant among non-Jews or would be if so many had not been seduced by the eternal malignancy of the Jewish community and its formidable power—so puzzlingly in excess of what its small numbers and complex internal divisions would lead one to expect—to determine world events in such a way that the good—as represented by the antisemite and his friends—inexplicably fail and the wicked equally inexplicably prosper.

These conclusions, if sound, are blankly incompatible with an account of the present prevalence of antisemitism widely accepted today. According to that account, the murderous antisemitism of the German National Socialist (Nazi) Party, whose fruit was the Holocaust, was an entirely and exclusively German phenomenon—one that dates from quite late in the nineteenth century, reached its murderous apogee during the brief twelve-year flourishing of the Third Reich (1933–45), and died absolutely and completely with the crushing of the Nazi regime by the Allies. In consequence, it is often suggested, all that remains of antisemitism today is a fading remnant of old prejudices that may reasonably be expected to die out entirely as liberal ideas continue their conquest of older ways of thought.

This latter, hopeful view can be found in two articles published in 2003: one by Anthony Lerman, then–chief executive of the Hanadiv Charitable Foundation, editor of *Antisemitism World Report*, and a former executive director of the London Institute for Jewish Policy Research, and the other, already cited, by Richard Bolchover, a leading City fund manager and author of *British Jewry and the Holocaust* (1993).

Bolchover begins his essay by noting that "in the spring of 2002, a time when synagogues were burning across France, and elements of the British media were given over to political pundits denouncing [*sic*] Zionist lobbies, London Jews reported that they faced very little antisemitism in the commercial workplace and their businesses."[10]

He cites a survey of three thousand members of the Jewish population of London and the Southeast, conducted by the Institute for Jewish Policy Research in collaboration with the National Centre for Social Research, and relates that "when asked about perceived levels of antisemitism in the British economy, only 34 respondents thought they had 'definitely' or 'probably' had 'business contracts or orders refused' in the past twelve months."[11] This is consistent with Anthony Lerman's claim of "a decline in anti-Jewish attitudes (a phenomenon noted in the United States)."[12]

These arguments, however, ignore the distinction between social and political antisemitism—between anti-Jewish attitudes and anti-Jewish *political theorizing*. The two are sufficiently different, after all, for a decline in the former to be entirely compatible with a simultaneous increase in the latter. And since, if we are right, political antisemitism is at present largely a phenomenon of the extreme left, and since the extreme left has very little influence in business circles, the results recorded by Bolchover, while gratifying, need not surprise us.

Lerman's argument, which also neglects the possibility that antisemitism comes in radically divergent varieties, is that antisemitism today, to the extent that it exists at all, is slight compared to its prewar prevalence, and that "the dangers of exaggerating the threat of antisemitism, even if the motive is just (though that is not always the case), are serious—you devalue the currency. And by making statements that imply antisemitism is as bad now as it was in the 1930s, we are sullying the memory of the millions of Jews who were dehumanized, persecuted and murdered at the hands of the Nazis and their associates."[13]

This, however, seems absurd. Whatever one makes of the alleged risks of devaluing the concept of antisemitism, it cannot be a necessary condition for protest against antisemitism that the disease must first reach the levels it attained in Europe in the 1930s. Nor is Lerman's position consistent with the facts, as he himself reports them, concerning the sharp rise in antisemitic incidents in Europe post–September 2001. "The Stephen Roth Institute at Tel Aviv University reported: 'Britain witnessed a 400 per cent rise in anti-Jewish incidents for the month of October compared with the same month in 1999.' An even sharper increase is reported in France."[14]

In fact, Lerman's concluding warning, that by exaggerating the impact of antisemitism, one risks devaluing the notion of antisemitism, does not go to the heart of his position. Earlier in the essay, he makes it clear that he shares the conviction universal among supporters of anti-Zionism/BDS, that all talk of "a new antisemitism" is disingenuous and that Israel itself is a new version of Nazi Germany.

So the "new antisemitism" is, in part, not new at all, but rather a device for de-legitimating any criticism of Israel and a political weapon in a global propaganda battle. The claim and counter claim in an unprecedented number of articles is testament to the power of that weapon and to a world that remains sensitized to antisemitism's dangers. But the antisemitism weapon is a blunt one, especially when used to refute comparison between the actions of Israel's army and the way the Nazis treated Jews. If such comparisons are antisemitic what about Israelis who describe other Israelis observing the actions of Israeli soldiers at checkpoints in the West bank as "kapos"? (kapos were Jews who acted as police for the Nazis in the death camps. Holocaust survivors lynched them). As Israeli journalist Akiva Eldar writes in Ha'aretz: Jews are allowed the liberty of likening Jews to Israel's worst enemies, while at the same time whining about those who liken Jews to Israel's worst enemies.[15]

Consistently with these elements in his view, he argues further that there can be nothing antisemitic about anti-Zionism:

> The anti-Zionism equals antisemitism argument drains the word antisemitism of any meaning. For it means that to be an antisemite, it is sufficient to hold any view ranging from criticism of policies of the current Israeli government to denial that Israel has a right to exist as a state, without having to subscribe to any of those things which historians have traditionally regarded as making up an antisemitic world view: hatred of Jews per se, belief in a worldwide Jewish conspiracy, belief that Jews generated communism and control capitalism, belief that Jews are racially inferior, and so on. Moreover, while theoretically allowing that criticism of Israeli government policies is legitimate, in practice it virtually proscribes any such thing. Following Sacks's reasoning, an Israeli soldier who sees elements of racism and the denial of human rights in policies towards the Palestinians must be antisemitic.[16]

I have spent the last eight chapters setting out the arguments for a conclusion diametrically opposite to Lerman's: namely, that tracing out the connections between anti-Zionism and earlier forms of political antisemitism, including the Nazis', far from draining the concept of antisemitism of any meaning, is the only thing that can make sense of it. Opposition to anti-Zionism/BDS in no way commits one to proscribing reasonable criticism of Israel, since all the "criticisms" of Israel that go to furnish the basic polemical armory of anti-Zionism, as we have seen, far overstep the bounds of reason and do so in all the ways Lerman lists as characteristic of traditional antisemitism.

The central tenet of political antisemitism is its *eliminationism*—the belief that the Jews cannot, realistically, be lived or compromised with: that there is simply no alternative to getting rid of them altogether. Eliminationism concerning the Jews is not of course antisemitic *taken in isolation*; taken in isolation, it is merely unintelligible—as unintelligible as such a claim would be if asserted of, say, Hoosiers or the Swiss. What makes it antisemitic is its connection to the reasons offered in its defense and the nature of those reasons: the imagined commitment of the Jews to iniquity, their allegedly terrifying

capacity for conspiratorial organization, and the vast secret control it supposedly enables them to exercise over non-Jewish life and institutions.

In an exactly parallel way, current anti-Zionism takes as its central doctrine
eliminationism with respect to the State of Israel. And it defends that doctrine
by appeal to precisely the same string of delusive supporting claims: the supposedly uniquely evil character of the Jewish state and the alleged ability of
the Jews to constrain, in Ahmadinejad's words, "the great people of America
and various nations of Europe . . . to obey the demands and wishes of a small
number of acquisitive and invasive people."

It follows that while, *pace* Lerman, criticism of the conduct of the Israel
Defense Forces, if factually, morally, and legally well founded, need in no
way be antisemitic, the denial of the right of Israel to exist, or what comes to
the same thing, the denial of the right of the Jewish people to political self-
determination, is indeed antisemitic.

Moreover, though it differs from Nazi Jew hatred in many of the specific
charges it levels at Jews, current anti-Zionism differs not at all from it in its
basic content and structure. Both represent versions of the same basic type of
antisemitism: antisemitism as a pseudo-explanatory political theory.

Contrary to the strand of current political folklore we have been discussing,
antisemitism of that type did not die definitively in 1945. Retreating from the
public domain into its many obscure redoubts in individual hearts and minds,
it passed for a time from the consciousness of political commentators. Over the
past twenty or thirty years, however, it has shifted from one end of the political
spectrum to the other, as its free-swinging lack of contact with reality allows it
to do, and reconstituted itself, as Alan Johnson and many others have noted, as
a publicly visible presence in certain sections of the extreme left.

Its reappearance also deals a blow to another element of the conventional
view—namely, the idea that antisemitism of the kind that leads to mass murder
was a peculiarly German phenomenon that, since German history has since
taken a different turn, may now be regarded as a purely historical phenomenon
of little relevance to the present day. German politics were indeed central to the
Holocaust; however, the Holocaust is only the greatest of many acts of mass
murder that have taken place against Jews in many centuries and in many countries. Isaac Babel's *1920 Diary* and Bela Szolt's *Nine Suitcases*, for example, offer
accounts, respectively, of Polish and Hungarian atrocities more than sufficient
to dispel the impression that such events are a uniquely German phenomenon.
And many other such memoirs exist.[17]

Attempts to explain the Holocaust in terms of the increasing influence
of German antisemitism from the 1870s onward, moreover, while unexcep-
tionably accurate as historical narrative, sometimes promote the misleading

impression not only that antisemitism in the period was an exclusively German phenomenon but also that antisemitism as a system of belief is a good deal more rational than in fact it is. Thus, for example, Albert S. Lindemann, in chapter 3 of *Esau's Tears*, devotes a good deal of space to the effect of a degree of Jewish upward mobility disproportionate to their numbers in encouraging German antisemitism in the later years of the nineteenth century.

> Banks, although less exclusively Jewish than elsewhere in central and eastern Europe, were still owned and operated by Jews (estimates range from forty to fifty per cent, whereas Jews were one per cent of the total population). The man reputed to be the richest in Germany was the Jewish banker Gerson Bleichröder.
>   Jews in Germany moved rapidly into the professions. Upwardly mobile Gentiles, or those who hoped for upward mobility in their children, encountered a most unwelcome competition to get into medical school or law school; Jews in those schools became overrepresented, often by ten, twenty, even thirty times their numbers in German society.
>   The liberal press was overwhelmingly in the hands of the Jews. It was an arena in which Jewish intellectuals could be active in an unhampered way.[18]

While this gives the initial impression of offering a concrete causal explanation, rooted in Jewish conduct, for the rising antisemitism of the times, a moment's thought is enough to show that it does nothing of the kind. Every profession, at all times and in all countries, selects from a pool of talent that may not only fail to be evenly spread over the population but that may often concentrate itself in some specific social or ethnic group. At present, in Britain, Indians of Hindu and Sikh religion are said to do considerably better in school and university, proportionately, than their native British contemporaries. It would not surprise me at all, therefore, if Sikhs or Hindus were to turn out to populate certain professions—medicine, say, or banking, or information technology—in numbers greater than could be justified by the proportion of Sikhs or Hindus in the general population. I have no idea whether this is in fact the case, because nobody has bothered to publicize the data, which are perhaps not even collected. And even if such data were collected and found to confirm these suspicions, I doubt if they would arouse alarm or even interest. Even if Sikhs turned out to supply some quite large proportion of a certain profession, say for the sake of argument, radiography, I cannot imagine anyone speaking of radiography being in danger of being "taken over" by the Sikhs, because the Sikhs, unlike the Jews, are not regarded by anybody as constituting an organized conspiratorial group aiming at a takeover of society through dominance of its institutions. They are just Sikhs: a collection of individuals

258

BLAMING THE JEWS

connected with one another in the popular British mind that knows nothing of Gurdwaras or the ten gurus, only by the sporting of curious and inexplicable top-knots and turbans.

Moreover, if any native British parent were to complain over the dinner table that her son was being crowded out of law school, or the local grammar school, by Sikh competition, I have a strong feeling that the response of her fellow guests, expressed or unexpressed, would be not only that she was a racist but that she was allowing her racism, possibly unwisely, to betray her into the admission that her son might not be the sharpest knife in the box.

In short, the discrepancies between the population size and the professional engagement of Jews in nineteenth-century Germany listed by Lindemann and many other historians do nothing to explain the incidence of antisemitism in Germany at the time. Rather, it is the incidence of antisemitism that explains why and in what way those discrepancies have been perceived, both at the time and since, as significant. And hence, antisemitism, German or otherwise, continues to stand in need of some deeper and more penetrating explanation.

POLITICAL ANTISEMITISM AND VIOLENCE AGAINST (AND ONLY AGAINST) JEWS

Today's anti-Zionism, I have argued, articulates a type of antisemitism that differs little from that of the prewar German Nazi Party, *at least in its fundamental claims and the relationships of mutual support and dependence holding between them.* Many will consider this assimilation alarmist. Anti-Zionism and BDS present themselves, after all, as left-wing, humanitarian, antiracist movements. Moreover, it will be said, Nazism both advocated and carried out acts of violence against Jewish institutions, businesses, and individuals; anti-Zionism, on the contrary, merely protests Jewish violence against Palestinians.

Unfortunately, these latter claims are no more resistant to critical scrutiny than anything else in the ideology of anti-Zionism.

Both anti-Zionism and BDS are movements whose leaders stop at nothing to convince their supporters, for the most part young and impressionable people, that Israel is guilty of crimes exceeding those of the Nazis. This equation has for more than twenty years been rendered visible at pro-Palestinian demonstrations by banners exhibiting the swastika and the Star of David connected by an "equals" sign. The message these signs convey is that anyone who supports Israel—which includes the vast bulk of Jews—is a supporter of evils dwarfing those of the Nazis and of a state that deserves to be annihilated. But its dissemination is not merely a matter of placards made and raised by student activists. A host of commentators and left-wing intellectuals with wide media access and influence have been pounding the same drum for at least two decades.

An example: on February 18, 2001, the liberal British Sunday newspaper *The Observer* published as its poem of the week, "Killed in the Crossfire" by the Northern Irish poet, academic, and broadcaster Tom Paulin. The poem itself, along with the long and ramifying collections of controversies prompted by its publication, can be followed to this day, over many pages on the web, by anyone with the patience to type "Tom Paulin, 'Killed in the Crossfire'" into Google. The controversy was further fueled by a later interview given by Paulin to the Egyptian paper *Al-Ahram Weekly* in which he was reported as having said that "Brooklyn-born Jewish settlers" should be murdered. "They should be shot dead. I think they are Nazis, racists. I feel nothing but hatred for them. I never believed that Israel had the right to exist at all."[19]

Given their circumstances, academics, poets, and media people are hardly likely to translate blood-curdling adolescent rhetoric of this kind into action. The trouble is that their words are widely read and circulated among people whose circumstances impose no such restraint. It is very difficult to imagine, therefore, that the incessant flow of violent propaganda of this type is not causally connected to the vast increase in attacks on synagogues and other Jewish institutions and attacks on individual Jews that has taken place across the Western world since 2001.

Nor is it the case, as is frequently asserted, that such attacks are entirely the work of Muslims. This is the line taken by Anthony Lerman, for instance, in the 2003 essay cited above: "France's 600,000 strong Jewish community has been especially hard-hit by attacks on synagogues. Some people link this to what they see as a cultural climate in which Jews are criticised for remaining 'different' and for refusing to accept the 'universal values' of French republicanism. But there is general argument that almost all the attacks were committed by young males of North African origin and are not the work of the traditional racist right."[20]

But this will no longer do for several reasons. Further research has shown that the idea that violence against Jews comes mainly or entirely from radicalized Muslims is at best only a half or quarter truth, while the idea that the only non-Muslim violence Jews have to fear comes from the "traditional racial right" is simply false. A widely cited 2016 Swedish study showed that, while a substantial proportion of attacks on Jews (53 percent in France, 51 percent in Sweden, 36 percent in the United Kingdom) were carried out by Muslims, a large number were not; and that among the latter, perpetrators of left-wing tendency nowadays massively predominate over the extreme right. In France, 4 percent of non-Muslim attacks on Jews were committed by right-wingers, 18 percent by left-wingers, while in Sweden the proportions are 5 percent to 25 percent and in the United Kingdom 7 percent to 14 percent.[21]

A second reason why Lerman is astray in his analysis is that anti-Zionism and BDS bring together representatives of radicalized Islam and the non-Muslim left with the common aim of eliminating Israel as a Jewish state. On university campuses, of which we shall have more to say in chapter 14, and at pro-Palestinian demonstrations, the atmosphere of violence and propaganda-fueled hatred toward Jews created by this combination can be terrifying.

But the fact that *Jews*, or people perceived as Jews, are the chief targets on such occasions itself calls into question the claim of anti-Zionism and BDS to be regarded as (normal) politics rather than as *politically organized antisemitism*. If Paulin and the rest of the anti-Zionist/BDS claque were right, and the conduct of Israel really were indistinguishable from that of the Third Reich, and the Israel Defense Forces from the SS, then fervent non-Jewish supporters of Israel, of whom there are no doubt a great many more than there are Jews *tout court*, would equally deserve the rage and hostility of the left. If anti-Zionism, that is to say, were a part of normal politics, one would expect to find it directing the greater part of its hostility against the vast body of non-Jewish pro-Israel center-left and center-right opinion that in Britain includes individuals on the left such as Alan Johnson and on the right such people as the Conservative politician Michel Gove, as well as the bulk of the membership of the Conservative and Labour organizations Friends of Israel. But this is not the case. Anti-Zionists and BDS supporters behave for the most part, with implications that we shall examine in the next chapter and in chapters 14–16, *as if it were the case that only Jews support Israel.*

The Norwegian ecologist and writer Eirik Eiglad gives the following account of the kind of violence to which this delusion is apt to lead in practice.

In January 2009 the Intifada came to Norway. The Israeli bombing and ground invasion of Gaza prompted thousands to demonstrate in all of Scandinavia's major cities. There were protests every Saturday in Oslo. The first clashes broke out on January 8th, when pro-Palestinian protesters attacked a pro-Israeli demonstration in front of the Norwegian Parliament with bottles and rocks, and scattered groups attacked individuals they believed to be Jews or Zionists. Later that evening there was a torch-lit "peace march" with thousands of people, but identifiably Jewish participants were told to leave; the march also displayed stark anti-semitic messages. The leaders of the Palestine movement in Norway refused to criticise the violent attacks, though they paid lip service to peaceful activism. Olav Svorstøl, the leader of the Coalition for Palestine, certainly made it clear that his organization "does not distinguish between worthy and unworthy demonstrations."

Two days later, the events were repeated on a larger scale. In Oslo the main demonstration that day brought a huge turnout; the thousands of protesters included prominent politicians, intellectuals, and artists, who had broad support from trade unions, community organizations, and political parties— although the demonstrations conveyed explicit anti-Jewish messages. People carried banners and posters identifying Israel with Nazism and Hitler and denouncing the Israeli "child murderers." "Death to the Jews" was heard repeatedly in Arabic, and walls in Oslo were painted with the unmistakable message: "Kill the Zionists." The main demonstration went from the Norwegian parliament to the Israeli embassy and subsequently disintegrated into smaller groups that attacked and vandalised presumably Jewish targets. Not only did they attack the Israeli embassy, but they also attacked the Masonic lodge, allegedly because it was considered an instrument for Zionist world domination. Five McDonalds' restaurants were smashed when text messages and social media spread a rumour that the McDonalds corporation would send their profits to support the Israeli invasion of Gaza. It was even reported that young children were told by older "activists" to "hunt Jews," and again rampant gangs attacked individuals in the streets because they were presumed to be Jews. Repeated clashes with the police during these several days resulted in 176 arrests.

The riots represented a historical watershed. Despite insistent attempts to explain away the radical anti-Israeli messages, the riots were not only the most violent street confrontations Norway had seen for decades, but the country had *never before* witnessed explicit anti-Jewish riots, *not even in the darkest years of our history*. The most frightening aspects of the riots, as I see it, were not the events themselves, but the complacency of the media, leading intellectuals and politicians, and particularly of influential spokespeople of the Left. During the Gaza war, a number of politicians posed in the Parliament with keffiyas to express where their sympathies lay.[22]

The telling thing to me about the violence displayed in these riots—the thing that places them outside the spectrum of normal politics and unites them instead with the attitudes and beliefs of prewar Nazism—is that it was not directed against just *any principled Norwegian opponent of anti-Zionism and disbeliever in the "Nazi" analogy* but specifically against *Jews*, as if supporters of Israel and opponents of anti-Zionism were only to be found in the tiny Norwegian Jewish community.

Eiglad provides a further example of the same obsession in Sweden.

Although the Oslo riots were particularly baleful, all major Scandinavian
cities displayed various ways to protest "Israeli aggression." Sometimes there
was violence similar to that witnessed in Oslo. A few months later, Malmø,
the third-largest city in Sweden, hosted the Davis cup match between
Swedish and Israeli teams. As the tennis match was threatened with mass
disruption, the organizers shamefully decided to close the event to the
public. Then, when the tennis match did take place, fenced off and without
an audience, six thousand angry protesters attacked the police barriers in
attempts to physically stop the match. Malmø has received much attention
lately, not least for the increasing harassment that has been marginalising its
small but long-standing Jewish community. On Holocaust Memorial Day
2010, when the Social democrat mayor, Ilmar Reepalu, was asked to comment
on the insecurity felt by Jews in his city, he obviously thought Malmø's Jewish
community was to be held responsible for Israeli politics, and considered
the hardships they faced quite understandable in light of the situation in
the Middle East. Reepalu challenged Sweden's Jewish citizens to distance
themselves more explicitly from Israel, and made it clear that in Malmø, "We
accept neither Zionism nor antisemitism."[23]

The absurdity as well as the political bankruptcy of the latter claim is evident
in the fact that *non-Jewish* supporters of Israel were not invited to distance
themselves from its politics, no doubt because that would involve admitting
that support for Israel is not a wholly Jewish concern.

Similar issues arise in connection with "Seven Jewish Children: A Play for
Gaza," a ten-minute playlet by the British playwright Caryl Churchill, staged at
the Royal Court Theatre in London on February 6, 2009. A controversy over its
alleged antisemitism then took place, in the *Independent* newspaper, between
Churchill and the Booker Prize–winning novelist Howard Jacobson. In it,
inter alia, Churchill commits herself as follows: "When people attack English
Jews in the street saying 'This is for Gaza' they are making a terrible mistake,
confusing the people who bombed Gaza with Jews in general. When Howard
Jacobson confuses those who criticise Israel with anti-Semites he is making
the same mistake."

There is a certain pathos in these words. Ms. Churchill plainly feels that the
main thing she has to establish, if she is to evade Jacobson's attack, is her own
moral purity: the moral purity, that is to say, of her intentions as a dramatist.
It is *other people*, people "making a terrible mistake," who attack English Jews
in the street in revenge for the bombing of Gaza. She is in no way to be held
responsible. She is not an antisemite. Her play criticizes *Israel*, not "Jews in

general." But the title of her ten-minute playlet is not *Seven Israeli Children* but *Seven Jewish Children*. Nor does it in any way concern, let alone impugn, those actually responsible for the conduct of the Israeli action in Gaza—that is to say, presumably the government and military establishment of Israel. Its action, brief as it is, presents in a way altogether free of political or historical context the more or less inadequate attempts of a group of Jewish parents to explain to their children the awkward "fact"—that Jews kill children. The play gains whatever power it possesses from tapping into one of the deepest motifs of Manichaean antisemitism: the motif of the blood libel. It is beyond belief to me, as a non-Jew, that those who clapped and cheered the play at the Royal Court Theatre were not cheering it for transgressing, with all the saving window-dressing associated with left-wing humanitarianism, a postwar veto which anyone who cares to chat to people in the bar parlor of a pub will discover to be widely felt and resented in England: not at all a veto on criticizing Israel but a veto on criticizing Jews.

So where is the terrible mistake? What, in fact, distinguishes the ethos of the play from, let us say, the ethos of the *Protocols*? Those who think they can make Manichaean antisemitism serve humanitarian ends are taking a very short spoon to sup with the devil. They must not be surprised if, when they protest the moral purity of their motives, the lips of that scrupulously amiable but vulpine gentleman curve into a smile.

NOTES

1. Sartre 1948, 41–42.
2. Austin 1962, 5.
3. Alan Johnson is currently senior research fellow at the Britain Israel Communications and Research Centre, having formerly been professor of democratic theory and practice at Edge Hill University. He has edited the journals *Democratiya* (2005–9) and *Engage Journal*, the former of which he helped to found. He is a scholar of the labor movement in Iraq and a founding member of *Labour Friends of Iraq*. He opposed the 2003 invasion of Iraq. He was one of the cosignatories of the 2006 *Euston Manifesto*, which combined a restatement of fundamental left-wing principles with an attack on forces on the left, which the authors considered to ready to weaken or abandon those principles.
4. David Hirsh, "Rebels against Zion," *Fathom Journal* 5 (2014): 68, http://www.fathomjournal.org/revies-culture/rebels-against-zion/.
5. Alan Johnson, "Intellectual Incitement: The Anti-Zionist Ideology and the Anti-Zionist Subject," 260–61, in Nelson and Brahm 2015, 259–81.

6. This and the following two citations are from Alan Johnson, "The Left and the Jews: Time for a Rethink," *Fathom Journal* (Autumn 2015), https://fathomjournal.org/the-left-and-the-jews-time-for-a-rethink/.

7. Bernard Harrison, "Anti-Zionism, Antisemitism and the Rhetorical Manipulation of Reality," in A. H. Rosenfeld 2013, 8–41.

8. John J. Mearsheimer, "The Future of Palestine: Righteous Jews vs. the New Afrikaners," in Loewenstein and Moor 2012, 140.

9. Neumann 2005, 3.

10. Richard Bolchover, "The Absence of Antisemitism in the Marketplace," in Iganski and Kosmin 2003, 267–74.

11. Bolchover in Iganski and Kosmin 2003, 267.

12. Anthony Lerman, "Sense on Antisemitism," in Iganski and Kosmin 2003, 61.

13. Lerman in Iganski and Kosmin 2003, 66–67.

14. Lerman in Iganski and Kosmin 2003, 57.

15. Lerman in Iganski and Kosmin 2003, 63.

16. Lerman in Iganski and Kosmin 2003, 59.

17. Babel 2002; Szolt 2005.

18. Lindemann 1997, 115.

19. *Al Ahram Weekly Online*, April 4–10, 2002, available at http://weekly.ahram.org.eg/2002/580/cu2htm. For further discussion of these remarks of Paulin's, see Harrison 2006, 108–10.

20. Lerman in Iganski and Kosmin 2003, 62.

21. Lars Dencik and Karl Marosi, "Different Antisemitisms: On Three Distinct Forms of Antisemitism in Contemporary Europe—With a Special Focus on Sweden" (Kantor Center for the Study of Contemporary European Jewry, 2016), http://kantorcenter.tau.ac.il/sites/default/files/PP%203%20Antisemitisms%20160608.pdf.

22. Eirik Eiglad, "The Resurgence of Antisemitism in Norway," in A. H. Rosenfeld 2013, 157–59.

23. Eiglad in A. H. Rosenfeld 2013, 159–60.

TEN

—᠅—

ISRAEL, THE LEFT, AND
THE UNIVERSITIES

An intellectual hatred is the worst.

—W. B. Yeats, "A Prayer for My Daughter"

ANTISEMITISM ON THE LEFT: WHY NOW?

I should like in this chapter to examine, and to make at least a tentative attempt
to explain, two curious facts of contemporary life. The first is that political
antisemitism has reappeared in force over the past few decades not as in the
1930s on the right of politics but on the left. The second is that a high proportion
of those who find the antisemitism of anti-Zionism/Boycott, Divestment and
Sanctions (BDS) not only attractive but—even more puzzlingly—persuasive
are intellectuals, many of them university academics.

Antisemitism, of course, was in earlier centuries never wholly confined to
the right of politics. From Marx onward, it has also enjoyed a substantial presence on the left. As Anthony Julius shrewdly observes:

Just as there were anti-Semites on the Right ready to identify Jews with
communist subversion, so there were anti-Semites on the Left who habitually
identified Jews with a sinister and predatory capitalism ... [while] ...
many leftists set their own values (secular, collectivist, internationalist,
universalist) against perceived "Jewish" values (religious, individualist,
nationalist, particularist), to the disadvantage of the Jews. They looked
askance at what they understood to be Judaism's merely national religion, its
merely national deity. They were affronted by that "collective subjectivity,"
the Jewish people. That to be an anti-Semite was not the very worst thing one

265

266					BLAMING THE JEWS

might be was something many on the left were quite ready to concede even in the late 1930s. *The Jewish Question*, a Left Book Club volume published in 1937 appealed to its readers: "Hate the Jews if you must, but do not allow your hatred to make you the victim of the fascist who, on the plea that he also hates the Jew, makes you his accomplice in worse crimes."[1]

If it comes to that, classical liberalism has never been without its antisemitic side. In 1834, when the Jewish Emancipation Bill had been passed by the House of Commons but rejected by the Lords, it failed to carry with it the great Thomas Arnold, headmaster of Rugby and intellectual leader in his day of the liberal or Broad Church wing of the Church of England.

Arnold took the view that the world is made up of Christians and non-Christians: with the former, unity was essential, with the latter, impossible, or where possible, deplorable. Parliament should be thanked for having achieved [in the Catholic Emancipation Act] the great liberal desideratum of doing away with distinctions between Christian and Christian. But "I would pray that distinctions be kept up between Christian and non-Christian." Jews, Arnold argued, had no claim whatsoever to political rights because "the Jews are strangers in England, and have no more claim to legislate for it, than a lodger has to share with the landlord in the management of his house. . . . England is the land of Englishmen, not of Jews . . . my German friends agree with me."[2]

Much water has run under many bridges since 1937, and even more since 1834, much of it stained with Jewish blood. No doubt then is then, and now is now. It remains true, however, as we have seen in the previous chapter and shall see again in chapter 14, that hostility to Jews, nominally motivated by hostility to Israel, and sympathy for anti-Zionism and the BDS movement is at present appallingly commonplace across a broad spectrum of left-liberal opinion. It is to be found particularly in the universities but also in much of the liberal media and in a host of governmental and nongovernmental organizations throughout the West. And if, as we have argued in preceding chapters, anti-Zionism and BDS are movements essentially antisemitic in character, then one must conclude that, after all, little has changed. The old nonsense is still up and running; behind liberal faces and left-wing sentiments still lurks the old fear that somewhere, in secret passages behind and inside the walls of the world, the Jew is still busily at work, running and ruining everything. Antisemitism, popular, at any rate acceptable on the left in 1937, appears once again to be acceptable on the left, a full eighty years later, and over seventy years after the Shoah, and particularly acceptable in the universities. What could account for that?

THE CRISIS OF SOCIALISM

In chapter 5, I argued that political antisemitism always arises in connection with some threat felt to be posed, at least *in principle*, by the deliberately and fiercely maintained singularity of the Jews to some movement aiming at the *total* reform and transformation of non-Jewish society. And I suggested that the temptation to invoke the imaginary explanatory resources of political antisemitism is generally greatest at points of crisis for the totalizing movement in question: points when the sweeping success in non-Jewish circles, in which its adherents trust, appears nevertheless to hang in the balance or, worse still, to be crumbling. Does the present popularity of political antisemitism on the left fit this pattern?

Left-wing movements over the past two centuries have taken many forms. But on the whole, these fall into two main categories. On the one hand, a multitude of campaigns and movements have sought the advancement of working-class interests as well as those of other oppressed groups through the pursuit of specific reforms. They include trade unionism in all its forms, women's suffrage, the cooperative movement, and many more. Such movements aim not at the wholesale overthrow of society but at versions of what the late Karl Popper called *piecemeal social engineering*.[3] The piecemeal social engineer, Popper says,

> may or may not have a blueprint of society before his eyes, he may or may not hope that mankind will one day reach an ideal state, and achieve happiness and perfection on earth. But he will be aware that perfection, if at all attainable, is far distant, and that every generation of men, and therefore also the living, have a claim; perhaps not so much a claim to be made happy, for there are no institutional means of making a man happy, but a claim not to be made unhappy, if it can be avoided. They have a claim to be given all possible help, if they suffer. The piecemeal social engineer will, accordingly, adopt the method of searching for, and fighting against, the greatest and most urgent evils of society, rather than searching for, and fighting for, its greatest ultimate good.[4]

Popper contrasts piecemeal social engineering with the utopian kind. The utopian social engineer does have the ultimate good of society in his sights and conceives of it on the grandest scale in terms of a blueprint for the total overthrow and remaking of society as a whole.

It is difficult to read *The Open Society and Its Enemies* now, seventy years after its first appearance, without the sense that Popper, in arguing against utopian social engineering, feels himself to be spitting against the wind. For at that point in time, the main body of left-wing thought and feeling in the Western world had for a century been committed to the vast project of utopian social engineering associated with Marxism ("utopian" in Popper's terms, of course; Marxists themselves detest the term). The mounting domination over left-wing opinion achieved by Marxist thought and Marxist movements throughout that century is a tribute to the apparent richness, the apparent comprehensiveness, of the answers offered by Marxism to the problems of the age.

Marxism draws strength, to begin with, from its ability to present itself, as it does in the title of a celebrated work of Friedrich Engels's,[5] precisely *not* as *utopian* but as *scientific* socialism. It sees itself as offering an account of social and economic life as firmly empirically based, as objectively correct, and as rigidly deterministic as the best accounts of the workings of physical nature offered by the natural sciences. According to its account, the course of human history is causally determined and cannot deviate from its ultimate destiny. For Marx, the necessity of historical causality is bound up with the notions of *surplus value* and *exploitation*. In all human societies above a certain level of technical sophistication, according to Marx, the products of labor are more than sufficient to sustain the lives and secure the replacement of the laborers and their families. In every such society, some set of social arrangements exists whose function is to transfer the *surplus value* thus created to the exclusive use of a small, socially dominant *exploiting class*. The engine of historical change is the fact that owing to the development of the technical resources of a given society, the processes of exploitation current in it become sufficiently inefficient and productive of conflict as to leave room for the introduction of the new and more efficient processes of exploitation characteristic of a new exploiting class. Thus, for example, industrial progress can be seen to have gradually undermined the position of the landowning nobility and gentry who make up the exploiting class under feudalism in ways that led to their replacement by a new exploiting class of capitalists, whose power was founded not on feudal rights over land but on finance and on the ownership of factories and other means of production and distribution of manufactured goods.

This grim vision of history, however, has another, brighter side. Capitalism must by its nature encourage the development of technical advances that, while they make money for the capitalists who finance their development, also vastly increase the productive power of labor. Capitalism as a system of social arrangements, however, systematically frustrates the enjoyment of this improved productive capacity by the mass of the population. It does so because the economic arrangements that define it tend inevitably to create an ever smaller and richer class of capitalists confronted by an ever vaster and more impoverished class of workers. The tensions resulting from these contradictions must lead to a revolution in which the possessions and powers of the very small remaining class of capitalists will pass into the *collective* control of the working class— which is as much as to say, given the fact that the development of capitalism will by this time have produced a working class embracing the vast bulk of the population, into the *collective* control of the population as a whole. Collective control, with the abolition of private ownership in the means of production and distribution, will enable the vast technical resources and productive capacity developed under capitalism to be put to work for the benefit of all sections of the community rather than for that of a small exploiting class.

In the late 1940s, when *The Open Society and Its Enemies* first appeared, communist parties were powerful in Western Europe, particularly in France and Italy. At the same time, the bulk of Eastern Europe was at that moment in the process of coming under the domination of the Soviet Union—at that point, since 1917, an expressly Marxist society, founded on the abolition of private property and state ownership of the entire economic machine, a society, moreover, that had just proved itself capable of playing a leading, not to say determining, role in the defeat of Nazism.

In these circumstances, despite a range of dissenting voices, including Popper's on the right and George Orwell's on the left, it was easy for a broad majority of opinion on the left to conclude that whatever minor defects might be discovered in the admittedly complex and eclectic, not to say esoteric, intellectual foundations of Marxism, it was, on the whole, on the right track. Its central arguments, at any rate, were simple and persuasive. They gave, many felt, ample warrant for the belief that a revolutionary transition from capitalism to socialism was indeed historically inevitable and must therefore eventually happen in all countries. When it did, it must introduce equally inevitably, many believed, a new order of society not only more just and equitable than the old but also far richer because far more rationally economically productive than could ever be achieved through the essentially unplanned and irrational operations of any system based on private ownership and free markets.

It would be false to the motives and virtues of the many who accepted it and who devoted their lives to attempting to realize it to deny that this is, at least, on the face of it, a generous and hopeful vision of the future. Unfortunately, since the late 1940s, events have conspired to destroy its plausibility.

Two connected difficulties, unforeseen by Marx, have played a major role in this process. The first concerns Marx's prediction that the development of capitalism would lead to the simultaneous enlargement and impoverishment of the working class to include the bulk of society. Notoriously, this has turned out in practice to be simply mistaken. Where socialist revolutionaries have achieved power, therefore, from 1917 onward, they have done so not, or not ultimately, through achieving popular consensus but by violently enforcing their program on a large and diverse range of politically organized groups opposed to them for a variety of reasons. Hence, "socialism," in the full sense of the abolition of private property and the control by the state of all economic activity, has invariably been achieved, where it has been achieved, only at the cost of concentrating all political power in the hands of an authoritarian regime operating a police state. The second, closely connected difficulty is that such states tend, in practice, to be both extremely corrupt and extremely hostile to criticism of any kind and in consequence, extremely economically inefficient.

Karl Popper foresees both these problems and their connection with one another in a passage that admirably combines clarity with brevity:

> As opposed to [piecemeal social engineering], the Utopian attempt to realize an ideal state, using a blueprint of society as a whole, is one which demands a strong centralized rule of a few, and which therefore is likely to lead to a dictatorship. This I consider a criticism of the Utopian approach; for I have tried to show, in the chapter on the Principle of Leadership, that an authoritarian rule is a most objectionable form of government. Some points not touched upon in that chapter furnish us with even more direct arguments against the Utopian approach. One of the difficulties faced by a benevolent dictator is to find whether the effects of his measures agree with his good intentions (as de Tocqueville saw clearly more than a hundred years ago). The difficulty arises out of the fact that authoritarianism must discourage criticism; accordingly, the benevolent dictator will not easily hear of complaints concerning the measures he has taken. But without some such check, he can hardly find out whether his measures achieve the desired benevolent aim. The situation must become even worse for the Utopian engineer. The reconstruction of society is a big undertaking which must cause considerable inconvenience to many, and for a considerable span of time. Accordingly the Utopian engineer will have to be deaf to many complaints; in fact it will be part of his business to suppress unreasonable objections. (He will say, like Lenin, "You can't make omelettes without breaking eggs"). But with it, he must invariably suppress reasonable criticism also.[6]

Anyone familiar with conditions in the Soviet bloc prior to the collapse of Soviet communism in 1988–91 is aware how central a part was played in that collapse by economic inefficiencies originating, on the one hand, in the power of the party to suppress criticism, and on the other hand, in the understandable unwillingness of subordinate authorities to advance it in the first place. In any command economy, a black market develops to supply demands that the official, state-run economy is either unwilling or unable to meet. Toward the end of the Soviet era, however, across the bloc, the black market was where many ordinary people actually conducted their economic lives, doing as little as they could during the day in their ill-rewarded state jobs, so that they could put more energy into the unofficial evening employments that actually supported them. That situation was encapsulated in two jokes I heard in Bulgaria in 1978: "They pretend to pay us, so we pretend to work," and "Bulgaria is a very rich country: people earn 500 leva a month but spend 1,000."

For whatever reason, however, the Soviet Union, and with it the socialist organization of the economies, not merely of Russia but of a broad swathe of Eastern European nations, came to an end in 1991. The consequences for left-wing parties and opinion in the West were necessarily traumatic. For many decades, the broad consensus of left-wing opinion on which political parties of the left depended for support had rested on two grand principles. The first was that socialist economies based on the abolition of private property and its replacement by centralized state control and rational planning, once brought into existence, must inevitably prove more efficient than capitalism in meeting human needs. The second was that for every country in the world, a transition from capitalism to socialism was not only inevitable, but once achieved must prove irreversible, since required by "laws of history" understood to operate with the same inflexible necessity as natural law.

The existence and comparative success of the Soviet Union had for seventy years served to provide concrete evidence that neither principle was badly at variance with reality and in particular that history, conceived not as a mere accumulation of accidents but as a law-governed natural force analogous to gravity or magnetism, was "moving in the right direction." Its collapse, correspondingly, threatened to reveal both as tissues of self-delusion and wishful thinking. Other models—other at least putatively successful instances of functioning socialist economies—continued to exist in the shape of China, North Korea, Cuba, and more recently Venezuela under Hugo Chávez and Nicolás Maduro. In the latter, at time of writing, economic mismanagement has led to mass hunger, the transport of food under armed guard, a government-declared state of emergency, and the flight of considerable parts of the population to other countries in the region. It is a measure of the present loss of faith by the left in its own traditional economic nostrums that the main left-wing British newspaper the *Guardian*, analyzing the causes of the disaster, writes:

> The Maduro government has blamed the crisis on the US and rightwing business owners who it accuses of cutting production to sabotage the

economy, but Maduro has inherited a ruinous state-run system from
Chávez, to which economists say he has added some damaging mistakes of
his own. Chávez built his popularity on oil money and foreign debt, using
both to fund consumption, while nationalizing 1200 companies deemed
not to be functioning in the public interest. But in 2015 the oil price was cut
in half and Venezuela's reckless public finances helped make it a high risk
debtor, cutting the country's access to international capital. The Maduro
government has responded to the consequent hole in public finances by
printing money, fuelling inflation. It's estimated that the cost of basic
groceries that would keep a family going through a week increased by
more than 25% between March and April, and now costs 22 times the state
minimum salary.[7]

Of the other existing potential models for socialist economics, Cuba is stable
but poor and has also suffered a substantial and continuing loss of population
to emigration. North Korea is a tyrannous, poverty-stricken police state. China
remains a one-party state with many state-owned enterprises, but it also has a
burgeoning private sector, and though the Chinese Communist Party retains
the name, it has retreated so far from the Marxism of the Maoist era that it is
attempting to revive Confucianism, formerly attacked and derided as a tissue
of nationalist and feudalist nonsense, as the philosophical and moral basis for
its continued dominance.

None of these states, in short, are capable of providing, for the Western left,
what the Soviet Union provided: namely, a concrete, existing instance of a socialist economy that could plausibly (though, admittedly, hardly conclusively)
be claimed to be outperforming capitalist economies in meeting human need,
and therefore to point the way toward the coming transition from capitalism to
socialism supposedly mandated by the laws of historical necessity.

THE MORALIZING OF LEFT-WING POLITICS

Left-wing politics in the West have always been doubly rooted: on the one hand,
in moral outrage at the present condition of society; on the other hand, in the
fabrication of detailed practical proposals for its radical reform. Central to the
second strand was the belief in socialism, state control, centralized planning,
and the rise to power of the industrial proletariat. That the collapse of Soviet
communism was so fatal to these beliefs is partly to be explained by social
changes in Western society that had for decades already threatened their plausibility. "The world that had defined the left since the 1880s, in which socialist
movements, in both trade union and parliamentary forms, campaigned for the

rights of working-class communities formed by mass industrialization, was beginning to crumble by the 1950s. Its political foundations were increasingly eroded on one side by rising post-war prosperity across Western societies, and on the other by radical, left-wing causes that did not fit within the old class politics."[8] These new "radical left-wing causes" arose, naturally enough, from the opposite side of left-wing consciousness—the side that deals not in the invention and rational assessment of practical proposals but in the articulation of moral outrage. In terms of a distinction proposed by the sociologist David Hirsh, "the politics of socialism, in its best form a positive constructive project," was in process of turning into a "politics of resistance" capable of "coexist[ing] easily with readiness to give up making the world better."[9]

A "politics of resistance" conceives its main business to lie with moral denunciation rather than with positive change. To those who think in this way, the fact that one has given up any serious possibility of replacing capitalism with something better does not, after all, alter the fact that capitalism is in itself an abominable system that oppresses many. If one cannot change it, such thinking goes, then at least one can range oneself on the side of the oppressed rather than on that of the oppressors.

The seeming moral reasonableness of this step in one's political thinking does not prevent some startling consequences when it is taken by enough concerned people for it to begin to constitute a major climate of opinion in left-wing circles. For a start, it radically changes the class character of left-wing politics, moving it, in effect, up the social scale. Dave Rich gives the following account of the transition, beginning in the 1960s, from the generations that had believed in the future of socialism to a new generation—the generation of the British New Left or the French student revolt of 1968—who no longer did.

The new political generation was marked by lack of deference for authority and an organizational fluidity that spawned a bewildering array of single-issue pressure groups and campaigns. The old left-wing politics of mass labour mobilization and class struggle were directly challenged, and at times replaced, by race, gender, sexuality, peace and the environment as the causes that shaped the New Left and continue to animate many left-wing activists today. . . . As New Left superseded Old, so identity politics replaced class politics as its primary mobilizing idea. It was all very different from the Old Left that was forged in the hardships of the 1930s and the sacrifice of the wartime struggle against fascism. Instead, the New Left effectively represented a new social class, rooted in intellectual and cultural professions, populated by public sector workers, and whose political agenda would come to be dominated by identity and iconoclasm.[10]

This "new social class" also distinguishes itself in a new way. The mostly working-class members of the Old Left thought of themselves as together *constituting* a sizable proportion of the oppressed. Supporters of the New Left, on the other hand, well aware that in most cases their economic status would render any such identification absurd, are therefore apt to identify themselves politically not as members of the oppressed but as concerned friends, helpers, and guardians of the oppressed. To think of oneself in this way is automatically to think of oneself as blessed with a higher moral consciousness than the benighted souls—members of left-wing groups closer to the Old Left or outright conservatives—who choose to disagree with one politically. As the sociologist David Hirsh notes, "The intense personal payoff of this variant of identity politics is a feeling of inner cleanliness. The world may be utterly compromised, and there may be nothing I can do about it, but it is not going to be my fault: my soul is clean. In this sense, while the Corbyn faction [the faction surrounding the current leader of the British Labour Party] loves to say that it doesn't do personal, in fact what it resists doing is 'political.'"[11]

What Hirsh means by "political" in this context is, of course, rational debate concerning the truth or falsity of politically relevant claims: debate such as I have tried to offer in this book. But once one moves to a politics founded solely on strongly felt prima facie moral response and the ideal of personal purity of motive, *argument* and *debate*, as Hirsh shrewdly notes, are likely to seem less and less important per se to political life. What is important is not *winning arguments* but on the one hand, preserving the purity of one's moral vision and on the other hand, excluding from the community of the progressive those who would pollute that purity. Hirsh underlines a remark of the American progressive academic Judith Butler that "understanding Hamas, Hesbollah as social movements that are on the left, that are part of a global left, is important." Butler, he notes, later amended this: "They are 'left' in the sense that they oppose colonialism and imperialism, but their tactics are not ones that I would ever condone." But the anodyne term *tactics* wildly understates the case. Hamas and Hezbollah represent versions of theocratic totalitarianism not only opposed root and branch to "Western values" but also opposed root and branch to a host of values formerly regarded as central by the Western left. Hirsh adds,

> Butler's distinction between their [Hezbollah's and Hamas's] positioning within the progressive movement on the one hand, and what they actually do and say, on the other, is significant . . . [because it shows that] who is considered to be part of the progressive movement and who is considered to be outside of the progressive movement is a judgment made independently of what people say and how they decide to mobilize their human agency. . . .

This "campist" worldview was marginal on the British left but has now
made significant strides into the mainstream political left. The way in which
positioning is taking precedence over debate in the British Labour Party is
indicative of its growing centrality.[12]

...

And "campism" has also been making significant inroads in public opinion
and attitudes. My hypothesis is that it is becoming standard within influential
liberal and left-liberal sections of the elite. In this milieu it is perfectly normal
to believe, for example, that Tony Blair is a war criminal, that Israel should be
boycotted, that America is responsible for most of what is going wrong in the
Middle East and that English teenagers who go to fight for ISIS are victims
of British foreign policy and were radicalized by efforts to stop them. In my
trade union, in my university, in my newspaper, in my Labour Party, on BBC
Radio 4, the unexamined assumptions of this variant of anti-imperialism are
to be found frequently repeated without critical assessment. They constitute
the warm background community-defining set of things that good people
are expected to believe. There are acknowledged and unwritten boundaries
which divide "us," the "good people," from them, the uncultured, the Tories,
the Americans, the Neo-Cons, the Blairites, the Islamophobes and, in
particular, the Zionists.[13]

THE NARROWING OF LEFT-WING HORIZONS

The effects of the transformation from an Old Left occupied with the pursuit of
working-class advancement in concrete terms to a New Left interested mainly
in its own moral concerns and its own moral purity have not been confined
to the devaluing of sound standards of argument in favor of moral hectoring
(and if that will not work, the exclusion and ostracism of the unpersuaded). The
new politics has also seen a remarkable narrowing of the range of topics that
excite moral concern within the large and influential sections of the left that
have espoused it. As affluence (and also, it must be said, the rising indifference
to working-class problems on the part of politicians nominally on the left that
has begun to create substantial working-class support for the likes of Donald
Trump and Marine Le Pen) has eaten away the traditional working-class constituency of the left, those sections of the left most profoundly skeptical of and
hostile to the present condition of Western societies have found themselves
searching for a new oppressed class in terms in which to define both the iniquities of capitalism and their own struggle against them. In recent decades, that
search has focused increasingly on the non-Western world with two consequences. The first is that the struggle of the left has ceased, in certain left-wing

circles, to be understood as a *class* struggle and has instead been reconstrued as
a struggle between good and evil fought out between *nations*. The second is that
in this struggle, while the nations of the third world are by and large conceived
as oppressed by capitalism, Europe and America are predominantly conceived
as the oppressors. As Alan Johnson puts it, the politics of the New Left has
increasingly "caused parts of the left to abandon universal progressive values
rooted in the Enlightenment and sign up instead as foot soldiers in what they
see as the great contest between—these terms change over time—'Progressive'
versus 'Reactionary' nations, 'Imperialism' versus 'Anti-Imperialism,' 'Oppressed' versus 'Oppressor' peoples, 'The Empire' versus 'The Resistance,' or
simply 'Power' versus 'The Other.'"[14]

Judith Butler's remark that "understanding Hamas, Hesbollah as social
movements that are on the left, that are part of a global left, is important" is,
of course, both a leading expression of this vision of the world and an attempt
to inculcate it.

A left-wing politics as narrowly focused as this raises problems, of course,
not only for conservatives but also for many less narrowly focused members
of the broad left. Earlier versions of left-wing politics, based on the idea of a
general movement of history toward socialism, had emphasized both equality
of suffering and equality of subjection to the causes of that suffering, between
the downtrodden of all races and nations, without regard to differences of race,
color, or culture. In contrast, the new politics of "anti-imperialism" tends, absurdly enough for a supposedly anti-racist movement, to equate the boundary
between oppressors and oppressed with that between "black" and "white" nations, without regard to the *internal* politics of either. Hence, *all* members of
the latter, rich or poor, powerful or powerless, are construed as equally guilty of
oppression and hence as equally valid targets for armed resistance. Conversely,
all members of the former, including people wealthy and powerful in local
terms, as well as people, often the same people, whose political commitments
and contempt for leading traditional principles of the left would formerly have
branded them as fascists, are construed as oppressed and hence, in Butler's
terms, as "part of the global left."

David Hirsh describes this situation as follows:

> With the post-war resurgence of democratic Europe and the rise of American
> power, much of the left began to downplay those of its core values which
> did not provide a defining contrast against the newly dominant democratic
> ideology. Democratic values were more and more subordinated to the
> principle of opposition to imperialism. Struggles for equality within nations,
> and solidarity between the powerless across national boundaries, were

sometimes sacrificed to struggles by "oppressed" nations and peoples against imperialist states. What is meant by "imperialist states" in the practical politics which flow from this discourse is "democratic states"—primarily Europe and the USA. What is meant by "oppressed nations" when this discourse is translated into worldly politics is the gangs of men who rule over them and speak in their name.

This set of developments has the potential to cause a splitting of the antiracist tradition. Any racism that was understood to be rooted in imperialism was vigorously opposed, while any racism that blurred the black/white binary was downplayed. Some of the peoples who tended to suffer most acutely as a result of the struggle against imperialism were those who were held to be compromised by their "collaboration" with imperialism: Tutsis, Tamils, Kurds, Baha'is, Yazidis, African Asians, Bosniaks, Armenians, Ukrainians and, of course, Jews. Some on the left are not as exercised as they might be by the oppression of these groups, because it is carried out by forces which they think of as broadly on the progressive side in the struggle against imperialism. The blood of those on the anti-imperialist left only really boils when it perceives white people, or people that it construes as white, to be the villains. The left can be so tied to this emotional framework that it comes to feel as though all bad things in the world are the work of white people. Sometimes, other people do bad things, but, at root, it is white people who are found to be responsible. In this way, a part of the left finds itself stumbling into a worldview in which the only significant social agents are white people, and all others are constructed as victims. This stripping of people who are thought of as non-white of social agency tends to infantilize them in the minds of the western left, reducing them to helpless children.[15]

In short, we confront the curious phenomenon of a new and allegedly left-wing political outlook, most strongly represented, not in the traditional working class, but among professionals in cultural and publicly funded organizations, whose adherents are accustomed to strike attitudes of uncompromising moral condemnation of relationships *between* notionally oppressed and oppressor groups or peoples, while freely tolerating the existence, *within* the former, of abuses and tyrannies that earlier versions of the left would have considered, and which many, both on and outside the left, still do consider, morally intolerable.

ISRAEL: FROM REASONABLE CRITICISM TO ANTISEMITIC CALUMNY

It is not difficult to see why those who share that outlook should nourish a particular detestation for the State of Israel, or why that detestation should display an inbuilt tendency to morph, through a process of gradual and possibly largely unconscious transformation, into the full-blown delusions of political antisemitism. A third of Israeli Jews are of European origin—enough, certainly, for it to be possible, by one of those sleights of ideological oversimplification so common in politics, simply to discount the even larger numbers of Israeli citizens, Jewish, Muslim, Christian, and others, whose roots are wholly in the region, and to talk henceforward as if all Israelis were European Jews. If one chooses to believe, moreover, that in any conflict between Europeans and non-Europeans, the former are always wholly in the wrong and the latter wholly innocent *whatever they may happen in practice to do*, then one will have left oneself little option but to regard the historic and ongoing conflict between Israel and the Palestinians as wholly the fault of the former. Doing that, as we have seen, obscures the actual history of relations between Jews and Arabs in Palestine to an extent that makes it easy to treat the establishment of Israel not as the seizure by a violently threatened national minority of the self-governing autonomy that earlier generations of the left would have considered the due of all such minorities but (implausibly, as we have seen) as a late exercise in European colonialism.

So far as the anti-imperialist left is concerned, imperialism *is* colonialism, and colonialism is racism in practice. And if imperialism, together with its concomitant racism, is the main global evil against which the left has to fight, the evil that embraces, supports, and engenders all other evils, then Israel, seen as a triumphantly and unashamedly imperialist and colonialist state is, a fortiori an evil state. Moreover, the evil that it does and represents is not *in the end* a matter of any *specific* thing it does or does not do (though the New Left sees plenty of those to complain about). Its evil is *intrinsic to its nature as a state*. What is ultimately evil about it, as the late historian Tony Judt was frequently at pains to claim, albeit in more modulated language, is that at this point in history, a point at which European colonialism is effectively a thing of the past, Israel has the gall to go on existing as *just such a state*. From its *essential nature* (as the New Left sees it) as a "colonial settler state," it necessarily follows, *morally speaking* (again, as the New Left sees it) that Israel should never have been allowed to come into existence in the first place and should cease to exist as soon as its demise can conveniently be arranged.

As the above suggests, it is important to note two things about the New Left's objection to the existence of Israel as a self-governing Jewish state. On the one hand, it is intensely *moral* in character. And on the other hand, it is—as Alan Johnson's work has abundantly demonstrated—*essentialist* and *ideological* in character. The nature of interaction between these two features in the thinking of the anti-Zionist left is also of interest. The violent moral condemnation central to the New Left position on Israel is in the last analysis driven *solely* by the essentialism equally central to that position. There is thus something decidedly odd about the claim of anti-Zionists and BDS supporters that what they are engaged in is *criticism* of Israel. Criticism in politics, whether of the policies of a given regime or of the customary assumptions of a nation or culture, always focuses on some specific policy, act, or abuse and seeks action to resolve that specific problem. But it seems clear that the hostility to Israel of today's anti-Zionists could not be assuaged by any conceivable action by Israel relative to any specific criticism. For that hostility is not *ultimately* motivated by moral outrage at any specific act of Israel but by moral outrage at the *very existence* of Israel, considered as a type of state that according to the anti-imperialist ideology of the new politics ought no longer to exist.

This in turn throws a lurid light on the attempt on the part of anti-Zionists to popularize an equation between Israel and the Nazis—an attempt symbolized by the image of the swastika and Star of David joined by an "equals" sign, an image not only widely seen at demonstrations against Israel but, according to Hirsh, also displayed by some of his university colleagues on the doors of their offices. No attempt is ever made by supporters of anti-Zionism to back up this equation in detail. And, in fact, it is childishly easy to demonstrate, on the one hand, that no significant parallel exists between the policies of Israel and those of the Third Reich and, on the other hand, that very significant parallels do exist between the conduct of the Third Reich and that of a number of other major actors in the region. But to the anti-Zionist (it is important to see), this is entirely beside the point. The little swastika/Star of David logo is not meant to introduce any serious argument in defense of such an equation; it is simply meant to dramatize what, for the ideology of the anti-imperial left, is the real heart of the matter, and of their opposition to Israel: that, as they see things, Israel and the Third Reich are both states in which an oppressive white majority (one that, in each case, allegedly conceives itself as superior to a degree that places itself above morality) oppresses a downtrodden, nonwhite Other.

It seems evident that once one has arrived at these moral-cum-political conclusions, one has begun to commit oneself to a version of political antisemitism. One has, in effect, taken on board its central contention, that Jews collectively constitute a force for evil in the world. Suppose Israel is an evil state in the sense of a state exercising a naked and blatantly oppressive power over an Other represented by the Palestinians considered, in effect, as an amorphous suffering mass whose "real" interests may be taken without the slightest critical hesitation to be perfectly comprehended and served by the leadership of such groups

as Hamas, Hezbollah, and Fatah. If one believes that, then one cannot avoid
holding that anyone who supports Israel and opposes the latter is, ex hypothesi,
supporting imperialism against the oppressed Other and hence is a servant of
evil. But although there exists an exceedingly vociferous minority of Jewish
supporters of anti-Zionism, an unspecifiable but certainly large and at any rate
in common belief overwhelming proportion of the world Jewish community
(along, of course, with a possibly very much larger number of non-Jews of conservative or democratic-left tendency) are supporters of Israel. Therefore—the
logic of anti-Zionist ideology allows no other conclusion—the Jewish community consists in the main of supporters of evil, friends of imperialism, and
enemies of progress.

Once one has persuaded oneself of this much, the other main contentions
of political antisemitism follow naturally. It will begin to seem plausible that
the tendency of leading political groups in America to be more supportive of
Israel than corresponding groups in Europe is to be explained not in terms
of obstacles to the penetration of left-wing ideology posed by the inherent
conservatism of most American elites outside the universities but rather
in terms of the machinations of the Israel lobby. Then it will begin to seem
natural to talk as if the Israel lobby itself were not merely one lobby among
others in the lobby-ridden American political system, and an entirely publicly visible one at that, but a secret, conspiratorial network aiming to take
secret control of major American institutions and public bodies and divert
their resources from the service of the American people to the service of the
Jews. To take such claims seriously is to begin to see merit in the basic fear,
not to say panic, that has dominated the mind of every political antisemite,
past or present: that the Jews are behind or beneath everything he takes to
be going wrong in the world. To cite Hirsh again: "Antizionism began as a
critique of the political movement for national self-determination. After the
Holocaust and the war of 1948, which radically transformed the material
basis of Jewish life, antizionism became something quite new, a movement
to abolish an existing nation state. It then matured into a worldview which
re-positions Jewish wrongdoing at the centre of all that is problematic in
the world."[16]

At this point, of course, it is only natural that people on the left who have
advanced step by step in this way toward the wholesale reinvention of the "Jewish problem," will begin to look askance at Jewish comrades in their own camp,
particularly ones inclined, however reluctantly, to see anti-Zionism as embodying elements of antisemitism. It is essential not merely to the self-image but
to the entire political stance of the present-day anti-imperialist left that both

its doctrines and its members are free of any taint of racism. Given that fact, accusations of antisemitism cannot but produce the vehement reactions of astonishment, intellectual rejection, and moral outrage that Hirsh documents in detail in his book. Hirsh, who is among other things the instigator and chief gadfly of the *Engage* website, has of course come in for a very great deal of that sort of thing himself.

When it comes to rebutting the accusation, however, the stock rebuttals available to the anti-Zionist are, as we have already seen, feeble and few in number. The two standardly used—and it is not easy to envisage others—are both defective, in the one case logically, in the other factually.

The first, to speak accurately, is not an *argument* at all but an instance of the "informal fallacy" known as ad hominem. I am grateful to the philosophy department at Texas State University for the following definition: "Ad Hominem (Attacking the person): This fallacy occurs when, instead of addressing someone's argument or position, you irrelevantly attack the person or some aspect of the person who is making the argument. The fallacious attack can also be directed to membership in a group or institution."[17]

In debates over antisemitism and anti-Zionism, the anti-Zionist retort I have in mind consists of accusing one's Jewish accuser of making his putatively absurd accusation merely in hopes of "silencing criticism of Israel" and of doing so *because* he is a Jew. The British left-wing politician Ken Livingstone has used this move in debate so often that, as noted earlier, David Hirsh refers to it as the "*Livingstone Formulation*—the counter-affirmation of Zionist conspiracy which treats discussion of antisemitism as though it were a vulgar, dishonest, and tribal fraud"[18]—devoting a whole chapter of his book to it under that title. But although it has been used, mostly to good forensic effect, not only by Livingstone but by a good many other participants in these tormented debates, including people of the kind that journalists like to dub "major public intellectuals," the "argument" itself is no more than an instance of a type of move in debate taught as a fallacy to first-year students of elementary logic in every philosophy department in America.

The second means by which anti-Zionists commonly seek to rebut the charge of antisemitism is at least an *argument*, but it is unfortunately one that founders on the rock of a false major premise. It begins by defining antisemitism as emotional antipathy toward Jews as Jews and proceeds to the conclusion that no anti-Zionist can possibly be antisemitic (however implausible that may seem in the face of many actual instances of conduct: a story touched on earlier and to be pursued further in chapter 14) by way of the subordinate claim that since all anti-Zionists, in virtue of being opposed to imperialism, are opposed

to racism in all its forms, no anti-Zionist could possibly harbor feelings of antipathy toward individual Jews qua Jews.

The trouble with this argument is, as we have seen in earlier chapters, that
it is not sufficient to the facts to define antisemitism as personal antipathy
toward individual Jews qua Jews. There is also political antisemitism. Political antisemitism is a bogus explanatory theory dealing in a range of delusive
beliefs concerning not individual Jews but the Jewish community as a whole.
It is a type of antisemitism into which *just because it need not involve feelings of
antipathy toward individuals on account of their perceived Jewishness*, it is very
easy for people to fall, step by plausible step, without clearly realizing that in
doing so they have become (political) antisemites. In any event, this is the kind
of antisemitism of which, for the most part, anti-Zionists stand accused. And
as we have argued here at length, the accusation has weight. It is particularly
ironic, given the tendency of present-day anti-Zionists to attempt to popularize analogies between Israel and the Third Reich, that the antisemitism of
which they stand accused should turn out be of exactly the type—political
antisemitism—patronized by the Nazis.

ISRAEL AND JEWISH OBSTINACY

In chapter 5, I suggested that political antisemitism becomes a temptation
when a political or social movement finds itself in an unexpectedly weak position that cannot be explained in terms of any deficiency of its own—except
for deficiencies so profound and central to its existence and coherence as a
movement that it can neither admit nor remedy them. In these circumstances,
it becomes tempting to look around for some alien force whose malignancy
might explain the reverses it deplores without the need for wrenching kinds
of self-examination.

The Jews, I suggested, have always provided the natural candidate for identification with the required malignant alien force simply because of their long
history of rejectionism. It is not merely that they regard themselves, as Deuteronomy 7:6–11 constrains them to do, as "a people set apart." More disturbing
still is their success in refusing to disappear as a distinct people, through total
assimilation to whatever non-Jewish political or religious movement happens
to hold sway in the world at this or that moment of history, no matter how
attractive the inducements held out to them for doing so or how terrible the
penalties threatened and exacted for not doing so.

This extraordinary history of survival in the face of impossible odds, I argued, has itself sufficed to identify them to superstitious eyes, in the successive

(and by contrast, in the historical time scale, fleeting and evanescent) cultures in which Jews have lived through the long history of the diaspora, not merely as an obstinate but as a quasi-magical people: a people so weak, dispersed, and few in number that extraordinary, not to say occult, capacities and sources of strength on their part must be invoked to explain their survival as a coherent culture. And the very invisibility to non-Jewish eyes of the actual sources of the capacity for survival displayed by Jewish communities (of which we shall have more to say in chapters 11–13) has functioned in turn to make the suspicion of secret and possibly malignant collective Jewish powers and purposes all the more plausible to troubled minds at moments of political crisis.

What ignites these slumbering suspicions into full-blooded political anti-semitism is, I suggested, the repeated refusal of substantial numbers of Jews (always enough to prevent Jews and Judaism disappearing into total assimilation) to abandon their history and Jewishness by immersing themselves, with others, in whatever messianic movement within the non-Jewish world happens, at a given historical moment, to be driven by the fear of marginalization to extend its membership and influence by any means possible and which therefore feels any rejection of its views as contempt, as rejection, as a threat—and of course (by its own standards) as profoundly immoral.

In the present chapter and the four immediately preceding it, I have argued, in effect, that these conditions for a recrudescence of political antisemitism are satisfied at present, on the non-Jewish side, by the current situation of left-wing or "progressive" political parties in the West, and on the Jewish side, by the equally anomalous but from a historical standpoint characteristically Jewish situation of Israel. In the non-Jewish world, we have a still-powerful movement, that of the utopian (Popper's term) or messianic left, that has largely lost its historic role as the defender and voice of the industrial proletariat. Its central political project in the past has been socialism: the project, conceived both in economic and moral terms, of replacing private with public enterprise. But the successive collapse of socialism in countries where it has been tried has made this difficult to defend. To continue to attract supporters, particularly among the young, the left has found itself in need of a new set of moral imperatives whose realization could be represented as demanding sacrifice, political organization, and struggle. In the 1960s, the movement found a new role of this kind consistent with its traditional values of equality and inclusion through presenting itself as the defender of a range of putatively oppressed groups—women, victims of racism, colonized non-European peoples, sexual minorities—whose interests came to replace, for it, those of the industrial proletariat. But of late years, this modest collection of causes has yielded center

stage to one: anti-imperialism or antiracism. Although these new commitments have brought it considerable influence, the movement is still intrinsically
marginal enough to feel that it must keep up the momentum of acceptance
and conversion. (It is curious, and mildly comic, from this point of view that
the movement founded to advance the cause of the British politician Jeremy
Corbyn, an elderly man deeply rooted in the politics of the New Left and in
his own words a "friend" of Hamas and Hezbollah,[19] should actually be called
Momentum).

On the Jewish side of the equation, we have Israel. The founding of Israel
was, as we saw earlier, in no sense an expression of Western colonialism. Apart
from its commitment to parliamentary democracy, freedom of speech and association, and the rule of law, Israel is not in any general sense an expression of
Western culture at all. It is almost wholly an expression of Jewish culture—the
culture that the Nazis almost, but not quite, succeeded in exterminating from
the face of the earth. It is an expression of that Jewish idiom that, in Cynthia
Ozick's words, frequently "goes against the grain of the world at large." In the
present case, the foundation and subsequent history of Israel has gone profoundly against the grain of late-twentieth- and twenty-first-century Western political culture. At a time when Europe has been withdrawing within
its pre-nineteenth-century borders, Israel has established what to many European eyes, especially on the left, can only appear as a European outpost in
non-European lands. Furthermore, at a time when Europe wishes to persuade
itself—in the face, it must be said, of a great deal of evidence to the contrary—
that it is loved, or at any rate tolerated, by all but a small and violent minority of
Muslims, Israel, at least as much of Europe sees it, is doing everything it can to
exacerbate already difficult relations with Islam. Worse still, from a European
standpoint, Israel stands as a beacon of Western political standards, of tolerance, democracy, and the rule of law. The defense of those standards against
fascism in the 1930s and 1940s plunged the continent into a vast and debilitating
war. For that reason, few in Western Europe wish to be forced to defend them
again—and particularly not in the context of the Muslim cultures of the Near
East with which many Europeans—and Americans—would dearly love to find
some accommodation that would allow them safely to leave the region to look
after its own affairs.

These discordances with the present political mood in the West echo, of
course, far beyond the limits of the Western left either in its hard or its liberal
versions. But from the point of view of large sections of the left, they make
it almost irresistible to find in the Israeli-Palestinian conflict precisely the
cause, and the set of associated rallying cries, that the movement needs both

to dramatize its new identity and to burnish its credentials as antiracist and an-ticolonial. A few Jews, mostly academics, have signed up for this program. But for the main body of the Jewish community, however constitutionally inclined to adopt liberal causes, it is manifestly impossible to do so.

The result can only be the present, very standard, recrudescence of political antisemitism in which we find people like John Mearsheimer (see chapter 9) drawing once again the standard distinction between the "good Jew," who has signed up for the bitter terms of non-Jewish acceptance—and the "bad" or reprobate remainder. These latter once again find themselves pilloried for their "obstinacy" in refusing to fall in with demands for the dismantling of their identity as Jews (remember Clermont-Tonnerre!) on the part of yet another non-Jewish messianic movement, and in consequence expelled from commu-nity with the very people whom they had imagined might provide their best bulwark against further persecution in the diaspora.

Adapting the Jews, or "Zios," to the role they at present serve in the demonol-ogy of sections of the left requires, of course, that the history and nature of the Israeli-Palestinian conflict be reinterpreted wholesale in ways that adapt it to fit the procrustean bed of the left's new concerns. That is, it has to be interpreted as a conflict between a group of land-thieving colonials and the colonized people whom they have expelled and impoverished; between racists and those they despise as racially inferior; between the vaunting industrial power of American capitalism and the impotence of a society of harmless traditional agricultural-ists; and last but not least, between "white" Europeans and a "brown" third-world people.

As I have tried to show in the preceding four chapters, and as many Arab commentators hostile to the left and its tendentious political narratives have themselves pointed out, this reinterpretation cannot be carried through with-out radically distorting both the history of the conflict and the present realities of Israeli and Palestinian society. Indeed, as I have tried to show, its distance from the awkward and idiosyncratic facts of the conflict is such that it cannot be carried through at all without embracing most of the doctrines and imagery characteristic of traditional political antisemitism.

In the literature of anti-Zionism and BDS, for that reason, we need hardly be surprised to encounter, as we do, the familiar figure of the arrogant, racially superior Jew with his absurd conviction of chosenness, or to find ourselves reacquainted with the Jew as inimical interloper, destructive of the economic life of non-Jewish societies, or as supreme conspirator adept at taking over from the inside such feeble goyish political constructions as the State Department or the White House in order to pervert them to his own malign purposes—in short, with all the familiar images and fantasies of Julius Streicher's prewar Nazi propaganda magazine *Der Stürmer*.

ANTI-IMPERIALISM ON CAMPUS

The new politics that, as Alan Johnson puts it, has "abandoned universal progressive values" in favor of a view of the world, starkly in black and white, that sees "progressive politics" primarily as a conflict between imperialism and anti-imperialism, power and "the Other" has enjoyed particular success in the universities. "In academia it has come to dominate disciplines such as Post-Colonial Studies and Middle East Studies, and is considered unremarkable and scholarly in a number of mainstream disciplines, including English, Sociology and Anthropology."[20]

It may therefore be worth pausing briefly in conclusion to consider why the universities, given their supposed institutional commitment to truth and sound reasoning, have proved so fertile a field for the kind of thinking we have been examining.

TWO CONCEPTIONS OF THE ROLE OF THE INTELLECTUAL

The Enlightenment initiated a gradual shift in the center of gravity of politics, from the courts of princes to the theater of public debate. It also introduced two distinct accounts of the relationship of intellectuals to the new public politics. It would not be too far from the truth to say that whereas the Enlightenment in France and Germany tended on the whole to see the intellectual as the natural master and director of public debate, the British, or more accurately the Scottish Enlightenment, tended, on the contrary, to see the intellectual as, broadly speaking, its servant.

The essence of the latter view is neatly caught by the Scottish philosopher David Hume in the following account of the modest but useful role in public affairs he felt should properly be assigned to the philosopher.

> Besides, we may observe, in every art or profession, even those which most concern life and action, that a spirit of accuracy, however acquired, carries all of them nearer their perfection, and renders them more subservient to the interests of society. And though a philosopher may live remote from business, the genius of philosophy, if carefully cultivated by several, must gradually diffuse itself throughout the whole society, and bestow a similar correctness on every art and calling. The politician will acquire greater foresight and subtility, in the subdividing and balancing of power; and the general more

regularity in his discipline, and more caution in his plans and operations. The stability of modern governments above the ancient, and the accuracy of modern philosophy, have improved, and probably will improve, by similar gradations.[21]

There is here no suggestion that the philosopher should go beyond articulating "the spirit of accuracy" in the interest of encouraging fidelity to truth and reason in the discharge of public business to the extent of *actually taking over, from the hands of the politician or the general, the concrete control and conduct of that business.* Abstract thought, according to Hume, has a valuable role in society, but that role is not the detailed direction of public affairs.

French and German philosophy from the seventeenth century onward took a very different turn. In the thought of both the major seventeenth-century rationalists Leibniz and Spinoza a central place is given to the idea that virtue and rational understanding are essentially connected: or to put it another way, that intellectual power equates with moral power, both in insight and action.

The idea of an equivalence amounting almost to an identity between reason and virtue was to bear a rich burden of fruit in the succeeding two centuries. The process of extracting from it a justification for assigning a central role in politics to the intellectual was begun by Rousseau. In *Du contrat social* (1762), he argues that a just society can only come about if each citizen is prepared to abandon any goal that he or she does not share with the generality of his or her fellow citizens. This is the celebrated "general will." But how is one to discover what is in fact in accord with the general will? Rousseau is clear that public debate in the ordinary sense is more likely to produce some sort of compromise or resultant of the private interests of individuals or interest groups rather than the desired revelation of what is strictly common to each and every one of the individual citizens. Nevertheless, some sort of public assembly must be trusted with the task of discovering the general will. But it will only succeed in doing so, Rousseau thinks, insofar as its debates are guided by an inspired "legislator" (*législateur*), envisaged for Rousseau's purposes as a figure capable of recognizing what, in any citizen's lexicon of desires, is of merely private significance, and what, on the contrary, unites him or her to the broad mass of his or her fellows.

Rousseau's description of his "legislator" was to prove prescient for the subsequent course of European politics.

> He who dares to undertake the making of a people's institutions ought to
> feel himself capable, so to speak, of changing human nature, of transforming
> each individual, who is by himself a complete and solitary whole, into part
> of a greater whole from which he, in a manner, receives his life and being;

of altering man's constitution for the purpose of strengthening it; and of substituting a subordinate (*partielle*) and moral existence for the physical and independent existence nature has conferred upon us all. He must, in a word, take away from man his own resources and give him instead new ones alien to him, and incapable of being made use of without the help of other men. The more completely these natural resources are annihilated, the greater and the more lasting are those which he acquires, and the more stable and perfect are the new institutions; so that if each citizen is nothing and can do nothing without the rest, and the resources acquired by the whole are equal or superior to the aggregate of the resources of all the individuals, it may be said that legislation is at the highest point of perfection.[22]

Intellectuals are people who live by and for the mind. To such people, it is an inspiring thought that dedication to the life of the mind might not only have as its grand aim the progressive transformation of man and society but that it might place in the hands of the dedicated intellectual himself precisely the powers needed to inaugurate and complete such a task. The French Revolution was led by the first major inheritors of this ideal—men like Robespierre and Saint-Just, who regarded their actions as both directed and justified by two intimately interconnected intellectual abstractions: reason and virtue.[23] There has followed a very long series of major intellectual figures, of both left and right, whose conception of the leading role of the intellectual in both conceiving and setting in train the transformation of man and society has followed the same pattern. The list includes Hammann, Fichte, Saint-Simon, Hegel, Marx, Nietzsche, and innumerable minor figures, down to such twentieth-century representatives of the tradition as Heidegger, Sartre, Althusser, Foucault, or Lacan.

It is this tradition that people primarily have in mind when they speak of the idea of the public intellectual, usually adding, with regret or satisfaction as the case may be, that such intellectuals are regarded with much greater respect in France or Germany than they are in Britain or America. If one were to ask why that is so, a simple and by no means misleading answer would be that English-speaking culture since the 1750s has tended to side with Hume against Rousseau. Anglo-Saxon culture, that is to say, has tended to regard intellectuals as the servants rather than as the inspired impresarios of public debate, and public debate itself rather than intellectual insight, as the source of moral progress.

This was very much the atmosphere of British and American philosophy in the 1950s, when I was moving from undergraduate work at the University of Birmingham in England to graduate work at the University of Michigan. I remember in particular a conversation with my thesis supervisor at Michigan,

C. L. Stevenson, whose defense of emotivism in moral theory, *Ethics and Language*,[24] a work deeply indebted to Hume's writings on moral philosophy, was a celebrated text at the time. Stevenson had been criticized for "irrationalism": for defending the view that there are no absolute moral standards in the sense of standards envisaged as capable of transcending the ebb and flow of public debate, because they are (supposedly) directly accessible to reason. His answer, as he put it to me in conversation, was that we come together in public moral debate with the primary end of "knocking the corners off one another." In such debate, that is to say, each of us is liable to hear reasons mooted why his own prejudices and idées fixes should be thought less persuasive by others than they are to himself. If he hears enough along these lines, he may even be led to drop or amend some of them—as may other participants to the debate. And in this way, Stevenson thought, we may be led to adopt common values that, whatever weaknesses may remain to be discovered in them, have at any rate more to be said for them than any untested moral prejudice evolved by the individual mind, however superior its intellectual gifts.

Views consonant with this outlook were in those remote days fairly general in the humanities departments of universities in the English-speaking world. Academic intellectuals, on the whole, saw their role in society not as that of managing or directing public debate but rather as leavening it, through the introduction of their students, and through them of the population at large, to higher standards of independence of mind and accuracy in reasoning and factual assertion.

THE AGE OF SUSPICION

From the start of the 1960s, however, a new and radically opposed climate of opinion began to dominate in the academy. It is commonplace to describe the change as involving the rise of a "hermeneutics of suspicion." The phrase is due to the French philosopher Paul Ricoeur, who introduced it in 1970, in a work on Freud.[25] Ricoeur defines it in terms of a parallel he finds to exist between three dominant intellectual figures of the nineteenth and twentieth centuries: Marx, Nietzsche, and Freud. In dealing with the role of religion in human life, Ricoeur suggests, each of the three distinguishes the apparent meaning of religion in the sense of the functions it serves in human life, from a "real" meaning, that appears only when the former is stripped away. For Marx, while the function of religion seems on the face of it to be that of acquainting its votaries with the divine, in reality it serves as a means of distracting the laboring poor from the inhumanity of their working conditions. Nietzsche undertakes a parallel "unmasking" of religion to reveal its true function of fettering the strong for the benefit of the weak, and Freud to reveal its real connection with infantile fantasies of a father god.

In *Culture and Anarchy*, Matthew Arnold (1869) had defined "culture" as the pursuit of human perfection through the communication and interpretation of "the best that had been thought and said in the world." The liberal humanism that prevailed in the academy prior to the 1960s took this definition, broadly speaking, at face value and regarded the function of humanities departments in universities as essentially that of interpreting culture, in this Arnoldian sense, to its students and beyond them to society at large. Into this humanist heaven the hermeneutics of suspicion introduced the intoxicatingly disruptive thought, that the bulk of the somnolent inherited cultural certainties currently ruling the academic roost might, one and all, be thoroughly fraudulent and in urgent need of interpretive ("hermeneutic") unmasking of broadly the kind visited upon religion by Marx, Nietzsche, and Freud.

The succeeding half century saw this vision of things become dominant, as to a considerable extent it still is, in department after department. It is a view that—very much in the spirit of Marx's theory of ideology—treats culture in the Arnoldian sense of the body of historic thought and writing that defines the nature and historical situation of a given nation less as a source of understanding and enlightenment than as a source of error and entrenched illusion: as something, therefore, that can yield understanding only if it is not taken at face value but rather critically dismantled and deconstructed in ways that reveal the pernicious nature of the functions that "in reality" it serves.

To understand culture in this way clearly yields an account of the role of the intellectual far closer to that associated with Rousseau's notion of the legislator than with the one defended by Hume in the passage quoted above. For suppose it is true—to a considerable extent anyway—that the character of a civilization or a nation is indeed defined by the nature of its historically accumulated cultural monuments: Arnold's "the best that has been thought and said in the world." And suppose even more plausibly that the link between a society and its cultural monuments consists of general belief in the validity of the vision of reality that they embody and communicate. Now suppose that a body of highly intelligent people—public intellectuals working in the humanities departments of universities, let's say—possess the means of demonstrating that that vision of reality is essentially fraudulent and that its general acceptance serves merely to blind the bulk of the populace to a deeper and darker reality. Must we not conclude that these highly intelligent people are in possession of insights—and beyond that, of sophisticated methods of inquiry capable of uncovering many more such insights—capable of overturning the present order of society and no doubt—since an order of society based on truth is always likely to be better than one based on fantasy and illusion—of replacing it with a better one?

The attractions—to intellectuals—of this account of the role of the intellectual in society, and more especially of the university professor, are, I think, evident enough. It transforms the cloistered scholar at one fell swoop from a passive conduit for cultural riches not of his creation, not only into a social revolutionary but into the possessor of precisely the combination of insight and expertise necessary for the successful direction and prosecution of social revolution: in short, into the impresario of historical change envisaged by Rousseau. Not surprisingly, it has proved since the 1960s popular not only among academics, but also among media pundits, whose trade also involves them in detailed analysis of the daily vicissitudes of political debate, while excluding them from any actual exercise of power.

It is primarily this, it seems to me, that explains the present reluctance of the university educated to describe themselves, as they would have done in the 1950s, as "liberal humanists" and their preference instead for the designation "liberal left." "Humanism," as a former Sussex colleague of mine said to me on a recent occasion, has nowadays become, as he put it, a "boo word." It captures in one word all that outmoded Arnoldian rubbish about sweetness and light and the best that has been thought and said. "Liberal left," on the other hand, has a forward-looking ring to it. It suggests that even though one may not be wholly in sympathy with Marx, Nietzsche, or Freud or for that matter with Foucault, with Derrida, with the "historicizing" of literary studies, or with any specific wind of change that has blown through the academy since 1960, one is nevertheless alive to the virtues of suspicion regarding the credentials of traditional certainties.

This shift in the self-image of large numbers of academics and university-trained intellectuals over the past half century, from a Humian to a Rousseauian conception of the function of the intellectual in society, goes far toward explaining the growth, both in the universities themselves and elsewhere in society, of a climate of opinion broadly oriented toward a version of what it is to be "on the left" defined centrally not in terms of detailed policy or immediate practicality but rather in the abstract moral and ideological terms with which such people feel themselves chiefly at home.

The new confidence of university-trained intellectuals in their own ability to see through and beyond traditional ways of thinking that still carry conviction to less well-educated compatriots, however, also goes far to explain, it seems to me, another salient feature of contemporary left-liberal opinion—namely, its rooted contempt for what media pundits nowadays call populism but that used in former days to be known as popular democracy or the will of the people.

Such contempt, and with it the sense that the speaker not only knows far better than his benighted compatriots what should be done, at least in the abstract, but knows it largely because he or she is also, morally speaking, a decidedly better person than they, often expresses itself in kinds of ranting moral hyperbole that as we have already seen, have become characteristic of the extremes of present-day left-wing discourse, particularly where Israel is concerned. The following passage from the London-based Israeli writer Gilad Atzmon, cited by David Hirsh, is typical.

> To regard Hitler as the ultimate evil is nothing but surrendering to the Zio-centric discourse. To regard Hitler as the wickedest man and the Third Reich as the embodiment of evilness is to let Israel off the hook. To compare Olmert to Hitler is to provide Israel and Olmert with a metaphorical moral shield. It maintains Hitler at the lead and allows Olmert to stay in the tail. . . . Israel has already established a unique interpretation of the notion of wickedness that has managed to surpass any other evil. It is about time we internalise the fact that Israel and Zionism are the ultimate Evil with no comparison. . . . Now is the time to stand up and say it, unlike the Nazis who had respect for other national movements including Zionism, Israel has zero respect for anyone including its next door neighbours. The Israeli behaviour should be realised as the ultimate vulgar biblical barbarism on the verge of cannibalism. Israel is nothing but evilness for the sake of evilness. It is wickedness with no comparison.[26]

This might, and no doubt does, pass in certain circles as high moral seriousness. But moral seriousness consists in part in the capacity to recognize both the diversity of our basic moral commitments and their inbuilt potentiality for conflict. The psychologist Jonathan Haidt, in a recent best-selling book, *The Righteous Mind: Why Good People Are Divided by Politics and Religion*,[27] argues that there are at least five types of fundamental moral concern, or as he explicitly terms them "foundations" (for morality/politics). They include the contrasts between care/harm, fairness/cheating, loyalty/betrayal, authority/subversion, and finally, sanctity/degradation. One might possibly add others: freedom/restraint and equality/inequality suggest themselves. Haidt argues that people on the left, liberals in American terms, attach value only to a small selection of these foundations: notably the contrasts between care and harm and that between fairness and cheating (I would add with reference to the British political scene, the contrast between equality and inequality).

Conservatives, on the other hand, he suggests, confer value in some degree on every member of his set of "foundations."

Haidt's analysis confirms among other things, the narrowing of both moral and practical concerns that Johnson, as we saw earlier, finds characteristic of recent developments on the hard left. It, together with the ranting moral hysteria that one finds in writing like Agnon's—common enough in anti-Zionist circles—cannot in the end be supposed to bode well for the left or for that matter, for any community over which such ideas manage to establish an influence.

The support rallied in such ways is largely, though by no means exclusively, juvenile, inexperienced, and richly ignorant of the real workings of human affairs either in the Middle East or in the world at large. Worse still, it consists largely of people interested only in facts that support their political stance. And these are considerations, among others, that that should give pause to any Arab who imagines that anti-Zionism and BDS constitute useful bodies of support for Palestinian interests. Rather, the truth is that both constitute tactical devices for ensuring continued support in the West for purely Western movements, whose interest in the welfare and future of the Arabs is as temporary and tactical as it is self-interested. Political anti-Zionism, as its dalliance with political antisemitism would tend to indicate, is a phenomenon not of glad confident morning but of the feared onset of darkness. And the ill consequences it threatens are not, as I shall argue in part 5, confined to Jews. They threaten all of us, and that includes Arabs and the Muslim world in general.

The reason for that is that political antisemitism is a delusive fantasy. Hence, whatever short-term political advantages may be conferred by its adoption, its essential delusiveness invariably denies it any good or lasting political result. In the present case, the main practical function served by anti-Zionism and BDS is that of giving aid and comfort to the various groups engaged in "armed struggle" against Israel. Their activities are in no way likely to lead to any good outcome, let alone to the absurd paradise of peace and mutual respect in a Muslim-majority successor state envisaged by protagonists of the "one-state solution." It is not difficult to envisage a possible way forward from the present situation. It might, for instance, as an Israeli friend once suggested to me, prove possible to establish a federal state, somewhat on the model of Switzerland involving Jewish, Arab Muslim, and Arab Christian cantons, with citizens free to settle in any canton but with intra-cantonal ethnoreligious political autonomy secured, say, by detaching voting rights from residence rights. But any such solution would require as a precondition the abandonment of all armed violence against Israel that Mahmoud Abbas has sometimes—but only sometimes—been brave enough to demand.

One must hope that something of the sort may eventually emerge. For those public intellectuals, leading academics, and media pundits who favor and promote the "anti-Zionist" and BDS narrative, on the other hand, the words that come most sharply to mind are perhaps those that Thomas Henry Huxley addressed to Bishop Samuel Wilberforce in Oxford in 1860, at the height of the controversy over Darwin's *On the Origin of Species*: "While it is no shame to have a monkey as an ancestor, I would be ashamed to be connected to a man who uses great gifts to obscure the truth."

NOTES

1. Julius 2010, 449.
2. Alexander 2003, 60.
3. Popper 1945, 1:158–60.
4. Popper 1945, 1:158.
5. Friedrich Engels, "Socialism: Utopian and Scientific," originally published in French in the March, April, and May issues of *Revue Socialiste* in 1880; an English translation by Paul Lafargue (1892), authorized by Engels, is available at https://www.marxists.org/archive/marx/works/download/Engels_Socialism _Utopian_and_Scientific.pdf.
6. Popper 1945, 1:159–60.
7. *Guardian*, June 22, 2016.
8. Rich 2016, 7.
9. Hirsh 2018, 50.
10. Rich 2016, 8.
11. Hirsh 2018, 51.
12. Hirsh 2018, 59.
13. Hirsh 2018, 59–60.
14. Alan Johnson, "No, Jeremy Corbyn Is Not Antisemitic—but the Left Should Be Wary of Who He Calls Friends," *New Statesman*, September 2, 2015, www.newstatesman.com.
15. Hirsh 2018, 57–58.
16. Hirsh 2018, 4.
17. Available in the "Student Resources" section of the philosophy department website at www.txstate.edu.
18. Hirsh 2018, 11–12.
19. Video of address by Corbyn, cited in Hirsh 2018, 43.
20. Hirsh 2018, 59.
21. Hume 1975, 10.
22. Rousseau 1913, 32–33.

23. See Blum 1986.

24. Stevenson 1944.

25. Ricoeur 1970.

26. Gilad Atzmon, "Beyond Comparison," *Peace Palestine* 2006, cited in Hirsh 2018, 235.

27. I am grateful to my friend Michael Leffell for introducing me to Haidt's work.

PART IV

JUDAISM DEFACED

ELEVEN

—ᴡᴧ—

A PRIMITIVE RELIGION?

The Jews, it is said, resisted the expansion of their own religion into Christianity; they were in the habit of spitting on the cross; they have held the name of Christ to be *Anathema*. Who taught them that? The men who made Christianity a curse to them: the men who made the name of Christ a symbol for the spirit of vengeance, and, what was worse, made the execution of the vengeance a pretext for satisfying their own savageness, greed, and envy: the men who sanctioned with the name of Christ a barbaric and blundering copy of pagan fatalism in taking the words "His blood be upon us and on our children" as a divinely appointed verbal warrant for wreaking cruelty from generation to generation on the people from whose sacred writings Christ drew His teaching. Strange retrogression in the professors of an expanded religion, boasting an illumination beyond the spiritual doctrine of Hebrew prophets! For Hebrew prophets proclaimed a God who demanded mercy rather than sacrifices.

—George Eliot, "Impressions of Theophrastus Such"

ANTISEMITISM AND THE COMMONPLACE DENIGRATION OF JUDAISM

In chapters 4 and 5, I suggested that there is certainly "something that Jews do" that accounts for the existence of political antisemitism. Unfortunately, that something is not ruling the world or even, as Hannah Arendt and many others have imagined, possessing the brilliant talent for business that most of the

Jews known to me so sadly lack. It is not something even that Jews could avoid doing, at least short of ceasing to exist as Jews. For what enrages the political antisemite is simply the "obstinate" refusal of the bulk of Jews to abandon Judaism and throw in their lot *en masse* with whatever political or religious nostrum the political antisemite happens to believe in.

Given the small numbers, the internal divisions, and the resulting political weakness of actual Jewish communities, the threat posed by Jewish obstinacy, could never be a practical one. Yet it can nevertheless be acutely felt, by a rising political movement, first as a political irritant and then as a heaven-sent means of both disguising and combatting non-Jewish opposition to its rule. On the one hand, a spurious unity can be claimed by representing opposition to the movement from within the non-Jewish world as coming exclusively from sources—Jewish ones—at least notionally outside that world. And on the other hand, non-Jewish opponents can be smeared and the threat they pose reduced by representing them as willing servants of disruptive alien forces: as, in effect, "dumb goys."

The various versions of cultural imperialism that have dominated over the past two millennia what was once the Greek and Roman world have all claimed final and universal validity for their founding ideas. A claim of universal validity is always somewhat weakened if it cannot in fact claim universal acceptance. Triumphalism, whether religious or political, thus requires that dissent, where permitted or accepted, be at least kept within bounds. The bulk of Jewish opinion over the centuries has made a habit of persistently transgressing such bounds. Not all Jews, of course: some always prove amenable to whatever is for the moment widely considered to constitute reason. But this only gives the political antisemite further grounds for resentment toward "bad Jews" for refusing to admit, as "good Jews" so freely do, the essential correctness of his vision of things. Nor, as we have seen, is the distinction between good and bad Jews dead in the twenty-first century. The political scientist John Mearsheimer, in a spirit of—no doubt unconscious—self-parody, has provided a recent, perfectly straight-faced instance of it, by distinguishing in both the title and the text of a recent article between "righteous Jews" and "the new Afrikaners."[1] "Righteous Jews," of course, are persons of Jewish descent who happen to agree with Mearsheimer and his friends. The "new Afrikaners" are the unregenerate remainder.

The steadfast resistance of the unregenerate Jew to seeing the reasonableness of what strikes his persecutors as unquestionable good sense of course requires explanation. The explanation chosen by the political antisemite is that the unregenerate Jew, known for short as "the Jew," is not with "us" because he is against "us." Moreover, he is not merely passive in his rejection of the light that "we" represent. He is actively plotting against it and plotting in underhand ways, using secret powers and resources whose existence goes far to explain how he is able to persist in his wicked ways. He can do so because he is a cog in a Jewish world conspiracy that besides working ceaselessly for "our" destruction supports in him a degree of recalcitrance otherwise inexplicable, given the apparent power of "the Jew" to resist levels of persecution that would break the spirit of any other people.

In one way, of course, the reasoning of the political antisemite is sound enough. The reluctance of Jews to cease to be Jews would be explicable if the practice of Judaism and membership of the Jewish community offered advantages so great as to outweigh both the fear and the reality of persecution. The antisemite assumes these advantages to consist of access to wealth and conspiratorially exercised power. But these assumptions sit ill with the individual poverty and the collective impotence, barring certain places and certain periods, under which the majority of Jews in most countries of the diaspora have labored on across the centuries.

Is it possible, then, that the rewards of remaining Jewish, as many Jews believe, and as we earlier in chapter 4 found Dennis Prager and Joseph Telushkin claiming in their *Why the Jews?*,[2] might be moral and spiritual, personal and familial, rather than material?

For the political antisemite to envisage *that* possibility would mean granting something destructive to his own position—namely, that the Jew who refuses conversion might conceivably possess, as a Jew, access to something better than the antisemite's own creed could offer him. Denigration of Judaism and of Jews for continuing to accept it is thus always an essential element in political antisemitism. That is why, since the analysis of political antisemitism is the central theme of this book, I shall be devoting this and the next two chapters to the nature of that denigration and more particularly to its claim to be factually based.

Surprisingly, the possibility that the climate of the moral and spiritual world generated by Judaism might *with good reason* be felt by the participant to be sweeter, saner, and generally more attractive than that of certain competing non-Jewish cultural and spiritual milieus, has seldom been entertained, let alone granted, even among those for the most part free from other aspects of antisemitic delusion. On the contrary, both Judaism and its obstinate adherents have found themselves consistently represented throughout the non-Jewish world, both by antisemites and by those preaching tolerance of the Jews' strange proclivities, as irrational, backward, superstitious, and certainly morally dubious, if not actually depraved. As David Nirenberg notes, the Enlightenment was in no way exceptional in this respect: "Because the Jews were imagined as the most fanatically irrational segment of the species (indeed as the very origin of fanatical irrationality), they provided the perfect proving ground for the powers of Enlightenment. Perfect because the Enlightenment won either way. If even the Jews could be 'regenerated,' then there were no limits to the emancipatory powers of Enlightenment anthropology. But if they could not, it simply meant that reason had reached the boundaries of its authority, and that the Jews lay on the other side."[3]

THREE GROUNDS OF DENIGRATION

The supposed deficiencies of Judaism most widely held up for reprobation among non-Jews are three in number. They concern, respectively, its supposed character as a religion, its alleged defects as a system of morals, and the support it offers to what is widely perceived as Jewish tribalism, or as it is usually more politely termed, particularism.

So far as the first is concerned, Judaism has been widely perceived among non-Jews, and to some extent still is perceived, as a primitive religion—a religion in which fear of divine vengeance, rather than the effort to emulate divine love and forgiveness, plays the principal part and in which much attention is given to absurd and fanciful observances in diet and dress supposedly designed to placate a terrifying deity. The second major ground of disapproval accuses the Jewish conception of morality of requiring the subjection of individual reason and conscience to a collectively imposed regime of unquestioning obedience to traditionally sanctioned rules of conduct whose moral authority is never queried, let alone submitted to rational scrutiny and criticism. The third line of objection is that Judaism involves a rejection of the generous universalism of the other major religions—their mission to speak to and for all humankind. In contrast, Judaism is held to be rootedly particularist in the sense of speaking to and for Jews alone. Worse still, the commandments of its God, expressly conceived as the God of a single, "chosen" people, interpose layers of unfortunate obstacles, of food, dress, marriage, and so on between observant Jews and non-Jews, reinforcing the tendency of Jews in the diaspora to live entirely within their own community and to occupy themselves solely with that community's affairs to the exclusion of the wider concerns of the surrounding, non-Jewish society.

The danger of these very widespread beliefs is that while they constitute standard components of antisemitic propaganda, they are by no means held exclusively by antisemites. Rather, they help to create among non-Jews an atmosphere, a climate of half-conscious denigration of Jews and Judaism, which while it may coexist perfectly easily in many cases with tolerance and even affection toward Jews, nevertheless keeps open the permanent possibility of a slide by reasonable-seeming stages toward far more explicit, consciously argued, and damaging forms of antisemitic delusion.

It is therefore a natural part of the task the present work has set itself, to do what can be done within reasonable limits of space to expose the confusions, misunderstandings, and errors of fact that underpin the above three commonplace and traditional lines of anti-Judaic denigration. We shall examine the first in the present chapter, the second in chapter 12, and the third in chapter 13.

One of the effects of the tide of commonplace defamation against which we shall be swimming in these chapters, according to the Jewish philosopher Franz Rosenzweig, is to reduce any discussion of Judaism to apologetics: "In 'Apologetic thinking,' Rosenzweig emphasized that . . . derogatory depiction of Judaism by Christian thinkers also has an impact on Jewish thought. . . 'Apologetic thinking remains dependent on the cause, the adversary. And in this sense Jewish thinking remains apologetic thinking.' . . . In his essay on 'The New Learning,' he argued that Jewish thought needs to find a path to the heart of Jewish life, instead of proving a relation between the Jewish (*Jüdischem*) and the non-Jewish (*Ausserjüdischem*)."[4]

The apologetic stance, that is to say, because it sees its primary task as that of replying to the critic's objections, all too easily ends by internalizing the concerns and outlook of the critic as a standard to which Judaism must at all costs be shown to conform, with the result that a truly radical defense, one that would work not by meeting the critic's demands but by showing those demands to be too ill-conceived and confused to be worth meeting, goes by the board.

It is a radical defense of Judaism of that kind, and not mere apologetics, at which I shall be aiming in these three chapters. So far as a non-Jew can hope to achieve such a thing, it is my intention here to do my best to follow Rosenzweig's demand and "find a path to the heart of Jewish life."

IN THE FOOTSTEPS OF TERTULLIAN

The main outlines of Christian opposition to Judaism were laid down in the second and third centuries CE, following the gradual, though at times bitter, separation that had occurred earlier between Jewish and gentile Christianity. The distinguished Canadian theologian William Nicholls, the founder and for several decades the head of the Department of Religious Studies at the University of British Columbia, offers a penetrating guide to the dialectics of this process of separation, which according to him still lie at the foundation of modern theological claims to the effect that Christianity has *superseded* Judaism.[5]

> The Christian literature of the second century onward has taken on a new tone, already foreshadowed in the later strata of the New Testament. The new tone is one of rejection of the Jewish people, based on the claim that God had himself rejected them because of their rejection and killing of their Messiah, Jesus. Christian writers now claim that the Church has altogether taken over the position of the elect people of God from the Jewish people. We are learning today to call this development *the theology of supersession* [emphasis Nicholls's].
>
> Israel has been rejected and displaced, superseded by the Church as the new Israel, which is also now the true Israel.[6]

This development was largely directed by the need of theologians representing a developing orthodoxy to find grounds for resisting the ideas of the heretic Marcion of Sinope (ca. 85–ca. 160 CE). Marcion held that the God from whom Jesus came was a different and far higher deity from the creating and law-giving God spoken of in the Jewish bible. Effectively, Marcion was claiming that Judaism and Christianity were simply different religions, having virtually nothing to do with each other—and by implication that the Jews deserved no special blame for refusing to accept Christ as their Messiah, since he was in fact no such thing. Hence, for Marcion, the Jewish bible was in no sense a Christian document and should simply be jettisoned by Christians.

Nicholls points out that had the church felt able to join Marcion in dispensing with the Jewish scriptures, it might have been able to adopt a position far less opposed to the Jewish people and their religion. And he notes in this connection how close modern liberal Christianity has come to Marcionism: "Looking back on the controversy from a modern perspective, it may not seem altogether clear why the Gentile church did not in fact simply cut its links with Judaism and approach the Gentile world as an entirely new religion. Modern liberal Christians are so convinced of the ethical inferiority of Judaism that it is hard to see what meaning the 'Old Testament' continues to have for them. Voices are occasionally heard suggesting it should now be dropped altogether."[7] Nicholls adduces a number of reasons why the early gentile church retained the Jewish scriptures and with them its connection to Judaism, none of them individually determining but in combination decisive. Some theologians at the time were indeed introducing the idea of Jesus as the divine word incarnate, yet to go all the way with this tendency, abandoning altogether the claim that Jesus was the Jewish Messiah, would have meant abandoning not only the Old

Testament but also large parts of the New Testament. To represent Christianity as an entirely novel religion, moreover, would have meant abandoning ground to pagan critics for whom its novelty was one of the main arguments against it. In addition, the gentile church also needed to resist the spiritualizing tendencies of Marcion and the Gnostics, for whom the created world was wholly corrupt because the creation of an inferior God, entirely distinct from the purely spiritual God whose representative they understood Jesus to be. To retain the unity of God and to avoid a complete rejection of the created world and the corporeal in general as corrupt and corrupting, the gentile church needed to take possession of the Hebrew scriptures. But to do so implied denying them to the Jews. Since the "right" of the Jews to their scriptures depended on their having been chosen by God to receive them, that in turn entailed giving grounds for believing that the status of chosenness had passed from the Jews to gentile Christians, who had thus become "the new Israel." It had done so, the developing Christian argument ran, because the Jews themselves had shown themselves so mired in iniquity that God had finally deserted them, with the result that the "old covenant" between God and the Jewish people had been dissolved, to be replaced by a "new covenant" between God in the person of Christ and the church.

The growing anti-Judaism generated by these debates comes to a head in the writings of Tertullian (ca.155–ca. 240). Tertullian was a North African, possibly a Romanized Berber, and a resident of Carthage. He was not only, among other things, a lawyer and professional rhetorician who made speeches for clients, but he was also an important theologian, whose "treatment of the problems of the Trinity effectively defined the terminology for succeeding western theology up to the present."[8] He codified, rather than invented, Christian ideas concerning the radical inferiority both of Jews and of Judaism. His powers as a rhetorician allowed him to present in vivid terms themes already to be found in Justin and Irenaeus. Indeed, as the Catholic writer Edward Flannery has shown, much early Christian invective against the Jews echoes the very similar invective to be found in earlier Greek and Roman writers—Cicero, Seneca, Apion, Tacitus—merely adapting it to Christian polemical purposes.[9]

If the Jewish scriptures are to be regarded, contrary to the advice of the Marcionites, as inspired by the unique God worshipped alike by Jews and Christians, rather than by the second, inferior deity of Marcion and the Gnostics, then plainly it needs to be explained why Christians no longer make any attempt to keep the laws laid down in those scriptures. "The pagan critic Celsus is scathing on the subject, and Origen, the Christian writer who replied to him, is in some difficulties with his reply."[10]

Tertullian's own reply is that the commandments of the Torah, "which pagans and Christians alike regarded as degrading and unworthy of enlightened people,"[11] were imposed on the Jews because of their criminal character and "tendency to idolatry, sensuality and greed"—a character not shared by the rest of the human race. The Jews were always unworthy of divine election, and now that their long trail of crimes has culminated in the murder of their Messiah, they have finally lost it.

The ingrained wickedness of the Jews also explains, for Tertullian, why God in the Old Testament appears primarily as a God obsessed with vengeance and justice to the exclusion of mercy, quite unlike the God of love and forgiveness to whom, he holds, the world was first introduced by Jesus.

Tertullian's explanation is not that God is harsh but that he had to deal with an impossible people with whom only hard measures would work. What God does with Christians is different from, and superior to, what he was able to do with Jews, because he has much more responsive people on whom to work.[12]

Nicholls cites an important study of Tertullian by a Catholic writer, David Efroymson:[13]

> In his careful investigation of Tertullian's writings against the Jews in various contexts, Efroymson found no less than twenty-four counts on which the Jews are accused of iniquity. They rejected or killed both Jesus and the prophets, they persecuted Jesus' disciples and later Christians. They spread calumnies against Christians. They displayed envy or jealousy against Christians or Gentiles. They were guilty of pride (national or ethnic). They were contentious about the meaning of the words of the bible. They committed idolatry. They forgot or were ignorant of God. They lacked faith or hope, and they were blind. They manifested *duritia*, hardness or stiff-neckedness. They were impatient and mocked God's own patience. They were ungrateful and senseless. They were generally disobedient and sinful. They were and are worldly, earthy, sensual and gluttonous. They indulged in empty ritual. Their religion was obsolete and sterile. They were unready for and unworthy the gifts of God. They were hypocritical and petty. They even aided and abetted the Marcionites.[14]

One would like to think that these antique controversies retain little hold on modern Christian thinking. However, that is not Nicholls's conclusion. For him, Tertullian is still very much alive.

> The shocking thing about Tertullian is not that he accused the Jews of things no-one else thought of, but that so much he said so long ago is still familiar to someone with a Christian education. How many modern Christians

have not heard that Judaism is a religion of vengeance and Christianity one
of compassion? How many have not heard that Christian worship is more
spiritual than the sacrifices of the Temple? How many have not heard that Jesus
brought a new teaching, superior to Judaism, and that the Jews hated him and
conspired to kill him because of it? Above all, how many millions up to our own
time continue to hear that the Jews killed Christ? To this day, and in peaceful
North America, innocent Jewish children are being confronted by their
Christian classmates with the same accusation. . . . Tertullian's ideas are not
dead, even if few, if any, responsible Christian writers would after Auschwitz
marshal them in the same organized and deliberate campaign of polemic.[15]

THE CENTRALITY OF *CHESED*

It would be difficult indeed to understand the attachment of Jews to Judaism
if this account were accurate. But, in fact, it is a travesty. Let us begin with the
claim that "Judaism is a religion of vengeance and Christianity one of compassion." The Gospels contain a story, repeated in Mark 12 and Matthew 22,
concerning Jesus's answer to the question, "Which is the great (or first) commandment in the Law?" In Matthew, the questioner is a lawyer, whose object
is to tempt Jesus on behalf of the "scribes and Pharisees," who, in this Gospel,
are taken to represent orthodox Jewry. In Mark, the questioner is a scribe but
one who appears close to Jesus in belief, as the latter commends him as "not far
from the kingdom of God." Here is Mark's version:

> And one of the scribes came, and having heard them reasoning together,
> and perceiving that he had answered them well, asked him, "Which is the
> first commandment of all?" And Jesus answered him, "The first of all the
> commandments is, 'Hear, O Israel; the Lord our God is one Lord: and thou
> shalt love the Lord with all thy heart, and with all thy soul, and with all they
> mind, and with all thy strength': this is the first commandment. And the
> second is like, namely this. 'Thou shalt love thy neighbour as thyself.' There
> is none other commandment greater than these." And the scribe said to him,
> "Well, Master, thou hast said the truth: for there is one God; and there is
> none other but he: and to love him with all the soul, and with all the strength,
> and to love his neighbour as himself, is more than all whole burnt offerings
> and sacrifices. And when Jesus saw that he answered discreetly, he said unto
> him, "Thou art not far from the kingdom of God." And no man after that
> durst ask him any question.[16]

Many Christians, in my experience, suppose that in thus giving a leading
place to love of one's neighbor, Jesus is introducing an altogether new idea of

his own: one foreign both to the questioner and to the Jewish community in general. But no: in the passage, Jesus is merely offering a brief summary of the standard Jewish answer to the question asked: the answer any observant and religiously informed Jew would have given, both before and after his time. It is the Torah, after all, that expressly commands such love, in the same breath forbidding (contrary to Tertullian) vengeance and grudge bearing, at Leviticus 19:17–18: "Thou shalt not avenge, nor bear any grudge against the children of thy people, but thou shalt love thy neighbour as thyself: I am the Lord." Moreover, it is entirely standard in Judaism, both before and after the rise of gentile Christianity, that this particular commandment (mitzvah) is not only central to the law but can in some sense be taken to summarize the law in its entirety. There is a celebrated story concerning the great Tannaitic rabbi Hillel (ca. 110 BCE–ca. 10 CE) in which Hillel is approached by a gentile who asks to have the essence of the Torah explained to him while he stands on one foot. The harsher sage Shammai calls the man a fool and refuses the question. Hillel, with the customary sweetness that clings to his name, accepts the question and replies, "What is hateful to you, do not do to your fellow: this is the whole Torah; the rest is the explanation; go and study."[17]

The Hebrew word commonly translated "love" or "loving kindness" is *chesed*. A saying of another Tannaitic rabbi, Simon the Just, recorded in the tractate of the Talmud known as the *Pirke Avot* (the Sayings of the Fathers) is: "The world rests upon three things: Torah, service to God and bestowing kindness (*chesed*)." But it is traditionally unclear in Judaism how distinct these three things are. Elsewhere in the Talmud, a midrash attributed to Rabbi Simlai holds that "the Torah begins with *chesed* and ends with *chesed*," a remark traditionally understood to imply that the ideal life envisaged in the Torah is, throughout, one characterized by mercy and compassion.

Simon the Just's maxim might at least be thought to imply the separateness, among the three things that sustain the world, of service to God and the bestowal of *chesed*. But that is not how Jews—including exceptionally observant (Hasidic or Haredi) Jews—read the passage. A Hasidic tale relates how the disciples of Rabbi Schneur Zalman of Liadi (1745–1812) asked their master: Which is the greater love—love of God, or love of one's fellow? "Rabbi Schneur Zalman replied, the two are one and the same. He then explained: G-d loves every one of his children. So ultimately love of one's fellow is a greater show of love for G-d than simply loving G-d. Because true love means that you love what your loved one loves."[18]

Further discussion of these issues must continue in the next chapter, where they will be dealt with in more detail.

THE ROLE OF LAW (HALAKAH) IN JUDAISM

It appears, then, that the image of Judaism, and Jews, as preferring justice and vengefulness over mercy and compassion, promulgated with such success by Tertullian and often considered to have been dramatized by Shakespeare in the figure of Shylock in *The Merchant of Venice*, is simply false. Nor is, or ever was, the actual Jewish preference for mercy and the avoidance of vengeance a matter merely of pious moral hand waving. At times when Jewish courts tried actual criminal cases, it made it extremely difficult to secure a sentence of death.

> Capital offences were tried by a specially composed court of twenty-three judges, known as a Sanhedra Ketana (Small Sanhedrin).... Since there were standing instructions to courts to refrain, insofar as possible, from passing the death sentence, it was customary to remove from the bench any man who was believed incapable of maintaining an impartial attitude towards the defendant. For example, if the members of the court had witnessed the crime with their own eyes, they were forbidden to try the case, on the assumption that their personal resentment would destroy their ability to pass fair judgment. Childless men or aged persons were also disqualified from serving on such courts, since, as the Talmud said, "They have forgotten the sorrow of raising children," and therefore might be more eager to apply the letter of the law than to consider the motives and emotions of the defendant.[19]

The idea that Judaism is a "religion of vengeance" seems to have had two intuitive sources. The first is the number of references to divine vengeance in the Old Testament: for example, Deuteronomy 32:35: "To me belongeth vengeance and recompense." The other is the idea, developed in Tertullian and other early Christian writers, that the commandments delivered in the Torah were imposed by God on the Jews as a punishment for and as a means of restraining their supposedly exceptional wickedness.

Vengeance, as we have seen, is in fact forbidden to Jews by Leviticus 19. That is why it must be left to God. On the other hand, forgiveness in Judaism is not the exclusive province of the deity. At Yom Kippur, the observant Jew is required to seek pardon and make restitution to any man or woman whom he or she may have wronged. So the granting of pardon, forgiveness, is abundantly possible in Judaism. The Jewish notion of forgiveness and of what conditions should govern it, on the other hand, is complex. In my experience, Christians sometimes talk as though it makes sense to forgive an offender who neither admits nor regrets what he or she has done. Forgiveness in this sense begins and ends within the mind of the person who forgives. Judaism has no such conception of forgiveness. For pardon to be appropriate, the remorse of the offender must be sincere, and he or she must fully understand as well as regret the precise nature of what he or she has done. He or she can't just wave in its general direction and say, "Sorry about that!" Another necessary sign of sincerity is that, confronted with the same temptation in future, he or she will not repeat the offense. The offended person cannot know that ahead of time and hence cannot forgive as if he or she did know. In general, the one appealed to for pardon can pardon only on the basis of what he or she knows about the offender. And there can be no forgiveness, from God or man, that simply *wipes out the offense*, irrespective of what the offender knows and feels about it.

Jewish religious writing is certainly consistent in treating both vengeance and forgiveness—the latter in the sense of a free act on the part of an offended person, which goes beyond reconciliation by *unilaterally* canceling or wiping out the guilt of the offender *irrespective of any remorse or regret on the offender's part*—as uniquely divine prerogatives. But by reserving them to God, it precisely forbids both, as usurpations of divine power, to human beings.

The second notion, that the mitzvoth constitute a kind of moral yoke *imposed on the Jews by divine fiat*, radically misconstrues—or to put it bluntly, misrepresents for polemical ends—both the Jewish understanding of the relationship of halakah to Jewish life and still more seriously the Jewish understanding of the relationship between God and man in the constitution of halakah.

Let us take the first of these misunderstandings first. For a start, the mitzvoth as Judaism understands the matter, were not *imposed on* the Jewish people but rather *offered to and accepted by* them. At Exodus 19:6–24:7, God makes, through Moses, an offer to the Jewish people. The terms of that offer are not, as antisemites sometimes like to suggest, that if the Jews will only do what He commands, God for His part will see to it that their enemies receive a bloody quittance for their temerity. The offer is rather (if we stick to the text of Exodus) that if the Jewish people will accept God's commands, He will "make them a kingdom of priests and a holy nation." This offer the Jewish people accepts, at Exodus 24:7, in the remarkable words, of which we shall have more to say in the next chapter, "*Na'aseh v'nishma*" ("We will do and we will hear").

Hence, it is axiomatic in Judaism that the Torah, and the law (halakah) constituted by its commandments, are not a burden or a punishment imposed by God but rather a gift from God and, as such, a reason for rejoicing. This thought expresses itself, for instance, in the title of the festival Simchat Torah ("Joy/Rejoicing in/with the Torah"), which each year celebrates the conclusion of the cycle of Torah readings in the synagogue. (*Simcha* in Hebrew means happiness or joy and also a party or celebration.) It is further axiomatic in Judaism that a mitzvah is not adequately performed, performed as God intended it to be performed, if the performer takes no pleasure, feels no joy, in its performance.

All of this might be dismissed as empty piety were it not for the uncomfortable fact that we have set ourselves to explain: namely, the will of a substantial fraction of Jews, over centuries of persecution, and in the face of, at times, very real offers of an easier life upon conversion, to retain, openly or in secret, their fidelity to Jewish observance. If halakah were indeed merely a burdensome and degrading imposition, such fidelity would be difficult to understand. Its existence leaves one little option but to conclude that Jewish observance does powerfully impress the participant as something of intrinsic value in itself. Very little inquiry among Jews will suffice to establish the extent to which Jewish observance is perceived as something that, to a greater extent than any alternative, on the one hand sustains a satisfying, meaningful, and mutually supportive communal life, and on the other hand strengthens the individual in the vicissitudes of existence.

Now for the second misrepresentation: that concerning the relationship of God to man in the constitution of halakah. Tertullian, and much Christian opinion still influenced by him, takes the book of Exodus, in effect, to record the self-revelation of an omnipotent God, who then proceeds to get the Jews to accept the unquestioned rule of His irresistible power as a preliminary to obtaining the same acceptance from humanity at large. That is not how Judaism sees it. In Jewish thought, the effect of the Covenant is not to make man arbitrarily subject to God's power but rather to open both a channel and a process of communication and cooperation between God and man in which the voices of both can, and will, make themselves heard.

Nowhere is this spirit of give and take more evident than in the constitution of the Talmud. The Talmud, "the classic text of Judaism, second only to the Bible,"[20] is a vast and complex collection of documents whose nature and origins are too complex to enter into here. Useful brief accounts are easily available.[21] What concerns me here is the purpose of the Talmud as a whole, which is, roughly speaking, to work out the bearing on all the vicissitudes of everyday life of the divine commandments contained both in the Torah and in the so-called oral law that preceded its composition, while at the same time rendering them as far as possible consistent with one another. In this project, as the American literary critic Geoffrey Hartman drily observes, "Non-Jews were taught to see only a crass and stubborn literalism, rather than what David Weiss Halivni has called the predilection of Midrash [halakic commentary] for justified law."[22]

A presupposition of the entire Talmudic enterprise is that divine power cannot, in the last analysis, ride roughshod over human reason. Nowhere is this more evident than in a famous passage of halakic midrash (see below) in the Talmudic tractate *Bava Mezia* (The second gate), 59b. The sages are discussing whether a certain clay oven, which has become ritually impure, could be purified. All except Rabbi Eliezer, a great scholar, agree that it cannot be. When the other sages refuse to accept his arguments, Rabbi Eliezer says (and as a veteran of professional philosophical debate, I feel keen sympathy with this plainly much-tried man), "If the halakah is according to me, let that carob tree prove it." The carob tree duly moves from its place a hundred cubits. This opening miracle is promptly followed by a stream of water running uphill and finally by the intervention of a divine voice that says, "What have you to do with Rabbi Eliezer? The halakah is according to him in every place."

At this point—and this is the point at which midrash enters the story—another rabbi, R. Joshua, rises and says, "It is not in the heavens" (Deuteronomy 30:12). The Talmudic passage continues: "What did he mean by quoting this? Said Rabbi Jeremiah, 'He meant that since the Torah has been given already on Mount Sinai, we do not pay attention to a heavenly voice, for You have written in Your Torah, 'Decide according to the majority'" (Exodus 23:2).

Something now needs to be said about the methodology of midrash of which the above is an example. *Midrash* means, roughly speaking, "interpretation." A midrash is any interpretation of the meaning of a biblical or Talmudic text. It is no doubt that this is what Tertullian (see Efroymson's catalog above) had in mind in accusing the Jews of being "contentious about the meaning of the words of the Bible." The accusation, however, misses its mark. There are, in fact, rules not only generally understood but actually formulated for the conduct of midrash. Embedded in those rules is a set of distinctions concerning different kinds of meaning, or levels of interpretation. The two levels that most concern us are, respectively, *p'shat*, pronounced *pehshaht* and meaning "simple," and *d'rash*, pronounced *dehrash* and meaning, effectively, "drawing out" or "what is drawn out." *P'shat* is the plain, literal meaning of the words and sentences of the text. A central principle of midrashic interpretation is that you must not monkey with *p'shat*. Whatever interpretation of a text you may "draw out" under color of *d'rash* must respect the plain literal meaning of the text from which you "draw" it.

It might be asked how, if the meaning of the passage under interpretation is not to change, "new meaning" can be found in it. "Meaning," of course, can mean various things. It is common in English, for instance, to speak on the one hand of "the meaning *of* X," where X is a linguistic expression of some sort, and on the other hand of "the meaning *of* X *for* Y" where neither X nor Y need be linguistic expressions, though either or both may be. Examples of the latter use might be, "We have to decide what the new rules on borrowing are going to mean *for* the council's expenditures" or, "It'll be interesting to see what some of these discoveries of papyri at Oxyrhynchus are going to mean *for* our understanding of αἰτία." One might speak, for short, of *meaning-of* and *meaning-for*. Equally, the job of "meaning" in *meaning-for* contexts is often done by the term *bearings*. Thus, "I wonder what the *bearings* of the Oxyrhynchus papyri are going to be on. . . ."[23]

It seems to me that in the instance above, Rabbi Joshua is in no way meddling with the *meaning-of* Deuteronomy 30:12. Rather, he is pointing out its *meaning-for* (its bearing on) the matter at hand. Let us look again at Rabbi Joshua's citation. The passage in Deuteronomy from which the citation is taken begins with God's promise to reward the keeping of His commandments. It continues: "For this commandment which I command thee this day, it is not too hard for thee, neither is it too far off. It is not in heaven, that thou shouldst say: 'Who shall go up to heaven, and bring it unto us, and make us to hear it, that we may do it?'"

The bearings of the passage in Deuteronomy are thus homiletic and pastoral. It argues, against those who want to find reasons for avoiding the performance of the mitzvoth, that they cannot complain that the law is ineffectually laid up in heaven. What Rabbi Joshua has seen is that despite this, the passage *also* has—just as it stands and without the need to do any violence whatsoever to its *p'shat*—a powerful bearing on the issue of whether one can, or should, treat miracles as arguments in determining questions of halakah. Rabbi Joshua's point is that were we to treat miracles as arguments, we should be treating the law as indeed "in the heavens," at which point we should have simply to abandon Deuteronomy 30:12, since we should, in effect, have declared it (a declaration, incidentally, tantamount to apostasy) to be false. Rabbi Jeremiah then drives home that argument by pointing out that not only Deuteronomy 30:12 would have to be abandoned but also Exodus 23:2; and the matter is settled.

The passage is plainly important for the general character of Judaism in at least three ways. First of all, it divests the notion of miracle of any serious epistemic role in religious debate—any role in determining the content of the central moral and doctrinal claims of the religion—in a way in which, it has to be said, Christianity does not. There would be no need, in other words, for a Jewish David Hume to write chapter 10 of the *Enquiry concerning Human Understanding*. Rabbis Joshua and Jeremiah have already done its main work for him on grounds, indeed tangentially related, via Rabbi Jeremiah's adaptation of Exodus 23:2, to Hume's own. Second, the passage presents a formidable obstacle to the idea of a human being's claiming either divine powers or direct personal access to divine authority—perversions, again, to which Christianity has over the centuries proved from time to time dismayingly receptive. Judaism here opts definitively, with Hume, for the rule of rational argument and majority decision over mystery, magic, and personal charisma. Third, to return at last to the theme of this section, it represents revelation and reason, God and man, as joint and equal participants in the determination of what obedience to halakah is to require *in concrete terms*. The Talmudic passage ends with a little dramatic coda in which the embattled rabbis finally learn, through the mediation of the prophet Elisha, the response of the maker of the universe to Rabbi Joshua's intervention: "Rabbi Nathan met [the prophet] Elisha, and asked, What did the Holy one, blessed be He, do when that happened? [Elisha] replied, He laughed, and said, My children have outvoted Me, My children have outvoted Me."[24]

ACTION AND BELIEF IN JUDAISM

The emphasis in Judaism on *action* and *observance* as the primary modes through which human beings relate to God has a further consequence, in sharply reducing the role played by *belief* in that relationship. We normally think of a religion, or of a developed political outlook, for that matter, as consisting of, primarily or fundamentally, a set of *beliefs* or *doctrines* having to do with God, or social organization, or history and only *secondarily and derivatively from those founding beliefs* in a set of moral or legal commitments. We think of belief, as one might put it, as *logically prior* to moral commitment. This, it seems to me, is not a particularly useful way of thinking about Judaism. Indeed, it would be a step closer to the truth, even if not yet quite the whole truth, to say that *in Judaism, moral commitment is logically prior to belief.*

That is not to say that Jews do not believe in God or address Him in prayer. The fundamental prayer of Judaism, the *Shema*, asserts the existence and unity of God: *Shema Yisrael, Adonai Elohenu, Adonai echad* (Hear, O Israel, the Lord our God, the Lord is One). Such prayers, especially when heard in context, such as the brief *Baruch dayan ha-emet* (Blessed be the just judge) spoken unanimously at a certain point in the funeral service and expressing the resignation of the congregation in accepting the will of God, can be extremely moving, even to a non-Jew. Fear of God goes so far among observant Jews, even as to proscribe in ordinary discourse the very word *God* in favor of the indirect expression "The Name" (*Hashem*).

At the same time, it is axiomatic in Judaism that merely *believing* in God, without the accompaniment of systematic observance, has no spiritual value whatsoever. This is the drift of a frequently cited and very early passage of midrash on Jeremiah in the Jerusalem Talmud (*Yerushalmi*): "R. Huma and R. Jeremiah said in the name of R. Hiyya B. Abba: It is written, They have forsaken me and not kept my law [Jeremiah 16.11]—i.e., would that they had forsaken me and kept my law, since by occupying themselves therewith, the light which it contains would have led them back to the right path."[25]

The sense of the midrash is sometimes taken to be that it is fine to be an atheist as long as one observes the law. Closer attention to the text, however, suggests a different and more canonical paraphrase: that it is impossible to *be* an atheist *and live in accordance with the law*, because the law itself is not a mere compendium of arbitrary rules but contains or embodies a "light" that will lead the observant back to God.

The thought suggests a parallel with Plato's distinction in the *Republic* between true belief (*doxa*) that something is the case, and knowledge (*episteme*) of why it is the case.[26] Belief may be correct, but without the knowledge of why it is correct, it is at best unstable and easily overthrown in debate.

But the parallel with Plato fails at a point crucial for the understanding of Judaism. The midrash seems, indeed, to echo Plato in suggesting that belief, even if correct, may not be enough; it may require, to render it stable, the support of something further. But whereas in Plato that "something further" is conceived in purely intellectual terms, as the ascent to a higher kind of *knowledge*, in the midrash, as in Judaism generally, it is conceived as a passage from the mere entertaining of belief to *action*: to the living attempt to shape life in conformity with the law.

A basic tenet of Judaism is, after all, that God's object in giving the Jews the commandments that form the divine basis of the law is to help them, and by extension humanity, to lead a fully human life. The values—and value—of such a life can be determined only by attempting to lead it. But if a life so led turns out to be valuable and valued, then a fortiori the laws that govern it cannot be regarded, as so many critics of Judaism have suggested, as an arbitrary and inhuman imposition. And plainly, a great many Jews over the centuries have felt a Jewish life to be sufficiently valuable for them to be extremely reluctant to give it up.

The claim of *Eichah Rabbah, Pesichta 2* that the law "contains a light" (i.e., is, in effect, self-validating) connects closely, in other words, with Prager and Telushkin's claim, noted in chapter 4, that as a result of their commitment to Judaism, Jews have led "higher-quality lives" than their non-Jewish neighbors.

Again, because the law is in this sense self-validating through practice, it would be difficult from a stance entirely within Judaism to make sense of the remark that Dostoevski puts in the mouth of Dmitri Karamazov, Без бога всё позволено: "Without God everything is permitted."[27] What that famous tag says, in effect, is that unless we have some grounds for belief in the existence of God, we have no grounds either for belief in the validity of moral distinctions. It would be *almost* faithful to the spirit of Judaism to say in response to this, following the lead of *Eichah Rabbah, Pesichta 2*, that it is *because* we have grounds for belief in the validity of moral distinctions that we have grounds for belief in God!

Only that way of putting things would not in fact be quite faithful to the spirit of Judaism. It would fall short of entire fidelity because in Judaism—as Buber, Lévinas, and others have pointed out—the link between man and God is conceived less by analogy with the relationship between a true belief and the natural circumstances that make it true, than by analogy with the relationship between persons who are acquainted with one another. So a better—a more Jewish—way of putting it would be to say that it is through discovering that they have grounds for belief in the validity of moral distinctions that people enter—sometimes—into a relationship of trust and love with *Hashem*.

Another way of putting the same point would be to say that whereas "faith" in the sense of *belief*, both in the truth of doctrinal claims and in that of canonical narratives such as the New Testament accounts of the miracles of Jesus, plays a major role in Christianity, and with respect to other articles of faith in most other religions, *faith* in that sense, in contrast to the *trust* in *Hashem* that grows out of religious and moral *observance*, plays a relatively diminished part in the life of Judaism. In *Must a Jew Believe Anything?*, for instance, Menachem Kellner opens his discussion by denying that the very notion of "faith" as ordinarily understood by Christianity and many other religions has much to do with Judaism. He distinguishes two senses of the Hebrew term *emunah*, usually translated as "faith": "belief" and "trust." He then argues that the second of these is the more fundamental for Judaism: "The point I am making here about the meaning of *emunah* is neither new nor controversial; it is just not often noticed. Yet perusing a concordance and examining the verses in context is enough to convince any reader that the basic root meaning of *emunah* is trust and reliance, not intellectual acquiescence in the truth of certain propositions."[28] Suppose, in accordance with this reading of *emunah*, we reinterpret the expression "belief in God" as "trust in God" and combine that thought with the idea—implicit in the midrash on Jeremiah discussed a moment ago—that the law is also "trustworthy" in the sense that it contains an inbuilt "light" that can only lead the observant toward God. Then "belief" (i.e., trust) in the law and "belief" (i.e., trust) in God become mutually self-supporting—with the consequence that, at least for the observant Jew, Dmitri Karamazov's problem evaporates—or rather, from the standpoint of Judaism, persists as a problem only for those for whom belief, and not trust, is what primarily constitutes "faith."

Bearing that in mind, it should come as no surprise that Judaism is inhospitable to the notion of *belief*—whether religious or ideological—per se. Hyam Maccoby, writing about the three great medieval disputations between Jews and Christians, which began with the Barcelona Disputation of 1263, notes, in a passage that will bear quoting at length, how much confusion was introduced into these debates by the Christian failure to grasp the Jewish distinction between halakah (law) and Aggadah (narrative, story).

> But there is also here a more fundamental point, relating to the difference between Judaism and Christianity. In Judaism the Aggadah is subordinate, whereas in Christianity, the Aggadah, or what corresponds to the Aggadah, is central. Christianity is an Aggadic religion. This difference accounts for the basic lack of rapprochement and mutual understanding in the disputations.
>
> In Judaism the centre is occupied by the Law, which regulates the behaviour of the community and the individual. It is in the sphere of law that the serious effort towards definition and precision occurs. Here it was that methods of formal logic and dialectic were developed, in order to arrive at hard-and-fast solutions of any problems that arose. But there was no such logic or dialectic for dealing with matters that Christians would have called "theological" (there is in fact no word for "theology" in Hebrew). Here the methods used by the Jews were literary, aphoristic, parabolic, intuitive.[29] . . . The point is that, precisely because of its profundity, the Aggadah could not be quoted in support of hard-and-fast doctrine. It would be like quoting a Keats sonnet in support of a theorem in geometry.[30]

Maccoby's description of the treatment in Judaism of aggadic passages in scripture as "literary, aphoristic, parabolic, intuitive" reminds one that it would be an oversimplification to describe halakah as *central* and Aggadah as *marginal* to Judaism. The difference is rather that, while there is an obligation to *act* in response to the former, there is no obligation—as in Christianity—to *believe* the latter. But stories that are in no way, as we say, "taken as gospel" may nevertheless possess profound spiritual significance; and that is how it is with Aggadah in Judaism. As a friend of mine put it, "Judaism, in its refusal to proceed 'philosophically,' harbored a recognition that what one might call

imprecision may be closer to the truth (of man and God) than conceptually
rigid doctrine can possibly be."

JEWISH "MATERIALISM" AND "COLLECTIVISM"

The reason for the greater emphasis on belief in Christianity is, of course, that in
Christianity, belief is a necessary and, on some doctrinal accounts, a sufficient
condition for personal salvation. We learn from Saint Paul "that if you shall
confess with your mouth the Lord Jesus, and shall believe in your heart that
God has raised him from the dead, you shall be saved" (Romans 10:9). For the
Christian, to be "saved" is to be released from the power of sin in general and
from original sin in particular, and with that liberated from the power of death
into eternal life. For the Christian, in other words, salvation, the possibility of
change brought about by Christ's sacrifice, is in the first instance a possibility
of *spiritual* change in the literal sense of a change affecting the individual *spirit*,
the individual *soul*. The thought—which is again Saint Paul's—is that inner,
spiritual transformation is worth far more than painstaking obedience to the
letter of pettifogging and detailed rules of outward conduct, set out in books
and intended to regulate the petty, concrete ("carnal") details of everyday life.
This is why Paul thinks of the "New Covenant" instituted by Christ as having
definitively abrogated the "Old Covenant" of the Book of Exodus and with it
the entire fabric of Jewish law (halakah). All this is implicit, for instance, in the
well-known text from Corinthians 3:6: "He [Christ] has made us competent
as ministers of a new covenant—not of the letter but of the Spirit; for the letter
kills, but the Spirit gives life."

From this Pauline vision of things spring two further elements in the belief
that Judaism is an outmoded, antiquated, and "superseded" religion. The first is
the idea that Judaism, because it concerns itself exclusively with "the letter," or
"the carnal," or the material—that is to say, with the concrete, detailed conduct
of everyday life in this world, to the exclusion of any "higher" or "ideal" aspirations, denies its adherents access to the Spirit. The second, connected idea
is that in Judaism, the achievement of an independent spiritual life is further
impeded by the tendency of Jewish ideas and practices to immerse Jews in a
species of primitive tribalism focused on the success and material advantages
of the Jewish community as a whole. This, of course, connects closely with the
idea of Jewish "particularism" of which we shall have more to say in chapter 13.

The short answer to the second of these charges is first, that Judaism conceives of the spiritual life as something that essentially concerns concrete relationships between the individual and the concrete, flesh-and-blood Other and

is therefore something that cannot be achieved by way of the kinds of private, *inner* transformation emphasized by many strands in Christianity. Second, in Judaism it is not possible either to distinguish the Jewish community from the network of relationships connecting its members or to distinguish its "success" from the moral health of those relationships. There isn't, in other words, an *abstract entity* called "the Jewish community" to which each individual Jew can be related *without reference to any other individual Jew.* The Talmud (*Shevuot* 39a), discussing the domino effect of sin, concludes with the Aramaic phrase *Kol yisrael arevim zeh bazeh,* "all of Israel are responsible for one another."[31] Jewish spirituality begins with the acceptance of this idea and the beginning of the effort to work out its implications and to live in accordance with them. Nothing more remote from Paul's idea of spirituality as a private interior transformation on the part of the individual soul, it would seem to me as a non-Jew, can readily be imagined.

Fuller development of this reply to the second branch of the Pauline critique must be deferred to the next chapter. The same is true of the reply to the first branch: that Judaism is a materialistic or worldly religion in the sense of being essentially concerned with the concrete conduct of everyday life in this world. But again, the outline of a reply can usefully be sketched in at this point.

The first point that needs to be established is that in Judaism there is no doctrine of original sin. Here is David Patterson, speaking of the Jewish conception of the Messiah:

> The one whom the Jews await is not the son of the Holy One any more than any other human being is a child of God. He is neither a divine incarnation nor part of a triune divinity: He is altogether flesh and blood. The Midrash, in fact, speaks of his mortal death, saying that when the Messiah dies, the World to Come will be ushered in (see *Tanchuna Ekev* 7). Further, he is not born of a virgin, who in turn requires an immaculate conception. Indeed, from a Jewish standpoint, the conception of any human being can be "immaculate," because in marriage the sexual union that produces a child is itself holy, as is the one born from that union. Because we do not inherit Adam's sin, we are born innocent and untainted. Therefore, the one whom we await is not one whose blood will be offered up in order to cleanse us of our sinful essence; rather, through his teaching concerning our actions, we become cleansed through our actions.[32]

In other words, to a Jew, it is action alone, and not the material world, or the human essence, that it makes sense to characterize as "evil," or "flawed," or "unholy." The world, and for that matter living human beings, remain holy

BLAMING THE JEWS

because they are God's creation. Because of that, there can be no ultimate distinction in Judaism between this world, viewed as essentially flawed, and thus a mere vale of tears that we must pass beyond, and another, which is our true and final destination. Here, on this question, is Martin Buber: "Some religions do not regard our sojourn on earth as true life. They either teach that everything appearing to us here is mere appearance, behind which we should penetrate, or that it is only a forecourt of the true world, which we should cross without paying much attention to it. Judaism, on the contrary, teaches that what a man does now and here with holy intent is no less important, no less true—being a terrestrial, but none the less factual, link with divine being—than the life of the world to come."[33]

GETTING PERSONAL

The issue of Jewish materialism and collectivism came to a head a year or two ago in a correspondence between myself and an American Jewish philosopher, Professor Abigail Rosenthal. Rosenthal is the author of the Pulitzer Prize–nominated *A Good Look at Evil* and also of a memoir, *Confessions of a Young Philosopher*, both of which occupy themselves in part with matters related to those issues.[34]

When one is trying to grasp how the elements of an alien vision of life hangs together, it can prove helpful to have before one not only the formal statements of recognized authorities but also some samples of unscripted personal utterance composed either in the heat of debate or in reflection on the course of a life actually lived by ordinary holders of the views whose inner logic one is trying to unravel. As novelists know well, the structure of a religious, political, or moral outlook often reveals itself most plainly in the way such an outlook determines the life choices of a real or fully imagined individual.

I shall therefore end this chapter with some extended comments on the work of Professor Rosenthal. I'll begin with the following long extract, printed here with her permission, from the correspondence noted above. In context, she is arguing against my suggestion—a foolish one, I now think—that Judaism might be regarded as dealing in collective rather than individual salvation.

Leaving aside chosenness, whether primarily social or not, for the nonce (I hadn't asked myself *that* question!) let me get back to your earlier email of May 25. I'm now looking at what you say about Paul.
Let me try to state my disagreement in as straightforward a way as I can. The letters attributed to Paul include some beautiful & profound lines, but

I agree that his lines about Judaism are not among them. I certainly agree that Paul misrepresents Judaism when he claims that no forgiveness or atonement is possible within the Jewish frame. And I agree that "salvation" in Paul's sense is not even a Jewish theme or concern. Nevertheless, the explanation you offer (that Judaism's kind of deliverance is collective) does not seem quite on target, in my view.

The thing to look at is *why* Paul cares about "salvation" at all. What is it that we are to be saved *from*? So far as I know, Paul has the theological problem of explaining the crucifixion of Jesus. Plato had no comparable problem re the execution of Socrates. There was nothing to "explain." Some people are intolerant of goodness and truth. That's real life. But if Jesus is God incarnate, there *is* a problem. Why did God-as-Jesus *permit himself* to be crucified? Paul's solution: assign to humankind a generic condition of Original Sin, which would be the inability properly to connect with God *via* anything we human beings can do or say or think. Then impute this doctrine to Judaism (which of course has no such doctrine). Then make God's incarnation and crucifixion the vicarious payment on humanity's otherwise unpayable debt.

Since neither the Religion of Israel nor rabbinic Judaism has Paul's problem, neither needs to offer "salvation" from the damnation that, for Paul, is our default position. Neither in Hebrew Scripture nor for the rabbis does the Righteous Gentile have anything to fear from God. Hebrew Scripture does not deal with any of its characters as if he or she were struggling with sin as a *generic* condition. Nor, so far as I can see, did Jesus. Neither is rabbinic Judaism made uncomfortable by the fact that each of us is *created* with a good and an evil impulse. Nobody (that I know of in all that literature) wishes that his evil impulse would disappear! Instead, the rabbis say realistically, "Without the evil impulse, nothing would get done." The *yetzer hara* can't be eradicated but it can be *rerouted* so that we come to serve God with all of our complex nature, not just the "pure" side.

It follows that Judaism *has no need* to turn from the individual to the collective to cure a problem that, in the first place, it does not have. To be sure, there must be some reason why God chooses a people, but I cannot agree that Jewish experience foregrounds the collective *at the expense* of the individual. There are very sharply delineated individual characters in the Tanach. Auerbach, the critic, notes that Homer's characters have one dimension (the "wily" Odysseus is always wily), while someone like David is shown in all his inconsistencies and complexities. There are a number of characters who stand out as persons: Jacob, Joseph, Moses, Job, Esther to name just a few. Job's concern to get reconciled with God is urgent for him as a person. The psalms deal with *the psalmist* as he wrestles with God while also trying to live his own life. Although the Song of Songs has been allegorized by the rabbis and by Christianity, it expresses the erotic landscape as only the individual desirer can feel it. The importance given to personal life continues in rabbinic Judaism. To a congregant who laments that he's no Moses, a rabbinic response is that God won't ask him why he wasn't Moses, only why he wasn't *himself*. If merging into the collective were the ideal, such tales would be puzzling. If the collective were paramount, "two Jews, three opinions" would not be repeated as often as it is.

Since the human condition is not per se "fallen," the Religion of Israel is the only one I know of that doesn't try to escape from real space, linear time and the cultural surroundings that (up to a point) can still be excavated! Rather, its relation to actual history is intrinsic. God's "deliverance" of the Israelites takes them out of Egyptian bondage, not out of the human condition![35]

Rosenthal's response here moves from the second to the first of the two objections to Judaism that have concerned us in this section and will continue to concern us in chapter 12: that Judaism subordinates the individual to the collective and that it is exclusively concerned with this world and hence, in Pauline terms, with the letter over the spirit, the carnal and worldly over the eternal and otherworldly. Her argument in reply to the second is that Judaism cannot be said to subordinate the deliverance of the individual to that of the people—the collectivity—since Judaism affords no doctrinal foothold to the idea of *deliverance*—of salvation—per se. And in fact, Judaism richly celebrates the particularity of the concrete individual person.

But these reflections, by their nature, lead her naturally, and in a way that seems to me entirely true to the inner spirit of Judaism, to what amounts both to a reply to and a critique of the first of the Pauline objections mentioned above: that Judaism concerns itself solely with the concrete, the material, the carnal, the fleshly, and leaves no place for the spirit.

Her reply is, in effect, that it is difficult to see how to get Paul's distinction between the "world and the flesh" on the one hand and spirit on the other hand off the ground in the first place if the world is not, in fact, "fallen"! And the position of Judaism is that the world is in no sense fallen. Rather, it is simply the world that God has given to us to live in, along with some instructions concerning how to set about living in it.

Of course, life in this world is often hard, and of course, as she says, the human heart is inhabited by both a good and an evil impulse, the *yetzer hatov* and the yetzer hara. But the yetzer hara (the bad impulse) is not a demonic impulse from whose influence the individual needs to be "saved." It is simply a drive toward pleasure, property, and security. If unchecked by the *yetzer hatov* (the good impulse), it can certainly lead to evil, but if brought under the control of the yetzer hatov, it can equally lead to good.

Hence, for Judaism, our business as human beings is to accept the world as we find it and to improve it as best we may through both collective and individual action in light of God's commandments. In Judaism, the point of performing a mitzvah is not to sanctify or redeem the individual soul that performs it: rather, it is to sanctify or redeem *the world*. The natural world, that is to say, is not seen, in Judaism, as a place of uncorrupted innocence, as in Rousseau or in many of the forms of ecological romanticism popular today. But it is not "corrupt" either. It is simply real. It is our world—but it is also God's world; and it is our business to invite—to draw—God into it: to make it still more His world. Every mitzvah further sanctifies the creation.

The focus of Judaism, in short, is upon the redeemed, the sanctified *world*, not the redeemed and sanctified *soul*. This is why in Judaism, the figure of the saint, the person who has achieved a state of personal grace or holiness, is replaced by that of the teacher (which is what "rabbi" actually means): the person who, through knowledge and sound argument, is able to interpret God's commandments to the people.

THE CONCRETE WORLD, "REAL TIME," AND THE MEANING OF LIFE

In conclusion, I would like to look more closely at the opening sentence of the concluding paragraph of Professor Rosenthal's email: "Since the human condition is not per se 'fallen,' the Religion of Israel is the only one I know of that doesn't try to escape from real space, linear time and the cultural surroundings that (up to a point) can still be excavated!"

What is it to "try to escape" from real space and linear time? In part, she is thinking, no doubt, of the pervasive sense in Christianity that this is a corrupt and fallen world, relative to a better one that lies beyond the grave. But Christianity is not the only source in Western culture for feelings of alienation from the physicality, the carnality of the natural world. It is commonplace to be told that the world revealed by natural science is without meaning for human beings. Bertrand Russell, for instance, in a celebrated passage of his essay "A Free Man's Worship" writes in elevatedly gloomy terms of the loneliness of human consciousness in a physical world empty of meaning for it.

> Even more purposeless, more void of meaning, is the world which Science presents for our belief. . . . That Man is the product of causes which had no prevision of the end they were achieving; that his origin, his growth, his hopes and fears, his loves and his beliefs, are but the outcome of accidental collocations of atoms; that no fire, no heroism, no intensity of thought and feeling, can preserve an individual life beyond the grave; that all the labours

of the ages, all the devotion, all the inspiration, all the noonday brightness
of human genius, are destined to extinction in the vast death of the solar
system, and that the whole temple of Man's achievements must inevitably
be buried beneath the debris of a universe in ruins—all these things, if not
quite beyond dispute, are yet so nearly certain, that no philosophy which
rejects them can hope to stand. Only within the scaffolding of these truths,
only on the form foundations of unyielding despair, can the soul's habitation
henceforth be safely built.[36]

It would not be a gross oversimplification to suggest that philosophy and
religion in the West have offered over the centuries two types of reply to
pessimism of this peculiarly bleak type. The first, characteristic equally of
Christianity and of many philosophical worldviews, including that of Marxism, is that the natural sciences are not to be regarded as having the last word
on the nature of reality and that from some higher, metaphysical or theological standpoint, objective reality is not without kinds of objective, nonimaginary meaning intelligible to human beings. The other, favored by Russell
but with its ultimate roots in Roman Stoicism, is that, though—since there
is no source of truth other than natural science—whatever meaning is to be
found in life is to be found merely in the indomitable will of the individual
mind to pursue the projects which commend themselves to it, some of these
projects—such as the pursuit of truth or moral virtue—may nevertheless
possess objective value. The stir created in intellectual circles just after the
war by Jean-Paul Sartre's *Being and Nothingness* was in large part due to that
work's apparent demonstration that both these supposed ways of equipping
life with objective, nonimaginary meaning are alike in their impotence to
do any such thing.

Judaism, on the other hand, idiosyncratic as ever, takes a different line
from either of these. It holds that meaning in human life comes into being
largely through relationship between persons. David Patterson puts the point
as follows:

> The question of meaning in our lives has to do neither with essence nor with
> belief but with the act of murder. . . . Meaning can be generated only through
> a relation to another, only through and oriented toward someone outside
> ourselves, an orientation that is commanded from on high and not decided
> by me, neither through my reason nor through my resolve. To have a sense
> of mission is to have a sense of calling, which means: I must answer to and
> for another, for the sake of another, even to death. Otherwise my life has
> no meaning. And if my life has no meaning, I have no reason not to kill by
> being.[37]

Jewish friends tell me that this overstates the case in several ways. Personal relationship is not in Judaism the *sole* source of meaning. There is, for example, a long Jewish tradition of finding wonder in the natural world and joy in the natural powers of human beings. Nor is it true that in Judaism, as we have already seen, that the moral agent has his course laid down for him absolutely by divine command, with no possibility of answering back. Again, as a friend put it, "Rabbinic responsa during the Holocaust forbade students to give their lives for their teachers, despite their fervent willingness to do so." But leaving these entirely valid objections aside, it is nevertheless true that according to Judaism, personal relationship is the *preeminent* source of meaning in life.

The idea that personal relationship is, ultimately, what contributes meaning to life is, of course, by no means unique to Judaism, but within the Western tradition, outside Judaism, it is mainly in literature, and particularly in the novel, that its traces are to be found. In a letter in which he speaks of his university days at King's College, Cambridge, the novelist E. M. Forster writes, "King's [College, Cambridge University] stands for personal relationships, and these still seem to me the most real things on the surface of the earth."[38]

Many writers would agree. And so, it would seem, would the bulk of Jews with any clear sense of the content of their own traditions. But much turns on the word *real*. For relationships to be a source of meaning in our lives—of objective, nonimaginary meaning, that is to say—one must be able to believe in the reality of the relationships in question. One needs love to be genuinely love, commitment to be genuinely commitment, trust and trustworthiness to be those things in reality, not merely phantom or pretend versions of the real things. And for that, one must have some means of distinguishing between pretense and reality, the true from the false coin.

One could argue now that it is precisely the unforgiving solidity of the real world, the iron connections it forges between cause and effect, act and consequence, the steely indifference of its times and seasons to human desire and human fantasy that make it possible in real life to distinguish between the true and the false, the genuine and the pretense, in our dealings with one another. And one could argue further that it is precisely in its solidity, in its power to make truth verifiable and fantasy detectable, that "holiness" of the created world affirmed by Judaism in part consists.

In other words, it is precisely those features of the natural world that lead Russell to despair of the natural world as a source of transcendent meaning for human beings, that make it possible for human beings to discover *grounded*, solidly based meaning in relationships with one another,

Abigail Rosenthal's memoir, *Confessions of a Young Philosopher*, it seems to me, explores precisely this set of insights concerning the connections between relationship, truth, and what it is to find meaning in a human life. The narrator looks back on a difficult period of her youth, living through two episodes that promised to deliver alternatives to the Jewish way of facing reality. Each has its appeal. The first, during a Fulbright year in Paris, is a classic seduction—the seducer, a Greek communist she names "Pheidias," who holds out the promise (as old as Tristan and Iseult) of a self-enclosed world where the rules for living in real space and time don't apply. The second alternative—prompted by the predictable disappointments of the first—invites her into a Gnostic-Christian thought-world. Her second persuader she names "Suzanne," a fellow graduate student in London, a young Afro-American who credits Gnosticism for the striking skill with which she navigates a milieu in which her race and femininity might otherwise be disabling handicaps. For the author, weighed down not only by disappointments of the heart but also by the burden of having concealed the Parisian digression from the closest people in her own world, and by the trials of navigating the world of professional academic philosophy in the prefeminist era, Suzanne's denial of material reality—as a mere mask for something more spiritual—seems to offer a new method for dealing with the besetting impasses of her life. Unfortunately, the relationship with Suzanne develops into a series of assaults on her independence and personal identity that in reality force her to serve as the chief means by which Suzanne is enabled to evade the demands of reality, and finally require a rescue organized by her intrepid father and mother, involving the US State Department and the Portuguese Polícia Internacional.

These two experiences lie, for Rosenthal, at the origin of her ideas—mainly expressed in the concluding section, "Aftermath"—concerning the relationship of Judaism to the way human beings conceive their relationship to time. They throw a penetrating light on what she meant, in her email to me, by her suggestion that, for her at any rate, Judaism is the only outlook that does not try in some way to escape from "real space and linear time." Her argument precisely contrasts the real, or natural, time in which our actions and their consequences actually unfold *in verifiable ways*, with the imaginary time in which our self-protective fantasies about ourselves and about others situate themselves. "What counts in a life is how one lives the tenses. If one has the chronology of one's passionate life lined up accurately in sequence—event, matching purpose and the actions it prompted—and if those purposes were the best accessible (or were corrected when they no longer seemed best), then one has lived the timeline of one's years optimally. One hasn't had a regrettable life. One has a record to stand on."[39]

Rosenthal holds this vision of life to be essentially, if perhaps not exclusively, Jewish. "Everybody is best at something. Jews were best (or at least first) at lining up the partnership with God in real time."[40]
But living this way is evidently, not easy. It is easier to fall victim to

a rather particular failure, which I'll call *scrambling the tenses*. One sets out in life. Things are encountered. One responds to the encounters. Effects follow. This is the natural, serial course of any life running along its timeline.
Sometimes, however, a deflection is seen. One decides to pretend that something consequential has not happened or that one has not reacted as one did. One fakes it. The memory mismatch occurs because it flatters the mis-rememberer or allows her to dodge some painful awareness. One lie requires a second or a third, each one designed to protect the lie that came before. The scaffolding erected on this basis feels rickety to the builder—even if others fail to notice how it shakes and cracks in the wind.
This is how the tenses get scrambled and one loses track of the "before" and "after." Is this trivial? If there is an Ultimate Witness who sees one's course over tine accurately, such a deflection can only be momentous. One's partnership with the Ultimate becomes a cheat. One is then estranged from the beat of the heart or the personal metronome that one shares with God.[41]

For Rosenthal, Pheidias and Suzanne stand in the book as instances of opposing ways of easing the pressures of consecutive life by "scrambling the tenses." Pheidias, the Marxist, thinks in terms of the imaginary chronology of Hegelian *Geistesgeshichte* in its "materialist" redaction by Marx, according to which individual human beings stand, in effect, in an imaginary temporal landscape constituted by Marx's stages of socioeconomic development, each collapsing into the next until the final redemption form time offered by the revolution. Here is Rosenthal again:

I came to Paris, a city that consecrates its erotic vectors, as an intellectual, a romantic and a virgin. I wanted to respond appropriately to the demands of such a city. At the same time, I was looking for a way to start my life journey by locating its place on the map of passionate history. That was the Jewish part of me, though I didn't necessarily think of it that way.
The young man I met and loved in that city represented himself as someone who had dealt authoritatively with the problems of history. His family was shattered by the Nazi occupation of Greece. The cruelties of that occupation had caused his mother to die prematurely. He could not sympathize with the establishment represented by his prominent father. He told me that he had fled the communists in adolescence, when they were kidnapping Greek

children to indoctrinate them. Since he did become a communist later,
I don't know if that part was true. The part about his mother and father was
more serious, and likely true. In any case, his was the report of a life whose
jagged fault lines intersected with the political accounts of those times.
His leap, or backflip, into the communist mindset substituted a ready-made
ideology for the life story he might have worked his own way through. It was
understandable. It gave him a manly ferocity. But it was not a sign of inner
courage. It was a simulacrum of real retrospection.

By making his approach to me equally ready-made—the generic one of
the predator—he made himself incalculably older than me, though in fact we
were both young. Thus he became unimaginable as the partner with whom
I could share an accurate place in space and time. Every seductive move was
crafted; the freshness was out of it. To his mind, both love and history were
scripted. The manipulative way he handled me was, among other things, a
refusal of the joint venture that we might have chosen to try.

Of course, he wanted to be rid of me as soon as he "had" me. To indulge a
longing for me—anticipatory or nostalgic—belonged to his decision to step
back from life's edge, so as to live comfortably inside a simulacrum instead.
Nevertheless, the love between us was not an imitation.[42]

Suzanne, the Christian Gnostic, according to Rosenthal practices an opposite strategy for avoiding the challenges of living. Far from opting into a ready-
made, scripted simulacrum of history, she abolishes history and other people
altogether by treating the physical world as an illusion, and the Spirit—her
spirit—as the only reality.

She categorically denied the reality of the life I was trying to have. She had
adopted the Gnostic strategy—treating all the resistance factors of her
experience as illusions. Behind the illusions, she *affirmed* the existence of a
hidden reality where she was free: of racial rejections, of any kind of scarcity,
of envy, of fear—of any powers to which she was unequal—free of the whole
burden of history. She acted as though she were above it all, instantly and
unconditionally.

At first, barriers seemed to give way before her. I thought I could try her
Gnostic path. As a thought experiment initially, but the kind you had to live
in order to think it. Perhaps, on this untried avenue, I might acquire some of
her freedom. She seemed to offer another way.

The trouble was, there really isn't another way. By the time we were
traveling, I was the one *modelling* the reactions she wanted our drivers to
produce. So her daring social moves were made feasible by me—not by her
Gnostic affirmations. I was being exploited, as her banker, translator and
touchstone of normality—for her to soar above on Gnostic wings. I was the

one keeping this theatrical production going. . . . But the more such advantage she gained, the more sanity she lost. By the end she had cut the last ligaments that could connect us to an accurate view of the conditions in which we were living.

Our rescue wasn't magic. It depended entirely on people of good will who coolly assessed the worldly powers available, the methods that could appeal to those powers, and the dangers if nothing were done. My parents and the unnamed others were heroes of historical intelligence. The gift of the Jews is to combine that with hope, because—behind the scenes—there is still God, the partner.[43]

And, of course, there is also the real world: the unfallen, "holy" world of Judaism, created by *Hashem*, whose unforgiving, blank solidity—so disturbing to Russell—assures, among other possibilities, the possibility of truth; of arriving at an objective determination of the meaning of our actions, and thus, by way of what Eliot called "the rending pain of reenactment," the possibility of renewal.

THE MYSTERY OF JEWISH SURVIVAL

The peculiarities of Judaism that have occupied us in this chapter as well as the nature of Rosenthal's reasons for returning to Judaism may also throw some light on a question to which my argument has forced me to return a number of times already in this book: how has Judaism managed to survive, against the pressures of persecution and the temptations of assimilation? In chapter 5, I distinguished between two kinds of social homogeneity: *natural* and *project-driven*. And I suggested that while Jewish flouting of conventions of the former kind may expose them, in common with many other groups, to social prejudice (Langmuir's "ethnic prejudice"), it is the refusal of an irreducible core of Jews to participate in large-scale enterprises of the latter kind that has exposed them, and them alone, to the system of delusive claims, clustered around the "disease" metaphor, that jointly constitute political antisemitism. It is both the determination *and the ability* of Jews to stand apart from projects—Islam, the Christianization of Europe, the Enlightenment, fascism, socialism—that both their instigators and masses of their followers hold to be both unarguably correct and crucial to the salvation of humankind, I argued, that makes Jews appear to such minds a source both of wonder and of alarm. For groups and movements that find political antisemitism a temptation, there are two mysteries at stake: the first, *why* the Jews hold back from joining "us" since "we" are so obviously in the right; the second, *how* they have been and are able to get away with it in the face of the powers of persecution that "we" now wield and that others before us have wielded to as little ultimate effect.

The present chapter has begun the work of examining these mysteries in hopes of making them a little less impenetrable. I set out by restating the arguments of the Christian claim to have superseded Judaism, as those descend from Tertullian, and by examining some possible lines along which these arguments might be rebutted from a Jewish standpoint. I began the latter process, naturally enough, by emphasizing the similarities between Christianity and its parent religion that arise from the centrality to both religions of love, or *chesed*. But from that point onward, the idiosyncrasies of Judaism have begun— despite the sketchy and preliminary character of the chapter—to reassert themselves in ways tending to confirm the remark of Cynthia Ozick that I took as an epigraph to chapter 5, that "most of the essential ideals of Judaism" are "uniquely antithetical to the practices and premises of the pre-Judaic and non-Judaic world" and go "against the grain of the world at large."

The "antithetical" character of Judaism cuts both ways. It means on the one hand that Jews, their concerns, and their conduct very often present themselves to non-Jews as a source of mystery and puzzlement. To non-Jews lacking any close acquaintance with the complexities of Jewish traditional thought and feeling—which is to say, to the bulk of non-Jews—it is evident that Jews are, often rather radically, "not like us," without its being at all clear, either what precisely the difference consists of or from what it arises. From an informed Jewish perspective on the other hand, the gulf that separates Jewish from non-Jewish ways of thinking and feeling means, to put it bluntly, that non-Jewish ways of thinking are apt to seem, to say the least, uninviting. Earlier, I suggested that Judaism in effect reverses the logical priority of doctrine over moral commitment that characterizes not only most other religions but also most developed systems of political and philosophical theory. For most of us, what gives solidity and direction to our lives is primarily a collection of beliefs, which could well, of course, be partly or wholly erroneous. Certainly, that is true of all the attempts to weld humankind into project-driven unanimity to which an obstinate core of Jews have, in effect, given a Bronx cheer over the past two millennia. What gives solidity and direction to the life of the observant Jew, on the other hand, is observance. Belief, by its nature, is vulnerable to the vicissitudes of experience. Collective observance, on the other hand, justifies itself daily by its fruits, by the experienced values of the collective life to which it gives access. One reason, I take it, for the power of Judaism to endure is that, whereas any system that accords logical priority to belief must tremble and possibly fall when that belief is shaken, either at the hands of events that call its doctrinal commitments into question or at those of mere rational scrutiny, a system that grants logical priority to observance does not face the same perils from either source.

That Judaism has survived may, in short, have much to do with the fact that its dependence, as a system of individual and collective *commitment*, on either factual misrepresentation or the abuse of reason, is minimal to nonexistent.

What about the celebrated "obstinacy" of the Jews? In the modern world, of course, sizable numbers of nonobservant Jews have left Judaism behind and become wholeheartedly engaged with revolutionary movements and often in leadership roles. But, as I argued in chapter 5, the puzzle here is not to explain why so many Jews convert but why a permanent and substantial core refuse that option.

I suspect part of the answer here once again lies with what Maccoby would have termed the *non-aggadic* character of Judaism: its inversion of the priority of belief over moral commitment observable in most other developed worldviews. If *belief* is what gives meaning and structure to one's life, then conversion is simply a matter of exchanging one belief for another. This may well involve profound personal change, but it does not strip the convert of everything that gives meaning to life. It is simply that the work done by the former belief in bestowing meaning on existence has now been transferred to the shoulders of the new belief, whatever that may be.

On the other hand, if what confers meaning on one's life is membership in a group united in trusting obedience to a system of moral commitments, and if belief—Aggaddah—per se is of marginal significance when viewed from within that system, then conversion to *any* outlook that consists primarily in a system of beliefs—of *mere* Aggadah, in Jewish terms, that is to say, will be experienced as entailing a profound loss of everything that gives meaning to life. It follows that when viewed from the interior of a nonaggadic system, conversion to *any* aggadic one, no matter how it may be accumulating mass converts in the non-Jewish world, will appear so uninviting as to occur, for the most part, only under explicit and severe threat, and to be accompanied, even under those circumstances, with constant backsliding and attempts to retain a living contact with the nonaggadic system, which, of course, is exactly what we observe in the long and sad history of forced conversion of Jews.

I am suggesting, I suppose, that on one level Jewish survival is explained, at least negatively, merely by the readiness of so many Jews to make any sacrifice rather than give up their Judaism.

But more is needed, perhaps, to explain the Jewish ability to survive in the face of the long history of persecution. Here, I think, the centrality of *chesed* to Jewish thought and feeling may have played an important part. To trace out the varied institutional implementation of *chesed* within Jewish communities would require another chapter. However, it has certainly meant that Jews in difficulty have very often, at least, been able to rely on Jews in better circumstances to help out.

The centrality of *chesed* has also meant that Jews, although Judaism has never been a unified religion, have never been decimated by internecine wars over differences between one sect and another. No Jew, that is to say, has ever said of other Jews the words attributed to Arnaud Amaury, abbot of Cîteaux and pontifical legate, before the siege of Béziers, during the first Albigensian Crusade in 1209: *Tuez-les tous: Dieu reconnetra les siens!* ["Kill them all: God will recognize his own!"] On the other hand, both the two daughter religions of Judaism have, in effect, said things that amount to that, and done so repeatedly, down to the present day. In the twentieth century, internecine bloodshed among Christians has been confined to the margins of Europe, to Northern Ireland and the Balkans; but that has perhaps more to do with the waning of Christian belief per se than with any waning of Christian sectarian animus. It cannot be said, though, that the wars between the Sunni and Sh'ia branches of Islam, which grew out of the Arab Spring of 2010–11, and continue to dominate the Middle East, have been in any sense marginal. They have been reported in the West largely in terms of terrorist attacks on European targets and the influx of refugees. For all that, the major costs of these wars, running into hundreds of thousands dead, millions displaced, and whole countries devastated, have been borne mainly by Muslims.

Considering these disparities, one cannot but wonder whether the time and energy expended over so long a period in denouncing Judaism as a primitive and superseded religion might not have been more usefully spent in inquiring how it has managed over so many centuries to avoid consuming its own children in this way? Why, we non-Jews might ask, have the sorrows of the Jews been for the most part of our making, while ours, for the most part, have been bred uniquely out of our own internecine discords?

NOTES

1. John J. Mearsheimer, "The Future of Palestine: Righteous Jews vs. the New Afrikaners," in Loewenstein and Moor 2012, 140.
2. Prager and Telushkin 2003.
3. Nirenberg 2013, 350–51.
4. Mack 2014, 129. For the references to Rosenzweig, see Mack.
5. Nicholls 1993.

6. Nicholls 1993, 172.
7. Nicholls 1993, 179.
8. Nicholls 1993, 181.
9. Flannery 1985. I am grateful to David Conway for drawing my attention to this neglected work.
10. Nicholls 1993, 185.
11. Nicholls 1993, 182.
12. Nicholls 1993, 183.
13. David P. Efroymson, "Tertullian's Anti-Judaism and Its Role in His Theology" (PhD diss., Temple University, 1977).
14. Nicholls 1993, 182.
15. Nicholls 1993, 186.
16. *The Reader's Bible* 1951, New Testament, p. 71.
17. Babylonian Talmud, Tractate *Shabbath*, Folio 31a. Available in translation at http://www.come-and-hear.com/shabbath/shabbath_31.html. The whole passage runs:

> On another occasion it happened that a certain heathen came before Shammai and said to him, "Make me a proselyte, on condition that you teach me the whole Torah while I stand on one foot. Thereupon he repulsed him with the builder's cubit that was in his hand. When he went before Hillel, he said to him "What is hateful to you, do not to your neighbour: that is the whole Torah, while the rest is the commentary thereof; go and learn it."

18. Yankl Tauber, "Love according to the Rebbe," TheRebbe.org, a section of the Lubavicher website Chabad.org. Rabbi Schneur Zalman was the founder of the Chabad branch of Hasidism. Zalman's son Rabbi DovBer settled in the town of Lubavitch: hence the name "Lubavitcher," by which followers of Chabad Hasidism are also known.
19. Steinsalz 1976, 165.
20. Solomon 2009, xi.
21. See, for example, either of the works cited in the previous two endnotes.
22. Geoffrey Hartman, "Midrash as Law and Literature," *Journal of Religion* 74, no. 3 (1994): 338.
23. For a fuller account of the distinction between meanings and bearings, see Harrison 2015, ch. 10.
24. Solomon 2009, 470.
25. *Jerusalem Talmud*, Eichah Rabbah, Pesichta 2.
26. See F. M. Cornford 1941, 175ff.
27. Dostoevski, *The Brothers Karamazov*, pt. 4, bk. 11, ch. 4. In Constance Garnett's English translation, the phrase becomes "Without God ... all things are lawful." For the location of the Russian text and for an excellent discussion of Garnett's and the other main English translations, I am indebted to Andrei

A. Volkov, "Dostoevski Did Say It: A Response to David E. Cortesi" (2011). This paper is to be found on a website, "The Secular Web," at infidels.org. Unfortunately, although Volkov's paper is available in full there, its presumed original print source is not given.

28. Kellner 2006, 15.

29. Maccoby 1982, 48.

30. Maccoby 1982, 44.

31. Website myjewishlearning.com; page on "All of Israel Are Responsible for One Another."

32. Patterson 2012, 35.

33. Buber 1965, 32–33.

34. Rosenthal 1987, expanded edition 2018; Rosenthal, forthcoming.

35. Rosenthal, correspondence with author, May 27, 2017.

36. Russell 1917, 47–48.

37. Patterson 2012, 40.

38. Cited in Furbank 1979, 2:124.

39. Rosenthal, forthcoming.

40. Rosenthal, forthcoming.

41. Rosenthal, forthcoming.

42. Rosenthal, forthcoming.

43. Rosenthal, forthcoming.

TWELVE

—⚮—

MITZVAH AND MORAL THEORY

The Jewish faith was, in its original form, a *collection of mere statutory laws*
upon which was established a political organization; for whatever moral
additions were then or later appended to it in no way whatever belonged to
Judaism as such.[1]

—Immanuel Kant, *Religion within the Limits of Reason Alone*

The antisemite, we have suggested, faces a puzzle: no persecution, no contempt,
no derision appear sufficient to induce an irreducible core of Jews, at any period,
to accept the evident superiority of "our" ways of thinking and doing things,
to give up their identity as Jews, in favor of joining the broad forward march
of humanity of which a given age likes to think of itself as constituting the
vanguard. Common opinion over the past three centuries has favored three
general explanations of the Jewish "obstinacy" that persistently refuses the call
of whatever happens to count, at a given historical moment, as modernity: the
antiquated and primitive character of Judaism as a religion, the clannishness,
the rejection of "universal" human sympathies that it supposedly encourages,
and perhaps worst of all, the way in which Judaism supposedly works to prevent
its adherents from becoming fully responsible and self-directing moral agents,
through its subordination of individual moral responsibility to communal observance of law: a subordination that, allegedly, prevents the Jew from rising
to the ennobling freedom of the autonomous, "self-legislating" moral agent.

335

The first charge, of religious obscurantism, we examined in the last chapter. The second, of the Jewish particularism that supposedly makes Jews incapable of rising to any of the various forms of universalism represented by Christianity, Islam, or the Enlightenment, we shall look into in the next chapter. The present chapter will be concerned with the third charge: that Judaism by its nature tends to deny its adherents the status of independent, fully responsible moral agents.

The form in which this charge is usually put owes much to the moral philosophy of Immanuel Kant (1724–1804) and in particular to Kant's notion of moral autonomy. Kant argues, plausibly, that if an act is motivated either by obedience to others, or by the agent's own appetites—concern for his or her own material interests—then it cannot be regarded as a *moral* act—that is, one springing from a purely moral impulse. If an action is to be considered moral, it must in some sense be directed by the agent's *reason*. Only then can it be *autonomous* in the sense of being an act of the agent himself or herself, rather than one forced upon him, or her, by pressure from others or by the urgencies of his or her appetites or desires for material things. If these conditions are not met, then, in Kantian terminology the act is *heteronomous*, and the agent is at best self-deluded concerning his or her own claim to *moral* virtue, at worst a conscious hypocrite.

The question of how action *can* be guided by reason was, of course, a burning issue for the Enlightenment, and one on which British and continental opinion found themselves sharply divided. Simply and bluntly stated, reason amounts to a set of formal rules for deriving true statements from other true statements. David Hume (1711–1776), the chief philosophical eminence of the Scottish Enlightenment, had argued that moral statements, such as "murder is wrong" or "promise-keeping is obligatory," fail to express *statements* at all, but are mere forms of words expressive of approval or disapproval. Such expressions of emotional attitude, however deeply felt, cannot significantly be said to be either true or false. Hence the rules of rational assessment are incapable of operating upon them, from which it appears to follow that morality falls *in principle* outside the sphere of reason. Following other ideas of Hume's, the fathers of the Utilitarian tradition of theorizing about morality, Jeremy Bentham (1748–1832) and James Mill (1773–1836), were beginning to speculate that the root of all moral conviction must lie in the desire to maximize pleasure and minimize pain—in other words, in familiar human appetites of the sort that for the Kantian constitute heteronomy of the worst kind.

Kant's resolute rejection of both these alien ways of thinking involves an interesting extension of the notion of reason itself. Deductive reasoning depends on the notion of contradiction in the following sense: that what forces one to accept the conclusion of a formally valid argument from true premises is that to deny it is to contradict oneself. Is there in *moral* reflection any analog of self-contradiction? Kant thought that there was. It comes into the picture, he thought, when one passes from thinking of oneself as a private person, whose pursuit of advantage in life concerns only himself or herself, to thinking of oneself as a universal legislator, disposing of the power to decree that every rational being shall adopt this or that given strategy for advancing his or her interests. Consider a specific strategy, say, that of obtaining money by borrowing on a false promise to repay it. So long as I consider myself as a private person, no "contradiction," in the sense of *no conflict in my will*, is involved in deciding to use this means of enriching myself. But now, suppose I adopt that same maxim as a universal legislator. In willing that every rational being should attempt to enrich himself or herself in this way, I am willing, in effect, that such promises should become worthless and the strategy itself become ineffective. I have thus uncovered a "contradiction" in the sense of a diametrical opposition between what I will as a private person (that I should become richer through false promising) and what I will when I adopt the same maxim as a universal legislator (that it should become impossible for anyone, including myself, to enrich himself or herself through false promising). And this contradiction, Kant thinks, is what shows that obtaining money through a false promise is *morally wrong.*[2]

It is important to see that Kant does not think that obtaining money on false pretenses is wrong *because it is likely to make the institution of promising collapse.* On the one hand, it isn't, and on the other hand, the issue is irrelevant to Kant's argument either way. The belief of many Anglo-Saxon commentators that Kant's argument collapses into some form of utilitarianism at this and related points is, it seems—not only to me but also to many Kant scholars—simply a mistake. What shows false promising to be wrong, in Kant's view, is not any *consequence* that it might be supposed to have but simply the contradiction—the conflict between the content of the two acts of will—that arises when one passes from adopting the strategy as a private person to adopting it as a universal legislator.

One might ask why this odd kind of contradiction should have any moral interest, should even be relevant to what we ordinarily think of as morality. But here, again, Kant has an answer that connects closely with everyday moral intuition. It is that the reason why a given strategy cannot be willed as valid for all rational beings by the act of a universal legislator is invariably that that strategy involves treating other rational beings not as "ends in themselves," as Kant puts it, but merely as tools to someone else's advantage. This, and not the contradiction itself, is ultimately, within the terms of Kant's theory, what makes the rejected strategy morally wrong.

MORAL THEORY AND THE JEWS

Kant is apt to strike the student on first acquaintance as offering an impressive, not to say grandiose, account of the nature of morality and beyond that even of the notion of Enlightenment itself. It appears to show how individual persons, by the private exercise of their own rational faculties, can raise themselves to the enjoyment of a moral vision that utterly transcends and leaves behind any concern with their own private desires and commitments. In effect, it offers a vision of humankind as constituting, in principle, a universal brotherhood of all rational beings, beings who abstain from treating one another as mere tools, but rather accord one another the dignity of being regarded, and treated, as ends in themselves; and who recognize the points at which action would overstep this mark not by appeal to desire, or "moral intuition," or social convention, but rather to their powers of abstract reasoning.

Vast numbers of intellectuals have found, and still find, Kant's moral vision compelling. As the Jewish philosopher Emil Fackenheim observes, "Kant's rational autonomy is the core of philosophical modernity."[3] At the same time, the vision of enlightened morality that Kant offers us is impossible to square with the moral outlook of Judaism. At the moral core of Judaism stands the notion of "observance": obedience to the commands of God. And while what an observant Jew takes to be the effective content of those commands may depend on the outcome of debate over many centuries, the processes of reasoning involved in the evolution of halakah are far removed from those advocated by Kant. For one thing, while they examine specific instances of moral dispute, they do so in light of a textual tradition; for another, they are *essentially collective in character*—ultimately responsive, not to Kantian standards of personal independence and moral autonomy, but to majority decision.

From a Kantian standpoint, therefore, the observant Jew has, in effect, set his face against the prospect of Enlightenment by deliberately cutting himself off from the liberating voices of reason, freedom, and moral autonomy. In doing so he appears to have aligned himself, when viewed from a Kantian standpoint, with the very impulses that on Kant's account it is the whole purpose of Enlightenment to transcend: those of mere personal and communal advantage. One can see how, at this point, these criticisms begin to merge with the Christian ones that we encountered in the last chapter. Just as the Christian sees the Jew as mired in a merely national cult that precludes his rising to the Christian

ideals of universal human brotherhood and love, so the Kantian sees the Jew
as obsessed with money making, trade, family, and tribe to an extent that cuts
him off from the exercise of rational moral autonomy that would enable him
to transcend these—in Kantian terms—essentially "heteronomous" concerns
and join the universal community of fully rational and therefore enlightened
moral agents. In short, Judaism locks the Jew, morally speaking, into a permanently infantilized condition, one that, because it denies him the possibility of
achieving the personal autonomy that characterizes adult moral responsibility,
permanently unfits him for membership of a fully enlightened civil society. In
his minor works, Kant fully elaborates these ideas into an extended critique,
on moral grounds, of Jews and Judaism.

> In Kant ... we find a collection of potent anti-Jewish concepts: Judaism
> is an *immoral* and *obsolete* religion; the Jews are an *alien* nation; the Jews
> are a nation of *traders* devoted to *money*. Unifying all these themes is the
> central Kantian revolutionary idea of moral freedom that sees the Jews as
> refusing to be free: they chain themselves to an external, irrational Law that
> reduces them in the end to being slaves to their own unenlightened egoism.
> It was this implicit notion of "egoism that was to receive an extraordinary
> elaboration and currency in subsequent philosophical critiques of Judaism.[4]

Post-Kantian philosophy in Germany, in the hands of Herder, Fichte, Hegel,
and others, did indeed further elaborate these ideas. For Kant, the ideals of
freedom, autonomy, and rationality find their primary locus in the individual
mind. In Hegel, their primary locus becomes the state. The state effectively
realizes the demand of Kantian moral rationality that individual desire is only
morally acceptable when it is universally compatible with the needs of others.
The state, for Hegel, both determines and enforces obedience to the demands
of just such a universal reconciliation of individual human wills. Hence, for
Hegel, the freedom of the individual comes to consist of a rationally justified
and willingly accepted obedience to the will of the state.

> For Hegel, to be fully satisfied is the mark of freedom. Man is fully satisfied
> when he knows what he wants, endeavours rationally to obtain it, and
> succeeds. But man cannot be free in society unless he desires to be just
> and his conception of justice accords with the existing order; and again, he
> cannot be free unless he desires justice as much as ends private to himself,
> and unless those ends accord with his notion of justice. Yet again, man cannot
> be free outside society, for it is in society that he acquires purposes which he
> can rationally pursue, and it is also in society that he comes to conceive of
> freedom and to desire it.[5]

In obedience to the state, according to Hegel, the individual also finds freedom from subservience to the prosaic conditions of his concrete, everyday life.

By compelling man to sacrifice his empirical well-being, the laws of
the state—being indifferent to particular characteristics—also realize
the absolute freedom of man from the material conditions of his
empirical life. Thus, as in Kant, positive law supports rather than conflicts
with transcendental philosophy as liberation from material existence.
     Significantly Hegel focused on war as the prime example of such realization
of the transcendental by means of the political, for in times of war the
state "puts its subjects into close contact with their master, death" (*in jener
auferlegten Arbeit ihren Herrn, den Tod, zu fühlen zu geben*) . . . [in a manner
that] . . . brings to the level "of Being and Consciousness" (*zum Dasein und
bewusstsein bringt*) the "nothingness of all these particles of immediate being."[6]

Once again, we have a parallel in German idealism with the Christian sense,
examined in the last chapter, that Judaism, in its commitment to redeeming life
in this world, lacks the spirituality that expresses itself in the yearning—which,
for example, permeates the hymns of John Wesley—to abandon this world for
the next. For exactly the same reasons, German idealism, from its inception in
the late eighteenth century, saw Judaism as the inherent enemy of its goal of
transcending and so redeeming the corrupt, self- and money-obsessed realities
of individual life by subordinating them entirely to the higher, universal reality
of the state.

The enemies of the Jews on the left . . . developed a revolutionary critique of
Judaism and Jewishness built on two interconnected notions: that the human
failing of "egoism" was embodied for the modern era in the economic system
of bourgeois capitalism; and that "money" was the supreme expression
of a self-interest and self-seeking that impeded the final emancipation of
humanity and the emergence of a genuinely social "new man."
     The basic idea was hardly new. In the guise of *amour propre* it had been
a central theme in Rousseau, but in Germany the insight was seized upon
and systematized with a grim determination that drained it of its original
spontaneity and turned it instead into a mechanical ideology, a set of
clumsy conceptual building blocks, More sinisterly, it was in Germany
that a specifically Jewish significance was injected into the general idea
that humanity was being alienated from its true loving social nature by an
egoism that was seen as essentially Jewish, being intrinsic to Jewish national
character.[7]

The role of this complex of ideas in the rise of German radical nationalism
during the nineteenth century has been amply documented since World War II.

Its success, as Karl Popper notes, was partly due to Hegel's good fortune in establishing himself as the official philosopher of the Prussian state. "It seems improbable that Hegel would ever have become the most influential figure in German philosophy without the authority of the Prussian state behind him. As it happened, he became the first official philosopher of Prussianism, appointed in the period of feudal 'restoration' after the Napoleonic wars. Later the state also backed his pupils (Germany had, and still has, only state-controlled universities) and they in turn backed one another. And although Hegelianism was officially renounced by most of them, Hegelianising philosophers have dominated philosophical teaching and thereby indirectly even the secondary schools of Germany ever since."[8]

As David Patterson shows, the resulting widespread familiarity of the Hegelian program, of political redemption from "egoism" through willing assent to the putatively universal institution of the state, allowed it in due course to flow naturally into the ideology of National Socialism. From this point of view, he says, "we need only recall a statement made by Dr. Walter Schultze at the June 1939 meeting of the National Socialist Association of University Lecturers: 'What the great thinkers of German Idealism dreamed of, and what was ultimately the kernel of their longing for liberty, finally comes alive, assumes reality.... Never has the German ideal of freedom been conceived with greater life and greater vigor than in our day.' A leading intellectual of Nazi Germany, Schultze saw as clearly as any of Nazi Germany's philosophers the link between the German idealism forged by Kant and National Socialism."[9]

The Kantian-Hegelian association of Jews with money as the essence of "egoistic self-seeking," of course, predated and has long outlived the Nazis. As David Nirenberg points out, and as we saw in an earlier chapter, it provides Hannah Arendt with an explanation of what she considers the shared "responsibility" (her word) of Jews for the Holocaust: "All economic statistics prove that German Jews belonged not to the German people, but at most to its bourgeoisie." As Nirenberg says, it is "a bit surprising" that the statistics in question are drawn from Nazi economists. But more telling still, perhaps, is her dependence on the tradition of German idealism for her distinction between "the people" and "its bourgeoisie."[10]

The Judaic conception of what connects individual to nation is indeed radically opposed to the account offered by idealist philosophy in the tradition of Kant and Hegel—or Marx. What divides them, however, is not that the Judaic understanding exalts money and self-seeking over social responsibility—though it does accept them as an irreducible part of life. To observant Jews with a sense of their tradition, self-seeking and the concern for economic security are, as we saw in the last chapter, certainly expressions of the evil impulse, the yetzer hara. But although such impulses need control at the hands of the good impulse, the yetzer hatov, they cannot be transcended or somehow written out of life, because then, as the rabbis say, "nothing would get done." That in turn points to the real reason why, with respect to the German idealist wing of the Enlightenment, just as to many strands in Christianity, Judaism stands, in Cynthia Ozick's words, as "dissenting, contradictory, frequently irreconcilable." It does so because of its rooted preference not for *transcending* the prosaic, difficult, often ambiguous life of this world but rather for *living* it. In Deuteronomy 30:19, "Moses our teacher," as a Jewish friend of mine recently put it to me, "offers his final oration to the children of Israel in which he presents the essence of his teaching": *I have set before you life and death, the blessing and the curse. Choose life.*

"Choosing life" is a central principle of Judaism, which even expresses itself in the conventional toast: *l'chaim* ("to life"). To "choose life" in Judaism is not, of course, just a matter of taking it as it comes but of attempting to live it in a way that permeates it with the spirit of God: that "draws God into the world," as it is sometimes put. From the point of view of Judaism, that effort is conceived as both permanently ongoing, from generation to generation, until the messianic age (which is also conceived as an age of *this world*) and as intrinsically communal in character. In the words of Rabbi Tarfon, recorded in the Talmud (*Avot* 2:21), "It is not your responsibility to finish the work of perfecting the world, but you are not free to desist from it either."

On such a view, what ultimately counts in the world is not the dramatic acts of personal transformation and self-transcendence celebrated by philosophers of the stamp of Kant or Sartre but rather those "unhistoric acts" of which everyone is capable, of which George Eliot speaks in the closing paragraph of *Middlemarch*: "[Dorothea Brookes's] finely touched spirit had still its fine issues, though they were not widely visible. Her full nature, like that river of which Cyrus broke the strength, spent itself in channels which had no great name on the earth. But the effect of her being on those around her was incalculably diffusive; for the growing good of the world is partly dependent on unhistoric acts; and that things are not so ill with you and me as they might have been, is half owing to the number who lived faithfully a hidden life, and rest in unvisited tombs."[11]

The sense of this passage is so close to that of *Avot* 2:21 that I think it unlikely that George Eliot, whose interest in Judaism is well documented, was not familiar with Rabbi Tarfon's version of her thought—or for that matter, with the opening passage of the *Amidah*, the great daily "standing prayer" of Judaism that blesses "God most high, who bestows acts of loving kindness and creates all, who remembers the loving kindness of the Fathers."[12]

Kant and Hegel, on the other hand, both conceive of moral redemption as something that can be achieved on an individual basis, through a process of radical renunciation of the ordinary conditions of life in this world: one that works by subjecting individual choice to the determinations of reason. In Kant's case, reason takes the shape of the categorical imperative, in Hegel's case in that of the state. To any reasonably observant Jew, this process must appear not as one that endeavors to redeem the world by drawing God into it but one that sets up a thin, abstract, and idealized conception of man—or at least of human rationality—in the place of God.

This is exactly the critique of German idealism advanced by the Jewish philosopher Franz Rosenzweig (1886–1929), both in his early *Hegel and the State* and in *The Star of Redemption*, the work for which he is chiefly remembered. "Instead of trying—in the eternity of philosophical thought or in the temporality of the historical process—to show the human under the might of the divine, one tries, on the contrary, to understand the divine as the self-projection of the human into the heaven of myth."[13]

Less has been written on the contrariety between Judaism and the two main British contributions to Enlightenment moral thought. But the contrariety is no less acute. Hume's skepticism sharply undercuts the idea that there is or could be such a thing as moral knowledge. From the point of view of any believer—Jewish or otherwise—in the superior moral adequacy of one tradition of moral response relative to others (of the moral outlook of Judaism relative to that of National Socialism, for example), a Humian outlook advances the dispiriting conclusion glumly echoed by the late Bernard Williams: "We must reject the objectivist view of ethical life as ... a pursuit of ethical truth."[14]

Utilitarianism, at least in a sense, turns its back on the relativism of Hume's position by proposing a general rational criterion for right action: the maximization of general welfare. But it is essential to utilitarianism that that criterion, once formulated, overrides the subordinate claims of any moral rule except in circumstances where the unthinking general observance of commonplace moral rules can plausibly be argued to work out in ways that tend to maximize general welfare. To the observant Jew, the mitzvoth certainly constitute rules to be obeyed. And there are plenty of well-known types of case, endlessly cited and argued out in philosophical dispute, between utilitarians and nonutilitarians in which moral principle and utility appear to conflict. May it not be, perhaps, as the Australian philosopher J. J. C. Smart suggests, that in some of these cases, "the conflict can be traced to some sort of confusion, perhaps even to some sort of superstitious rule-worship."[15] To the utilitarian following out the implications of that thought, the moral weakness of Judaism can easily appear to consist not so much, as Kant thought, in disregard for the values of autonomous reason but rather in its vulnerability to what they see as "superstitious rule-worship."

SOME LIMITATIONS OF ENLIGHTENMENT MORAL THOUGHT

The trio of opposing theories we have just been discussing—Humian skepticism, utilitarianism, and Kantian rational universalism—all saw the light between 1739 and 1785, in the remote heyday of the European Enlightenment. Each of them pretends to offer, at least at its simplest level, a rational reconstruction of everyday moral experience. Each pretends, that is, to make clear what ordinary, unphilosophical people *really mean* when they use moral terminology. Or to put it both more modestly and more arrogantly, each pretends to show what and how much, in ordinary people's moral thinking, actually *makes sense*—can be *rescued*, that is to say, *in rational terms*, from the supposed morass of confusion attending any attempt by the common man to think straight about anything.

Despite the relative remoteness, both historical and cultural, of all three accounts, they continue to dominate "mainstream" moral philosophy, as it is taught presently in the philosophy departments of English-speaking universities. Such teaching is apt, broadly speaking, to take at face value the claim of abstract moral theorizing to express all that can be rationally salvaged from the supposed confusions of our ordinary moral thinking and to proceed on the tacit assumption that anyone committed to serious thought about the moral life must, in the end, opt for one or other of the three types of theory bequeathed us by the Enlightenment.

At the same time, all three types of theory operate at some distance from the moral outlook of most ordinary people: a distance, one might think, sufficient to render problematic an uncritical or wholesale acceptance of any of them. To put it bluntly, we commonly assume the centrality to our everyday moral thinking of a range of concerns of which Enlightenment moral theory, if it does not ignore them altogether, can offer no very adequate account. Here are four of them.

Duties to Specific Persons

In ordinary life, we think of morality as to a great extent a matter of duties owed to other people in respect of specific, publicly established kinds of relationship in which we stand to them. Sometimes the relationships are of the kind we call "personal." These include those between wives and husbands, parents and children, friends and neighbors. But others, less "personal" in that sense, are nevertheless relationships between particular persons. I am thinking here, for example, of relationships between work colleagues, between teachers and students, between doctors and patients, between political representatives and their constituents, between shopkeepers and their customers (Kant's butcher, for instance), and so on. All of these, including the personal ones, might be termed person-to-person relationships. All of them give rise to specific structures of rights and correlative duties that in turn create moral demands requiring specific, named persons to treat, or refrain from treating, other specific, named persons in specific ways. In any complex society here thus comes into being a moral fabric, or web, or nexus, connecting persons to persons in a wide variety of interconnected ways, on a wide variety of interconnected levels.

Enlightenment moral theory, in all the three forms we have looked at, has little to say concerning specific, person-to-person moral relationships of this kind. On the contrary, it views the duties of the moral agent—call him A—as arising not from concrete relationships between A and other specific, named persons but rather from relationships holding *between the agent and "humanity" or "society" in general*, on one or another highly abstract theoretical account of how the latter terms are to be understood. Thus, for Kantians, moral concerns arise in virtue of a relationship between the individual and the abstract community theoretically constituted by the totality of rational wills. For utilitarians, moral concerns arise in virtue of a relationship between the individual and the abstract community of sentient beings capable of experiencing pleasure or pain. For the Humian skeptic, they arise in virtue of a relationship between the individual and the causal processes, biological or social as the case may be, that enter into the determination of his or her sentiments of approval or disapproval. This, of course, is an aspect of still deeper and explicitly political disagreements concerning the very nature of the social bond. It is characteristic of liberalism in all its forms, on both sides of the channel, to envisage the social bond, the fundamental relationship uniting men and women into a society, as running *vertically*, from each individual to the totality of individuals, and to share in some degree Rousseau's suspicion of what the latter called partial associations, including the family. Conservatism in all its forms tends, on the contrary, to view the social bond as propagating itself *horizontally* through a network of overlapping relationships between individuals and groups of individuals. Much to the irritation of liberal intellectuals, the thinking of ordinary, unphilosophical men and women tends, in this respect, to be for the most part rootedly conservative (with a small *c*).

Morality and Social Practice

The neglect of person-to-person relationship by all three of the main Enlightenment accounts of morality arises largely from the fact that all three
see it as their main task to address the central problem inherited by modern
philosophy from Descartes: that of giving some account of how the individual can determine *for himself* the truth of judgments, without appeal to
tradition, testimony, or hearsay. All three assume that the same problem
must be solved for moral judgments *if individuals are to have any reason for
taking them seriously.* For Kant, there must be some form of reasoning, accessible to every individual in the privacy of his or her own mind, by appeal
to which an individual can validate moral judgments without reference to
others, since otherwise morality would presumably remain, for each individual, an arbitrary imposition arising from some source external to that individual's mind. Utilitarianism, though radically opposed to much in Kant's
thought, agrees with it in this respect. In principle, utilitarianism grants to
individuals, in the shape of the principle of utility, a criterion they can use to
determine for themselves the content of right and wrong, without reference
to the demands and restrictions of "traditional" or "folk morality." Again,
for Hume, although individuals, he thinks, lack access to any rational means
of validating moral claims, what is to count as "right" and "wrong" is still
something to be settled *internally to the individual* mind by appeal to its own
moral *sentiments.*

The trouble with this feature of all three accounts of moral autonomy is that
it appears to divorce morality from any basis in common social practice and
mutual agreement. For all moral theorizing with roots in the Cartesian tradition, the central question we confront *as moral beings* is "what ought *I* to do in
this situation?" Equally, the central *theoretical* problem for moral theory so conceived is to show how this question can be answered *from within the standpoint
of each individual who confronts it.* Ordinary, unphilosophical minds, on the
other hand, tend to see the moral issues confronting them as arising not from
private speculation on their part but from public practices and conventions—
promising, marriage, friendship, property (private or public), the teacher-pupil
relationship, the conventions of military comradeship, and so forth—which
they did not invent but found already operative in society and whose rules and
conventions are in no way responsive to the private reflections of this or that
specific individual but apply, rather, to *anybody at all who happens to find himself
in this or that given situation.* As the Australian moral philosopher Julius Kovesi
notes in this connection:

a large number and surprising variety of moral philosophers seem to talk about our moral life and language as if each of us spoke a private language and yet lived in society, as if our moral notions were private notions that we try to make universal.

The fact that [Hume] regards the relationship of a son to a father as the same as that between an acorn and an oak tree shows that for him a moral agent does not live in society. The only sentiment he considers is his own disapproval in his own breast towards what is (apparently) an inanimate world.[16]

Trust

The notions of *trust* and *trustworthiness* play, obviously enough, a central role in our everyday moral thinking. Discussion of the nature and functions of trust in our lives, however, is virtually absent from the classical texts of the three versions of Enlightenment moral theorizing before us and almost absent from the mainstream of university studies in ethics that those traditions continue to dominate. (The one current, though very significant, counterinstance known to me is that of the eminent Oxford philosopher and public figure Onora O'Neill.[17]) It is important to see also that this sidelining of the notion of trust is not a mere accident or oversight but is an *essential* feature of the abstract moral theorizing bequeathed us by the Enlightenment. It is no use, after all, trusting someone to consider one's interests if that person considers himself or herself bound by higher moral demands that in his or her view override all considerations of person-to-person relationship. Notoriously, the convinced Kantian must truthfully inform the murderer of the whereabouts of his victim. Equally notoriously, the convinced utilitarian must sacrifice his friend—or for that matter, the perfect stranger—to the demands of the party, if he (the utilitarian) believes that the activities of the party conduce to the greater good of humankind. It was precisely E. M. Forster's sense of the dangers of imagining abstract aims or causes of this kind to be the source of the deepest and most serious moral demands that produced his famous remark, "If I had to choose between betraying my friend and betraying my country, I hope I would have the guts to betray my country."[18]

Motive

All three of the main Enlightenment accounts of morality leave it obscure why moral considerations per se should exercise any hold over us in the first place. It is one of Kant's major merits to have seen how sharply this problem arises for his own theory—and to have dismissed it, with striking honesty, as insoluble!

"How the bare *principle of the universal validity of all its maxims as laws* (which would admittedly be the form of a pure practical reason) can by itself—without any matter (or object) of the will in which we could take some antecedent interest—supply a motive and create an interest which could be called purely moral; or in other words, *how pure reason can be practical*—all human reason is incapable of explaining this."[19]

Kant's question arises with equal force, however, for utilitarianism and for Humian skepticism. Why, for instance—without there being, as Kant puts it, some other "matter (or object) of the will in which we could take some antecedent interest"—should anyone feel the slightest interest in the project of maximizing the abstract totality of human—or, still more grandly, sentient—happiness? Again, once one has been shown by Hume that all of the supposedly moral restraints under which one labors amount to no more than causally induced emotional incapacities to contemplate this or that course of action, why should one not endeavor, in the manner of Sade or Fielding's Jonathan Wild, to break the chains of causality and free oneself to commit any atrocity that may answer to one's desires, hampered neither by causally induced feelings of hesitation, nor by equally causally induced feelings of remorse?

THE COHERENCE OF OUR ORDINARY MORAL THINKING

How, in respect of these four considerations, does our ordinary, everyday moral thinking differ from these venerable Enlightenment attempts to disclose its rational basis? And is that everyday thinking coherent in the way, or ways, in which it does so? Is it perhaps perfectly "rational" as it stands but in ways, and in a sense, that the formal debates of academic philosophers fail to uncover?

Let us begin with the last and perhaps the most serious of our four issues: that surrounding the question of what it is that motivates people—as people clearly are motivated, every day and in very large numbers—to take the demands of morality seriously. The problem facing Kant, in the passage cited above, is that there cannot, in his terms, be any such thing as "an interest which could be called purely moral," because *interest* per se is in his terms *heteronomous* and thus nonmoral. But it is not simply the terms of Kant's philosophy that make it difficult to represent the desire to behave in accordance with the demands of morality—as a number of eighteenth-century British moralists attempted to do—as arising from self-interest. Even then, the novelist Henry Fielding was capable of delivering the coup de grace to such efforts in the following terse sentence: "There are a set of religious, or rather moral writers, who teach that virtue is the certain road to happiness, and vice to misery, in this world. A very wholesome and comfortable doctrine, and to which we have but one objection, namely, that it is not true."[20]

The difficulty upon which Fielding has here obliquely placed his finger is that when virtue is hostile to self-interest, as it often is, *people very often prefer to practice virtue and let self-interest go hang.* What could possibly *motivate* them to do that? This is the ultimate anomaly that, as Kant sees it, "all human reason is incapable of explaining."

Kant was wrong about that. Even in his age, an explanation had for some time been available, although not in a form readily accessible to philosophers, in hints and suggestions scattered through the work of some of the more philosophically attentive writers of the day.[21] Divested of its literary trappings, it comes down to a simple enough suggestion: that interests can influence action, not in one but rather in two distinct ways. One may be led at times to act in certain ways by one's need to *satisfy* some interest. Equally, at other times, one may be led to act in certain ways not by the need to *satisfy* an interest but merely by the need to *preserve it as one of one's interests.*

The distinction arises characteristically in the context of what I called above *person-to-person relationships.* Such relationships generate complex structures of pleasure, satisfaction, and meaning—structures that would, of course, collapse, as possible sources of direction and fulfillment in life in the event of a collapse in the relationships from which they arise and on whose continuing health they depend. If, therefore, one wishes to go on enjoying and anticipating such satisfactions, then one must look to the health of the relationships on which they depend. But at times, looking to the health of a relationship not only yields no satisfaction of the interests normally associated with it but actually impedes the satisfaction of other interests. A father, for example, loves his son and wishes to see him develop into a grown man with whom he will remain able to share the intimacy they now enjoy. The son is beginning to lead an independent life and wants to borrow the car some evenings. If the father agrees, no joy will come to him from the agreement, since he will not only lose the use of the car those evenings but will also worry terribly until the moment he hears the vehicle nosing finally into the garage at past eleven. But he also sees that if he were to refuse to license the use of the car, he would in effect be denying his son the right to achieve an independent life, and he sees also that this could only in the long run harm the relationship and possibly in time destroy it.

In effect, the term *interests,* when applied to the father in this prosaic example, covers three quite different kinds of thing. First, there are what one might call *purely personal* interests, exemplified by the father's desire to have the use of the car and to be free from worry. Purely personal interests can be specified without reference to anyone beyond the individual they concern. Then there are what one might call *impersonal interests*, including the father's interest in seeing his son become a successful and independent adult. Impersonal interests cannot be specified without reference beyond the individual: to other persons *to whom he or she stands in specific relationship.* Nor can they be felt as interests or desires *outside the context of that relationship.* The father feels the concern he feels for his son's future, because the latter *is* his son and because the relationship between them is one of close affection, involving the many kinds of meaning and satisfaction that such relationships introduce into the otherwise isolated and limited lives of the individuals involved in them. Third, and finally, there are what one might call *relational interests.* Relational interests are interests in preserving the coherence and functionality of relationships as sources of impersonal interests, together with the possibilities of meaning and satisfaction that impersonal interests contribute to the life of the individual.

Relational interests thus turn out, in the terms provided by Kant's remarks cited above, to "supply a motive and create an interest which could be called purely moral." For Kant, a motive is "purely moral" only if it prescinds entirely from any consideration of personal pleasure. But that is precisely what relational interests do. Like any other interest, of course, relational interests demand *fulfillment.* But *fulfillment* is not necessarily the same as *pleasure.* To do something because it must be done to secure the validity and health of a relationship is, as the above example shows, not at all the same thing as *doing it for the sake of the pleasure it provides,* and that remains true even when the protected relationship contributes much, in terms of pleasure and meaning, to the life of the agent in other ways.[22]

One might reasonably ask why this simple way of resolving the mystery of what could induce agents to set the demands of morality above those of self-interest should not have occurred to Kant. The obvious answer, it seems to me, is that Kant is committed, like most moral theorists from the Enlightenment to the present day, to deriving the demands of morality not from relationships between persons but from a relationship between each individual person taken separately and some grandly universal abstract entity: "the community of all pure rational wills," "the community of all beings capable of experiencing pleasure and pain," "society," "the nation," and so on. In consequence, Kant in particular faces a contradiction at the heart of his own moral theory. On the one hand, that theory affirms that an act to be moral, rather than self-interested, must be *autonomous* in the sense of springing entirely from the unconstrained will of the agent. On the other hand, it sees the demands of morality as originating in a formal feature of "pure practical reason"—"the bare *principle of the universal validity of all its maxims as laws"*—that cannot conceivably "supply a motive and create an interest which could be called purely moral"! One or other of these two demands, it seems, must be dropped. Either one asserts the autonomy of moral action but denies the possibility of explaining its motivation—which is Kant's own choice—or one does what many non-Kantian moralists have done before and since—namely, one attempts to explain moral action as in some sense motivated by pleasure, thereby abandoning the Kantian claim of autonomy.

As we have just seen, there is a way out of, or around, this dilemma. Distinguishing, in the way we have suggested, between different senses of interest allows one to have this particular cake and eat it. It allows one, that is, to represent moral impulses as arising wholly from the rational will of the moral agent without that step compelling one to abandon the distinction between moral agency and the pursuit of pleasure. Moral action, in other words, becomes action designed not to *gratify* specific desires of the agent but merely to secure the ground conditions for the *possibility* of their gratification by avoiding injury to concrete, person-to-person relationships on whose health that possibility depends. But this way out comes at a price—namely, that of being prepared to locate the source of moral demands not in some abstractly specifiable relationship between the individual and *humanity* (or *sentient beings*) *in general* but rather in concrete relationships between one flesh-and-blood individual and another.

A main reason why Kant, like other Enlightenment moralists, failed to see this possibility is no doubt that, like them, he sees morality as something that serves the collective rather than the individual. All these writers, of course, admit the existence of warm personal affection between individuals. Yet either they regard it, like Hume, as having little to do with the morality of principle and law, or like Kant—as in his famous example of the butcher who gives fair weight not because of any abstract reasoning concerning the *universal validity of maxims as laws* but merely because he likes his customers and values his relationships with them—they regard it merely as one more instance of self-interested conduct.

This way of looking at things might perhaps be defensible if what I have called *person-to person relationships* were sufficiently secured, as we often imagine what we nowadays call personal relationships to be, solely by the existence of warm feelings of love and affection between the participants. Hume, for instance, often talks as if this were the case. Such views have doubtless been encouraged by the wide influence in Western culture of Christian

antinomianism: the notion that love alone is sufficient to prompt virtuous action without the intervention of mutually understood rules and conventions
requiring, among other things, the observance of types of self-restraint specific
to each given type of relationship.

Antinomianism of that type stands open, however, to obvious counterar-
guments. Social life is a web of person-to-person relationships of all kinds,
stretching far beyond those based on warm personal affection. Such relationships subsist, for example, between teachers and pupils, doctors and patients,
representatives and their constituents in a democracy, vendors and purchas-
ers, police and public, and so on. Entering into any such relationship involves
the risk of abuse by other participants. Such risks can only be avoided if each
such relationship proceeds on terms understood by all the participants, involving the acceptance and observance of certain specific types of restraint upon
self-interested action (in the sense of "self-interested" defined above), and if
participants can, in general, be trusted to abide by those rules and observe the
associated restraints upon action. This is why the notions of trust and trustworthiness are, as the philosopher Onora O'Neill has recently done us the service
of pointing out, as central to the morality we actually live by every day, as they
are absent from the abstract speculations composing, since approximately 1650,
both main Western traditions of moral philosophy.

It follows that from the standpoint of everyday morality, it is absurd to suppose, as philosophers down to the present day have been prone to do, that the
content of morals—the actual knowledge of which actions, in given contexts
of moral concern, are morally permissible, and which are not—could possibly
be excogitated, in accordance with the Cartesian ideal, through a process of
private reflection taking place within the mind of a single individual. Learning
the difference between right and wrong, from the standpoint of everyday morality, is a matter of learning, for each of a multitude of specific relationships, the
exact nature of the specific patterns of restraint and trustworthiness exacted
by that relationship as the price of entering into and engaging successfully in
it. Armchair reflection, *pace* Descartes and the entire subsequent tradition of
"moral philosophy," both Anglo-Saxon and continental, will not help us here.
A grasp of the distinction between right and wrong can be acquired only from
the experience of actually engaging in relationship with others, and from reflection not upon the "universalizing" abstractions of the philosophers but *upon
that experience.* And until that experience has been acquired and the necessary
reflection upon it performed, it may well be wise for the tyro in the moral life
simply to take the advice of those more experienced in these matters and better
able to judge. Descartes himself, to do him justice, explicitly says as much,[23]

however much his intellectual successors may have departed in spirit and in practice, from that wise advice.

THE JUDAIC CHARACTER OF OUR
ORDINARY MORAL THINKING

Judaism, while it has virtually nothing in common with the intellectualizing moral philosophy that has dominated European intellectual and political life for the past four centuries, has a great deal in common with the everyday moral thinking of most ordinary Europeans and Americans, Jewish and non-Jewish alike.

That such a community of thought and feeling exists is not hard to demonstrate. At the center of the moral universe of Judaism sits an idea of relationship. But the relationship in question is not that between the individual and some collective abstraction ("society," or "humanity," or "the state," or the abstract community of rational beings, or the total community of beings capable of experiencing pleasure and pain). Nor is it even the relationship between the individual and God. The relationship Judaism treats as *ultimately* morally significant, as we briefly noted in the last chapter, is that between one person *and another person*. For Judaism, even the relationship between the individual and God is secondary to relationship with the concrete, individual, flesh-and-blood Other, because rightly ordered relationship with the flesh-and-blood Other is one of the main things that *constitutes* relationship with God. It isn't the *only* thing, because Judaism (certainly in its Orthodox or Modern Orthodox versions) does not conceive of God as *constituted* by consensual human relationship but as an independent player in human affairs. But in most ordinary circumstances, it is a central element in the human relationship with Hashem. As David Patterson puts it, "The root of the Hebrew word for 'commandment,' *mitzvah*, is *tzavta*, which means 'connection.' A commandment, then, is not a rule, or a dictate that must be followed; rather, it is a means of connecting with God. As we have seen, the most fundamental means of connecting with God lies in our connection with other human beings."[24]

Patterson's point concerning the semantic relationship between *tzavta* ("connection") and mitzvah goes far, it seems to me, toward answering the commonplace charge that Jews conceive of morality as consisting in the mechanical and habitual observance of a collection of arbitrary commandments, supposedly imposed by a jealous God upon their forbears for reasons apparent only to Himself. On the contrary, if the point of performing a mitzvah is, by and large, to connect fruitfully with God by connecting fruitfully with

354

the concrete, individual Other, then we are, curiously enough, in the presence of a moral outlook not all that far removed from that of E. M. Forster, whose watchword, "only connect!" springs, in his case also, from a preference, at the heart of morality, for personal relationship over generalizing moral abstractions.

Both Lévinas and Rosenzweig also make connection with the concrete, individual Other central both to their moral and to their religious thought.

> Rosenzweig calls for a new method of thinking: In contrast to the abstraction and isolation of thought ruled by reason, Rosenzweig posits the concrete, time-bound interrelations of human beings in what he calls "new thinking" or "speaking thinking," which is essentially Jewish thinking. In accordance with Jewish teaching, like Maimonides, he sees the human being not so much as a thinking being as a speaking being. "The difference between the old and the new" thinking, as Rosenzweig describes it, "does not lie in the sound and silence, but in the need of the other and, what is the same thing, in taking time seriously."[25] Here we see what indeed makes Jewish thought Jewish: It is about a concrete relation here and now—not everywhere and at all times—with this flesh-and-blood human being who stands before me now, as that relation is manifest in the word. "Mankind is always absent," says Rosenzweig. "Present is a man, this fellow or that one," with whom we stand in a speaking relation, a giving relation, through which a Third who is beyond the categories of speculation is manifest in the word.[26]

Lévinas, similarly, "sees the ethics of Judaism as an ethics of heteronomy that is not a servitude, but the service of God through responsibility for the neighbour, in which I am irreplaceable."[27]

I would disagree with Lévinas only that an ethics so conceived is necessarily an "ethics of heteronomy." I have tried to show above, in effect, how a distinction between heteronomy and autonomy can quite easily be reconstructed, within the context of an ethics of person-to-person relationship, in terms of the notion of relational interests.

At this point, one can begin to understand why Judaism should have developed the concern, discussed in the last chapter, with redeeming this world rather than abandoning it for some higher realm, a concern that has repeatedly exposed it to the charge—variously developed by Christian, Hegelian, or Marxist critics—of materialism. Essentially, one must accept life in this world, because it only is in this world, for better or worse, that the encounter between self and Other central to Jewish ethics can occur. This is how Patterson puts the matter in discussing the Hebrew phrase *tikkun haolam* (literally "repair of the world"):

The centrality of *tikkun haolam* in Jewish thought underscores the concrete accent on this realm. From the standpoint of such thinking, we do not go to a better place when the soul leaves this world; *this* is a better place, precisely because only in this realm are we able to enter into a concrete, flesh-and-blood relationship with our fellow human being, hence the teaching concerning the resurrection of the body. Although they may have a similar teaching, Christianity and Islam labour more to get into God's kingdom than to get God into this kingdom, insisting, as Jesus does, that "my kingdom is not of this world" (John 18:36). . . . As soon as we disparage this world as unreal or vile . . . we devalue not only this world but those who would dwell in it, beginning with the stranger. The regard for one is tied to the regard for the other.

   Tikkun haolam is the opposite of the *contemptus mundi* found in Christianity and Islam. The Christian contempt for this world is not merely a contempt for worldliness, for power and pleasure, prestige and possessions; no, it is a contempt for this concrete, physical reality. "Only one who hates his life in this world shall keep it unto life eternal" (John 12:25). But if I hate my life in this world, I am apt to have little regard for the physical lives of others. . . . Although in the Hebrew bible one can find passages disparaging those who thrive only by the material goods of this world (for example Psalms 12:2), much more frequently we have the affirmation that "the earth is the Lord's, and the fullness thereof. . . . Indeed how can a world that God has created through his wisdom (see Jeremiah 10:12) be an object of contempt? But that is just what one finds in many of the Christian scriptures.[28]

In terms of the Jewish rejection of *contemptus mundi*, when that is taken as "contempt for this concrete physical reality," one can also begin to see more clearly what Rosenzweig, when he speaks of "taking time seriously," or Abigail Rosenthal when she speaks, as we found her doing in the last chapter, of the attempt to live well in "real time" or "passionate history," are getting at.

   What Rosenzweig fundamentally objected to in Hegelianism, both in its right-wing phase as nationalism and in its left-wing phase as Marxism, is that it offers the believer the apparent possibility of vaulting out of the time in which day simply succeeds day, each with its new array of problems and botched or semibotched relationships to be dealt with, into another kind of time altogether: a time divided not into the humdrum, meaningless progression of day into night and back again but into a vaster, intrinsically meaning-charged progression from stage to theoretically revealed stage of historical progress, culminating in the arrival of a new order in which the tedious problems of everyday life will all be magically solved.

   Christianity in its more theologically developed forms also offers the believer the sense that the ordering of time as it unfolds in day-to-day existence has been superseded by a higher ordering, from the fall of man into original sin, through suffering and Christian struggle in this world, to an eventual redemption offering the same promise of final release from the problems and struggles of everyday life.

Judaism "takes time seriously" in that it fundamentally rejects the idea that one can hope to live well by attempting to vault in this way out of the duties and challenges of everyday life: life lived sequentially in "real time," by contrast with the theoretically or theologically organized time of Hegelian *Geistesgeschichte*, or dialectical materialism, or the Christian historical drama of fall and redemption.

Judaism is content with the *open-endedness* of lived time in this world. By contrast, metaphysically or theologically organized conceptions of time are apt to be cyclical in character and necessarily so, since half the point of such theories is that they offer the believer *closure* in the sense of an end to human struggles and striving. They present history as a story with a beginning, middle, and end in which initial problems proceed by way of intermediate struggles to a satisfactory conclusion.

Judaism, by contrast, not only remains content with the open-ended projection into the future displayed both by life and by real time but also makes that openness, that absence of closure, a central pillar of its account of what the right living of life consists of, whether that account is summarized in Lévinas's sense of the absolute openness, the *unlimitedness*, of the demands made on the self by the gaze of the Other, or in Rabbi Tarfon's "It is not your responsibility to finish the work of perfecting the world, but you are not free to desist from it either" (*Avot* 2:21). One is not free to vault out of real time because it is only in real time that the real Other, as distinct from the imaginary Other (the worker, the bourgeois, the reprobate, the savage, the kaffir, the Jew) inhabiting the imaginary time of this or that tendentious political or theological narrative can be encountered.

In earlier chapters, I argued that political antisemitism is fundamentally a response to the rejection by an irreducible core of Jews, in any age, of vaunting political messianism of any kind. We are now getting perhaps a little closer to seeing why a rooted skepticism of this kind, reminiscent of a variety of secular Jewish or non-Jewish figures from E. M. Forster to Orwell to Popper, should lie so close to the heart of religious Judaism.

In the "Coherence of Our Ordinary Moral Thinking" section above, I argued that Kant's problem of what motivates people to do the right thing even when it conflicts with their private interests can be solved, without abandoning a Kant-style distinction between moral autonomy and heteronomy, provided one is careful to distinguish between different kinds of interest; and in particular between relational interests (interests in merely securing the continued health of relationships that contribute much in the way of meaning and value to one's life) and interests of other kinds.

To see the force of the latter distinction is, in part, a matter of noticing the extent to which even those relationships traditionally considered personal require of us not merely warm affection but also willingness to accept, and trustworthiness in observing, certain types of restraint on action specific to this or that type of relationship, even when those restraints conflict painfully with other, perhaps more immediate and more pressing, interests of ours. And I suggested that these features of relationship—which most of us would be prepared, even if at times ruefully, to admit as all too real—stand in sharp conflict with the idea, characteristic of "moral philosophy" since Descartes, that it must be possible, if morality is to be shown to have any sort of rational foundation, for each moral agent to enjoy the capacity to work out for himself or herself, by appeal to the resources of his own reason (and thus without reference to others, whether in the shape of tradition, or authority, or custom, or merely in that of sound advice) which things he or she ought morally to do and which avoid.

This philosophical picture (resembling in this respect, as Wittgenstein taught us, most philosophical pictures) seems to me entirely false to the way in which we actually set about determining the limits of right and wrong. We do so by gradually learning, from childhood onward, both through experience and through attending to and reflecting on good advice, what is actually required for the successful conduct of this or that type of relationship.

This conclusion has two consequences. The first is that it is neither irrational nor an abandonment of personal moral responsibility for an individual to pay attention to the results of collective and cooperative rational reflection on questions of morality. The second is that because some experience of life may be needed to teach one the reasons why it is wise to observe certain kinds of moral restraint, and since the observance of those kinds of restraint may be a necessary prerequisite for obtaining the relevant experience, it may at times be the part of wisdom to observe those restraints even without a clear sense of why they are to be recommended.

A further parallel between our ordinary moral outlook and that of Judaism is that most versions of the latter take for granted both these consequences of placing person-to-person relationship and its requirements at the center of the moral life. In developing the moral critique of Judaism along the lines pursued at the start of the present chapter, it is often cited as a particularly gross medieval absurdity of Jewish thinking that the people of Israel, at Exodus 19:8, accept obedience to the mitzvoth with the words *Na'aseh v'nishma*: "We will do, and we will hear/understand." The absurdity, to any mind formed in the Cartesian tradition of critical rationality, consists in the commitment to obey a command *before one fully understands its implications*. Is this not both an abandonment of any fully adult conception of individual moral responsibility and a craven sinking on one knee before a deity who expressly demands that very sacrifice as a condition of taking the people of Israel under his wing?

So it may appear from the standpoint of Enlightenment moral theory. But Enlightenment moral theory offers us, when it comes down to it, no more than an attempt—or rather a series of related attempts—to represent the moral life in a manner that conforms to the presuppositions of a certain philosophical outlook. No doubt that outlook is an important one—one that sits, as we earlier found Emil Fackenheim observing, at "the core of philosophical modernity." But for all that, it is in the end no more than an intellectual construct: a toy of the mind. From the standpoint of our actual experience of the way in which morality intervenes in our lives, things may look different. From that standpoint, what exactly is supposed to be wrong with accepting an invitation to live by certain rules, with the proviso that later one will wish not merely to act but to understand, to look more deeply into how they hang together and what sense they make: questions, after all, far more likely to be pursued successfully when people have had some experience of attempting to live by the rules in question? As Rabbi Jill Jacobs puts it, "While emphasising deed over study, the rabbis appear wary of promoting a religion by rote, in which people perform rituals without any understanding of the significance of these actions. In claiming that 'understanding things leads to action,' the rabbis can prioritise action without negating the meaning of one's actions. The insistence that 'na'aseh' precedes 'nishma' also allows for the creation of a coherent community unified by its practice, even while allowing for discussion about the details and significance of this practice."[29]

To supplement *na'aseh* (do) with *nishma* (hear, understand) is also, in effect, to reject the idea, characteristic of a certain kind of Christian antinomianism, that to be in a position to obey the command "Love thy neighbor as thyself," it is enough to be in a sufficiently elevated spiritual state (to be "in a state of grace," as it was put to me in my youth). In the Talmud (*Shabbat* 31a), the sage Hillel, mentioned earlier, is approached by a would-be convert, whose condition for converting is that Hillel teach him Torah in its entirety while he, the prospective convert, stands on one foot. Famously, Hillel answers, "What is hateful to you, do not do to your neighbor. That is the whole torah; the rest is explanation of this—now go and study it." The mere injunction, in other worlds, is not enough; what is also needed is explanation.

The extent of the explanation that has emerged over the centuries, including the *Mishnah*, both Talmuds, the *Zohar*, and a multitude of minor works down to and including such things as Martin Buber's collections of Hasidic stories, is now vast. While the average non-Jew is likely to gape at its extent, its existence does at least accord with the average non-Jew's commonsense belief that there is more to morality than warm feelings or elevated sentiments and that a little careful thought about the practical details of the thing can at least do no harm.

But matters are more complex, even than that. In Judaism, the relationship between thought and action is always reflexive: if action is merely mechanical without thought, then, equally, thought—study, explanation—is empty and fruitless without action, without actual moral experience. Elsewhere in the Talmud (*Avot* 1:2) stands the well-known saying of Simon the Just (*Shimeon ha-Tzaddik*), encountered earlier, that the world stands upon three things, upon Torah, upon the divine service, and upon acts of faithful love. Here is what Jonathan Wittenberg, the senior rabbi of Masorti Judaism in Britain and rabbi of the New North London Synagogue, has to say about the connection between Torah and acts of love:

[Judaism] educates us to respond to the whole world with the whole person. In order that we should be equipped to do this, it endeavours to foster in us certain sensibilities, notably greater awareness of the moral, and deeper consciousness of the spiritual aspects of life. This cannot be achieved by simply telling us that these dimensions exist; we have to be put in touch with the actual experience of such matters. What Judaism wants to teach us is therefore something which we have to be led to discover, an understanding of which we must arrive at, for ourselves. Hence the challenge Judaism faces is not merely that of informing its adherents of the truths in which it believes but, far more significantly, of guiding them to perceive these matters for themselves. This, from one point of view, is the purpose of what in Judaism has always been *the* path *par excellence*, the way of the commandments. Through the commandments, the mitzvot, the framework is created by which we make ourselves available to certain experiences that have the power to educate our spirits and refine the manner in which we live our lives. "To say that the Mitzvot have meaning is less accurate than saying that they lead to wells of emergent meaning, to experiences which are full of the hidden brilliance of the holy, suddenly blazing in our thoughts," writes A. J. Heschel. Thus we set aside the Shabbat, make it holy, protect it from invasion by the quotidian concerns of money, manufacture and chores. We enter its special world, within time but outside ordinary time, "partaking of the nature of the world to come," as our rabbis put it, not to act but to be acted upon. For the end to which we observe its special laws is certainly not so that we can show off our own scrupulousness. It is rather to follow in a sacred tradition which has taught, with an insight refined over millennia, how a day can best be protected and made special, so as to make ourselves accessible to the opportunities for spiritual growth which such sanctified time can offer. As for what we will actually learn or gain from the experience, that is, in the very nature of things, a matter we cannot know in advance.[30]

CONCLUSION

I have tried to show in this chapter that, and why, the commonplace moral critique of Judaism is without foundation. In sum, it represents the observant Jew as a slave to the mechanical observance of arbitrary rules, hence unable to think for himself or herself and hence incapable of rising to the challenges of an adult, fully autonomous conception of moral responsibility. Its primary origin is to be found in Kant and in the subsequent development of German phi-losophy, though similar kinds of charge can be found in the British empiricist tradition, particularly in connection with utilitarianism. Against such views I have argued, first of all, that the theories characteristic of academic, or as Kant would have said, "speculative" philosophy, proceed on a level rather remote, in a number of specific ways, from the common experience and thinking of ordi-nary people, Jewish and non-Jewish, concerning morality and the moral life. In particular, such theories represent moral demands as arising from a "vertical" relationship between each individual moral agent and some abstract totality: the community of all rational beings for Kantians; for utilitarians, the totality of all beings capable of experiencing pleasure and pain, and so on. In our ordinary moral thinking, I suggested, we see, on the contrary, moral demands as arising not from our relationship to any such abstract totality but rather from the terms of the *horizontal* propagation of the social bond through specific relationships between actual, concrete persons or groups of persons.

On the basis of these arguments, my next move was, in effect, to mount a two-pronged defense of Judaism against the critique summarized above. On the one hand, I argued that the moral outlook of Judaism, though very remote from and sharply at odds with the speculations of philosophical moralists, is rather close, both in its fundamental assumptions and in its way of develop-ing those assumptions, to the outlook of ordinary, unphilosophical men and women, Jewish or non-Jewish. On the other hand, I argued that the specific claims of the moral critique of Judaism can be very easily refuted. There is, for instance, no need for observant Jews to see the Kantian distinction between autonomy and heteronomy, crucial as that has been to the moral critique of

Judaism over the past three centuries, as posing any threat to their position, since a workable analog of that distinction can perfectly easily be reconstructed in terms of an ethic of person-to-person relationship, provided one is sufficiently careful to distinguish between different types and levels of self-interest. Again, the idea that Jews are committed by their religion to the rote, mechanical observance of rules, not only without question but without any attempt at rational debate, stands refuted not only, as we found Rabbi Jill Jacobs arguing above, by the pairing of *na'aseh* and *nishma* (acting and understanding) in the original reception of the mitzvoth but by the extent, the intellectual intensity, and the commitment from the earliest times to democratic principles of majority decision, exhibited by the debates among Jews to which the pursuit of *nishma* has led.

These arguments once again connect back, in yet another way, to one of the central claims of this book, advanced in chapters 4–5: that political antisemitism is to be understood as a response to the refusal of Jews to accept, as a body, the ideas of whatever revolutionary system of ideas happens to be sweeping the world at a given time and to dissolve themselves obediently into the ranks of its supporters. One of the advantages of this way of understanding antisemitism is that it allows one to make sense of the otherwise puzzling fact, that we have already examined in chapter 2 and to which we shall return in chapter 14, that antisemitism has exercised such power over the minds of intellectuals, from Voltaire and Clermont-Tonnerre, to Dr. Walter Schultz of the National Socialist Association of University Lecturers, down to the young gentlemen and ladies of the Oxford University Labour Club. The reason, if we have argued correctly, is, on the one hand, that political antisemitism is by its nature a response to the stoic resistance of an irreducible core of the Jewish community to the blandishments of revolutionary movements and nostrums of all kinds, and on the other hand, that intellectuals are characteristically the originators and self-elected guardians of such movements.

The German philosophical romanticism, within which the moral critique of Judaism examined in this chapter was mainly developed, was just such a movement. It is tempting to see, in the antisemitism of all its main protagonists, from Kant to Marx, a characteristic expression of the baffled fury occasioned in these profoundly engaged intellectuals by what they felt as the brute hostility not just of this or that aspect of Judaism but of the entire Jewish outlook on life to ideas which they themselves—however strange that may seem to us now that those ideas have dried and shriveled under the stress of time and terrible events into little more than toys of academic debate—credited with the power to bring about a fundamental transformation of humanity into something godlike.

Leaving that aside, the present chapter has also uncovered another cultural continuity requiring explanation. If I am right, there is much conformity between the moral outlook of Judaism and that of most ordinary non-Jewish men and women in Europe and America. How, given the small numbers and the ghettoization, not to mention the often fearful self-isolation of most historic Jewish communities in the diaspora, could such a conformity possibly have come about?

The answer, of course, lies with Christianity and returns us to the discussions of chapter 11 and in particular to the work of Professor William Nicholls. In Nicholls's view, Christianity, in the light of recent scholarship,

> now appears to the critically alerted eye as an amalgam and not a pure substance. Its Jewish origins have been adulterated at an early stage with much that is not only non-Jewish but inherently antithetical to the Jewish spirit so purely embodied in Jesus himself. Is it possible that Christian humanism, the passion for truth, justice, and human brotherhood in which Christians rightly rejoice, and its compassion for sinners, belong to the Jewish element transmitted through Jesus himself, whereas the power-seeking, the cruelty, the support of and connivance at injustice and oppression, and above all the antisemitic and racial hatred that can, even today, successfully invoke the Christian name, represent pagan pollution of that original pure stream?[31]

I share Nicholls's sense of the Jewish/pagan duality within Christianity. But, of course, his conclusion cuts both ways. It is commonplace to speak of the nations of Europe, and particularly Britain, as to a great extent "post-Christian." And no doubt the past century has seen both immense falls in church attendance and a general waning of the influence of many aspects of Christianity in people's lives. Yet when pollsters ask people to name their religious affiliation, if any, a surprisingly large number still answer "Christian." My sense is that when one probes a little deeper, what one finds is that the ideas such people continue to entertain of Christianity, while making very little reference to those elements that most sharply distinguish the religion as unique, identify it very strongly with precisely those that link it most strongly to Judaism and most notably with the commandment to treat others—in the shape of the concrete, individual Other celebrated by Jewish moralists from Hillel or Shimon Ha-Tzaddik to Rosenzweig or Lévinas—with love and justice. Paradoxically, that is to say, Christian persecution of Judaism over the past two millennia has been accompanied by the equally vigorous implantation in the hearts and minds of Christians of some of the most central and essential features of a Jewish outlook on life. As the unique theology and the associated world picture of Christianity fade gradually from the public mind, that, it seems, is what remains.

NOTES

1. Italics mine.
2. For Kant's treatment of this example, see Paton 1948, 89–90. For a fuller version of the present interpretation of Kant, see Bernard Harrison, "Kant and the Sincere Fanatic," in Brown 1979, 226–61.
3. Fackenheim 1996, 46.
4. Rose 1990, 96–97
5. Plamenatz 1963, 2:218–19.
6. Mack 2014, 51. The Hegel citation is from *Grundlinien der Philosophie des Rechts*, 491.
7. Rose 1990, 44–45.
8. Popper 1945, 2:29.
9. Patterson 2012, 50.
10. Nirenberg 2013, 463.
11. Eliot 1895, 621.
12. Singer and Sacks 2007, 75.
13. Rosenzweig 2000, 17.
14. Williams 1985, 152.
15. J. J. C. Smart, "An Outline of a System of Utilitarian Ethics," in Smart and Williams, 1973, 5–6.
16. Kovesi 1967, 57–58.
17. Onora O'Neill, Baroness O'Neill of Bengarve, see, in particular, her *Autonomy and Trust in Bioethics, the 2001 Gifford Lectures* (Cambridge: Cambridge University Press, 2001); *A Question of Trust: The BBC Reith Lectures* (Cambridge: Cambridge University Press, 2002); and *Justice, Trust and Accountability* (Cambridge: Cambridge University Press, 2005).
18. Forster 1951, 68.
19. Paton 1948, 129.
20. Henry Fielding, *Tom Jones*, bk. 15, ch. 1.
21. On the literary sources for the ideas that follow here, see, for instance, Harrison 1975, especially ch. 7, and "Sterne and Sentimentalism," in Harrison 2015, 368–413.
22. Earlier and fuller versions of the arguments concerning interest and morality offered here can be found in Bernard Harrison, "Moral Judgment, Action and Emotion," *Philosophy* 59, no. 229 (July 1984): 295–321; "Morality and Interest," *Philosophy* 64, no. 249 (July 1989): 303–22; "Moral Theory and the Concept of Trust," *The Philosopher* (June 2011).

23. See, for example, the opening paragraphs of part 3 of the *Discours de la méthode* (1637): Anscombe, Geach, and Koyré 1968, 24–25.

24. Patterson 2012, 79.

25. Compare Abigail Rosenthal's remarks on time in the last chapter.

26. Patterson 2012, 25–26.

27. Patterson 2012, 26.

28. Patterson 2012, 82–83.

29. Rabbi Jill Jacobs, executive director of Rabbis for Human Rights–North America, writing on the website www.myjewishlearning.com.

30. Wittenberg 1996, 39–40.

31. Nicholls 1993, 432.

THIRTEEN

—⟋⟍—

WHAT'S WRONG WITH UNIVERSALISM?

If I am not for myself, then who will be for me? But if I am only for myself,
then what am I?

—Hillel the Elder, c.110 BCE–10 CE (*Pirkhe Avot*, 1:14)

ACCUSATIONS AND ASSUMPTIONS

I come now to the third and last of what one might call the three great canards
concerning Judaism. It is not uncommon for people to say, in most cases evok-
ing the wise nods that acknowledge statements of the obvious, that Judaism is
peculiarly and narrowly *particularist* in character and hence altogether lacks
the generous *universalism* to be found in Christianity or for that matter in the
leading ideas of the Enlightenment.

Such remarks carry with them the unspoken assumption that to be generously universalist is an unqualified good, while to be narrowly particularist is
an equally unqualified evil. But is there truth in any of these claims? And if so,
how much? These are the questions that will occupy us in this chapter.

While any of the great canards may find its way as a tool of defamation into
antisemitic discourse of any type, irrespective of whether it be religious or political in character and whether it comes from the right, the left, or the liberal
center, each has its own originating constituency. The charge of "materialism"
or "carnality"—of inability to move beyond the concerns of life in this world—
is Christian in origin. The charge of heteronomy finds its origin in German
idealist moral philosophy. The charge of Jewish "particularism" arises from the

365

tradition of humanitarianism, of internationalist moral concern for humankind in general, that begins with the French Revolution and subsequently becomes part of the ideology of most branches of the left.

The treatment of the terms *universalism* and *particularism* by the *Oxford English Dictionary* (OED) displays most of the implications and connotations that they and their main cognates have acquired since 1789. For *particularism*, the OED offers the following: "**Particularism:** Exclusive attachment to one particular party, sect, nation, &c.; exclusiveness."

For *universalism*, the most relevant passages of the lengthy entry for the term are perhaps the following two definitions: "**Ethical universalism:** Insistence on the treatment of all men by the same generalised, impersonal standard; **Universalist:** One who believes in the brotherhood of man in a manner not subject to national allegiances."

Among its samples of exemplary usage, the entry also offers the following, which neatly allies it with "humanitarianism," while contrasting it with "particularism": "The humanitarian theme of the preceding centuries certainly continued, but universalism yielded step by step to national particularism."

Putting together these dictionary definitions and explications, one can see clearly enough what critics of Jewish particularism have in mind. Judaism, as such critics see things, encourages Jews to develop an attachment to their own "party, sect, nation" so all-consuming as to exclude any interest in the sufferings and fate of the rest of humanity. Hence, Jews, the complainant continues, tend to concern themselves not with the establishing of common standards of just treatment for all humankind but merely with the formulation of rules, often merely formal or arbitrary ones, concerning the treatment of Jews by other Jews or with parochial struggles to secure Jews against ill-treatment by their non-Jewish neighbors.

Polemic from voices on the radical left against Jewish particularism, so conceived, dates at least from Voltaire and Clermont-Tonnerre. For both, the price of full French citizenship is that each Jew must give up everything that belongs to his Jewishness. Jews, Clermont-Tonnerre demands, "should not be allowed to form in the state either a political body or an order. *They must be citizens individually*" (my italics). As he famously put it, commencing his summing up of his speech to the National Assembly of December 23, 1789, "We must refuse everything to the Jews as a nation and accord everything to Jews as individuals."

The 1790s might be considered too remote an era to mine for evidences of antisemitism likely to have any bearing on the present day. Yet we find exactly the same attitudes, surviving unchanged the passage of almost two centuries, expressed by the British historian Hugh Trevor-Roper, in controversy with his Princeton homologue Arthur Hertzberg over the latter's book *The French Enlightenment and the Jews*. Here is Hertzberg's summary of their differences:

What I find most surprising, in purely historical terms, in Mr Trevor-Roper's review is his shrugging off my assertion that Voltaire was the major source in his own time and during the Revolution of both the rhetoric and the authority in the name of which left-wing, secular Jew-haters spoke. In his review Mr Trevor-Roper concluded his essay by praising me for writing a book which is "full of interesting information about the debate concerning the Jews." . . . Yet two paragraphs earlier, in order to deny my charge that the doctrinaire side of the Enlightenment is a major seed-bed of modern secular anti-Semitism, Mr Trevor-Roper brushed this aside by saying that I make too much of the occasional uses, as he would have it there, of Voltaire's nastier quips by some anti-Jewish writers.

Mr Trevor-Roper certainly does not need to be told that the heirs of Rome, Sparta, and even Athens, and of the Gallic and Teutonic tribes, did not have [as Voltaire alleges] to go to Jerusalem to learn bloodthirstiness. He must at some time have read that we are enjoined in the Bible to love our neighbour, to respect the rights of the stranger, and to do justice and to love mercy. Does Mr Trevor-Roper really believe that whatever faith there is in these values in the Western tradition owes nothing to the Bible? Voltaire was indeed sure that the mediaeval and contemporary Jews were a spiritual desert, but one is most surprised to find that Mr Trevor-Roper is no more in doubt. There is no point in my invoking here a list of "Jewish contributions to civilization," from the Talmud through Maimonides to Israel Baal Shem Tov, for the issue between us is not the evidence, but the deeper categories of moral judgment.

On all these issues of historical evidence and interpretation—and more could be mentioned—differences between the reviewer and myself are still within the bounds of normal argument. My problem with Mr Trevor-Roper, and his with me, is more fundamental. He has found my reading of the evidence unconvincing because he asserts "that there is an objective basis for anti-Semitism in the continuing Jewish life." Mr Trevor-Roper agrees with Voltaire that the Jews were inferior to the Greeks, that the major source of bloodthirstiness in Christianity is the Bible; that Judaism is an inferior spiritual tradition, and that "tolerant cosmopolitans through the ages" have rightly been angered by "their [the Jews'] intolerant defense of their own singularity." This, as Mr Trevor-Roper will have it, is "fair comment on matter of fact." He suggests that I refuse to consider these "truths" and I am, therefore, driven to looking for the sources of modern anti-Semitism "not in objective Jewish fact but in subjective Gentile illusion."[1]

Trevor-Roper here confirms, conveniently for me, one of the major theses that I have been laboring to establish in this book, that the main source of political antisemitism is indeed the Jews' resolute, and as I see it entirely reasonable, "defense of their own singularity."

Hertzberg's 1968 response to all this is well worth reading, not least because it also is entirely in accord with everything I have been attempting to establish in the present work and is so in ways that make it an excellent introduction to the arguments I shall pursue in the remainder of the present chapter.

> Mr Trevor-Roper has erred in assuming that I disagree with him on one fundamental point. Yes, he is right, and so was Voltaire before him, that *anti-Semitism is generated among Western Gentiles, be they pagans, Christians or secularists, by the fact that Jews continue to exist, in all their permutations, as a recognisably separate entity* [my italics]. The trouble is in what Mr Trevor-Roper has made of this observation. Styling himself as a "tolerant cosmopolitan," he has no more doubt than Voltaire before him that this Jewish singularity ought to cease existing, for assimilation into the modes of Western secular culture is the necessary entrance fee the Jews must pay for personal equality. This is a secular version of mediaeval enforced apostasy. Such a proposition is culturally and morally outrageous.

What Hertzberg omits to mention, at least explicitly, is the bare-faced impudence with which Trevor-Roper reserves the epithet "tolerant" for an alleged "cosmopolitanism" so "angered" by the very existence of the Jewish community and its continued religious life as to demand its immediate dissolution, while describing as "intolerant" the not unreasonable preference of Jews for the preservation of their own culture and outlook. Such insolent upending of the normal meanings of words is characteristic of George Orwell's Newspeak in his novel *1984*. Orwell intended Newspeak, of course, as a satire on the language of fascism. Are we to say that Trevor-Roper's adoption of what are effectively the methods of Newspeak, in his bizarre disposal of the epithets "tolerant" and "intolerant," betrays a similar orientation?

A clue, perhaps, lies in the play Trevor-Roper makes with the word *cosmopolitan*. That Jews are "rootless cosmopolitans" was a standard accusation of Nazi antisemitic propaganda. Trevor-Roper attempts, in effect, to stand this claim also on its head, by offering himself, presented as an heir to the glories of Western civilization, as the true cosmopolitan, and the Jews as crabbed outsiders who carry on their "singular" affairs in the shadows of this great tradition while, in effect, contributing nothing of value to it. But this in turn offends against the ordinary meaning of the term *cosmopolitan*. The true cosmopolitan, as we normally understand the term, is one who, having traveled widely, has seen enough of the varieties of human experience to recognize as valid and acceptable ways of conducting and understanding human life very different from those accepted in whatever narrow national or provincial milieu he or she happens to have been born and brought up in. The position outlined in the above controversy by Trevor-Roper is in no way cosmopolitan in that sense. It is one based on the rejection of any reading of the content of the Western tradition contrary to his own and on resentment of the very existence of any way of life that calls that reading into question. In much the same way, the Nazis rejected cosmopolitanism (in the ordinary sense of the term) in favor of imposing universal adherence to "Aryan" culture and Aryan ways and demanded the liquidation of any culture—not only that of the Jews but also those of gypsies, homosexuals, and others—that failed to fit that pattern. We know from the above what Trevor-Roper made of the Jews: one wonders what he made of the gypsies, say, or the Irish?

We are dealing here, in short, with a further manifestation of the demand for what in chapter 5 I called *project-driven homogeneity*: the demand that everyone fall into line behind some project, some unifying intellectual vision of what society is, or could be, or ought to be, whether that happens to be the Nazi project of restoring alleged Aryan values and supremacy in Germany and Europe or merely the Enlightenment vision of what European civilization has been, and might become, that Trevor-Roper shares with Voltaire. Someone like Trevor-Roper, who by his own admission believed in such a project with sufficient force to feel "rightly angered" by the mere existence of an organized group of people who view things differently and wish to defend their own "singularity," is to my mind quite as "particularist" as the Jews have been alleged to be but with this one significant difference: that Jewish particularism such as it is has never issued, and does not now issue, in a desire to ram the favored way of looking at things down dissenters' throats by force.

I introduced the Trevor-Roper–Hertzberg controversy by way of beginning the process of bringing the charge of Jewish particularism down to the present. That charge is, as I noted earlier, peculiarly associated with the growth of radically internationalist forms of humanitarianism on the left or radical wing of politics since 1797. Karl Marx's critique of Judaism marks an influential stage along that path. Although Marx's family was of Jewish origin, his father, Heinrich, a lawyer, converted to Lutheranism to advance his career. It is hard to say whether the young Marx's views on Jewish matters, common enough in the Germany of his day, were in part directed by a felt need to further dissociate the family from its origins. Those views are to be found most fully expressed in

his essay *On the Jewish Question* [*Zur Judenfrage*] (1843). The following passage
from that essay gives concise expression to precisely the accusation, of Jewish
particularism, and consequent lack of universal sympathies with humankind
in general, that we are examining in this chapter: "He [the Jew] considers it his
right to separate himself from the rest of humanity; as a matter of principle he
takes no part in the historical movement and looks to a future which has nothing in common with the future of mankind as a whole. He regards himself as
a member of the Jewish people, and the Jewish people as the chosen people."[2]
    It is worth noting that Marx's main charge against the Jews, that they imag-
ine themselves to have the right to *separate themselves from the rest of humanity,*
only makes sense if there is such an entity as "mankind as a whole," whose history it is intelligible both to record and to predict. If there is no such thing as
"mankind as a whole" but only the innumerable tribes, nations, religions, and
sects into which humanity is to all appearances divided, from the Germans or
the French to the Dani of the Baliem Valley in New Guinea or the reindeer-
herding Sami of Lapland, then, evidently, particularism becomes not some
strange obsession peculiar to the Jews but a universal conviction common to all
humankind. Common observation teaches us, after all, that everyone regards
himself or herself not as a member of mankind as a whole but as a member of
some specific nation or tribe—a Swede, a Frenchwoman, a Dani, a Hindu, and
so on—and so far as he or she looks to the future, "looks to a future which has
nothing in common with the future of mankind as a whole."
    To point this out, of course, is merely to point out the extraordinary cultural
provinciality of the concept *mankind as a whole.* It is not to be confused with
the essentially biological concept *humanity.* That concept embraces every member of the species *Homo sapiens.* And, of course, it is *biologically* impossible for
any human being to "separate himself from the rest of humanity," *if one takes
"humanity" in the biological sense.* It goes without saying, however, that that is
not the kind of "separation" that Marx takes "the Jew" to be effecting between
himself and "the rest of humanity." For Marx, the separateness of the Jew from
the rest of humanity is not a biological but rather a *cultural* separation.
    But are humanity (excluding the Jews) or the rest of humanity the sort of
entities to which a distinct culture can be intelligibly attributed? No doubt
the members of any collection of human beings must be admitted to possess a common culture if they possess a common history. And the claim that
humanity at large possesses a common history plays an essential part both
in the philosophy of Hegel and in the system of revolutionary political ideas
that Marx was at that point beginning to build on the disparate foundations
provided by Hegel and the classical economists. It is essential to Marxism

WHAT'S WRONG WITH UNIVERSALISM?

that the categories and stages of economic history can be presumed to apply indifferently to all Europeans without regard to national boundaries or differences and by extension to all humankind. In Marxist theory, in effect, history and economics transcend everything that we ordinarily consider to constitute cultural differences for the simple reason that according to Marxist theory, history and economics are real, while cultural differences are illusory. What are real are the economically founded distinctions of class that divide capitalists from proletarians. What are illusory are the differences of national culture that divide proletarian from proletarian and prevent workers of different nations from recognizing the essential community of their interests as proletarians. Marxism, in short, *supplies all humanity with a common culture*—once proletarians of all nations can be brought to recognize the essential correctness of Marx's analyses and thus the essential applicability to their common situation of its defining categories.

For the Marxist, then, there is both a history and a culture of mankind as a whole—namely, the "objective" history and culture defined in terms of Marxist theory and its conceptual categories. Thus, when Marx speaks of "the future of mankind as a whole" from which the Jews have—scandalously, as he sees it—claimed the right to exclude themselves, what he has in mind is *the future projected by Marxist theory*.

But if *this* is what is meant by "the future of mankind as a whole," the future from which "[the Jew] considers it his right to separate himself," then Marx's objection to Jewish particularism is merely that Jews, as a breed, fail to be impressed by the philosophical project—of *Geistesgeschichte*—which Marx shares with Hegel. And this interpretation is confirmed by the reformulation of the complaint which follows immediately: "he [the Jew] takes no part in the historical movement"—that "movement" being, precisely, the project of philosophically reformulating the history of humankind (in strikingly Eurocentric terms) which Marx at this point takes himself to share with Hegel.

That, of course, is not at all what the phrase "separating himself from the rest of humanity" would ordinarily be taken to mean in English (or in its German equivalent). One would ordinarily take someone who accused the Jews of "separating themselves from the rest of humanity" to be accusing them of lacking concern for the sufferings or fate of anybody non-Jewish. Whether *that* accusation has weight is something we shall consider later. It is certainly an accusation Marx is prepared to make and makes at length elsewhere. But at this point in *Zur Judenfrage*, the accusation his words actually articulate is a weaker one: that Jews are difficult to mobilize in support of certain principles that Marx himself, like many other young Germans of the period, happens to consider to be on the side of progress. Anyone skeptical of the intellectual, moral, and political credentials of Marxism, and for that matter Hegelianism, might find in *that* accusation less an attack on Judaism than a compliment to its general sagacity.

Before leaving Marx's diatribe, we also need to ask ourselves at this point what it is exactly in Marx's mind that excludes Jews from participation in "the future of mankind as a whole" as he conceives it. Given the abject poverty in which the bulk of Jewish inhabitants of the Pale of Settlement existed in 1843, Marx can hardly have supposed that there were no Jewish proletarians. Why, then, should membership of the Jewish people present more of a bar than membership of any other people to the recognition of the essential community of proletarian interests?

The answer is, I suggest, that Marx's ultimate target in this essay, despite its title, is not the Jews taken in themselves but rather the Jews *taken as an emblem and instance of the nature and workings of civil society*—the kind of society, variously announced by the 1793 Declaration of the Rights of Man and the American Declaration of Independence, that guarantees freedom to the individual, within a framework of law, to pursue his or her private goals in life. Marx's dismissal of this vision of life is caustic: "In civil society [man] acts simply as a private individual, treats other men as means, degrades himself to the level of a mere means, and becomes the plaything of alien powers. . . . None of the supposed rights of man, therefore, go beyond the egoistic man, man as he is, as a member of civil society; that is, an individual separated from the community, withdrawn into himself, wholly preoccupied with his private interest and acting in accordance with his private caprice."

The case against the Jews that Marx advances in *Zur Judenfrage* is in fact merely an extension of his case against civil society. In essence, it is that both the Jewish outlook on life and the religious Judaism from which that outlook ultimately derives its power enshrine the very convictions central to the revolutionary French and American ideal of civil society: that the proper business of the individual, once he or she has fulfilled the duties prescribed by religion, is simply the conduct of his or her own private or family life. "What is the profane basis of Judaism? *Practical* need, *self-interest*. What is the worldly cult of the Jews? *Huckstering.* What is his worldly god? *Money*."

This joint attack, on civil society and on Judaism, manifestly draws on the ideas originating with Kant and characteristic of later German idealism that we examined in the last chapter. Civil society, with its emphasis on individual liberty and self-interest, forces people, in defiance of the demands of Kant's moral philosophy, to "treat other men as means" rather than, in Kantian terms, as "ends in themselves" and prevents them from rising above their own petty concerns to make their private good subordinate to that of humankind—or in Hegelian terms, of the state—at large.

It appears, then, that the ultimate problem presented, for Marx, by Jewish national identity is that Jewish national identity *consists* not of some collection of peculiarities of national character and history that can, so far as Marx is concerned, be cast aside as trivial or "illusory" but in fidelity to an organized outlook and system of thought intrinsically contrary, for reasons we have ex- amined in the last two chapters, not only to Marx's ideas but to those of the entire German Enlightenment. This is what distinguishes Jewish identity, for him, from all the other national identities whose illusory cultural shibboleths are to be transcended by the international proletarian revolution.

With other nationalities—English, French, German, say—there is no unique system of ideas and observances that defines what it is to be English, French, or German and whose observance tends to turn people into recogniz- ably English, French, or German specimens of the human race.

With Jewish nationality, there is. And the system of ideas and observances in question happens—for reasons we have already partly encountered and shall develop in more detail and from a new direction in this chapter—to be intrinsically hostile to vast political programs for the wholesale transforma- tion of human affairs, Marx's included. Judaism *is*, as Marx dimly but correctly perceives, somehow hand in glove with the French or American ideals of civil society—with "capitalism," in Marxist terms—that he detests.

But that is not because all Jews are really capitalists (tell that to a poor Jewish peasant in the Pale), or because money is actually the god of the Jews (tell that to all the Jews I have known with a hopeless head for business). It is because, like the philosophies that—mainly under the influence of John Locke—gave rise to the ideas and ideals of civil society, Judaism enshrines a horizontal rather than a vertical conception of how moral demands arise: not, that is, through a relationship between individual men and women and some speculative human totality born of abstract theory but through the vast and diverse network of concrete relationships that actually connect individuals into families or groups. But of course if *that* is what Jewish particularism is supposed to consist of, then, as I argued in the last chapter, it is a particularism that connects Jews with, rather than divides them from, the non-Jewish remainder of the human race—theorists and political nostrum peddlers aside.

NATIONHOOD AND THE JEWS

Since the arrival on the scene of a Jewish national state, accusations of par- ticularism, though that term is still used, have tended to focus on the allegedly exceptional and obsessive *nationalism* of majority Jewish support for Israel. At the same time, with a splendid disregard for consistency, the very people who most affect to find the supposedly unique nationalism of the Jews offensive are also ready to accuse it of being *fraudulent and illegitimate* by contrast with *other, putatively more legitimate kinds of nationalism*: those exhibited by the French or the Germans, for instance. In both respects, since the turn of the twenty-first century and a little earlier, Israel and the Jews have begun to fall particularly foul of both left-wing and liberal/centrist opinion in Europe.

That has had a great deal to do with the rise of the European Union (EU) and that in turn with the fear and dislike of nationalism created in influential sections of the European elites by the two world wars of the twentieth century. That fear has largely eroded—at least among European opinion formers in politics, the universities, and the media—the climate of moral approval dominant in the West at the end of World War I for the cause of national autonomy and independence.

The failure of the governing institutions of the EU to support the recent vote of a majority of Catalans for the independence of Catalonia from Spain, and for that matter to support demands for Kurdish or Tibetan independence, has made it clear that the EU is now an imperial entity with little patience with demands for national independence, either within its own frontiers or within those of other imperial blocs with which it has economic and diplomatic dealings. It has been normal for many years to meet well-meaning middle-class supporters of the EU who regard the foundation of Israel as a late and disreputable manifestation of the same kind of nationalism as that which, in their view, led to so much bloodshed in Europe. Many such people hold that it would be better if Israel had never come into existence, and some hold also that the collapse of Israel, if it were to occur, would be in some sense a good thing, not least because it would involve giving the land back to the Arabs.

I tried in chapters 6–10 to indicate some of the difficulties, practical, moral, and intellectual, attending this collection of political sentiments, and I shall not return to those issues here. But there are still one or two things to be said. The first is that it is hardly defensible to accuse Israel, or the bulk of Jews, of nationalism *as if either were somehow exceptional in this respect*, when nationalism of all kinds has never ceased to appeal to the bulk of citizens in Europe outside the opinion-forming elites, and is in any case on the rise again in Europe, and not merely in suppressed national minorities such as the Catalans or the Corsicans (or the Basques, or the Bretons, or the Scots, or the Welsh) but in major components of the union. Britain, after all, has voted decisively to leave the union, and the new president of France, Emmanuel Macron, has conceded that if they were offered a referendum, the French would probably do the same. If *nationalism* is what Jewish particularism is fundamentally supposed to amount to, then the Jews, in opting for particularism, are merely following the crowd to the ballpark.

A further difficulty with this version of the particularism canard is, of course, that most of those concerned to attack the Jews of Palestine for defending their lives and property by establishing a national state are also stout supporters of the establishment, if necessary by force, of a national state for Palestinian Arabs.

Something must clearly be done to somehow neutralize these unhappy facts. What is in fact done on the left, as noted above, is to argue that *Jewish* nationalism, in contrast to that of other, non-Jewish peoples, has something fishy about it—something so fishy, in fact, as to cancel any right the Jews might be thought to possess to a national state of their own.

It would naturally be ideal, from this standpoint, if Jewishness itself, the idea that there is such a thing as Jewish national identity, analogous to British, French, or American national identity, could somehow be shown to be illusory, a mere appearance with no reality whatsoever behind it. Just such a line of argument originates, as so often, with Marx, again in *Zur Judenfrage*: "The Jew . . . can only adopt a Jewish attitude, i.e., that of a foreigner, towards the state, since he opposes his illusory nationality to actual nationality, his illusory law to actual law."[3]

Marx held the Jewish nationality to be "illusory" because, on his account, Judaism and the egoistic commercial cupidity that, for him, functions as the presiding spirit of civil society and its economic counterpart, capitalism, are one and the same thing: "The *chimerical* nationality of the Jew is the nationality of the merchant, of the man of money in general."

Both Judaism and Jewish identity are on this account merely expressions of the corrupt and corrupting nature of capitalism. "It is from its own entrails that civil society ceaselessly engenders the Jew." But for that very reason, as Marx sees things, antisemitism cannot survive the collapse of capitalism, for with that collapse Jews themselves, and Judaism, as a mere fetid outgassing of the spirit of capitalism and civil society, will cease to exist. "Once society has succeeded in abolishing the *empirical* essence of Judaism—huckstering and its preconditions—the Jew will have become *impossible*, because his consciousness no longer has an object, because the subjective basis of Judaism, practical need, has been humanized, and because the conflict between man's individual-sensuous existence and his species-existence has been abolished. The *social* emancipation of the Jew is the *emancipation of society from Judaism.*"

The essence of the "Jewish question" for Marx is, as we saw above, that "[the Jew] considers it his right to separate himself from the rest of humanity; as a matter of principle he takes no part in the historical movement and looks to a future which has nothing in common with the future of mankind as a whole." Marx's extraordinary "solution" to that "problem" is that it doesn't matter, *because, in effect, there are no Jews.* That is to say, the Jews have no ideas, no project, of their own. Jewish life and society are merely outgrowths of the worst aspects of *non*-Jewish life and society and will therefore not only vanish but also stand revealed as having been illusory in the first place, when those aspects of non-Jewish life and society are removed in the course of the revolutionary transformation of both.

In chapter 3, I suggested that the project of eliminating Jewish influence on non-Jewish affairs invariably appears as a leading element of political antisemitism. This is because the main claim of the political antisemite is that whatever offends him in the present conduct of non-Jewish life or society is not intrinsic to non-Jewish affairs but results entirely from the influence of the Jews, with the consequence that things must inevitably return to whatever the antisemite thinks of as normal once the Jews have been got rid of. Marx's argument beautifully illustrates this immemorial play of longing and delusion. What Marx conceives of as repellent in *non*-Jewish affairs—civil society and the small-minded, egoistic pursuit of individual advantage it encourages, is first reconceived as intrinsically *Jewish* in character. Next, Jewishness itself is reconceived as essentially *non*-Jewish in character so that finally, with a flourish worthy of a stage magician, *the emancipation of society from Judaism* can be represented as constituting nothing less than "the *social* emancipation of the Jew." The concrete, the actual Jews of Marx's day, with a culture and life of their own, have been made by Hegelian rhetorical magic to vanish in a puff of smoke, in a chilling metaphorical rehearsal of the actual fate that overtook their descendants a century later.

Almost exactly a century after the publication of *Zur Judenfrage*, the same bizarre logic of *ideal* or *virtual* elimination governs Sartre's treatment of antisemitism in *Réflexions sur la question Juive* (1944), published in English under the title *Antisemite and Jew.* Famously, Sartre held that "it is the antisemite who creates the Jew." On one level, this looks like a positive assertion of the common humanity of Jew and non-Jew, physical differences apart ("the sole ethnic characteristics of the Jew are physical").[4] But by denying in this way the Otherness of the Jews, it denies also their integrity as a people possessing a culture and a history of their own. Sartre sees antisemitism as a revolt against the division of society into economic classes—a revolt that becomes antisemitic only when it takes the Jews as a mythic representation of all that is evil about those divisions. "This means that antisemitism is a mythical, bourgeois representation of the class struggle, and that it could not exist in a classless society. . . . In a society whose members feel mutual bonds of solidarity, because they are all engaged in the same enterprise, there would be no place for it. . . . What is there to say except that the socialist revolution is necessary to and sufficient for the suppression of antisemitism."[5]

Sartre follows Marx, in short, in denying that there is any such thing as a coherent Jewish national identity. The idea that there is any such thing, according to him, is an illusion arrived at by misconstruing the nature of certain conflicts within *non-Jewish* society. When those conflicts evaporate with the arrival of the socialist revolution, so will antisemitism; *and so will the Jews themselves*, since their apparent existence as a presence, a collective Other separate from the non-Jewish world, was always an illusion. Convenient as this story is for the radical left, it sheds very little light on the curious fact that twenty-first-century antisemitism is in large part a phenomenon of those sectors of the left that still believe in the socialist revolution.

Twenty-first-century attempts to demonstrate the fishiness of Jewish national aspirations usually stop short of dismissing the very existence of Jews as illusory. They grant that Jews possess a common culture and history whose distinctness derives from specific features of Judaism, and rest their case on the denial that the culture and history in question, while sufficient to constitute the glue of a religious community, are insufficient to constitute the glue of a *nation*. Nations, they then argue, have a right—in principle at least—to political autonomy; religious communities do not.

I shall consider two such attempts, one due to the late distinguished European historian Tony Judt, the other to the Israeli historian Shlomo Sand. In a much-cited 2003 article in the *New York Review of Books*, the former suggested that Israel "is an oddity among modern nations not—as its more paranoid supporters assert—because it is a *Jewish* state and no one wants the Jews to have a state; but because it is a Jewish *state* in which one community—Jews—is set above others, in an age when that sort of state has no place."[6]

It has become perfectly clear since 2003 that a great many people—the bulk of the Boycott, Divestment and Sanctions (BDS) movement, for a start—object strongly to the Jews having a state *because they are Jews* and allegedly guilty of evils and abuses beside which those of the Nazis pale into insignificance. And even in 2003, such views were already being expressed with a degree of vehemence sufficient to make it scarcely paranoid to draw attention to them. But not to "want the Jews to have a state," while granting the right of national autonomy to virtually every other group contesting such a right, is to adopt a position not easy to distinguish, to put it delicately, from antisemitism. Hence, Judt, if he is to avoid accusations of antisemitism, must distance himself from any suggestion that the objection to a Jewish state is that it is a *Jewish* state.

The necessary distance is supposed to be created by the shift from *"Jewish* state" to "Jewish *state*," with the supporting arguments that in the latter, "one community—Jews—is set above others" and that in the age we now live in, "that sort of state has no place."

The trouble for Judt is that that shift, taken together with its supporting arguments, entirely fails to create the required distance. Judt does not tell us why the "age" we presently live in "has no place" for states in which "one community is set above others," but a shrewd guess would be that it is the age inaugurated by the French Revolution and the temporary triumph that accompanied it of Rousseau's ideal of a society bound together solely by common acceptance of the general will and entirely lacking in subordinate loyalties. It is an ideal that has haunted the European radical imagination ever since. It is echoed by Marx's enthusiasm for a society in which the petty concerns of private interest are entirely superseded by concern for the communal good and by Sartre's talk of "a society whose members feel mutual bonds of solidarity, because they are all engaged in the same enterprise." It is difficult to see what other aspect of political modernity Judt might have in mind.

If this *is* the direction in which Judt's mind was moving, what is problematic about it is that the Rousseauian ideal in question has never, over the almost three centuries that separate us from its author, in fact progressed beyond left-wing political fantasy. It has failed to do so for the evident reason that any national state, any state, that is, that serves to realize and implement the right to political self-determination of a coherent community, must *in some sense* set that community "above others." The foundation of the Republic of Ireland, initially as the Irish Free State, in December 1922, for example, effectively brought to an end what had been known as the Protestant Ascendancy in Southern Ireland, replacing it, from that point onward, with what might be termed a Catholic ascendancy. From that point onward, that is to say, the Catholic community in the republic—the majority—found itself "set above" the residual Protestant community in the obvious sense that it acquired overwhelming power to determine the character and direction of national life in its broadest aspects, and for that matter, in many of its more detailed ones. That kind of "setting above" is, after all, what the nation-state is about. There is no point in a community's seeking political autonomy by way of the foundation of a state unless it is to be

reasonably anticipated that once the state is achieved, the community in question will find itself in a position to largely direct its own affairs.

In the same way, if the Palestinians were to defeat the Jews in battle, as so
many wished them to do in 1948, and as many on the left still wish they had
done, the only possible result would be the founding, upon the present territory of Israel, of a Palestinian-majority state. In that state, Palestinian Muslims
would be, de facto, set above all other groups. From it, indeed, if the character
of the present Palestinian leadership and the appalling savagery of recent intra-
Muslim conflict in the Middle East is to be taken as a guide, Jews and no doubt
other non-Muslim groups would swiftly find themselves eliminated either by
the kind of semiforced migration that has already robbed the region of the bulk,
not only of its former Jewish but also of its former Christian population, or in
the case of the Jews, by actual extermination.

If the setting of one community above another is inseparable from the idea of
the nation-state, then, trivially Judt's ingenious attempt to avoid the antisemitic
implications of opposing Jewish political self-determination by shifting the focus of criticism from the idea of a *Jewish* state to that of a Jewish *state* collapses,
leaving those implications still clinging to his position. It is acceptable, it seems,
for Irish Catholics, or for that matter Palestinian Muslims, to be set above other
communities in the manner characteristic of a nation-state. Why not for Jews?

The only counterargument available to Judt at this point, so far as I can see,
would be that the Irish Catholics and the Palestinian Muslims each constitute
a nation, with an in-principle right to the political autonomy conferred by an
independent state, not because they are *Catholics* or *Muslims* but because they
are *Irish* and (Palestinian) *Arabs*, respectively. For a group to count as a nation,
the argument would go, it needs more than *religious* community; it also needs
genetic unity—the unity of a *race* or *people*.

This argument in turn, however, runs afoul of the obvious fact that Jewish
identity involves both a religious *and* a genetic component. To be a Jew, one
must *either* be the child of a Jewish mother *or* a convert. This is why Jews constitute a *people* rather than a religious community. They do so because most Jews
are actually related to one another and to the remote ancestors of the community,
and can very often trace that ancestry.

Unsurprisingly, the claim of genetic nationhood has also has been questioned by left-wing critics of Israel, most notably by the Israeli historian Shlomo
Sand, who provides my second and last example of a twenty-first-century attempt to show the claim of Jewish nationhood to be somehow faulty, and to
whom I now turn.

Sand is a professor of history at Tel Aviv University, at present emeritus. His experience in the Israel Defense Forces at the time of the Six-Day War in 1967 left him with a profound sympathy for the Palestinians and an equally profound distaste for what he saw as the arrogance of Israeli society. In 2014, he gave an interview—well worth reading for its biographical details—to the British left-wing *Guardian* newspaper, affirming among other things his "wish to resign and cease considering myself a Jew."[7]

Sand objects powerfully to what he sees as the high-handed and historically ill-founded Jewish claim to be the rightful owners of the land of Israel. He has published two immensely controversial books attacking the historical basis of such ideas: *The Invention of the Jewish People* (2010) and *The Invention of the Land of Israel* (2014). As the titles suggest, his claim is that *both* the claim of the Jews to be a people *and* the claim of that supposed people to constitute the original population of the land of Israel are *historically* unfounded. At the same time, Sand rejects the BDS objective of "delegitimizing" and destroying the State of Israel, though "not because of historical right, but because of the fact that it exists today and any effort to destroy it will bring new tragedies." He opposes the law and the right of return but still holds that "Israel has to be the state of Israelis. That is the only way we can continue to live in the Middle East."

There is much to discuss in Sand's work, but what interests me here are his reasons for denying that Jews collectively constitute a *nation*, a *people*. The introduction to his second book provides the best source for these, since it is here that Sand restates his position on this particular issue, as that has emerged from the intense controversy unleashed by the first book. It is clear from what Sand says here that for him, a "nation" is *a body of people united by a history that recounts the circumstances of remote ancestors of whom they are the genetically related descendants*. One of the theses developed in *The Invention of the Jewish People*, and one that provoked howls of protest when that book first appeared, is that modern Ashkenazi Jews have no genetic relationship to the people who figure in the stories of the Old Testament but derive either from the mass conversion of an ancient non-Jewish people, the Khazars, or from a series of conversions among a variety of ethnic groups in medieval Europe. This is still a main claim of Sand's in the second book.

My aim in writing it [*The Invention of the Jewish People*] had been mainly to use historical and historiographical sources to question the ethnocentric and ahistorical concept of essentialism and the role it has played in past and present definitions of Judaism and Jewish identity. Although it is widely evident that the Jews are not a pure race, many people—Judeophobes and Zionists in particular—still tend to espouse the incorrect and misleading

WHAT'S WRONG WITH UNIVERSALISM? 381

view that most Jews belong to an ancient race-based people, an eternal "*ethnos*" who found places of residence among other peoples and, at a decisive stage in history, when their host societies cast them out, began to return to their ancestral land.[8]

This claim, that the Jews constitute a group entirely constituted by relatively recent religious conversion, then fuels Sand's main ground for denying nationhood to the Jews, which is in effect that the Jews are not a distinct *ethnos*, a race, but merely a religious denomination.

My previous book employed one basic working premise: that a human unit of pluralistic origin, whose members are united by a common fabric devoid of any secular cultural component—a unit that can be joined, even by an atheist, not by forging a linguistic or cultural connection with its members but solely through religious conversion—cannot under any criteria be considered a people or an ethnic group (the latter is a concept that flourished in academic circles after the bankruptcy of the term "race").

If we are to be consistent and logical in our understanding of the term "people" as used in cases such as the "French people," the "American people," the "Vietnamese people" or even the "Israeli people," then referring to a "Jewish people" is just as strange as referring to a "Buddhist people," an "Evangelical people," or a "Baha'i people."

... Even if human society consists of a linked collection of multifaceted complex experiences that defy all attempts at formulation in mathematical terms, we must nevertheless do our utmost to employ precise mechanisms of conceptualization. Since the beginning of the modern era, "peoples" have been conceptualised as groups possessing a unifying culture (including elements such as cuisine, a spoken language, and music). However, despite their great uniqueness, Jews throughout all of history have been characterised by "only" a diverse culture of religion (including elements such as a common nonspoken sacred language and common rituals and ceremonies).[9]

This passage announces itself with a flourish as an exercise in precise conceptual analysis ("if we are to be consistent and logical"; "we must do our utmost to employ precise mechanisms of conceptualization," etc.). Nevertheless, it is precisely as conceptual analysis that it fails altogether to persuade. Let us examine it in detail. The first thing that is wrong with the Jews' claim to constitute a nation, Sand argues, is that they are not (as he believes many Zionists suppose them to be), a "pure race," "an ancient race-based people, an eternal 'ethnos.'" It is not entirely clear what he means by a "pure race," but one can take a stab at guessing. Here's my guess. A "pure race" is a tribe of people—call them "the

Puritans"—whose gene pool has from immemorial antiquity remained closed off from the remainder of the human gene pool. In all that time, the Puritan population has been augmented only by the addition of children of Puritan fathers and mothers. In all that time, that is to say, no non-Puritan applicant for membership of the Puritan tribe has been allowed to join or for that matter allowed sexual favors. It hardly needs saying that no nation—with the (just) conceivable exception of the Japanese up to the point at which Commodore Perry and the Treaty of Kanagawa put an end to their self-imposed isolation (and even then, there are the Ainu to consider)—meets this exacting requirement. There just are no pure races, and there's an end of it. Our concept of a nation certainly requires *genetic continuity*, but that is a much weaker requirement. Genetic continuity requires only that *some* of each individual's genome connect that individual to the historic ancestors of the nation. Take me, for instance. I stand before you an Englishman: a very English one indeed, painfully English, some would say. But what do we take that to mean in genetic terms? Some of my genes no doubt do actually derive from fifth-century members of the group of Germanic tribes who at that remote period laid the foundations of the English nation. But I know for a certainty that a lot of them don't. Quite a lot of them carry my ancestry back into Wales (and *walha* in Old English means not just "foreigner" but "member of an inferior tribe ripe for enslavement"). Some must be Norse, since my name ends in "son," while between 1 percent and 6 percent (I am told by geneticists) will certainly be of Neanderthal origin. But that's OK: *enough* of my genes come down to me from genuine ax-bearing, slave-taking, mass-butchering Angles and Saxons, the terrifying pagan people against whose incursions the forts of the Saxon Shore were so unsuccessfully reared by the Romans, to make me an entirely authentic Englishman.

Genetic continuity as the glue of nationhood, in other words, allows for an awful lot of conversion and marrying-in. I had a friend who was even more painfully English than I am, but one of his grandmothers was in fact a West African. So what? In eighteenth-century Britain, there were a host of resident Africans, some slaves, some free. Where were they by 1900? Gone, married-in, their children's children unrecognizable as of partly African descent. But their genes are still there to this day in the British gene pool.

What does that mean for the claim of the Jews to be a nation? Quite a lot. Sand makes great play with the fact that much conversion into Judaism has taken place. And he is right. The Czech writer Ivan Klima, for instance, explains how his mother's originally Protestant family became Jewish in the seventeenth century. At that point, only two religions were permitted in Bohemia—the Jewish and the Roman Catholic—and many Protestant congregations were advised to become Jewish on the understanding that they could always change back later: they never did.[10] But so what? If genetic *continuity*, rather than genetic *purity*, is all that is required for nationhood, then the arrival of such converts marks only a temporary interruption in that continuity: the moment the convert marries into the community and has children, the required continuity is restored *in them*.

What Sand needs to demonstrate historically, in other words, if he is to establish his claim that modern Jewry lacks the kind of connection with biblical Jewry needed to establish the two as composing a single nation, is not a failure of genetic *purity* but rather a failure of genetic *continuity*. And the latter, it seems to me, would be *extremely* hard to demonstrate. One would need, in effect, to demonstrate somehow that *all* descendants of the biblical people of Israel died *without Jewish issue* before *any* of the ancestors of the modern people of Israel became Jews. And given the enormous forced distribution of members of the ancient community across the ancient world, first into the Babylonian and later across the Roman Empire, I cannot see how one could possibly hope to do that with any plausibility.

Related difficulties also attend Sand's other main argument, that the Jews can't be a nation because, since the "common fabric" uniting them is "devoid of any secular cultural component," talk of a "Jewish people" is as absurd as talk of a "Buddhist people" or an "Evangelical people."

Much here hangs on Sand's play with the term *secular*. According to the OED, the term derives from the Latin *saeculum* ("generation," "age") and in Christian Latin means "concerned with the world," as opposed to the higher, otherworldly matters that occupy the church. The secular is also at times equated with the temporal and contrasted with the spiritual. According to that distinction, secular (or temporal) concerns are occupied with events "in the world" in the sense of events *in time*, while spiritual or religious concerns are occupied not with *time* but with *eternity*.

The trouble with Sand's attempt to make Judaism out to be a religion *in exactly the same sense in which Buddhism and Christianity are religions* is that the *spiritual* element in Judaism, though present, is by comparison very much reduced. Judaism is minimally concerned with the eternal and maximally concerned with the temporal, with the conduct of everyday life *in this world*—which is to say, *with the secular*. That, of course, is why Jews have found themselves exposed to precisely the criticisms that we have spent the last two chapters examining: why Christians have accused Jews of worldliness and lack of spirituality, and why the leading figures of the Enlightenment, at least in its French and German manifestations, so readily accused them of an inability to raise their minds from the petty concerns of everyday existence to contemplate the future of humanity.

I happen to possess the T-shirt of an American university's Jewish Studies program. It bears on its back the legend, "Wisdom from the past: Leaders for the future." That, in a way, says it all. What it reminds one is that Judaism, though it has aspects that entitle one to call it a religion, has other aspects that incline one to think of it not so much as a religion but rather as what one might call a *wisdom literature*. The peculiarity of this literature is that the wisdom it embodies, while *potentially universal*, is conceived as the wisdom of a specific nation whose members have the responsibility to preserve it and to live by it, and in living by it to demonstrate its virtues (that is what being a "chosen" people *means*; that is *what the Jews have been chosen to do*, that is what they have been *about*, all these many centuries). That is why becoming a Jew, *pace* Sand, is not in the least like becoming a Christian or a Buddhist. Normally, joining a religion is a matter of acquiring certain beliefs (the divinity of Christ, the Enlightenment of the Buddha) plus certain hopes (of eternal life, of release from the wheel of birth and death), and accepting a few specific prohibitions (one wife only, no meat on Fridays). Becoming a Jew, on the other hand, is a matter of joining what is essentially a *national* project, built around a *national* wisdom literature, one requiring considerable expenditures of study, observance, and commitment. That is why Judaism is not, or not just, a *religion* but rather *the glue that holds a nation together.*

Sand could retort that while this, or something along those lines, may be the case, building a nation around the "glue" provided by a wisdom literature introduces a special, Jewish concept of nationhood having nothing to do with our ordinary concept of nationhood.

Unfortunately for Sand, his chosen instances of groups to which he takes the term *nation* to apply include one that conforms exactly to the Jewish model: namely, the United States of America. American nationhood is built in exactly the same way as Jewish nationhood around a wisdom literature, one constituted in the first instance by the Constitution and beyond that by all the many prior and consequent documents necessary to its full understanding. Terms such as *the English* and *the French* locate bodies of people united as nations by their descent from founding collections of tribes and by the subsequent history that forged those tribes into political unity. By contrast, the term *the Americans* locates a people "of pluralistic origin" as Sand would put it, united only by common fidelity to a system of ideas. So it is with the Jews.

It might be objected that many Jews know less than nothing of Judaism. This is true: I lunch regularly with an amiable lawyer who abundantly satisfies this description. But experience has also taught me that a great many Jews turn out to be rather deeply versed in the literature and outlook of Judaism and that quite often they are people of whom one might not expect that. And in any case, when it comes to determining the identity of a nation across time, culture obeys the same requirements as genetics: what is required, that is to say, is not purity but merely continuity.

In any case, these abstract criteria of identity fail to go entirely to the heart of the matter. In the end, it is hard to find a better account of what constitutes a nation and of what constitutes Jews as one than the philosopher Henry Sidgwick's: "What is really essential . . . to a Nation is. . . that the persons composing it should have a consciousness of belonging to one another, of being members of one body, over and above what they derive from the mere fact of being under one government; so that, if their government were destroyed by war or revolution, they would still hold firmly together."[11]

THE AMBIGUITIES OF UNIVERSALISM

Criticism of Judaism as particularist in character proceeds, generally speaking, against the background of the assumption that "universalism" affords a better, more virtuous, more humane outlook on life. Is that necessarily so?

For a start, what exactly do we mean by "universalism"? As with any other complex term, its meaning, implications, and connotations vary with context. One thing we may have in mind in speaking of a religion or system of belief as "universalist" in character is simply that it *addresses itself*, at least in principle, to all humankind rather than to a select group of initiates. Let's call this "universalism of address" or "universalism$_A$." In this sense, Christianity and Islam are both universalist$_A$ in character, while Shintoism and Wicca, say, are equally clearly not. One of the things people often have in mind in speaking of Judaism as particularist is that it has no universalist$_A$ dimension. In one sense, this is true, at any rate up to a point; in another, it is entirely false as we shall see in a moment.

We also deploy the term *universalism* to distinguish political movements that aim—in principle, at any rate—at extending their rule over all humankind, or some substantial section of it, from those with no such aim. Let us call this "political universalism" or "universalism$_P$," to distinguish it from universalism of address. In this sense, the political version of Islam represented by movements such as ISIL, Marxism in its original form, Nazism, Roman imperialism, and the EU are or were movements with a strong dose of universalism$_P$ in their makeup. Equally, Sinn Fein or the Scottish Nationalist Party, having no ambitions beyond a united Ireland and an independent Scotland, respectively, are movements in which a commitment to universalism$_p$ plays a minimal role. If having no truck with universalism$_p$ is one way of being particularist, then *in that sense,* Judaism is certainly particularist. Jewish religious laws (halakah), with certain exceptions that we shall examine in a moment, are supposed to apply to Jews and to nobody else.

Used in the second of the above two senses, universalism contrasts sharply with nationalism. It is in the context of this contrast that universalism, meaning by that political universalism (universalism$_p$) has in many liberal, or progressive, or humanitarian minds acquired an aura of warm moral approval, while nationalism, in contrast, has taken on sharply pejorative overtones. The primary reason for that is that in many such people's minds, competition between nation-states has come to be seen as the main cause of war. This is particularly true of European opinion at the present time. The increasingly appalling series of wars, 1870–71, 1914–18, 1939–45, all of which could be seen as resulting wholly or in part from the long-standing conflict between France and Germany for leadership in Europe, convinced many that a radical retreat was needed not merely from aggressive, jingoistic national sentiment but from the very idea of the nation-state itself. After 1945, it was thus possible for the project of tying the nations of Europe into some kind of supranational organization, which would at least serve to contain their rivalries from breaking out in armed conflict and possibly even lead ultimately to their disappearance as distinct political entities to achieve widespread support, at least among influential political and social elites. The establishment in 1951 of the European Coal and Steel Community began the process of formal integration that led to the present EU. The widespread support for the values and integrity of the EU that now exists throughout Europe in certain influential sections of European society correlates closely with dislike of any expression of national sentiment. "Jewish"—that is to say, Israeli—national sentiment, as I noted earlier, is often felt to be particularly repellent by this strand of opinion, since it is felt that "the Jews should have learned from the Holocaust" how dangerous nationalism and national sentiment can be.

This sense, dominant in certain quarters, that a reformed, redeemed, and politically purified Europe has now definitively outgrown errors in which the Jews are still floundering, is closely connected with the equally widespread desire felt by people in broadly the same sectors of opinion to dissociate oneself from the abuses of nineteenth-century European colonialism. This desire all too often translates into uncritical support for any movement that can with any color of plausibility be represented as "anticolonial." These two attitudes of mind, operating in combination, no doubt go far to explain the popularity of BDS and BDS-leaning attitudes in left and left-center European circles today. Unfortunately, such attitudes, never entirely in tune with reality, are nowadays increasingly parting company with it. A powerful vein of argument has always held the values of classical liberalism to be inseparable from those of the nation-state. Those values, according to the British political philosopher David Conway, "include, most importantly, private property rights, strictly limited government, and hence, maximum possible freedom of thought, expression, activity and association, together with constitutional representative government, division of powers, and the rule of law."[12]

Of these, constitutional representative government is perhaps the most important, since it is the key to the maintenance of the rest. And it is a general presumption of such systems of government that both representatives and those they represent are alike members of the same people and jointly responsible for the welfare of that people. Representatives and represented, that is to say, must share the consciousness of which Sidgwick wrote in the passage cited above, of "belonging to one another, of being members of one body, over and above what they derive from the mere fact of being under the same government." If those in charge of the government under which I live are not linked to me by any such consciousness, then in what sense can they be said to represent me?

This is the difficulty that according to many observers accounts for the mounting tally of crises and internecine conflicts under which the EU, both politically and economically, has begun to labor during the past decade. According to the French political philosopher Pierre Manent, a fundamental error of the EU has been to attempt to construct a political order faithful in intention to the ideals of liberalism and democracy without the support of a nation-state. Manent puts the problem sharply in his preface to the American edition of his best-selling book: "What the Europeans are trying to do is to separate the democratic regime completely, or rather the machinery of democratic politics (composed of "institutions" and animated by "values") from any underlying conception of what it means to be a *people*."[13]

There is, of course, a European Parliament bringing together representatives of all twenty-eight nations, organized among themselves into the usual ideological groupings. The parliament supposedly controls the activity of the European Commission, the vast body of unelected bureaucrats and technicians that actually originates most of the projects and legislation that make up the now immense body of supposedly binding laws, principles, and conventions that constitute the so-called European *acquis* and that all candidate countries have to agree to accept on joining the union. But since the European Parliament

is, as might be expected, too diverse and too little rooted in any of the peoples
it supposedly represents to exercise more than minimal control over the commission, the commission has always risked appearing to a substantial segment
of opinion in the component states of the union as an alien, unelected, technocratic power insusceptible of democratic control. These risks were sharply
exacerbated by the introduction of the euro in 1999. The use of a common
currency with a single external exchange rate by regional communities with
vastly different economies and cultural traditions inevitably leads to problems
of economic and fiscal divergence. The external rate of exchange, wherever it is
set or settles, will prove advantageous for some regions and disadvantageous to
others. Within a nation-state, these problems are invariably solved by centrally
organized fiscal transfers, often on a large scale, from more prosperous to less
prosperous regions. But since the EU remains a union of sovereign states, such
transfers have proved politically impossible to organize. As a result, the introduction of the euro has led to Germany and certain others in the northern tier
of member states running immense and permanent surpluses, while the entire
southern tier of nations—Greece, Italy, Spain, Portugal—have faced severe
deficits that can only be corrected by policies of internal austerity that have led
to immense economic hardship, including unsustainably high levels of youth
unemployment. The resulting conflicts have been further exacerbated by high
levels of immigration from Africa and the Middle East, particularly resented by
the formerly communist states of Eastern Europe but also by Italy. All of this
has led to a steep rise in political influence in a number of member states, of
nationalist parties opposed to EU membership, and to the 2016 majority vote
in the United Kingdom to exit the EU altogether.

It is conventional, in media and some political circles sympathetic to the European project and especially in the heated atmosphere produced in Britain by
the popular majority in favor of Brexit, to speak of its opponents as "nationalist"
or "populist" or "right wing." Such language suggests that national sentiment
of any kind can be dismissed as atavistic, actually or potentially racist, doomed
to disappear with the progress of society and history toward world government
and, while it still persists, to be found only among the people viewed in this
context as an ignorant and ill-educated rabble, or in political movements so
right wing as to be to all intents and purposes fascist.

It would be nearer to the truth to recognize, it seems to me, that national
sentiment, in one form or another—that "consciousness of belonging to one
another, of being members of one body" of which Henry Sidgwick spoke—is
so fundamental to the human condition as to render it futile to imagine a possible world without it.

There is an analogy to be drawn here, perhaps, between cultural and bio-logical evolution. Evolutionary biologists recognize the role of contiguity and distance in what is called *speciation*. Animal and plant species, if successful, often create populations spread over very wide geographical ranges. Mere dis-tance then works to ensure that the members of the species at the far ends of such ranges mate only with one another. That, together with the drift of chance mutation, is sometimes enough to bring about the splitting of the species into two whose members are no longer able to mate to produce fertile offspring. It seems obvious that distance and contiguity operate in much the same way as the motor of cultural differentiation in human groups. People who live close together, who see each other frequently, come to see things similarly in ways increasingly important for their relationships to one another. Over time, they devise social and political conventions and institutions—the Icelandic thing, shari'a law, Athenian democracy—that reflect these similarities and outlook: arrangements with which they feel happy and at home but which divide them increasingly sharply from neighboring societies and still more from remoter ones. Around these specific institutions, and the still more specific ways of feeling and thinking that go with them, grows up Sidgwick's "consciousness of belonging to one another"—that consciousness that provides, if Sidgwick is to be believed, the glue of peoplehood. The existence of *peoples*, in other words, is not some kind of moral aberration but the consequence of a process, cultural speciation, that appears on the face of it too deeply rooted in the human condi-tion for there to be any obvious means by which it could be removed, or any obvious way of determining how much would be left of human life, or what human life would still be worth, if it were to be removed.

Political universalists, universalists$_p$, employ various means of persuading themselves that cultural speciation presents no insuperable obstacle to the success of their various projects. Classical Marxism, for instance, solves the problem by arguing that cultural difference is illusory. Only economic rela-tionships, according to Marxists, are real in the sense of causally efficacious. Culture in all its forms—literary, religious, political, social—is insofar as it conflicts with the Marxist deliverance merely a tissue of obscurantist myth de-signed to protect the ruling class by concealing the real nature and sources of its power. Hence, cultural difference insofar as it amounts to anything more than charming folkloric oddity may therefore be expected to disappear as history proceeds to its terminus in a new order ushered in by the revolution. In much the same way, as we saw in chapter 3, Clermont-Tonnerre confidently expected such quaint peculiarities of Jewish life as respect for the laws of kashruth and dislike of intermarriage to disappear with the assimilation of the Jews into postrevolutionary society. Again, supporters of the introduction of the euro seem confidently to have anticipated that any divisive economic difficulties that might emerge, in view of the vast national cultural differences dividing the continent, would be solved by the rapid disappearance of the latter: in effect, by Greeks, Italians, and Spaniards metamorphosing overnight into Germans.

In fact, the forces of cultural speciation constitute a potent and permanent obstacle to any project of political universalism. In practice, there are only two ways of dealing with it. The first is to find some way of uniting culturally diverse communities under the umbrella of some wider *national* sentiment, as has been achieved in the United States. The other—contrary to the opinion of those universalists who imagine war to be uniquely associated with nationalist particularism—is war.

Rather evidently, war has historically provided the main means by which universalist$_p$ projects have achieved success. The rise of Islam was virtually entirely a process of armed conquest, as was that of the Roman, Austro-Hungarian, Ottoman, czarist, and British Empires. In the same way the Christianization of Europe was largely forced, first by Roman imperial fiat and later, as often as not, by mass conversions achieved through war. Structures achieved in this way tend to be stable only if they result in the effective formation of a political order with many of the leading characteristics of a *nation*: a larger-scale community in which people feel as connected to one another as members of the new imperial order as they did in their former, preimperial groupings. The Romans, the Muslims, and the Ottoman Turks proved remarkably adept in replacing former loyalties with new ones. The Austro-Hungarian Empire, less adept in this respect, fell apart because ultimately none of its subject peoples felt sufficiently at home in the institutional and cultural structures it provided to want to keep it going. The EU represents an altogether new and remarkable attempt to found a pan-European, quasi-imperial order not by war, as in the past, but through the mutual consent of its component nations. It aims, in effect, at the creation of a version of the Austro-Hungarian Empire but without the emperor. Unfortunately, however, what has taken the place of the emperor is not a genuinely representative democracy but—in too many eyes for the issue to be readily dismissed or papered over—merely an inaccessible and ultimately unaccountable technocratic bureaucracy. The problem of national difference thus remains a running sore for the union: one at present unaddressed and very possibly in the longer run unaddressable.

Nor do the problems created for political universalism by cultural speciation end there. There remains the possibility of cultural fragmentation within the ranks of the universalist$_p$ project itself: of religious schism or political factionalism. When this happens, each schismatic group is liable to regard itself as the true inheritor of the universalizing$_P$ project of the original movement. This leaves it little choice but to regard members of the other faction as enemies of human progress whose resistance deserves to be dealt with as vigorously as that of the mass of recalcitrant souls who stand outside the movement altogether. At this point, too, internecine war remains the only likely outcome.

A series of recent wars of this kind, between various representatives of the main factions, Shi'a and Sunni, of schismatic Islam, have to date killed hundreds of thousands and displaced many millions more, most of them Muslims, in Iraq, Syria, and Yemen. This, together with the more limited but equally bloody effects of Islamist terror in the West, has led some Western journalists to talk as if such events were characteristic of Islam alone and arise from the supposed nature of Islam as a "death cult." One problem with this is that Christianity itself is not without a certain degree of obsession with death. There is, for instance, the famous, possibly apocryphal story of an abbot of Ampleforth, an English Catholic boys' school, addressing a headmasters' conference with the words "Other schools pride themselves on preparing boys for life. At Ampleforth we prefer, rather, to prepare them for death." Among the major religions, only Judaism, to my knowledge, urges its members to follow the sound advice of Moses and "choose life."

More seriously, the history of Christianity includes, quite as much as that of Islam, a history of warfare between schismatic sects each presuming to offer the salvation of humankind at large and each taking this goal to justify any brutality whatsoever. These wars were, in their time, quite as destructive as what is taking place at present in the Middle East. The Thirty Years' War (1618–48), for instance, so reduced the population of the German-speaking states that it was not until just prior to World War I that it recovered to the level at which it had stood in 1617.

In any case, it would be equally mistaken to associate such wars uniquely with religion. Secular movements aimed at uniting large segments of humanity behind a common project, in defiance of the workings of cultural speciation, have proved as guilty. The philosopher Ernst Cassirer once justly observed that World War II could be described as a battle between left and right Hegelians.[14] Marx's ideas, which still enjoy widespread support in the West, have led successively not only to the gulag, whose horrors, generally underestimated in the West, are comparable to those of the Holocaust, and to the mass starvation, including the Ukrainian Holodomor, occasioned by Stalin's policies of forced collectivization but also successively to equally disastrous episodes of mass starvation in China under Mao and to the policies of extermination of "class enemies" adopted by the Khmer Rouge in Cambodia. The same policies, under Hugo Chávez and Nicolás Maduro, are presently producing the same results in Venezuela. Even the French Revolution, which founded the modern tradition of universalist political reform, immediately produced a genocide in the shape of the Wars of the Vendée, in Brittany and northwestern France, a region in which peasants and townsfolk alike continued to support the monarchy. Robespierre, then at the head of the revolutionary Comité de Salut Publique, was responsible for the law of October 1, 1793, which declared, "Il faut que les brigands de la Vendée soient exterminés avant la fin du mois!" ("It is necessary that the brigands of the Vendée be exterminated by the end of the month!"). The excellent French Channel 3 television documentary *L'Ombre d'un doute* (The shadow of a doubt)—at present available in full on YouTube—caused a media furor in France in 2011 when, in an edition titled *Robespierre, Bourreau de la Vendée?* (Robespierre, executioner of the Vendée?), it revealed that more than 170,000 civilians had been massacred in the resulting campaign and that recent investigation of mass graves from the period had found them to contain individuals killed without distinction of age, sex, or social class, at least 30 percent of them women and children. The subject had long been politically untouchable in France, though in 2008 leading voices in the Vendée called for the episode to be recognized as the first genocide in modern history.[15]

So much for the modern faith in universalist solutions to the world's problems, given the ease with which any project, religious or political, of making humanity one, once it has gained political traction, transforms itself into that of exterminating anyone, including former comrades, seen as hostile or merely indifferent to the project.

WHERE DOES JUDAISM STAND?

In terms of the distinctions proposed above, Judaism, I want to suggest, is both particularist and universalist in character. From the standpoint of universalism of address (universalism$_A$), it is universalist. From the standpoint of political universalism (universalism$_P$), it is resolutely particularist.

In the last section, I suggested that universalist schemes for the salvation of humankind are at permanent odds with those features of human life— by analogy with evolutionary biology I called them the forces of cultural speciation—that tend toward cultural, social, and political diversity. Matters are in fact worse than this. Essential to universalism is the idea that humanity, or some substantial section of it, can fruitfully be brought together under one banner, one cause, one collection of ideas. That implies that the favored outlook captures the essence of what it is to be fully human at the present time. And that in turn implies that whoever obstinately resists being brought under that banner is resisting the call of full humanity—is, in fact, less than human or perhaps not human at all, and so fit to be discarded, for whatever reason of *realpolitik* or eugenics may arise or be imagined, from the long march of human progress. As the last century demonstrated and the present one is continuing to demonstrate, nothing more is needed to set, sooner or later, the wheels of genocide in motion—whether against Jews or others.

By contrast, Judaism is perfectly happy to admit the unavoidable facticity of human diversity. "Two Jews, three opinions" is less a joke than a wry recognition that human life by its nature tends to disagreement. Judaism, shockingly to those whose idea of religion assigns a central place to doctrinal agreement, thrives on argument—is, indeed, "the only religious culture all of whose canonical texts are anthologies of arguments."[16]

Judaism not only accepts and privileges human diversity, however; it regards it as holy. The Babylonian Talmud (Sanhedrin 37a) argues that the reason Adam was created alone was to teach us that a single person can contain an entire world so that whoever destroys a single soul is as guilty as if he had destroyed a whole world, while the merit of saving a life is indistinguishable from that of saving a world.

The idea of Jewish chosenness also works to save Jews from the common delusion that the world would be saved if only everyone would cease being themselves and become somebody else: if the Greeks, say, would only be more German, or the Americans more European. The point of chosenness is that to be a Jew is to be committed to higher standards of behavior than other people. According to Jewish tradition, there are laws—the seven so-called Noahide Laws—given to all humanity, but the prohibitions they enjoin—to abstain from murder, idol worship, cursing God, adultery and sexual immorality, theft and the eating of flesh from a living animal, and to establish courts of justice—fall far short of the supposedly 613 mitzvoth imposed on Jews. For this reason, conversion to Judaism has never been easy. According to the Talmud (Yevamoth), "the rabbis taught: When someone nowadays presents himself for conversion, we say to him: Why do you wish to convert? Are you not aware that nowadays Israelites are careworn, stressed, despised, harassed and persecuted? If he responds, 'I know, and I feel unworthy to share their troubles,' we accept him at once."

Even unconverted, however, the non-Jew is still, to the Jew, a child of Adam and as such partakes of the holiness of created life. "Because Judaism does not subscribe to the doctrine of original sin and takes every soul that enters this world to be free of any blemish, the phrase 'child of Adam' connotes the holiness of one who, like Adam, is created in the image and likeness of the Holy One."[17]

From these two principles, that humanity is always and inevitably going to be divided into Jews and non-Jews and that the non-Jew is also a child of Adam, depends an elaborate collection of Jewish views on how one should conduct oneself toward the "stranger," the non-Jew. For a start, these include the principle that justice is indivisible: "You shall not pervert the justice due to the stranger" (Deuteronomy 24:17). There is also the requirement to seek peace with other nations: "Be among the disciples of Aaron, loving peace and pursuing peace, loving people" (*Mishna Avot* 1:12). As David Patterson reminds us:

> What must be kept in mind ... is that in these commandments of Torah the word for "stranger" is *ger*: A *ger* is a non-Jew who dwells among the Jews, seeking only peace, only to be a good neighbour, and only the human-to-human relation that makes dwelling possible. Two other words for "stranger" are *zar* and *nakhar*. *Nakhar* simply refers to one who is foreign and unfamiliar, but with whom one might become familiar. The *nakhar* is one who might become a *ger*. *Zar*, however, refers to one who is utterly alien, who is beyond anything that can become familiar, as in *avodah zarah*, the alien worship that is "idolatry." The height of idolatry is found among those who make their children "pass through the fire" (Deuteronomy 18:10), either through child sacrifice or by strapping bombs to their children, making them into murderers whom they regard as "martyrs." According to Jewish teaching, there is no obligation to the "stranger" as *zar*, that is, as one who is bent on your extermination or the extermination of others.[18]

To everyone except the *zar*, Judaism recommends open-mindedness. Hence Lévinas, "the presence of the Other is a presence that teaches" and the *Pirkhe Avot*, "Who is wise? He who learns from every person." Once again, the idea that every person has something to teach is inseparable not only from the acceptance of human diversity but also from its positive glorification. It is this feature of Judaism that no doubt accounts for the tendency, noted by Isaiah Berlin in a celebrated essay, for diaspora Jews brought by the Enlightenment into close proximity to the alien culture around then to fall in love, particularly in Germany, with that culture: an affection largely unrequited and too often in time bitterly rewarded.

> So much labour and devotion to the life and outlook of other people must in time induce a natural affection for, and devotion to it.... The strangers become primary authorities on the natives: they codify their language and

their customs, they compose the tribe's dictionaries and encyclopedias, they interpret the native society to the outside world. . . . In the end they are prepared not merely to live but to die for it and, if need be, with it, no less bravely, and perhaps with greater passion, than the natives themselves.[19]

What are we to make, then, finally and by way of conclusion, of the accusation of Jewish particularism? The complaint usually voiced in these terms has two components. The first is that Jews are unsociable: that they hold themselves apart from "the rest of us." The second is that Jews, driven supposedly by pride in their own superiority as "the chosen people, desire to rule the world." The second of these is precisely what is ruled out by the respect in which Judaism genuinely is particularist: that is, in its inbuilt hostility to political universalism (universalism$_p$). Becoming masters of the world is an essentially non-Jewish project, because it is a project that essentially entails contempt for the singularity of the Other and, in the last analysis, the destruction of the Other. Jews, as long as they remain Jewish, are not interested in ruling the world: they are interested in ploughing their own furrow in life and in harvesting what it may yield (when that crop has not been burned by the malice of others).

That does not mean, however, that they are indifferent to the nature and fate of the Other. Here, we encounter the other side of the Jewish coin: the respect in which Judaism is universalist in character. Its universalism is of the first of our two kinds: universalism of address (universalism$_A$). And it is a universalism of address that runs both ways. Jews keep the outlook and traditions of Judaism available to non-Jews—who in my opinion and in that of the Christian theologian William Nicholls, of whom we saw a good deal in chapter 11, stand at times sorely in need of it. At the same time Judaism has led Jews to the extraordinary receptivity to the ideas, art, science, and culture of non-Jews that has placed them over the past three centuries among the chief benefactors of Western and world civilization.

The contrast between a culture weak on universalism$_p$ but strong on universalism$_A$, and one displaying the opposite proclivities, can be seen at present tragically displayed in the Middle East. On the one hand, we see a Jewish state within which Jews, Arab Muslims, Arab and other Christians, Baha'is, and others live, for the most part, at peace with one another under a law that, again for the most part, does not "pervert the justice due the stranger." Among other things, Israel has recently shown its concern for the plight of the Other by offering free treatment in its hospitals to thousands of wounded refugees from the wars across its border in Syria.[20] Outside Israel, we see a profoundly schismatic civilization, each faction committed to dominance over the other, to be achieved if necessary by extermination, slowly tearing itself apart in a series of wars marked by what Amnesty International recently described with remarkable understatement as "flagrant war crimes" and by the regular opening of new fronts and new grounds of dispute. It is a leading symptom of the present moral and intellectual collapse of the Western left that large sections of it wish to "correct" this situation by bringing about the destruction of Israel.

NOTES

1. Arthur Hertzberg, "The Chosen People," *New York Review of Books*, October 24, 1968, https://www.nybooks.com/articles/1968/10/24/the-chosen -people-1/.
2. Karl Marx, "On the Jewish Question," in Tucker 1978.
3. Marx in Tucker 1978.
4. Sartre 1948, 118.
5. Sartre 1948, 149–50.
6. Tony Judt, "Israel: The Alternative," *New York Review of Books*, October 23, 2003, https://www.nybooks.com/articles/2003/10/23/israel-the-alternative/.
7. "Shlomo Sand: I Wish to Resign and Cease Considering Myself as a Jew," *Guardian*, October 10, 2016, theguardian.com.
8. Sand 2014, 11.
9. Sand 2014, 11–12.
10. Klima 1974, 12.
11. Sidgwick 2014, cited in Conway 2004, 82.
12. Conway 2004, 81.
13. Manent 2006, vii.
14. Cassirer 1946, 249.
15. Henry Samuel, "Vendée French Call for Revolution Massacre to Be Termed 'Genocide,'" *The Telegraph*, December 26, 2008, https://www.telegraph .co.uk/news/worldnews/europe/france/3964724/Vende-French-call-for -revolution-massacre-to-be-termed-genocide.html.
16. Rabbi Jonathan Sacks, "The Genesis of Jewish Genius," *Slate*, slate.com.
17. Patterson 2012, 78.
18. Patterson 2012, 80.
19. Isaiah Berlin, "Jewish Slavery and Emancipation," in Berlin 2001, 166.
20. Sam McNeil, "Israel Treating Thousands of Civilians Injured in War," *The Independent*, April 8, 2017, https://www.independent.co.uk/news/world/middle -east/israel-syria-assad-treating-airstrikes-military-wounded-injured-war -a7673771.html.

PART V

ANTISEMITISM AS A PROBLEM
FOR NON-JEWS

FOURTEEN

JEW BAITING ON CAMPUS

A University should be a place of light, of liberty, and of learning.

—Benjamin Disraeli (Speech in the House of Commons, March 11, 1873)

WHY SHOULD *WE* WORRY?

It is usual, and very natural, to assume that the costs of antisemitism are paid in their entirety by the Jewish people. This seems to me another of the many illusions surrounding the master delusion that whatever is going wrong in the world, and whatever the scale on which it is going wrong, "the Jews" are to blame for it. The price paid over the centuries by Jews for that delusion is in sum, of course, beyond reckoning. But it is false to imagine that the antisemite exacts no price at all from his fellow non-Jews, or that the price he exacts is a small one.

It is a price exacted primarily by political antisemitism. Political antisemitism is, as we have already seen at length, to be sharply distinguished from social antisemitism. The latter is a form of ethnic prejudice, which in turn is an emotional disposition on the part of individuals, marked by dislike and contempt felt toward members of a socially despised and excluded group. The latter is not an *emotional disposition* of any kind. On the contrary, it is a delusive, pseudo-explanatory *theory* about how the world works and is constituted. It belongs with other delusive systems of alleged explanation, such as astrology or phrenology.

Belief in such theories may not harm the believer but always has the power to do so, simply because it is profoundly unsafe to suppose that one understands

the workings of the world, or society, or politics when in fact one has a grip on
no more than a nebulous collection of fantasies. Delusion unhinges and derails
judgment.

In the case of political antisemitism, in any of its versions, there are two ways
in which this derailing can occur. First, political antisemitism by its nature
disinclines the sufferer to examine his own follies, errors, or misdeeds in search
of an explanation for whatever distressing fate has overtaken him. Why should
he after all? The fault lies not with him but with the obscure and conspiratorial
machinations of the Jews.

Second, by establishing in the foreground of the sufferer's view of events the
threatening but essentially imaginary figure of "the Jew," and thereby grossly
exaggerating the significance of actual Jews in national and world politics, political antisemitism serves to obscure from him important features of the real
world—features that, in his position, he might do well to give some attention to.

Political antisemitism in the specific form that it most commonly takes at
present—namely, the idea that the crimes of Israel outweigh those of any other
nation and that the very existence of Israel is a crime against humanity—poses
additional dangers for those foolish enough to believe it. These additional dangers arise from the ease with which it allows believers to persuade themselves
that their hatred of Israel—and Jews—arises not from any *personal* dislike of
Jews but rather from moral impulses of a generously altruistic and humanitarian character. Persons who think in this way commonly fail to see that antisemitism can have either of the two forms we have examined in this book, the
first an emotional disposition, the second a delusive explanatory theory. They
are thus rendered unable to recognize their antisemitism for what it is: not an
antisemitism of emotional dislike and contempt but rather an antisemitism of
belief, and thus an antisemitism of the most potentially lethal kind.

This initial failure to grasp the force of this evident distinction carries along
with it two other important kinds of blindness. First, it makes it impossible for
believers to grasp *as antisemitism* the political antisemitism presently rampant
in the Muslim world, since that involves attitudes toward Israel and the Jews
indistinguishable from their own and thus presumably, from their point of view,
equally humanitarian in character. This allows many on the left to accept as
brothers in a common cause Arab movements such as Hamas whose policies
can lead only into darkness and whose antisemitism, as we saw in chapter 2
and subsequently, is of exactly the same type as that of the prewar German
Nazi Party.

Even more seriously, it makes it impossible for the believer to see that Muslim
attacks, in Western countries, on Jewish citizens of those countries who have

no personal connection with the government of Israel and hence no responsibility for its policies or actions, are motivated not by political resentment or moral outrage but by antisemitism of exactly the type that motivated attacks on Jews in the Europe of the 1930s. Given the wide diffusion of anti-Zionist views in Europe at present, extending far outside the boundaries of the hard left for which they serve as a central, unifying principle of political faith, this blindness can, and does, make it very hard for Jews who suffer such attacks to present themselves to society and its institutions as what, in fact, they are: victims of antisemitic prejudice. Jews are thus left to feel both endangered and excluded by a society who seems inclined to regard them not as fellow citizens and innocent victims of prejudice but as somehow responsible for their own sufferings.

This is particularly unfortunate, given the extent to which the media and other would-be molders of opinion in Western societies stand at present opposed to racism and—in principle at least—the exclusion or victimization by the matrix society of any minority group. These concerns are generous and sound. It is necessary to the health of a civilized society for all its citizens to be assured of full participation, without sectional exclusions or penalties, in all social and political institutions. But political antisemitism, like other forms of sectional prejudice, works not to create but to destroy that assurance. It works to damage, debauch, and delegitimate any consistent opposition to racism in any public institution it affects.

The fruits of that debauch have recently been making themselves evident in a number of ways. One of them is the steady shrinking of the Jewish community in France as more and more of its members decide that France is no longer a safe place for Jews. Another is the extraordinary climate of hostility to Jewish students and faculty being orchestrated in universities on both sides of the Atlantic at present. This is not only damaging to Jews; it is damaging to the idea of the university as—in Disraeli's terms—"a place of light, of liberty, and of learning." That is an idea that matters—or ought to matter—to all of us, Jew or non-Jew. I shall devote this chapter simply to documenting some of the ways in which the current threat posed to that ideal by supporters of Boycott, Divestment and Sanctions (BDS) and anti-Zionism reanimates those posed in the last century by Nazism and other forms of European fascism.[1] Chapter 15 will examine why it is that the growing atmosphere of hostility to Jews in political, media, and university circles in Western countries revealed by these events has proved so difficult to combat. Finally, in the concluding chapter, I shall consider a more fundamental threat, again to all of us, and not just to Jews, posed by political antisemitism in any of its forms: its power—noted by E. M. Forster among others—to derange the judgment of ostensibly rational people.

THE MANY FACES OF THE UNIVERSITY

For the most part, universities are still centers of Disraeli's light, liberty, and learning. But, of course, they are, and have always been, a good many other kinds of things as well. For a start, they are businesses focused on their own survival. Then again, they are, as Matthew Arnold reminded us, homes "of lost causes, and forsaken beliefs, and unpopular names, and impossible loyalties!"[2]—places, in short, where people go to lick their wounds and regroup. They also have a political life of their own, both student- and faculty-oriented in which parochial issues and divisions are fought out, often with surprising ferocity. And while the issues that animate campus politics, both student and faculty, often cut very little ice in the larger political world outside the campus, there is some overlap. Many graduates, when they leave university behind, leave behind campus politics, but others do not. For them, issues and attitudes learned in youth on campus become part of their adult political identity. That makes campus politics a fruitful recruiting ground for anyone from the larger political world with a message difficult to sell to an adult audience but easy to sell to a student one, some of whose members, at least, will then carry it on with them into adulthood.

If some of these political salesmen are peddling antisemitism, then we have reason to be concerned—and not just if we happen to be Jewish. The transformation of our universities into cultural battlefields in which campaigners with dubious political axes to grind strive not only to harass but also to demonize, silence, and exclude members of specific ethnic or religious groups is not a development that any of us in the wider society should welcome. These are places that our children, Jewish and non-Jewish, are going to find themselves inhabiting at an impressionable age. One would prefer the impressions and habits of mind they pick up there not to include blinkered, violent, and self-righteous hostility to minority groups.

At the same time, we should neither demand that the universities themselves deal with such issues without outside guidance nor imagine that they are fully capable of doing so. First, university administrations naturally value the smooth running of the institutions they govern. Hence, they can hardly not be committed, among other things, to keeping the lid on any disturbance that might arise from campus politics even if that involves turning a blind eye to the unsavory character of certain of its manifestations. Second, they tend to be committed to preserving the freedom and the finance necessary to the continuing conduct of significant research even if that again should turn out to involve accepting certain unpleasant political facts. Both impulses are visible in the following reminiscence of Peter Drucker, an Austrian economist, concerning a meeting of faculty he attended at the University of Frankfurt in 1933, to meet the university's first Nazi commissar. The arrival in power of the Nazi-led government that year had already been welcomed by many university professors and students, and many student fraternities and other student groups had already banned Jews. Here is Drucker on the meeting:

> The new Nazi commissar wasted no time on amenities. He immediately announced that Jews would be forbidden to enter university premises and would be dismissed without salary on March 15; this was something that nobody had thought possible despite the Nazis' loud antisemitism. Then he launched into a tirade of abuse, filth, and four-letter words such as had been heard rarely even in the barracks and never before in academia.... [He] pointed his finger at one department chairman after another and said, "You either do what I tell you or we'll put you into a concentration camp." There was a silence when he finished; everybody waited for the distinguished biochemist-physiologist. The great liberal got up, cleared his throat and said, "Very interesting, Mr. Commissar, and in some respects very illuminating: but one point I didn't get too clearly. Will there be more money for research in physiology?"
>
> The meeting broke up shortly thereafter with the commissar assuring the scholars that indeed there would be plenty of money for "racially pure science." A few of the professors had the courage to walk out with their Jewish colleagues, but most kept a safe distance from these who only a few hours earlier had been their close friends. I went out sick unto death—and I knew that I was going to leave Germany within forty-eight hours.[3]

HARASSING "ZIONISTS"

In chapter 10, I examined some of the stranger aspects of the hothouse climate of political opinion concerning Israel now current in universities on both sides of the Atlantic. We now have to consider whether Jewish students and faculty are not having to pay an altogether unreasonable price for the political rancor it engenders. There is abundant evidence that Jewish students and faculty in our universities are presently suffering kinds of antisemitic harassment not wholly different from those cataloged by Drucker: harassment for which they find it difficult or impossible to obtain redress. It runs the entire gamut from verbal abuse by way of threatening behavior to actual physical assault.[4] In October 2016, for instance, the London *Daily Telegraph* reported:

> Dozens of police officers were called to one of the country's top universities to quell a "violent" anti-Israel protest which left Jewish students barricaded in a room after being told their safety could not be guaranteed if they left alone.
>
> Attendees at University College London (UCL) were forced to remain in a lecture room after hearing a talk by Israeli activist Hen Mazzig, as they waited for police to escort them through the crowd of around 100 demonstrators who had gathered outside.
>
> Police are investigating after two female Jewish students reported that they were assaulted during the evening. One was knocked to the ground when protesters broke into the lecture room through a window and jumped in, while another was pushed against a door causing her to have a panic attack.
>
> Mazzig, a former IDF commander, had been invited to speak by UCL Friends of Israel about his humanitarian work in the West Bank, building medical facilities, schools, roads and water infrastructure.
>
> Craig Dillon, a recent graduate from Westminster University who attended the event said the protesters were aggressive, violent and threatening. "Protesters were outside chanting and banging on windows, coming close to breaking them," he said.
>
> Liora Cadranel, president of UCL Friends of Israel society, said that students were left "shaken" by the evening's events. "At the time, I and many others were concerned for our physical safety—we were also just in shock that an event like this all about bringing a better understanding and therefore future for Palestinians and Israelis alike, could be hijacked in such a manner," she said.[5]

Similar events had already taken place at King's College, London, on January 19, 2016:

> Kings College London (KCL) has announced it is undertaking an "urgent investigation" after the building had to be evacuated on Tuesday night when a pro-Israel talk turned violent, reportedly at the hands of a pro-Palestinian group.
>
> Esther Enfield, of the KCL Israel Society, had organised an event which played host to Ami Ayalon, former head of the Israeli secret service Shin Bet and commander-in-chief of the navy.
>
> Enfield issued a lengthy statement in the aftermath of the incident, which began: "Never did I ever think that I would have to write a post like this but, in life, sometimes you do things that you never expect."
>
> Describing how KCL is meant to be "one of the global universities in the world," she claimed to have been assaulted when demonstrators from the KCL Action Palestine (KCLAP) group stormed the event—attended by

more than 200 people—and began throwing chairs, smashing windows, and setting off the fire alarm more than 15 times.[6]

Social media also serve as a potent device for antisemitic harassment and denigration. Lesley Klaff, an academic lawyer at Sheffield Hallam University, writing in the *Jewish Political Studies Review*, tells the story of "Brian, a disabled student who identifies as Jewish," who submitted a complaint to the university concerning the social media activity of the student Palestine Society, a group affiliated with and approved by the student union. The university dismissed his complaint. A year later, however, it was upheld by the Office of the Independent Adjudicator for Higher Education, which ordered Sheffield Hallam to pay Brian £3,000 in compensation for failing to give the complaint proper consideration. The Facebook posts and tweets by the Palestine Society, about which Brian complained,

accused Israel and Israelis of genocide, deliberately killing Palestinian children, deliberately killing other Palestinian civilians, war crimes, atrocities, using chemical weapons, ethnic cleansing, inhumanity, cruelty, behaving like Nazis, sexual and other abuse of Palestinian children (including abduction and human trafficking), stealing Palestinian organs, being racists and fascists, and rejoicing in Palestinian deaths.... Brian complained that these posts contributed to "an intimidating campus climate" and that he felt "intimidated and afraid to mention Israel on campus or to wear my Star of David or my skull cap for fear of being picked on." He said that "they are based on lies and half-truth about Jews, invoking blood libel motifs, stereotypes and defamations on campus and online, creating a threatening mob mentality.[7]

Harassment and intimidation also figured large in the proceedings of the Oxford Labour Club, which came to light as a result of the resignation of its cochair Alex Chalmers. According to the report in the center-left British newspaper the *Guardian*,

Alex Chalmers' resignation statement was clear, emphasising that "A large proportion of both OULC and the student left in Oxford more generally have some kind of problem with Jews." The Oxford Jewish Society noted that "it was not the first time that it has had to deal with antisemitic incidents within the student left, and it will not be the last." The Labour MP John Mann, chair of the all-party parliamentary group against antisemitism, has called for the party to sever all ties with the club.

Following Chalmers' resignation, further allegations have appeared. Other OULC members, including past executive officers, approached Oxford

University Jewish Society with a list of antisemitic incidents they had recorded. One OULC member argued that Hamas was justified in its killing of Jewish civilians, and that all Jews were legitimate targets. A committee member stated that all Jews should be expected to publicly denounce Zionism and the state of Israel, and that we should not associate with any Jew who fails to do so. It has been alleged that another OULC member organised a group of students to harass a Jewish student and to shout "filthy Zionist" whenever they saw her.

This type of rhetoric is not confined to the OULC. Leftwing student leaders have rallied against "any Rothschild" and "Zios" in their Facebook statuses. One of Oxford's online political forums removed members with Jewish sounding surnames from the group. In another group, a member called for Jews to pack their bags and leave the Middle East. One notable far-left student politician said, "I don't like being smeared as antisemitic, but I don't bleed for it, either."[8]

The above cases offer merely illustrative examples of a problem that informed sources now assert to be widespread in UK universities. Baroness Ruth Deech is a distinguished British academic lawyer. She sits as a crossbench peer in the House of Lords. A former principal of St Anne's College, Oxford, she has served in a number of roles in British public life, including those of chair of the Human Fertilisation and Embryology Authority (1994–2002), chair of the Bar Standards Board (2009–15), and independent adjudicator for higher education (2004–8). In 2016, she felt it necessary to take a public stand on the harassment of Jewish students in British universities. The London *Daily Telegraph* reported her statement as follows:

> Some of Britain's leading universities are becoming no-go zones for Jewish students because anti-semitism is so rife, the first ever higher education adjudicator has warned.
>
> Baroness Ruth Deech, a cross-bench peer who formerly held the highest office dealing with student complaints, said that institutions may be failing to combat hatred against Jews as they are "afraid of offending" their potential benefactors from Gulf states.
>
> Her comments come after a series of high-profile incidents at top universities where Jewish students claim they were verbally abused or physically attacked. The academic community is in the forefront of calls to boycott Israel.
>
> In an interview with the *Daily Telegraph*, Baroness Deech said that the extreme levels of hostility to Israel at universities across the country can at times go so far as to equate to anti-Semitism.
>
> Many universities are in receipt of or are chasing very large donations from Saudi Arabia and the Gulf states and so on, and maybe they are frightened of offending them, she said. "I don't know why they aren't doing anything

about it, it really is a bad situation. . . . Amongst Jewish students there is gradually a feeling that there are certain universities that you should avoid," Baroness Deech said. "Definitely SOAS [School of African and Asian Studies, University of London], Manchester I think is now not so popular because of things that have happened there, Southampton, Exeter and so on."

Earlier this year students at Exeter were photographed wearing T-shirts displaying racist and anti-Semitic slogans at a sports club social event. Phrases photographed included: "Don't speak to me if you're not white," and "The Holocaust was a good time."[9]

Similar events have been, and are, widespread at university and college campuses across the United States. In October 2016, *Newsweek* carried a piece by Tammi Rossman Benjamin, then a faculty member in Hebrew and Jewish Studies at the University of California at Santa Cruz, protesting against the tendency of university administrators to "misidentify the harassment, intimidation, suppression of speech and ethnic discrimination of Jewish students" as "incivility," which she defines as "rude or unsociable speech and behavior" rather than as "intolerance," defined as "unwillingness to accept views, beliefs, or behavior that differ from one's own." She cites a pattern of events in relation to which the point seems entirely just.

When more than a dozen Jewish student events about Israel were violently disrupted at schools from coast to coast this year, including San Francisco State University, University of California Irvine and Davis, University of Maryland, Boston University, University of New Mexico, University of South Florida, University of Georgia, University of Chicago, Ohio University, UC Santa Barbara and University of Illinois, is it "incivility" or "intolerance"?

When Jewish students who attempt to express their opposition to anti-Israel boycott resolutions are viciously mocked, vilified and heckled during student government meetings at schools such as Vassar College, Ohio University, UC Santa Barbara and University of Illinois, is it "incivility" or "intolerance"?

When Jewish students are shunned from participating in student government, rejected from progressive social justice activities such as pro-choice rallies, anti-rape demonstrations, Black Lives Matter events and racial justice conferences and ostracised from areas of campus life because of their "Jewish agenda" or presumed support for Israel at schools such as Stanford University, San Diego State University, UCLA, UC Santa Cruz, Northwestern University, Brooklyn College and SUNY Albany—is it "incivility" or "intolerance"?[10]

In 2011, Rossman Benjamin and Leila Beckwith, the latter an emeritus professor in the Department of Medicine at UCLA, cofounded AMCHA Initiative

BLAMING THE JEWS

(from Hebrew "amcha," a term meaning "your people" but connoting ordinary people, the grassroots, or the masses), a nonprofit organization "dedicated to investigating, documenting, educating about and combating antisemitism at institutes of higher education in America." AMCHA's published list of "Categories of Antisemitic Activity" reads as follows:

PHYSICAL ASSAULT—Physically attacking Jewish students, or causing them to fear that they are about to suffer physical harm.

DISCRIMINATION—Unfairly treating individuals because they are Jewish.

DESTRUCTION OF JEWISH PROPERTY—inflicting damage or destroying property owned by Jews or related to Jews (eg. vandalising a menorah outside a Chabad house).

GENOCIDAL EXPRESSION—Using imagery (eg. swastika) or language that expresses a desire to, or will to, exterminate the Jewish people.

SUPPRESSION OF SPEECH/MOVEMENT/ASSEMBLY—Preventing or impeding the expression of Jewish students, such as by removing or defacing Jewish students' flyers, attempting to disrupt or shut down speakers at Jewish events, or blocking the entrance to a Jewish student event.

VERBAL ASSAULT—Verbally insulting or abusing Jewish students.

INTIMIDATION—Intentionally frightening Jewish students in order to force them into or deter them from some action.

HARASSMENT—Intentionally disturbing or upsetting Jewish students.

DENIGRATION—Unfairly disparaging, vilifying or defaming Jewish students.[11]

Since 2015, the organization has maintained a database of activity at US campuses falling under the above descriptions. It lists 469 incidents in 2015, 639 incidents in 2016, and 600 in 2017, at major campuses from coast to coast across the United States.

POLITICS, FREE SPEECH, AND RACISM

The level and kinds of harassment directed at Jewish students, on both sides of the Atlantic, on the one hand by anti-Zionist student groups organized by the BDS movement, on the other by alt-right or other extreme right-wing groups, is alarmingly reminiscent of the drive to demonize and exclude Jews in prewar Nazi Germany. This is particularly true of repeated attempts to exclude Jews from participation in student government and to harass, or close down entirely, Jewish student organizations on campus. AMCHA, for instance, records "the shutdown of a pro-Israel event by protesters at the University of California, Irvine, who entered the event and shouted loudly and continuously, explicitly stating to speakers, 'You people ... should not be allowed on this f***ing campus!' The event was effectively ruined, and attendees and speakers had to be escorted safely out by police."[12]

Given the nature of the behavior displayed in demonstrations of this kind, it is apt to seem surprising that university administrations, again on both sides of the Atlantic, find themselves regularly accused of doing little or nothing to put a stop to them. At the time of the Oxford Labour Club scandal in 2016, Baroness Deech expressed personal outrage and distress at the failure of the university authorities to embark upon a full inquiry. "Baroness Deech said she felt compelled to speak out about her concern at the way Oxford has handled the allegations of anti-Semitism, despite her strong attachment to the university. 'I find it personally very difficult. I've been at Oxford 45 years or something, and I owe my career to Oxford,' she said. 'But I can't believe that my own university is not setting up an investigation and being pro-active about this.'"

The same *Telegraph* article concludes with a series of responses to journalists' inquiries from the authorities of universities named in Baroness Deech's public stand on antisemitic harassment. They display bland bureaucratic self-protectiveness of the kind familiar to observers of state-supported institutions in Britain that aims to suggest that criticisms are misplaced while studiously avoiding addressing their actual substance.

A spokesman for Exeter university said it is "completely untrue" that it is not a welcoming place for Jewish students. "Anti-semitic and racist behaviour in any form is not tolerated by the university" the spokesman said.

Exeter has philanthropic supporters of many faiths, including Jewish, Christian and Muslim, the spokesman added.

A spokesman for Southampton University said they are "home to a supportive, friendly and inclusive community that welcomes staff, students, alumni, collaborators and visitors from a wide variety of backgrounds, including people of all faiths and none."

A spokesman for SOAS said the university "does not permit the expression of anti-Semitic or other views that are illegal or inspire racial hatred."

Manchester University could not be reached for comment.[13]

In the United States, university administrators have been somewhat more proactive in addressing the problem. In September 2015, the Regents of the University of California publicly acknowledged for the first time the necessity of addressing the problem of antisemitism on campus and announced the formation of a working committee to draft a new Statement of Principles against Intolerance addressing the issue. But it has to be said that they did so only "after hearing from dozens of students, faculty, alumni and Jewish groups yesterday at the meeting, and more than 3,000 University of California stakeholders over the past six months."[14] In fact, it had taken a prolonged campaign, vigorously fought and widely recorded in the press, a full account of which would require a chapter of its own. And it would be false to suggest that this success has created a radical change of climate for Jewish students.

No doubt Baroness Deech was right to suggest that the unwillingness of university administrations to address complaints of antisemitism on campus is at times connected with funding and endowment concerns. It doubtless also creates difficulties that BDS and anti-Zionist activity among student groups is often supported and encouraged both by individual faculty members and at times, for that matter, by entire departments that not only attract outside funding but contribute to the overall teaching and research effort of the university.

But that is still only part of the picture. There are other considerations quite as capable of darkening counsel, bedeviling committees, and inclining harassed university administrators to ignore the issue unless and until it degenerates into actual violence and then leave it to the police to sort it out. We shall look at these more closely in the next chapter.

NOTES

1. It will be impossible for me to give here more than a sampling of the facts concerning campus anti-Zionism. A full and richly informative account is to be found in Pessin and Ben-Atar 2018. On BDS activity, see also Nelson and Brahm 2015.

2. Arnold 1966, first series, preface.

3. Drucker 1994, 161–62.

4. For a very much fuller account of current harassment of Jews on US campuses, see Pessin and Ben-Atar 2018.

5. Camilla Turner, "Police Called to UCL over 'Violent' Anti-Israel Protest Which Left Jewish Students Barricaded in Room," *Daily Telegraph*, October 28, 2016, https://www.telegraph.co.uk/news/2016/10/28/police-called-to-top-university-over-violent-anti-israel-protest/.

6. Aftab Ali, "Kings College London Launches 'Urgent Investigation' after Pro-Israel Event Attacked by Pro-Palestinian Group," *Independent*, January 21, 2016, https://www.independent.co.uk/student/news/king-s-college-london -launches-urgent-investigation-after-pro-israel-event-attacked-by-pro-palestine -a6825116.html.

7. Lesley Klaff, "Contemporary Antisemitism on the UK University Campus: A Case Study and Context," *Jewish Political Studies Review* (Spring–Summer 2017): 19–25.

8. Aaron Simons, "It's Time We Acknowledged that Oxford's Student Left Is Institutionally Antisemitic," *Guardian*, February 18, 2016, https://www .theguardian.com/commentisfree/2016/feb/18/oxford-student-left-antisemitic -university-antisemitism-jewish-progressive-politics.

9. Camilla Turner, "Some of Britain's Top Universities Are Becoming No-Go Zones for Jews, Baroness Deech Claims," *Telegraph*, December 23, 2016, https:// www.telegraph.co.uk/education/2016/12/22/britains-top-universities-becoming -no-go-zones-jews-baroness/.

10. Tammi Rossman Benjamin, "Anti-Semitism on Campus Is Not Just Uncivil, It's Intolerant," *Newsweek*, September 28, 2016, https://www.newsweek .com/anti-semitism-campus-not-just-uncivil-its-intolerant-503491.

11. AMCHA website at https//amchainitiative.org.

12. "Protecting Freedom of Expression on Campus in the Face of Intolerant Behavior: A Conceptual Model for University Administrators." Available on the AMCHA website, www.AMCHAinitiative.org.

13. Turner, "Some of Britain's Top Universities Are Becoming No-Go Zones."

14. AMCHA Campaign Update, September 18, 2015.

FIFTEEN

—∭—

DEFAMATION DISGUISED

Thou shalt not bear false witness against thy neighbor.

—Exodus 20:13

OBSTACLES TO REDRESS

There are two main reasons why it is not easy for Jewish individuals or groups to obtain redress, or even to marshal much in the way of sympathy at any rate from official bodies, for the kinds of abuse cataloged in the preceding chapter. The first is the problem of saying precisely what legally specifiable offense the abusers are supposed to be committing other than (in a minority of cases) riot, public disorder, and attempting to suppress others' freedom of expression.

It would be natural at first sight to accuse them of racism. Unfortunately, the wording of present legislation on race relations, on both sides of the Atlantic, fails to support such an accusation. In the United States, the relevant legal instrument is Title VI of the Civil Rights Act of 1964. Title VI Section 601 reads: "No person in the United States shall, on the ground of race, color or national origin, be excluded from participation in, be denied the benefits of, or be subjected to discrimination under any program or activity receiving Federal financial assistance." In Britain, the relevant instrument is the Race Relations Act of 1965, which also outlaws discrimination in private businesses on grounds of "colour, race, or ethnic or national origins."

For those hoping to represent Boycott, Divestment and Sanctions (BDS)/"anti-Zionist" action or discourse as racist, the difficulty lies in the

412

terms of the phrase "race, color or national origin," or the only syntactically differing one in the British act. Jews were at one time, in the nineteenth and early twentieth century, considered in some circles to be "colored" but are now generally accepted to be white—unless they happen to be black or brown, as many non-Ashkenazi Jews of course are. Similarly, Jews are no longer often spoken of, at least in respectable circles, to constitute a race—any such suggestion being considered, no doubt justifiably, to carry Hitlerian overtones. And Jews certainly share no common national origin. Hence, one seems left with no category under which hostility to Jews and their causes could be classified as racist in character. It is true that in the United Kingdom, the Equality Act 2010 makes Jewish a "protected characteristic" in terms of both race and religion under section 26.[1] However, this recent legislation, as we shall see later in this chapter, has not proved easy to appeal to in practice.

IS *ANY* CRITICISM OF ISRAEL ANTISEMITIC?

The second, and possibly a more important, obstacle to obtaining redress or sympathy for harassment of Jews by opponents of Israel is the ease with which all such harassment can at present be passed off not as racial or ethnic hostility of any kind but rather as the expression of a purely *political* and therefore entirely legitimate opposition to the policies of Israel. Such responses find support in the present popularity, on the left or liberal left of Western politics, of the view that accusations of antisemitism against anti-Zionists or BDS supporters are not only without foundation but represent disingenuous attempts to silence all criticism of Israel: a claim heard so frequently from the maverick British hard-left politician and former mayor of London Ken Livingstone, as to have been baptized "the Livingstone formulation" by the British sociologist David Hirsh.[2]

In the real world, the debate divides otherwise. On the one hand stand those, including many Jews, who hold that while some criticisms of Israel indeed belong in the arena of legitimate critical debate, others display antisemitic prejudice. On the other stand those who find any such distinction bogus. According to them, *all criticism of Israel whatsoever* is political and deserves the legal protection that law in a free society accords to political discourse.

This second and more extreme view, far from being confined to the hard left and the BDS movement, presently commands wide support on both sides of the Atlantic from a much broader range of liberal-left opinion. In Britain, support for it extends even to senior members of the legal profession. The eminent

Court of Appeal judge Sir Stephen Sedley, for example, embraces it in an essay, "Defining Antisemitism," in the *London Review of Books*.

> Shorn of philosophical and political refinements, anti-Semitism is hostility towards Jews as Jews. Where it manifests itself in discriminatory acts or inflammatory speech it is generally illegal, lying beyond the bounds of freedom of speech and of action. By contrast, criticism (and equally defense) of Israel or of Zionism is not only generally lawful: it is affirmatively protected by law. Endeavours to conflate the two by characterising anything other than anodyne criticism of Israel as anti-Semitic are not new. What is new is the adoption by the UK government (and the Labour Party) of a definition of antisemitism which endorses the conflation.[3]

THE EUROPEAN MONITORING CENTRE ON RACISM AND XENOPHOBIA/INTERNATIONAL HOLOCAUST REMEMBRANCE ALLIANCE DEFINITION

The specific "conflation" with antisemitism of "anything other than anodyne criticism of Israel or of Zionism," to which Sir Stephen Sedley here objects, is that allegedly created by the acceptance in 2016, first by the British government and then, subject to certain reservations, by the British Labour Party, of the so-called International Holocaust Remembrance Alliance (IHRA) definition of antisemitism.

This document has a brief but complex and interesting history. It belongs to a family of proposed definitions of antisemitism, all of which derive from what has become known as the international working definition, or the European Monitoring Centre on Racism and Xenophobia (EUMC) definition of anti-semitism. This was originally published in January 2005 by the Fundamental Rights Agency (FRA) of the European Union (EU). It differed from the multitude of previous definitions, for the most part formulated by individual scholars and writers, by having emerged from lengthy discussion by teams of scholars, government officials, and representatives of community and civil rights organizations. No doubt because of this, the definition broke new ground in recognizing for the first time that antisemitism "could also target the State of Israel, conceived as a Jewish community."[4] This has since made it and all its subsequent versions intensely controversial.

In 2013, the FRA quietly removed the working definition from its website during a remodeling of the site. Under pressure from Jewish organizations, the FRA's spokesperson at the time, Blanca Tapia, dodged the issue, emphasizing that the working definition had never been sanctioned within the EU. Her statement maintained with questionable logic, and contrary to earlier declarations by the FRA of the urgent practical need for such a definition, that "the agency does not need to develop its own definition of anti-Semitism in order to research these issues."[5]

Despite this, the working definition has been enormously influential. Versions of it have been adopted by the US Department of State, the US Commission of Civil Rights, the Organization for Security and Co-operation in Europe, and other agencies. At its conference in Ottawa, November 7–9, 2010, the Inter-parliamentary Coalition for Combating Antisemitism, an international body composed of parliamentarians of many countries, urged universities to "use the EUMC Working Definition of Antisemitism as a basis for education, training and orientation."[6] In November 2016, Senators Bob Casey and Tim Scott introduced, and the Senate passed, the Anti-Semitism Awareness Act, a bipartisan bill aimed specifically at combating campus antisemitism. The bill's effective clauses are also based closely on the international working definition.

In summer 2016, a version of the international working definition was adopted by the Berlin-based IHRA. Later that same year, the British government announced its decision to formally adopt the definition in its IHRA version. According to a statement from the prime minister's office at the time, the intention of adopting the definition was to "ensure that culprits will not be able to get away with being antisemitic because the term is ill-defined, or because different organisations or bodies have different interpretations of it."[7]

All versions of the international definition share the same format. Each begins with a formula, essentially unchanged from the EUMC version, intended to establish the *nature* of antisemitism: to say *what antisemitism is*. In the IHRA version, this reads: "Antisemitism is a certain perception of Jews, which may be expressed as hatred toward Jews. Rhetorical and physical manifestations of antisemitism are directed toward Jewish or non-Jewish individuals and/or their property, toward Jewish community institutions and religious facilities."

The importance attached to the above statement is often indicated by enclosing it on the page in a printed box. This is followed by a brief further elucidation of the above and by a series of "examples" that, it is proposed, "may serve as illustrations." The further elucidation reads:

> Manifestations might include the targeting of the state of Israel conceived as a Jewish collectivity. However, criticism of Israel similar to that levelled against any other country cannot be regarded as antisemitic. Antisemitism frequently charges Jews with conspiring to harm humanity, and it is often used to blame Jews for "why things go wrong." It is expressed in speech, writing, visual forms and action, and employs sinister stereotypes and

negative character traits. Contemporary examples of antisemitism in public life, the media, schools, the workplace and in the religious sphere could, taking into account the overall context, include, but are not limited to ...

The list of "contemporary examples" then follows. It includes the following (numbers added):

1. Calling for, aiding, or justifying the killing or harming of Jews in the name of a radical ideology, or an extremist view of religion.
2. Making mendacious, dehumanising, demonizing, or stereotypical allegations about Jews as such, or the power of Jews as a collective—such as, especially but not exclusively, the myth about a world Jewish conspiracy or of Jews controlling the media, economy, government or other societal institutions.
3. Accusing Jews as a people of being responsible for real or imagined wrongdoing committed by a single Jewish person or group, or even for acts committed by non-Jews.
4. Denying the fact, scope, mechanisms (e.g., gas chambers) or intentionality of the genocide of the Jewish people at the hands of national socialist Germany and its supporters and accomplices during World War II (the Holocaust).
5. Accusing the Jews as a people, or Israel as a state, of inventing or exaggerating the Holocaust.
6. Accusing Jewish citizens of being more loyal to Israel, or to the alleged priorities of Jews worldwide, than to the interests of their own nations.
7. Denying the Jewish people their right to self-determination, e.g., by claiming that the existence of a state of Israel is a racist endeavour.
8. Applying double standards by requiring of it [Israel] a behavior not expected or demanded of any other democratic nation.
9. Using the symbols and images associated with classical antisemitism (e.g., claims of Jews killing Jesus or blood libel) to characterise Israel or Israelis.
10. Drawing comparisons of contemporary Israeli policy to that of the Nazis.
11. Holding Jews collectively responsible for actions of the state of Israel.

The definition plainly singles out as prima facie antisemitic several types of claim (e.g., 2, 6, 7, 10, 11) that, as we have seen in earlier chapters, make regular appearances in propaganda, demonstrations, and campaigns conducted in universities and elsewhere by agencies, including the BDS movement, opposed to Zionism. It is mainly these clauses that have made the definition politically controversial.

THE IHRA DEFINITION IN RECENT BRITISH POLITICS

Between 2016 and 2018, a series of political scandals erupted in Britain over alleged institutional antisemitism in the Labour Party, the main political organization of the left. This began with the row in the Oxford University Labour Club covered in the previous chapter but soon widened to include, among other things, virulent social media attacks, including death threats, by Labour activists on Labour Members of Parliament (MPs) of Jewish descent. As one result of this, the Jewish (Labour) MP Luciana Berger was forced by threats of this kind from "activists" on social media to request police protection at the Labour Party Conference in 2018.

These events produced intense political and media pressure on the Labour Party to follow the lead of the Conservative government of the day by adopting the IHRA definition. In July 2018, after much public criticism, Labour's National Executive Committee (NEC) did finally endorse the IHRA definition. However, its endorsement excluded several of the examples, notably the following: accusing Jewish people of being more loyal to Israel than to their home country, claiming that Israel's existence as a state is a racist endeavor, and likening Israeli politics to those of the Nazis. In September, the NEC revisited the issue and, this time, accepted the IHRA definition in full but with a caveat asserting the need to preserve free speech on controversial issues to do with the Israel-Palestine conflict.

LEGAL CRITICISM OF THE IHRA DEFINITION

In 2016, the year before the *London Review of Books* published Sir Stephen Sedley's article pouring cold water on the IHRA definition, various interested organizations,[8] concerned about the impact the definition might have in the future on the conduct of public authorities, had sought legal advice of their own. They requested opinions from two senior lawyers specializing in human rights legislation: Hugh Tomlinson, QC,[9] of Matrix Chambers in Geneva and Gray's Inn, London, and Geoffrey Robertson, QC, founder and joint head of Doughty Street Chambers, London. The texts of both opinions are available in full on the internet.[10]

Both opinions stress the obscurity and imprecision of the opening formula of the IHRA definition. Tomlinson finds the language of the definition "vague and unclear"[11] in ways that make it "very difficult to use as a 'tool.'"[12] These problems of language come to a head in the definition's fundamental character-ization of the *nature* of antisemitism, as *"a certain perception of Jews, which may be expressed as hatred towards Jews."* The word *may*, he suggests, is confusing, since if understood in its usual sense of possibility, it suggests that while it is *possible* that the "perception of Jews" that supposedly constitutes antisemitism may be expressed as hatred of Jews, it is also *possible* that it may be expressed in other ways that the IHRA definition leaves entirely unspecified.[13]

The very least that is needed to clarify matters, Tomlinson continues, is to reformulate the first sentence to read: *Antisemitism is a particular attitude towards Jews, which is expressed as hatred toward Jews.*[14]

But even thus amended, Tomlinson argues, the definition remains obviously unsatisfactory in general terms. "The apparent confining of antisemitism to an attitude which is 'expressed' as a hatred of Jews seems too narrow and not to capture conduct which, though not *expressed* as hatred of Jews is clearly a manifestation of antisemitism. It does not, for instance, include discrimina-tory social and institutional practices."[15] This last point is echoed by Robert-son, who points out that hatred is a "very strong word . . . [that] . . . falls short of capturing those who express only hostility or prejudice, or who practise discrimination."[16]

"I don't like Jews and never employ them, but I don't hate them."—this speaker is anti-Semitic, but it does not seem included in this definition. Similarly, "I am prejudiced against Jews because they are not 'one of us' and their religious practices are ridiculous, but I don't hate them." Or "I think we should deport all Jews to Israel, because they would be happy there. It would be in their own interests—I certainly don't hate them, I just think they don't fit in here in England." Under the IHRA definition, these anti-Semitic comments would not be deemed "anti-Semitic." This consideration, above all others, convinces me that the definition is not fit for purpose, or any purpose that relies upon it to identify anti-Semitism accurately.[17]

According to both Tomlinson and Robertson, the obscurity of the opening clauses of the IHRA definition extends to the identification *as antisemitic* of at least some of the eleven examples offered—not, it must be said, to all eleven. Robertson finds examples 1, 3, 4, 5, 9, and 11 "unexceptionable,"[18] or virtually so, as offering instances of antisemitism. But as far as the remaining five examples are concerned, including all those explicitly mentioning Israel, Robertson's view is that while conduct covered by any of them could amount to antisemitism, it need not necessarily do so.

Tomlinson, similarly, argues that a number of types of act widely criticized as antisemitic could not be properly described as antisemitic *by the criteria established by the international definition.* He gives it as his opinion[19] that if a university or public authority were to ban an event on such grounds, justifying it by appeal to the IHRA definition but without providing such further evidence, the ban would be unlawful. The examples he suggests[20] include the following:

- Describing Israel as a state enacting policies of apartheid
- Describing Israel as a state practicing settler colonialism
- Describing the establishment of the State of Israel, and the actions associated with its establishment, as illegal or illegitimate
- Campaigning for policies of boycott divestment or sanctions against Israel, Israeli companies or international companies complicit in violation of Palestinian human rights (unless the campaigner was also calling for similar actions against other states)
- Stating that the State of Israel and its defenders "use" the Holocaust to chill debate on Israel's own behavior toward Palestinians

The chief difficulty identified by Tomlinson as obstructing appeals to the IHRA definition to justify describing this or that kind of conduct as antisemitic is that the initial identification of antisemitism *as a form of hatred* necessarily constrains the legal interpretation of the examples offered in the remainder of the definition. "These examples must be read in the light of the definition itself and cannot either expand or restrict its scope. All of them must be regarded as examples of activity which can properly be regarded as manifesting 'hatred toward Jews.'"[21]

Thus, an accusation of the type cited in example 6—that Jews are more loyal to Israel than to their nation of citizenship—could be classed as antisemitic according to the terms of the definition only if it could be shown to be motivated by hatred of Jews in general. If motivated by a reasonable belief that the actions of a particular Jewish citizen or group had indicated such a shift of loyalties, then the accusation would not be antisemitic.[22]

Robertson makes essentially the same point: "It must be said that all eleven examples are of conduct that 'could' amount to anti-semitism, so long as the core definition is applied, namely that they express hatred toward Jewish people as a race.... If the extended definition (i.e. core definition plus examples) were ever put into a law, a court would doubtless find that the core definition must control each example."[23] Hence, he argues, it cannot be established by appeal to the IHRA definition that, in the words of example 10, "drawing comparisons of contemporary Israeli policy to that of the Nazis" is necessarily antisemitic.

> It will usually be an exaggeration, or else inappropriate, and will inevitably give offense to many Jewish people, but that does not make it anti-Semitic unless the Nazi comparison was intended to show contempt for Jews in general. In the early years of Hitler governance, Nazi anti-Semitic policy took the form of discrimination which made it more difficult for Jews to find employment or enter the professions: it would not be anti-Semitic to liken current Israeli policy to these measures (however inappropriately) unless it displays hatred to all Jews or the intention was to manifest hostility to all Jews, and not just the present Government.[24]

In addition to concluding, for all the above reasons, that obscurities of drafting and related shortcomings render the IHRA definition virtually useless as a legal instrument, both lawyers nevertheless join Sedley in arguing that the adoption of the definition by government, and by such nongovernmental institutions as universities, trade unions, and political parties, poses a grave threat to freedom of speech. Robertson usefully defines the present state of the law on these matters as follows:

> Anti-Semitic utterances, unless intended or likely to foment hatred against Jewish people, do not amount to an offence under English law. But this discreditable and indeed contemptible behaviour may result in disciplinary action, expulsion from organizations, and a loss of the right to practise certain employments or professions. To accuse someone wrongly of anti-Semitism is defamatory and would incur damages in a civil action.
>
> The position taken by British law differs from that in certain European countries with historic experience of Nazi repression, which have stricter laws against racism and genocide denial. Even so, all European countries are subject to the Convention, Article 10 of which lays down:
>
> "Everyone has the right to freedom of expression. This right shall include freedom to hold opinions and to retrieve and impart information and ideas without interference by public authority and regardless of frontiers."
>
> This principle may only be overborne a) by a precise law, which is b) necessary in a democratic society either in the interests of national security, the prevention of disorder or the protection of the reputation and rights of others, and c) counts as a proportionate measure to achieve these legitimate aims. But the need for restrictions must be established convincingly and they must be "clear, certain and predictable"—i.e. formulated with sufficient precision to enable citizens to regulate their conduct. The European Court of

Human Rights has also held that they must be a proportionate response to a pressing social need. The right may be availed of by those whose utterances "offend, shock or disturb." The scope for criticism of states and statesmen is wider than for private individuals because of the need for free and open discussion of politics.[25]

The problem created by widespread governmental and nongovernmental adoption of the IHRA definition, as Robertson sees it, is that the costs of invoking Article 10 in defense of freedom of speech may be such as to render such a defense nugatory.

While it is true that the European convention protects free speech, that is a protection offered by the courts in what is termed judicial review of the actions of public authorities. Like all cases that end in court, this can be very expensive even if you win—costs cover only part of your legal expenses. For cash-strapped nongovernmental organizations and student organizations, this is obviously a deterrent when faced with threats of legal action that require an expensive legal defense to protect their fundamental right to criticize Israel when it is unjustifiably limited by the application of the application of the IHRA definition and its examples.[26]

KINDS OF ANTISEMITISM

Tomlinson's and Robertson's opinions on the legal merits of the IHRA definition both tend to support Sir Stephen Sedley's main contention: that the adoption of the IHRA definition by governmental and nongovernmental bodies is to be regretted on the ground that it "endorses the conflation" of criticism of Israel with antisemitism. Of the two possibilities before us—that is to say, that some criticism of Israel is antisemitic and some not, or that no criticism of Israel whatsoever is antisemitic—all three tend to support the second and more extreme option.

All three arguments, however, depend for their force on a certain interpretation of the *nature* of antisemitism: of what one supposes "being an antisemite" to *consist of.* All three legal critics in effect share the interpretation advanced in the opening sentence of Sir Stephen Sedley's *London Review of Books* essay: "Shorn of philosophical and political refinements, antisemitism is hostility towards Jews as Jews."

If one accepts this thumbnail definition as adequate, then it follows necessarily that no criticism of Israel or Zionism can be antisemitic unless it can be shown to express, or to be motivated by, not merely hostility to the State of Israel, or to its government, or to its founding beliefs, *but also hostility to individual Jews in general as Jews.* And it appears, at least, as if any such imputation can be avoided simply by formally disowning it: by distinguishing one's own, legitimate (because purely political) hostility to Israel or Zionism, from the undoubted antisemitism of someone who, holding similar views about either, makes those views an excuse for attacking, physically or otherwise, individual Jews "as Jews."

This is the central point, also, that animates both Tomlinson's and Robertson's opinions. They take the opening clauses of the IHRA definition to specify the nature of antisemitism as hatred towards Jews, and argue, reasonably enough, that on such an account political opposition to Israel or Zionism can hardly be construed as antisemitic unless for some reason it can also be shown to involve hatred of Jews in general.

So far so good, then—both for our legal critics and for the BDS movement— *provided Sedley's thumbnail definition is both sound and exhaustive.* But is it? A definition of a general term, such as *antisemitism*, is sound if it identifies a kind of thing justly describable by that term. It is exhaustive if it identifies the *only* kind of thing justly describable by that term. No doubt Sedley's definition is sound: one of the kinds of thing we use the term *antisemitism* to describe is indeed a certain kind of mental state or disposition—one consisting in settled hostility to Jews as Jews.

But is Sedley's definition exhaustive? Are there perhaps other sorts of entity, not mental states or emotional dispositions, but quite other kinds of thing, that the term *antisemitism* may *also* justly be held to describe or designate?

Here, the plot thickens. For there exists, as I have argued throughout the foregoing chapters, just such an entity. The word *antisemitism* has been used indifferently since its invention by the German agitator and publicist Wilhelm Marr (1819–1904) to designate two quite different kinds of thing. One is indeed an emotional disposition: one consisting in hostility to individual Jews as Jews. The other is a body of pseudo-explanatory theory concerning the Jewish community considered as a supposedly coherently organized and unified political force, "the Jews," and the supposedly crucial role holders of the theory imagine this force to play in the direction of world affairs.

The main lines of the theory, as we saw in earlier chapters, are familiar enough. The Jews are an alien people with a profoundly particularist religion that attaches supreme cosmic significance to the welfare of Jews and none at all to that of non-Jews. Jews are gifted with immense financial acumen and conspiratorially organized in ways that allow them to employ that acumen to hollow out and seize control over a multitude of non-Jewish organizations— among them, in antisemitic imaginings, the banks, Hollywood, the US State

Department, and the US presidency. These organizations, although they may continue to appear to the trusting and simple-minded non-Jewish in character and goals, have actually been perverted, the theory maintains, to serve the purposes of the Jewish conspiracy. Those purposes are profoundly evil and utterly destructive to the peace and welfare of the non-Jewish world. Jews have been single-handedly responsible for all the wars, revolutions, and economic crises that the non-Jewish world has suffered for centuries. It follows—so the theory teaches—that if only the Jews could be got rid of, non-Jewish life would immediately return to the permanent state of peace, order, and economic success to which the evident virtues of non-Jews plainly entitle them.

I have called this theory "political antisemitism" to distinguish it from what I have called social antisemitism, which is not a *theory* of any kind but rather a state of mind: Sedley's "hostility to Jews as Jews." Political antisemitism, as we have seen, has an emotional tone of its own, but it is a different emotional tone from that of social antisemitism. Social antisemitism feeds on personal dislike and contempt for individual Jews but seldom involves *fear* of Jews as a group. Natural self-regard, after all, disinclines us to *fear* those we regard as grossly inferior to ourselves. Political antisemitism, on the other hand, feeds precisely on fear, not to say panic: fear of the hidden threat constituted by the arcane financial and conspiratorial power wielded by Jews considered not as a mere collection of unpleasant and contemptible individuals but as a supposedly collectively organized force in world affairs. Sartre, as we saw earlier, writing in *Antisemite and Jew* of the antisemitism of the French writer Louis-Ferdinand Céline, nicely captures this brooding sense of imminent peril. "Antisemitism is . . . a form of Manichaeism. It explains the course of the world by the struggle of the Principle of Good with the Principle of Evil. . . . Look at Céline: his vision of the universe in catastrophic. The Jew is everywhere, the earth is lost, it is up to the Aryan not to compromise, never to make peace."

That the Nazis both accepted and vigorously disseminated the main doctrines of political antisemitism, as summarized above, can easily be verified from the Nazi propaganda sheet *Der Stürmer*. No doubt, to the Nazi sympathizers who formed the main readership of *Der Stürmer*, what it offered was not propaganda but rather a fair and timely exposé of the dangers facing Germany from the imagined power of international Jewry. We, enjoying the gift of hindsight, can see that they were wrong. Political antisemitism is a fantasy. The Jews are a small people, deeply divided in both political and religious terms. There neither is nor could be any such thing as the vast, organized Jewish conspiracy imagined by the political antisemite. Jewish influence over world affairs was and is minimal. The absence of the Jews, though it might well diminish the

BLAMING THE JEWS

splendors and pleasures of the non-Jewish world, would make no difference whatsoever to its miseries.

Nevertheless, the leading doctrines of political antisemitism were widely believed. And the wide belief they enjoyed proved fatal to the vast majority of European Jews. Political antisemitism, in other words, is potentially lethal in ways in which a merely social antisemitism is not. One does not go to the expense and trouble of liquidating very large numbers of people because one happens to dislike and despise them. One does it because one fears them. The growth of political antisemitism in Europe from the late nineteenth century onward gradually fixed in many simple people's minds the insane idea that their Jewish neighbors belonged secretly to a worldwide conspiracy whose activities threatened everything that they, the simple people, believed in. Without the spread of such mass delusions, not solely the work of the Nazis but industriously encouraged by them, it is difficult to see how the Holocaust could have taken place.

WHAT KIND OF CRIME?

It seems not unreasonable, therefore, to describe as criminal the deliberate elaboration and dissemination of such delusions. But what sort of crime is involved? Is it an instance of what we have come to call hate crime? According to the website of the (British) Citizens Advice Service, "Hate incidents and hate crime [sic] are acts of violence or hostility directed at people because of who they are or who someone thinks they are."

The trouble with this is that the political antisemite in search of converts to his view may be too smooth a character to offer "acts of violence or hostility" to any individual. Such acts may even be foreign to his nature. His purpose is not to abuse or affront anyone but simply to awaken his fellow citizens to the alarming nature of the threat he and they face from the activities of the Jewish conspiracy. Hence, though belief in the doctrines of political antisemitism may be plentifully productive of hate crimes, it is difficult to see how the mere defense and encouragement of such beliefs could reasonably be construed as *itself* constituting a hate crime.

If the dissemination of political antisemitism cannot, or cannot necessarily, be construed as a hate crime, does it then follow that it must be construed as a political act deserving the protection that the commitment of British and US law to freedom of speech affords to political discourse in general? Again, not necessarily. Both common and statute law limit freedom of speech in the case of defamation. Consulting the internet, one finds the following brief guide to the tort of defamation, which a senior legal friend assures me is entirely accurate:

Defamation occurs when there is a publication to a third party of words or matters containing an untrue imputation against the reputation of individuals, companies or firms which serve to undermine such reputation in the eyes of right thinking members of society generally, by exposing the victim to hatred, contempt or ridicule.

The tort of defamation acts to redress unjustified injury to the claimant's reputation and can be divided into two areas, slander and libel. Slander is the publication of defamatory words or actions in a temporary form, for example by spoken word. Libel is the publication of defamatory materials in permanent form.

Political antisemitism is plainly a tissue of defamatory falsehoods. Its dissemination, whether as slander or libel, plainly exposes an entire community not only to hatred and contempt but also to personal attack from those who take it seriously. A clear line separates it, as collective defamation, from rational political discourse deserving the protection of legislation guaranteeing freedom of speech.

It has become conventional to assume that political antisemitism, as sketched above, was a delusion confined to the Nazi Party: one that for that reason became briefly significant in the '30s and '40s of the last century but that has since ceased to play any important role in world affairs. That comforting illusion can be dispelled in many ways: for example, by close attention to the speeches of Mahmoud Ahmedinejad, president of Iran (2005–13). But it is more or less true that until quite recently, political antisemitism, with the exception of certain tiny groups on the extreme right and left of politics and a certain number of writers and intellectuals, played very little part in British life. For the most part, British antisemitism has generally taken the form of social antisemitism: hostility to Jews as Jews.

Of late years, that has changed. Since 1967 and the Six Day War that left in Israeli hands what was then Jordanian territory but has since been known as the Occupied Territories, or the West Bank, hostility to Israel has, as we noted in earlier chapters, become a defining characteristic of left-wing opinion across the West. Given the nature of left-wing politics, any issue important to the left tends to take on the status of a moral crusade. A further incentive to moralize the question of Israel stems from the wide appeal, to many and perhaps most sections of the Western left, of the proposition that Israel is in some sense an illegitimate state, one that should never have been allowed to come into existence. Much evidence suggests that those who favor that view would not find any difficulty in welcoming the existence of a state within the same borders as Israel, provided it were one possessing an Arab-majority, and presumably also

Muslim-majority, population and government. What is supposedly illegitimate about Israel therefore comes down to the fact that it is a Jewish-majority state.

Some plausible backing must plainly be found for the claim that the continued existence of Jewish majority rule in Israel is morally intolerable. Matters here are complicated by the fact that Israel is the only state in the world whose right to exist as a state is seriously questioned by a substantial body of opinion. Hence, it will not do merely to claim that whatever crimes are alleged of Israel be grave ones. What is required is that they be worse—much worse—than those of any of the many states whose legitimacy is never called into question by the Western left or for that matter by anybody else.

This proposal, as we have seen, numbers among its supporters some distinguished academics in literary studies. Jacqueline Rose, for instance, professor of English at Queen Mary College, University of London, catches the general spirit of this line of anti-Zionist rhetoric on pages 115–16 of her 2005 *The Question of Zion* (Princeton University Press): "How did one of the most persecuted peoples of the world come to embody some of the worst cruelties of the modern nation-state?" But the dedicatee of Rose's book, the late Edward Said, had already upped the ante still further—indeed, to the limit—in an interview published in 1989 in the journal *Critical Inquiry*, describing Israel's occupation of the West Bank and (at that time) of Gaza, as "in severity and outright cruelty more than rivaling any other military occupations in modern history."

"Modern history" and "the modern nation-state," however, offer, as we have seen, panoramas of tyranny and cruelty wide enough to render difficult any rational defense of claims as global as this concerning one small state in the Middle East. Much is made of the civilian losses entailed by the repeated small wars, none lasting more than a few days or weeks, in which Israel has been required to engage in in order to defend itself from attack in Gaza, Lebanon, and elsewhere. But, as we have seen, nothing of this nature of which Israel can plausibly be accused comes anywhere near approaching, let alone exceeding, the levels of atrocity attributable to other actors in the very much vaster, more enduring and more savage conflicts—the Iran-Iraq War, the first and second Iraq Wars, the Syrian Civil War, and now the war in Yemen—that have consumed the entire region with increasing frequency since the abrogation by Iraq in 1980 of the Algiers Accord.

No doubt because of this, what one might call the thesis of the *moral exceptionalism* of Israel is never advanced on the back of factually detailed comparisons with the conduct of other states in the region, let alone with the broader perspectives offered by the modern nation-state or modern history in general. Rather, it is advanced by means of the constant repetition, in political literature and speeches, along with the text and iconography of banners carried at demonstrations, of a small set of essentially formulaic accusations associating Israel with things widely accepted, across broad swathes of left-wing opinion, as constituting the depths of human depravity. Thus, for example, as we have noted at length earlier, Israel is accused of being a Nazi state, an apartheid state, a racist state, and (both in its origin and in its present conduct) a colonial settler state.

Considered as a candidate for any of these descriptions, as I have argued in detail in chapters 6–8, Israel falls at the first hurdle. Israel is not a Nazi state because its government (unlike that of the late Saddam Hussein in Iraq, for instance, or for that matter that of Bashar al-Assad in Syria) is not in the hands of a single political party obedient to an inspired leader and committed to enforcing policies in broad alignment with those of the former Nationalsozialistische Deutsche Arbeiterpartei. It is not an apartheid state because it altogether lacks the legal and social apparatus of racial separation that characterized the apartheid regime in South Africa. It is not a racist state because its Jewish population embraces Jews of all racial origins and colors, and for that matter because its citizens are only about 70 percent Jewish, the remainder being Arab, both Muslim and Christian, Druse, Circassian, and others. There are Arab Israeli members of the Knesset and Arab ministers of government. Many Druse, some Christian Arabs, and a few Muslims choose to serve in the Israel Defense Forces. It is not a colonial settler state because it did not come into being as a result of any European project of colonialism but as the result of the Jewish population of Palestine establishing its right to political autonomy in the face of an attempt, from which the European powers stood aloof, to exterminate it or drive it from the land by military force.

These accusations, in short, make no contribution to serious political debate. Rather, they are sonorous but empty phrases, good only for hurling at demonstrations or the rowdier kind of meeting. They are also defamatory in the strict legal sense of falsehoods calculated to undermine the reputation of the victim and to expose him or her to hatred and contempt.

But might one not argue that even if such accusations are, strictly speaking, defamatory, those defamed by them are not *Jews as such* but rather *supporters of Israel*, be they Jewish or non-Jewish? Sadly, the forensic plausibility of this objection greatly exceeds its contact with reality. Polls show in the United States a large proportion of evangelical Christians and Republicans, as well as a smaller proportion of Democrats, and in the United Kingdom a large proportion of Conservative voters as well as smaller numbers of Labour and Liberal Democrat voters to be supportive of Israel. Hence, very possibly, the numbers of pro-Israel non-Jews may greatly exceed those of pro-Israel Jews. Furthermore,

on both sides of the Atlantic, a certain stratum of Jewish opinion is hostile to
Israel, even to the extent of sympathizing with BDS.

Possibly, these facts are not widely understood. In any event, their influence on public opinion seems slight. Israel is generally, and more particularly
on the left, perceived as a Jewish enterprise, enjoying overseas support virtually exclusively from Jews. To those who perceive supporting Israel as to all
intents and purposes equivalent to supporting Nazism, racism, colonialism,
and apartheid, those whom they see as manifesting this strikingly unpleasant
combination of commitments are virtually exclusively Jews! When, in 2016,
Alex Chalmers, the cochair of the Oxford University Labour Club (OULC, the
largest student Labour group in the country) resigned, he did so because according to his widely published statement, both OULC and a large proportion
of the student left "have some kind of problem with Jews." Not, that is to say,
with "supporters of Israel" but with Jews viewed as intrinsically in league—as
Jews—with the evils that wide sections of the left perceive Israel as representing and promoting.

In effect, we have here a recrudescence of the central thesis of political antisemitism: that the goals pursued by "the Jews" are profoundly evil and destructive ones. When to this one adds to this three other claims that presently
attract support not only on the remoter tracts of left-wing opinion but on the
liberal left in general—

- that the Israel lobby in the United States is so strong and so
  well supported by Jewish money that American political
  institutions, including the State Department and the Oval
  Office, are powerless against it (in other words, that a Jewish
  conspiracy actually exists);
- that the existence of Israel represents a permanent threat to
  world peace (in other words, that a new world war, if it were to
  occur, would be, like all wars, the fault of the Jews); and
- that the existence of Jewish political autonomy in Israel
  represents the only serious obstacle to a peaceful settlement of
  the Israeli-Palestinian conflict that would protect the rights of
  all participants, including Jews (in other words, that if it were
  not for the obstinacy of the Jews in their eternally particularist
  pursuit of their sectional interests, there would have been no
  problem in the first place)

—there seems, as we argued at length earlier, little option but to conclude that
we are witnessing a recrudescence of a version of political (i.e., theoretical,

pseudo-intellectual) antisemitism that differs little in its main theses from the version disseminated by the Nazis. The new version represents itself, it is true, as directed not against Jews *as such* but rather against the existence and the legitimacy of *the Jewish state*. And in this way, it is thought to allow its supporters to claim that they are not *antisemites*, at least in the sense identified by Sir Stephen Sedley, of persons animated by "hostility to Jews as Jews."

Three things, however, as we have seen, obstruct the passage of this disclaimer. First, given that Israel is in fact supported by many Jews and is in any case widely believed to be supported by most Jews, one cannot, in both spoken and written material of a defamatory character, identify support for Israel with support for Nazism, racism, colonialism, and war without publicly defaming at least a great many Jews who in fact support Israel and defaming them for supporting a cause widely publicly believed to be dear to the hearts of all Jews! Hence, someone who is an antisemite in the second of the two senses we have distinguished here—someone accustomed to circulate defamatory falsehoods concerning Jews—can hardly avoid *also* being an antisemite in the first sense—Sedley's sense—of being someone hostile to Jews *as Jews* (that is to say, hostile to Jews on grounds either actually or widely believed to be intrinsic to their nature *as Jews*).

Second, political activity, some of it threatening or actually violent, on the part of student groups and others politically hostile to Israel, tends in fact, as we saw in the previous chapter, to target Jewish rather than non-Jewish supporters of Israel. This was evident enough in the barrage of abuse on social media, death threats, and so on endured at the height of the recent controversy over antisemitism in the Labour Party by various Jewish Labour MPs. It was, for instance, the Jewish MP Luciana Berger, mentioned earlier, who was forced by threats of this kind from "activists" on social media to request police protection at the Labour Party Conference in 2018. Not one of the many non-Jewish members of Labour Friends of Israel was given reason of that kind to seek similar protection.

Third, if what we are dealing with is *political* antisemitism, antisemitism as a type of pseudo-explanatory theory, then to establish that this or that act, speech, pamphlet, or tweet is antisemitic *in that sense*, it is quite unnecessary to inquire into the motives, or more generally the mental states, of the actor or writer (to inquire, for example, whether his/her acts were motivated by a private and inner hostility to Jews as Jews). All that need be established, as in any case of slander or libel, is that the matter concerned involved the circulation of falsehoods likely to be publicly understood, if believed, as defamatory, and that the falsehoods in question were specifically defamatory to Jews as Jews.

FREE SPEECH AND THE IHRA DEFINITION

Where do the above arguments leave the "controversial" examples offered by
the IHRA definition: those, that is to say, that in one way or another equate
certain kinds of criticism of Israel with antisemitism? The position of our three
legal critics is, first, that no criticism of Israel can be antisemitic unless it derives
from or explicitly expresses a felt hostility to Jews as Jews on the part of the
critic, and second, that to brand any criticism whatsoever of Israel as antisemitic cannot but pose a grave threat to freedom of speech. We have seen that,
and why, the first of these claims is without foundation. What about the second?

The six examples listed by the IHRA definition that in one way or another
allude to features of current political debate concerning Israel read as follows:

> 2. Making mendacious, dehumanising, demonizing, or stereotypical
> allegations about Jews as such, or the power of Jews as collective—such as,
> especially but not exclusively, the myth about a world Jewish conspiracy
> or of Jews controlling the media, economy, government or other societal
> institutions.

> 6. Accusing Jewish citizens of being more loyal to Israel, or to the alleged
> priorities of Jews worldwide, than to the interests of their own nations.

> 7. Denying the Jewish people their right to self-determination, e.g., by
> claiming that the existence of a state of Israel is a racist endeavour.

> 8. Applying double standards by requiring of it [Israel] a behavior not
> expected or demanded of any other democratic nation.

> 10. Drawing comparisons of contemporary Israeli policy to that of the Nazis.

> 11. Holding Jews collectively responsible for actions of the state of Israel.

Evidently, these examples are far from disallowing all but anodyne criticism
of Israel, let alone criticism of Israel per se. The list of things they identify as
prima facie antisemitic is in fact a very short one: denying the right of the Jewish
people to exercise political autonomy; describing Israel as an essentially racist
or Nazi state; asserting the existence of a Jewish conspiracy; asserting support
for Israel on the part of non-Israeli Jews to argue disloyalty to their actual nations of citizenship; and finally, the singling out of Israel for condemnation in
respect of conduct passed over or condoned in other nations.

For the reasons examined earlier—essentially, the extreme generality of
these charges, together with their incompatibility with evident matters of fact
concerning Israel—I suggest that what we confront in these criticisms is not

political debate but rather political defamation. More specifically, they represent types of defamatory falsehood characteristic of political antisemitism. It is, after all, only intelligible to deny the right of the Jewish people, alone among the nations of the world, to exercise political autonomy if there is some good reason why they should be denied it. That reason can only rest in the supposed commitment of Jews to harming the interests of others on an altogether overwhelming scale that has always formed the central plank of political antisemitism considered as a delusive explanatory theory. Other claims in the short list stigmatized as antisemitic by the IHRA examples, such as the claim that Israel is a Nazi or racist state, are a familiar element in efforts on the part of present-day anti-Zionists to persuade sympathizers of the possibility of rooting that central contention in reality. As we have already argued, none of these claims can be defended by the sober recitation of facts. Hence, the goal of delegitimating Israel can only be pursued by means of the remaining two elements in Natan Sharansky's famous "3 Ds" test for distinguishing legitimate criticism of Israel from antisemitic defamation. Delegitimation, that is to say, can only be made plausible by way of demonization and double standards. Similarly, belief in the existence of a Jewish conspiracy, rehashed of late years as the claim that the activities of the Israel lobby in the United States are (a) conspiratorial in character and (b) opposed to the national interest of the United States, is a familiar element in any version of political antisemitism, as is the closely related belief that Jews *by their nature* operate, in effect, as agents of a foreign power.

To conclude, one may grant to the legal critics that the opening preamble of the IHRA could, at least for legal purposes, be better drafted. But there seems no reason to dissent from the implied claim of the definition that the examples it offers genuinely are, one and all, examples of *antisemitism*. Nor is there any reason to suppose, pace Sir Stephen Sedley et al., that acceptance of the definition by public bodies poses any threat to freedom of speech. What the definition disbars as antisemitic amounts without exception, as we have seen, to collectively defamatory falsehood; and the utterance of defamatory falsehood neither is—at least in Great Britain—nor should be protected by laws guaranteeing freedom of speech in political debate.

OFFENSE

It is often asserted that Jews object to the propagation of such views either because they wish to silence "all criticism of Israel" or because they simply find such criticism "offensive." If either were true, it would be entirely correct to conclude that no valid argument can justify denying their propagators the protection of the law governing freedom of speech. Thus, Sir Stephen Sedley, noting in passing that the right of free expression under Article 10 of the European convention is not absolute or unqualified but "can be abrogated or restricted where to do so is lawful, proportionate and necessary for (among other things) public safety, the prevention of disorder or the protection of the rights of others," is careful—and of course correct—to add that "these qualifications do not include a right not to be offended."[27] The latter point is entirely sound: to allow claims of mere offensiveness to stand as grounds for restricting freedom of speech would be tantamount to abandoning the right to freedom of speech altogether.

For that reason, it is important to note that for concerned Jews (and others) where the types of criticism of Israel singled out by the IHRA examples as prima facie antisemitic are concerned, offensiveness is not the issue. The problem is, rather, that in the case of charges of the kinds thus singled out we are dealing, not with valid political debate concerning the rights and wrongs of Middle Eastern politics but rather with the collective defamation and demonization of the Jewish community, by its being represented, in effect, as a community united in support of Nazism, racism, colonialism, and war and as a potentially traitorous Israeli fifth column. These are exactly the kind of charges that fueled in prewar Europe the widespread climate of hostility to Jews that culminated in the Holocaust; and many Jews, having understandably long memories, see no reason why they should not do so again.

The British Labour Party is presently accused of institutional antisemitism for a number of reasons, but prominent among them is the jolt that its recent actions gave to precisely such memories. In July 2018, after much public criticism, Labour's National Executive Committee (NEC) endorsed the IHRA definition. But its endorsement excluded several of the examples to which I have devoted space here, notably the following: accusing Jewish people of being more loyal to Israel than to their home country, claiming that Israel's existence as a state is a racist endeavor, and likening Israeli politics to those of the Nazis. In September, the NEC revisited the issue and this time accepted the IHRA definition in full but with a caveat asserting the need to preserve free speech on controversial issues to do with the Israel-Palestine conflict.

By that point, the damage had been done. That same month (September), a poll by the London *Jewish Chronicle* found that 38.53 percent of British Jews would seriously consider emigrating if Jeremy Corbyn were to become prime minister. This extraordinary statistic is enough on its own, I suggest, to demonstrate that offense is not the issue. One does not consider emigrating because one is offended by this or that line of political rhetoric. One does so because history has shown that when certain familiar lines of defamation of the Jewish community take hold in a society and do so to the extent not only of being tolerated over respectable dinner tables but to that of being masked and excused by senior lawyers on subtle but specious legal grounds, then Jews have reason to be afraid.

The reason non-Jews should also be concerned, I suggest, and concerned not merely for the welfare of the Jews but for their own, is that the legal and political institutions thus debauched are, like the universities, institutions upon whose proper functioning all of us in one way or another depend. If the politics of angry delusion gain a sufficient hold over society to make it difficult or impossible for some of our fellow citizens to gain legal redress for injury, it may not be long before others find themselves in the same position.

THE RONNIE FRASER CASE

A disturbing recent British case in point, which returns us to the issues of university-based harassment of Jews raised in the preceding chapter, is that of Ronnie Fraser versus the University and College Union (UCU).

The UCU is the main trade union representing British academics. The political atmosphere internal to the UCU is sharply left wing and at times extremely heated. In 2011, it was strongly committed to BDS, the campaign to boycott, divest, and sanction Israel. At the UCU Congress of that year, a motion to reject the EUMC working definition (as it was called at that time) was proposed and passed. The events that followed this decision are fully and fascinatingly described in chapter 6 of a recent book by the sociologist David Hirsh, then a member of the union and an observer of events for the website ENGAGE. I shall let him take up the story. "By the time of the UCU Congress of 2011, as we have seen, opposition to the boycott campaign within the union was almost wholly silenced and defeated. The boycott campaign brought forward a motion to disavow the *EUMC Working Definition* of antisemitism. Rather than stop doing that which could be judged antisemitic under the definition, Congress preferred to disavow the definition. Congress is the sovereign body of the UCU, and it acts as the UCU."[28]

A teacher of mathematics named Ronnie Fraser spoke in the debate against the motion. His speech included the following remarks: "The overwhelming majority of Jews feel that there is something wrong in this union. They understand that it is legitimate to criticise Israel in a way that is, quoting from this definition, 'similar to that levelled against any other country' but they make a distinction between criticism and the kind of demonization that is considered acceptable in this union."[29]

In terms of the dispute between those who think no criticism of Israel is antisemitic and those who think that while some is not, some is, Fraser was here, in effect, defending the second, less extreme, and more plausible of the two options, and doing so on behalf of what he considers "the overwhelming majority of Jews."

Hirsh, who knows Fraser well, and had always thought of him as "somebody with a very thick skin and . . . very tough," affirms, and later gave it in evidence, that Fraser was heartbroken by the result of the debate because, as Hirsh puts it, "he had just experienced an antisemitic response, from a big hall of his trade union colleagues, to his speech."[30] We will consider in more detail in a moment—though we have already largely explained in general terms— in what the "antisemitism" of that response consisted.

Later, in October 2012, Fraser sued the UCU. Asserting that the union had created and allowed to flourish within it a culture of institutional anti-semitism, he argued that this constituted antisemitic harassment against him under the Equality Act (2010). He was represented on a pro bono basis by the eminent lawyer Anthony Julius—also an authority on the history of anti-semitism in Britain[31]—who had previously represented Princess Diana in her divorce from Prince Charles, and Deborah Lipstadt in the unsuccessful libel case brought against her by the writer David Irving, whom she had described as a Holocaust denier. Fraser's case was heard at London Central Court in October–November 2012, before an Employment Tribunal whose chair was employment judge A. M. Snelson and whose members were Mr. A. Grant and Lady Sedley.

Evidence on behalf of Fraser at this lengthy hearing was offered, Hirsh recounts, by an extensive group of supporters. "Thirty-four witnesses: union activists, scientists, sociologists, historians, lawyers, philosophers, Members of Parliament, Jews, Christians, Muslims, atheists, academic experts on anti-semitism and Jewish communal leaders. Witnesses gave written statements and were subject to cross-examination."[32]

Hirsh provides extensive extracts from these statements of which I shall confine myself to the following by my fellow philosopher Professor David-Hillel Ruben of Birkbeck College, University of London. Ruben resigned from the UCU in 2011, outraged, like Fraser, by the refusal of the union's rejection of the EUMC definition. His resignation letter, to Sally Hunt, the general secretary of the UCU, is worth citing in full.

Dear Sally Hunt,
As a life long socialist and a member of the AUT/UCU for almost 42 years,
I could not have imagined that anything could have made me resign from

the union. I have grown accustomed to the UCU's annual adoption of illegal Israel boycott motions. But my imagination was obviously limited: the official UCU rejection of the European Union Monitoring Centre on Racism and Xenophobia (EUMC) working definition of anti-Semitism has accomplished just that. It has brought about my resignation from the union.

One part of that working definition rejected by the union stands out: it is anti-Semitic to "deny the right of the Jewish people to self-determination," within some borders, unspecified as to what they might be. It is hard for me to comprehend how anyone could consider this relatively anodyne claim as unacceptable, let alone reject it as a current form of anti-Semitism, which it most certainly is.

I have no doubt that there remain some individual Jewish members of the UCU. Many publicly identify as Jews only for the purpose of opposing Israel "as Jews" and at no other times. But I can no longer allow my dues to support a union that is institutionally racist and that has demonstrated its anti-Semitism so repeatedly and unashamedly. I am therefore resigning my membership of the union with immediate effect.

David-Hillel Ruben, Professor of Philosophy, Birkbeck, University of London[33]

Professor Ruben's written statement to the tribunal in the Fraser case contained the following remarks:

I attended a general, London-wide meeting at SOAS [School of Oriental and African Studies] called by the union on Israel, and was laughed at and harangued. If anyone thinks these special meetings are places where open-minded discussion occurs, he should attend such a meeting in order to be disabused. They are meetings where the true believers speak to one another about Israeli imperialism and aggression. The narrative from one side only is heard. No one can seriously take these meetings to be balanced. They have in fact a threatening effect on those who have anything positive to say about Israel.

It was impossible for me to feel that this was any longer "my" union, one to which I was welcome to belong. Here is what a member of the national executive committee wrote to me recently:

"I don't want to re-enter this debate, but Israel is subject to a delegitimation campaign precisely because apartheid and racism is unique to the very fabric of Israel."

If Zionism is racist, then I am being told that I, my family, my friends, are racist. As Director of a small university campus from 1999–2011 (NYU [New York University]), I tried to encourage union membership amongst our part-time academic staff. I failed. No-one wanted to join. I spoke time and time again to many, Jews and non-Jews, who had already resigned from the union out of disgust over their policies on Israel.

In truth, although I resigned from the union, it felt much more like my union having been taken away from me. Over the years I have watched the anti-Israel sentiment in the union grow from a peculiar occupation of the union, though well within the bound of political legitimacy, to what it is today: a fetish that has crossed the line into anti-Semitism. I appreciate that a few of the union anti-Israel activists are themselves Jewish, but the appellation of anti-Semitism is an objective one and I believe it accurately describes the union today.[34]

In both statements, Ruben makes it very clear that he is not objecting to the actions of union on the grounds that those actions have *offended him personally.* His grounds of objection are essentially that those actions, in sum, involve the collective defamation of *the Jewish community* as a *racist* community ("If Zionism is racist, then I am being told that I, my family, my friends, are racist").

We learn from section 30 of the tribunal's report that the notion of harassment is defined in section 26 of the Equality Act 2010, under which Fraser's case was brought, as follows: "(1) A person (A) harasses another (B) if—(a) A engages in unwanted conduct related to a relevant protected characteristic, and (b) the conduct has the purpose or effect of—(i) violating B's dignity, or (ii) creating an intimidating, hostile, degrading, humiliating or offensive environment for B."

Most people would, I think, consider the charge made in the letter received by Professor Ruben from a member of the UCU's NEC, that "apartheid and racism is unique to the very fabric of Israel," to be a very serious one. It is, rather evidently, a charge that unless it can be shown to be in some reasonably uncontroversial sense simply true, is defamatory. It is specifically defamatory to Jews like Professor Ruben who are known to be supporters of Israel. But since Jews are widely believed to be in general supporters of Israel, it is also more widely defamatory of Jews as a recognizable community. Its constant reassertion can therefore only be regarded as harassment in the terms set out by section 26 of the Equality Act 2010. It certainly tends to create an "intimidating, hostile, degrading, humiliating or offensive environment" for Jews, given the widespread, and to some extent well-founded, assumption that support for Israel is an intrinsic component of Jewishness.

And there can be no doubt, as section 18 of the report of the tribunal grants, that under the act of 2010, Jewishness counts as a "protected characteristic." Both factually and legally, therefore, as critics like Lesley Klaff[35] have pointed out, one might have expected the case to go against the UCU. But that is not what happened. Despite Ruben's evidence and much other evidence of similar purport from equally distinguished supporters, Fraser's case went against him. The tribunal found no merit in anything said by Fraser or any of his witnesses. They concluded that everything that in the opinion of those witnesses constituted antisemitic harassment constituted, in fact, an entirely legitimate exercise by union officers and members of rights protected under legislation guaranteeing freedom of speech on political questions. Paragraph 178 of their judgment adds: "Lessons should be learned from this sorry saga. We greatly regret that the case was ever brought. At heart, it represents an impermissible attempt to achieve a political end by litigious means. It would be very unfortunate if an exercise of this sort were ever repeated."[36]

For David Hirsh, the tribunal, in effect, consciously aligned itself with the bulk of BDS supporters in dismissing any suggestion that the UCU could be in any way guilty of antisemitic harassment as a disingenuous attempt illegitimately to silence legitimate criticism of Israel. As Hirsh disgustedly summarizes his view of the matter: "The tribunal responded with a legally binding *Livingstone Formulation*."[37]

Although this is perhaps not entirely correct—I gather from legal friends that there is nothing legally binding about the report of such a tribunal—it is hard not to agree with the remainder of Hirsh's conclusion.

Among other things, the tribunal implicitly determined that there is nothing antisemitic about denying the right of Israel to exist on the grounds that "racism and apartheid" are "unique to its very fabric" (whatever that may mean). That implicit choice is no doubt partly explained by paragraph 147 of the tribunal's report. This makes it clear that for the members of the tribunal, what is fundamentally at stake in the case is not the mendacious collective defamation of the Jewish community in Britain by a handful of sectarian hard leftists occupying positions of power in a public institution but merely offended pique on the part of weak-minded people who want to intervene in the politics of their trade union but cannot stand up to the cut and thrust of vigorous debate. It reads in part:

"The Claimant is a campaigner. He chooses to engage in the politics of the union in support of Israel and in opposition to activists for the Palestinian cause. When a rugby player takes the field he must accept his fair share of minor injuries (see *Vowles*, para 35, citing an earlier Court of Appeal authority). Similarly, a political activist accepts the risk of being offended or hurt on occasions by things said or done by his opponents (who themselves take on a corresponding risk)."

We have already seen, I think, why "being offended or hurt" cannot be an issue, let alone *the* issue here. The issue is one of defamation, specifically, the defamation of Jewish members of the UCU, and of the British Jewish community generally, in terms not seen since the 1930s. The specific content of the defamatory lies faced by Ruben and Fraser are different, of course. But in their general character, they reanimate, as we have argued in other chapters, familiar components of the tradition of political antisemitism common to both Nazism and contemporary anti-Zionism. The specific differences of content merely reflect the fact that contemporary antisemitism nowadays infects the extreme left as well as the extreme right. To employ freedom of speech legislation—in this context, for the reasons we have shown, a legal red herring—to disguise this lamentable fact serves neither the country nor the tribunal's ostensible goal of keeping law separate from politics.

SAFEGUARDING FREEDOM OF POLITICAL DEBATE

It would be sad to end this chapter with either the conclusion that nothing can be done to protect Jews in the West from 1930s-style violence and harassment or the conclusion that something *can* be done about it—but only at the cost of severely restricting political debate concerning Israel.

If we are to safeguard both Jewish rights and freedom of speech, the first thing we need, of course, is a hard and fast distinction between honest political debate, and what used to be called in the 1930s "Jew baiting." That is one of the things that this book was designed to provide. We have argued that it is sufficient for a claim concerning Israel to be *antisemitic* if is (a) demonstrably false and (b) reanimates one of the standard traditional claims of political antisemitism. Both (a) and (b) hold, for instance, for the small collection of claims concerning Israel marked by the IHRA definition as exemplifying current antisemitic discourse: that Israel as it stands is an "illegitimate" state (but would be perfectly legitimate if it were a Muslim-majority state), and that it is illegitimate because, *in consequence of its status as a Jewish state*, it supposedly embodies the evils of racism, colonialism, apartheid, Nazism, and warmongering.

But if all that the box marked "antisemitic defamation" contains is this small collection of vacuously general and empirically unwarranted claims, then we seem left with a wide range of criticisms of Israel that are more or less empirically warranted and the pros and cons of which can be argued by assorted critics and defenders of various political leanings without any suggestion at all of antisemitism. Necessary freedoms of political debate are preserved, while the way is left open for vigorous opposition to illicit attempts to defame, harass, and exclude Jewish fellow-citizens.

What forms ought, and can, that opposition take? In Britain, as the academic lawyer Lesley Klaff has argued,[38] adequate statute law already exists, not only to allow but to require institutions—universities or trade unions, for instance—to take steps to prevent politically organised groups from creating work environments hostile and intimidating to Jews. The Equality Act 2010, for instance, prohibits discrimination in respect to "protected characteristics" that include race and religion. Recent precedent has established that Jewishness attracts the protection of the act on both counts. It follows, Klaff argues, that antisemitism constitutes both racial and religious discrimination under the provisions of the act. The act, therefore, specifically protects Jews from "hostile environmental harassment," and defines "harassment" of B by A (Section 26) as, inter alia, the creation by A of "an intimidating, hostile, degrading, humiliating or offensive environment for B." The relatively new phenomenon of online antisemitism, in social media and elsewhere on the internet, is similarly already covered by the Malicious Communications Act 1988 and the Communications Act 2003. The former makes it an offense to send indecent, grossly offensive, threatening, or false electronic communications the object of which, or one of the objects, is to cause distress or anxiety to the recipient. Section 127 of the latter Act makes it an offense to send a message (or other matter) that is grossly offensive or of an indecent, obscene or menacing character, or to send a false message "for the purpose of causing annoyance, inconvenience or needless anxiety to another."

The legal difficulty Sedley and others perceive, in applying the provisions of these and related acts of Parliament to any dispute involving criticism of Israel is, of course, that the general stance of British law and political/cultural tradition in favour of freedom of speech makes it imperative to ensure that it remains possible publicly to advance factually well-grounded criticism of Israel without thereby inviting legal action on grounds of antisemitism. The answer to that objection, I have suggested here, is that what is at issue in cases such as that of *Fraser v. University & College Union* is not factually well-grounded criticism of Israel, but rather the violent and belligerent repetition of a small range of entirely factually ungrounded but profoundly defamatory charges to the effect that Israel is a racist, apartheid, or Nazi state whose crimes outweigh those of any other existing or recent political entity. Discouraging such abuses does no harm to the cause of ensuring the conditions for free and unimpeded political debate; on the contrary, it advances that cause.

It is tempting to draw the same conclusion from current debates in the United States over the merits of the IHRA definition. In December 2019, President Trump signed an executive order designed to combat antisemitic harassment on American campuses. The order directs federal agencies to take the

IHRA definition into consideration when evaluating complaints of discrimination under Title VI of the 1964 Civil Rights Act, which prohibits discrimination
"on the ground of race, colour or national origin" but not religion.

The order proved violently controversial on two grounds. Liberal Jewish
opinion has always found the Trump administration's attitude toward antisemitism ambiguous, to say the least. It suspects the administration of having
links to the alt-right, and also of being willing, at least, to see American Jews
as primarily loyal to Israel, rather than to the United States. Weaponizing
Title VI as a means of combating antisemitism on campus has thus seemed
to many to play into the second of these worries. At the same time many
commentators, including many distinguished Jews, have attacked the IHRA
definition, much as has happened in Britain, for posing putative threats to
freedom of speech and academic freedom. From this point on, the whole
issue has developed, as so frequently in recent politics on both sides of the
Atlantic, into a dialogue of the deaf between the political Right and the political Liberal-Left.

One possible way of moving beyond these sterile divisions is offered by the
Academic Engagement Network, founded in 2015, a national organization of
faculty and staff on American campuses. It cites its aims as to "oppose efforts
to delegitimize Israel; promote campus free expression and academic freedom;
support research, education, and robust dialogue about Israel in the academy;
counter antisemitism where it occurs."[39] Its programs concentrate on opposing BDS on campus by financing speakers and courses committed to reasoned
argument and truth concerning Israel.

What is fruitful about this approach, I take it, is that, consistent with the
central place of the first amendment in American political culture, it sees no difficulty in combining the defense of Israel with the defense of academic freedom
and freedom of speech. That approach implicitly recognizes two weaknesses of
BDS-style anti-Zionism that I have been at pains to emphasize in this book. The
first is that BDS characteristically operates on campus by attempting to close
down, violently if necessary, any discussion of Israel that fails to conform to its
own political line. Fighting BDS is not, therefore, *the same thing as fighting freedom of speech*; on the contrary, fighting BDS is fighting *for* freedom of speech.
"The Academic Engagement Network [AEN] began, you should know"—I
quote the eminent Holocaust scholar Kenneth Waltzer, in correspondence—
"not as a lobby for Israel (our members are diverse on Israel) but as a lobby for
the idea of the university as an arena of open exchange, for academic freedom
and freedom of speech, and so on. We used A. Bartlett Giamatti's phrase about
the university as a free and ordered space."

In effect, Waltzer and the AEN are appealing beyond the bizarre collection of special-interest groups and purveyors of this or that version of identity politics currently competing for influence in our universities, to an older and better liberal idea of the functions of the university in a free society.

The reason BDS-inspired groups tend to work by attempting to restrict and close down the range of opinions that can be freely and safely expressed on campus, is of course, that the central claims of BDS—that Israel is a criminal, Nazi, racist, apartheid—are incapable of surviving calm and detailed critical examination, because they belong, not to the *genre* of reasoned political debate, but rather to that of politically motivated defamation. When screamed out or brandished on placards at a demonstration, or when presented in carefully selected contexts from which opposing evidence has been excluded, they will make converts, but not otherwise. This is the second of the two weaknesses of BDS, mentioned above, that the AEN approach intrinsically addresses. What I have tried to offer, in the present chapter and elsewhere in this book are, in effect, two supplementary observations. The first is that whatever doubts liberals may nourish concerning the claims of the Trump administration to be opposed to antisemitism, they need have no doubt that Trump's executive order is on firm ground in proposing the IHRA definition as a safe guide to contemporary antisemitism. As I have tried to show in the present chapter, the small set of central doctrines of BDS-style anti-Zionism that the IHRA definition stigmatises as antisemitic are indeed antisemitic. What I have tried to show elsewhere in this book are that these central claims of BDS are neither new, nor pulled out of the air at random, nor peculiar to current debate concerning Israel. They represent a mere rehashing, to fit the terms of contemporary debate concerning peace and war in the Middle East, of claims as old, and as constantly renewed over the centuries, as political antisemitism itself; the very claims, in fact, that in their most recent iteration provided the main conceptual spine of the Nazi antisemitism that produced the Holocaust. This needs to be clearly understood, it seems to me, by university and other administrative and legal authorities debating whether to take a stand, and which stand to take, in the current culture wars over Israel.

NOTES

1. Lesley Klaff, "Using Section 26 Equality Act to Combat Institutional Antisemitism: A Critical Race Perspective on *Fraser v University and College Union,*" in Campbell and Klaff 2019, 81.

2. David Hirsh, *Contemporary Left Antisemitism* (Abingdon, UK: Routledge, 2018), 6 and passim.

3. Sir Stephen Sedley, "Defining Anti-Semitism," *London Review of Books* 39, no. 9 (2017), https://www.lrb.co.uk/the-paper/v39/n09/stephen-sedley/defining -anti-semitism.

4. Marcus 2015, 18.

5. Marcus 2015, 22–23.

6. Marcus 2015, 20.

7. Peter Walker, "UK Adopts Antisemitism Definition to Combat Hate Crime against Jews," *The Guardian*, December 12, 2016, https://www .theguardian.com/society/2016/dec/12/antisemitism-definition-government -combat-hate-crime-jews-israel.

8. Free Speech on Israel, Independent Jewish Voices, Jews for Justice for Palestinians, the Palestine Solidarity Campaign, and the Palestinian Return Centre.

9. In British law, the appellation Queen's Counsel (QC) is a distinction awarded to senior lawyers, usually barristers (advocates), on grounds of merit.

10. Tomlinson's can be found at the website of Free Speech on Israel (https:// freespeechonisrael.org.uk/ihra-opinion). Robertson's can be found at the website of Doughty Street Chambers (https://doughtystreet.co.uk).

11. Tomlinson, 2.

12. Tomlinson, 3.

13. Tomlinson, 2.

14. Tomlinson, 2.

15. Tomlinson, 3.

16. Robertson, 6.

17. Robertson, 6–7.

18. Robertson, 13.

19. Tomlinson, 6–7.

20. Tomlinson, 7.

21. Tomlinson, 3.

22. Tomlinson, 3.

23. Robertson, 18.

24. Robertson, 17–18.

25. Robertson, 1–2.

26. Robertson, 23.

27. Sedley, 2.

28. Hirsh 2018, 155.

29. Hirsh 2018, 156.

30. Hirsh 2018, 156.

31. Anthony Julius, *Trials of the Diaspora: A History of Antisemitism in England* (Oxford: Oxford University Press, 2010).

32. Hirsh 2018, 157.

33. Text as published subsequently on the ENGAGE website.

34. Hirsh 2018, 162–63.

35. See endnote 1.

36. Report of Employment Tribunals case number 2203290/2011, available at the website judiciary.gov.uk.

37. Hirsh 2018, 163.

38. Klaff in Campbell and Klaff 2019; Harrison and Klaff, "The IHRA Definition and Its Critics," in A. H. Rosenfeld, 2021.

39. https://academicengagement.org.

SIXTEEN

JUDGMENT UNHINGED

To me, anti-Semitism is now the most shocking of all things. It is destroying much more than the Jews; it is assailing the human mind at its source, and inviting it to create false categories before exercising judgement.

—E. M. Forster, *Two Cheers for Democracy*

DANGEROUS OBSESSIONS

Forster was clearly right to see in the kind of antisemitism that deals in "false categories"—the antisemitism of *theory* rather than of mere dislike or contempt—an assault on the integrity of the human mind: on human reason at its source. At the start of chapter 14, I suggested that it is this assault on reason, this power to unhinge both the thinking and the political responses of anyone who takes it seriously, that makes political antisemitism—antisemitism as a pseudo-explanatory theory—not only a threat to Jews but a threat to all of us, Jew *and* non-Jew. Political antisemitism is no mere collection of abusive stereotypes; rather, it is an internally connected and endlessly self-reconstituting *system* of malicious lies about Jews and Jewish institutions. Such lies have, of course, the power to damage those of whom they are told. But if they are actually believed by those who circulate them, then they have in addition the power to damage the teller.

Hitler's delusions, which became those of the Nazi Party, offer a case in point. Hitler believed that Germany had lost World War I because the Jews had brought about the collapse of the monarchy and the poisoning of the national consciousness. The German historian Joachim Riecker[1] dates the genesis of these ideas to Hitler's experiences of November 9, 1918, in Munich, where a number of Jewish figures were prominent in the revolt against the monarchy, but that ideas of this type played a central role in Hitler's thinking is not in doubt. Such beliefs chimed with a general desire in Germany to believe that the blame for defeat in World War I did not lie with any inadequacy in German arms. It was thus a comforting thought that "the Jews" might be to blame, rather than any failure of German soldiers to sacrifice all in the defense of the fatherland or any weakness in German strategy. The belief in the intrinsic invincibility of German arms could thus continue to play an unquestioned role in sustaining national pride and self-confidence.

At the same time, the idea that Germany lost the war because it was stabbed in the back by Jewish money and Jewish disloyalty threatened rational reflection on the real causes of the debacle. A major reason why Germany lost World War I, and would proceed in due course to lose World War II, lay, evidently enough, in the intervention of the United States. Germany in 1914 was a major European power with a population of approximately 82 million and a land area of about 540,000 km^2. This is substantial enough by European standards but not substantial when one adds to the equally substantial forces of France and the British Empire the over 100 million population and continental resources of the United States at that time. In any European war in which the United States chose to intervene on behalf of one side, in other words, the other side, in this case Germany, was bound to lose.

After 1933, the idea that the Jews had engineered the defeat of 1918 became holy writ. Its evident implication was that if the Jewish poison could only be cleansed from the German soul, then German victory in a renewed European war, given the unquestioned invincibility of German arms when wielded and backed by a nation renewed and freed at last from the Jewish disease, was more or less inevitable.

Guided by these unhinged doctrines, the German government then embarked simultaneously on a campaign to rid Germany of Jewish influence and on preparations for a second world war that, as hindsight teaches us and as rational reflection at the time might have persuaded them, Germany was not in the long run likely to win any more than the first. Things went very well for a time, but then, as is generally the case in war, not quite as well as expected. Reichsmarschall Hermann Goering's Luftwaffe proved, to everyone's surprise, incapable of establishing German air superiority over the British Isles. America began to change its mind about entering the European theater. And in 1941, driven by the very belief in the invincibility of German arms that the political antisemitism central to the outlook of Nazism helped to sustain, there began the hubristic assault on the Soviet Union that was to lead, in August 1942–February 1943, to the catastrophe of Stalingrad.

Meanwhile, the war against the Jews was proving as successful as a war of extermination fought with modern weapons and organization against a bewildered, ill-informed, uncomprehending, and disorganized collection of civilians must inevitably prove. On the other hand, it was not doing much to help the progress of the war against Germany's actual enemies. The philosopher Berel Lang notes the extraordinary persistence with which the Nazi government continued to implement the Holocaust even when the necessary diversion of manpower and material was in sharp conflict with urgent military needs.

> The evidence is clear that the Nazi genocide against the Jews proved costly to the Nazis in the more general war they were waging at the same time. It may be excessive, and it is in any event unprovable to claim that the resources expended by the Nazis in the effort to annihilate the Jews were a decisive factor in their own defeat. But in a country facing the prospect of defeat (and certainly by 1943 this prospect was clear to virtually everyone in the Nazi hierarchy), it might be supposed that all the means available would be used to avert that defeat. There was, furthermore, no practical reason that this could not have been done—but it was not. Up until the last days of the War, in May 1945, the extermination of the Jews continued, with the diversion this entailed of material resources (trains, supplies) and of personnel.[2]

Lang suggests that the fact that, for the Nazis, even in the face of imminent defeat, the extermination of the Jews took priority over the war effort, "contradicts the justification proposed by the Nazis, that the Jews were a threat to the survival of Germany," suggesting instead that the extermination of the Jews was their primary aim, since they showed by their actions that, for them, "German survival was to be sacrificed or at least risked for the destruction of the Jews."

Lang is clearly right about this, but what it may show, I think, is not that the Nazi high command clearly distinguished the goal of exterminating the Jews from that of ensuring German survival and consciously decided to put resources behind the former even at the cost of sacrificing the latter. What is more likely, I suspect, is that by this late stage in the war, the Nazi high command was no longer capable of distinguishing between the two. Political antisemitism—the belief in the demonic power and world historic significance of the Jewish threat to humanity—can be sustained after all, as I have tried to show at length in the foregoing chapters, only by a continual effort to believe intrinsic absurdities. In that enterprise, mere credulity is not enough. What is required is the active and systematic neutralizing of inconvenient matters of fact, either by tendentious reinterpretation or by outright dismissal, and the equally systematic blurring or ignoring of distinctions essential to the maintenance of a firm grasp on reality.[3] Of course things of that nature enter into all politics. But in normal politics, they are kept within limits. Sustaining a commitment to political antisemitism requires by contrast that those limits be rapidly transgressed and never again mentioned within the movement. For the believers, keeping up the credit of what has become the founding delusion of their movement and the raison d'être of their political existence rapidly becomes their main aim. To that end, everything—national survival, victory, or defeat in war, every real and *non*delusive goal, in other words—must ultimately give way.

Even before the war, however, the Nazis had shown their disregard for national survival in an even more direct way. Earlier, at the start of chapter 14, I suggested two distinct ways in which a society infected with political antisemitism may suffer in consequence. The first is that political antisemitism disinclines believers to examine the possibility that their own errors and delusions, rather than the imaginary machinations of the Jews, may have played some part in bringing about whatever displeases them. The second is that the obsession with the Jews may obscure aspects of reality that the sufferer would do well to pay attention to. A third, however, is obvious enough: such a society is all too likely to suffer as a result of the loss of its Jews and of the many benefits conferred by a thriving Jewish community. For a regime with the strikingly ambitious war aims of the Nazis, including the millennial domination of Europe in its entirety by the German people in the Wagnerian role of the Aryan master race, it was surely scarcely a wise move to begin preparing for war by dispossessing and expelling, by murder or by forced emigration, half a million of the country's most loyal and useful citizens. Yet this is precisely what the Nazi regime immediately set about doing in 1933.

It is not my business to recall here either the vast human cost of the Holocaust or the cost to European culture in general of the abrupt extinguishing of the immensely rich Jewish contribution of the immediate past. My point is a much simpler and cruder one: that the half-million people of whose services the German nation was thus abruptly deprived were among its most loyal and devoted citizens—people whose help in wartime would have been generously and abundantly offered and could ill be done without.

Everyone who has known émigré German Jews or even their children knows how very German prewar German Jews were. Jews had lived in German lands, after all, since the Dark Ages. To quote Isaiah Berlin, writing in 1951:

> In a sense no community ever succeeded in identifying itself more closely with the nation in which it lived. When a German Jew, shortly after Hitler's rise to power, declined to go to France, saying, "I cannot go to the country of our enemies," the pathos of the situation which this underlined could not, perhaps, be paralleled in any other country. . . . Walther Rathenau once wrote, "My people are the Germans, no-one else. For me the Jews are a German tribe, like the Saxons, the Bavarians or the Wends." No sensitive person— particularly if he is German—can read this without embarrassment. And when he was killed by the kind of young German nationalist whom, in some moods, he seemed to admire most, his assassination was doubtless a great crime and a tragedy for his country, but it had a dreadful pathos about it too—since it was something which Rathenau himself was all his life too blind, or too self-blinded, to allow even to be possible.[4]

Joseph Roth, writing before World War II, tells the same story: "Most German Jews regarded themselves, despite an abundance of clearly threatening evidence of anti-Semitism, as perfectly good Germans; on High Holy Days, at most, they thought of themselves as Jewish Germans. They took great pains either to take no account of latent anti-Semitism, or to overlook it altogether."[5]

The love toward Germany felt by German Jews even extended at times to sympathy with Nazism itself.

> The architectural historian Nikolaus Pevsner had converted to Lutheranism in 1921, but, like other converts, was categorized by the Nazis as a "non-Aryan." In the spring of 1933 he said: "I love Germany. It is my country. I am a Nationalist, and in spite of the way I am treated I want this movement to succeed. . . . There are things worse than Hitlerism." Pevsner sided with Goebbels against the conductor Wilhelm Furtwängler, who wanted to employ Jewish musicians. All this availed him nothing: his application for admission to the *Reichskulturkammer* (the state-controlled "cultural chamber" set up by the Nazis) was rejected and he was compelled to leave Germany.[6]

Not only was the help of such fellow Germans disdained; wherever possible, they were expelled or butchered, to the abiding loss, both cultural and strategic, of the nation. Once again, the point I am making is a prosaic, brutal but very simple one. The delusions of political antisemitism have their uses in non-Jewish political maneuvering. But they carry correlative costs: for Jews certainly *but also for non-Jews*. There is always a price to be paid for conducting one's affairs at arm's length from reality, and in politics it can be a severe one.

For all that, the lesson of the 1930s is not one that Europe shows very much sign of having learned. In present-day France, a country that has yet to overcome its own traditions of Jew hatred, Jews in considerable numbers have for a number of years now begun leaving for good. In Britain, in early 2018, Jews were sufficiently alarmed by the rising antisemitism of the Labour Party under the leadership of Jeremy Corbyn to demonstrate in large numbers in Parliament Square. And as we saw in chapter 15, according to a recent poll, a high proportion of British Jews are contemplating emigrating if Corbyn's Labour Party should come to power.

FAILING TO PAY ATTENTION TO CAUSES OF CONFLICT IN THE MUSLIM WORLD

The worst turn political antisemitism does to those who consciously or unconsciously acquiesce in its main doctrines is to persuade them that the Jews are the key to understanding what is going on whenever things appear to be falling apart.

In recent years, the focus of this delusion has shifted from Europe to the Middle East. At the same time, it has ceased to be the sole property of the European mind. During the twentieth century, power in the main states of the region fell increasingly into the hands of authoritarian regimes all of which (whether secular fascist, like the Ba'ath regimes in Iraq and Syria, or committed to religious authoritarianism in the manner of Wahhabism in Saudi Arabia, or that of its Shi'a version in Iran, or those of the various movements, including al-Qaeda, or ISIL, or Hamas, that descend from the ideas of al-Banna and the Muslim Brotherhood) gave a central role in their thinking to the ideology of political antisemitism in its most ripely European form.[7]

According to that ideology, when entertained from a Muslim perspective, the West, and particularly America, is under the secret and absolute control of the Jews. This is helpful for the movements concerned when it comes to generating and maintaining popular support, since among other things it allows opponents to be represented as in the pay of the Jews and critical debate outside prescribed limits more easily suppressed. But insofar as it is widely believed—and it appears to be widely believed—it promotes the depressing image of Muslims in general and Arabs in particular as eternal victims, facing enemies so strong and so mysterious in their mode of operation as to leave open

450 BLAMING THE JEWS

no possibility of response beyond the hopeless, arbitrary, and utterly unproductive small-scale violence of terrorism.

The attacks of September 11, 2001, made the intensity of Islamist hatred
toward the West in general and America in particular too evident for Western
politicians and media pundits to ignore. Liberal and left-wing opinion in the
West, however, proved deeply unwilling to admit that any serious political
force or forces in the Muslim world could possibly nurse any very deep hostility to Western values. Instead, it reacted in a manner characteristic of minds
open to the consolations of political antisemitism. The main utility of political antisemitism in non-Jewish political life, as I argued in earlier chapters, is
that it enables one to ignore the reality of sharp conflict between non-Jewish
groups by reinterpreting it as a conflict between both groups and "the Jews,"
which would naturally end in a renewal of unity, peace, and mutual respect
within the non-Jewish world, if only the malign and divisive influence of Jewish interference in non-Jewish affairs could only somehow be brought to an
end. In short, a broad consensus of left-wing and liberal opinion in the West
preferred to believe that what might appear on the surface to be Muslim hatred of the West and its "values" per se was really only hatred of the Jews and
in particular hatred of Israel. It came to be widely believed, therefore, (a) that
what was unsettling "the Arab street" in Middle Eastern countries was largely,
or only, the absence of a peace settlement with Israel; (b) that the actions of
the government of Israel constituted the main obstacle to such a settlement;
and therefore (c) that the main obstacle to the ending of conflict and mutual
misunderstanding between the West and the Islamic world must therefore lie
with the obstinacy and fanaticism of the Israeli right. It followed—or seemed
to follow—that the increasing difficulties experienced by Western countries
in their relations with the Islamic world of the Middle East could be entirely
explained on the one hand by the intransigence of one "shitty little country"
and by the remarkable success of a well-financed Jewish cabal in the United
States—the so called Israel lobby—in preventing Israel from being brought to
heel by successive presidents and secretaries of state.

Suppose, now (ran the story—a story still widely believed on the extreme
left), that the sinister power of Jewish money could be somehow defeated. Suppose that, as a result, the Israel lobby were to be brought to heel, and Israel forced
on the one hand to bring to an end the crimes of which the Palestinians and its
Arab neighbors complained, and on the other hand to begin serving the goals of
US foreign policy instead of the other way around. Then, undoubtedly—a great
many respectable commentators were ready to give out as their opinion—an
era of peace would descend upon the entire Middle East—a peace in which

there need no longer be any serious difficulty in getting the Muslim world and the Western world to see eye to eye. That this story contains virtually all the traditional components of political antisemitism will be evident enough to the reader. Like earlier versions of the theory, it offers a convenient and plausible narrative in which evil and con-spiratorial Jews organize themselves collectively to create for the non-Jewish world problems that despite their appearance of extreme gravity could be re-lied on to vanish abruptly into thin air if only the malign Jewish collectivity in question—in this case the state of Israel—could be removed from the scene.

Nevertheless from well before 2001 until very recently, interpretations of events all roughly along these lines provided the dominant narrative in main-stream Western politics and the media. Following the logic of this narrative, Israel came to be regarded almost universally as the ultimate key to political advance in the Middle East, and the major—indeed on some accounts the sole—threat to peace in the region.

In consequence, while representatives of news organizations and nongov-ernmental organizations flocked in large numbers to Israel, very few spent much time in other parts of the Middle East. As a result, very little news capable of conflicting with the received narrative on Middle Eastern affairs reached the West for the simple reason that very little was being gathered. A different and more balanced view could be gleaned from academic studies and from a range of Arab and Palestinian commentators sharing a broadly liberal and pro-Western stance, but these lacked wide diffusion.

Mainstream Western liberal opinion was thus left secure in the conviction that Arab Muslim opinion, while deeply hostile to Israel—and with reason, it was felt, given the supposed Nazi-like iniquities that the Jews in Israel, having "learned nothing from the Holocaust," had felt themselves free to inflict on the Palestinians—could hardly be supposed to entertain any hostility to such cen-tral and self-evidently desirable Western values as freedom of speech, religion and assembly, female emancipation, economic progress, and parliamentary democracy.

In due course, as we know, the secular Ba'ath government of Saddam Hus-sein in Iraq and the somewhat more idiosyncratic one of Muammar al-Gaddafi in Libya managed to make themselves deeply objectionable to a number of Western politicians equipped at the time with the above mind-set. Several ma-jor Western powers—the United States, Great Britain, France—took it upon themselves to overthrow the two tyrants in question on the assumption that the populations they had ruled would be happy to accept—much as Euro-pean populations had done following the then fairly recent fall of European

dictatorships of both the right and the left—new constitutions and representative institutions conceived on a liberal Western model.

It is now more than fifteen years after the start of the second Iraq War and
eight since the outbreak of the so-called Arab Spring, both of which were widely
welcomed in sections of the Western media as opening a new era in which a
new relationship between the Muslim world and the West might be confidently
expected to blossom. The emptiness of these hopes is now apparent. As things
have turned out, Israel did not, after all, constitute the one vital key to the
future of the Middle East. When it came to determining the course of major
events across the region, Israel has not even been a serious actor. As Jews have
always done, Israel has confined itself to creating a safe space in a dangerous
world for the Jewish minority—and while it was at it, for a number of other
minorities—Arab Christians, Baha'i, Druse—now at serious risk in the remainder of the region.

The most serious error planted by the dominant narrative, however, has
turned out to be the idea of Israel as the key to peace both in the Middle East
and in the world generally. Far from being "the main threat to peace in the
world," as 60 percent of media-led European poll respondents thought in 2003,
Israel has turned out to be not much of a threat to peace at all, even in the
Middle East, let alone in the world. There were always, it now appears, many
far graver threats in the Middle East, from the popular appeal of the ideas of
the Muslim Brotherhood and its multitude of offshoots, to the ancient rivalries
between Sunni and Shi'a Islam, between Shi'a Iran on the one hand and Sunni
Saudi Arabia on the other, and between Turkey and the Kurds.

All of this was foreseeable. Some of it might even have been foreseen, and
wisely acted upon, with considerable savings in blood and treasure to non-Jews
of many nations, *if* the response of the liberal West and its media organizations to the straws that began in 2001 to blow in the wind had not been so
dominated—sometimes consciously, often unconsciously—by the ancient,
culturally imprinted image of the Jew, striding immense, hook-nosed, vast and
threatening across the political-cum-military theaters of the world, wielding
darkly incalculable financial and conspiratorial powers, reeling from the recent
Nazi onslaught, no doubt, but using his survival only to re-create Nazism over
again in his new third world redoubt, and so on.

The time-honored delusion that our troubles, whatever they may be, are
not actually ours at all but are in reality foisted upon us by the Jews and would
vanish if only the Jews could be got rid of, still has plenty of life in it. When
adjusted for civilized consumption—often merely by being put more politely,
or by way of readily understood winks and nudges—it can make fascinating

journalism, that really does sell copies and build ratings. But since it is from start to finish utterly without foundation, actually believing it has the power to derange, sometimes fatally, any mind that gives it a moment's houseroom. The deranged mind makes mistakes. Those mistakes, like others, entail costs. And while some of those costs will inevitably be absorbed by Jews, many may not.

ANTI-ZIONISM AS A TOOL OF SELF-DECEPTION

Contemporary anti-Zionism is the latest Western movement to fall for the ancient idea that the Jews are solely to be blamed for whatever, in terms of current perceptions of the world, most troubles us. One reason I have expended so much space on anti-Zionism and BDS in this book is that the label "the new antisemitism" that generally attaches to it[8] is in one sense singularly appropriate. Anti-Zionism is indeed a new version of Jew hatred in that it is the first version of political antisemitism to have succeeded in defining itself in such a way that its own nature *as a form of antisemitism* becomes not only invisible but actually *conceptually inaccessible* to those foolish enough to accept it.

This last is by no means a thought original to me. In a recent article in the *Times of Israel*, Fred Maroun, a Canadian journalist of Arab descent, recounts the experience of a friend of his—call him David—who was recently invited to speak about antisemitism at a left-wing rally in a major Canadian city. His speech was well received. As Maroun notes, "A young Palestinian even approached David after the speech to shake his hand. This event confirms that much of the left, even the modern left, is friendly and even welcoming towards Jews."[9]

The speech that David gave, however, was not the speech he originally wrote. His original draft speech had included the claim, rejected by anti-Zionists, that it is antisemitic to believe that every ethnic group has the right to self-determination except the Jewish people. "Unfortunately," says Maroun, "when the organizer read the draft speech, David was told that his safety would be at risk if he delivered the speech as it is"—a warning that was no doubt all too credible given the kinds of events recorded in chapter 14. David had a choice: not to speak at all or to deliver a politically bowdlerized speech. He chose the latter course. Maroun concludes:

> Unfortunately, the fact that David was forced to change his speech indicates that while the left is not anti-Jews, it is virulently anti-Israel. The left tolerates and even welcomes Jews so long as they do not do what all other peoples on earth have the right to do: pursue self-determination. The left accepts Jews as

long as Jews renounce their connections to their past, to their present, and to
the land that has always been at the center of their religion and culture.
In other words, the left accepts the Jews as long as they are no longer
Jewish. It is a form of "Jew-friendly" anti-Semitism, which is a contradiction
in terms. By refusing to boldly stand for the right of self-determination for the
Jewish people, the left is marching hand-in-hand with anti-Semites. Unlike
more traditional anti-Semites, they do not see themselves as anti-Jewish,
which makes them incapable of seeing their own biases and their own problem
[my italics].
Consequently, the left's anti-Semitism is the most insidious and the most
resilient anti-Semitism of all.

One might ask, of course, whether in suggesting that "the left is not anti-
Jews," Maroun is not granting too much. Possibly, there is irony at work here,
given Maroun's further observation that "the left accepts the Jews as long as
they are no longer Jewish." There is a long tradition on the left, going back at
least to Clermont-Tonnerre, of granting everything to the Jews *provided they
show themselves prepared to stop being Jews.* The continuation of this tradition
into the present is evident in much of the left's current rhetoric, including, as we
noted in chapter 11, John Mearsheimer's distinction between "righteous Jews"
(those who despise Israel) and "new Africaners" (the rest). Many in that tradition imagine, as we have seen, that there is a sharp distinction to be drawn between being anti-Israel and being anti-Jew. In chapter 15, I offered some reasons
for regarding that conviction as built on sand. I shall return to this and related
questions one last time in the penultimate section of this concluding chapter.

WHITEWASHING MUSLIM ANTISEMITISM

Be that as it may, many continue to be persuaded by the claim of the anti-Zionist
left to be opposed not to Jews but merely to the Jewish state and on that ground
to represent a "legitimate" political stance, rather than a racist campaign aiming
at the exclusion and persecution of Jews in Western societies. The persuasive-
ness of anti-Zionism in this respect is important not only because it serves to
mask its own antisemitic tendencies, but because it also serves to make many
otherwise reasonable and well-meaning people incapable of recognizing for
what it is the open and rabid antisemitism active in much of the Muslim world
at present. In particular, such people fail to grasp the leading role played by
versions of political antisemitism in all the various Islamist movements originating from the Muslim Brotherhood[10] and in all the Palestinian resistance
movements, including Hamas and Fateh. To leave Arab antisemitism out of

the equation makes it impossible, of course, to understand the course taken by relations between Israel and the Arabs over the past century and more.

Worse still, it makes it difficult for many otherwise well-meaning people in the West to recognize as expressions of murderous Jew hatred rather than as the acts of presumed freedom fighters actuated by political resentment against Israel the many violent and often murderous attacks by Muslims on vulnerable individual Jews that have been taking place in Europe with horrifically increasing frequency over the past two decades.

Such cases are typified by the torture, murder, and defenestration, on April 4, 2017, in Paris, of an elderly retired physician, Sara Halimi, by a Muslim neighbor who shouted, "Allahu Akbar" ("God is great"). Halimi had several times reported to the police that she had received antisemitic threats but without receiving assistance or protection. Moreover, the French authorities, including the judge in charge of the case, went to considerable lengths to deny the antisemitic character of the attack, presumably in the fear of otherwise offending the Muslim community and inviting the charge of Islamophobia.[11] (It is worth noting that a year later, the very similar murder of Mireille Knoll was immediately admitted by the authorities to be motivated by Jew hatred.)

Here, once again—as in the case of the harassment of Jewish student societies and individual students in universities and in that of the legal administration of British equality legislation, dealt with successively in the previous two chapters—the unwitting and largely unperceived commitment to political antisemitism masked by the pieties of current left-wing opinion works to corrupt and disrupt the functions of major non-Jewish institutions, much as Nazi antisemitism did in Germany in the 1930s.

THE ANTI-ZIONIST LEFT AND THE PALESTINIANS

What makes it so difficult for anti-Zionists to grasp the community between their discourse and that of earlier manifestations of political antisemitism is primarily, as I argued in chapters 6–10, their blindness to the factual hollowness, not to say the absurdity, of their primary political characterizations of Israel—as a Nazi state, an apartheid state, a colonial settler state, and so on.

What, in turn, sustains them in that blindness is no doubt the belief, widespread in all forms of politics, that lying is no very terrible thing, provided it is for a good cause. The good cause in this case is supposedly the liberation and general advancement of the Palestinian people.

This comforting belief is unhinged from reality in two ways. First, there is the uncomfortable fact that the rise of anti-Zionism to its present position as a central concern of Western left-wing movements has more to do with the local political difficulties faced by such movements in the past few decades than with any deep concern with or knowledge of the actual circumstances, present or historical, of the Palestinian people. In chapter 10, we considered at some length the problems caused for the Western left by the failure of communism and the ways in which parts of the left have attempted to find a new political role by, in effect, narrowing their political focus: replacing a diverse range of traditional socialist values and concerns with the sole function of opposition to the supposed evils of Western "imperialism" and support for "anticolonialist" revolt.

Second, it is utterly unclear what good such political activity in the West does or could conceivably do to further the political or economic advancement of the Palestinians. On the one hand, it is powerless to harm or to influence Israel; on the other hand, through its uncritical support for the present— essentially, fascist—Palestinian leadership, it works powerfully to confirm the broad masses of the Palestinian people in their present state of economic distress and political impotence under the control of armed gangs whose leaders deserve to be prosecuted for war crimes rather than feted by Western leftists and liberals.

For one thing, it perpetuates and reinforces the self-image of the Palestinians as perpetual victims. As the Israeli historian Benny Morris noted long ago,

> One of the characteristics of the Palestinian national movement has been the Palestinians' view of themselves as perpetual victims of others—Ottoman Turks, British officials, Zionists, Americans—and never to appreciate that they are, at least in large part, victims of their own mistakes and iniquities. In the Palestinian *Weltanschauung*, they never set a foot wrong; their misfortunes are always the fault of others. The inevitable corollary of this refusal to recognize their own historical agency has been a perpetual Palestinian whining—that, I fear, is the apt term—to the outside world to save them from what is usually their own fault.[12]

The immediate origin of the Palestinians' present situation is the defeat of 1948, which they call the *Nakba* or "disaster." The war that preceded that defeat was instigated first by the Palestinian Higher Committee, dominated by the Husseini clan, and then by the surrounding Arab nations with the announced purpose of ending Jewish settlement in Palestine altogether by expelling or exterminating the entire Jewish population.

The Arabs did not expect to lose the war of 1948. They were, after all, vastly in the majority. On the other hand, they took the risk of attacking a determined and entrenched minority population, some members of which had just survived the Holocaust and all members of which knew what had just taken place in Europe. The Jews knew that their backs were against the wall, and they knew perfectly well what would happen to them in Palestine if they lost. Under such circumstances, faced by opponents with no such threat hanging over them, nations are apt to secure surprising victories. This the future Israelis duly did.

Even so, there was as yet no reason for the Arab side to imagine that the position in which they found themselves was irrecoverable. As we know, the war aims of the Yishuv (the Jewish community in Palestine) were very different from those of the Arab Higher Committee and the surrounding Arab states. Far from setting out to exterminate or expel the Arab population, the Yishuv conferred citizenship in the new State of Israel on the 150,000 Palestinian Arabs who chose to remain within its borders. Arab representatives of their descendants now sit in the Knesset. The Yishuv certainly refused to allow those who had fled to return, as the government of Israel does to this day, but that is surely hardly surprising given the threat to their existence that the Jewish population survived in 1948 and the unbroken history of terrorist attacks by Arab infiltrators that followed.

It would have been perfectly possible in 1948, in other words, for the Palestinians to make peace with the Israelis and to usher in a mutually supportive relationship based on the founding of a Palestinian state, possibly in some kind of federal relationship with Israel. In fact, the Palestinian leadership rejected this solution in 1948. It chose instead to follow a policy of low-level guerilla warfare against Israel in hopes of somehow overturning the historic consequences of the 1948 war. Nevertheless, in a series of peace negotiations, Israel repeatedly offered to cede territory to a future Palestinian state. In 2008, Prime Minister Ehud Olmert offered a near-total withdrawal from the West Bank. The offer proposed that Israel should keep 6.35 percent of the West Bank to retain control of major Jewish settlements but should compensate the Palestinians with Israeli land equivalent to 5.8 percent of the West Bank, along with a link to the Gaza Strip, Israeli withdrawal from Arab neighborhoods of East Jerusalem, and the placing of the Old City and sites sacred to all three major religions it contains under international control.[13]

All these offers were refused by the Arab side, the earlier ones by Yasser Arafat and the 2008 Olmert offer by the present leader of the Palestinian Authority, Mahmoud Abbas. The unilateral and unconditional Israeli withdrawal from the Gaza Strip in 2005 led only to the bloody and still-unhealed split between Fateh and the Islamist movement Hamas. At time of writing, the Gaza Strip remains controlled by Hamas and several other, smaller Islamist groups, all owing ultimate allegiance to the Muslim Brotherhood. These rule the strip by the usual arbitrary and violent methods of authoritarian groups the world over and wage a permanent war of sorts against Israel, largely by means of rockets or incendiary balloons or kites but occasionally by armed infiltration through tunnels. The conduct of this campaign by the various Islamist groups currently ruling Gaza has demonstrated complete disregard for the interests and safety of the civilian population of the strip (just under two million souls), who are also debarred from travel to Egypt by reason of the politics of their "leaders." Hamas is financed by Iran, as is the Shi'a group Hezbollah, which threaten Israel from the north. Despite being effectively at war with Hamas in Gaza, Israel continues to maintain the supply of electricity and other utilities to the strip.

A major plank in the propaganda of all the various Palestinian armed factions is that it is useless for the Palestinians to lay down their arms and sue for peace with Israel, because Israel is merely the visible face of a world Jewish conspiracy that controls the United States, directs the spread of capitalism in the world, and is devoted root and branch to the total destruction of the Palestinians, as of all other "oppressed nations" in the world. On this basis, suicide bombings and other ways of murdering civilians in Israel, in Europe, and elsewhere in the world are considered by the perpetrators to be justified on the grounds that they offer the only remaining means of struggle against the quasi-mystical tentacular power of world Zionism and that, in consequence, anyone who fails to join the struggle against Zionism becomes by that fact a legitimate target. Such acts are in reality war crimes, however much certain Western political and media organizations may dislike being reminded of the fact.

Considered as war, such a stance is futile; considered as politics, it is manifestly completely mad and utterly counterproductive. It is politically mad because it is politically fruitless. It cannot achieve the end it notionally proposes to its followers, of improving the present, often miserable, conditions under which the Palestinian people live. Peace with Israel would do that, and only peace with Israel could do that. Israel, in fact, is the only power *with a substantial body of opinion willing to give the Palestinians a state of their own.* The war of 1967, which secured Israeli control of the West Bank, in fact marked the first point since the partition proposals of 1947–48 at which a Palestinian state began to be on offer as a real possibility. In the intervening two decades, 1948–67, when the West Bank was under the control of Jordan, there was absolutely no talk on the Jordanian side of setting up an independent Palestinian state on these territories.

It is not, of course, *quite* true that the politics of self-embraced victimhood and eternal rejectionism are entirely useless. They are extremely useful when it comes to maintaining the control of David Hirsh's "gangs of armed men" over the broad masses of the "oppressed peoples" whom they notionally represent and actually exploit and bleed, both financially and literally, for their own purposes. The old question cui bono?—who benefits?—is as useful in politics as it is in detective fiction. Who benefits from the failure of attempts to negotiate peace between Israel and the Palestinians? Israel? I would be interested to have it explained how. The armed groups that at present dominate Palestinian politics? That is an altogether different matter. The economic progress that would inevitably accompany real peace would very rapidly break the power of the armed groups to control the Palestinian population and relegate them to a backwater of history.

Be that as it may, this—the politics of victimhood and rejection, and the accompanying vision of the world as dominated by "international Jewish interests"—is the politics that the anti-Zionist left, along with a good many of its self-described liberal fellow travelers in the media and the universities, wishes to represent as a politics of liberation directed toward the advancement of the Palestinian people. In fact, it is a politics that promotes the continued enslavement of the vast mass of the Palestinian people to the political fantasies of the armed gangs that have come to control them.

As earlier chapters of this book have shown, it is also a politics whose vision of reality is profoundly infected with the delusions of political antisemitism. Its eternal refrain—that the Jews are absolutely bad and the Palestinians and their leadership absolutely good—is a simple reiteration, when it comes down to it, of the central plank of political antisemitism. Here as elsewhere, those delusions have demonstrated the power they exert, when they are genuinely believed by those who propagate them, to work not only to the destruction of the Jews but also to the destruction of the propagators themselves. In the present case, we are faced with the unedifying spectacle of a soi-disant left diverted by its own unrecognized antisemitism from the pursuit of its original goals of democracy, liberation, and human fulfillment to the pursuit of their exact opposites: permanent war, the whitewashing of war crimes, and the subordination of masses of ordinary people to the fantasies of the armed fascist groups who control them.

COMING INTO THE OPEN

Since the beginning of the present century, it has become progressively harder to ignore the increasing ease with which people on the extremes of left and right, both in Europe and America, have taken to giving vent, on social media and elsewhere, to the kinds of abuse of Jews hitherto unheard since the 1930s.

Many people on the left and liberal left, as we saw earlier in this chapter in the case of Fred Maroun's "David," would like to persuade themselves that it is possible to be both hostile to Israel and friendly to individual Jews. But as we saw in the previous chapter, the nature of the left's hostility to Israel makes this stance difficult to sustain. Anti-Zionists on the left persistently state as their reason for denying the Jewish people the right to self-government that Israel is responsible for crimes not only equaling but outstripping those of the Nazis. But if one really *believes that* and if (as happens to be the case) large numbers of Jews support the right of Israel to exist as a self-governing polity, then one has no choice in logic but to accept the conclusion that at least large numbers of Jews must be as much enemies of humankind as were the Nazis, since they support, and are therefore presumably accessory to, the commission of these putatively equally egregious crimes.

Most of the "public intellectuals" who have occupied themselves with pro-claiming, over the past decade or two, the absolute Nazi-style wickedness of Israel have tended prudently to ignore the force of this simple syllogism. Standing in the public eye and having a literary or academic reputation to defend does, at least in most cases, make one relatively circumspect about such things, though there have been exceptions.

On the other hand, the horde of young, deeply radical people who have since 2016 joined the British Labour Party to celebrate the sudden and surprising rise to the post of party leader of the hard-left Islington MP Jeremy Corbyn have shown by the nature and tone of many of their posts on social media that its force is by no means lost on them.

This problem came to a head in the House of Commons on April 17, 2018, during a debate on antisemitism in the new Corbynite Labour Party. The report on the front page of the London *Daily Telegraph* the next morning is graphic enough to be worth quoting at length:

> Labour MPs have turned on Jeremy Corbyn over his "betrayal" of Jews as they described rape and death threats they had received for speaking out against anti-Semitism in their party.
>
> Mr. Corbyn sat in the Commons in silence as his MPs read out hate mail they had received from his supporters. Others received standing ovations for calling out the "bullying and intimidation" in the party as the Labour leader was told: "Enough is enough."
>
> One Labour MP was moved to tears as Luciana Berger, her colleague, described the "torrent" of abuse she had faced for being Jewish in a party in which Mr. Corbyn has allowed anti-Semitism to become "more commonplace, more conspicuous and more corrosive."
>
> The extraordinary scene erupted after months of discontent over his handling of anti-Semitism in Labour, which many MPs claim has been

tolerated or even encouraged by sections of the party sympathetic to the leader.

John Mann, the Labour MP, said members of the Corbyn-supporting Momentum group had targeted him for showing solidarity with Jewish Labour members. He said his wife had been sent a dead bird in the post and received rape threats and his son and daughter had had contact with the bomb squad and "special branch" after death threats to the family.

Dame Margaret Hodge, whose family were caught up in the Holocaust, was applauded as she said: "I have never felt as nervous and frightened as I feel today at being a Jew. It feels that my party has given permission for anti-Semitism to go unchallenged. Anti-Semitism is making me an outsider in my Labour Party. To that I simply say, enough is enough."

... Ms Berger fought back tears as she said: "I have no words for the people who purport to be both members and supporters of our party, who use that hashtag JC4PM [Jeremy Corbyn for Prime Minister], who attacked me in recent weeks for speaking at the rally ... who said I should be deselected."

Detailing other examples of anti-Semitic abuse, she said, voice shaking: "They have called me Judas, a Zio-Nazi, and told me to go back to Israel."

... Ruth Smeeth, her colleague, reached out and squeezed Ms Berger's hand during her emotional speech, for which she was given a standing ovation as MPs ignored Commons conventions banning applause in the chamber.

Ms Smeeth, who was moved to tears by Ms Berger's words, received a similar ovation as she read abuse she had received, such as "hang yourself you vile treacherous Zionist Tory filth, you're a cancer of humanity."[14]

There can be little serious question of these being attacks on *Israel*. Not at all: they are attacks on Jews. Nor are they attacks on Jews for being supporters of Israel, despite that being the ostensible ground of hostility. If support for Israel were the real bone of contention here, then as I pointed out in the last chapter, anybody who supports Israel, Jew or non-Jew, could expect the same kind of public attack on social media, including death and rape threats. But in fact, the only non-Jews who receive this kind of abuse are those, like John Mann, who receive it not for supporting *Israel* but for supporting Jews. What we are witnessing here, in twenty-first-century Britain, is in cold fact a resurgence of the old, prewar antisemitism: antisemitism of exactly the type exhibited by the German Nazi Party.

This kind of antisemitism is also on the rise elsewhere in Europe, partly in consequence of the vast wave of Syrians and others seeking refuge in Europe since 2011. Merkel's 2015 invitation, perceived as the main cause of hundreds of thousands of Syrian and other refugees entering Germany, has, according to the leading German newspaper *Die Zeit,* "cast a shadow over Merkel's political future, boosted the right-wing populist Alternative for Germany party... and poisoned the political climate to such a degree that politicians are routinely insulted as 'traitors to their people,' even during the recent Day of German Unity celebrations in Dresden."[15]

The rise in Muslim immigration to Europe, while itself fueling a rise in incidents of antisemitism, has also produced a powerful right-wing backlash in Eastern European countries, particularly those, like Hungary, with a history of armed conflict with the Ottoman Empire. A number of governments in Eastern Europe now appear determined, in conflict with the desire of the European Commission to spread the refugees across Europe, to resist any influx across their borders. In the resulting heated political climate, hostility to Muslim immigration mutates naturally into hostility to Jews, perceived as eternal aliens.

In Poland, in particular, it is no longer politically taboo to express prewar attitudes to Jews. Mark Weitzmann, director of government affairs at the Simon Wiesenthal Center, recently had this to say at a hearing of the Committee on Foreign Affairs in Washington, DC:

> I think recent events have forced upon us the realization that while much of antisemitism, especially violent and murderous antisemitism, today is indeed filtered through anti-Zionism, a disturbing trend has emerged in which a new form of classical antisemitism itself has re-entered the main institutions of civil society in certain areas.
>
> This regeneration of traditional antisemitism is all the more dangerous because, unlike the violent extremists of both left, right and radical Islam, it is now found in government circles and halls of power in countries that we define as Western democracies.
>
> In many ways it is also connected with attempts to distort the history of the Holocaust by whitewashing local collaborators or minimizing or even removing the Jewish identity of the victims. Often this is connected to a political agenda that is concerned with creating a traditionalist national narrative that wants to look back to an idealized past for heroes and models. And since many of these societies have emerged from both Nazi and Communist occupation and oppression, the past that they glorify is frequently the last period of home rule before World War II, and the ideals that they glorify can include versions of the traditional antisemitism that was prevalent before the war.
>
> Perhaps in no country today is the situation more acute than in Poland. There we find senior government officials, such as Minister of Defense Antoni Macierewicz claiming in 2002 that he had read the infamous

Protocols of the Elders of Zion and that "Experience shows that there are such groups in Jewish circles." He has never publicly retracted that statement, and two other cabinet members, Foreign Minister Witold Waszcykowski and Culture Minister Piotr Glinski, have also declined to condemn the Protocols when asked to do so.

Macierewicz's original 2002 statement was given to Radio Maryja, the notorious antisemitic radio station that has been condemned by the Vatican for its anti-Jewish remarks. Radio Maryja's history of antisemitism is both well documented and current. Already in 2008 the State Department's *Global Anti-Semitism Report* called Radio Maryja "one of Europe's most blatantly anti-Semitic media venues." More recent examples abound. In September the founder and head of Radio Maryja, Father Tadeusz Rydzyk berated an unruly audience by telling them that they should not be indulging in "synagogue-type behavior."

In November one commentator on the station stated that "the Jewish Lobby in Poland demonstrates its racial solidity with the Ukrainian oligarchs." In December he made the blatantly antisemitic claim that "The U.S. media and entertainment industry are dependent on the Jewish lobby. It is similar to the Stalinist terror, which was organized and implemented by Jewish communism." And in the same month he made a trip to the US where he spoke in New York, New Jersey and Massachusetts and among other antisemitic remarks referred to the "Jewish faction" which allegedly is ruling Poland.

It is bitterly ironic, then, that this allegedly Jewish run government has become a huge subsidizer of Radio Maryja. According to news reports the government has paid out the staggering sum of over seven million dollars to Radio Maryja, and was even issuing a postage stamp to commemorate the station's twenty-fifth anniversary.[16]

More recently still, Dr. Moshe Kantor, president of the European Jewish Congress, summarized the present situation in these terms: "If in previous years we saw different types of anti-Semitism—anti-Semitism of the far-Right, anti-Semitism of the far-Left, and an anti-Semitism masked as anti-Israel— now it has transformed more openly into classic anti-Semitism. There has been an increase in open, unashamed and explicit hatred directed against Jews. The Jew as exploiter, the Jew as killer, the Jew as banker. It is like we have regressed 100 years."[17]

If we are to be guided by Forster's remarks on the power of antisemitism to corrupt judgment that serve as the epigraph to this chapter, then it would appear that not only the safety of European Jews but also the sanity of the European mind are once again under serious threat.

CONCLUSIONS

The train of argument followed out in this book has been long and complex. It will do no harm, therefore, to look briefly again in conclusion at the main stages of the argument and at the ways in which their separate conclusions fit together. The central claim of the book has been that antisemitism has two basic forms. It can manifest itself either as ethnic prejudice against any individual Jew or as an elaborate and delusive pseudo-explanatory theory concerning the supposed role of the Jewish collectivity in determining events in the wider, non-Jewish world.

I have defended two main claims concerning this second form of antisemitism. The first is (1) that it has over many centuries served a very specific set of functions in non-Jewish political life. It has offered a means by which putatively redemptive non-Jewish political or religious projects, finding themselves under threat from within the non-Jewish world, have been enabled to represent that threat as coming, not from the non-Jewish community whose unanimous allegiance defenders of the project are anxious to secure but from a conspiratorially organized alien force, "the Jews": a force hostile to whatever putatively redemptive project happens to feel, at a given moment, the ground shifting beneath its feet because, allegedly, it is hostile to the interests of the non-Jewish community as a whole.

The second main claim I have defended is (2) that antisemitism in this second form is, and always has been, unique to the Jews. They, and they alone, have always been cast as the conspiratorially hostile alien fifth column required by the above non-Jewish political scenario.

Two questions naturally arise: Why should this have been so? That is, why should the Jews have so consistently found themselves cast in this role by elements in the non-Jewish community? And does the explanation lie in something the Jews themselves have done?

I have answered this last question in the affirmative: yes, something the Jews have done has led to their playing the perennial role that they have played in a certain fabric of non-Jewish delusion. But this "something the Jews have done" is not being good at business, or at handling money, or at passing more examinations with higher marks than their unfortunate non-Jewish fellows. The crucial something, according to me, is nothing the Jews could *not* have done *other than by ceasing to be Jews*. What they have done, what has brought antisemitism of the second kind down on their heads, is simply to refuse, generation after generation, century after century, to do what a long series of putatively redemptive non-Jewish political or religious movements have demanded of them: to give up *entirely* their commitment to Judaism and Jew-ishness, to fade untraceably into the general population and become "like everybody else."

Why, it might be asked, have only the Jews displayed this indomitable will to remain themselves when other diasporic groups holding, one would have thought, equally unique and specific systems of belief and value have long since vanished, through total assimilation, from the pages of history? The reason I of-fered, in chapters 11 and 12, was, in effect, that Judaism is not in the ordinary sense a system of beliefs or values. What holds the Jewish community together as a community is neither common adherence to certain *doctrines* nor com-mon agreement in attaching *value* to certain abstract notions. Rather, what holds the community together, and gives meaning to the lives of individual members, is common involvement in a vast and richly intelligible system of *observances* and *practices*. Judaism, unlike Christianity or most other religions, turns not on *belief* but on *agency*. People whose sense of the meaningfulness of life is underpinned by a specific system of *beliefs* can quite easily transfer that function, by conversion, to some different set of beliefs. People whose sense of the meaningfulness of life is sustained, on the contrary, not by *belief* but rather by membership of a community committed in common to a vast and coherent system of observances and habits of agency, will be likely to find the loss of membership in that community, and its replacement in the role of meaning-bestowing substratum by some collection of more or less arbitrary and implausible beliefs difficult to bear.

In addition, the present book has offered itself as a study of contemporary antisemitism. But unlike many sociological and historical studies of this sub-ject matter, it has endeavored to place and to understand recent phenomena in the context of the above account of what sort of thing, or things, antisemitism *is*, of what *functions* it serves in non-Jewish political and cultural life, and of why, given what it is and what functions it serves in non-Jewish societies, it has shown itself so protean in its ability to reconstitute itself in new forms, with new slogans and new obsessions, as century has succeeded century. By doing so, I hope I may have been enabled to shed new light on a number of the vexing questions that have animated recent debate on the new antisemitism.

In particular, I have tried to show that, and why, the anti-Zionism so popular with large parts of the Western left at the moment is—and it really *is*, no doubt about it—antisemitic. Until very recently, it has been standard to accuse those who have made this accusation of doing so disingenuously, out of a desire to silence legitimate criticism of Israel. I hope I have shown that, and why, such accusations are not only false but themselves disingenuous.

I have also taken issue with the idea that those who entertain sincerely antiracist sentiments, and who entertain no hatred for individual Jews, are therefore justified in regarding themselves as incapable of committing an antisemitic act. Antisemitism, if I have argued correctly here, does not solely or necessarily manifest itself in *racial hatred*. It also manifests itself in the mendacious propagation of the tenets of a delusive explanatory theory. Industry in the elaboration or propagation of those tenets is therefore antisemitic *irrespective of the motives, sentiments, or self-image* of the person who exhibits it.

I further take the above arguments to have shown why the fact that antisemitism *in the form of ethnic prejudice* is—if it is—relatively in abeyance need not and does not mean that antisemitism per se is in abeyance.

Finally, last but by no means least, I hope to have provided some reasons for resisting the idea that antisemitism, while a very bad thing, is a thing that chiefly concerns Jews and can therefore safely be left to Jews to obsess about. In the last three chapters, I have argued that antisemitism is as dangerous (though in different ways) to non-Jews as Jews, and I have done so on two main grounds. The first (chapters 14 and 15) is that antisemitism corrupts institutions: the universities, the law, political parties. The second (chapter 16) is that believing nonsense is unsafe, because it leads to bad decisions. That is true in all contexts and of nonsense of all types. Since antisemitic nonsense has the power to radically corrupt and derange the workings of political intelligence, however, the bad decisions it promotes may be catastrophic, for non-Jews as well as Jews.

I hope therefore that the arguments of this book may have done something to lead at any rate a few people to see more clearly that, and why, the rabid dog of antisemitism is a beast that needs shooting before it bites, not only our Jewish fellow countrymen and countrywomen, but the rest of us as well.

NOTES

1. Joachim Riecker, *Hitlers 9. November: Wie die Erste Weltkrieg zum Holocaust führte* (Berlin: Wjs Verlag, 2009).
2. Lang 1990, 39.
3. On the details of this process in the propagation of contemporary anti-Zionism, see Bernard Harrison, "Anti-Zionism, Antisemitism and the Rhetorical Manipulation of Reality," in A. H. Rosenfeld 2013.
4. Isaiah Berlin, "Jewish Slavery and Emancipation," in Berlin 2001, 169–71.
5. Roth 2001, 121 (preface to the new edition, 1937).
6. Wasserstein 2012, 215–16.
7. See Küntzel 2007.

8. First used, I believe, by the late Robert Wistrich during the 1980s but now commonplace.

9. Fred Maroun, "The Jew-Friendly Anti-Semitism of the left," *Times of Israel*, January 16, 2018, https://blogs.timesofisrael.com/the-jew-friendly-anti-semitism -of-the-left/.

10. See, in particular here, Küntzel 2007.

11. Robert Sarnier, "Journalist Investigates wholesale denial of pivotal anti-Semitic murder in Paris," *Times of Israel*, September 16, 2018, https://www .timesofisrael.com/journalist-investigates-wholesale-denial-of-pivotal-anti -semitic-murder-in-paris/.

12. Benny Morris, "Rejection," *New Republic* (April 21–28, 2003): 37.

13. Joseph Fererman, "Abbas Admits He Rejected 2008 Peace Offer from Olmert," *Times of Israel*, November 19, 2015, https://www.timesofisrael.com /abbas-admits-he-rejected-2008-peace-offer-from-olmert/.

14. Gordon Rayner and Anna Mikhailova, "Enough Is Enough: Labour Fury at Corbyn over Anti-Semitism," *Daily Telegraph*, April 17, 2018, https://www .telegraph.co.uk/politics/2018/04/17/labour-mps-tell-jeremy-corbyn-enough -enough-partys-corrosive/.

15. Philip Faigle et al., "It Really Wasn't Merkel," *Zeit Online*, October 11, 2016, https://www.zeit.de/politik/ausland/2016-10/angela-merkel-influence-refugees -open-borders-balkan-route.

16. Available at the website of the US House of Representatives, http://docs .house.gov/meetings/FA/FA16/20170322/105755/HHRG-115-FA16-Wstate -WeitzmanM-20170322.pdf.

17. Report: "Anti-Semitism Mainstreamed and Normalised," Israelnationalnews.com, November 4, 2018.

SELECTED BIBLIOGRAPHY

Alexander, Edward. 1994. *The Holocaust and the War of Ideas*. New Brunswick, NJ: Transaction.

———. 1998. *The Jewish Idea and Its Enemies*. New Brunswick, NJ: Transaction.

———. 2003. *Classical Liberalism and the Jewish Tradition*. New Brunswick, NJ: Transaction.

Alexander, Edward, and Paul Bogdanor. 2006. *The Jewish Divide over Israel*. New Brunswick, NJ: Transaction.

Allport, Gordon. 1954. *The Nature of Prejudice*. New York: Basic Books.

Anscombe, E., P. T. Geach, and A. Koyré. 1963. *Descartes: Philosophical Writings*. London: Nelson.

Arendt, Hannah.1976. *The Origins of Totalitarianism*. New York: Houghton Mifflin Harcourt.

———. 2007. "Antisemitism." In *The Jewish Writings*, edited by Jerome Kahn and Ron H. Feldman. New York: Schocken.

Arnold, Matthew. 1966. *Essays in Criticism*. London: J. M. Dent.

Austin, J. L. 1962. *Sense and Sensibilia*. Oxford: Clarendon.

Babel, Isaac. 2002. *1920 Diary*. Edited by Carol J. Avins. Translated by H. T. Willetts. New Haven, CT: Yale University Press.

Bachi, Roberto. 1974. *The Population of Israel*. Jerusalem: Institute of Contemporary Jewry, Hebrew University.

Bauer, Yehuda. 1978. *The Holocaust in Historical Perspective*. Seattle: University of Washington Press.

Begin, Menachem. 1951. *The Revolt: Story of the Irgun*. New York: H. Schuman.

Ben Atar, Doron, and Andrew Pessin. 2018. *Anti-Zionism on Campus*. Bloomington: Indiana University Press.

Berlin, Isaiah. 2001. *The Power of Ideas*. Edited by Henry Hardy. London: Pimlico.

Blum, Carol. 1986. *Rousseau and the Republic of Virtue: The Language of Politics in the French Revolution*. Ithaca, NY: Cornell University Press.

Brown, S. C., ed. 1979. *Philosophers of the Enlightenment: Royal Institute of Philosophy Lectures 1975–6*. Brighton, UK: Harvester Press.

Buber, Martin. 1965. *The Way of Man*. London: Routledge.

Campbell, Jonathan G., and Lesley D. Klaff. 2019. *Unity and Diversity in Contemporary Antisemitism: The Bristol-Sheffield Hallam Colloquium on Contemporary Antisemitism*. Boston: Academic Studies Press.

Cassirer, E. 1946. *The Myth of the State*. New Haven, CT: Yale University Press.

Cheyette, Bryan. 1993. *Constructions of "the Jew" in English Literature and Society: Racial Representations, 1875–1945*. Cambridge: Cambridge University Press.

Chomsky, Noam. 1992. *Chronicles of Dissent: Interviews with David Barsamian*. New York: Common Courage Press.

Cohen, Avner. 1998. *Israel and the Bomb*. New York: Columbia University Press.

Conway, David. 2004. *In Defence of the Realm: The Place of Nations in Classical Liberalism*. Aldershot, UK: Ashgate.

———. 2015. "Review: *Raphael Lemkin and the Struggle for the Genocide Convention*." *Jewish Chronicle* (October 29). https://www.thejc.com/culture/books/review -raphael-lemkin-and-the-struggle-for-the-genocide-convention-1.61350.

Cooper, John. 2015. *Raphael Lemkin and the Struggle for the Genocide Convention*. London: Palgrave Macmillan.

Cornford, F. M. 1941. *The Republic of Plato*. Oxford: Clarendon.

Dershowitz, Alan. 2003. *The Case for Israel*. New York: Wiley.

Drucker, Peter F. 1994. *Adventures of a Bystander*. New Brunswick, NJ: Transaction.

Eliot, George. 1895. *Middlemarch: A Study of Provincial Life*. London: William Blackwood.

Eliot, T. S. 1934. *After Strange Gods: A Primer of Modern Heresy*. London: Faber and Faber.

Fackenheim, Emil J. 1996. *Jewish Philosophers and Jewish Philosophy*. Edited by Michael J. Morgan. Bloomington: Indiana University Press.

Flannery, Edward. 1985. *The Anguish of the Jews*. New York: Paulist Press.

Forster, E. M. 1951. *Two Cheers for Democracy*. London: Edward Arnold.

Foxman, Abraham H. 2007. *The Deadliest Lies: The Israel Lobby and the Myth of Jewish Control*. London: Palgrave Macmillan.

Furbank, P. N. 1979. *E. M. Forster: A Life*. Oxford: Oxford University Press.

Glock, Charles Y., and Rodney Stark. 1966. *Christian Beliefs and Anti-Semitism*. New York: Harper and Row.

Harrison, Bernard. 1975. *Fielding's Tom Jones: The Novelist as Moral Philosopher*. Brighton, UK: University of Sussex Press.

———. 2006. *The Resurgence of Antisemitism: Jews, Israel and Liberal Opinion*, Lanham, MD: Rowman and Littlefield.

———. 2011. "Appropriating the Holocaust." *Israel Affairs* 17, no. 4 (October): 644–50.

———. 2013. "Anti-Zionism, Antisemitism and the Rhetorical Manipulation of Reality." In *Resurgent Antisemitism: Global Perspectives*, edited by Alvin H. Rosenfeld, 8–41. Bloomington: Indiana University Press.

———. 2015. *What Is Fiction For? Literary Humanism Restored*. Bloomington: Indiana University Press.

Hersh, Seymour M. 1991.*The Samson Option*. New York: Random House.

Heinsohn, Gunnar. 2000. "What Makes the Holocaust a Uniquely Unique Genocide?" *Journal of Genocide Research* 2, no. 3: 411–30.

Hirsh, David. 2018. *Contemporary Left Antisemitism*. London: Routledge.

Hume, David. 1975. *Enquiries concerning Human Understanding and concerning the Principles of Morals*. Edited by L. A. Selby-Bigge and P. H. Nidditch. Oxford: Clarendon.

Iganski, Paul, and Barry Kosmin. 2003. *A New Antisemitism? Debating Judeophobia in 21st Century Britain*. London: Profile Books.

Isaac, Rael Jean. 2009. Review of B. Harrison, "The Resurgence of Anti-Semitism: Jews, Israel, and Liberal Opinion." *Society*, January.

Josephus, Flavius. 1971. *The Destruction of the Jews*. Translated by G. A. Williamson. London: The Folio Society.

Julius, Anthony. 1993. *T. S. Eliot, Anti-Semitism and Literary Form*. Cambridge: Cambridge University Press.

———. 2010. *Trials of the Diaspora: A History of Anti-Semitism in England*. Oxford: Oxford University Press.

Kant, Immanuel. 1953. *Prolegomena to Any Future Metaphysic Worthy to Be Considered a Science (1781)*. Translated by P. Gray-Lucas. Manchester, UK: Manchester University Press.

Karsh, Efrem. 2010. *Palestine Betrayed*. New Haven, CT: Yale University Press.

Kellner, Menachem. 2006. *Must a Jew Believe Anything?* Oxford: Littman Library of Jewish Civilisation.

Klima, Ivan. 1974. *The Spirit of Prague*. Translated by Paul Wilson. London: Granta Books.

Kovesi, Julius. 1967. *Moral Notions*, London: Routledge and Kegan Paul.

Küntzel, Matthias. 2007. *Jihad and Jew-Hatred: Islamism, Nazism and the Roots of 9/11*. Translated by Colin Meade. New York: Telos.

Lang, Berel. 1990. *Act and Idea in the Nazi Genocide*. Chicago: University of Chicago Press.

Langmuir, Gavin. 1990. *Toward a Definition of Antisemitism*. Berkeley: University of California Press.

Laqueur, Walter. 2008. *The Changing Face of Anti-Semitism*. Oxford: Oxford University Press.

Lévinas, Emmanuel. 1990. *Difficult Freedom: Essays on Judaism*. Translated by Seán Hand. London: Athlone.

———. 1994. *Outside the Subject*. Translated by Michel B. Smith. Stanford, CA: Stanford University Press.

Lindemann, Albert S. J. 1997. *Esau's Tears: Modern Anti-Semitism and the Rise of the Jews*. Cambridge: Cambridge University Press.

Locke, John. 1924. *An Essay Concerning Human Understanding*. Edited by A. S. Pringle-Pattison. Oxford: Clarendon.

Loewenstein, Antony, and Ahmed Moor. 2012. *After Zionism: One State for Israel and Palestine*. London: Saqui Books.

Maccoby, Hyam. 1982. *Judaism on Trial: Jewish-Christian Disputations in the Middle Ages*. London: Littman Library of Jewish Civilisation.

Mack, Michael. 2014. *German Idealism and the Jew*. Chicago: University of Chicago Press.

Manent, Pierre. 2006. *A World beyond Politics? A Defense of the Nation-State*. Translated by Marc LePain. Princeton, NJ: Princeton University Press.

Marcus, Kenneth. 2015. *The Definition of Anti-Semitism*. Oxford: Oxford University Press.

McCarthy, Justin. 1990. *The Population of Palestine*. New York: Columbia University Press.

Mearsheimer, John J., and Stephen M. Walt. 2007. *The Israel Lobby and U.S. Foreign Policy*. New York: Farrar, Straus and Giroux.

Morris, Benny. 2001. *Righteous Victims*. New York: Vintage Books.

———. 2008. *1948: The First Arab-Israeli War*. New Haven, CT: Yale University Press.

Nelson, Cary, and Gabriel Noah Brahm. 2015. *The Case against Academic Boycotts of Israel*. Chicago: MLA Members for Scholars' Rights.

Neumann, Michael. 2005. *The Case against Israel*. Petrolia, CA: CounterPunch and AK Press.

Nicholls, William. 1993. *Christian Antisemitism: A History of Hate*. Northvale, NJ: Jason Aaronson.

Nirenberg, David. 2013. *Anti-Judaism*. New York: Norton.

Paton, H. J. 1948. *The Moral Law, or Kant's Groundwork of the Metaphysic of Morals*. London: Hutchinson.

Patterson, David. 2012. *Genocide in Jewish Thought*. Cambridge: Cambridge University Press.

Pessin, Andrew, and Doron S. Ben-Atar, eds. 2018. *Anti-Zionism on Campus: The University, Free Speech and BDS*. Bloomington: Indiana University Press.

Plamenatz, John. 1963. *Man and Society: A Critical Examination of Some Important Political Theories, from Machiavelli to Marx*. London: Longman.

Pollack, Eunice G., ed. 2016. *Anti-Zionism and Antisemitism: Past & Present.* Boston: Academic Studies Press.

Popper, K. R. 1945. *The Open Society and Its Enemies.* London: Routledge and Kegan Paul.

Prager, Dennis, and Joseph Telushkin. 2003. *Why the Jews?* New York: Simon and Schuster.

Rich, Dave. 2016. *The Left's Jewish Problem.* London: Biteback.

Ricoeur, Paul. 1970. *Freud and Philosophy: An Essay on Interpretation.* New Haven, CT: Yale University Press.

Rose, E. M. 2015. *The Murder of William of Norwich: The Origins of the Blood Libel in Mediaeval Europe.* Oxford: Oxford University Press.

Rose, Jacqueline. 2005. *The Question of Zion,* Princeton, NJ: Princeton University Press.

Rose, Paul Lawrence.1990. *German Question, Jewish Question: Antisemitism from Kant to Wagner.* Princeton, NJ: Princeton University Press.

Rosenbaum, Alan S., ed. 2009. *Is the Holocaust Unique? Perspectives on Comparative Genocide.* Boulder, CO: Westview.

Rosenbaum, Ron. 2011. *How the End Begins: The Road to a Nuclear World War III.* New York: Simon and Schuster.

Rosenfeld, Alvin H. 2011. *The End of the Holocaust.* Bloomington: Indiana University Press.

———, ed. 2013. *Resurgent Antisemitism: Global Perspectives.* Bloomington: Indiana University Press.

———, ed. 2015. *Deciphering the New Antisemitism.* Bloomington: Indiana University Press.

———, ed. 2021. *Contending with Antisemitism in a Rapidly Changing Political Climate.* Bloomington: Indiana University Press.

Rosenfeld, Gavriel D. 2014. *Hi Hitler! How the Nazi Past Is Being Normalised in Contemporary Culture.* Cambridge: Cambridge University Press.

Rosenthal, Abigail. 2018 [1987]. *A Good Look at Evil.* Eugene, OR: Wipf and Stock.

Rosenzweig, Franz. 2000. *Philosophical and Theological Writings.* Translated and edited by Paul W. Frank and Michel L. Morgan. Indianapolis: Hackett.

Rossman-Benjamin, Tammi. 2015. "Interrogating the Academic Boycotters of Israel on American Campuses." In *The Case against Academic Boycotts of Israel,* edited by Cary Nelson and Gabriel Noah Brahm. Chicago: MLA Members for Scholars' Rights.

Roth, Philip. 2001. *The Wandering Jews.* Translated by Michael Hoffman. London: Granta Books.

Rousseau, Jean-Jacques. 1913. *The Social Contract.* Translated by G. D. H. Cole. London: Dent.

Russell, Bertrand. 1917. *Mysticism and Logic.* London: George Allen and Unwin.

Sand, Shlomo. 2014. *The Invention of the Land of Israel: From Holy Land to Homeland.* Translated by Geremy Forman. London: Verso.

Sartre, Jean-Paul. 1948. *Anti-Semite and Jew.* New York: Grove.

Selby-Bigge, L. A. 1897. *The British Moralists.* Oxford: Clarendon.

Sidgwick, H. 1891/2014. *Elements of Politics.* London: Macmillan.

Singer, Rev. Simeon, and Sir Jonathan Sacks. 2007. *The Authorised Daily Prayer Book of the United Hebrew Congregations of the Commonwealth.* London: Collins.

Smart, J. J. C., and Bernard Williams. 1973. *Utilitarianism For and Against.* Cambridge: Cambridge University Press.

Solomon, Norman. 2009. *The Talmud: A Selection.* Selected, edited, and translated by Norman Solomon. London: Penguin Books.

Steinsalz, Adin. 1976. *The Essential Talmud.* New York: Basic Books.

Stevenson, C. L. 1944. *Ethics and Language.* New Haven, CT: Yale University Press.

Szolt, Bela. 2005. *Nine Suitcases.* Translated by Ladislas Löb. London: Pimlico.

Tauber, Eliezer. 2017. *Deir Yassin: The End of the Myth.* Kinneret, Israel: Zvora-Bitan.

The Reader's Bible. 1951. London: Oxford University Press, Cambridge University Press, Eyre and Spottiswood.

Tucker, Robert, ed. 1978. *The Marx-Engels Reader.* New York: Norton.

Wasserstein, Bernard. 2012. *The Jews of Europe before the Second World War.* London: Profile Books.

Williams, Bernard. 1985. *Ethics and the Limits of Philosophy.* London: Fontana Paperbacks.

Wittenberg, Jonathan. 1996. *The Three Pillars of Judaism: A Search for Faith and Values.* London: SCM Press.

Wittgenstein, Ludwig. 1980. *Culture and Value.* Edited by G. H. von Wright. Translated by Peter Winch. Oxford: Blackwell.

Wolf, Aaron T. 1995. *Hydropolitics along the Jordan River: Scarce Water and Its Impact on the Arab-Israeli Conflict.* Tokyo: United Nations University Press.

Yakira, Elhanan. 2010. *Post-Zionism, Post-Holocaust.* Cambridge: Cambridge University Press.

INDEX

apartheid: and Israel, 142, 163, 201, 207, 214, 217, 231, 246, 247, 419, 427, 428, 435, 436, 437, 438, 439, 441, 455; in South Africa, 145, 163, 166, 171, 196, 201, 217, 225, 250, 251, 427. *See also* Israel, Israel Apartheid Week

Arab Higher Committee, 179, 180, 181, 206, 247, 457

Arab League, 180, 185, 206, 209

Arab Spring, 154, 191, 232, 332, 452

Arendt, Hannah, 86–88, 89, 90, 92, 132, 133, 299, 341

Armenians, 41, 85, 146, 190, 277; Ottoman massacre, 41, 43

Arnold, Matthew, 290, 402

Arnold, Thomas, 266

Aryans, 70, 100, 241, 245, 423, 447; Aryan myth, 57–58; Aryan values, 369

assimilation, 190, 207, 465; Jewish resistance to, 114, 115, 116, 117, 126, 127, 128, 130, 131, 134, 282, 283, 329, 368, 389

atrocities, 200, 233, 256, 348; Arab, 200. *See also* Israel, Israeli atrocities; Nazism, Nazi atrocities

Atzmon, Gilad, 292

Austin, J. L., 22, 26, 242

Avishai, Bernard, 146

Ayalon, Ami, 404

Azm, Khalid al-, 188

Azzam, Abdul Rahman, 185, 203n37

Ba'ath Party, 235

Babel, Isaac, 256

Bachi, Roberto, 175–76

Baghouti, Mustafa, 221

Balfour Declaration, 19, 178, 227

Banna, Hassan al-, 18, 234, 449

Barak, Ehud, 211, 214, 229

Barghouti, Omar, 201, 232

Baskin, Gershon, 229

Bauer, Yehuda, 31, 35, 37, 38, 45

Beckwith, Leila, 407

Begin, Menachem, 183, 209

Ben-Gurion, David, 187, 189

Ben-Menashe, Ari, 25

Bennett, Naftali, 193

Berger, Luciana, 417, 429, 460–61

Berlin, Isaiah, 394, 448

Bernard, Daniel, 4–5, 7–8

Bible, the, 91, 172, 304, 306, 311, 312, 355, 367

bin Laden, Osama, 160

Bishop, Julie, 228

Blair, Tony, 275

blood libel, 22, 72, 86, 221, 240, 263, 405, 416

Bodi, Faisal, 144, 147, 167n5

Bogdanor, Paul, 146

Bolchover, Richard, 161–62, 253–54

Bonnier, Elisabet Borsiin, 150

Bormann, Martin, 96

Boycott, Divestment and Sanctions (BDS) movement, 2, 10, 11, 141, 144, 145–46, 153, 154, 166, 170, 172, 186, 188, 190, 207, 213, 214, 220, 232, 239, 243, 245, 252, 258, 260, 265, 266, 293, 377, 380, 387, 401, 408, 410, 412, 417, 422, 428, 433, 441, 453; campaigns, 200; literature of, 163, 285; narrative, 175, 196, 294; opposition to, 168n25, 255, 440; politics of, 137, 251; supporters, 160, 164, 180, 201, 225, 230, 254, 260, 279, 413, 437

Britain, 25, 47, 66, 130, 158, 177, 179, 180, 182, 234, 257, 258, 260, 286, 362, 374, 375, 382, 409, 412–13, 424, 439, 451, 461; and antisemitism, 1, 112, 145, 162, 254, 406, 413, 417, 420, 425, 434, 437, 438, 440, 449; British army, 179, 186, 223, 224, 235; British economy, 162, 253; British Empire, 8, 112, 390, 445; British Foreign Office, 176; British foreign policy, 275; British government, 18, 173, 178, 414, 415, 455; British imperialism, 75, 112; British Jews, 126, 142, 432, 449; British journalism, 167n5; British left, 145, 273, 275; British Mandate, 171, 174, 187, 227; British media, 5, 161, 253; British politics, 103, 292, 388; Britons, 85, 118, 128, 179. *See also* British Broadcasting Corporation; Labour Party (British)

British Broadcasting Corporation (BBC), 4, 5, 6–7, 9, 161, 167n5, 181–82, 184, 188, 195, 220–21, 275

Bruckner, Pascal, 47

Buber, Martin, 127, 316, 320, 359

Budick, Emily, 201

Bush, George W., 149

Butler, Judith, 242, 243, 274, 276

480 INDEX

Hobbes, Thomas, 99, 144, 206

Hodge, Margaret, 461

Holocaust, 32, 33, 34, 37, 39, 40, 42, 43–44,
47, 48, 90, 96, 97, 107, 144, 149, 161, 197,
198, 200, 207, 280, 325, 341, 386, 391, 407,
416, 419, 424, 446, 447, 451, 461, 462;
and antisemitism, 4, 8, 244, 253, 256, 432,
441; commemoration of, 34, 49–50; as a
crime, 35, 47, 48, 49–50; denial of, 1, 32,
105–6, 416, 434; hagiographers, 41, 42, 43,
47; Holocaust industry, 49, 51; Holocaust
studies, 31, 43; Jewish ownership of, 36,
44, 46, 47; Jewish suffering in, 39, 40,
41, 42, 46, 49, 50, 55; survivors of, 25, 255,
456; uniqueness of, 25; 10, 18, 31, 33–34, 35,
36–39, 40–41, 42, 43, 45–47, 48, 49, 52n28,
68, 97; universalizing of, 35, 38, 45. See also
genocide, and Holocaust

homogeneity, 105, 110–11, 112, 122, 123, 136,
243; cultural, 105; ethnic, 170; natural,
111, 112–13, 123, 134, 329; project-driven,
111, 112–13, 114, 116, 123, 329, 369; religious,
105, 170

Horowitz, Irving Louis, 44

human rights, 18, 45, 76, 77, 144, 201, 225,
231, 246, 250, 255, 417, 419; Universal
Declaration of Human Rights, 41. See also
Europe, European Court of Human
Rights; Human Rights Watch

Human Rights Watch, 220

humanitarianism, 263, 366, 369

Hume, David, 32, 105, 286, 287, 288–89, 290,
291, 313–14, 336, 343, 346, 347, 348, 351;
Humian skepticism, 344, 345, 348

Hussein (king of Jordan), 207, 209

Hussein, Saddam, 200, 427, 451

Husseini, Amin al-, 180, 177, 188, 235, 236

Huxley, Thomas Henry, 294

Hyndman, H. M., 112

ideology, 61, 62, 107; and antisemitism, 61, 62,
69, 73, 74, 416, 449; and Zionism, 166, 189,
242, 243, 258, 280

immigration, 174–76, 178, 189, 196, 197, 199,
388, 462; immigrants, 78, 173, 174–76,
191, 196, 197. See also Muslims, Muslim
immigration

imperialism, 19, 166, 171, 274, 276–77, 278,
280, 281, 286, 300, 385, 435, 456; anti-
imperialism, 275, 276, 277, 278, 279,
280, 284, 286. See also Britain, British
imperialism

Index of Arab-Jewish Relations in Israel, 195

indigeneity, 38, 165, 166, 170–71, 172–73,
174, 176

Institute for Jewish Policy Research, 162, 253

intellectuals, 11, 39, 107, 127, 130, 134, 149, 286,
289, 291, 324, 338, 345; and antisemitism,
71, 94, 147, 162, 246, 259, 261, 265, 281, 361,
425; Arab, 234; Jewish, 116, 130, 160, 257;
public, 147, 152, 160, 162, 281, 288, 290,
294, 460; Western, 42. See also Europe,
European intellectuals

interests, 21, 336, 337, 347, 349, 350, 356, 431,
458; Arab, 193, 197; Jewish, 9–10, 19, 21,
68, 87, 156, 245, 250, 416, 418, 428, 430,
459; non-Jewish, 9, 27, 68, 86, 156, 464;
proletarian, 267, 371, 372; purely personal,
349; relational, 350, 354, 357. See also
Palestine, Palestinian interests; Zionism,
Zionist interests

intermarriage, 126, 389

International Holocaust Remembrance
Alliance (IHRA) definition of
antisemitism, 414, 415, 417–19, 420,
421–22, 430–31, 432, 438, 439–40, 441

Inter-parliamentary Coalition for
Combating Antisemitism, 415

Iran, 20, 21, 25, 76, 154, 191, 199, 200, 218, 232,
246, 250, 425, 449, 452, 458

Iran-Iraq War, 23, 154, 426

Iraq, 21, 24, 148, 149, 154, 184, 187, 194, 199,
222, 224, 235, 236n1, 246, 263n3, 391, 427,
449, 451; Iraq Body Count, 222; Iraq Wars,
154, 426, 452

Ireland, 150, 151, 332, 378, 386; Irish, 85, 94,
150, 241, 369, 379

Irgun Zvai Leumi, 179, 181, 182–83, 186

Irving, David, 434

ISIL, 148, 159, 200, 225, 232, 235, 275, 385, 449

ISIS. See ISIL

Islam, 11, 111, 154, 234, 235, 284, 329, 336,
355, 385, 391; anti-Islamists, 168n25; and
antisemitism, 17, 18, 234; conversion to,

126, 173; Islamic Caliphate, 19, 20; Islamist fundamentalism, 159; Islamist groups, 232, 234, 247, 457, 458; Islamist movements, 18, 159, 233, 454, 457; Islamists, 3, 10, 17, 29n1, 31, 154, 160, 190, 212, 234, 391, 450; radical, 260, 462; Shi'a, 24, 191, 222, 332, 391, 452; Sunni, 24, 191, 222, 332, 391, 452

Israel, 1, 29, 194, 220, 230–31, 283, 293, 304, 305, 379, 395, 403, 416, 418, 426, 452, 455, 456, 458–59; boycott of, 2, 142, 192, 275, 406, 407, 419, 433, 435; as colonial settler state, 166, 167, 170, 178, 196, 207, 214, 243, 247, 278, 419; compared to Nazis, 149, 150, 200, 254, 279, 282, 417, 420, 427, 429, 430, 431, 432, 439, 441, 455, 460; criticism of, 148, 160–61, 162, 240, 242, 243–44, 247, 255, 262–63, 279, 281, 292, 379, 406, 413–14, 415, 421, 430, 432, 433–34, 437, 438, 465; and defamation, 163, 431, 439; and democracy, 21, 146, 159, 194, 195, 207, 225, 231, 243, 248, 284, 361, 416, 430; demonization of, 76–77, 168n25, 239, 431; elimination of, 28, 74, 188, 213, 256, 260, 278, 374, 396, 451; hatred of, 27, 234, 277, 400, 450, 454; history of, 11, 27, 48, 151, 166, 172, 175, 176, 180, 186, 187, 197, 198, 200, 247, 284, 457; hostility toward, 4, 18, 76, 125, 141, 240, 261, 262, 266, 279, 406, 422, 425, 428, 429, 451, 460, 461; Israel Apartheid Week, 1, 144; Israel Defense Forces (IDF), 155, 181, 193, 209, 210, 212, 213, 224, 228, 256, 260, 380, 404, 427; Israel Democracy Institute, 195; Israel Labor Party, 211, 227; Israel lobby, 86, 135, 156–57, 158, 160, 240, 250, 251, 280, 428, 431, 450; Israeli atrocities, 144, 147, 148, 152–53, 181, 182, 183, 184, 186, 200, 405, 426; Israeli citizenship, 145, 146, 184, 189, 190, 191, 207, 214, 457; Israeli crimes, 163, 186, 207, 211, 225, 226, 258, 400, 405, 426; Israeli economy, 159, 219; Israeli government, 21, 149, 151, 195, 209, 227, 229, 250, 401, 450; Israeli involvement in wars, 23–24 149, 153–54, 164, 201, 206–7, 208–9, 211–13, 218, 221–22, 223–24, 426; Israeli military forces, 193, 207, 209, 210–11, 227; Israeli people, 3, 189–90, 192, 217, 233, 278, 381,

383, 393; Israeli policies, 142, 150, 160–61, 171, 216, 255, 413, 416, 420; Israeli politics, 21, 229, 262, 417, 432; Israeli power, 8, 26, 171; Israeli society, 192, 193, 195, 248, 380; as Jewish state, 2, 4, 5, 6, 24, 25, 27, 145, 146, 153, 212, 213, 214, 232, 233, 248, 249, 278, 377, 414, 415; legitimacy of, 145, 147, 170, 186, 226, 240, 425–26, 438; and nuclear weapons, 24–25; opposition to, 6, 17, 76, 137, 142, 143, 195, 404, 413, 453, 454; and racism, 27, 142, 163, 166, 240, 243, 412, 416, 417, 427, 428, 429, 430, 431, 432, 435, 437, 438, 439, 441, 454; right to exist, 148, 155, 166, 167n5, 208, 220, 255, 256, 259, 437; support of, 5, 21, 28, 125, 142, 156, 157, 158–59, 164, 166, 168n25, 193, 194, 195, 196, 214, 258, 260, 261, 262, 280, 374, 407, 409, 427, 428, 429, 436, 437, 461; as threat to world peace, 20–21, 23, 24, 26, 153, 428. See also American-Israel Public Affairs Committee; apartheid, and Israel; evil, and Israel; Friends of Israel; Gaza Strip, Israeli occupation of; genocide, and Israel; Index of Arab-Jewish Relations in Israel; Israeli-Palestinian conflict; Middle East, and Israel; United States, and Israel; West Bank, Israeli occupation of

Israeli-Palestinian conflict, 4, 11, 27–28, 40, 142, 149, 158, 159, 163–64, 165–66, 170, 172, 184, 192, 193, 208, 211, 212, 213, 215, 226, 229, 230, 236, 242, 243, 248, 251–52, 278, 279, 284, 285, 379, 417, 419, 428, 432, 456, 459

Jabari, Ahmed, 213
Jacobs, Jill, 358, 361
Jacobson, Howard, 262
Johnson, Alan, 239, 242, 244, 246, 248, 256, 260, 263n3, 276, 278, 286, 293
Jordan, 146, 171, 187–88, 194, 206–7, 208–9, 214, 219, 227, 228, 425, 458
Jordan River, 163, 207, 227, 230, 231, 232
Josephus, Titus Flavius, 117, 118
Judaism, 11, 27, 59, 87, 89–92, 93, 97, 101, 110, 114, 120, 122, 123, 125, 126, 128, 129, 130, 131, 132, 133, 265, 301, 302, 303, 308, 310–11, 313, 314–17, 318–19, 323, 326, 329, 330–31, 332, 340, 342, 354, 356, 359, 360, 367, 369,

Maccoby, Hyam, 317, 331
Machiavelli, Niccolò, 170
Macierewicz, Antoni, 462–63
Maduro, Nicolás, 271–72, 392
Maimonides, 354, 367
Manekin, Charles H. (Jeremiah Haber), 231
Manent, Pierre, 387
Mann, John, 405, 461 ·
Marcion of Sinope, 304–5; Marcionites, 306
Marcus, Kenneth L., 53, 55, 56, 61–62, 63, 69, 71, 73, 74, 77, 80n3, 141
Maroun, Fred, 453, 454, 459
Marr, Wilhelm, 57, 422
Marx, Karl, 94, 243, 265, 268, 269, 288, 289, 290, 291, 327, 341, 361, 371; and Jews, 370–71, 372, 373, 375–76, 377. See also Marxism
Marxism, 61, 115, 165, 186, 268, 269, 272, 324, 354, 355, 370–71, 372, 373, 385, 389; Communism, 18, 75, 88, 111, 124, 134, 190, 199, 255, 265, 269, 270, 272, 326, 327–28, 388, 456, 462, 463; Marxists, 61, 116, 268, 327, 371, 389. See also Marx, Karl
Massing, Michael, 156
materialism, 102, 243, 327, 356; Jewish, 103, 105, 319, 320, 354, 365
Maurras, Charles, 105
Mazzig, Hen, 404
McCarthy, Justin, 175–76
Mearsheimer, John, 155–57, 158, 160, 161, 162, 250, 285, 300, 454
Meir, Golda, 209
Middle East, 5, 8, 23, 154, 155, 208, 218, 230, 262, 275, 293, 332, 379, 388, 391, 395, 426, 441, 449; and antisemitism, 27, 222, 234, 235, 251, 406; and Israel, 166, 167n5, 190, 191, 194, 380, 450, 451, 452; Middle Eastern Jews, 173, 190, 196, 199; Middle Eastern politics, 26, 135, 154, 432; Middle East policy, 135, 250; nations of, 26
midrash, 308, 311–12, 315, 316, 319
Mill, James, 336
mitzvah, 131, 308, 311, 323, 353
Montesquieu, 101
Moor, Ahmed, 230
Moorhead, Alan, 42
morality, 131, 146, 279, 292, 336, 337, 338, 344, 346, 347, 351, 354, 357, 358, 360; demands of,

348, 350; everyday, 352; Jewish, 120, 131, 302, 353, 359; moral agents, 325, 335–36, 339, 345, 347, 351, 357, 360; moral autonomy, 336, 338–39, 346, 356; moral capital, 43, 45; moral knowledge, 343; moral responsibility, 131, 164, 335, 339, 357, 358, 360; political, 74; public, 74. See also Enlightenment, moral theory of; Judaism, moral outlook of; Kant, and moral autonomy, and morality, and moral rationality, and moral reasoning, and moral redemption, and moral responsibility
Morris, Benny, 181, 182, 185–86, 188, 203n37, 236n1, 456
Morsi, Mohamed, 194, 216
Motassadeq, Mounir el-, 159
Muslim Brotherhood, 18, 154, 159, 194, 216, 234, 236, 449, 452, 454, 457
Muslims, 17, 24, 28, 48, 60, 147, 150, 168n25, 173, 174, 180, 184, 189, 194, 198, 199, 201, 211, 217, 231, 234, 235, 236, 278, 284, 332, 390, 391, 409, 426, 434, 449; Arab Muslims, 190, 193, 195, 231, 293, 395, 427, 451; intra-Muslim conflict, 191, 222, 379; and Jews, 17, 48, 88, 177, 178, 259, 400, 450, 454, 455; Muslim community, 18, 455; Muslim immigration, 462; Muslim state, 213, 231, 293, 438; Muslim world, 27, 78, 125, 154, 196, 217, 293, 400, 450, 451, 452. See also Islam; Muslim Brotherhood; Palestine, Palestinian Muslims

Nadaf, Gabriel, 193–94
Nasser, Gamal Abdel, 165, 206–7
National Centre for Social Research, 162, 253
nationalism, 231, 355, 386; Jewish, 91, 243, 374, 375. See also Germany, German nationalism
National Socialist German Workers' Party. See Nazism, Nazi Party
Nazism, 17, 29, 31, 34, 35, 38, 55, 101, 111, 135, 197, 235, 244, 246, 258, 261, 269, 341, 343, 385, 401, 428, 429, 432, 438, 448, 452; and antisemitism, 20, 37, 38, 44–45, 46, 88, 155, 189, 233, 234, 254, 255, 256, 282, 368, 403, 420, 423, 429, 438, 441, 445, 455; Nazi atrocities, 45, 46; Nazi era, 38, 200;

BERNARD HARRISON was born in Bristol, England, in 1933. He is at present Emeritus E. E. Ericksen Professor of Philosophy in the University of Utah and Emeritus Professor in the Faculty of Humanities, University of Sussex, UK. He is the author of *The Resurgence of Anti-Semitism: Jews, Israel, and Liberal Opinion* (2006). Other recent books include *Word and World: Practice and the Foundations of Language* (coauthor Patricia Hanna, 2004); and *What Is Fiction For?: Literary Humanism Restored* (2015). Further information is available at http://bernardharrison1.academia.edu.

CPSIA information can be obtained
at www.ICGtesting.com
Printed in the USA
JSHW020543130123
36216JS00001B/4